100 Years

of

Nose Creek Valley History

Editor-in-Chief: Stephen Wilk
Assistant Editor: Valerie Jobson
Consulting Editor: C. Redvers Perry

Nose Creek Historical Society Book Committee:
Floyd Reynolds
Eleanor Meyer
Leighton Perry
Howard Pole

Published by the
Nose Creek Historical Society
First Edition (2,000 copies)

1997

Printer: A to Zee Printing, Calgary, Alberta

ISBN 0-9681412-0-X   Bar Code 9 780968 141205

Hey man·
♡ you!

This book is dedicated
to the pioneers who laid the
foundations of this great country

ACKNOWLEDGEMENTS

The production of a book of this scope was not the work of a single individual, but involved a large number of people and institutions who contributed materials and expertise to make this historical anthology possible. All of those from whom the editorial committee sought assistance willingly cooperated. The main response was: "this book is long overdue."

The editorial assistance and computer skills of Valerie Jobson proved most valuable in the preparation of the manuscripts for this anthology. Valerie, a freelance historical researcher, holds Bachelor degrees in Biology and History and an M.A. degree in History from the University of Calgary.

The editorial and local news reporting labours of Redvers Perry, local historian, provided the inspiration for this book project. He has contributed a wide range of historical data for this anthology.

The many persons who submitted articles and pioneer manuscripts are also acknowledged here; those who wrote articles for Society pamphlets over the years and those who wrote articles or loaned us memoirs for this book. They include a large number of people who live in Nose Creek Valley, and academic historians.

The work of other members of the book committee is gratefully acknowledged. Floyd Reynolds' public relation experience, assistance in collecting photographs and information, and attention to administrative detail have helped make the complex aspects of this book much easier. Eleanor Meyers' dedicated and untiring efforts to this book project. Howard Poles' fine spirit in recording the financial support and promotional program was extremely helpful in bringing the project to a successful conclusion. The leadership of Leighton Perry who, with his keen business sense, headed up the ways-and-means committee is also acknowledged. His many hours of contacting members of the community helped provide the financial backing necessary to publish this volume.

The initiative and support of the Nose Creek Historical Society's Executive not only started this book project, but their personal, financial, and moral support for it provided the example for others to follow.

Our sincere appreciation is extended to the contributors and supporters for their donations and pre-orders for the book. Their backing made it possible for the editorial committee to proceed with confidence in carrying out the enormous task of editing, co-ordinating, and publishing this anthology. Among the donors in support of the book project, we make special mention of the Historic Resources Foundation of Alberta and the various corporate and individual donors who are acknowledged in the back pages of this book.

Research was facilitated by the use of several published history books, articles, theses, and other secondary sources. Primary sources included published interviews of pioneers and their descendants, private papers, and photograph collections. The Glenbow Archives, the Calgary Public Library, and the University of Calgary Library were all important sources of information. I wish to thank Dr. Robert MacDonald who was consulted at various stages of the project.

Over 640 historic photographs, 30 maps and charts, and artists sketches have been included with written or verbal permission. (See Photo Credits' Section). Special mention in this regard is made of the Glenbow Library and Archives and other public and private collections: The Ranchman's Club, Redvers Perry, Florence Walker, Marilyn McCall, Peter J.M. Pallesen, Rino Basso, and Dorothy Tilleman collections to name only a few.

The co-operation of the Nose Creek Valley Museum, Glenbow Library and Archives, Heritage Park, and Fort Calgary Historical Park has proved very helpful to us in this endeavour.

We also thank the *Airdrie Echo*, the *Five Village Weekly*, *Alberta Museums Review*, Alberta Wheat Pool and others, for their assistance in the advertising and pre-sale of the book.

Finally, I wish to make special mention of the support of my wife Reta Wilk, who sacrificed countless hours of family time to make this book possible   — Stephen Wilk

Table of Contents

List of Maps, Charts, and Illustrations

PREFACE

The Nose Creek Historical Society with its many members has been active over the years in stimulating interest in Nose Creek Valley history.

Our Society has undertaken a variety of historic projects such as suitably marking historic sites, sponsoring historic programs, supporting the Nose Creek Valley Museum, collecting, and storing historic artifacts and documents, and initiating the publication of the *Nose Creek Story* as well as this historic anthology.

On behalf of the Society, we make special mention of the major contribution made by the Rev. Dr. Stephen Wilk, Editor-in-Chief, in designing, compiling, editing and preparing this book for publication. His study of the history of Calgary and area produced his two published books, *Pioneers of the Faith* in 1962 and *One Day's Journey* in 1963, his Bachelor of Divinity thesis in 1965, and his Doctoral Dissertation in 1978. These have all been useful sources for this anthology. His leadership over the years has also inspired our historic endeavours. He not only spear-headed the research, writing, compiling, editing, publishing, and production of this book, but has also spent countless hours coordinating every aspect of its creation, including the development of its funding base. His many years of editing and publishing a wide variety of publications across Canada and his wide interest in Canadian history has been helpful in designing this anthology.

Our Society is also grateful to Dr. Wilk's Assistant Editor, Valerie Jobson, who helped type and edit the manuscripts. The contribution of Consulting Editor, Redvers Perry, whose untiring efforts to continue the work begun by his father, Clem, in preserving the history of the region over the years, is appreciated.

Our Society is thankful for the co-operation of those who willingly contributed articles and photographs which helped animate the entire anthology.

Other members of the Book Project Committee have spent many hours behind the scenes to make this book possible. Of special mention are the work and devotion of Eleanor Meyer (Secretary), Leighton Perry (Ways and Means Co-ordinator), and Howard Pole (Treasurer), without whose efforts this project would not have come to a successful conclusion.

We appreciate the many financial donations and pre-orders of the book by members and friends, and formally acknowledge the generosity of corporate and individual donors (listed at the back of the book).

We invite you all to read and enjoy the memories of the past recorded here. It is our hope that these memories may help in making decisions for the future.

We hope that the many historic themes not included in this book will be covered in future historic projects.

Floyd Reynolds
President of the Nose Creek Historic Society

FOREWORD

In this anthology we celebrate the history of the Nose Creek Valley district, as experienced by the people living here in the past and present. On its way to join the Bow River at the original site of Fort Calgary, Nose Creek drains an area of approximately 900 square miles north of the Bow River, including Crossfield and Airdrie districts.

The book had its origin in the historic pamphlets produced by the Nose Creek Historical Society. From 1972 to the present, the society has held annual interdenominational church services to celebrate historic events and aspects of settlement history in the Nose Creek Valley district. At each service, the Society distributed a pamphlet explaining the tribute for that year's theme. Local historian C. Redvers Perry researched and wrote many of the pamphlets and edited the remainder, compiling submissions from a wide variety of people.

For the 25th anniversary of the historic celebrations, the Society decided, on the suggestion of the editor, to publish these collected pamphlets as a book. While planning the book, the editorial committee concluded it should also include accounts of recent events, in order to update previously published histories of the area. We sought contributions from local people, businesses, amateur historians and professional historians, and received many submissions of high quality.

It became evident to the editors that a thematic approach would provide a framework for the varied contributions included herein. Rather than the usual approach of including accounts about each family in a community history, we have included representative stories about the kinds of activities which have taken place in the Nose Creek Valley in the past and present. The reader will float down a multitude of thematic trickles, all of which empty into a stream of holistic experience and understanding of the history of the Nose Creek Valley.

The material has been divided into six parts for ease of access. Part I describes the recent growth of local interest in the history of the area, and the search for and preservation of knowledge, artifacts, and historic sites. Part II describes the formation of the valley and its geography; also the lifestyle of the native peoples, who lived and travelled freely in this area long before immigrants came and settled on particular pieces of land. Part III contains the pamphlets produced by the Nose Creek Historical Society in their original order and enriched by some new material. Most of the themes of these chapters deal with preparations for permanent settlement of the area or with aspects of settlement life. Part IV includes articles on the more recent history of the urban centres, the city of Airdrie and the town of Crossfield, as well as the impact on the valley of its proximity to Calgary. Part V describes agricultural and business activities as well as many organizations which have served the needs of people in the district. Part VI contains reviews of books and previously unpublished material about the history of the area.

End notes and a bibliography are included in the final section of this book. This includes a list of supporters. An index of photo credits should be invaluable in aiding the researcher. A list of museums connected with this book is also published. Finally, the customary index of names, places and major subjects closes out this book.

Throughout this anthology the reader will note different spellings of proper names. McPherson's Coulee was originally named MacPherson's Coulee on the official Dominion Land Agency map in 1887, and was spelled that way until around 1925. It was named for Addison McPherson, sometimes called "Ad" or "Add" McPherson. What is usually spelled now as Symon's Valley was named after the local postmaster, W.E. Simons. Over time the original Simons' Valley took on the "y" spelling and lost or moved the apostrophe. Also, while the editors have tended to use British spellings, in some cases we retained American spelling preferences to maintain the integrity of an article.

INTRODUCTION

When standing on Nose Hill looking southwest to the tall buildings of Calgary's city centre, one cannot help but be impressed by the Bow Valley Corridor, cut by the waters of the Bow River with its tributaries, the Elbow River and the Nose Creek. Each of these flow into the city centre and meet at their confluence a short distance from the historic Fort Calgary (constructed by the North West Mounted Police in 1875) and flow on to join the South Saskatchewan River near Medicine Hat.

Looking east from Nose Hill, one sees the valley of Nose Creek with its tributaries, flowing through the north part of the sprawling city. Nose Creek waters arise in the spring fed Nier Lakes and flow through McPherson Coulee and south-easterly into the Nose Creek Basin. Another branch originates a few miles northwest of Crossfield, and joins Nose Creek to flow south through Airdrie, Balzac and Beddington on its way to meet the Bow River in north Calgary. Other tributaries add to the Nose Creek waters on their way to meet the Bow; an important one drains through Symons Valley and north Calgary to join Nose Creek. The drainage basin of the Nose Creek waters covers approximately 900 square miles (2340 square kilometres).

The first impression of the physical features of metropolitan Calgary is that the city settled mainly along the Bow Valley and Elbow River corridors. An aerial view of Calgary and its surrounding regions, however, makes it abundantly clear that the Nose Creek Valley corridor historically has played a distinctive role in the development of the region covered by this book.

Nose Creek Valley blends into the scenic foothills of the Canadian Rockies. Early explorers named the hills along the eastern slopes of the Valley northeast of Balzac "The Butte Hills", which is French for a hill or mound. From these hills one observes the spectacular beauty of the foothills and snowcapped mountains while overlooking the Nose Creek Valley with its characteristic scenery. Also called "Sharp Hills" or "The Buttes" over the years, they provide a unique vantage point to view the city of Airdrie and the mouth of McPherson Coulee stretching towards the west.

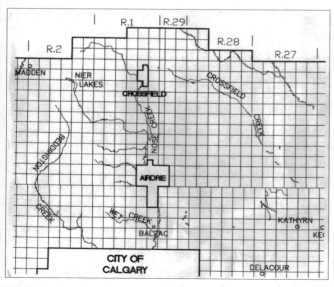

In the main Nose Creek Valley and part way up Beddington Creek, Wet Creek and Symons Valley are small basins of heavy textured soils. These soils determined the route of the trails, railroad and highway, and the difficult conditions and distances between settlements. The Valley also produced sandstone from which public buildings in Calgary and some pioneer homes were built.

The climate affecting economic and community life here is classed as "Cold Temperate". The Chinook wind from over the mountains modifies most winters considerably and is a striking feature of the weather in this region. The cool air off the mountains keeps the climate pleasant and cool as compared to the hot, dry summers of the prairies to the east.

A newcomer or visitor to the Calgary might wonder how many of the streets, hills and valleys received their names, such as "Deerfoot Trail", a portion of the Number 2 Highway, historically known as the Calgary-Edmonton Trail. The trail, passing along the Nose Creek corridor on its way to Edmonton, was named after a Blackfoot Indian runner named A'pikaiees, Scabby Dried Meat, whose professional racing name was Deerfoot. Other trails in Calgary were named after Blackfoot tribes such as the Sarcee, Peigan and Blackfoot Trails.

How Spy Hill and Nose Hill got their names is less commonly known. Spy Hill was used by Indians to spot buffalo herds and other wild animals, and later they used mirrors to signal across the valley. The names Nose Creek and Nose Hill had a unique origin, coming from the Blackfoot Indian tribes who frequently camped in the area. It was customary for Indians to give places names according to topographical features. One theory suggests that because the Bow River flows on one side of Nose Hill and Nose Creek on the other that the protrusion of the hill was referred to as an "The Nose". Another myth about the origin of the name suggests that during a whiskey-induced brawl a Blackfoot man bit off the end of a Blackfoot woman's nose. The most likely explanation was given by Frances Fraser, a student of Indian lore, and by George H. Gooderham, former Indian agent to the Blackfoot, in an interview with Stephen Wilk in 1960. Fraser and Gooderham concurred that the name originated in a Blackfoot custom that a women who was found to be unfaithful to her husband might have her nose cut off as an example to the others. An anecdote supporting this explanation was told by Gooderham, who in the early 1900's met a Blackfoot woman named Mrs. Skunk whose nose had been cut off. After having been such an example, she could no longer marry anyone with a high class name, such as Sun, Moon, Star, Tree or Bear, but could only marry a man named Skunk.

In this anthology we describe recent efforts to preserve the heritage and history of the evolution of the Valley through the Nose Creek Historical Society and the Nose Creek Valley Museum. Through these organizations, historic sites were marked and historic resources preserved, and a variety of historic themes were celebrated over the years.

The reader will gain an appreciation of the geological formation of the Nose Creek Valley, of the earliest people to live here after the ice age, and of the lives of the Blackfoot, who found the Valley with its protective coulees and ridges a haven from the harsh winter climate. The abundance of food for animals and the regular water supply made possible human existence. The features which sustained early tribal life also attracted early ranching, the Canadian Pacific Railway, agricultural settlement, and later industrial development in the Valley.

After the Indians with their distinctive culture, folkways and mores were placed on reserves, the squatters, ranchers and settlers brought their cultural heritage from their original homelands. These traditions blended over the years in the Valley through interaction and inter-marriage into what today may be described as a typical Canadian population mix. We have given some examples of how cultures of other countries have made a distinctive contribution to the development of the community by looking at Scandinavian and British influences.

The Nose Creek Valley area, like all of Alberta, underwent a vast number of economic and social changes as a result of settlement. The fur traders and the missionaries began the immigration which continued in waves before and after the first World War. The population in Alberta increased 500% from 73,022 in 1901 to 374,663 in 1911 and was close to 900,000 by 1947. With the influx of settlement into this area, with its variety of soil types, the Valley produced some of the finest grass and field crops in Western Canada. The soil has supported some of the largest buffalo herds, outstanding beef and dairy cattle, as well as purebred horses, sheep and grain.

Besides covering some historic aspects of the growth of Crossfield and Airdrie, we have shown how some of the major institutions of Calgary historically served the Nose Creek Valley. Here we have selected educational institutions such as Mount Royal College, the Southern Alberta Institute of Technology and the Universities of Alberta and Calgary, and medical services of the hospitals over the years.

As the Valley increased in population and its ranching and agricultural enterprises advanced technologically, a variety of specialized business enterprises developed. We have recorded the history of a series of large and small business enterprises: construction, dairy, meat, mushroom, seed, grain, gardening products, sheep, cattle, breeding, aviation, and utilities. The discovery of oil and gas added another aspect of industrial development. We have also attempted to show not only how these businesses provided the raw materials but also how they prepared their products for the market. The Co-operative movement produced many large and small co-ops serving rural needs. Aspects of social interaction are featured, such as settlement by families and ethnic groups, and how organizations and clubs were part of building community life.

We have included descriptions of major historical books and other works related to the Nose Creek Valley. We review their contents and show how some of them came to be written. In the endnotes we have provided suggestions for further reading and research on various topics.

A major feature enhancing this anthology is that each of the themes presented in this book is animated and enriched by the lavish use of illustrations.

Submitted by Stephen Wilk, 1996

The Valley and its Environs

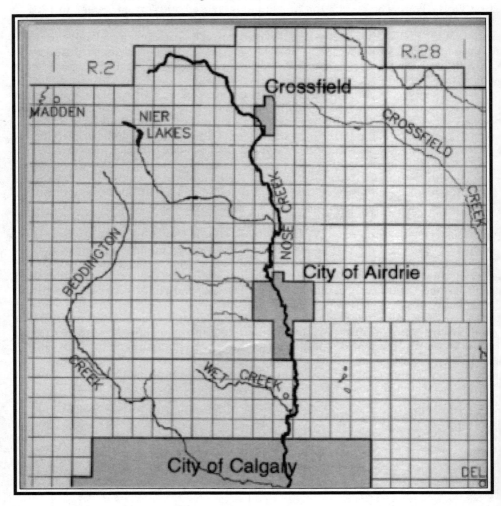

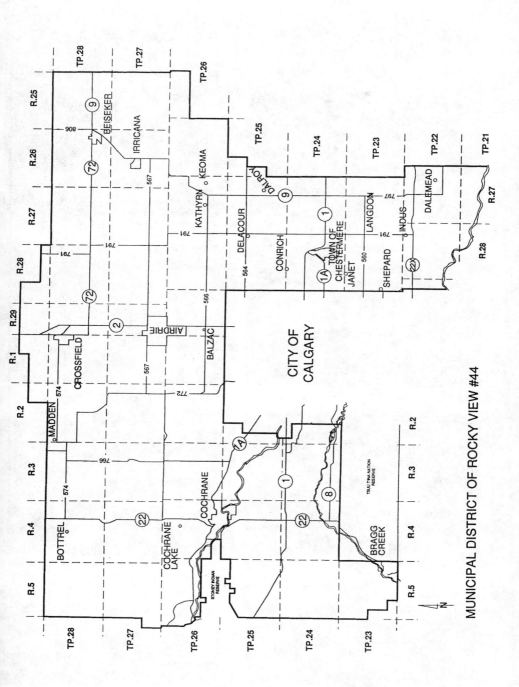

MUNICIPAL DISTRICT OF ROCKY VIEW #44

Typical Valley Scenes

A view of historic McPherson's Coulee looking west.

An interesting geological formation.

Looking northeast at Butte (Sharp) Hills.

An historic passageway made modern.

Nose Creek providing fodder for contented horses.

Ranching along McPherson's Coulee.

Nose Creek winds its way into Calgary city centre.

Nose Creek flowing through scenic Airdrie.

Courtesy: Peter Saunders, Click Photo Design Inc. and Mach 2 Stock Exchange Ltd., Calgary.

PART I: CELEBRATING THE HISTORY OF NOSE CREEK VALLEY

INTRODUCTION

Part I of this historical anthology gives a brief sketch of the growth and development of the Nose Creek Historical Society together with the Nose Creek Museum Heritage Foundation Society. Both societies have their roots in the pioneer settlement of the Nose Creek Valley.

Many of the families in the district arrived during that first wave of immigration in the early 1900s. These pioneers knew that they were part of a major historical movement. They brought sweeping changes to this land, and in turn the land changed the shape of their lives. It is little wonder that many of their children and grandchildren are fascinated by their stories; their lives then were so different from our lives today. As the world changed more and more quickly, the pioneers and their children recognized the need to preserve their memories of the past we all share.

The Nose Creek Historical Society generated the enthusiasm to discover, preserve and celebrate the district's history and heritage. This enthusiasm expressed itself in a variety of imaginative activities which have kept the movement alive to this day.

On the other hand, the prime movers of the Nose Creek Museum Heritage Foundation Society worked to collect and preserve the artifacts of our forebears for present and future generations. They built the museum which stands in the heart of the City of Airdrie, a credit to the thousands of volunteer hours spent and the generosity of its supporters.

Many places in the Nose Creek Valley still hold memories of the past. The Government of Alberta has designated two sites as Registered Historic Resources; the Nose Creek Historical Society has marked others with plaques and cairns; and local people have named parks as a memorial to deceased members of the community.

CHAPTER 1: NOSE CREEK HISTORICAL SOCIETY

The people who settled Western Canada at the turn of the century played an important part in the history of Canada, and many of them realized this. They passed on their memories of pioneering by writing diaries, letters and memoirs, but most of all by telling stories to their children and grandchildren. The story-tellers vividly recalled joyful events and tragedies, awe-inspiring natural calamities and wondrous changes in technology. As time went on and the pioneers grew older and passed away, younger generations became aware of the need to preserve the stories before they were lost forever. The Nose Creek Historical Society has worked to preserve the history of the area and its settlers.

After World War II ended, Alberta's population and economy grew rapidly and the province became much more urbanized. Several writers and institutions demonstrated their interest in the early and rural past of Alberta and Western Canada. Grant MacEwan published his first of many history books in 1948, and James MacGregor followed suit in 1949. The growing Historical Society of Alberta began to publish the *Alberta Historical Review* in 1953, and Hugh Dempsey became its editor in 1958. The celebration of Alberta's Jubilee Year in 1955 caused people to reflect on Alberta's past and its pioneer roots. Also in 1955, Eric Harvie endowed the Glenbow Foundation to house his collection of historical artifacts and of art. Employees of the Glenbow Foundation included Dempsey and others who collected historical papers, books and photographs to build up the Glenbow Library and Archives. The Foundation was also involved in creating Calgary's Heritage Park in 1964. Yet another source of interest in history was Canada's Centennial year in 1967, which inspired many local history projects.

Beginning in the 1950s, many districts in Alberta produced local histories, which usually consisted of many short pieces about individual families or about local institutions. In the late 1950s, the Rev. Stephen Wilk, then minister of the United Churches in Airdrie and Balzac, began to interview pioneers in the district for their memories of the early days. He published *Pioneers of the Faith*, a church history in 1962 and *One Day's Journey*, a local history of the Airdrie district, in 1963. Wilk put much more research and scholarship into writing *One Day's*

Journey than most local history committees were able to do.

People in the Nose Creek Valley area shared this increased interest in the history of their area. At a meeting around 1950, the Beddington chapter of the United Farm Women of Alberta (U.F.W.A.) first thought of writing a local history. One of the members at the meeting had told about how her family left England in the early 1900's to settle in Alberta. From this interesting story came the idea of a history of Beddington and its old-time residents. For some time the group discussed the possibilities of writing a history of Beddington.

The U.F.W.A. and U.F.A. (United Farmers of Alberta) became the F.W.U.A. and F.U.A. (Farm Women's Union of Alberta and Farmers Union of Alberta). Ruth Sandgathe, Margaret Bushfield and W.H. Evans were appointed as the book committee, with the later addition of Vivian Pole. In 1957 the Balzac and Beddington groups united to form the Nose Creek F.U.A. and F.W.U.A. Interest in the book went beyond the Beddington district, and Eileen Beaton, Gladys Campbell and Redvers Perry joined the committee to help produce a book covering the Nose Creek district from Calgary north to Airdrie. By late 1959 work on the book was well underway.

The F.W.U.A. organized an interesting Historic Program on December 14, 1960 to launch *The Nose Creek Story*. Redvers Perry described the events around the book launch in his diary:

...December 13th, 1960 - Fair and sunny. [Went] to Calgary to meet Buster Elliot and Jimmy Jones where the three of us appeared on CHCT Television to make a presentation on behalf of the Nose Creek Story. Apparently satisfactory according to local viewers. I [went] to Fred and Gladys Campbells to make up the program for tomorrow's Book Presentation. Heavy north west winds all night. Power disrupted, chores as usual.

December 14, 1960 - Had a huge crowd at Beddington Hall on this the opening night of the Nose Creek Story's Grand Presentation. Standing room only in some instances. I was chairman, and what a task!! I had to introduce all old timers of the past prior to 1905 and there were many present at that time. Also numerous thank yous for contributions well done. There were no end of program items. Then the Grand Presentation to the McDougall Church at Morley and the receiver was Chief Jacob Two Young Men where Mr. Bill Evans passed it on to him, with all the best wishes. The Chief made an outstanding acceptance address. His dancers did a war dance on the stage and the "Tom-Tom" drummer chanted a tune in Stoney language while they danced in gaily decorated leather and feathered headdress. Mother and Dad were there and Uncle Joe Davy. Kelly Davy was the photographer, with thanks. Leighton was an usher, and Doreen was in charge of Balzac's effort. The program ended at 12:30 am, with a delicious lunch served and sociability unending amongst us all.

December 15th, 1960 - Fair and mild. I made another appearance on Ruben Ham's farm breakfast for 5 minutes, relating the presentation of the Nose Creek Story Book at Beddington. Dorothy and I with Janet and Neil got groceries at the newly formed Co-op store on 16th Avenue and 5th Street NE, Calgary. This is the second Co-op store now in Calgary. I sold 3 more books today. I [went] down to Gladys Campbells at Balzac for a full report on sales. 300 sold, 100 more to be covered at once...

The 400 copies sold very quickly, at $4.00 each, and the book created a great deal of enthusiasm for preserving the history of the Nose Creek area.

At a meeting on April 4, 1963, the members of the Nose Creek Story Committee decided to change its name to the "Nose Creek Old Timers Historical Society", with ongoing business to be continued by the Society. A further name change took place afterwards, when Hugh Dempsey of the Glenbow Foundation was consulted on the matter. He pointed out that the Old Timers Association basically focused on social activities, and that the name "Historical Society" would include those interested in learning about the history of the area. He discouraged mixing of the two organizations and suggested that a Historical Society could have a broad spectrum of historic programs. A rural museum, picnic gatherings at historical places, and production of inexpensive maps were some of the ideas that could be developed under the new incorporated name.

Canada's Centennial in 1967 provided the opportunity to celebrate history in all sorts of ways. Many Nose Creek area groups collaborated to organize a large celebration on July 1st.

As well, undertakings which had been in the works for some time were completed as centennial projects, such as the society's historical map.

The Nose Creek Historical Map Project had started in 1959, and much of the information was collected around that time from oldtimers. Redvers Perry, Harry Pole, and Albert Anderson researched the map with a good deal of help from the oldtime families in the community. Their original research records are unique, having been written on anything that was handy at the time; for instance a researcher might talk with a farmer out in his field, who would pull an old cigarette box out of his pocket and write the information on it.

The map's area was expanded from the original size, and as printed in 1967, it covered about the same area as *The Nose Creek Story* and showed physical features, historic sites, and names of the owners of each quarter section. The mapmakers squared it off in the hope that neighbouring communities would produce their own matching maps, but this did not happen. Unfortunately, it is probably too late now to make more maps in such detail, as the oldtime informants have passed on. The Society originally sold copies of the map for $2.50 each, and had to reprint it to meet the demand. *A reproduction of the map is included in the back cover pocket of this book.*

Another centennial project completed by the Nose Creek F.U.A. originated in 1963, when the F.U.A. endorsed the concept of unveiling a plaque to honour the pioneers and settlers of the area. They did this at a dedication ceremony on November 2, 1968. The cairn stands on land in Huntington Hills in the northwest corner of the city of Calgary. This land was provided and improved by Carma Developers, who named the site Nose Hill Springs Park. The F.U.A placed the following items in the cairn: a scroll by Redvers Perry describing the history of Nose Hill Spring; some current newspapers, coins and stamps; photographs of the area before development; a Calgary Historical Society notice; a document signed by three oldtimers who were present; samples of wheat, oats and barley; and a copy of the Nose Creek Historical Map. Several groups, including Cub Scouts and Girl Guides, planted Colorado spruce trees to enhance the park, in a project sponsored by the City of Calgary Parks Department. After the Nose Creek F.U.A. disbanded, the Nose Creek Historical Society followed its example by unveiling 15 plaques to date, to honour various people or recall historic events.

On January 19, 1969, the Society met at the home of Redvers and Dorothy Perry, with Harry Pole as President. After a great deal of discussion, they agreed to initiate the process of incorporating the Nose Creek Historical Society, and took formal steps under the Societies Act of Alberta. The final incorporation was completed on September 17, 1969.

Another significant event occurred when the Beddington F.U.A. Co-op disbanded and turned over the residue of their money to the Nose Creek Historical Society. This generous gesture afforded the Society the opportunity to provide a scholarship or bursary throughout the schools in the area to promote history in the community. The approximately $2000 from the Beddington Co-op was invested, and the interest was to provide the funding for this project.

The accumulation of Historic Documents and Artifacts caused the Historical Society to purchase a fireproof vault for their permanent security. It remained at the home of Redvers Perry until the Society decided to transfer the vault with its contents to the Nose Creek Valley Museum. According to his diary:

Saturday April 4th 1970 - Fair, sunny, pleasant and mild. Chopped two mixers of grain for laying hens. Unloaded truck of barley, so we can go to Calgary for the vault.

Jack Osborne and I [went] to West End Auction for the $91.00 safe of the NCHS. Ralph Northcott, Walter Bushfield, and Harry Pole helped us load it. We took the safe doors to Head's Lock & Key and had the lock combination changed - cost $5.00.

Had a dinner of Chinese food and drove home very carefully in the old 1950 Mercury One-ton. The safe weighs 1000 pounds and has six shelves and a set of six drawers. It's a beautiful buy; an 1858 lock mechanism, and built in 1900, and so real Quality...

Another activity of the F.U.A. which the Historical Society continued was holding annual interdenominational church services. These services had their beginnings during the early settlement years.

The Dry Creek School was the site of the first local interdenominational services in 1905 and following years. Many of the pioneer residents at the time helped set in motion these services in the schoolhouse, which was later moved to Balzac to become St. Clement's Anglican Church. The pioneer families of Osia Rosenberger, William Northcott, Frank Davy, and Clem Perry were among the first to gather for worship. Clem Perry's diary states that he was lay reader for such services from 1905 to 1908. The interdenominational services were usually held around Thanksgiving time, after the harvest was gathered in.

In the 1950's the Beddington chapter of the United Farmers of Alberta held interdenominational services. The Beddington U.F.A. amalgamated with the Balzac chapter in 1957 to form the Nose Creek Farmers' Union of Alberta (F.U.A.), which carried on the services. Speakers gave sermons on various economic and political topics. As time went on, it was decided that these talks were more appropriately given at gatherings on Sunday afternoons at Balzac, Beddington or Airdrie, rather than at regular church services. The places of worship used for the gatherings later included Crossfield as part of the community interested in these services.

In 1972, the Nose Creek Historical Society held its first interdenominational service in tribute to Colonel Robertson-Ross, who visited the district in 1872. This was the first of a series of annual commemorative services which have continued to the present day, honouring a wide variety of people and events in the Nose Creek Valley area. These services alternated between Beddington, Balzac, Airdrie and Crossfield, however since 1988 they have been held at the Nose Creek Valley Museum. In a traditional fashion, the women of the community provided excellent refreshments. Various clergy, laity and speakers, were invited to provide leadership at the services. A number of Society members worked to create and install the plaques and cairns, including Jack Osborne, who also restored the sandstone quarry winch and a historic school bell. For each service, the Society produced and distributed a historical pamphlet; these were the original foundation for this book. Several members helped produce these pamphlets; some were researched and written by Redvers Perry, others compiled by him from the contributions of many local residents.

In recent years the Society has engaged in activities such as giving awards for historical essays by schoolchildren, organizing bus trips to historic sites and museums, and decorating prize-winning floats for the July 1st parade at Airdrie. Annual general meetings have included catered dinners and entertainment; music, poetry readings, and skits.

The Society promotes other historical undertakings. At the 1980 annual meeting, Dick Clayton gave a report on the local interest in a museum. The Nose Creek Historical Society voted to endorse the Museum Project, and many of its members worked on this project, which was completed in 1988. In 1990, the sites of the first schools were identified and they are now identified on the Topographical Diorama in the Nose Creek Valley Museum.

In 1992, Alice Hays requested that her road be named "Butte Hills Drive" for the hills which had been levelled to widen the Number 2 Highway. The Butte Hills (or Sharp Hills) had been landmarks and viewpoints for Indians and pioneer travellers for centuries. The Municipal District acknowledged the name and a sign was posted. The next year, Redvers Perry collected the names and pictures of the Councillors of the Rocky View Municipal District from 1904 to 1960. These were unveiled at the Rocky View Municipal District Office in northeast Calgary.

At the 1994 annual meeting, the Society unanimously endorsed a proposal to update the local histories and to combine the annual service pamphlets into a published book. A committee was struck to edit and produce a suitable book. Redvers Perry, Valerie Jobson and Stephen Wilk were named to the committee, and Floyd Reynolds and Eleanor Meyer joined it to assist in the production. A great number of people contributed the articles and photographs in the book.

Submitted by the Editorial Committee, Nose Creek Historical Society, 1996

(Left) Farmer's Union of Alberta Inter-denominational Service bulletin. (Above) Nose Creek Valley Museum: Part of the audience at the Nose Creek Historical Society's 23rd Annual celebration of Historic Themes, held June 26, 1994. Below: A typical Order of Service in which congregation participation is encouraged. Below right: The announcement page covered both church and FUA activities within the Valley.

```
              SERVICE OF WORSHIP
              3.00 P.M. Dec.14th
              1958.......Balzac

CALL TO WORSHIP: "This is the day that the Lord
hath made, let us rejoice and be glad in it".
HYMN#1 (In both Anglican and United Hymnaries)
INVOCATION PRAYER AND LORD'S PRAYER(Said byall)
THE MAGNIFICAT (READ RESPONSIVELY)Page 25 Ang.
                       &#747 United.
THE GLORIA PATRI (Said by all)
THE SCRIPTURE LESSON:St. Mathew 13:1-23 (The
                   Parable of the Sower).
AIRDRIE UNITED CHURCH OF CANADA CHOIR...ANTHEM
PRAYERS OF THANKSGIVING AND PETITION
ANNOUNCEMENTS
OFFERTORY HYMN#343 Ang. & #19 United.
DEDICATION OF OFFERING
REV. MR.E.A.JUSTICE ..............SOLO
HYMN#566 Ang. & 662 United.
ADDRESS: MR ROY FARRAN Editor of the North Hill
        News and the Rocky View News.
HYMN#514 Ang. &58 United.
BENEDICTION
         #       #       #       #
Mrs. E.Shuttleworth............Pianist
Mr. F.T. Pole.....................Usher
Mr.Cliff Rush.....................Usher
Mr.C.R.Perry.......................Usher
Rev.Mr. E.A.Justice B.A.,B.D. Minister of
Anglican Church in Canada at Balzac Alta.
Mr. Marvin Pickering Lay Minister of the
United Church of Canada at Beddington.
Rev. Mr. S.W.Wilk B.S.A., M.A.I.C. Minister
of the United Church of Canada Airdrie-Balzac
Columbia Pastoral Charge.
         #       #       #       #
JUBILEE GUEST BOOKS ON DIPLAY
We are greatful to have    pioneers exibit
the Balzac and Beddington Jubilee Books.They
are Mr.W.J.Church who pinneered in the early
1900's and Mr.P.C.Lewis who pioneered here in
1887. We extend to them many years of health,
wealth and every spiritual blessing as they
represent amony us many fine things of the
past.
```

```
              Announcements To Remember

Thanks: Our thanks to Mr. Gordon Church for
acting as Janitor for this occasion.
Our deepest appreciation to Mr. Roy Farran who
took time out of an already busy schedule to
bring us the address . We extend to him our
support and loyalty as he continues to contri-
bute to the life and work of our community.
To everyone who helped to make this event a
success we say thanks.
         #       #       #       #
THE OFFERING TO-DAY will be divided evenly
between the participating congregations as
they did not hold services to facilitate this
co-operative service. Envelopes will be given
to the respective treasurers and the loose
collection divided equally. GIVE GENEROUSLY as
the work of Christ in this area depends on you.
         #       #       #       #
TIMES OF SERVICES AND CHURCH SCHOOLS
BALZAC ANGLICAN CHURCH IN CANADA: WORSHIP 3.00
P.M. each Sunday the 1st and 3rd Sunday of each
month.Church School-Children retire before the
sermon.
BALZAC UNITED CHURCH OF CANADA: Sunday Church
School 2.00 P.M. Worship at 3.00 P.M. Every
Sunday.
BEDDINGTON UNITED CHURCH OF CANADA: Church
School at 1.30 P.M. Worship at 2.00 P.M. Each
Sunday.
         #       #       #       #
THE AIMS AND OBJECTIVES OF THE F.U.A.
        FOR    THIS    WE    STAND
PARITY FOR AGRICULTURE AND PRESERVATION OF THE
FAMILY FARM.
        OUR   OBJECTIVES   FOR 1959
Implementation of the Provisions contained in
the Price Support Legislation to the full mean-
ing and interest of the Legislation ---A new
Farm Credit Program - - -Long Term, intermediate
and short term financing.--Comprehensive Crop
Insurance program.-- Lower Freight Rates-----
These objectives change as needs arise.1959
Officers:Mr.Howard Pole-Pres.,Mr.Myrl Beaton-
Soc Treas. Past Pres.Mr. Dick Kibolewhite.
```

(Left) A Tribute to the Horse at the 3rd Historical Celebration, held at the Crossfield United Church, November 3, 1974. Stuart Walker, a Grade XII student at George McDougall High School reading his prize-winning essay.
(Right) At the N.C.V. Museum, Alice Hays, President, opens the 21st Anniversary celebrations of 'Tribute to Community Halls' June 21, 1992.
(Below)Congregation witnessing the unveiling of the plaque dedicated to the 'Hay Trail,' July 28, 1985. The Balzac United Church is in the background.

Executives of the Nose Creek Historical Society

Floyd Reynolds, 9th President.

Alice Hays, 8th President

Bill Walker, 7th President

Ray Howden, 6th President

Albert Anderson, 5th President

Jack Osborne, 4th President

Walter Bushfield, 3rd President

Harry Pole, 2nd President

Redvers Perry, 1st President.

The Nose Creek Historical Society float —dedicated to 'Pioneer Men' took first prize in the 1995 Airdrie Parade.

6

Walter Bushfield (left) presenting a Nose Creek Historical map to Earl Olson, a representative of C.P.R., October 20, 1991 on the occasion of the celebration of 'Tribute to the Calgary-Edmonton Railroad (1891-1990)' held at the Nose Creek Historical Society Museum, Airdrie, Alberta.

Paul Bertholet and Sharon Polk of the 'Wild Rose Blue Grass Society' entertain at the 1992 Annual Meeting of the Society.

The late Stan Anderson and Eleanor Meyer (above) do a duet at the Nose Creek Historical Society Banquet and Annual Meeting, February 24, 1992.
Stan and Chris Anderson take a bow (above right) after a performance at the Nose Creek Historical Society Banquet and Annual Meeting, February 24, 1992.

Bobby Turner (right) strums and sings at the October 20, 1991 celebration. He regaled the audience with songs of the railroad, including 'The Wreck of the Old '97.'
Redvers Perry (left) paying tribute to the six community halls in the Nose Creek Valley, June 21, 1992.

7

Celebrating Historic Themes

1. ***Prairie Mountain Fiddlers*** *entertaining after the Annual Supper meeting of the N.C.H. Society, February 20, 1995 at the Balzac Hall.*
2. *Stephen Wilk introducing the* ***Renfrew Ramblers****, a band he started 20 years ago, at the Annual 1996 meeting of the Society. He is still active in the band.*
3. *The* ***Renfrew Ramblers*** *provide entertainment at the 1996 Annual Meeting of the N.C.H. Society. Historically, Renfrew district was the location of the Canadian Air Training Plan airport during World War*

II. It is now a housing development. The airport hangar, currently the Calgary Boys' and Girls' Club, is being considered for designation as a historic site.
4. *The Nose Creek Historical Society float entered the Airdrie Parade paying tribute to community halls.*
5. *Bob and Betty Collier (Ballroom winners) dancing to the music of the* ***Prairie Mountain Fiddlers*** *at the Society's February 1995 Annual Meeting at the Balzac Community Hall.*

Celebrating Historic Themes

Above left, A plaque marks the original Johnston-Stevenson Stopping House (1879-1900). The marker was fashioned by Colin Fraser and Alan Horne by welding a plate bearing the message onto a steel base.

Above right, Redvers Perry deposits a time capsule at the RCMP Centennial Cairn, Aridrie October 19, 1974. (l-r) Ray Howden, Redvers Perry, Walter Bushfield.

Left: Col. Robertson Ross Memorial Cairn dedicated in Airdrie, November 2, 1974. (l-r) RCMP Officer, Mrs Louise Dorval of Castor (daughter of the late Johnston Stevenson), Hon. Clarence Copithorne, Minister of Highways. Unveiling the cairn is the Mayor of Airdrie, Darrel Bennett.

Below: Marker commemorates Rev. George McDougall's untimely death. This plaque is located in the Beddington area, off Centre Street North, Calgary.

Historic Themes

Three plaque site erected 1988 to mark the Johnston Stevenson Stopping House site , 4 miles north of Airdrie.

Leighton Perry and Betty Cardiff standing by grave marker for Bessie and William Stevenson and an unknown stagecoach passenger

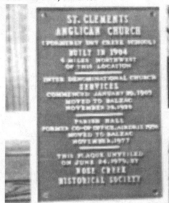

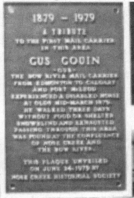

The three plaques on church cairn. Erected between the Anglican and United Churches, Balzac.

At the top of Nose Hill: (Left to right) Albert Anderson, Redvers Perry, and Harry Pole display the Nose Creek Historical map.

10

1. *R.C.M.P. Sgt. Lawrence Bracewell relates history of the force at the unveiling ceremony at the Airdrie Cairn, November 1, 1974.*
2. *Don Beddows boom truck lowers Cairn rock at Airdrie Water Tower site, October 1974.*
3. *Preparing a site for the plaque dedicated to unmarked graves at the Stopping House of Johnston Stevenson, 4 miles north of Airdrie.*

Plaques for Posterity

This page, clockwise from top left: Presentation of the Nose Creek Historical Map at the Balzac Community Hall, December 10, 1967: (Left to Right) Albert Anderson, Harry Pole, Lt. Governor Grant MacEwan, Redvers Perry, and Keith Rosenberger.

Top right: Nose Creek Historic Society flag stand. Designed and erected by Jack Osborne and daughter-in-law, Merle, it was donated to the society, January 26, 1976.

Below: 1902 pioneers, Harry and '28' Bill Northcott as they welcome a 42-car convoy at the first stopping house (Johnson Stevenson) north of Fort Calgary, November 3, 1974.

Left: President of the Society, Ray Howden, Darrel Bennett, Airdrie Mayor, Louise Dorval, a daughter of the late Johnston Stevenson, participate in the unveiling of the plaque. Clarence Copirthorne MLA, Alberta Roads Minister is in the background.

Plaques for Posterity

Top Left: *Jack Leslie, Mayor of Calgary officiates at the Nose Hill Spring Cairn Ceremony, November 2, 1968. Mr. & Mrs. Clem Perry and Mr. & Mrs. Art Bushfield were the last of the pioneer homesteaders of the Valley to sign the document placed in the time capsule.*

Above: *The Airdrie water tower provides the backdrop for the historic cairn.*

Left: *Citizens of the Valley gather to witness the unveiling of the Nose Hill Spring ceremony, November 2, 1968*

Nose Hill Springs Cairn, November 2, 1968: (l to r) Clem Perry, Harry Pole, Arthur Savill, Redvers Perry, Albert Anderson, and Walter Bushfield.

Honours and Awards

NCHS EXECUTIVE BOARD OF DIRECTORS, 1996: *Holding up certificates awarded in recognition of their leadership and support for the goal of launching of this book project are: (back row, l to r) Harold Watters, Lorne Fowler, Earl Northcott, Bill Lawson, Leighton Perry, Howard Pole, Don Copley, Valerie Jobson. (Front row, l to r) Alice Hays, Floyd Reynolds, Stephen Wilk, Erma Lawson, Eleanor Meyer, Redvers Perry. Anne Hollands (inset, right), and Bobby Turner, (inset top left) are also on the Executive, but were absent when this picture was taken.*

President Alice Hays presenting Life Membership to Bill Walker at the Annual Meeting, February 24, 1992

Balzac Community Hall, after the Banquet, Annual Meeting, and Concert: *Bill Walker, Merle Osborne (standing in for Jack Osborne) and Ray Howden after receiving their Life Membership certificates, February 24, 1992.*

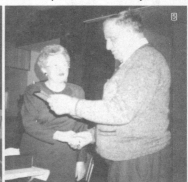

After years of dedicated service: *Lorne Fowler receives a certificate of recognition.*

President Alice Hays presenting Life Membership to Ray Howden at the Annual Meeting, February 24, 1992

14

CHAPTER 2: THE NOSE CREEK VALLEY MUSEUM STORY

As can be seen in the story of the Nose Creek Historical Society, the idea of a museum came up a considerable time before the actual down-to-earth movement got under way. At Unifarm meetings in the 1970's, it was discussed informally by Lorne Fowler, Bert Clisdell, Dick Clayton, Ellen Johnston, Harry Pole, Don Copley, Don Evans, and Jack Osborne. From its inception, the purpose for developing a museum was to preserve and display materials dealing with the Human and Natural History of the area of Balzac, Nose Creek, Airdrie, and Crossfield.

The first correspondence concerning the formal establishment of the museum was sent on March 14, 1980, when Dick Clayton, a prime mover in establishing the museum, made contact with the Province of Alberta's Historical Resources Foundation in Edmonton.

Ian Patterson, Museum Advisor for the Community Recreation and Cultural Division of the Government of Alberta, accepted an invitation from Dick Clayton to attend an organisational meeting in Airdrie. The meeting was held at 7:30 pm on April 22, 1980 at the Airdrie Regional Agricultural Centre. Ken Reid, President of the Airdrie and District Agricultural Society, welcomed 25 attendees. Redvers Perry chaired the meeting and Grace Fowler acted as secretary. Patterson shared his expertise in every area, from canvassing for funds to the problems and pitfalls of establishing a museum.

The first people elected to the Board of Directors of the Museum were Dick Clayton as Chairman and Grace Fowler as Secretary/Treasurer. Also attending were Jack Osborne, Bert Clisdell, Walter Bushfield, Ray Howden, Ken Reid, Don Copley, Redvers Perry, Harry Pole, and Ellen Johnston.

The operation of the museum was seen as the main concern. On June 2, 1980, a Museum Board meeting was held at the home of Dick and Alma Clayton, with 13 in attendance. These included Jack Osborne, Bert Clisdell, Walter Bushfield, Ray Howden, Ken Reid, Don Copley, Redvers Perry, Harry Pole, Grace Fowler, Lorne Fowler, and Ellen Johnston. Some attendees were present as interested individuals; others represented Airdrie Unifarm Local, Nose Creek Historical Society, Airdrie Chamber of Commerce, or Airdrie & District Agricultural Society. Walter Bushfield moved that a Museum be established in Airdrie. The motion was seconded by Ray Howden and carried unanimously.

On October 28, 1980, Chairman Dick Clayton asked to be relieved of his duties due to ill health; consequently, Walter Bushfield was elected as Chairman. The board met regularly every month at the Airdrie Information Centre, where they had lengthy discussions about how they were going to finance the museum; they did not have a bank account at that time. They were also concerned about finding a location which would meet the approval of everyone.

In 1981, at the Airdrie Trade Fair, the Museum Board had a booth where they displayed interesting artifacts and a suggestion box for people to submit names for the museum. The board then had a short list of 17 names to choose from. They agreed on "Nose Creek Valley Museum", because the area around the museum, from Crossfield to the Bow River, drains all waters into the Nose Creek.

The Nose Creek Valley Museum Society was created in order to achieve the following objectives:
1. To encourage the preservation of the Nose Creek Valley Heritage
2. To encourage the accurate recording of pioneer life in the Nose Creek Valley Region
3. To encourage and assist residents to share their accumulated knowledge in languages, music customs, crafts, and their special skills with others
4. To encourage instruction in 'Heritage' arts
5. To encourage and provide the opportunity to display collections of articles having historical significance

6. To encourage the assembly of accurate archives
7. To encourage the recording in various forms of stories and tales of pioneer life in the Nose Creek Valley region
8. To encourage community participation
9. To encourage and promote a better appreciation of the Nose Creek Valley region through meetings, lectures, and demonstrations
10. To encourage exhibition of the crafts and special skills of residents of the region
11. To encourage the restoration of artifacts

On August 18, 1982, the Society opened its first bank account, depositing $183.15 to the account of the Nose Creek Valley Museum. The additional monies received came from various government agencies, business donations, a canvas of the rural people who resided in the Crossfield, Airdrie, and Balzac areas as well as a door to door canvas of the people who resided in Airdrie. These funds were enough to build the museum.

Denise Boutin, Manager of the Tower Land Mall, gave the Museum the use of unrented retail sites where artifacts on display generated a lot of interest and the Board were able to hold their meetings. John Graham, Director of Parks and Recreation for the City of Airdrie, addressed the board on different occasions in regard to possible available sites for the Museum within the city. Linda Manarin, Recreation Director of Programs for Airdrie, made recommendations on how to operate a museum.

The Museum Society considered many sites in Airdrie in their search for a suitable location. These included a place near the Scout Hall close to Fletcher Park and the Modular Home Park, the west side of Main Street in Summerhill district; the Spens Jensen farm, the old Royal Canadian Mounted Police (R.C.M.P.) building on First Avenue Northeast, a site on the old secondary highway, the current site of the R.C.M.P. detachment, and a site near the twin arenas.

After thoroughly discussing the pros and cons of every suggested location, the Society finally decided to build on Main Street in the Summerhill district. This site had the advantage of easy access from the main highway, enough space for a rest area and picnic tables, and a bus line which ran nearby. It offered the possibility of renting meeting rooms to the community and was a good location for a tourist information centre.

Soon the actual construction got underway with six construction companies submitting their bids. After lengthy discussions the board decided to accept the Provincial Steel Building bid. One persuading factor in their bid was that the company would hire many of their subtrade workers from Airdrie. The Beddoes Construction Company offered to reduce the cost of stripping and levelling the museum site as their contribution and the Bushfield family donated the gravel. Thus, these two companies were engaged.

The Sod Turning was held October 15, 1986, attended by Mayor Ron Davidson, the city aldermen, Ian Patterson, representing the Community Recreation and Cultural Division of the Provincial Government, and Connie Osterman, M.L.A. After the ceremony the shovel was duly chromed and displayed.

On February 28, 1987, the 8400 square foot building was completed, and in 1993, a 4000 square foot addition was built. Over half a million dollars were spent in building the museum; a grant from the Provincial Government covered about half of it, while federal and municipal grants plus other generous donations covered the rest. These donations from individuals, businesses, and the City of Airdrie helped to build the museum and continue to support its operation. In the future, as in the past, this investment will continue to yield returns to the community and future generations by helping to record its history and collect and animate an accurate portrayal of pioneer life.

On June 11, 1988, the original building was officially opened with a ribbon cutting ceremony by Mary Bushfield, age 89 (mother of Walter Bushfield). A pair of hand sheep shears had been diligently polished and sharpened for the occasion, however they would not cut the ribbon. The ever resourceful Mrs. Bushfield produced from her handbag a pair of scissors; she had put them in her bag that morning, just in case. The scissors did in fact cut the ribbon, officially opening the Nose Creek Valley Museum.

Redvers Perry wrote in his diary for that day:

...Sunny westerly winds, pleasant.

Rose at 4:45 am. Cultivated on summerfallow; finished at 10:45; hurried home to make ready the old 1925 Dodge to go to the Museum grand opening.

Gordon Taylor, MP; Connie Osterman, MLA; His Worship Mayor McLean, Airdrie; Deputy Reeve Konchuk; all there to give an address and presentations, plaques, flags, etc. Mr. Howard Pole gave an opening blessing, and most fitting remarks. They even had myself as one of the honored platform guests, and asked if I would say a few words about the capsule contents, etc. Mr. Jack Osborne was a very good chairman. Mrs. Mary Bushfield cut the ribbon to open the Museum, and made a nice address, brief and most fitting for an 86-year-old lady [89]. Walter Bushfield gave an address as the devoted chairman of the museum for many, many, untiring years. He sure has put many hours in there, and mile upon mile of back and forth travel. In that regard I sincerely thanked him, with crowd applause, and a hand shake.

The RCMP color party was present in NWMP antique uniforms, and the current full dress of 1988 on the second member, as two were on duty for the occasion, and escorted each one of us guests to the platform and respective seats. With the Flag Flying and O Canada, the ribbon was cut by Mrs Bushfield. The museum had a large attendance. Christopher Minhinnett came home with me in the 1925 Dodge down Highway #2. Floyd and Nan Reynolds invited us up to their home, as members of the board, an evening of fun and laughs until 12:15 am; and home.

A most memorable day!

An article in the *Five Village Weekly* about the opening described some of the exhibits:

...To say the least the museum is impressive as it honors not only the pioneers of the area but the native Indian tribes of Blackfoot, Blood and Peigan. It houses one of the largest displays of Indian artifacts in Western Canada. Most of these artifacts were donated by Brian Gablehouse and Dick Buchanan.

About one-third of the floor space is represented by the Crossfield district. Among the displays is a blacksmith's shop, which contains the original equipment of Gus Rettschlag, a Crossfield blacksmith. There is also an impressive display of a house, once owned by Crossfield residents Mr. and Mrs. Bill Walker, who are active members of the Nose Creek Historical Society, the group most responsible for collecting the artifacts for the museum. Furniture in the house display was gathered mostly from Crossfield and district residents.

A display of A.E. Bowers and Company, General Merchants, depicts the warm atmosphere which was enjoyed by the early pioneers when they went shopping.

A tribute to those area residents who fought in both World Wars is also on display, as well as artifacts commemorating the early farmers within Nose Creek...

On June 18, 1988 the Society sealed a Time Capsule containing reports of the official opening and other historic items, to be opened on June 11, 2088. We hope that future generations will reflect on the community's past and will perpetuate the knowledge of the foundations laid by their ancestors.

Julian Fell was the first curator and had the difficult task of planning the layout, choosing and co-ordinating exhibit content and displays, creating a topographical diorama of the area recognized by the Nose Creek Valley Museum and all the minute details of beginning a museum. He was followed by Gideon Smith, whose many interests included the geological display. More recently, Colleen Granda has maintained the founding spirit of the Museum, further developed the displays, and promoted every interest of the many segments of the community.

The Museum boasts over 9000 Indian artifacts which were collected by Brian Gablehouse over a period of 27 years. This represents a significant contribution to the museum and is of such calibre that it is a major historical resource for the native community and for those with an interest in prehistoric and native artifacts.

An outdoor display of the Calgary & Edmonton Railway was set up to recognize the importance of the railroad to the history of the Valley. The caboose, rails, and ties were brought to the site on December 2, 1991, free of charge by Finnie Trucking and D.B.C. M.M. Stroick and Earl Olson of the Canadian Pacific Railway (C.P.R.) and Museum Curator Colleen Granda obtained this display for the Museum. John Baisch obtained a railcar from the C.P.R., supplied most of the furnishings for the caboose, and put together the telegraph exhibit which visitors find so interesting.

The Airdrie Artists Guild, formed in September 1988, has used the Museum meeting rooms for classes, sessions, seminars, and a twice yearly Art Show and Sale. In return the Artists Guild has provided a velcro hanging system for changing displays in the Museum.

The Nose Creek Valley New Horizons group was formed September 20, 1988. The first government grant, for $5,236.00, purchased wood-working tools for the workshop, two spinning wheels, and a previously owned 45 inch weaving loom. The New Horizons group and the Museum Board members restored artifacts, built swings, lawn chairs and tables, and completed many other projects in order to help meet the Museum's operating expenses. In 1993 the New Horizons provided the funds to finish the interior of the new addition.

In February 1989, the Nose Creek Museum Heritage Foundation Society was established with the long range purpose of providing operating funds for the Museum.

The Museum Board of Directors has been very active over the years in establishing suitable policies and directions with the help of volunteers. In 1994 and 1995 the Board added garage and bake sales to their fund raising repertoire, in order to augment the Museum's funds. The Board has been responsible for operating the Museum on holidays and weekends.

The Museum has had many volunteers since its inception. Nan Reynolds has catalogued the donated items; Sunni Turner worked on brands; Walter Saville programmed the computer; Karen Copley worked on the computer; Alma Clayton, Fred Bushfield, Phil Klassen, John Sylvester, Don Drebit, Leighton Perry, Bernie Knittle, John Church, Dick Clayton, Walter Bushfield, Albert Gibeau, Harry Pole, and Ross Giles are just a few of the many people who have donated their time and talents towards operating the Museum.

The first officers of the Society were Dick Clayton as Chairman, Roger Lee and Harry Pole as Vice Chairmen, Grace Fowler as Secretary, and Elaine McCracken as Treasurer. Other board members were Jack Osborne, Dolly Dunne, Redvers Perry, Ben Abramson, Lorne Fowler, Ellen Johnston, Bert Clisdell, Ken Reid, Eldon Stafford, Ralph McCall, Ken Howe, Ray Howden, Clay Cathcart, Irene Echlin, and Andrew Benedix. The 1995 board consists of Walter Bushfield as Chairman, Earl Northcott as Vice Chairman, Erna Klassen as Secretary, and Marge Uhrich as Treasurer; other board members are Don Copley, Albert Gibeau, Floyd Reynolds, Bobby Turner, Ross Giles, Mary Hickley and Nick Visser.

Since its inception the Nose Creek Valley Museum has been an important source of information for schools and everyone interested in the early history of the district. It has also been an attraction to people residing in or visiting Airdrie, and a repository for many things that are dear to the memories of our first residents.

Submitted by Walter Bushfield, Don and Karen Copley, Margaret Giles, Mary Hickley, Earl and Ronnie Northcott, and Floyd and Nan Reynolds; additional information from Dick Clayton, Redvers Perry and *Five Village Weekly.*

How the Gablehouse Collection Evolved

As a boy, Brian Gablehouse was keenly interested in nature, Indians, and collecting rocks, fossils and minerals. These were his boyhood hobbies. He constantly watched the ground while out hiking through the hills along the Bow River Valley around Bowness, on the west edge of Calgary where he grew up. Brian had always wanted to find a real Indian artifact such as an arrowhead or a stone hammerhead. In March of 1963, quite accidentally, he found an excellent stone hammerhead protruding from the bank of the lagoon in Bowness Park. The park area held a series of old Indian campsites and buffalo drives, and Brian and his friends had already discovered numerous buffalo bones near the Wood's Christian Homes. In the 1950's, the father of a friend had found several arrowheads and scrapers in his yard in this same area of Bowness, while putting in his lawn. Brian recalls looking with envy at these artifacts many times, and wondering if and when he would find a real Indian artifact of his own.

Brian's first find launched him into a hobby that would literally sweep him away over many years and consume most of his spare time. Throughout the middle to late 1960's, he scoured the Bowness, Bearspaw Dam, Springbank, Montgomery and Silversprings areas. He combed any exposed soil on dirt roads, trails, cowpaths, cut-banks, and in the few cultivated fields of the region. He found numerous stone scrapers and broken arrowheads and, finally, his first complete arrowhead, all within the first year of collecting. An iron arrowhead, two musket flints, some trade beads, all from the Indian Fur Trade period; a perfect stone drill, another stone hammerhead, two nearly-whole buffalo skulls, and several more intact arrowheads were amongst his Bowness and area finds during his first few years of collecting.

In the following years Brian expanded his field of operations over large areas of Southern and Central Alberta, and parts of Saskatchewan and Montana. He also made a few finds in more distant regions: in parts of British Columbia, Manitoba, North Dakota, Indiana and Florida. He collected actively whenever time permitted in literally hundreds of locations, usually in cultivated fields. Over the years the collection grew to some thirty thousand items, all found by him personally. His best finds, some six thousand in number, are on permanent display in the Nose Creek Valley Museum.

A number of the artifacts exhibited are from areas near Airdrie, and are labelled as comparatively local finds. Artifacts from Symons Valley, Balzac, West Nose Creek and Madden areas are identified in the displays. Included are several very ancient, rare and exceptionally well-made artifacts of several different types. He has attempted to make the labelling in the displays as interesting and informative as possible.

The section of the Gablehouse Collection containing Indian craftwork, such as weapons, costume items, regalia and tipi furnishings of local tribes, all consists of replicas made by Brian over a twenty year period. He made all of these as authentic and faithful as possible to the traditions of these tribes, giving special consideration to bead colours and designs, types of feathers and featherworking methods, overall composition, form and appearance. They were researched from original specimens in numerous museums and collections in Alberta, Montana and Saskatchewan, and from many early photographs of Indians in those regions. All of the articles in the displays are of his own composition, adapted from originals. Brian made them to look typical of the more spectacular and visually appealing Indian implements and regalia of the 1840's to early 1900's era. This span of time was the most colourful of Plains Indian history, including the late part of the fur frade era, the end of the nomadic buffalo hunting days and the inter-tribal wars, ending in the early reservation times.

In these displays, he has attempted to convey some of the artistry and flamboyance of the regalia of local tribal groups such as the Blackfoot, Peigan, Blood, Sarcee and Stoney tribes, and of some other tribes who at times forayed into Southern Alberta, such as the Gros

Ventres, Plains Cree, and Kutenai. In the labelling of these items, he has pointed out various typicalities of some, and unusual features of others, as well as the tribes they represent and the time periods when the original artifacts were made and used.

"Many of these replicas took scores of hours to complete, particularly the heavily-beaded items. The making of Indian crafts such as these is very painstaking, time consuming, and is not recommended for those lacking patience or long-range work habits," says Brian. "Come to think of it, I'm not certain I would want to do it all again, but if others enjoy it, I will consider it my reward."

Submitted by Brian Gablehouse, 1996

Brian Gablehouse was born in Victoria, B.C. in 1947, and grew up in Calgary. He attended King George School and Bowness Composite High School until 1966, and worked at various jobs, including topographical and geological drafting, taxi-driving, and construction. He worked for many years for Calgary Handi-Bus Association, a transportation service for disabled people.

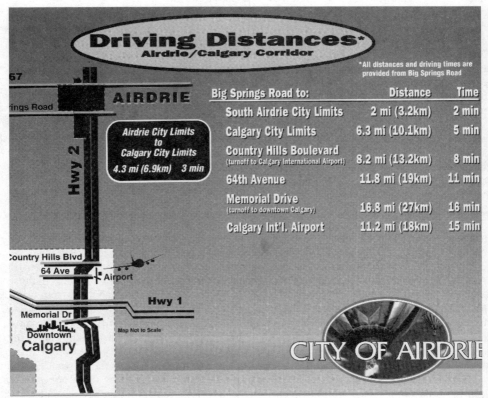

Driving Distances*
Airdrie/Calgary Corridor

*All distances and driving times are provided from Big Springs Road

Airdrie City Limits to Calgary City Limits
4.3 mi (6.9km)   3 min

Big Springs Road to:	Distance	Time
South Airdrie City Limits	2 mi (3.2km)	2 min
Calgary City Limits	6.3 mi (10.1km)	5 min
Country Hills Boulevard (turnoff to Calgary International Airport)	8.2 mi (13.2km)	8 min
64th Avenue	11.8 mi (19km)	11 min
Memorial Drive (turnoff to downtown Calgary)	16.8 mi (27km)	16 min
Calgary Int'l. Airport	11.2 mi (18km)	15 min

Map Not to Scale

CITY OF AIRDRIE

Courtesy, City of Airdrie. 1996

Official opening of Nose Creek Valley Museum, Airdrie, June 11, 1988

At the opening (left to right): Julian Fell-Curator; Redvers Perry-Historian; Howard Pole-Prayer leader and blessing; Mayor McLean-Airdrie; Government representative, Mrs Raymond (Mary) Bushfield-Ribbon Cutting; Connie Osterman-M.L.A.; Gordon Taylor-M.P., Ottawa; Jack Osborne-M.C.

Walter Bushfield, President, sod breaking at the Museum, October 25, 1986.

21

Dick Clayton, First Museum President.

Walter Bushfield, present Museum President

Nick Visser replaced Ralph McCall on the Board of Directors.

Original Museum Board of Directors, 1988-89 *(left to right): Albert Gibeau, Earl Northcott, Walter Bushfield, Harry Pole, Marg Uhrich, Don Copley, Julian Fell, Elaine McCracken, Bobby Turner, Mary Hickley, Dick Clayton, Jack Osborne.*

Present Board of Directors *(left to right): Walter Bushfield, Nick Visser, Dick Clayton, Mary Hickley, Coleen Granda (Curator); Back Row: Don Copley, Marg Uhrich, Erna Klassen, Bobby Turner, Floyd Reynolds, Albert Gibeau, Earl Northcott, and Ross Giles.*

Lorna Switzer of Melody Makers supplies the entertainment at the 1996 Annual Meeting of the Museum Association.

The Yankee Valley Room of the Museum, 1996: audience at the Museum's Annual Dinner meeting being entertained.

Ralph McCall, on behalf of the museum archives, is seen receiving a donation of an original Stock Show Advertisement. (Redvers Perry, who preserved the valuable article and laminated it for extra protection, is making the presentation.)

Rose Grisdale plays the accordion for the Annual Meeting audience.

Walter Bushfield chairing the Annual Meeting, aided by Erna Klassen, Secretary

23

Float in the July 1, 1982 parade promotes the museum project.. C.R. Perry is driving the 1947 "2" Minneapolis Moline. Harry Pole and Ray Howden are the passengers.

Celebrating the Museum's 1ˢᵗ Anniversary in period costumes and vintage cars. Museum building is in the background.

May Fraser Standing beside her car and (inset) cutting the 1st Anniversary cake, June 11, 1989

Sunni & Bobby Turner, and Tony Turner do some entertaining at the museum's 1st Anniversary, June 11, 1989.

Muriel (Mason) Clayton was the first school teacher north of Fort Calgary. Her children (pictured right) donate her piano to the museum, September 11, 1988. (L-R) Earl, Joe, Eddy, and Dick Clayton. Gwen Copley is seated on the piano stool.

Nose Creek Valley Museum Displays

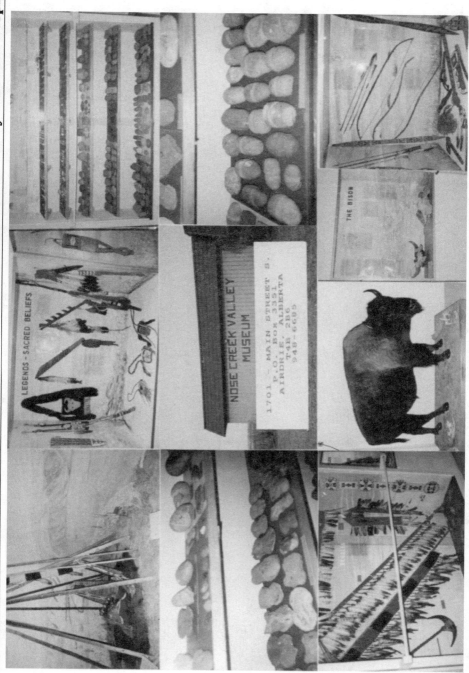

NOSE CREEK VALLEY
MUSEUM

1701 - MAIN STREET S.
P.O. BOX 3551
AIRDRIE, ALBERTA
T4B 2B6
948-6685

LEGENDS - SACRED BELIEFS

THE BISON

Courtesy Nose Creek Valley Museum

Courtesy Nose Creek Valley Museum

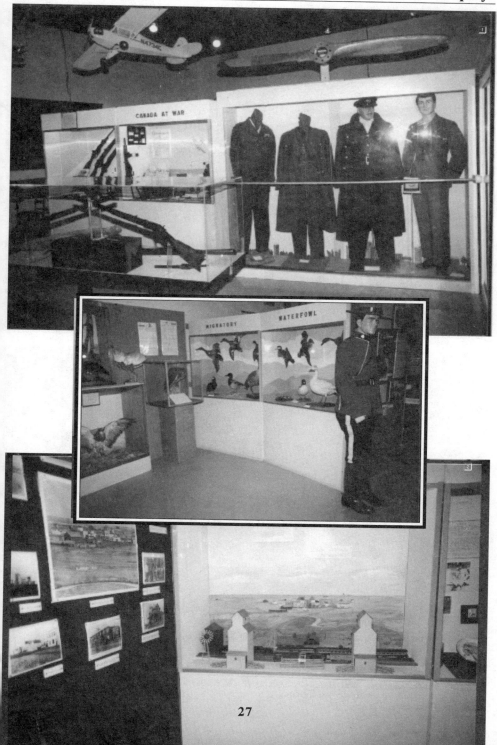

Sundry art on display.

A secretive denizen of the Foothills, and sometimes of the Valley

Nose Creek Valley Museum: a variety of brands, along with tools, harnesses, and implements.

LIST OF CONTENTS PUT IN CAPSULE JUNE 6, 1988

1. Rockyview Square Dance Club material.
2. United Church, St. Clements Anglican Church of Balzac, Nose Creek Historical Society.
3. Balzac Hall history and pictures and Balzac 4H Club.
4. Material relating to Rocky View School District.
5. Brochures on Western Breeders, Balzac.
6. Material relating to Airdrie and District:

Local Historian Redvers Perry placing time capsule at the Nose Creek Valley Museum, Monday June 25, 1988 at 9:20PM.

- Faith Community, Anglican, Balzac and Beddington, Airdrie United Church.
- Northern Trails Riding Club.
- Airdrie Museum, known as Nose Creek Valley Museum consisting of the original letterhead and envelope and Museum Badge.
- Airdrie and District Rodeo Posters and Pamphlets.
- West Airdrie R.E.A. information.
- Goldenrod 4H Club booklet.
- Airdrie Wheat Pool literatures, coins and pin and Rockyview M.D. Badge.
- *Airdrie Echo*, relating to Olympics '88 contributed by Pat Clayton.
- Crossfield newspaper—*The Chronicle*—and Fire Service Awards brochure contributed by Mr. & Mrs. Bill Walker.
- 1987 Big Game Regulations contributed by Bob Turner, Cochrane, Alberta.
- Calgary and Canmore & District Brochures.
- Nose Creek Historical Society Brochures for 1977, 1978, 1981, 1983, 1984, 1985, 1986 and 1987.
- *Western Farm Leader* (newspaper) donated by Annie Clark.
- Calgary Heritage Network 1987 Directory.
- Assortment of current stamps donated by Redvers Perry, Balzac.
- The Canadian Dollar (the Looney) 1987 donated by Redvers Perry, Balzac.
- The Nose Creek Historical Map.
- Assortment of current Canadian coins: 1-5-10-25 cent pieces and a paper $1.00 bill. Donated by C.R. Perry.
- Stamps: 1-2-3-5-10-25-37; larger 37-50-57 and 74 cents.
- Knights of Columbus material including coin of "Alberta Papal Visit".
- Short history of Casa Loma Community Association. Short history of Casa Loma School.
- The "Enoch Anderson" History.
- "My Story" by Berenice Shuttleworth.
- The Scottish Society of Airdrie Executive June 1988—Goal, including sample of tartan and pin.
- R.C.M.P. - 4 badges and shoulder crest.
- Nose Creek Valley Museum Commemorative Brochure official opening June 11, 1988.
- Paper cuttings of Museum Opening from *Airdrie Echo, Rocky View Times* and *Rockyview Five Village Weekly*.
- Other paper cuttings of current local and world interest.
- 1st Sept, 1905 Tax Receipt from Local Improvement District 13-A-5 ($2.00 for 1/4 section)
- Canister with numerous slides of Airdrie & District—by Curator Julian Fell
- Introduction and Background of Museum March 14, 1980. Mr Ryan Patterson Guest Speaker
- May 13, 1986 *Blizzard Story* by Floyd Reynolds
- Colour snapshot of Olympic Torch being carried in Airdrie
- Message from Mayor Grant McLean of Airdrie
- Message from Mayor Curtis of Crossfield
- Piece of Blue Ribbon Cut During Opening Ceremony
- Wheat Pool Budget Copy, June 1988
- Municipal District of Rocky View Statistics & Map #44
- Colour photograph of Nose Creek Valley Museum Executive 1988
- Autographed copy of all in attendance at Grand Opening June 11, 1988
- Final Letter Outlining the Current Day's Activities From Us All, With Best Wishes From 1988 to Residents Here In 2088

Signed June 27, 1988 just previous to final drop at 9:20PM
Signed C. Redvers Perry

CHAPTER 3: HISTORIC RESOURCES PRESERVED

Alberta Provincial Historical Resource crest incorporates the Alberta Coat of Arms..

The Nose Creek Valley is a fascinating region, recognized for both its unique natural features and rich history. The commemoration of the Valley's heritage began over three decades ago and the tradition then established has been maintained by the Nose Creek Historical Society. The Society is joined and supported in its endeavours by the Province of Alberta which officially recognized the importance of its heritage resources in 1973 with the passage of the Alberta Heritage Act. This legislation not only reflected the need to preserve, study, and interpret Alberta's historic resources, but also to promote public appreciation of our heritage. Today the legislation is called the Historical Resources Act (as revised in 1980); the Ministry of Community Development is responsible for preserving, protecting, and presenting Alberta's unique cultural and natural history; and the Historic Sites Service, created in 1974 as a Branch of the Department, oversees the heritage resource work of the Province.

In the Nose Creek Valley, the influence of the Historic Sites Service is most obvious at the Dickson Rest Area south of Crossfield on Highway 2. It is here that a piece of the history of the Valley is presented to travellers who stop to rest on their journeys south. Panels with historic photos interpret early settlement in the area, the McPherson Coulee, the Calgary-Edmonton Trail, and the Dickson-Stevenson Stopping House. While the Service presents the story of the Valley's best-known stopping house to the general public, the Nose Creek Historical Society ensures that the location of the Dickson-Stevenson Stopping House will not be forgotten. The Society installed a ground-level plaque in 1975 to mark the site of the popular rest stop and in 1981, it also recognized the Trail at the same location by erecting a plaque commemorating the last used portion of the original Calgary-Edmonton Trail. Known as the Dickson-Stevenson Trail, this portion of the familiar route was used until 1931.

As transportation routes in the Valley changed over time, so too did the cultural landscape of the area. While remnants of many historic trails, pathways and railbeds are still visible in the Nose Creek Valley, only long-time residents remember the Old Rocky Mountain House Trail, the well-worn path leading from the Symons Valley sandstone quarry site to the City of Calgary, and the Beddington rail siding, to name but a few. Without a record of what once was, important aspects of our history can be neglected and ultimately forgotten. For example, Lackner, that city surveyed for development in an area very close to the Beddington siding and widely promoted in 1912, ended up as a small cluster of commercial structures of which no evidence exists today.

The Historic Sites Service began the Provincial Historical Resources Inventory Programme in 1976 with the specific purpose of providing a photographic and location record of sites and structures generally constructed before 1940. In the Nose Creek Valley, the Inventory documents the historic buildings and structures of Beddington, Balzac, Airdrie, Crossfield, and Madden. The Inventory reveals, for example, that Crossfield has maintained its historic character. Its main street is built on a pattern typical of many rural Alberta communities that came into existence because of the railway. The commercial buildings are located on one side of the street; on the other is the railway right of way which borders the tracks and the grain elevators. The buildings on Crossfield's main street include the Oliver Hotel and Canadian Imperial Bank of Commerce constructed in 1928 and a food store, garage, and lumber yard also of pre-1935 construction. In the residential area of Crossfield, the Inventory shows a variety of architectural styles that were used in the building of houses. Osler Avenue offers a particularly good selection of residences built between 1904 and 1935.

The Inventory of Crossfield also includes a structure not common to the typical rural town, the 1932 flat-roofed Baptist Church on Strathcona Street. While the architectural style of the Crossfield Baptist Church stands out, the very number of churches recorded in the Inventory reveals the importance of religion to the lives of Nose Creek Valley settlers. The Madden United Church was constructed in 1942. The Airdrie United Church, built in 1922, boasts a spire that is 19 metres high. In Balzac, the 1928 St. Clement's Anglican Church and the 1945 Balzac United Church share not only a common church yard, but also a similar history. Both buildings were redundant district school houses moved to the community for renovation and reuse.

The strong religious traditions of the Nose Creek Valley settlers were officially recognized by the Province with the designation of the Reverend George McDougall Cairn as a Provincial Historic Resource in 1976. Provincial Historic Resource designation indicates that the site has received the highest level of recognition awarded by the Province. It is acknowledged as being of outstanding provincial significance; it is associated with an important aspect of Alberta's natural or human pre-history or history (an event, a theme, or a person); and/or it is of outstanding palaentological, archaeological, or architectural merit. The Nose Creek Valley has one other Provincial Historic Resource within its boundaries, a natural feature that was designated in 1979. The Airdrie Erratic, commonly referred to as the "Twin Rocks", is part of the Foothills Erratics Train which stretches from Jasper to Montana. This massive split rock was likely deposited by a glacier advancing eastward and southward from the Jasper area some 50,000 years ago.

The Province has a second level of designation, the Registered Historic Resource. Registered Historic Resources are significant to the region or community in which they are located and provide good examples of an aspect of Alberta's natural or human prehistory or history. While there are no Registered Historic Resources acknowledged in the Nose Creek Valley at this time, the region possesses a wealth of heritage resources. The Madden Buffalo Jump reveals the natural features of the coulees which were used by First Nation populations in Alberta's pre-history era. Many farmsteads in the Valley possess original buildings from the first days of settlement. There are rural homes such as the Frank Collicut house in McPherson Coulee and the Beaton home in Symons Valley which were constructed of sandstone quarried in the region. The community centres of the Valley speak of the active social lives of the residents. There are also the regional landmarks such as the Big Rock just east of Centre Street in Calgary, an erratic that acted as a beacon to travellers in poor weather conditions.

The Nose Creek Valley is a region with a long, interesting past that combines natural and human history. The Nose Creek Historical Society is to be commended for its efforts in commemorating the history of the Valley and the Historic Sites Service will continue to join with the Society and area residents in projects which preserve, protect, and present the Valley's heritage resources.

Submitted by Judy Bedford, Planning Advisor,
Alberta Community Development, Historic Sites Service

Memorial Parks in Nose Creek Valley

Charles Butler Memorial Park - Symons Valley

In the summer of 1980 the Charles Butler Memorial Park was dedicated to the memory of Charles William Butler, who was killed on January 1, 1980 in a sour gas well accident. Born and raised two miles north of the park location, he was a well respected and dedicated farmer who enthusiastically supported community projects, one being the working alongside other far-sighted individuals to establish this recreational park in Symons Valley.

Although it was in its early stages of development at the time of his death, he had enjoyed many baseball games and times of great fellowship here with the community friends he held so dear. Today the park is well maintained and enjoyed by the Nose Creek Community Club and surrounding neighbours.

Submitted by Mrs Doris Butler

Morley James Park

Morley James Park was created after Jim Creasser had the idea to use a municipal reserve parcel that seemed to be destined to be sold to the highest bidder. Donations were solicited from the Municipality, the Lottery Foundation through the local MLA, Connie Osterman, and local Airdrie businesses. A non-profit group, the Butte Hills Park Association, was formed and several volunteers in the neighbourhood got together and decided what they wanted. They built the playground after leasing the four acres from the municipality and providing liability insurance.

The Park would probably have been called "The Buttes Park" except for the untimely death of Calgary Firefighter Morley James. Morley had worked with Jim Creasser and was a friend of Jim and of all Calgary Firefighters. He had been raised in the area, and his wife Debbie was raised only one half mile from the Park. The Morley James Park is a perfect memorial to a loved and respected man who was taken from his family, friends and fellow Firefighters while performing his duty to the citizens of Calgary and working at the job he loved.

A large rock was dug from an adjoining field and placed at the corner of the Park. Ken Bilben, a longtime friend, placed a plaque on the rock, and another Firefighter engraved the name Morley James Park on the face of the rock.

The ongoing maintenance of the park, including grass cutting, is done by local residents. Trees and shrubs have been donated and as donations are received, more will be added. Many children are enjoying these facilities that were needed in the area.

Submitted by Jim Creasser

Text of the Plaque:

This Park is Dedicated in Memory of MORLEY JAMES, Calgary Firefighter, who gave his life in the line of duty July 13, 1992. Morley grew up in the Balzac area, attending school in Airdrie, and served his community as a volunteer firefighter before joining the Calgary Fire Department in 1975. He will always be remembered by his family, friends and fellow Firefighters. Those who met Morley were fortunate to have had the opportunity of his friendship. His dedication to duty is an inspiration to us all.

Knud Jensen Park

This park began in 1967 as a Centennial Project with a tree planting program and a wading pool was added. It was named after Knud Jensen, a Village Councillor for 18 years, who had died suddenly in 1965. A wading pool had been added to the park, and in 1975 a skating arena was built there.

CONCLUSION TO PART I

We have seen how two separate organizations with an active, overlapping membership have worked together like a team of horses pulling a load up a hill toward common goals and objectives. They have brought the memories and artifacts of past generations to places where present and future generations can learn about and reflect on the history of the people of the Nose Creek Valley. In turn, we see that these organizations are part of a larger effort to understand the history of our province and nation. The written chapters and the photographs of these activities have underlined the importance of remembering and preserving our heritage and historic resources.

A northern view of the Bewes Trail.

A memento of the Ice Age: *scarred by time, elements and graffiti, Big Rock is located north on Centre Street in an area called Harvest Hills.*

A typical farm in Symons Valley, 1996.

This erratic rock doubles as a signpost for Morley James Park, located northeast of Balzac. (1996 photo).

The 1996 photo represents a view of the Beddington siding. A water tower for steam locomotives used to be located here.

This plaque is dedicated to Morley James, a Balzac firefighter who died in the line of duty.

A general view of the Beaton farmyard, including what is considered the oldest barn in the area.

A close-up view of an Airdrie erratic rock, split by forces of nature. Picture taken from the south end of the site

PART II: THE ORIGINS OF THE VALLEY
INTRODUCTION

Part II of this anthology describes some of the early history of the Nose Creek Valley. Because there are no written records, we rely on the physical evidence as interpreted by geologists and archaeologists. Thus we learn how the valley was formed by melting glaciers as the Ice Age ended, and how people moved into the area perhaps 10,000 years ago. We can observe how these first people found food and shelter, but can only guess at other parts of their lives; their beliefs, feelings and social interactions.

We know more about the people who lived in this area within the past few centuries; they have strong oral traditions about their beliefs and way of life. They often named sites in their long-time home for important historic events that had occurred there. They kept winter counts by memory; lists of years, with each year remembered by a local incident or a significant event. They sometimes drew pictures on a buffalo robe to tell an individual's life story, or painted pictures on rock walls. As well, we have written records about the Indians from fur traders, missionaries, and others who traded or dwelt with them.

A brief summary of the archaeology is included to give some perspective of early human activity in the area. Many more archaeological sites have not yet been excavated to reveal the riches of the Valley's prehistoic past. We have also included a 1960 geological map to indicate the many geological formations under the surface of the Valley, which gave rise to the gas and oil industries of today.

CHAPTER 4: GEOLOGY OF NOSE CREEK AND ITS TRIBUTARIES

Nose Creek and its tributaries, McPherson Creek and Beddington Creek, lie neatly in a rectangle defined by Townships 25-1-W5 and 28-2-W5 (*see geological sketch map*). Very simply, the bedrock of the whole area was buried under a mantle of material left by melting glaciers at the end of the Ice Age about 15,000 years ago. Torrents of melt water from melting glaciers further to the west cut the deep channels of McPherson Creek and Beddington Creek through the mantle of glacial material and into the sandstone bedrock. Blocked by an ice mass to the east, the McPherson and Beddington melt water resulted in a lake or series of lakes along what is now the north-south valley of Nose Creek. Draining of these lakes cut the steeper sided lower reaches of the Nose Creek valley between the mouth of Beddington Creek and the point where Nose Creek joins the Bow River. The upper reaches of Nose Creek west of Crossfield were formed by normal drainage since the Ice Age.

The bedrock is spectacularly exposed in sandstone cliffs along the rims of McPherson and Beddington Creeks. Geologists know these rocks as the Porcupine Hills Formation because those hills are made of the same rock. Some 55 to 60 million years ago, before the Rockies had been pushed up, rivers flowing eastward from central B.C. brought great quantities of sand and silt to what is now western Alberta, where these sediments were laid down to become the Porcupine Hills Formation. At that time Alberta was part of a vast low-lying area of forests, lakes, swamps, sluggish rivers and deltas which extended northwards from the Gulf of Mexico. The Rockies were formed later when great pressures from the west caused hard, deeply buried sediments to buckle and fracture into sheets which rode up on one another. The low plains on which the Porcupine Hills Formation had been laid down prior to the rise of the Rockies were also raised to approximately their present elevations.

After the uplift of the Rockies, the land surface of Western Canada was and remained much as it is today, that is with high mountains in the west and a general slope down towards Hudson Bay in the northeast. Rivers such as the Bow eroded valleys which wended to the northeast. Before the Ice Age, neither Nose Creek nor its tributaries existed in their present form. In fact, when we study the courses of McPherson and Beddington Creeks and the course of Nose Creek south of Crossfield, we notice that the trend is most decidedly not to the northeast. A drastic modification of normal downslope drainage must have taken place. The present configuration of these valleys is almost entirely due to events which took place during and subsequent to the Ice Age.

Nobody knows for certain why the Ice Age began or what set of geographic and atmospheric factors combined to initiate the accumulation of ice in the Northwest Territories and in the Rocky Mountains about a million years ago. We do know that in these regions more snow fell each winter than melted the following summer. The increasing weight of snows caused the lower layers to become solid ice. With further increases in the overburden of snow, the ice began to flow towards areas of less weight or pressure. Thus the glaciers of the Ice Age were formed, and thus they started to flow. The glaciers pushing out in all directions from north central Canada formed an enormous, thick ice sheet which geologists know as the Laurentide or Continental Ice Sheet. The tongues of ice pushing out through the mountain valleys of the Rockies coalesced when they reached the plains to form the Cordilleran or Mountain Ice Sheet. Inevitably the two sheets met. Of particular interest to us is the fact that a section of the meeting line lies just east of the north-south portion of Nose Creek Valley.

Glaciers have enormous destructive and carrying power. They break off pieces of the rocks over which they pass and carry these pieces with them as they flow. Some of the pieces of rock transported by the ice are large, even house-sized, but most of the material is in the form of tiny grains. Eventually, when a glacier melts, it releases its load of silt, sand, pebbles and boulders and this material forms a mantle known as glacial till over the surface of the bedrock. Typically the till is rather like a plum pudding with larger pieces lying in a fine grained matrix *i.e.* there has been none of the sorting one might expect if the material had been laid down by flowing water. In addition the pieces are quite angular in outline. The glacial tills left by the melting Continental ice to the east of Nose Creek contain numerous boulders of granite and other crystalline rock which were carried by that ice from the Northwest Territories. To the west of Nose Creek the boulders are seen to consist of sandstone, quartzite and occasionally limestone, which were carried here by ice from the Rocky Mountains. Boulders which were carried by ice to be laid down far from their sources are called glacial erratics or just erratics. Harder rocks are more commonly found as erratics. Although limestone makes up a major portion of the Rocky Mountain ranges, limestone erratics are rather rare in the till left by the mountain ice. Limestone is a relatively soft rock and is easily ground down to fine particles by glaciers. These particles do make up much of the till matrix, with the result that soils to the west of Nose Creek are often quite limey.

A very distinctive group of erratics is well represented in the Nose Creek area. These erratics are formed of extremely hard quartzite which originated in the mountains close to Jasper. Many of the fused quartz grains are quite pink in colour and as a result the rock is easily identified. In addition the extremely tough nature of this rock has resulted in very large erratics and the course of Jasper ice is easily traced eastward to Edson and then southeastwards and southwards as far as the US border. It appears that the Jasper ice met the Continental ice somewhere in the vicinity of Edson. The stronger Continental ice deflected the Jasper ice southeastwards and coalesced with it along its edge.

Further south, other streams of ice from the mountains met the coalesced Jasper/Continental ice and were in turn deflected to the south. This more southern mountain ice did not contain distinctive erratics and as a result its course cannot be so easily traced. The Jasper erratic train is so well known that it has been given the name "Foothills Erratic Train". Its most famous example is the Big Rock near Okotoks, but the Nose Creek area also contains some fine examples. Numerous medium sized erratics of the Foothills Train lie on the surface in Sections 9 and 16 of 28-1-W5. A very large example lies close to Nose Creek and the C.P.R. track in L.S.D. 6, Section 26-25-1-W5. Another large one, known locally as "Split Rock" lies in the bed of Nose Creek just east of Calgary's 4th Street extension (*see illustration*), and yet another a little over a mile north of there in the Northwest corner of Section 22-25-1-W5. This excellent example lies in a hollow, but its flat top is easily seen as one drives by. Not surprisingly it has been given the name "Flat Top" by local residents. If interested people examine these examples, they will be able to recognize others when they come across them.

When the climate improved about 15,000 years ago it was Rocky Mountain ice which began to melt first. The Continental ice, having a more northern source, continued to accumulate and push out. Its edge presented a north-south barrier of ice just east of present day Nose Creek. The flow of melt water from the west was blocked by this barrier and as a result a lake or series of glacial lakes developed along much of the north-south portion of the Nose Creek Valley *i.e.* the portion between Crossfield and the mouth of Beddington Creek. The scene at the time would have been one of great wonder, with dirty melting glaciers visible as thick caps on hills to the west, raging torrents of melt water flowing out wherever they could find passage between the melting masses of ice, and Lake Nose reflecting the high wall of Continental ice which formed its eastern shore. Perhaps icebergs dotted the surface of the lake. Two especially tumultuous torrents rushed into the lake from the valleys of what are now called McPherson Creek and Beddington Creek. At first these valleys were quite shallow but the torrents of melt water quickly cut through the unconsolidated glacial till and deep into bedrock below. When we look at a map showing these channels we are struck by the sinuous pattern they form. To fully interpret the sudden changes in course is not possible now. One can only assume that the streams found routes where thinner ice occurred and that they hastened the melting along these routes. Thus the sinuous courses may have had their initiation on the surface of the melting Mountain Ice Sheet. There can be no doubt, however, that these channels were formed by much more powerful streams than those which now occupy them. This is also the case along the lower reaches of Nose Creek south of the mouth of Beddington Creek. The waters of the glacial lake eventually became so deep that they topped the barrier at the south end of the lake and rushed southwards, cutting the lower Nose Creek valley and joining the melt water in the Bow valley at a point where the Bow River takes an abrupt course change from east to south. This deflection of the Bow is another result of the Continental ice barrier to the east.

The Continental Ice Sheet started to retreat sometime after the north-south course of Nose Creek had been cut. As it melted it left its own features on the surface of the prairies to the east of our area. Most of these have no bearing on Nose Creek, but the beautiful group of hillocks just east of Highway 2 near Balzac should be mentioned. These unfortunately consist of gravel and are being steadily excavated and removed. They used to present the only beautiful scene along a very monotonous stretch of highway.

It is believed that plant life returned quite quickly to the barren landscape left by the retreating ice and that the prairies soon attracted herds of grazing animals together with their predators, including humans. It is likely that humanity first came to Nose Creek as early as 10,000 years ago.

One last geological event left an interesting if not very visible mark on our area. Approximately 6850 years ago a violent volcanic explosion occurred in Oregon. More violent than the event at Mount St. Helens during recent times, the Oregon explosion left a large crater now occupied by Crater Lake. Geologists and archaeologists have given the name "Mount Mazama" to that old volcano, and the layer of ash that it produced is known as the Mazama Ash. Unlike the Mount St. Helens ash, the Mazama Ash did reach our area, and a thick layer of white dust fell from the sky. Occasionally one can find this layer of ash a foot or two below the present surface or exposed in river banks. It has become a useful time marker for archaeologists, who can immediately assign an age greater than 6850 years to human artifacts found below the layer.

Who knows what future geological events will affect our area? Some believe that we are merely enjoying a respite from prolonged cold weather and that the glaciers will come again. If they do come back, one wonders whether or not humans will be able to stop them from destroying everything in their paths as before. Meanwhile, let us be thankful for our beautiful environment and continue to enjoy our Nose Creek valleys.

Submitted by Desmond Allen; Artwork by Elizabeth Allen, 1966

Desmond Allen was born in Ireland and attended Kings Hospital School in Dublin. During World War II he lived in London, England and later served in the Royal Navy. After the war he took his degree in Geology at the University of London. After a spell of teaching in London he and his wife Elizabeth, who is an artist, came to Alberta where he worked in various geological, geophysical and management positions until his retirement in 1990, and where Elizabeth became well known in her field. He is an avid gardener and naturalist.

Archaeology in the Nose Creek Area

A number of archaeological sites have been identified in Calgary, including a campsite in Hawkwood which was first used over 8000 years ago. Situated along the Bow River Valley in Calgary, the Happy Valley bison kill site and many others have been studied by archaeologists. The evidence indicates that buffalo hunters used the river valley almost continuously from 4000 years ago to roughly 200 years ago. Nose Hill has at least 42 sites, includings tipi rings, a stone cairn, and stone tool workshops.

At least one site in the Nose Creek Valley has been studied. The H.M.S. Balzac Site (EhPm-34), between Balzac and Beddington, was first identified in 1978 during a Historic Resources Impact Assessment. In 1982, Thomas H. Head excavated it as part of his Master of Arts in Archaeology degree program. He found hundreds of stone tools including projectile points and scrapers, thousands of bison bone fragments, as well as bone tools, ceramics, and a couple of beads. The site had been in use for at least the past two millenia, as a campsite and a processing site for buffalo which had probably been killed nearby. In a 1985 article, Head concluded:

...the site is one of the best Late Prehistoric campsites presently known. It affords a unique opportunity to examine cultural changes as well as indications of site patterning that continue through time and possibly across stylistic boundaries for the majority of the Late Prehistoric Period.

Other sites in the Nose Creek Valley which may be more recent include the buffalo jump and rock paintings at Madden.

Submitted by Valerie Jobson. 1996

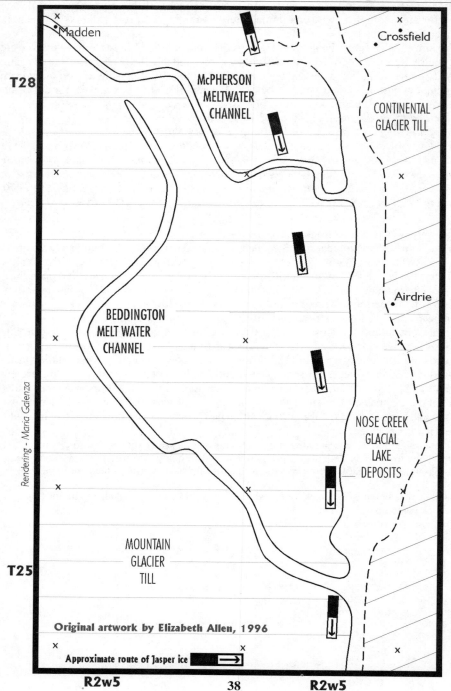

Madden

Crossfield

T28

McPHERSON
MELTWATER
CHANNEL

CONTINENTAL
GLACIER TILL

Airdrie

BEDDINGTON
MELT WATER
CHANNEL

NOSE CREEK
GLACIAL
LAKE
DEPOSITS

MOUNTAIN
GLACIER
TILL

T25

Original artwork by Elizabeth Allen, 1996

Approximate route of Jasper ice

Rendering - Maria Galenza

R2w5   38   R2w5

Big Chief Symon Rock located on the east side of Country Hills Golf Course. General view faces north west. Courtesy Nose Creek Valley Heritage Resources Photo Report by Rino M Basso, Senior Preservation Advisor, Alberta Community Development (1966).

The 'Split Rock,' Beddington Creek: Artist's concept by Elizabeth Allen, Calgary, Alberta.

40

Chapter5: The Indians in the Nose Creek Valley

by Hugh A. Dempsey

The area along Nose Creek has been associated with the Blackfoot Indians from the time of recorded history. The three tribes of the Blackfoot Nation -- the Bloods, Peigans, and Siksika—camped, hunted, and travelled through the area. The creek provided a good camping place where water was readily available and in winter they moved into the foothills for protection from winter storms. Nose Hill (or "The Nose" as it is shown on early maps) was an excellent vantage point to search for buffalo herds.

McPherson Coulee was a favourite winter camping place. There is a buffalo jump near Madden which dates back hundred of years. Nearby is a shallow cave where a number of faded rock paintings can barely be seen. Archaeologists believe these were made by Shoshoni Indians who, in the 1600s, probably occupied part of the Alberta plains as far north as the Bow River. The Madden site is the most northerly evidence of a Shoshoni presence. The belief is that the Blackfoot tribes moved to the easterly part of their hunting grounds in the 1600s and in their absence, tribes from across the mountains filled the void. In the latter part of the century they returned and drove the enemy tribes away.

Interestingly, McPherson's Coulee's name in Blackfoot, "namahkanes", means " weapon entrenchment" or "gun entrenchment," indicating that a fierce battle had occurred there.

Of the three Blackfoot tribes, the Siksika are the ones most readily identified with the Nose Creek and Calgary areas. For example, in the winter of 1871-72, Big Swan of the Bad Guns band was camped south-east of Nose Hill while Many Necklaces, leader of the Strong Ropes band, was just across the river. Sometimes the Bloods, under their leader Rainy Chief, also camped in the area. The Stoneys, who now have a reserve at Morley, seldom ventured farther east than the Big Hill at Cochrane, unless they knew the Blackfoot were off hunting on the plains.

Of all the creatures in the Blackfoot hunting grounds, the buffalo was the most important to the Blackfoot. Its flesh was called "real meat" to distinguish it from all other flesh, which was believed to be inferior. In addition to its use for food, the buffalo provided many articles of value, such as clothing, lodges, tools, drinking vessels, and storage containers.

In the years before horses, the Blackfoot had several methods of hunting buffalo. One of the most popular was the surround, where hunters encircled a small herd and systematically killed them with lances and arrows. Another method was for a hunter to cover himself with the skin of a calf or wolf and approach close enough to the herd to kill an animal. In winter, he might wear snowshoes and trap a buffalo in deep snow.

But perhaps the most successful method was know as the buffalo jump, or "piskun." In the autumn or early winter, hunters enticed a herd to the edge of a cliff -- such as the one at McPherson's Coulee -- and then stampeded them over the precipice. Those not killed by the fall were slain with arrows and spears. In this way, a Blackfoot band might gather enough food to last for several weeks. Buffalo jumps usually had a northern exposure, so that the carcasses remained in the cool shade where they could methodically butchered and the meat dried for later use.

When a jump site was chosen, rocks or other materials were formed into piles, creating two drive lines which extended for a mile or more back from the cliff, diverging like the arms of the letter V. The piles were high enough for a man to hide behind during the actual hunt. Once the buffalo had been herded within sight of the drive lanes, hunters took their places behind the rock piles. As the buffalo entered the wings of the drive lines, they suddenly jumped up, waving robes and shouting. As the buffalo stampeded forward, they plunged over the cliff to their death.

About 1725, the Blackfoot obtained their first horses. These were descendants of those brought by the Spanish to Mexico which over the years had passed northward from tribe to tribe. Freed from the confines of foot travel, the Blackfoot expanded their methods of hunting, changed their concept of wealth, and increased their personal possessions. The horse enabled them to hunt buffalo by the chase, to carry more objects in their travels, and to move greater distances in a day. Their tipis increased in size, winter pasturage became a consideration, and more leisure time became available to develop artistic and religious pursuits.

Next to hunting, the most important change in daily life caused by the acquisition of the horse was in the rapid escalation of warfare. Not only were incursions by hunting parties more frequent, particularly from across the mountains, but horses, themselves became source of plunder. Small raiding parties coursed the plains in the summer, seeking out enemy camps and attempting to run off their horse herds.

The annual movements of a Blackfoot band were governed by the climate and buffalo. In winter, the tribes gathered in small camps along the wooded river bottoms, such as the Bow, where they were within reach of the buffalo. In such winter camps, lodges were strung out for miles among the protective cottonwoods of a river valley. In spring, the people scattered out onto the prairies, hunting, gathering new tipi poles from the foothills, visiting trading posts, and replacing worn out lodges and equipment. In early summer they congregated for their Sun Dance and other ceremonies. From there they again drifted onto the open prairies, sometimes staying in large camps if there were enough buffalo to support them. In the fall, they again made their way to the foothills and their winter camp-sites.

In daily life, there was a clear division of labour between men and women. The wives were considered to be the owners of the tipis and furnishings. Their duties included the pitching and striking of the lodge, packing, cooking, making most clothing, caring for infants, training girls, and the general maintenance of the lodge. The men provided food, protected the camp, manufactured certain religious and war objects, looked after the horses, trained boys for manhood, and carried our raids upon enemy tribes.

In their cycle of life, at the time of birth, the father arranged to have a child named by an elder or an important person in the camp. For a girl, the name would remain with her for life. If the name was chosen by a man, it usually related to his own war experiences, so many Blackfoot women's names were of a warlike nature, i.e., Good Gun Woman, Attacked at Home, or Nice Killer. Others were religious names, i..e., Giving to the Sun Woman, Buffalo Stone Woman, or Morning Star Woman, while a few were purely descriptive, i.e., Pretty Woman.

Boys were given their first names in a sweatlodge ceremony when they were a few weeks old but they could earn a succession of new names as a result of their own war exploits, hunting prowess, or religious experiences. Thus, Blackfoot chief Crowfoot was known successively as Shot Close, Bear Ghost, Packs a Knife, and Crowfoot. Boys might be named for an elder's war experiences but more often a family name no longer in use would be passed down to them. Typical names are White Bull, Calf Chief, Running Wolf, Weasel Horse, and Falling Over a Bank.

Boys and girls played together until about five years of age, when a male relative began training the boy and older sisters or the mother began to give chores and to teach the girl. At an early age all children were taught to be obedient, to respect the numerous religious taboos, and to be quiet in the presence of elders. Boys were taught to use the bow and arrow, to guard and round up horses, to follow game trails, and to be warriors. Girls began by collecting firewood and water, and learning the arts of cooking, tanning, sewing and packing.

Boys often joined war parties at the age of thirteen or fourteen, acting as servants in making fires, cooking and looking after the camp while the warriors scouted and raided enemy camps. This was considered to be part of a boy's training and he did not expect to share in the booty. After two or three trips as a servant, he could expect to be invited to join a raiding party as a full member.

Marriages were arranged between the father and his prospective son-in-law or between the two male parents. Polygamy was common, with the number of wives being limited only by a man's wealth. Several men were said to possess four or five wives while one Blood reportedly had 23 wives kept in two separate tipis. Normally the first wife was the senior member of the female household and was referred to as the "sits beside him" wife. Often she was consulted about additional marriages or sometimes took the initiative in encouraging her husband to take further wives to share the work load. It was common for a man to marry one or more sisters or to marry the widows of his brother.

When a man was near death, he was dressed in his best clothes and his personal possessions were placed around him. After he died, the camping place was abandoned as the Blackfoot believed his spirit would remain in the area before leaving for the sand hills. The tipi which the man died was sometimes sewn up and used as a death lodge; otherwise the body was placed on a scaffold, in a tree, or on a high hill. A man's horse might be killed to provide him with transportation to the sand hills.

In 1874, the North-West Mounted Police came west and a year later they built Fort Calgary. Such was the respect that the Indians held for the Mounted Police that the Canadian government was able to arrange for a treaty in 1877. Through this treaty, the Indians surrendered their hunting grounds of approximately 50,000 square miles in return for reserves, treaty money of $5.00 a year, as well as an assortment of farming implements, cattle, tools, flags, medals, and ammunition.

By 1880, the last buffalo herds were virtually destroyed and the Blackfoot were forced to go onto their reserves. The Siksika moved to Gleichen, the Bloods to Standoff, and the Peigans to Pincher Creek. By the 1990s, these Blackfoot tribes have come a long way in becoming part of Canadian society. Many have entered the profession, including law, nursing, education, administration, social welfare, and agriculture. Many graduates have returned to their reserves to utilize their education while others gravitated to the cities. However, agriculture continues to be the primary occupation available on most reserves.

FOR FURTHER READING

Hugh A. Dempsey, *The Amazing Death of Calf Shirt, and Other Blackfoot Stories.* Saskatoon: Fifth House Limited.

Hugh A. Dempsey, *Indian Tribes of Alberta. Calgary:* Glenbow Museum.

John C. Ewers, *The Blackfoot: Raiders on the Northwestern Plains,* Norman: University of Oklahoma Press.

George Bird Grinnell, *Blackfoot Lodge Tales. Lincoln:* University of Nebraska Press.

KEY TO RESERVES

Blackfoot
1. Blood
2. Peigan
3. Blackfoot

Sarcee
4. Sarcee

Stoney
5. Eden Valley
6. Stoney
7. Bighorn
8. Paul
9. Alexis

Plains Cree
10. Sunchild
11. O'Chiese
12. Montana
13. Samson
14. Ermineskin
15. Louis Bull
16. Saddle Lake
17. Goodfish Lake
18. Frog Lake
19. Kehiwin

Woodland Cree
20. Enoch
21. Alexander
22. Duncan
23. Sturgeon Lake
24. Grouard

25. Sucker Creek
26. Driftpile
27. Swan River
28. Sawridge
29. Lubicon Lake
30. Whitefish Lake
31. Wabasca
32. Beaver Lake
33. Heart Lake
34. McMurray
35. Cree
36. Cree
37. Little Red River
38. Tallcree
39. Tallcree

Chipewyan
40. Fitz/Smith
41. Chipewyan
42. Fort McKay
43. Janvier
44. Cold Lake

Beaver
45. Boyer River
46. Clear Hills
47. Horse Hills

Slavey
48. Upper Hay River
49. Upper Hay River
50. Upper Hay River
51. Upper Hay River

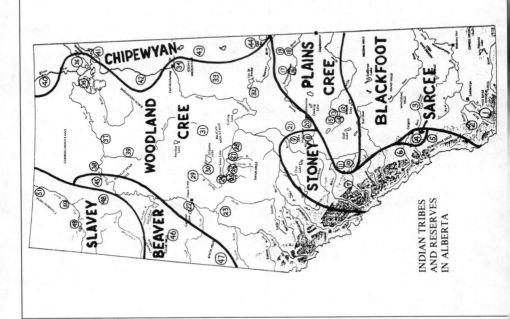

INDIAN TRIBES
AND RESERVES
IN ALBERTA

From *Indian Tribes of Alberta*, by Hugh A. Dempsey. pp. 86 & 87, Glenbow Museum, 1979

44

After the Riel Rebellion of 1885, Father Lacombe took some of the "loyal" Indians to Montreal and Ottawa. He is seen here with Crowfoot (left) and Three Bulls at Montreal.

Photographed in the 1880s, Bear Shield, a Blackfoot Indian, wears a "war shirt" which indicates his prowess in battle.

Rev. John McDougall, Chief Samson, Chief Pakan, Robert B. Steinhauer, and Chief Jonas Bigstoney travelled to Ontario in support of the missionary enterprise and a peaceful settlement of the west.

Artist Frederic Remington depicted a famous battle between the Crees and Blackfoot in 1866. Father Lacombe had been in the Blackfoot camp and was wounded when he tried to stop the fighting.

Artist Sydney Hall recorded this meeting between Crowfoot and Canada's Governor General, the Marquis of Lorne, in 1881. It took place at Blackfoot Crossing, south of Cluny.

Leading chiefs of the Blackfoot nation were painted by artist Paul Kane in 1848. **Left to right:** Little Horn, an unidentified chief, White Buffalo, Big Snake, another chief, and Iron Collar.

A Blackfoot man and woman are seen here with a horse travois.

The Blackfoot were still nomadic buffalo hunters when this picture (above) was taken by the Royal Engineers in 1874.

In 1881, an artist sketched (right) the river flats at Blackfoot Crossing, south of Cluny. The Marquis of Lorne, Governor General of Canada camped on this side of the river. The Blackfoot camp is on the far side.

Chiefs of the Blackfoot nation were photographed on a visit to Regina soon after the CPR was built in 1883. Front row left tor right, are Crowfoot, Sitting on an Eagle Tail, and Three Bulls. Back, interpreter, Jean L'Heureux, Red Crow, and Constable Piercy.

A Blackfoot woman, the wife of White Horn, carries her baby on her back. This picture was taken in Calgary about 1886.

Blackfoot horse racers at High River in the 1890s.

This view of a Blackfoot camp shows a tepee painted with a deer design.

46

CONCLUSION TO PART II

We have seen that the Nose Creek Valley was formed by retreating glaciers, and that afterwards humans gradually moved into the area. For thousands of years, these people travelled over the plains, relying on the buffalo for almost all of their needs, and seeing gradual changes in technology. Those who lived here in the 1700's and 1800's saw enormous changes take place as a result of contact with immigrating Europeans; changes in technology and lifestyles, and population decreases because of epidemics. The disappearance of the buffalo was the greatest change; the Indians were forced to settle on reserves in order to survive, and the prairies were left empty.

There was room now for the immigrants to move in, and first the large ranchers came in with their herds of cattle. After a couple of decades, many circumstances caused the ranchers to be displaced by settlers: the filling of free land in the United States, farm technology more suitable to Canada's climate, the Canadian government's encouragement of immigration, and higher wheat prices and wages.

We shall now turn to Part III to see how the variety of themes celebrated by the Nose Creek Historical Society helps us to grasp the significance of the many elements influencing the establishment of the Nose Creek Community.

This model depicts a typical buffalo jump—a method Indians frequently employed to obtain food. Picture courtesy Luxton Museum, Banff, Alberta.

PART III: CELEBRATING 100 YEARS NORTH OF THE BOW

INTRODUCTION

The first five chapters of this book laid the foundation for presentation of a series of historic themes which have been celebrated by the Nose Creek Historical Society. Part III is based on the Society's annual interdenominational services to celebrate centennials and anniversaries of historic events. These services, which began in 1972, continued a tradition of holding interdenominational church services which dates back as far as 1905, when Alberta became a province. The Society's 25th celebration will be in November 1996, at which this history book will be launched.

As we turn to this section of the book we are especially indebted to the historic interest and enthusiasm of Redvers Perry, following in the footsteps of his pioneering father Clem Perry. Clem, his wife Lucy and Redvers all kept diaries, scrupulously recording events and circumstances, as history unfolded in their experiences as pioneers and citizens of the valley.

For its interdenominational services, the Nose Creek Historical Society focused on one theme each year, often related to a centennial. Redvers, with the assistance of other Society members, carefully researched and prepared a historic sketch of each theme reflecting on one hundred years of Nose Creek Valley history. Hence, the title of this book was inspired from his devoted efforts, which provided the inspiration for this anthology. He wrote many of the thematic sketches and also got contributions from many other writers. The Society thus produced a printed historic pamphlet for each service of worship based on the theme for that year. The illustrations within this book help to animate the story of the Valley.

While the Society celebrated a particular theme each year, sometimes it dedicated two or three different plaques, and some pamphlets included small articles on other topics. Each chapter of Part III is based on a pamphlet. They were edited to be faithful to the authors' concepts, with some standardization in style. A few repetitive sketches were cut out, and a number of items of interest have been added to enrich the presentation of some themes.

Local histories in Western Canada tend to focus on the pioneer settlement era, showing a natural fascination with the great historic movement which produced our modern society. Some themes in Part III deal with preludes to settlement: the arrival of traders, missionaries and police; the Indian treaties; the land surveys; and the development of travel and communications. Other themes portray many and varied aspects of a frontier prairie society, from horses and cattle to hay and prairie fires to the growth of towns and social institutions.

CHAPTER 6: THE JOURNEY OF COLONEL P. ROBERTSON-ROSS

FIRST LOCAL CENTENNIAL: 1872-1972

Canada celebrated its centennial in 1967, but 100 years ago the west was young. The Indians roamed the entire countryside at their will to hunt, fish, participate in tribal skirmishes, and worship the Great Spirit as they chose. The influence of the white man in many cases worked hardship on the natives, both directly and indirectly. The introduction of the horse resulted in ruthless slaughter between tribes over territorial ambitions, and the buffalo were killed in thousands to satisfy the greedy racketeers of the fur trade. Worst of all, the unscrupulous whiskey traders ruined the existence of the Indians by selling no end of fire water, as it was termed, which added to the decline of the great Indian culture of Western North America. Something had to be done, and numerous western white missionaries and influential sound-thinking western pioneers pleaded with Ottawa to send a force to see justice done to the natives and whites alike.

To make a long story short, Colonel Patrick Robertson-Ross, Adjutant-General of the Militia of Canada, was ordered to make a reconnaissance of Western Canada. He left Ontario in July 1872 with his 16 year old son, a guide, and a Saulteaux Indian boy, travelling from Fort Garry (Winnipeg) to Edmonton and Rocky Mountain House on his way to Wildhorse B.C. Many colourful events took place but space permits only his diary account of his journey from Wednesday September 17th when he arrived in the McPherson Coulee area northwest of the present town of Airdrie. An extract from the colonel's personal diary follows, as provided by Hugh A. Dempsey, a noted western Canadian historian.

Journey of Robertson-Ross, September 1872

...Tuesday September 17th - Rose about 5 a.m. slight rain, started from the Clearwater Camp about 6:40 a.m. passed a small stream called Cree's Creek where Munroe and I saw the track of a bear. Passed a curious looking tree a "great medicine tree" of the Blackfeet and halted for breakfast at a few minutes before 12, about 2 miles from the Red Deer River. Started again at 1:45 p.m. and crossed the Red Deer River (forded it). It was up to our horses' bellies and is a fine stream. About 10 miles further on we crossed the little Deer River and leaving the woody country came out on the open plains and camped for the night early at 5 p.m. at a pool of water on the edge of the plains at a point about 10 miles south of the junction of the Medicine River with the Red Deer River. I shot four prairie hen or ducks this day.

Wednesday September 18th - Rose at 5 a.m. started at 7:40 and travelled over bare open plains until 12:40 when we halted for breakfast in "Writing Creek". We had to go on all this distance for water. We had a splendid view of the Rocky Mountains this day, far finer than any we have hitherto had. Started again at 3 p.m. and camped for the night at 5:45 p.m. about 10 miles further on in the same valley or "canyon", Writing Creek. There was no water to be had for the horses but they had water twice today and we have taken precaution to bring some water along with us from the last halting place for ourselves. We had an alarm today on the march of a grizzly bear, so we all prepared for the battle but on a nearer approach what was thought to be a grizzly turned out to be the shaggy head of an old defunct buffalo bull that had been killed last fall. All this day we have been on the open plains in full view of the glorious mountains, and all over the plains are the track and sign of buffalo.

Thursday September 19th - The place we camped in last night is called "Writing Creek". It blew a gale of a wind last night and it snowed with a cold wind. Awoke early and was very cold. Tent nearly blown down. Some of my blankets wet. Did not rise till 6:30 a.m. and did not start till 8:30 a.m. being now about 20 miles from Bow River and it blowing a perfect gale of wind. Arrived at the Bow River, alias the south branch of the Saskatchewan, at 2 p.m. in exactly three days from the Rocky Mountain House. On our way we saw several antelope and three wolves. Had a shot at one antelope but missed it. On reaching the Bow River it came on sleet and snow and bad weather so we camped for the night.

Friday September 20th - This is the anniversary of the Battle of Alma. What changes since then! Ah me! Rose about 5 a.m. beautiful morning, calm and serene after yesterdays storm. The Rocky Mountains are all white with snow sparkling in the fine clear blue sky and the sun is shining brightly. A glorious sight. We started from camp at 8:30 a.m., not being able to manage to get off sooner. Just as we were starting our Indian Guide "Benjamin" took offence at something and went off in a huff apparently meaning to desert, but we took no notice of him and went off without him and before we had crossed the "Bow River" he had come back. We had some difficulty in finding a Ford and when we crossed our feet were wet and cold so we had to change our boots and socks (water up to saddle girths). Water very cold. We passed Moose Creek (2) and Sweet Creek (1) today and halted for dinner at 12:30, the sun having come out and the weather become fine we spread out our blankets todry whilst at dinner. Yesterday we passed "Nose Hill" and today "Moose Hill". We saw several antelope and one wolf on the plains. Some of the creeks or rivers running through valleys are very pretty. Started from the halting place at 2:45 p.m. and proceeding over some hilly ground but bare and open we crossed about 10 miles further on the "Sheep Creek" and camped at 5 p.m. for the night on the south bank of the stream on the top of the hill in full view of the Rocky Mountains. A party of four American Smugglers wintered here on the Sheep Creek some time ago. Very fine pastural and agricultural country all round. Some good timber in the valleys...

From here on the Robertson-Ross expedition continued to Wildhorse, B.C. He made his way back to the east by way of an American railroad and made a strong recommendation that the Canadian Government send a mounted force of militia to restore law and order to the west. In 1873, the North-West Mounted Police force (N.W.M.P.) was assembled and in 1874 it arrived in the west and built Fort Macleod. Another N.W.M.P. headquarters, Fort Calgary, was established in 1875 at the junction of the Bow and Elbow Rivers on what is now 9th Avenue East, Calgary.

This fact finding journey of Col. Robertson-Ross was the beginning of a great era in the west - one of law and order. The N.W.M.P. of 1874, now the R.C.M.P. (Royal Canadian Mounted Police), indeed provides the present generation a heritage of tremendous value. In what better way could we begin the era of centennials than by paying our respects to the Mounted Police past and present.

Submitted by C. Redvers Perry, 1972

Editors' Additions: *[The place Robertson-Ross called "Writing Creek" is now named McPherson Coulee, and the creek is Nose Creek.]*

McPherson Coulee as seen from Dickson Rest Stop

Six kilometres to the southwest, across from the location of the original Dickson-Stevenson Stopping house, you can see the deep cut of the McPherson Coulee. It is perhaps the most dramatic geographical feature in the vicinity. Out of it rises the main channel of Nose Creek, once a source of sweet, fresh water, that flows from two small lakes lying deep within the confines of the coulee walls.

The Coulee has been the scene of human settlement in one form or another for hundreds, perhaps thousands, of years. Within its recesses, and protected by Provincial law, lies one of Alberta's most important buffalo kill sites, made even more interesting by the presence of native rock art on the cliff face. Near this focus of native activity, toward the north end of the Coulee, "Fort" McPherson was built by the pioneer trader and entrepreneur, Addison McPherson, some time in the 1870's. It is thought that, despite the official spelling of the name, the coulee was named after "Add" McPherson, and the Geological Survey of Canada first identified it as "McPherson's Coulee". McPherson is generally given credit as the first "settler" north of Calgary, and at one point he is supposed to have run sheep in the lush grass of the valley. He later acquired land in Calgary where Nose Creek meets the Bow with his father-in-law, the Metis freighter Cuthbert McGillis. For some time he operated a lucrative coal mine near Black Diamond south of Calgary, and later drilled one of the pioneer wells in the Turner Valley oil field.

McPherson's presence on the Coulee was followed by John Dickson and Johnston Stevenson, who homesteaded at its eastern end in the Nose Creek Valley. They ran what came to be known as the Dickson-Stevenson Stopping house (or "Stopping Place"), which also served as the local post office. In 1885, a year before the arrival of Dickson and the Stevensons, Amelia Vanasse, a Metis, had settled deeper into the coulee, and later took up land near Stevenson's property along with another Metis, Victor Laurence. These were the sole settlers in the area until the serious ranching families began to move in in the 1890's, although extensive settlement did not begin to surround the coulee until the minor land rush in 1902.

A healthy blend of mixed farming characterized the early farm settlement after the turn of the century, but on McPherson Coulee ranching was the order of the day. With the head-start that had been established in the nineties, three impressive ranches were formed through separate land consolidations, each family buying up cancelled homesteads, open Metis lands, and the CPR land grant sections that sold rapidly in 1902. The Grasley Ranch became the Fraser Property in 1903; the William MacKenzie Ranch engulfed most of the land that you can actually see near the Coulee from this vantage point. Probably the most well known of the three operations was Frank Collicutt's Willow Springs Ranch, which he established about seven kilometres into the Coulee itself.

McPherson Coulee had given shelter, water, fuel, and food to native bands, traders, Police patrols, travellers, settlers, and ranchers for centuries. It is, in fact, one of our truly neglected geographical features that marks the interesting history of this rolling prairie land north of Calgary.

From a panel at the Dickson Rest Stop, by Community Development Display Department, Historic Sites Service, Province of Alberta

Addison McPherson

The Rev. John McDougall recalled that he, his brother and a Stoney man were travelling north in March 1876:

...By the evening of the first day we found ourselves travelling with great difficulty through deep snow. That night we camped with Ad McPherson, a pioneer frieghter and trader. He had married a daughter of Cuthbert McGillis, one of the noted men of the old days of tribal war and fur trading. Ad and his native wife welcomed us into their large one-room shack and treated the party with genuine hospitality. From this family wintering here has come to us the place-name McPherson Coulee, a well known physical feature of this part...

According to Hugh Dempsey, McPherson was a Virginian who came to Edmonton in 1869 as a gold prospector, then worked as a freighter, trader, and wolver, poisoning wolves for their pelts, and moved to Calgary after the N.W.M.P. arrived in the west in 1874.

This raises the possibility that he was one of the whiskey traders who brought so much misery, vice and violence to the Indians of southern Alberta between 1869 and 1874. When the N.W.M.P. arrived and closed down the liquor trade, a number of the traders became solid, respectable citizens who later denied, played down or did not mention their disreputable past.

At least one oldtimer, Mrs Benars of Turner Valley, stated in the 1950's that McPherson had traded mostly rum for fur. It is also possible that he or someone else in the district ran an illicit still to make bootleg whiskey while the mounted police were working to curtail the trade in alcohol. In a 1939 speech, Muriel Clayton recalled; "Not far from Fort McPherson in a branch of the coulee is a large cave, which is supposed to have housed a moonshine still, and giving to the branch coulee the name of Whiskey Coulee."

Submitted by Valerie Jobson, 1996

With Law and Order, Ranching Gained Momentum

Cochrane Ranche Company

Leased Acres	Cattle	Horses	Sheep
204,500 (north) 130,000 (south)	10,400	1,000 800	8,000

The Cochrane Ranche Company which commenced operating on leases on the Bow River in 1881, was the first of the large ranches. After bringing over 10,000 head of cattle north in two great drives, Senator Cochrane and his manager, Colonel James Walker, suffered very serious stock losses through two unfortunate winters, so Cochrane decided to move the herd to more southern ranges. Ranching continued with some 8,000 sheep and 1,000 horses on the reinstituted northern holdings for a few years. In 1903 Cochrane died and the Mormon Church bought the southern ranch three years later.

Oxley Ranche Company

Leased Acres	Cattle	Horses
253,000	6,500	150

John Craig, an Ontario farmer/stock breeder, obtained the backing of Alexander Stavely Hill and other British investors to form the New Oxley Canada Ranche Company in 1882. Consolidating his and other leases on Willow Creek and the Porcupine Hills, he arranged for the arrival of 3,500 head of cattle in August 1883 and commenced using the "OX" brand, although this was not registered until 1885. Management troubles plagued the operation, Craig left after stormy disagreements with Hill and the second manager, Stanley Pinhorne committed suicide in 1892. W. R. Hull bought the properties in 1903.

Walrond Ranche Company

Leased Acres	Cattle	Horses
216,000	13,000	300

Donald McEachran, Dominion Veterinary Surgeon, attracted British capitalists, notably Lord Walrond and established the Walrond Ranche on the Old Man River and west slopes of the Porcupine Hills in 1883. Cattle came up from Montana, bulls from the U.K. and their progeny was exported back to the U.K. After the terrible winter of 1906-07, Pat Burns purchased the cattle and Wm. R. Hull the leases. Today local ranchers operate a community grazing syndicate on these lands.

North-West Cattle Company

Leased Acres	Cattle	Horses
158,000	10,400	800

Montrealer Fred Stimson, influenced by his brother-in-law, William Winder, and backed by the Allans of Allan Steamship Line, formed the North-West Cattle Company in March 1882. This ranch, the Bar U, became perhaps the best known and most successful of the early ranches. John Ware, George Lane and other notable ranchers rode in the early days for this Highwood spread. George Lane, manager from 1902 and eventually sole owner, died in 1925 and the following year Pat Burns purchased the Bar U.

Stimson, a most colourful character, who served as the ranche's first manager, was a charter member of the Ranchmen's Club.

This picture were taken from a mural in the Glenbow Room, Ranchman's Club, Calgary. Reproduced with permission. Photography by Mach II Exchange Ltd., Calgary.

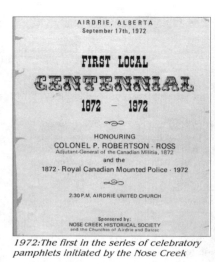

AIRDRIE, ALBERTA
September 17th, 1972

FIRST LOCAL
CENTENNIAL
1872 – 1972

HONOURING
COLONEL P. ROBERTSON - ROSS
Adjutant-General of the Canadian Militia, 1872
and the
1872 · Royal Canadian Mounted Police · 1972

2:30 P.M. AIRDRIE UNITED CHURCH

Sponsored by:
NOSE CREEK HISTORICAL SOCIETY
and the Churches of Airdrie and Balzac

1972:The first in the series of celebratory pamphlets initiated by the Nose Creek

COLONEL P. ROBERTSON-ROSS

IN THE FALL OF 1872 COLONEL P.
ROBERTSON-ROSS, ADJUTANT-GENERAL
OF THE MILITIA OF CANADA, CAMPED
IN THE McPHERSON COULEE AREA
WHILE ON A TRIP TO STUDY THE NEED
FOR A MOUNTED POLICE FORCE IN
THE WEST

ERECTED BY THE NOSE CREEK HISTORICAL SOCIETY

— JIM WELLS, Calgary Sun

The establishment of Fort Calgary in 1875 by the N.W.M.P. was enacted in 1994 when riders wearing period costumes crossed the Bow River.

52

CHAPTER 7: THE ARRIVAL OF CATTLE IN THE CALGARY AREA
SECOND LOCAL CENTENNIAL: 1873-1973

With the cattle industry of such major importance in Western Canada it seems hard to believe that only 100 years ago Townships 25, 26 and 27 West of the 5th Meridian had never a cow hoof print upon them. In the publication Blazing the Old Cattle Trail, Grant MacEwan states that eleven cows and one bull were brought from Fort Edmonton to Morley by the Rev. John McDougall and his family. This marked a historic occasion when in November of 1873, the seeds of a multi-million dollar industry had been established. The relations between the McDougall missionaries and the Indians, so numerous around the prairies and woodlands, were friendly. The whiskey traders from over the border were having a terrifying effect on the natives, enticing them into acts of violence which had been heretofore rare occasions. In short, Colonel Robertson-Ross's recommendation that a mounted force of militia be sent out to subdue the illicit traders resulted in the N.W.M.P. quelling the trade and making peace with the natives.

Thus, in 1874, the police brought law and order and made the ground safe for farmers and ranchers to own and expand herds of domestic cattle. The disappearance of buffalo herds in 1879 made it compulsory to turn to the alternative of domestic cattle. The Indians were being set up on reserves in the early 1880s, leaving land unoccupied for settlers to establish farms and ranches on. So commenced the cattle industry which expanded in rapid succession; especially in extreme southern Alberta. One of the early ranches in our area was the Cochrane ranch of 100,000 acres stocked in 1881. Two of the early farmers and no doubt cattle owners were John Glenn of irrigation fame, living near the Lacombe Home in Midnapore, and Sam Livingstone, whose land now comprises Heritage Park. So commences an endless list of devoted, hard core men of the land - our pioneers, of whom words cannot express their contributions to Canada and the world.

The official voice of the stockman today is the Western Stock Growers Association (W.S.G.A.). This organization grew out of a number of small associations which started in Southern Alberta from 1882 until 1896 at which time the W.S.G.A. was officially formed.

The first stock association in Alberta was the Pincher Creek Stock Growers Association, formed in 1882. Its purpose was basically to decide the date of the roundups, the location of holding areas, and the disposition of mavericks. The Fort Macleod Gazette of July 1, 1882 stated that that year's roundup was the first regularly organized one. The newspaper expressed the hope that a strong and compact Cattle Association such as existed in Montana would result. A number of cattlemen's associations were formed, including: the South Western Stock Association, April 1883; the North-West Stock Growers Association (High River-Calgary area), September 7, 1885; the Alberta District Stock Association, later Canadian North West Territories Stock Association, April 20, 1886; the Alberta Stock Growers Association, second annual meeting May 4, 1887; the Stockman's Committee, June 1892; the Southern Alberta Stock Growers Association, November 1894. Meetings held in October and December 1895 and April and December 1896 eventually resulted in the Western Stock Growers Association, 1896. The Cattleman's Protective Association of Western Canada was formed in 1919, changed in 1920 to the Stock Growers Association of Western Canada, and later absorbed into our present day Western Stock Growers Association. It's been a long history of associations, each playing a vital role in the immense cattle industry of today's Alberta.

Submitted by C. Redvers Perry, 1973

Brands Arrive in Alberta

According to a memorandum from the Brand Office, the first cattle came from Montana during the early 1870s and were the property of Joe McFarlane, near Fort Macleod, with brand "J.O." on the left hip. After this, American ranchers came along with brands registered in the U.S.A. Not until 1876 did anyone keep a record of brands, this being done by the N.W.M.P. C.E.D. Wood of Fort Macleod was appointed the recorder of brands, with a committee of three ranchers to assist and examine applications and to allot brands. No legal status was accorded to these brands. In 1897 the first Brand Act was introduced. This Act provided for the compulsory recording of brands allotted to cattle owners under government supervision. Some early brands were: "A.B.2"; "A.2.B"; "2 A.B." Brands have played a vital part in identifying cattle on huge government leases and community pastures down to the lowly little cattle owner with a few head which still make a vital contribution to his every day way of making a living. Indeed, brands have assisted immeasurably in tracking down the old time cattle rustler who worked from horseback, to the modern day rustler in truck or camouflaged van, swiftly moving down the blacktop highway to dispose of his loot and make illicit financial gain.

Submitted by C. Redvers Perry, 1973

Non-denominational Church Services

The history of local non-denominational church services in our area goes back as far as a service held in 1903 [1905] in the Dry Creek School house. The Beddington U.F.A. continued the practice when their organization was in full swing, prior to their amalgamation with the Balzac U.F.A. in the 1950s. The Nose Creek F.U.A. became the new organization in 1957 and again annual church services continued, each year alternating between Balzac and Beddington. Since the Nose Creek F.U.A. disbanded, the Nose Creek Historical Society has continued the practice of annual services of a non-denominational character. This was our second centennial service and indeed an honour to pay tribute to the coming of cattle to this area and our local detachment of the R.C.M.P. in Airdrie.

Submitted by C. Redvers Perry, 1973

The Origins of Western Ranches 1873-1885

Superintendent William Winder — NWMP

An original officer of the North West Mounted Police, Supt. Winder trooped west in 1874 in charge of 'C'' Troop (Artillery) and for six years commanded the S.W. portion of Alberta, out of Fort Macleod. Returning home to the Quebec Townships in 1879 for a holiday, his family connections permitted him to convey first hand information to Senator Cochrane and other wealthy individuals concerning the golden opportunity for establishing a great ranching industry in the vast new grass frontier of the West. No doubt he must be given key credit for the ensuing development.

He in fact registered the first brand /1'' to fellow policemen P.R. Neale and S.B. Steele, and the second ''double crank'' in his own name.

Resigning from the force in 1881 he acquired his own 50,000 acre lease on Willow Creek and with eastern backing purchased 1,200 cattle and settled down as a respected and progressive rancher living in Fort Macleod. Four years later, he died.

Senator M. H. Cochrane — (1823 - 1903)

Making his fortune in the leather and shoe business, Cochrane settled on a purebred Shorthorn, Hereford and Angus cattle and horse farm near Compton, Quebec. He became a non-active senator in 1872 and was later persuaded through the vision of Wm. Winder and others to use his connections and influence in Ottawa to change the existing policy and regulations to permit and encourage western large scale ranching. He successfully negotiated directly with John A. MacDonald, the Prime Minister, and in return for a $125,000 cattle purchase commitment was given preferred "first lease" selection on the Bow Valley, west of Calgary.

He clearly was the prime negotiator, financier and breeder behind this great dream for our West.

These pictures were taken from a mural in the Glenbow Room, Ranchman's Club, Calgary. Reproduced with permission. Photography by Mach II Exchange Ltd., Calgary.

BEDDINGTON, ALBERTA
November 4th, 1973

SECOND LOCAL

CENTENNIAL

1873 — 1973

HONOURING

ARRIVAL OF CATTLE IN CALGARY AREA

Leaving Edmonton Oct. 22, 1873 arriving in Morley in November,

and the

1873   Royal Canadian Mounted Police - 1973

2:00 P.M. BEDDINGTON COMMUNITY HALL

Sponsored by:
NOSE CREEK HISTORICAL SOCIETY
and the Chamber of Airdrie and Balzac

Fraser cow/calf pairs.

Fraser purebred and commercial replacement heifers.

Livestock awaiting the auctioneer's block.

(Below) Rollie Bilben and a cousin moving cattle to a new range. (1961).

A modern corral

Chronological Record of Earliest Cattle Drives into Southern Alberta 1873-1885

1873	John McDougall, a Methodist missionary and his trader brother David brought the first breeding herd of cattle (12 animals) south from Fort Edmonton to Morleyville on the Bow River.
1874	K. Mackenzie brought a larger herd from Montana to Morleyville and the N.W.M.P. arrived in Fort Macleod with 235 head of cattle.
1875	J. MacFarland brought a small herd of Montana cattle to Fort Macleod; also John Shaw trailed 456 head from the Kootenay to Morleyville.
1876-79	Various cattle herds came north from Montana to supply police and Indian markets and replace the massacred buffalo. Two Government owned ranches were stocked near Fort Calgary and Fort Macleod. By 1879, a number of small ranches were operating in the foothills, particularly around Pincher Creek and Fort Macleod.
1880-81	Influence and politics persuaded the Government to pass an Order in Council permitting the allocating of 100,000 acre ranch leases at a cost of .01cent per acre per year.
by 1884	The four "big ranches" (referred to on page 54) held almost 1/3 (900,000 acres) of all land in S.W. Alberta used by ranchers or settlers. The rationale was that large area ranches permitted controlled identification and breeding management of the cattle populations and through mass production of beef obtained greatest financial returns from the western grasslands. Many of the smaller ranchers and settlers operated on the fringes of the better lands and as settlement progressed, pressure for the release of leased lands for homesteading mounted.
	During the 1870's the stage was set for the forthcoming rapid development of the western ranches. The early settlers chose first the better and closer farm lands of the eastern prairies. The negotiation with the nomadic Plains Indians removed the potential of conflict with the allocation of reserves. The Mounted Police offered protection and controlled the American liquor traders. The CPR promise of a rail connection to the Pacific opened communication. Finally the destruction of the vast buffalo herds created available grass and local market opportunities. It was clearly good Government policy to attract Canadian/British citizens and capital in order to hold the vast foothills country against an expected American thrust northward. The ranchers filled this gap admirably for most of the 1880-90 period.

Transcribed (with permission) from the Glenbow Room mural, Ranchman's Club. Photography by Mach II Exchange Ltd., Calgary.

CHAPTER 8: THE HORSE IN ALBERTA

THIRD LOCAL HISTORICAL COMMEMORATION: 1754-1974

According to the World Book Encyclopedia, ancient tablets reveal man first rode horses 5000 years ago in Southwestern Asia. The Hittites trained horses for sport and war in 1400 B.C. and from then on horses have been used by man continuously for tasks of burden and pleasure. Their existence in Asia, Europe and Africa was enjoyed for centuries until a Spanish conqueror named Hernando Cortes came to America in 1519 and used horses for his purposes of conquest. The Indians there were horrified at the enormous beast ridden by an armoured soldier, so the Spanish had an easy time achieving their ambitions. However, in the 1600's the Western Plains Indians took advantage of the swift method of travel and used the horse to hunt buffalo and play war games. Space will not permit the full tale of the colourful part horses have played in the Americas, but in 1788 explorer David Thompson recorded a story told him by a Peigan Indian of some 80 years of age. The man recalled that in his youth, around 1730, the Snake Indians were the first to possess horses. The Peigans shot a horse with a Snake Indian riding on it. The rider ran away, and the Peigans had their first close up glimpse of a horse somewhere in southwestern Canada.

Our first record of a white man possessing horses in what may be Alberta or the west was the son of La Verendrye, who had two horses purchased from Missouri in 1741. Some 13 years later, Anthony Henday, who came to the Red Deer-Innisfail area in 1754 referred to horses in his writings. It would be a reasonable assumption that Henday was the first white man to use a horse north of the Bow, some 220 years ago.

From records it could also be said that the horse dealing and stealing was in full swing in the mid-1700s. The first record of horse brands was by Edward Umfreville in 1785, when he mentioned that the Plains Cree Indians had horses with Spanish brands, or at least with Roman capitals in the brands. In the early 1800s horses were quite common amongst northwestern prairie Indians, and to this day the relationship still remains, though modern machines continue to make inroads on the customs of yore. The Palliser Expedition of 1857, a fact-finding mission to investigate weather and general conditions which would influence agriculture, was conducted west from Lake Superior deep into Alberta, using 30 horses.

Horses have played a major part in making Alberta what it is today. Their early role was as a means of transportation by saddle and wheeled vehicle. As time went on, their burdens were added to. In order of seasons they were used for plowing, disking, harrowing, seeding, haying, and harvesting. Many would have the added task of a month on the local threshing outfit. During the winter farmers and ranchers would go to the bush for lumber and firewood. In early years a trip to the Carbon coal fields for winter fuel would be undertaken. One of the main sources of income for local farmers was the Calgary hay market; the faithful teams of horses delivered this hay. There were stories of hardship and cruelty to the horse from a merciless master, while on the other hand the affectionate master would forfeit every comfort for that of his horse. We recall many heated arguments in the school yard as to who had the best horse. The one with the loudest voice usually won, though his horse could be not quite the finest on the road!!

From the explorers of the 1700s to when agriculture depended on horse power, and on to the present day when the horse is strictly a pleasure or race animal, we pay our hearty tribute on this day of November 3, 1974.

Words cannot express our indebtedness to the intelligent beast and friend of man— THE HORSE—may they rest in peace.

Submitted by C. Redvers Perry, 1974

Colonel P. Robertson-Ross 1872

Col. P. Robertson-Ross, Adjutant General of the Canadian Militia, was ordered to make a reconnaissance of Western Canada. He left Ontario in July 1872 with his 16 year old son, a guide, and a Saulteaux Indian boy, travelling from Fort Garry (Winnipeg) to Edmonton and then to Rocky Mountain House on his way to Wildhorse, B.C. Many colourful events took place but space permits only slight comment. On Wednesday, September 18, 1872, he arrived at McPherson's Coulee northwest of the present town of Airdrie. The overnight stay was an unpleasant one with gale force winds and snow. The following day the small party proceeded south and arrived at the Bow River at 2 p.m. They reported seeing three wolves and numerous antelope. Another night of gale winds and sleet greeted them where now the big city of Calgary is located. The horsemen were exactly three days since leaving Rocky Mountain House and arriving on the banks of the Bow. From here on the Robertson-Ross expedition continued to Wildhorse, B.C. He made his way back to the east by way of a U.S.A. Railroad, making a strong recommendation to the Canadian Government to send a mounted militia to restore law and order to the west. In 1873 the force was assembled and in 1874 (100 years ago) established a headquarters at Fort Macleod. On November 3rd, 1974, the Nose Creek Historical Society and the R.C.M.P. Centennial Committee were proud to unveil a plaque in his memory, which marked an era of law and order in the west.

Submitted by C. Redvers Perry, 1974

R.C.M.P. Centennial Cairn

This field rock was located 2½ miles west of its present site, the R.C.M.P. Detachment Barracks in Airdrie on the property of Lorne Fowler; the southeast quarter of Section 10, Township 27, Range 1 West of the 5th Meridian (Section 10-27-1-W5). It was moved to its cairn site on October 17, 1974 by eight-wheel stack mover and tractor and erected on site by J. Osborne, W. Bushfield, R. Howden, and R. Perry on October 19, 1974.

Submitted by C. Redvers Perry, 1974

Editors' Additions: A Horse Roundup

The Mayhood family settled on the northwest quarter of Section 10-26-2-W5M on the West Branch of Nose Creek in 1889, when Samuel E. Mayhood was about three years old. In his memoirs of the pioneer years, he recalled how as a teenager, he went on a roundup with "Tom Reynolds, probably in his late thirties, who always seemed to be chewing tobacco when he was not eating." Reynolds was the manager of the Parslow and Hamilton Ranch. Mayhood wrote:

> ...R.G. Robinson, who owned a lot of horses, had on his ranch, located about six miles northwest of Dad's place, two adjoining large, round corrals made of large logs, with pole gates so horses would not injure themselves, which were usually used for the roundup...
>
> ...One year Tom Reynolds asked me if I would help him with about ten other cowboys round up horses. I had a good saddle horse and was glad to go, though Dad never had any horses outside our fences. I rode with Reynolds and picked up the first horses about 9 a.m. on the hill just north of Hillhurst and gradually picked up horses as we moved westward and joined other riders driving horses toward the Robinson ranch where the round corrals barely held the estimated 800 head which had been gathered off the open range. After lunch in the house, prepared by a male cook, we all returned to the corrals to sort out, cutting out we called it, the horses belonging to each rancher that he wanted to take home and keep them

separate to be driven home. The cutting out was done by an owner, usually with two other men, all on horseback, riding among the horses in the corral, reading the brands and driving one at a time to the swinging gate where a man would open the gate enough to let the one horse out. Because there were so many horses cutting out was slow and not completed until late afternoon. Reynolds had cut out maybe 30 head which I helped him drive into one of the fields on the Parslow and Hamilton ranch, to be broken to work and sold to settlers...

...As soon as the horses were put in the field I rode on home. My horse was tired. That day I had worked with cowboys, ate with cowboys, heard many arrangements of swear words, heard several smutty stories, cowboys did not seem to tell any other kind, my horse was tired, I was tired but I felt quite grown up.

Reynolds would take those horses, maybe three or four at a time, put halters on them and tie them to a manger in a single stall, teach them to drink, never raise his voice, pat them on the neck and around their ears and gradually use a brush on their body and legs, sometimes get them to eat oats out of his hand, put harness on one at a time, hitch it to a California cart, a two-wheeled cart with long shafts, so the horse could not kick the driver, and after it was broken to be guided by reins, hitch it with a well broken mare to a wagon and drive the team around in a field a little each day until it was broken so a settler could work it and ready for sale. Sometimes if he had two horses that looked alike a matched team was put together and sold for more money than singly. I think the usual price was about $125 per horse.

I might add that Reynolds loved horses, always treated them gently, never rode on exhibition, and was recognized as the best horse handler and had as good a memory for horses as most people have for humans. Stories were told of him seeing, working in some settler's field, a horse that had disappeared several years before, one of Parslow and Hamilton's horses and [he] was able to prove ownership...

From S.E. Mayhood's Recollections, 1977; courtesy of Cyril Woolliams

Tribute to the Horse and Horse Farmer

This is dedicated to the memory of the faithful, hardworking horses that pulled the wagons, bringing the homesteaders to the Prairies; that supplied the power to break the sod and till the land; the power to pull the lumber wagons to build the homes and haul supplies to comfort and feed the families;- and after the prairie soil was producing grain, to the horses that pulled the wagons loaded with grain to town, and home loaded with coal to warm the homes.

To the buggy horses that brought the doctors to deliver the babies or to administer to the sick and dying; the horses that took the families to church and social gatherings; that brought the eggs and cream cans to town and the groceries home.

To the trustful, gentle horses that took the children of the pioneers safely to and from school.

To the dedicated, intelligent horses that found their way, bringing their masters home, through a raging blizzard.

Along with the horses that did their work so well, a tribute of reverence and respect to the farmers who appreciated their horses, treating them with care, love and kindness, with the end result - the prairie was tilled and the crops were grown, the railways were built, the villages and towns arose and roads were built all by horse power.

Because of the horse and the skilled horsemen, the horse-farming era gave rise to the thriving prairies over a period of more than thirty years, until mechanized farming took over.

May the pioneers and their horses hold a valued place in the history of our country.

*From the Brisco, BC, Riding Club's **Scrapbook**; author unknown*

HISTORICAL COMMEMORATION
"THE HORSE" TO ALBERTA
1754 — 1974
HONOURING
TRIBUTE TO THE HORSE
in conjunction with interdenominational
Church Service at Crossfield
2:00 p.m. Crossfield United Church
and the
UNVEILING OF CAIRN AT AIRDRIE
1874 - Royal Canadian Mounted Police - 1974
1872 - Col. P. Robertson-Ross - 1972
1880 - Johnston Stevenson Stopping House - 1900

4:00 P.M. AIRDRIE R.C.M.P. DETACHMENT

Sponsored by:
NOSE CREEK HISTORICAL SOCIETY
and the Churches of Airdrie, Crossfield and Balzac

The horse reigned supreme in the process of taming the West.
1. Two horses pulling a load at the Calgary Stampede.
2. The buffalo hunt.
3. Until the thirties, children customarily rode to school.
4. A 4-horse team at the Calgary Stampede.
5. The late Georgia Jarvis painted this mural of a 4-horse team pulling a binder.

One word described the horse in in the West : *INDISPENSABLE.*
1   Robin Burwash riding '**78 Gunsmoke** at the Crossfields Rodeo
2   Chuck waggon races at the Calgary Exhibition and Stampede
3   Four matched Percheron beauties line up at the Calgary Horse Sale.
4   Eight horses in tandem taking part in the Calgary Stampede Parade.

1   A rodeo in 1906: at the Charlie Lewis farm.
2   Calgary-Edmonton horse-drawn stage coach. Picture
    can be seen at the Calgary Ranchman's Club.
3   Spruce Meadows exhibit at the Calgary International
    Airport lobby, 1996.
4   Ann Hollands with her Arabian yearling, 'Montana
    Fire.'
5   Ann Hollands riding her Arabian gelding, 'Buddy.'
6   Ann Hollands and 'Cherokee' a half Arab yearling.
    Farm house in the background.

CHAPTER 9: THE JOHNSTON STEVENSON STOPPING HOUSE
FOURTH LOCAL HISTORICAL COMMEMORATION: 1879-1900

A fascinating account of what eventually resulted in the establishment of Fort Brisebois (later Fort Calgary) is recorded in the history of the N.W.M.P. A brief summary follows, but by no means relates all of the interesting facts of what took place 100 years ago in 1875.

Apparently the Dominion Government approved the establishment of a fort between the U.S.A. border and the North Saskatchewan River. So in August, Inspector E. Brisebois and fifty mounted men of "F" troop were fully equipped and, under the expert guidance of a halfbreed named Jerry Potts, set out northwards from Fort Macleod. Meanwhile Major-General Selby-Smyth of the Canadian Militia sent a message to Assistant Commissioner James Macleod of the N.W.M.P. that he wished to meet with him at a Red Deer River crossing south of Fort Edmonton.

Macleod and his party soon overtook Inspector Brisebois at the Bow River around the present Blackfoot Reserve area. After a hazardous crossing, the party proceeded to the Red Deer River, through pleasant scenes of scattered buffalo herds, ducks, and fascinating interests in the wide open prairies, picturesquely spotted with lakes, streams and tree bluffs. The only pest mentioned was the infernal mosquito— and evening smudges had to be arranged to keep the little 'miseries' away!!

Six days north of the Bow they arrived at Buffalo Lake and Tail Creek (near the present town of Nevis). The only residents there were a halfbreed and his daughter and son-in-law. Their hospitality of fresh fish and game was ever so welcome, and their canoe met the travellers' convenience. Days were spent keeping the troop and equipment in all excellence for Major-General Selby-Smyth's inspection. However, word came from Fort Saskatchewan by courier that they were to meet Selby-Smyth near Wolf Trail, so Jerry Potts again made no mistakes in his excellent guidance, and, pushing through mud and tangled wood, they arrived just in time. The Major-General's party fared no better, and were quite agreeable and glad to meet the troop in the wilderness and wilds of the west. One must remember the Metis and Indians were quite uneasy, and caution was needed in considering the safety of one's path and exposure. After the horses were rested and views exchanged, Selby-Smyth, Macleod, and Potts departed for the south somewhere west of Three Hills and south to Blackfoot Crossing, meeting some 200 Indians and their Chief Crowfoot, prior to returning to Fort Macleod. The Major-General's party moved on to Montana, then to British Columbia and back to the U.S.A. to return to Ottawa by railroad.

Meanwhile, Inspector E. Brisebois doctored the ailing horses from Edmonton which Selby-Smyth had used, and returned them from whence they came by another party. Then "F" troop pulled out to seek the post at Bow River. Without the guidance of Jerry Potts, they followed the McDougall Trail at a leisurely pace, hunting and making observations on the way. This also known as the Wolf Trail, and passed through Olds and Lone Pine areas, wending its way in a southwesterly direction to where the Ghost River and the Bow River meet. At this point they paid a visit to the nearby McDougall Methodist church mission. From there they proceeded eastward towards what was to be Fort Calgary, staying on the north bank of the Bow River until they reached a point where 4th Street East now exists. They forded the river and established a fort site. A messenger was sent to Fort Macleod requesting the I.G. Baker Company to at once erect a fort. The only residents at the lonely but beautiful site, with lush prairies and scattered buffalo herds to the east and the Rockies snow-capped to the west, were Father Doucet and Father Alexis, who in a rough residence carried on their Roman Catholic mission. The police soon helped them re-establish a new home near the fort. The fathers and the Rev. George McDougall contributed much to relieve the loneliness at the post, but on January 24, 1876, George McDougall lost his life in a blizzard while on a buffalo hunt in our district. This ended his good work amongst the mounties and indeed the Indians at Morley. A cairn has been erected in tribute on the farm of F.T. Pole, the southwest quarter of Section 33-25-1-W5.

While no one knows the exact path that "F" troop took, we surmise it was west of our Nose Creek Map area. However, as Section 4-25-2-W5 on the north side of the Bow is marked as the path they took to view at first hand the fort site, they did pass through the Nose Creek Map Area.

We are pleased to mark the Johnston Stevenson Stopping House site to honour their passing through our district - on many occasions the mounties made overnight stays at this location registered in N.W.M.P. files as "One Days' Journey North of the Bow".

Submitted by C. Redvers Perry, 1975

Johnston Stevenson Stopping House

In Edmonton coach road days of the 1880s, a stopping house was what would be called a hotel or motel today. Originally at this site, the S.W.¼ of Section 36-27-1-W5, the stopping house was owned by John M. Dixon [or Dickson] and listed by the N.W.M.P. in their table of distances from Calgary as "one day's journey north". This stopping house could have been in operation in the late 1870s, but on July 23, 1886, it was registered in the name of J.M. Dixon. Records reveal that Johnston Stevenson obtained title to it on December 9, 1895, and quite likely he resided on this property for some time prior to receiving title. It remained as a stopping house until 1900 when the Airdrie Hotel came into operation, thus ending a colourful 20 years of accommodation for northern travellers. As items of interest, we read of Johnston Stevenson's participation in the Riel Rebellion and receiving a wound to his lung, and then returning to carry on with the stopping house. He also operated a ferry across the Bow River in Calgary, prior to any bridge being constructed.

In 1891 when the Calgary and Edmonton railroad was in operation, mail was dropped off opposite the stopping house. At times when the water was too high, he used to paddle across the marsh in the water trough to secure the bag of mail. Later a mail catching tower was installed at the crossing, and from 1900 to 1903 he was appointed postmaster at the stopping house. In 1903 a post office was set up in Airdrie.

If one could see the variety of overnight visitors at the stopping house over the years, indeed it would be a sight to behold. N.W.M.P. constables with handcuffed prisoners. A bull train with some of its personnel in comfortable warm log cabin quarters, and the tough rugged bullwackers rolled up in blankets under the crude heavy-duty cargo laden wagons. There could be a homesteader and his family, or just a lonely traveller on horseback - one with a friendly talkative attitude, or the quiet mysterious type of few words. Ministers of many faiths were on the trail, and on numerous occasions they conducted services of worship. "Gus" the mailman, who carried mail to the north long before the C.P.R., no doubt paid visits there too. Records reveal a bull team would only make a few miles per day, so from Calgary their first stop was at the Sharp Hills (Buttes Hills) one mile northeast of Balzac, where there was a flowing spring and a shack.

On November 3, 1974, the Nose Creek Historical Society is proud to unveil a plaque in tribute to the proprietors of the First Stopping House north of Fort Calgary. [see also "The Dickson-Stevenson Stopping House" below]

Submitted by C. Redvers Perry, 1975

Memorial to the Unmarked Graves of Nose Creek

While the first settlers came into our area in the early 1880's, countless explorers, fur traders and just plain adventurers or even men of mystery also roamed the prairies, on missions known only to themselves and those who may have been in pursuit. Regardless of who they were or where they were going, one often ponders how many of them are buried on the prairies. Unattended while suffering untold agony, broken of heart from the pangs of homesickness, perhaps even the slightest medication or doctor's assistance could have prevented their tragic death, but they passed on, and only by the efforts of a friend or a passing fellow man would their pathetic bodies be laid to rest.

Days, even months, would elapse before some of the West's true pioneers would be discovered after their day's work was ended.

More recently, when numerous settlers had arrived it was quite common to bury a loved one in a selected place within the confines of the home grounds. We can personally walk to such sites, unmarked by name but by a tree or shrub. On the Nose Creek Historical Map, Number 44 marks the graves which were brought to our notice in 1960; more have since been located. On this property within a few yards of the marker is the resting place of two young children of the Johnston Stevenson family. In 1980, we also dedicated a marker in memory of the unmarked graves of the Nose Creek District at this site.

From authentic reports, the Stevensons held church services at their stopping house home. In keeping with their faith in God, we all joined in a service of worship at St. Clement's Church, Balzac, prior to this most memorable occasion of unveiling the Nose Creek Historical Society's tribute to the Johnston Stevenson Stopping House.

Submitted by C. Redvers Perry, 1975

The Boiler Plate Plaque

The Nose Creek Historical Society president and board of directors deeply regret that we are forced to abandon the attractive bronze plaques used at Nose Hill Spring in 1968, also the R.C.M.P. cairn at Airdrie in 1974, and resort to a more durable material and welding bead inscription. Vandals have maliciously mutilated the plaque at Nose Hill Spring on 75th Avenue and 7th Street N.W., Calgary, and 96 bullet holes are to be seen on the Rev. George McDougall's Provincial Government Cairn in the Beddington area. However, we shall continue to honour our pioneers, so that the more appreciative generations of the future will be able to observe how the west was won.

Submitted by C. Redvers Perry, 1975

Marker for Johnston Stevenson Stopping House

This site is the first shelter for overnight accommodation north of the Bow River on the Calgary-Edmonton Trail in the 1870s. The heavy boiler plate markers with welding bead inscription thereon was completed by J.B. Horne and Colin Fraser of Balzac West. The marker was located and constructed and the concrete material contributed by Ray Howden, Jack Osborne and Redvers Perry. Donald Copley gave the Society permission to place the historical marker on his property.

Submitted by C. Redvers Perry, 1975

Editor's Additions: Livery Stables

Historian Grant MacEwan, in a newspaper column, described Calgary's livery stables, which appeared there in 1883 and were in decline by 1919. He noted that there was at least one stable in every urban centre that served prairie farm communities, and wrote:

...as institutions offering welcome warmth for humans and horses and never locking their doors, the stables in towns and villages became more conspicuously the "nerve-centres" of their areas and endeared themselves to pioneer residents. There a driver from the rural part could buy shelter for a single horse and find a sheaf of feed oats in the manger for a cost of 25 cents, or a double stall and two sheaves for a team of horses at a cost of 35 cents.

But that small town livery stable was much more than an escape for tired and hungry horses. The big waiting room with a potbellied heater in the middle was where town and country people met to transact much of their business; it was where the local veterinarian made his headquarters and where he could be reached for consultation; it was where horses were often bought and sold or traded; a box stall at the rear was one of the few places to which a man with a bottle might retire with his friends for a short celebration.

The stable represented an almost constant market for farm hay, oat sheaves and feed grain. More than that, the stable owner was generally ready to sell feed from his loft if he saw a profit, just as he might deal in fence posts, used saddles and harness, second-hand wagons and buggies and

65

even field machinery...

...As a meeting place the old livery stable was better than the pool hall because women and children did not enter the latter. The warmth of the big room attracted everybody, including the ne'er-do-wells who spent their winters telling stories and trying to protect their claims to the chairs next to the stove - that big round stove that might have been seen as the real pivot point of the urban-rural community.

From a column by Grant MacEwan, 1988

The Dickson-Stevenson Stopping House

In the early years of horse travel, before trains and automobile traffic made them unnecessary, travellers relied on the presence of stopping houses along the way for meals, a night's rest, or shelter from the severe weather that can sweep down upon the prairie. These were often commercial efforts, much like modern hotels or motels, established on well worn travel routes. Frequently, they were simply homestead structures that happened to be near a new trail and were then opened to people on the trail because of the generosity or the entrepreneurial spirit of the owner.

In the mid 1880's, John Dickson from Calgary was drawn to a point on the Calgary-Edmonton Trail, near the mouth of MacPherson Coulee and close to Nose Creek, because of the steady supply of fresh water. It seems clear that the steady traffic using the trail after the Canadian Pacific Railway reached Calgary in 1883 enticed Dickson to establish his complex of log structures to serve as a stopping house. The first true settler in the area, Dickson filed his homestead in 1886. He was joined in the territory later that year by another settler also interested in the Trail, Johnston Stevenson, who had given up land he had squatted on in what is now north Calgary to take up a homestead just north of Dickson's. Along with two Metis families who took up "North-West Half Breed" claims on the coulee to the southwest, Dickson and the Stevensons had anticipated the great rush of settlement into the area by some sixteen years. If you visit the trails above the Centre and look toward MacPherson Coulee to the southwest, you will be looking across the site of the old stopping house where it nestled near the main channel in the Nose Creek Valley.

Little is actually known about the Dickson Stopping House except that the North West Mounted Police used the facility while passing their patrols and thought that the feed and water supply was 'good'. Located about thirty-five kilometres from Calgary, it became a favoured first stop for the passenger coaches whose speed allowed them to make this kind of distance each day. In the end, however, the lifetime of the stopping house was determined by the success of the Calgary and Edmonton Railway which opened in 1891. Sudden disuse spelled the end of Dickson's along with many other stopping places along the route. Some were moved to became homestead buildings elsewhere, others continued to serve as local centres at least until the new railway towns grew large enough to replace these functions, and others were simply abandoned. Eventually John Dickson moved on. He had never "proven up" his homestead and it was cancelled, thus opening the land for Johnston Stevenson who by virtue of his service during the North-West Insurrection of 1885 was able to file a "Military Homestead" on both Dickson's quarter and the one adjacent to it on the east. Finally, the Stevensons had access to Nose Creek. The transfer was not without its rancour, however, and Stevenson was required by the Dominion Lands Office to reimburse Dickson for the stopping house structures that he was taking over in the process. Despite the apparent quarrel between the two men, the site came to be known in the local area as the Dickson-Stevenson Stopping house after 1895. Ninety years after the stopping house had become the Johnston Stevenson farm, the new Dickson Stevenson Stopping House, on the new Calgary-Edmonton Trail, was opened not far from the original site, to provide highway travellers with rest, refreshment, and information. The camaraderie of overnight stays at the old places may now be lost, but the invitation is here to stop and enjoy the views of our farm and ranch land that has been under settlement for almost a century.

By the Historic Sites Service

[After the Nose Creek Historical Society held its celebration in 1975, the Province of Alberta's Historic Sites Service set up the Dickson Rest Area, near the old stopping house site, south of Crossfield on Highway 2. The Historic Sites Service did further research to clarify and expand upon what was known about the area's history; a panel at the rest stop contains the above information.]

View of Calgary, looking west from Elbow River
Photo courtesy of Glenbow-Alberta Institute.

Balzac, Alberta
Sept. 7th, 1975
NORTH OF THE BOW

FOURTH LOCAL

HISTORICAL COMMEMORATION
MARKING SITE OF JOHNSTON STEVENSON
STOPPING HOUSE
1879 — 1900
ALSO
MEMORIUM TO UNMARKED GRAVES
OF NOSE CREEK DISTRICT

In conjunction with Interdenominational
Church Service at
St. Clements Anglican Church
Balzac   1:30 p.m.

and the

UNVEILING OF MARKER AT SITE OF
JOHNSTON STEVENSON STOPPING HOUSE
3:30 p.m, 4 MILES NORTH OF AIRDRIE ON
OLD EDMONTON COACH ROAD (Still in use)
Sponsored by:
NOSE CREEK HISTORICAL SOCIETY
and Churches of Airdrie, Crossfield and Balzac

Dickson's Stopping House - North of Fort Calgary

Fourth historical Commemorative pamphlet (left) and Alan Hamilton (right) pipes the congregation out of St. Clement's Anglican Church at a service sponsored by the Nose Creek Historical Society, and the churches of Airdrie, Crossfield, and Balzac. A ceremony was later held to mark the site of the Johnston Stevenson Stopping House

Dickson's Stopping House was sold to Johnston Stevenson. Many ministers stopped over and held services here.

Wick's Livery Barn.

The Old Hotel, located at 105 Main Street, Airdrie, has served as a stopping place for travellers since 1912.

Unveiling Ceremony at the first stopping house north of Fort Calgary. (There were five such houses between Fort Calgary and Fort Edmonton). The saddle, hat, and rope symbolize the era of the horse and ranching. (l-r) Jack Delorne, and Bill Walker.

Vice President Bill Walker (l) greeting Dr. Hugh Dempsey (r) at the Johnston Stevenson Historic Site.

Placing a saddle at the marker commemorating the site of the Johnston Stevenson stopping house.

Sandy Van Dongen and Debbie Lake, Crossfield horse riders at the 4th local commemoration of the Johnston Stevenson stopping house, September 7, 1975

Positioning a buffalo robe as part of the dedication ceremony of the Johnston Stevenson stopping house.

CHAPTER 10: THE DEATH OF THE REVEREND GEORGE MCDOUGALL
FIFTH LOCAL HISTORICAL COMMEMORATION: 1876-1976

The full account of the Methodist Church missions on the prairies would far exceed the brief space on this brochure. A brief summary follows of some of the stout-hearted missionaries who first came to the prairie west, an untamed and fascinating challenge to many, the church being no exception. In 1840, the Rev. Robert Terrill Rundle arrived in Fort Edmonton from London, England, appointed by the Wesleyan Society and supported by the Hudson's Bay Company. The first settled mission of any church had been realized. Banff's Mount Rundle bears his name, and no doubt he passed over our area of Nose Creek many times on his missions. In 1862, George and John McDougall arrived in the west near Smoky Lake, Alberta, then named 'Victoria', on the north bank of the Saskatchewan River. They established the Morley Mission in 1873 which, we recall, is when the first domestic cattle were driven through our district enroute from Fort Edmonton. Despite many hardships endured during the establishment of the mission, the McDougalls no doubt derived endless satisfaction from their good work amongst the Stoney Indians, teaching the Bible, administering help to the sick, and contributing better living techniques to the natives.

In winter 1875-76 meat rations were running low and a buffalo hunt at once had to be organized. George and son John, and a nephew from Eastern Canada named Moses set out on the buffalo hunt, and killed two buffalo cows prior to running on to a herd of choice buffalo in a preferred hunting position, of which they managed to lower six head of excellent animals. Having been skinned and quartered, they were securely loaded on the sleds drawn by one horse each, and proceeded in the direction of base camp, where Moses had remained due to a slight illness. The night was clear, and a slight ground snow blow was in evidence. George told his son John he would proceed to base camp a half hour further on to make supper, and overnight preparations. He rode off cheerfully at full gallop to the west, while John and a Wood Stoney assistant followed with the valuable cargo loaded on the four sleds.

Little did John know that the sight of his father, fading over the hills of our Nose Creek district, would be the last time he would see him alive. Shortly after, the four sleds pulled up to base camp, and John's father was not to be seen. Moses was aroused from sleep and said he had heard nothing from the older missionary. Calls were frantically sounded and rifle shots fired to no avail. John rode all next day searching the vicinity - still no clues. Upon the hunting party's return to Morleyville, optimism that he would be there turned to deep concern and frustration. A search commenced from Fort Calgary, but was hampered by cold weather. Some Indians reported seeing a man leading a horse which answered the description, but the search revealed nothing. A more intensive search was organized. A half-breed who had shot a buffalo for his own consumption and was making a beeline for it came across the body of our servant, put it on his sleigh and called the search party to his camp. In sorrow, an Indian lady had covered the body with her shawl, and on removing it, the sons recognized their father. The reverend gentleman's face was peacefully composed, his arms folded across his chest and legs straight as though ready for burial. Birds nor animals had disturbed his body during the twelve days of being unaccounted for. His body was placed on a sleigh and taken home to Morleyville. He was buried in the western hunting clothes which he had worn on his "Last Roundup", and peacefully composed as he had prepared himself. Burial services were conducted at the Morleyville cemetery, which he had previously selected as a cemetery, and which today is still used for those he loved and respected, who loved and respected him.

So concluded the colourful life of one of Western Canada's many missionaries. His untimely death at age 54 left many worthwhile plans yet unfulfilled. His efforts, however, will live long in records, with his son carrying on where he left off. Our Lord had called him home; his journey's end, the foothills of Nose Creek in the shade of the towering Rockies beyond the sunset.

Submitted by C. Redvers Perry, 1976

Plaque dedicated
REV. GEORGE McDOUGALL 1821-1876
Rev. George Millward McDougall, Pioneer Methodist Missionary, perished at this site on January 24, 1876. He had been buffalo hunting, apparently suffered a heart attack and did not return to his camp. He had come west in 1860 and had devoted his life to the Indians. The whole west mourned his passing. Erected by the Province of Alberta

Editors' Addition: Missions to Western Canada
Several denominations sent out missionaries to what was the Hudson's Bay Company Territory until 1869-70. These people ministered to the Indians as well as to Hudson's Bay Company [H.B.C.] employees and other early settlers. In 1820 there were Roman Catholic and Church of England missionaries at Red River. In what is now Alberta, the early missionaries were either Methodists or Roman Catholics, and the determined rivalry between the two spurred them to establish competing missions throughout Alberta.

The British Wesleyan Methodist Robert Rundle arrived in the H.B.C.'s Fort Edmonton in 1840, and travelled from there to visit the Cree and Stoneys. He was followed by the French Canadian Catholics Jean-Baptiste Thibault in 1842 and Father Bourassa later, to Rundle's dismay. He no doubt felt quite out-numbered when Father Jan de Smet passed through in 1845, but the story-telling Jesuit priest from the U.S.A. charmed Rundle out of his initial prejudice.

After Rundle left in 1848, his work was carried on by the native lay assistant Benjamin Sinclair in Cree settlements in central and northern Alberta from 1847 to 1884. In 1852, the French-Canadian Oblate priest Father Albert Lacombe came west to replace Thibault; he spent much of his time with the Cree and Blackfoot. A convent of Grey Nuns settled at Lac-Sainte-Anne in 1859, and they moved to Lacombe's new settlement of Saint Albert in 1861.

More Methodist missionaries came along, Canadian instead of British Methodists: in 1855, Thomas Woolsey and Henry Bird Steinhauer, an Ojibway Indian; in 1860, George McDougall with his family, including his wife Elizabeth who was raised a Quaker, and his son John who was ordained as a minister in 1872. The Methodists followed Rundle's footsteps in working mostly with the Cree and Stoneys. In 1873, the McDougalls established a mission for the Stoneys in the vicinity of Morley, west of Calgary. They also intended to start a mission further south in 1876 for the Blackfoot, but were prevented by the death of George McDougall. In the course of their extensive travels, visiting Indians, traders, settlers and N.W.M.P posts, the McDougalls passed through Nose Creek Valley a number of times. The valley was the scene of George McDougall's death while hunting buffalo.

Constantine Scollen, an Irishman, came west as an Oblate layman in 1862, and in 1873 he was ordained and sent to replace Father Lacombe who went east for 10 years. Father Scollen set up his mission to the Blackfoot on the Elbow River, where Oblate Fathers E. Bonnald and Leon Doucet joined him in 1874. In the summer of 1875, Scollen went travelling with a newly arrived Oblate, Father Zacharie Touze. They left young Father Doucet camping at the junction of the Elbow and Bow rivers, alone with an Indian boy until the North West Mounted Police came along and started building their fort right there.

The Anglicans and Presbyterians were slower at establishing their presence in what is now Alberta. By 1875, Anglican Canon William Newton was at Edmonton, and Presbyterian Dr. A.B. Baird arrived there in 1881. As more settlers came with their varying beliefs and loyalties, many more denominations and religions developed in Alberta. Some missionaries ministered to the urban and rural settlers; a number of the early missionaries stayed with the Indians on their reserves for many years.

Submitted by Valerie Jobson, 1996

Chapter X   The Tragic Death of George Millward McDougall

BEDDINGTON, ALBERTA
January 25th, 1976

NORTH OF THE BOW
* * *
FIFTH LOCAL

HISTORICAL COMMEMORATION
In Recognition of 100 years plus one day
The Death of Rev. Geo. McDougall

1876 - 1976

also

*PLAQUE ERECTED ON SITE
AS TRIBUTE ANNIVERSARY
in conjunction with Interdenominational
Church Services at
Beddington Hall
3 Miles North of Calgary
2:00 p.m.*
and the
UNVEILING OF MARKER AT SITE OF
TRAJIC DEATH OF
REV. GEO. McDOUGALL
While on Buffalo Hunt

3:30 p.m. - 1 mile due west
of Beddington Hall.
S.W. ¼ Sec. 33, Twp. 25, R-1, W-5th
Sponsored by :
NOSE CREEK HISTORICAL SOCIETY
& Churches of Balzac & Airdrie

"THE BUFFALO HUNT"

A reproduction of the souvenir pamphlet published in honour of the 100th Anniversary of the death of George McDougall. Above right, monument (located in the Beddington area, off Center Street North, Calgary) marks the spot where George McDougall's body was discovered.

McDougall Memorial United Church: *Built in 1875 by Rev. George McDougall and son John, pioneer Methodist missionaries on the eastern edge of the Stoney Indian Reserve, Morley, Alberta. This was the first Protestant church in Southern Alberta and is maintained by the McDougall Stoney Mission Society, Calgary and named Provincial Historical Resource in 1979. The site is located about 7 miles west of Calgary.*

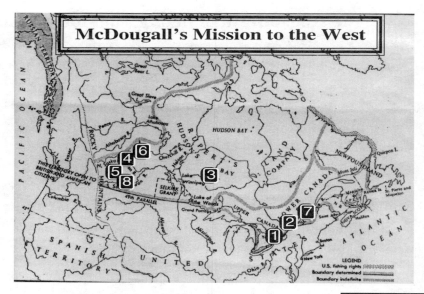

McDougall's Mission to the West

1. 1821 George Millward McDougall born at Kingston, Upper Canada. (September 9). Married Elizabeth Chantler in 1841.

2. 1842 John Chantler (son of George) McDougall born at Owen Sound, Upper Canada.

3. 1860. The George Millward McDougall family move to Norway House, north of Lake Winnipeg.

'Young' John Chantler McDougall

4. 1862. Trip to Fort Edmonton. Remained with Rev. T. Woolsey. Founded Victoria Mission.

5. 1865. John married Abigail Steinhauer (no photo available). Whitefish Lake. Honeymoon cart to Pigeon Lake. Three daughters born in this marriage.

6. 1871. Abigail died suddenly at Victoria. John later transferred to Victoria.

7. 1872. Conference of Western Missionaries, Winnipeg. John ordained. Travelled to Upper Canada. Married Elizabeth Boyd in August.

8. 1873. Mission opened on Bow River. John and Elizabeth moved to Morley Settlement west of Calgary. Six children born from this marriage. John died in 1917.

Adapted (with permission) from McDougall Reflections, McDougall Stoney Mission Society, Historical Booklet No1, 1996, pps 10& 11.

Rev. George Millward McDougall

Elizabeth Chantler McDougall.

Rev. John Chantler McDougall

Elizabeth Boyd McDougall.

CHAPTER 11: TREATY NO· 7 AT BLACKFOOT CROSSING
SIXTH LOCAL HISTORICAL COMMEMORATION: 1877-1977
[ALSO AIRDRIE SCHOOL'S FIRST BELL 1907-1957]

From a copy of the famous Treaty No.7, signed at Blackfoot Crossing entitled "Articles of a Treaty between Her Most Gracious Majesty the Queen of Great Britain & Ireland and her representatives Hon. David Laird Lieut. Gov. and Indian Superintendant accompanied by J.F. Macleod C.M.G. Commissioner of the North-West Mounted Police" this brief account follows.

The Indian tribes involved were the Blackfeet, Blood, Piegan, Sarcee, and Stoney tribes living in the general area bordered by the U.S.A. border to the south, the Rockies to the west, and the northern and western plains not involved in previous treaties.

Accounts tell us that the Blackfoot speaking tribes were in an irritable and tough mood and didn't hesitate to show their anger at the foreigners encroaching on their territory. On the other hand settlers and government authorities were reluctant to go too far from armed protection because of the Indians' attitude. Hence the necessity for some amiable agreement acceptable to both sides. The Blackfoot Tribe was deemed the most influential of all the Alberta tribes and a settlement with Crowfoot, one of their important chiefs, would accomplish so much, in fact it would be regarded as a successful exercise if his signature could be on the treaty, as others would likely follow. Crowfoot demanded the treaty discussion be held at Blackfoot Crossing and not as originally planned at Fort Macleod. The wish was granted.

The Blackfoot and Stoney Indians were on time, in fact ahead of Colonel Macleod and his party of 80 mounted men. The Bloods, Piegans and Sarcees, not concerned about time schedules, gradually arrived later. It must have been a most colourful event with the top administrators of each tribe all arriving from various directions in full native costume, such a proud people they were.

Through interpreters, the Treaty Commissioners announced the terms of the proposed treaty. Food rations were present in abundance for the Indians, though Crowfoot was independent and would accept no bribes or government gifts. The chiefs studied treaty terms over the late evening camp fires, while younger warriors rode wildly up and down the hillsides, making warlike gestures and shooting at a full gallop. Fear was expressed by Macleod's men. No serious incidents occurred, fortunately, or a slaughter would have resulted.

Indian Chiefs and Government Authorities sat in front of some 4,000 visiting Indians, which was the largest gathering of native people known up to that time on the prairies. Each chief spoke on his tribe's behalf. Chief Crowfoot was highly regarded, and has great respect for his philosophies in life to this day. He was at the forefront during all negotiations and when the final document was presented he said he would be the first to sign and the last to break a promise. This he lived up to, to the last letter, until his death.

Reserve sites were named in the treaty, though some boundaries and sites were later quite controversial. The one-time payment of treaty money was popular: $25.00 to each of 10 chiefs, $15.00 to each of 40 minor chiefs and councillors, and $12.00 each to 4,342 men, women, and children. A grand sum of $52,954.00 was the total issued to 4,392 Indians of the five tribes represented.

It was, I suppose, a sad day for the Indians in many respects, their greatest concern was the progressive loss of the buffalo which basically sustained their very existence. The Whites would be moving in in great numbers; the freedom of the prairies was soon to be lost. Time had marched on to many saddened hearts - we hope they rest in peace now in the Happy Hunting Grounds of the Great Spirit they held so much faith in. What a change on the prairie scene in just a short hundred years.

Submitted by C. Redvers Perry, 1977

The Airdrie School Bell

The school in Airdrie was opened in the spring of 1904 with the minimum number of students required by the Department of Education for forming a new school district.

In those good old days little was supplied to the schools by the trustees and Department of Education; just the bare necessities such as a few library books, chalk, pointer ruler, the old double desks and possibly a strap.

In the fall of 1906 the teacher, Mr. R.J. Hawkey, decided that he and the students would put on a concert and box social to raise funds for a few 'extras'. This was held in the Bowers' hall and a record crowd turned out, especially the bachelors of the community. They, of course, hopefully expected to buy the lunch box of some fair young lady. Much to their chagrin some of them ended up eating supper with a little school girl.

The program consisted of various items by the students and the reading of essays written on the topic, "The World Fifty Years from Now".

Soon after the big event the teacher proceeded to spend the money for things he wished to have for the school, which included pictures for the walls, window curtains, a flag, and the school bell.

The bell was ordered from the American Foundry Company in Michigan and it took some time in being delivered. A belfry with flag pole attached was built atop our little gray school house presumably in the fall of 1907. When the bell arrived it was placed in position and it remained there until the old school was demolished in 1957.

Some little incidents in regard to the bell are as follows: In February of 1908, one of our school boys was dragged by a horse and killed. The day of the funeral the bell was tolled, the flag flown at half-mast and the pupils marched in a body to the cemetery which was then at the northern end of Airdrie's present Main Street.

The bell was of great interest to the smaller children who would often stand in the hall all recess for a chance to ring the bell which was done by means of a long rope. Older boys also enjoyed this job as by some foul means they were able to overturn the bell and it couldn't be rung again until someone went up on the roof and turned it back.

One very gallant principal wouldn't allow the boys to go up on the roof but procured a ladder and went up himself. Some of the students, not all boys, removed the ladder and left the blustering gentleman stranded there for some time.

When the bell was removed from the old building in 1957 it was stored at the farm of Mr. Ken Neil for safe keeping. Now twenty years later it is returned 'in state' to the Town of Airdrie and placed in the new Airdrie Town and Country Centre.

Could it but talk our bell could tell of the wonderful progress made in our community, especially in our schools during the last seventy years. The little one-room country school has through the years developed into three ultra-modern buildings with almost every modern educational need.

Submitted by Lillian Edwards, 1977

Editors' Addition:
The Meaning of the Indian Treaties

Treaty Seven between Canada and the First Nations in southern Alberta meant different things to the parties involved, who came from two different cultures each with a long history: one based on individual ownership of land and resources, using set boundaries and written agreements; the other based on group sharing of resources in a large territory with fluid boundaries, and reaching a spoken consensus.

For Canada, the treaties were part of a long process of preparing for the settlement of the West, which was necessary for the new country of Canada to grow and prosper. Thus in 1869-70, Canada bought Rupert's Land and the Northwest Territories from the Hudson's Bay Company (leading to the Metis Resistance in Manitoba - no one had consulted them or the Indians); in 1871, the colony of British Columbia agreed to enter Confederation on several conditions, including a promise of a railroad across Canada; from 1871 to 1877, Canada made seven treaties with the First Nations living in parts of what are now Ontario and the Prairie Provinces; from 1871 to the mid 1880's, the prairie west was surveyed for homesteading; in the early 1870's the government started working on building a railroad to the Pacific Ocean, which was completed in 1885.

To the Canadian leaders then, obtaining title to the land and clearing it for settlement was the most important issue. The treaties were a way to get the Indians to settle down peacefully on lands reserved or them, while ceding their claim to the rest of the land. The Government of Canada expected the ndians to become farmers and eventually to break up the reserves into individual land holdings and hus assimilate into Canadian society. Treaty Seven as written concentrates on the land to be ceded, the ands to be reserved for the Indians, and the payment for the land cession, including money, agricul-ural tools and livestock.

The emphasis was much different for the First Nations who accepted Treaty Seven; the Siksika Blackfoot); Kainai (Blood); Pikuni (Piegan); Tsuu T'Ina (Sarcee); and Stoney (Assiniboine). The irst three tribes were closely related, spoke the Blackfoot language, and formed what is sometimes -alled the Blackfoot Confederacy, along with their allies, the Tsuu T'Ina, who came originally from urther north and had their own language and traditions. The Stoneys were related to the Sioux; they ravelled north and south along the Rocky Mountains, west across the mountains, and east into the voods of central Alberta; some Stoney bands signed Treaty Six which covered central Alberta. The itoneys tended to be friendly with the Cree and hostile to the Blackfoot; at Treaty Seven they camped . couple of miles down river from the other tribes.

The First Nations lived as nomadic hunters, mostly following the buffalo herds, and adapting their ifestyle to the movement of game and the requirements of the weather. A tribe would fight to protect ts territory from encroachment by other tribes, but the concept of individual ownership of a piece of and was foreign to them. If a prairie Indian decided to measure off a piece of land and sit there all year ound, he would quickly starve to death; the way to survive was for a group of people to work together ɔ use the resources in the area, sharing all of the food with all of the group and fighting to protect their erritory and its resources from strangers.

To the native leaders, Treaty Seven was about peace; about not attacking the whites who wanted to ome into this territory and share the resources. In return, the Indians hoped for help when they needed ɔod, for they saw that the buffalo were disappearing. Most Indians did not realize that they were ·ading the right to travel and hunt over a vast territory for having to stay always on a small reserve and ɔllow a totally different way of living. A few Stoneys may have had some understanding of what was eing decided; for years the McDougalls had been telling them that eventually settlers would come and ιe Indians would have to settle down and farm. Controversy still rages over the location and size of the eserves.

During the treaty discussions, one Blood leader tried to negotiate better terms, but the Commission-rs dismissed his counter-offer; the treaty terms had already been set by the Canadian government. he First Nations had little choice about signing the treaty; the Blackfoot Confederacy tribes had been veakened by the smallpox epidemic of 1869-70, and the depredations of the whiskey traders; they vere grateful to the N.W.M.P. for stopping the whiskey trade, and fearful of a future without buffalo. hey were well aware of the terrible wars that had been fought between Indians and settlers and ɔldiers in the United States; possibly some of the Piegans present were survivors of an 1870 massacre y American soldiers in Montana. The Canadian representatives also desired to promote peace and the ɔoken words at the treaty emphasized this.

While the treaties were important to Canada as a condition for settlement, they were and are impor-ınt to the First Nations as a statement of some of their rights as the original people in this country. ince the treaty was made between a literate culture and an oral culture, both the written provisions and ιe spoken promises need to be taken into consideration. It is necessary to consider what each party nderstood, given the difficulty of translating the words and concepts of one culture so that people from ιother culture can understand them. Today the treaties are still a major factor in deciding native aims, and the meaning of the treaties is still a hot topic for discussion.

Submitted by Valerie Jobson, 1996

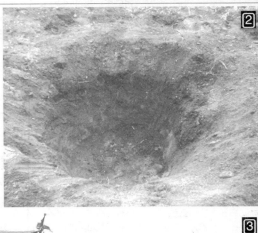

Airdrie, Alberta
November 13th, 1977
NORTH OF THE BOW

SIXTH LOCAL

HISTORICAL COMMEMORATION

IN RECOGNITION OF THE 100th ANNIVERSARY
OF
TREATY NO. 7 AT BLACKFOOT CROSSING
SEPTEMBER 22, 1877 – 1977

ALSO

THE OFFICIAL UNVEILING AND PRESERVATION
OF AIRDRIE SCHOOL'S FIRST BELL
1907 – 1957

*in conjunction with Interdenominational
Church Service at
Airdrie United Church*

and

UNVEILING CEREMONY AT
TOWN AND COUNTRY CENTRE

at

2 p.m. SUNDAY, NOVEMBER 13, 1977

1. Cover of the brochure commemorating three separate historical occasions.
2. Historic Indian sweat oven located N.W. 1/4, S. Tsp 26 - R ? W of 5th. The hole is 2'6" deep and 2 to 3' in diameter. Red rocks piled nearby were apparently fired and, on application of water, used to create the steam necessary.
3. Crowfoot speaking at the Blackfoot Treaty Number 7, September 22, 1877.
4. The Morris family with the historic school bell: (l to r) Gordon, Norman, Mabel, Jim and Spence.

CHAPTER 12: 100 YEARS OF PRAIRIE FIRES
SEVENTH LOCAL HISTORICAL COMMEMORATION: 1878-1978

Looking back over our brief history of a mere one hundred years one is amazed at how history repeats itself. From the Annual Report for 1878 of the North West Mounted Police, I quote a portion extracted from the Commissioner's Report:

...The state of affairs existing during the early part of the year 1878, in the south-westerly districts of the North-West Territories were entirely different from any we experienced since the arrival of the force in the country. The winter was extremely mild, week following week with the same genial sunshine, the mild weather being interrupted only by an occasional cold day; there was little or no snow, so that the grass of the prairie from one end to the other being dried up, easily took fire, and only required a spark to set it in a blaze for miles in every direction. Unfortunately nearly all the country out from the mountains, the favourite haunt of buffalo during the winter season, was burnt over, so that from this cause, and also on account of the mild weather, the herd did not come into their usual winter feeding ground; but remained out in the plains to the north and south of the Saskatchewan. The Blackfoot Indians who had as usual moved up towards the mountains in the fall, and formed their camp along the river bottoms, which had for years back afforded them fuel and shelter, and easy access to a supply of meat, were forced to take long journeys of seventy and one hundred miles, to secure the necessary supply of food for themselves and families, and eventually moved their camps out to where buffalo were to be got, with the exception of a few small camps, who were in an almost starving condition several times during the winter.

The result of this condition of things was a large band of Blackfeet were gradually getting closer and closer to the Sioux who were, by degrees, making their way up from the south-east in pursuit of buffalo, while other bands of Indians and half-breeds were pressing in both from the north and south...

Further on in this report he wrote:

...On my way to Battleford last summer I met a band of Crees who were in a very poor plight; they said, in answer to my question as to what they lived on, that they seldom had anything but berries; as for the occasional buffalo they managed to kill, it was so poor that it hardly supplied them with any meat...

Hugh Dempsey, in his book *Indian Tribes of Alberta*, states:

...Then, during the winter of 1877-78 prairie fires raced across the Blackfoot hunting grounds, driving the buffalo far to the south and east. By the following summer, some of the people were beginning to starve, and everyone could see that the buffalo had almost all been destroyed. At last, in a futile effort to hold onto their freedom, the Blackfoot followed the last buffalo herds into Montana and remained there from the fall of 1879 until the spring of 1881. When they returned to Canada, the last buffalo had been killed, and the Blackfoot were starving and confused. Some people blamed the treaty for wiping out the buffalo; others said that the Sun spirit had opened a hole in the ground and driven the buffalo into it because he was angry at the Indians for letting the white people come in...

This refers to the Blackfoot Tribe, while Dempsey also writes, about the Blood Tribe:

...The government had expected that the Indians could live off the buffalo for another ten years, but events moved too quickly. In 1878 a devastating prairie fire swept across the territory, driving the buffalo herds into Montana. By the following spring the entire Blood tribe had crossed the line and was engaged in the last great buffalo hunt. Then it was all over. Starving and bewildered, the Bloods began drifting back to Canada early in 1880 and camped near Fort Macleod...

With a Blood Indian population nearing 2200 and 550 of them husky warriors, the N.W.M.P. felt grave concern. Nothing can be worse than for a poor human being or even a lowly animal to be hungry and starving. Violence could happen, and much of this was due to prairie fires in 1878.

As settlers moved in, the danger of camp fires also increased. A fireguard around a new homestead was of paramount importance, both to confine a blaze on site or to prevent prairie fire from sweeping in on an entire family's accumulations.

The arrival of the railroad builders and cook camps, with fires to carry on various heating projects, also caused numerous prairie fires and brush fires, but this was minor compared to the fires started when the railroad was completed and the steam engines commenced to leave a trail of smoke along the railways. From the smokestacks of those labouring little steam engines came cinders or wood sparks, depending on what they were burning. These falling on the parched dry prairies, would cause fires in proportions far beyond the imagination of anyone today. Fires would sweep through hills, valleys, woodlands, until finally they came to a river, or a thunder shower or snow squall occurred.

The fear and terror of a prairie fire was uppermost in the minds of all the early settlers and their wives and children. There are stories of untold hardships in every local history book of the prairies from ravaging prairie and bush fires. This continued well into the 1920s, when sufficient land and fireguards had been broken to assist in quelling a blaze out of control.

One of the major fire control methods adopted by the railroads was to plow a fireguard of some six to eight furrows a hundred or so yards on each side of a railroad where pasture of prairie wool hay fields existed. Indeed, it was a welcome method for local farmers to earn few dollars hard cash to cover their numerous expenses, to plow fireguards along the railroads this I can remember well into the 1930s. Furrow traces still remain on the pasture land north and south of Balzac.

As a small boy I recall the telephone ringing in a general call for help; a prairie fire was out of control. Wet sacks and scoop shovels were gathered and away the adults would go. Vivid still is the memory of the Brushy Ridge Fire in Springbank on November 19, 1936 smoke billowed up well in view of our district. That fire started from lightning in a marsh or a campfire which smouldered in the muskeg and was fanned by 94 mph winds. A most tragic report of entire families wiped out and devastated agricultural areas, the full story is told in Chaps and Chinooks.

Most recently in our district, a major prairie fire occurred January 24, 1944, when smouldering strawpile at Silver Springs set a fire which came to its end near the 4th Street NW road and the CPR tracks in the Nose Hill areas. In the mild winter, tractors were used to plow fireguards and the Calgary Fire Department and local farmers helped quell the blaze.

So the story could go on and on. It seems strange that in 1877-1878 so many fires caused untold hardship for the Indians, and 100 years later we find that in the Rockyview District generally the same area, history has repeated itself. 1977 saw endless prairie and stubble fires in a dry April, and in 1978 the tallest grass we have known since 1902 has caused many fire outbreaks in harvest fields, causing endless concern.

To the Indians, the N.W.M.P., those hardy pioneers with their faithful wives who ever faced the terror and untold hardship of prairie fires, we who are gathered here at St. Clement Anglican Church, Balzac today, November 19, 1978, pay our unfailing respects to those who braved the elements and laid the foundation for the luxury and life of plenty we enjoy today.

May they rest in peace and heavenly care.

Submitted by C. Redvers Perry, 1978

Editors' Additions: Other Natural Hazards

Dust Devil near Balzac

An article in the *Calgary Herald* in April 1995 described a dust devil about half a kilo metre high that was photographed near Balzac. Allen Browarny, a livestock photographer said "I am out in that area every week but have never seen a dust devil that big. It was amazing." He had thought at first it was a tornado but it was dark at the bottom and the sky was blue, whereas a tornado is dark at the top and connected to a cloud. The article con cluded that most tornados occurred in Camrose area, but were rare in Calgary, "because the area is too dry and too close to the mountains."

From article by Paul Drohan, *Calgary Herald*

S.E. Mayhood Recollections:

[The Mayhood family moved from Ontario to California, then settled on the northwest quarter of Section 10, 26-2-W5M, on the West Branch of Nose Creek, in April 1889, when Samuel E. Mayhood was 3; his older siblings were Minnie, Frank, and Fred. These selections from his memoirs include many experiences, including flood, fire, and the effects of poor weather. His introduction explains why so many settlers and their children want to remember their history.]

...I have been persuaded by my three sons to write the story of my life. Unfortunately I have kept no diary but my father, named by his parents, Samuel Mahood, who changed his name to Samuel Harrison Mayhood, because of some confusion of names at one post office in California, had made some records which I have, so the statistical records are correct. There was no official registration of names, marriages, births, or deaths at the place where my father lived in his youth.

There seems to have been no time in history when there were such rapid changes in traveling facilities, the science of use and control of electricity, communication, advance in medical and surgical science, and the manner of living as has taken place during my lifetime, particularly in the development of Western Canada.

By briefly narrating some of the experiences of my parents, about which I have been told and some of my own experiences, I have tried to illustrate some of the changes which have taken place during my lifetime.

[Samuel was saved from drowning at age 3 by a brave Chinese man in California, who jumped in the river and dragged him out and would accept no recompense]

...I have often wondered if that incident has had anything to do with the kindly feeling I have for the Chinese who have proved themselves good citizens, helped to build our railways, and especially in the small towns and villages provided a restaurant with the best food obtainable and were so anxious to please where a white man could not exist...

...I think I was about ten years of age when Dad and Mother took all of us in a wagon box on a bob sleigh to a party at the Fletchers who lived on a farm about four miles west of Airdrie, and about 12 miles from our place.

For the occasion the Fletchers had rented a gramophone, made by Edison, and one of the first talking machines, so a great novelty. The records were cylinders put on a shaft and long rubber tubes with earplugs and only one at a time could listen. Being the youngest guest at the party I had to wait until all the other guests had a turn before I was allowed to listen to the screechy voice, but it was a marvelous invention...

...At one place behind our horse barn the creek made a sharp 'S' turn making a large pocket of deep water in one bend, and just downstream the banks were quite high and against a steep hill. A few years before the flood, Frank, Fred, and I had worked very hard making a dam and spillway, which made the creek from six feet deep at the bend gradually down where it was too shallow to swim. In the summer the water got comfortably warm. The flood washed out the dam, which was not rebuilt

Dad had learned to swim when a boy, could make a short run, leap and dive into the water, had three attentive pupils who learned to swim, and anyway stay afloat for quite some time. I was never very keen about being in water but could swim about 100 yards.

The Calgary School Board built a heated swimming pool and had an instructor, and notified the schools when each class could use the pool. I think I was 15 when it came the turn for the class I was in and all the boys went one afternoon. The pool varied in depth from about 3 to 6 feet of water and because I had been told the water was heated, I did not test it with my hand and jumped in the deep end. To me the water was cold and I was suddenly so paralyzed that I had difficulty in reaching the side of the tank and getting out.

The Cave and Basin at Banff is the only place I have been swimming since.

Dad had always been determined that his family would have a good education, which he had missed in his own life. Mother may not have attended high school but seemed to me to be well educated as compared to most people I associated with, and certainly was very wise as regards bringing up a family.

I suppose I was six, maybe going on seven, when the addition was built on the north end of the house. This addition provided a bedroom for the school teachers Dad hired, and a large room in which the three desks Dad had made from scraps of boards for Frank, Fred, and me. The school teachers, men, helped some milking the cows and doing outside chores outside school hours. The teachers got the regular school curriculum and as we reached the higher grades we boys were driven into Calgary and wrote our exams in Central School. There was so much work to be done in the fall in preparation for winter that we did not get started to school until late October or November. When Frank and Fred reached high school grades a house was rented in Calgary where sometimes Minnie kept house and sometimes we boys batched, being taken home to the ranch after school on Fridays and returned late Sunday or early Monday morning with bread, vegetables and meat enough to last us five days. I failed two subjects of my Grade 9 exam and never went to school again. I was needed to work full time on the ranch. Stanley had board and room in a private home when attending the higher grades and high school...

...By the year, I think it was 1900, Dad had plowed fireguards, a strip about 12 feet wide, from the northwest corner of our Section 10 to the valley of Big Hill Creek, about 10 miles west and south to the Morley Trail, a well beaten trail from Calgary to Cochrane suitable for backfiring, thus providing some protection from prairie fires destroying our possible hay and grazing land in any one year.

I have mentioned that Dad had given up trying to grow grain because of dry seasons and this year was so dry that the grass would burn any time after June. In order to secure hay to feed our milk cows and calves, Dad and Frank set up a tent on the shore of a large slough about 10 miles northwest of our home where Dad and Frank stayed from Monday to Friday, stacking the hay that grew on the foreshore of what had been a large, shallow slough, each taking a load of hay home each weekend and haying was finished early in June.

In July I had gone, just for the ride, with Frank to the stacks around the slough and we were on our way home and north of the fireguard to Big Hill Creek when we saw smoke from a prairie fire to the south of us. That fire had started north of the Morley Trail and west of the fireguard Dad had plowed from our place to the Morley Trail. There was not a strong wind, the fire burned out the whole area bounded by Dad's fireguards, the Morley Trail and Big Hill Creek. As a result of the drought cracks had formed in the earth, the fire caught in the grass roots and burned in some quite large areas about 10% of the turf. For some weeks Dad rode along his fireguards. In some placed the turf was burning for months. Frank had to drive over this burning land for about two miles, keeping to the trail where traffic had kept the grass too short to burn. We saw several grown cattle burned so they were blind and died in a day or two. Many cattle had perished in that fire.

I think it was the following year that the land Dad had plowed and given up cultivating because of dry seasons, was so wet that cattle avoided walking on it. To my personal knowledge that cultivated land has since had sufficient moisture each year to produce a fair crop and some very bountiful crops.

For two years or more southwest winds blew clouds of dust from those burning roots over our place, sometimes reducing visibility to less than a quarter of a mile. A northwest wind produced the same effect over the City of Calgary. It took over ten years for grass to grow in the burnouts. After a fire it was three years before that bunch grass or prairie wool as it was commonly called produced a crop worth cutting for hay. From a grazing standpoint cattle, and especially horse, preferred grazing where there was not much old grass.

Fires started from campfires not carefully extinguished, settlers burning the grass off land they intended to plow break away caused by a sudden change of wind direction, whirlwinds were common, hot cinders from locomotives, maybe a careless smoker and some horse ranchers were accused of starting fires to burn off the old grass and make better pastures for their horses which ran at large on the open range, and lightning. In some unsettled areas the fires burned until they came to a barrier like a creek.

By the time I was about 14 a foreign, I think Hungarian, family had taken a homestead about two miles south of the northwest corner of Dad's homestead, and burning some grass off some land they intended to break and on which a narrow strip had been plowed around, a wind got up, the fire jumped the fireguard and the fire came running toward Dad's homestead. Fred and I saddled our horses and met the fire just as it passed the corner of our land, and another change of wind direction forced the fire toward our home at such speed that Fred and I had to gallop our horses to keep in front of the fire until we reached the steep hill with a dim trail leading down to our house where the grass was too short for the fire to run but needed watching in case a bit of dry manure would blow across the trail. The smoke was so dense we had to lay flat on the ground with our faces down in order to breathe. Fred and I were the only ones home at that time...

...There had been an unusual amount of rainfall during the spring of 1902, after a heavy winter snowfall, when beginning in the morning of, I think, May 10, a very heavy rain started. The ground was soaked, the sloughs mostly filled, and with rain falling at our place, calculated by a pail in the yard, at about 1 inch per hour, the stream in the creek began to rise rapidly and by 2 p.m. was beginning to flood our barnyards and the rain had not let up.

It was decided that the milk cows in the cow barn, the calves in the frame addition to the cow barn, and the pigs, some half dozen in a log barn, should be driven to higher land. The five horses in the horse barn would not be in danger even if they had to stand a short time in a little water. Dad was crippled, we had no hired men, so it was up to Fred and I to move the animals.

Right away Fred and I became aware that as soon as the water flowed over the banks of that crook creek the stream bed did not carry the water which began to rise rapidly. To reach high ground the animals had to face a heavy wind and were reluctant to go, so we were about two hours getting the cows, calves and pigs to safety. We found in order to get to the horse barn we had to wade around 30 to 40 feet through a fast-running stream and found the force of the water made our feet slip on the ground where there was no grass. For a distance of about 10 feet I was slipping so I was frightened that I would be carried downstream and was greatly relieved when I got to where the current was blocked by the shed attached to the barn, which made it easy to walk through knee-deep water into the barn.

The water was still rising rapidly so instead of staying in the barn that night it became necessary to saddle the two saddle horses in the barn, ride them out, and lead the others. There was no hope of the water receding so we could get back to the house that night. In fact we discovered that a high level bridge, built a year or two before, had been struck by a small bridge built of planks nailed to logs, belonging to a ranch about 6 miles upstream had struck our bridge broadside and both bridges floated away.

The only place where Fred and I could find shelter for the night was where Walter Harrison had lived, which he had sold to George Simpson, a bachelor who lived in the one-room shack. Gates had been made so our two places were only a mile apart to walk or ride. Fred and I decided to ride.

A sharp-sided, deep coulee intervened, which drained a large area, but had never had more than a little spring-fed stream of water. We found a deep, fast-running stream, impossible for horses to cross, and had to ride over 8 miles around the coulee to get to Simpson's, long after dark.

As was customary at that time, Simpson took us in, stabled and fed our horses, made us a good supper, kept a good fire in his cookstove to help dry our soaking wet clothing. Simpson had only a bunk bed against one end of the shack and no extra bedding. Fred and I brought in the blankets we used under the saddles, spread the blankets on the floor, did not remove our clothing and soon fell asleep.

Next morning the sun was shining, the creek had mostly receded within its banks, Fred and I rode home crossing the coulee as usual, the cows were waiting to be milked to relieve them of much pain because they had not been milked the evening before. After shouting a few words to Mother and Dad we milked the cows on the ground, collected enough logs and boards left by the flood to tie together with ropes to make a raft on which we crossed the creek, which was still about 25 feet wide, and joined our parents for lunch and talk about what we should do. The milk house was gone, there had been over three feet of water in the basement and cellar, leaving a heavy coating of muck over the butter-making equipment and floors. In places the banks of the creek eroded and exposed numerous buffalo bones, indicating that there had been previous floods, and we were told several beaver dams near the headwaters of the creek had washed out, which caused the extremely high water and might happen again...

...After the flood only the log pig house, the frame cow barn and the addition to the cow barn had washed away, and the log horse barn and adjoining log shed were maintained, and from the salvage picked up and new boards, rails posts, providing shelter for stock and corrals for hay, were built on the leased quarter section...

...Immediately after the flood we made a small wire corral near, and on the same side of the creek, as the house, where we milked the cows outside and soon decided to give up the dairy business, keeping only two cows milking to provide milk and butter for ourselves and feed for the pigs and poultry. Partly because Fred had sold his homestead, I think for $600, and decided to study law at the University of Michigan, Ann Arbor, when the fall term started.

As a result of the flood the dairy business could not be continued without hired help, and men willing to milk cows were either undependable or high priced. Dad was unable to do any outside work so decided the best thing to do was to give up making butter for sale and sell the ranch. I think partly because of improved varieties of seeds and several consecutive good growing seasons farming was becoming more attractive. Increased settlement was encroaching on open grazing ranges and I think partly my lack of enthusiasm of the prospect of carrying on much as we had been doing. I became 16 that year, did not like any part of the life I had been living, except being outside, but I knew I could not leave Dad and Mother as long as they stayed on the ranch, so gave up any thought of going to school again...

From S.E. Mayhood's *Recollections*, 1977; courtesy of Cyril Woolliams

Sunday November 19th, 1978

NORTH OF THE BOW

SEVENTH LOCAL

HISTORICAL COMMEMORATION

IN RECOGNITION OF 100 YRS. OF PRAIRIE FIRES

1 8 7 8 - 1 9 7 8

in conjunction with Interdenominational

CHURCH SERVICE

(Left) Pamphlet commemorates various natural disasters the Valley has lived through. (Above) Smoke, flames and utter horror as a Prairie fire descends on settlers, destroying everything in its path and (below, left), a scene of total devastation: all that was left of the Arnell Ranch at Brushy Ridge, south west of Cochrane, in November 1936 after a Prairie fire.

3. *1929: The Hansen family inspects the hail damaged crop.*
4. *Cumulonimbus cloud formation.*
5. *1935: With an old Ford as a backdrop, mother and son pose for a photograph while surveying hail damage.*
6. *A squall enters town, preceded by blowing dust.*

A former RCAF fuel tender serves as the first Airdrie fire truck (circa 1968)

Fire consumes the first Scout Hall in Airdrie, circa 1972. St. Francis Anglican Church occupies a site nearby.

Girls learn fire drill as part of Babysitting Course, 1975. (l-r) Pat Saurette, Laurie Russel, Kelly Echlin, and Janet McCall. Members of the Airdrie fire department gave talks on home fire escape.

Wet Creek 1941: Spring thaw flows down past C. Perry's stooks and into the Bow River.

Early winter snow cloaks Clem Perry's stooks in the fall of 1943.

Above: a massive dust devil swirls ominously across field near Balzac. April 23, 1995.

Typical Weather Headlines.

1 Friends share homes, hot meals *(May 16, 1986)*

2 Calves Feared Buried in Snowdrifts

3 Blackfoot Band Still Huddling in Sleeping Bags

4 Snowstorm Forces Vehicles into Ditch

5 Rural Area Bore the Brunt of Storm

6 Airdrie Residents Come to the Rescue

7 Hundreds Stranded by Storm

8 Many Rural Residents Without Electricity

9 Poor Visibility and Slippery Runaways Kept Airport Closed Wednesday

10 Walking Home a Cold, Wet Experience.

What a mess! Leighton Perry helps clear snow from Redvers Perry's driveway, March 1988.

CHAPTER 13: ANNIVERSARY OF MAIL SERVICE PASSING THROUGH THE AREA

EIGHTH LOCAL HISTORICAL RECOGNITION: 1879-1979

50TH ANNIVERSARY OF BALZAC HALL: 1929-1979

Gus the Mail Carrier

It seems hard to realize that 100 years ago there was only a trace of a two-wheel cart path through our district. It generally followed a random course dodging sloughs, steep coulees, or rough areas from Ft. Edmonton to the trading areas of the south and eventually to Ft. Benton, Montana. Today's railroads, modern blacktop highways and airlines with their ever-increasing use constantly remind us of the solitude and loneliness of not so long ago. Those hardy pioneers just carried on as part of daily living, and the following relates one episode of life in the western plains.

Looking back, we quote from an item in the Saskatchewan Herald dated May 5, 1879:

...Gus, the Bow River mail carrier, who left here with the mail about the 12th of March, had a rough trip. His horse gave out at One Pine (Olds), near the edge of the woods, about seventy miles from the Elbow (Calgary). He left the horse and mail there and started on foot to cross the seventy miles of bare plain. On the way he got snow-blind and when found he was on the Nose Creek, which comes into the Bow River at the Elbow, following the ice down. He had been three days without food and two nights without fire. The mail was subsequently brought in and forwarded to Fort MacLeod...

Just a simple little item in the prairie press, caught by someone who related it almost three months later; I suppose a rather common occurrence at that time, but taken in its stride. Having researched some material kindly made available by Father E.O. Drovin, O.M.I. of Edmonton, Alberta, we were able to relate the following;

Gus Gouin's full name was Augustin Gouin, the son of Antoine Gouin and Catherine Boucher. Gus was born in 1840 or 1841 and was one of eight children. He was the second oldest son. He married Emilia Monroe who was the daughter of Felix Monroe and the granddaughter of the famous Hugh Monroe who was one of the first white men to live among the Blackfoot.

From the material submitted one can only conclude he was born somewhere on the western plains and probably was unaware of the location himself, as those hearty frontier men were ever on the move. There are no records of where the 38-year old mail carrier carried on his career afterwards or indeed where he was buried; just another mystery in western plains history.

As Gus Gouin cautiously wended his way towards Calgary following Nose Creek and passing the Sharp Hills (Buttes Hills), and at last reached the welcome of towering Nose Hill, he little thought that a vigorous settlement was less than ten years away.

Settlers for many years received their mail from Calgary box numbers or general delivery. Later on in the 1890s some mail was available for Airdrie settlers at the Johnston-Stevenson Stopping House, until the 1900s when Airdrie received a post office. Some eastern settlers' mail was held at Freshfield Post Office some six miles southeast of Balzac for pick-up service. Beddington siding had post office service at the proposed Lackner townsite in 1913, where the former Vestrum home still stands in 1979. The first postmistress was Mrs. Johnston, followed soon after by R.F. Tindal. The last postmaster at Beddington and the first at Balzac was George Washington, and during his term a mail delivery commenced, by team and democrat or team and sleigh, whichever conditions warranted. As an added source of revenue, groceries and confectionary were sold at the post office, and some were carried on the mail route.

Mr. Halford was the second postmaster, retaining that position until he traded the business for a farm three miles northwest with E.D. Evans, who became postmaster number three. During his term he added farm supplies, gas and oil to his wares. At first he used horses and a sleigh or democrat, which were neatly constructed with complete cabs for inclement weather conditions; Evans was also the first to use an automobile to transport mail.

In approximately 1935, Gladys Barker took over the post office as a fourth postal offical at Balzac, assisted by her sister Ida Barker; their father had settled in Beddington in 1887. Severe road and weather conditions in 1936 are still remembered, when the service of two extra teams and an auto for highway deliveries were put into full use. In 1936, Gladys Barker married Fred Campbell, continuing as postmistress.

We well recall the severe winter of 1948 when the first four-wheel drive vehicle was pressed into service, a Willys Army Jeep that fearlessly challenged all drifts dauntlessly for miles. Postmaster number five in 1948 was Jim Kirby with his wife Jennie, an ex-RCAF couple; he was the son of John and Jean Kirby, who came to Balzac in 1912. The Kirbys carried a full line of supplies for rural use and sold out to another native son, C.J. Davy, whose wife became the postal official in 1951. The Davy family had been in the vicinity since 1902. Davy increased his stock of local service supplies, and added a farm fuel delivery service, a new residence, and numerous other attractive improvements.

On December 15, 1962, Bill and Stella Murphy took over the post office as the seventh operators - again with full local service of agricultural needs. It was on October 1st, 1966, that the Murphys sold out to Jean and Winston McElroy. On March 1st, 1976 they sold out to James and Karen Roberts; he is the son of Jean McElroy, and continues to carry on inmuch the same manner as previous recent managers.

Mails to Beddington and Balzac were delivered by Canadian Pacific Railway until 1954, when Dench Cartage of Canada began to deliver them by mail van. The mail was picked up at the No. 2 highway by the postmaster, and outgoing mail was sent by the same method. Nowadays Her Majesty's Royal Mail truck delivers it to the Post Office vaults outside the premises where the outgoing mail is under lock and key for pickup.

Indeed quite a change from the early days when if no fragile large cartons were to be delivered, mail was literally kicked off a speedy, spotlessly clean, sixteen coach train along the railroad ditch. I personally recall picking up mail bags for 150 yards prior to putting them on a cart to go to the post office. I also recall seeing a mail tower 50 yards south of the main crossing where the bag of outgoing mail was placed waving in the breeze. As the speedy mail train passed, a mail coach employee would catch it by a hook and drag it in. A miss would mean stop by a much aggravated train engineer— and an amused school-bound audience who hoped such an act would be repeated to add excitement to the monotonous four-mile trek to the Buttes School.

So ends the Balzac Post Office story and 100 years of hardship, development and progress passing through our district. The writer dedicates this little account to the hard working civil servants of Her Majesty's Royal Mail at Balzac 1879-1979.

Submitted by C. Redvers Perry, 1979

Balzac Hall: 1929-1979

At the turn of the century, when settlement began in the Balzac district, the prairie consisted of grazing grass and a railroad winding through. There was one house between Balzac and Calgary. The first community effort was the building of Beddington and Buttes Schools. Art Robinson and George Jones organized dances that were held in Buttes School. From this they developed the idea of building a hall for dances and other community activities.

The first meeting to decide upon the community hall was held on December 6, 1928. The community hall was placed on a two-acre parcel of land; one acre was donated by G. Barker, and the other was purchased for $60.00. The first board of directors elected were: George E. Church, A.E. Robinson, Oliver R. Ingraham, Ed Rosenberger, Herbert J. Jobson, E. Sireni, W.J. Davy, and J. Weir. Balzac and area were divided into four districts, and various directors appointed to canvas each district. Many community members and businesses gave donations. The coming of electricity through the district in 1929 enabled the hall to have power. Volunteers built most of the building with Mr. Nels Keddy, a carpenter, acting as overseer. The actual cost of the building was $2,578.50.

A Gotfriedson truck was used to haul gravel for the concrete work. The hall was completed in June 1929, and the grand opening was held on June 6, 1929 [July 5], with the Hon. J.E. Brownlee, premier of the U.F.A. Government of Alberta, attending.

In 1951, the name U.F.A. Community Hall Association was changed and the hall was registered as Balzac Community Hall.

86

The hall sponsored many dances through the years, as well as housing many community functions. A $1 admission was charged for the early dances. Ladies of the community brought lunch. The dances apparently became boisterous at times, so the following rules were printed and posted:

1) No dancing without coats;
2) No smoking near stage or front of main dancing hall;
3) No drinking allowed on the premises;
4) No excessive noise or shouting in the hall.

Police were also requested to attend at unexpected times.

The hall also served as a clinic; in 1932, tonsil and adenoid patients were housed overnight. Seed fairs were held in the early 1930s. Dominion and provincial elections were voted upon and counted there. Church and Sunday School services were held in the hall until 1945, as well as interdenominational services. Sports days were quite frequent.

A baseball diamond was located on the hall grounds and in constant use from 1929-1940. Leagues from Beddington, Balzac, Airdrie, and Airdrie West competed, giving the community hours of enjoyable entertainment. The hockey rink was built on the hall grounds as well. Many exciting hockey games and skating parties occurred.

Over the years, many hours of volunteer labour have been donated to maintain, rebuild, and repair the building. The floor has been rebuilt twice and refinished. The stage has been rebuilt. The oil heating system was installed in the late 1950s. Supporters sponsored many activities to help maintain and improve the hall. Some activities of interest during the early years were: sports days, oyster suppers, Junior U.F.A. activities, and plays. One year a Stampede Queen contest was sponsored.

It was not always easy to keep the hall running. For example, in 1955 some suggested that grain be stored in the hall to bring in revenue, but this idea was rejected. Another time, closing the hall was contemplated; at times like these, however, community members always prevailed to overcome the emergency.

In the 1960's, the nature of the community changed again, with many people building small acreage holdings in the district. They too became involved in community affairs. In the 1970's, one noted helper, Doug Ekman, directed and helped to build the new addition to the hall.

The idea of adding to the hall was formulated in 1974 by the executive: Vicky Rewita, Ron James, Lorne Howell, Wayne Ham, Gordon Duce, Ed Holmes, and Earl Northcott. The hall sponsored a miscellaneous auction sale to raise funds for the new addition. Approximately $6,000 was realized from this sale, and there were many donations from the community. The executive applied to the Provincial Recreation Board and received $5,000 for the new addition. After many hours of volunteer labour from the community, with Doug Ekman and Earl Northcott having their second home at the hall, the addition was completed at an approximate cost of $24,000. We now celebrate the 50th Anniversary of the Balzac Hall. From pioneer days to the present, the hall continues to be a viable and active part of our community. May it so continue in the years ahead.

Submitted by C. Redvers Perry, 1979

Balzac United Church

In the early days church services were first held in homes, then in both Dry Creek School, northwest of Balzac, and Buttes School, east of Balzac. Services were sometimes taken by student ministers sent out from the east, and later by the Airdrie minister. The Dry Creek and Buttes School congregations joined to form the Balzac United Church.

In 1929 the Balzac Hall was built and Balzac United Church held services there until 1945. The church service was held in the main hall and Sunday School in the basement, with Alexa Church as Superintendent.

W.J. Church and Osia Rosenberger (both Elders) approached the congregation about purchasing a building and met with unanimous approval. They bought McPherson Coulee School and moved it to its present location on December 15, 1944. Volunteer work progressed rapidly and on January 14, 1945, the first service was held. The Rev. J.W. Smiley was minister at that time. On Easter Sunday, April 16, 1945, the Rev. Thomas Powell led the dedication service, assisted by J.W. Hallett, lay minister from Calgary. Osia Rosenberger, the first treasurer, reported on the contributions received, including a piano from Oliver Ingraham which is still in use today, and debts paid. During this period Sunday School was held at 2 p.m. and Church at 3 p.m.

In 1949, Gothic windows were installed and the building was stuccoed and redecorated. A propane floor furnace replaced the wood and coal heater, which added greatly to our comfort. Power was installed in 1954.

The Beddington Church building was moved to Balzac in March 1968, during the Rev. Norman Radway's ministry. Money was raised for renovations, and volunteers working under one paid supervisor made the building ready for its re-dedication on September 29, 1968. We invited all the former congregation of Beddington to join us. With the two buildings we were now able to have Sunday School at the same time as the church service, which had been changed to 9:45 a.m. in 1966. In 1970, the two structures were joined with a common entrance and cloak room.

The first pianist was Annie Rosenberger, then her daughter Lorna from 1928 to 1934. Berenice Shuttleworth began playing the piano in 1934 and is still organist today. She took a few years off from 1968 to 1970, when Betty Lamb played. Betty Lamb began a Junior Choir which sang at all special services from 1968 to 1973. These girls still get together once in a while and favour us with their music. Jean McElroy had a younger choir in 1974-75. An electric organ was purchased and dedicated on March 25, 1973.

The Sunday School has continued throughout the years, under several superintendents and teachers, sometimes with almost too many children for the space but in later years not so many but still very active. Last year carpet was laid to soften the noise level and make it warmer for the little ones. We enjoy programs put on by them for Family Services.

Annie Rosenberger organized and then for many years chaired the Ladies Aid. This group has always been active in the community although known by different names, from Ladies Aid to Women's Association and United Church Women (U.C.W.).

Not many of the original congregation are left but we do have children, grandchildren and great-grandchildren of these pioneers, along with newcomers, who still enjoy the fellowship of a small community church.

Submitted by Janie Church, c.1960, (revised by Jack Osborne, 1979)

Beddington United Church

The original history of the Balzac United Church dates back to 1900 or earlier. Among the earliest settlers to the Beddington area were the Lewis family, and as soon as their pioneer home was built the door was open for church services as this was an essential part of a law abiding community.

In 1902 Beddington School was built and sometime later church was held in it as the congregation was becoming too large for the Lewis home. On July 2, 1911, at a congregational meeting, it was decided to form a Ladies Aid Society. On July 19, the first meeting of this new group was held at the home of Lizzie Barker; the ladies helped in canvassing for funds to build a church and never ceased their efforts to maintain it in all the years that followed. The new church was built and was dedicated on February 23, 1913, Elizabeth Lewis' birthday. Throughout the years dedicated ministers and members carried out their duties, such as the organists: Helen Pole, Elsie Bushfield, and Faye Bushfield. Tom Pole, Lizzie Barker, and Verna Pole acted as Sunday School Superintendents, and there were many Sunday School teachers. At this time the Lewis family gave willingly of their musical talent with instruments and voice. During the late 1920s Beddington became United in name; it had been Presbyterian, but really had been United through these years as all denominations had built and worked for this church.

On November 27, 1949 a service of re-dedication was held as the church had undergone a facelift under the supervision and work of the Rev. R. Upton and the men of the community. The building walls had been lowered and stuccoed, the inside lined and painted. New pews and a communion table were added, which much improved the appearance and comfort of the building.

The next highlight was the 50th Anniversary, held on April 19, 1963, with a buffet supper and program of local talent followed by a church service on April 21, with a capacity crowd in attendance. The church carried on until January, 1968, when the congregation voted to close its doors and possibly burn it. However, much to the satisfaction and happiness of many of us, we learned of Balzac's desire to move it to the present site, and thus April 1968 ended an era but was also the beginning of a new.

Submitted by Doris Evans, 1979

The Anglicans of Balzac, Beddington and Symons Valley

The absence of an Anglican Church or mission in the Nose Creek area and so far north as Crossfield, where the next Anglican church was located, was felt by many families of Anglican faith. They wanted their children to have a religious education and to grow up with the church, and we see that many have done so and remain interested in and faithful to the church.

When Bishop Sherman became the Bishop of Calgary he deplored the absence of Anglican Churches in rural areas of Alberta. This business-like, ambitious church leader left no doubt in the minds of Anglicans of Canada that they must establish their own houses of worship. Not to wane or slacken from their duties and thanks to God, Anglicans of the district took up the challenge and obtained what they had wished and hoped for.

Many items of interest can be found in the St. Clement's Anglican Church records, which are methodically ordered. The first meeting was held in the home of Mr. and Mrs. R.B. Marston. The Rev. Mr. Clay from Olds was one of the early ministers to get the church services under way at the old Airdrie I.O.O.F. Hall in 1927. The Rev. Adams-Cooper was actually the first minister who spent many years amongst the parishioners. He carried on services at Airdrie and was the first minister to take a service at Balzac.

The church services carried on at Airdrie for a year or so and then it was decided to establish a church at Airdrie or Balzac to be more permanent. A congregational meeting decided on Balzac as the location and the Dry Creek school house, which had been used as a school up until 1926, was purchased from W.J. Northcott for $250. A name was chosen, after St. Clement of Alexandria. It was soon moved in 1927 by Charlie Riddick's moving equipment and pulled by two tractors, a Wallis belonging to Jack Sheppard and an "L" Case belonging to Clarence Church. The building came across fields to its location 100 yards west of the railroad at Balzac on the north side of the road. A temporary foundation was soon installed and services commenced. For many years, improvements were made little by little and under a great financial strain, which occurred chiefly in the hungry thirties. It would be impossible to estimate the efforts of so many who contributed so much in volunteer labour and financial support, right up to the present day.

The minute book of the church reveals that Rev. Adams-Cooper carried on the ministry until 1931 when the Rev. A.D. Currie took charge. The first church warden was C.W. Perry and Frank Davy was the people's warden. Vestrymen were B.M. Woods, W.C. Davy, W.J. Davy, H. Davy, T.L. Perry, Major Keeling, R. Croft, J. Sheppard Sr., J. Sheppard Jr., R. Whittaker, J. Hamilton, and R. Talbot. James Baldwin was the first secretary. One of the first items of business was the buying of a parcel of land at Balzac on November 29, 1928, on which to place the old 1904 Dry Creek school house as a Parish hall. It was used to raise money to carry on improvements to the building and pay its way in church business. Dances and church teas were put on with great success, in the old building which many local old timers had attended school in. This was the building where a local homesteader named C.W. Perry (Layreader) held the first interdenominational church service on Sunday, January 29, 1905 at 3:00 p.m. Osia Rosenberger and Billy Northcott Jr. took their part in promoting services, as records reveal, thus showing a real community spirit. The colourful history of the little church in the community holds quite a contrast in 75 years of existence, being built as a school in 1904 originally.

Sunday School was first conducted in 1930, with Annie Shuttleworth as the first Sunday School teacher.

The Rev. Mr. Currie, who resided in Crossfield, was well-known throughout surrounding districts. He carried on until November 1944, and afterwards always remembered his old friends at Balzac and on occasions was called back to conduct a wedding or funeral. He passed away in 1958 and was buried in Red Deer. A memorial window in St. Luke's was installed in his memory.

Other ministers included The Rev. R. Gibney, who was a teacher at the Sarcee Indian Reserve, and who served at intervals in the 1930s. The Rev. Mr. Mussen served in 1945-46, The Rev. Mr. Roe in 1946-48, The Rev. Mr. Vance in 1948, and The Rev. A.B. Lea from 1948 to 1952 when he returned to England. In 1952 The Rev. E.A. Justice of St Gabriel's of North Calgary took charge until 1961, with The Rev. M.H. Fairbridge from 1961-63, and The Rev. J. Roberts from 1963-66. From 1966 to 1968 The Rev. D. Blackwell carried on with Cochrane and Balzac as his responsibility until he moved to North Battleford, Saskatchewan. The Rev. G. Heald and Dean Stiff took services in 1968, and in succeeding years Archdeacon Carter, his son Dean Carter, and The Rev. Mr. Parsk have faithfully conducted the services, filling the needs of our Church of St. Clement's at Balzac.

It is regretted that more cannot be learned about the historical organ. Old timers relate that it was moved from Winnipeg to Calgary by Red River cart and first played in the Pro Cathedral in Calgary. It remained in storage at Ellen Davy's farm for a number of years prior to being placed in St. Clement's church where it is in constant use. On April 13, 1969 a farewell service was held for the old Bell organ when it was sent to Glenbow Foundation. The memorable service was conducted by the Venerable Archdeacon Cecil Swanson, and was televised on that occasion. Clem Perry, who brought it out in a wagon on December 31, 1904, and conducted the first service, was in the truck which delivered it to Glenbow that afternoon in 1969. It is now ready to go back into the old Pro Cathedral on Seventh Avenue where the organ was ably played in the first church in the 1880's.

One of the early missionaries of the west, Archdeacon Tims, who carried on the work amongst the Sarcee Indians in the 1870s, related his experiences in the church on occasions. Bishops Sherman, Ragg, and Calvert, in order of succession as Bishop of Calgary Diocese, have conducted services in the church.

Many of the founders of St. Clement's have passed on, but new members continue to fill the vacancies. To all who still attend, pleasant memories of the old days and the church founders prevail, as familiar hymns are heartily sung to the music of the historical organ.

To all of the clergyment and community workers who have done so much to retain an active Anglican Church in this area, St. Clement's congregation extends its hearty appreciation. This little account is dedicated to them, many of whom have passed on to God's eternal peace.

Submitted by C. Redvers Perry, 1979

First Plaque
1879-1979 A TRIBUTE To the First Mail Carrier in this area GUS GOUIN
GUS - The Bow River Mail Carrier From Edmonton to Calgary and Fort McLeod experienced a disabled horse at Olds mid-March 1879. He walked three days without food or shelter Snowblind and exhausted passing through this area was found at the Confluence of Nose Creek and the Bow River.
This Plaque unveiled on June 24th, 1979 By Nose Creek Historical Society

Second Plaque
Balzac United Church
Services held in BALZAC HALL from 1929 to January, 1945
McPherson Coulee School moved here December 15, 1944
DEDICATED Easter Sunday, April 16, 1945
BEDDINGTON CHURCH moved here in March, 1968

Third Plaque
St. Clement's Anglican Church
(Formerly Dry Creek School)
BUILT IN 1904 4 Miles Northwest of this location
INTERDENOMINATIONAL CHURCH SERVICES
Commenced January 29, 1905 Moved to Balzac November 28, 1928
PARISH HALL Former Co-op Office, Airdrie 1958. Moved to Balzac, November, 1977
This plaque unveiled on June 24th, 1979, by NOSE CREEK HISTORICAL SOCIETY

Balzac Alberta
Sunday, June 24, 1979
1:30 p.m.
NORTH OF THE BOW

EIGHTH LOCAL
HISTORICAL RECOGNITION
OF THE 100th ANNIVERSARY
OF
MAIL SERVICE PASSING THROUGH THE AREA
1879 - 1979
in conjunction with
Interdenominational
Church Service
at
Balzac Hall
Celebrating its 50th Anniversary
1929 - 1979
and
UNVEILING CEREMONY
at
UNITED AND ANGLICAN CHURCHYARD
COMMEMORATING SERVICES OF WORSHIP
since
JAN. 29th 1905   3 p.m.

Sponsored by
NOSE CREEK HISTORICAL SOCIETY
in conjunction
Anglican and United Churches

Pamphlet cover *(far left)* pays tribute to the mail service.
Jean Wallace*(left)* became Postmistress at Delacour in 1976.
(Above) Hoops and other equipment, used to sweep up mail bags as express trains passed a station, are pictured above. These items are displayed at the Grain Academy, Calgary, Alberta.
(Below) The mail always got through.

GUS GOUIN

GUS — *The Bow River Mail Carrier*
From Edmonton to Calgary
and Fort McLeod
experienced a disabled horse
at Olds mid-March 1879.
He walked three days without
food or shelter.
Snowblind and exhausted passing
through this area was found
at the Confluence
of Nose Creek and the Bow River.

This Plaque unveiled on June 24th, 1979 By
Nose Creek Historical Society

75th Anniversary of the Balzac-Beddington Postal Service April 1, 1912-April 1987. *(l-r)* Jim & Jeannette Kirby, Kelly & Vi Davy, George & Stella Murphy, Jean & Winston McElroy and the present Postmaster, Karen & Jamie Roberts. Plaque at left honors heroism of the first mail delivery man.

TO THE MANY
UNMARKED GRAVES
OF
NOSE CREEK
BURIED HERE

Bessie Stevenson - 1889-1901
William Stevenson - 1887-1887
also
Male stage coach passenger

N.C.H.S. — 1979

To Commemorate
50 YEARS OF SERVICE
to the
Balzac Community
1929 - 1979

1929 Hall Board
G. Church, A. Robinson, O. R. Ingraham,
E. Rosenberger, H. J. Jobson, F. Sireni, W. J. Davy,
J. Weir

1979 Hall Board
E. Northcott, D. Eckman, C. Ham, B. Ham,
B. James, M. Neeley, L. Dillabaugh, L. Mangus,
W. Stacey, S. Hladych

Balzac, June 1979: 50 years of Balzac Hall,
Commemorative Services of Worship and the Unveiling
Ceremony.

BALZAC - JUNE, 1979
Buttes Hills in background.

Above: Zane Gayda describes how an automated sorting machine works (*inset*) a modern (1996) mail sorting plant in Calgary handles huge volumes of mail daily.
Left: State of the art technology takes the drudgery out of sorting out mail. This picture courtesy 1995 Annual Report of Canada Post Corporation.
Below: Conveyor belts in the Calgary Plant assist in moving tons of mail each day.

The different mediums of mail delivery. The original picture from which this picture was taken hangs in the Calgary Central mail depot.

CHAPTER 14: ALBERTA'S 75TH ANNIVERSARY
EIGHTH LOCAL HISTORICAL COMMEMORATION: 1905-1980
ALSO BEDDINGTON HOMECOMING: 1886-1980
AND THE SANDSTONE QUARRY WINCH

The Sandstone Quarry Winch

As part of our tribute to the old timers of the Nose Creek District and the pioneers of the sandstone building industry we have preserved and reconstructed a sandstone quarry winch. Found in Symons Valley on the southwest quarter of Section 15-26-2-W5, on the farm formerly owned by Captain D'Encourt, D. Shearer, Johnstone Brothers, and currently by Robert Johnston, this winch was probably last used in 1912. Covered with rust and lichen, it had been abandoned by the west branch of Nose Creek on the old Rocky Mountain House traders' trail, which wended its way to Fort Benton, Montana in years gone by.

This winch was manufactured by M. Beatty and Sons, the Welland Iron Works, established in the 1860's in Welland, Ontario. Landing in Calgary in the 1880s when the sandstone building industry commenced, it could have been in operation at many locations. Endless research has revealed few or no details of its whereabouts or operations - another secret hidden away in history and laid to rest with our pioneer settlers.

When the winch was discovered in 1968, the Nose Creek Historical Society began to consider how to preserve the antique machine. With the co-operation of Robert Johnston and the Calgary Co-op Stores, the wish became a reality. In October 1979, the Society made arrangements to move it from its long resting site to the shop of Jack Osborne, three miles northwest of Balzac, for complete restoration. The restorers carried out excellent work, spending many hours and much patience on the job. When the resoration was complete the Society displayed the winch in the Airdrie Arena Historic Section at Airdrie Homecoming Celebration days; in the July 1st parade, it was also favourably accepted. As a final resting place, the winch was placed at the entrance of the new Calgary Co-op Shopping Centre, Beddington Heights, in tribute to the old timers of Nose Creek and the sandstone building industry in Calgary 1886-1920. For a complete and well researched book on the local sandstone industry, see *Calgary in Sandstone* written by Richard Cunniffe.

Submitted by C. Redvers Perry, 1980

Memorial to the Unmarked Graves of Nose Creek

On the Nose Creek historical Map, number 44 marks the graves which were brought to our attention in 1960. More have been located since. On this property, within a few yards of the marker is the resting place of two young children of the Johnstone Stevenson family.

Hidden away in history a stage coach passenger passed away and was buried in the same area. There are no records as to who he was, what age or what caused his death; just one more secret of the past which was handed down by old-timers over the years.

We of the Nose Creek Historical Society warmly welcomed all who made a sincere effort to attend this informal unveiling ceremony in tribute to the many lonely unmarked graves all over the prairies and particularly the Nose Creek District.

It was indeed a pleasure to have as our guest of honour Mrs. Jessie (Stevenson) Anderson from Oakland, California, who officially unveiled the plaque; she is the granddaughter of Johnston Stevenson. Her Aunt Bessie Stevenson, who died at the early age of 12 years, is in one of the graves near this site, and was a twin to Jessie's father Jack Stevenson. Mrs. Anderson was assisted by Don Copley, whose family came west to the Olds district in the

1890s, and in 1917 to the Airdrie District. The plaques are currently installed on the Copley property.

Submitted by C. Redvers Perry, 1980

Homecoming

The Beddington Ladies have made an intense effort to extend invitations to all former and present members of the community who had close associations with the local schools, the church and the three community halls that have been in operation from the early 1900's onward. The original Beddington School is at Jack Evan's farm, used as a shop. The United Church dedicated in 1913 has moved to the Balzac Churchyard. The original Beddington Hall, moved from Beddington to the present hall site, was moved again to Harry Pole's where it burnt down in the 1950s. The second hall, built in 1929, burnt in 1932 from a lightning bolt. The present one was built in 1933. We welcome you home in this year of Alberta's 75th Anniversary as a Province. Come again.

First Plaque

THE SANDSTONE INDUSTRY 1886-1912

This Beatty & Sons Horse-powered winch, used to load sandstone in the Nose Creek Valley quarries northwest of here, was restored by the Nose Creek Historical Society and placed here in tribute to the pioneers of Beddington and Balzac Districts.

Dedicated 1980

Second Plaque

To the Many Unmarked Graves of Nose Creek Buried Here
- Bessie Stevenson - 1889-1901
- William Stevenson - 1887-1887
- Male stage coach passenger
N.C.H.S. - 1979

Editors' Addition:
Sandstone City
The City

November 7, 1886 marked the beginning of Calgary's "Sandstone Era". On this date, the small town was struck with a devastating fire which consumed much of the main street. Determined Calgarians rebuilt their town in sandstone, a more fireproof material.

Easily quarried and carved, this native stone would transform the pioneer settlement to an urban centre known as the "Sandstone City of the West". Prior to 1900, sandstone construction focused on commercial buildings. The solid and substantial appearance of the golden stone gave Calgary's streets an aura of prosperity which in turn attracted business and new residents.

From 1906 to 1913, the town experienced phenomenal growth. Sandstone was now primarily used in large public buildings, schools, churches and several private residences.

At the peak of activity small communities for workers and their families were established near the outlying quarries at Brickburn, Glenbow and Sandstone.

The Industry

During the "Sandstone Era", fifteen quarries operated in and around Calgary. Wesley Orr opened the first quarry in 1886. Other quarriers soon followed, carving the stone from rich seams exposed along the Bow and Elbow Rivers.

Calgary's largest and longest running quarry was the Bankview Quarry, operated by William Oliver from 1902 until 1915. This major quarry supplied stone to many of Calgary's landmark buildings, and was itself a landmark until being filled in for road construction. Initially, the quarries were located close to town, but by 1910 most were overrun by the rapidly expanding suburbs. With improved rail lines, the industry relocated from the city to sites further west along the Bow River.

Rising costs for stone carving, the failure of the quarries to supply desirable stone, and competition from other building materials led to the abandonment of the quarries. With the outbreak of World War I, the "Sandstone Era" came to an end.

The Art

Building the "Sandstone City" involved hundreds of workers. By 1890, over half of the city's skilled tradesmen were stonecutters or masons. Many were Scots and came from generations of stoneworking experience.

There were three phases of stoneworking: quarrying, cutting, and finishing. It was the final phase that illustrated the true art of the industry. Skilled artisans, with their traditional tools of mallet and chisel, adorned the city's buildings with delicate details in geometric and floral motifs.

Today almost all of the master craftsmen who produced Calgary's sandstone heritage are gone. But the pride in their skill and tradition lives on in Calgary, the "Sandstone City".

Courtesy of Heritage Advisory Board, City of Calgary; date unknown.

The Alberta Coat of Arms

The Armorial Bearings of Alberta are described by the Emblems of Alberta Act Chapter E-8 and authorised 30 May 1907 as follows with editors inserts.

(Revised statues of Alberta 1980)

Arms - Azure [blue], in front of a range of snow mountains proper a range of hills. Vert [green], in base a wheat field surmounted by a prairie both also proper, on a chief Argent [silver] a St. George's Cross [England].

Crest - On a helm [Helmet, tilted] with a Wreath Argent [Silver] and Gules [Red] a Beaver [Hudson Bay Company] couchant [lying] upholding on its back the Royal Crown both proper.

Supporters - On the dexter [right] side a Lion d'or [Gold, possibly Scotland] armed and langred [tongue out] Gules [Gold] and on the sinister [left] a grassy mount with the Floral emblem of the Province of Alberta the Wild Rose growing therefrom proper.

Motto - Fortis Et Liber [Strong and Free].

BEDDINGTON, ALBERTA
Sunday, July 27, 1980
2:00 p.m.
NORTH OF THE BOW

NINTH LOCAL
HISTORICAL COMMEMORATION
IN RECOGNITION OF ALBERTA'S 75th ANNIVERSARY
✦
AND
BEDDINGTON HOMECOMING WELCOME
1886 - 1980
Mr. & Mrs. James Parsons
confirmed settler 1886
on what is now the
International Airport
and
Plaque to Unmarked Graves
Church Service

Sponsored by
BEDDINGTON LADIES
and
NOSE CREEK HISTORICAL SOCIETY

*Calgary's first hospital, the General, was built with sandstone, 1911. The above photo hangs at the present Rundle Lodge. (**Below**): What remains of the old sandstone building, located on 12 Avenue S.E, Calgary.*

Sandstone Sundial: this Park, located on the grounds of the original General Hospital, was officially opened June 11, 1974 by Hon. Peter Lougheed, Premier of the Province of Alberta.

City Hall, Calgary: sandstone was the material of choice.

**TO THE MANY
UNMARKED GRAVES
OF
NOSE CREEK
BURIED HERE**

Bessie Stevenson - 1889-1901
William Stevenson - 1887-1887
also
Male stage coach passenger

N.C.H.S. — 1979

*Completely restored in July 20, 1980 by Jack Osborne, this horse propelled winch (**above**) was used to quarry sandstone until 1912. It had been abandoned by the west branch of Nose Creek, (pictured on cover of pamphlet) on the Rocky Mountain House traders' trail.*
Left: *Located 4 miles north of Airdrie on the old Edmonton-Calgary coach trail just east of McPhersons Coulee, this plaque is mute testimony of the hardships endured by our pioneers.*

McDougall School (1906). 412-7 Street S.W.

Cathedral Church of the Redeemer (1904) 602-1 Street S.E.

Lougheed House (1891) 707 13 Ave. S.W.

Land Titles Building (1907) 520-Avenue S.W. (demolished)

Court House (1914) 530-7 Ave. S.W.

Grain Exchange Building (1909) 815-1 Street S.W.

Knox United Church (1911). 506-4 Street S.W.

Royal Bank Building (1890), former Hudson Bay Company, 102-8 Ave. S.W.

CHAPTER 15: THE CALGARY-EDMONTON TRAIL
TENTH LOCAL HISTORICAL RECOGNITION: 1875-1981

Dr. Hugh A. Dempsey and Dr. Stephen Wilk have both written about the history of the Calgary-Edmonton Trail, showing the tremendous impact this travel route has had over the years. David Thompson, in 1800, was the first white man to travel a portion of the Calgary-Edmonton Trail. At that time it was known as the "wolf track" by the famous explorer. The Blackfoot and Peigan Indians called it the "Old North Trail", going back into ancient times. They declared that the north portion from the Bow and Elbow rivers where Calgary now stands led to the barren wastes of the north, and the southern part of the trail led clear down to Mexico. No doubt stories of trade communications, warfare and tribal relations all had a part in this historic trail.

The Methodist missionary John McDougall was one of the first to cut the line of travel to Fort Edmonton in 1873. He traversed the area with his brother David when journeying from Fort Edmonton to the Morley mission located 50 miles west of Fort Calgary. The original trail swung west from the Olds district, skirting the parklands to Morley. In 1875, when the North-West Mounted Police were established in Fort Calgary, Reverend McDougall established a track from Lone Pine (Olds) to Calgary. Over the course of time this became known as the Calgary-Edmonton Trail, prior to 1931 when the No.2 Highway came into existence.

For many years the Calgary-Edmonton Trail was used to transport goods of all types from Fort Benton, Montana to Edmonton, filling the needs of settlers in the north. Prior to that, barges were used on the North Saskatchewan River to bring essentials from the east; this was much more slow and expensive than the Benton-Calgary route. The alternative was to travel overland by Red River cart from Fort Garry (Winnipeg) which was equally slow, cumbersome and expensive. The routes from the U.S.A. started at the Missouri River. When the goods arrived at Fort Benton they were transferred to heavy-duty ox carts, and travelled up the Whoop Up Trail to Fort Macleod and on to Fort Calgary, where they were switched to light two-wheel Red River carts and sent on to Fort Edmonton. The heavy bog land and deep black soil necessitated the use of only the light wheeled vehicles over Alberta northern areas. Northern Alberta residents were jubilant at the success of this route. The trail saw many varied vehicles at that time; covered wagons, Red River carts, mule trains, and stage coaches. There would be a lonely rider passing through with little to say, his actions revealing nothing to the casual observer. Was he in pursuit or being pursued? An eager adventurer or a cautious traveller? It was anyone's guess.

In 1883 Calgary, till then only a tent town, boomed with the advent of the railroad, and so consequently did the use of the Edmonton Trail. For the next eight years it was the most well-beaten track in the Dominion. Calgary was a beehive of activity, with goods being brought in from the east and shipped north on the trail to numerous settlers and trappers. Likewise, furs from as far north as the Arctic were sent back south for trade, via the Edmonton Trail, and then shipped east by rail to the greedy European market. Airdrie's Addison McPherson was a freighter and one of the first sheep ranchers north of the Bow. He and a partner, John Coleman, obtained the contract entitling them to carry the Royal Mail every two weeks between Calgary and Edmonton. They also carried light freight and passengers. Soon after, a weekly passenger service was set up by stage driver Donald McLeod. Settlers in wagons, prospective business men and general store operators were frequent road users. Before long, the Calgary and Edmonton Railroad was proposed, surveyed, and brought into being. The sod was turned in 1890 and the railroad started operating in 1891. An abrupt end came to the colourful travel on the Calgary-Edmonton Trail, it took only 12 hours to cover the distance between Edmonton and Calgary by rail. The stage coach service stopped, unable to compete with the comfort and efficiency of the train. For the next couple of decades, there was a gradual decline in the use of the Edmonton Trail. Settlers' wagons, the odd buggy with a land dealer, quiet and observant mounted policemen, and every so often the mystic tight-lipped traveler, would use this well-known route. Then in 1908, the automobile made its appearance, and from here the story is familiar.

The old trail was graded, levelled and gravelled. Turns were eliminated, hills cut down, waterways re-routed, and bridges installed. Road signs and police car patrols became evident in the 1920s. Soon followed white lines, oil and then tarmac surfaces; and a multitude of regulations and reminders designed to alert us to the hazards of excessive speed and resulting carelessness.

What a past, what an exciting history, what stories can be told! What untold hardships were encountered when a stage coach made a five day trek to Edmonton with only 10 homes between the two centres to extend shelter. No doubt there were amusing times too, but the harsh Alberta climate can be ruthless. To illustrate the fact; a stage coach was lost in fog and snow for a day while enroute from the Dickson-Stevenson stopping house to a log cabin at the Sharp Hills (Butte Hills, east of Balzac). Gus the mailman suffered the ordeal of walking from Olds to Calgary in March, arriving weak and exhausted. The trail's history is unending.

To the local people, this small portion of the Edmonton Trail was referred to as the Dickson-Stevenson trail after the Dickson-Stevenson stopping house. These operators ran the first stopping house north of the Bow River, from 1879 to 1900. It proved to be a multipurposed dwelling. Not only did it provide overnight accommodation to travellers, but also it served as a school for local children and a post office, and occasionally a church service would be held there when a clergyman passed through.

The tales of this trail have been laid to rest - an epoch past; but to this era a tribute long overdue has been realized.

Submitted by: C. Redvers Perry, 1981

CROSSFIELD, ALBERTA
Sunday, Oct. 25th, 1981
2:00 p.m.

TENTH LOCAL
HISTORICAL RECOGNITION
of
CALGARY — EDMONTON TRAIL
and
NAMING OF A PORTION IN CONSTANT USE
1875 - 1981
The
DICKSON-STEVENSON TRAIL
1875 - 1931
Main Road To Edmonton
in conjunction with
INTERDENOMINATIONAL CHURCH SERVICE
at
CROSSFIELD
2 p.m. Sunday Oct 25th 1981
and
UNVEILING CEREMONY
3½ Miles South
at
JOHNSON STEVENSON STOPPING HOUSE SITE
Naming the
DICKSON-STEVENSON TRAIL
which passes through
Sponsored by
NOSE CREEK HISTORICAL SOCIETY
in conjunction with
UNITED CATHOLIC AND BAPTIST CHURCHES

This page, clockwise from top: Pamphlet celebrates Calgary-Edmonton traffic through the years; Modern equipment, modern roads ('x' indicates location of Balzac); A 1926 Ford, negotiates the Little Red River (circa 1938); The Calgary-Edmonton Coach Road, 1878-1891. The men pictured above marked the waning importance of this route. They were part of a Geological Survey team and were mapping a system of travel that quickly made coach travel almost obsolete—the railway.

Modern roadbuilding equipment sets up near Balzac, 1962.

The old Calgary-Edmonton Coach road. This picture was taken four miles south of Airdrie. Ray Howden is in the foreground.

The Dickson-Stevenson Trail (1875-1981) was officially recognized as a historical location October 25, 1987. (l-r) RCMP representative, Gwen Copley, and Peter Morrison, Council Member, Rocky View Municipality.

Preparing for the official ribbon-cutting ceremony of the Dickson-Stevenson Trail, Oct 25, 1987. Note RCMP cruiser in background.

Horse trails to vapor trails: Precision flying at the Penhold Air Show, August 1992. (Inset) Space technology.

Historic Trail Maps—Nose Creek Valley

Adapted from Glenbow Library maps
Source: *Pioneers of the Faith* by S. Wilk, 1962 (pg. 110)

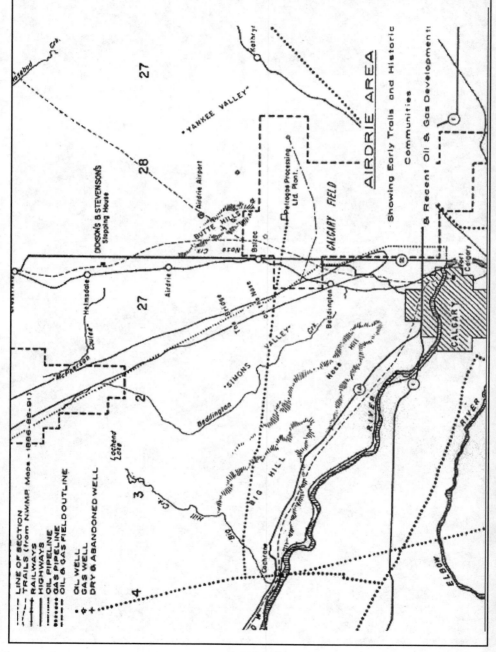

Fort Benton, circa 1878, as sketched by an army officer.
Prior to the arrival of CP Rail Calgary was a tent town punctuated by the odd wooden structure. This picture was taken east of the Elbow River, with Fort Calgary and the I.G. Baker store located on the west.
Oxcarts wend their way along the trail, hauling up to 400 tons of cargo at a time.
The Fort Benton (Montana) dock c. 1880. A newly arrived consignment of goods destined for distribution in the North West

Territories (Canada). In the pioneer era, this port was crucial.
5. A section of the old trail from Fort Benton to Fort Walsh, taken July 5, 1936
6. Fort Edmonton on the North Saskatchewan River. This sketch is taken from the **North West Passage** by Milton & Cheadle.
7. A view of Fort Calgary, facing north, August 1881. Picture taken by the Geological Survey of Canada.
8. Fort Macleod circa 1878.

CHAPTER 16: AGRICULTURE AND RANCHING IN THE NOSE CREEK AREA
ELEVENTH LOCAL HISTORICAL RECOGNITION: 1882-1982
ALSO PRESERVATION OF THE SANDSTONE ESCARPMENT

A century of agriculture in the Nose Creek country is described in *One Day's Journey*, by Stephen Wilk. On April 11, 1882, the following leases were granted by the Government of Canada:

Lease #42 Cochrane Ranch Co. 100,000 acres (stocked in 1881)
Lease #43 A.W. Ogilvie 34,000 acres leased but never ranched
Lease #44 E.M. Bains 55,000 acres
Lease #51 Duncan C. Plumb 88,000 acres
Lease #14 Thomas Temple 44,000 acres

Ranching was their main intention, in short to run a major cattle enterprise. The ups and downs of farming and ranching were as prevalent in those days as in all succeeding years. The ranchers were reluctant to see the homesteader arrive on the scene, viewing it as a move by the small operator to encroach on their leased ranchland. Squatters were watched with a stern eye too, for fear they might use the services of the rancher's bull to improve their little cattle herds; as well, there was the suspicion that they might nip a few rancher's calves as the year progressed. Be that as it may, settlers arrived in droves from 1882 to 1905, securing land by one means or other. There were four different ways settlers could obtain land as regulated by the government's order in council P.C.874:

1. By Purchase, at a price of $1.00 an acre up to a maximum of 640 acres, or one section per person.
2. By Pre-emption Rights, in the case of a settler having settled on the land previous to the survey, by paying $1.00 per acre in cash for a maximum acreage of 160 acres, or one quarter section, on proof of residence and being a British subject by birth or naturalization. The settler must be the head of a family or a single man over 21 years of age.
3. Homestead Rights. On the payment of a $10.00 fee, a settler could obtain 160 acres, and receive patent for the land after three years on proof of residence and cultivation of land. The settler must be the head of a family or a single man over 21 years of age.
4. Free Grant. Officers and men who were or had been in the Ontario or Quebec battalion of Rifles and stationed in Manitoba, were entitled to a free grant of one quarter section, without actual residence.

Slowly and surely settlement caught hold, though some failed to prove up and had to wend their way home from whence they came. The stalwarts braved the severe winters, the summer droughts, the fearful prairie fires, flu epidemics, shortage of ready cash, and the loneliness often mentioned in local history books. Family responsibilities soon led to the building of schools, community centres and churches, and good roads and bridges catered to increased traffic flow. Small towns flourished. Beddington, Balzac, Airdrie, and Crossfield were established before long. This year we salute the homesteaders and ranchers of our district who generally settled here in the 1880s to 1910, and are regarded as the pioneers. Agriculture, the backbone of our very existence, we acknowledge with the greatest respect and reverence for the part played in the Nose Creek area. Well done!

Submitted by C. Redvers Perry, 1982

The Lewis Trail

The first mention of this picturesque valley was on December 7th, 1792 when Peter Fidler, an employee of the Hudson's Bay Company fur trading post at Rocky Mountain House, made his way into what is now known as southern Alberta. He described the valley and a creek now called Nose Creek, even recording the temperature at 58 degrees Fahrenheit. It was on November 21st, 1800, that the west's most renowned explorer David Thompson passed through, according to the record of ancient maps. The trail was a popular fur trade route, providing shelter and food to early travellers, its natural course leading them to the excellent ford across the Bow River near where Langevin Bridge is today. It would only be natural to assume that pioneers wishing to settle close to the little town of Calgary would choose this spot with its fresh water and lush sheltered pastures. Settlers first arrived in the 1880s, and one family whom we particularly remember over the years was the Lewis family.

In 1889, Joseph and Elizabeth Lewis came from Peel County, Ontario to Alberta and settled in "the valley" on the advice of the Lougheeds and other friends from Ontario who had already been established in the North-West Territories as it was known then. On maps of the 1880s, the creek running in the valley was known as Lougheed Creek, later officially named West Nose Creek.

Over the years the Lewises took part in many community activities, of which some of the most outstanding follow. Elizabeth Lewis offered her home for church services soon after settling in the district and continued to be active all her life in church circles. The cattle dip, a device to control mange or louse outbreaks, was in the charge of one native son, Bill Lewis, for many years. In fact this part of the valley and the bridge over the creek was commonly called "The Dip". P.C. (Charlie) Lewis was a school trustee from 1907 to 1935 and also served as a conscientious councillor for many years with the M.D. of Beddington #250. Over these hills the same Charlie Lewis herded horses and corralled them just south-west of where the Nose Hill cairn is now located (75th Ave. and 7th St. NW, Calgary) for overnight safety. Everyone knew of the Lewis orchestra of violins and harmonicas. They gave freely of their time on many occasions, and played at the Palliser Hostel during the Southern Alberta Old Timers Association dances. On reading the Nose Creek Literary Society minute books from 1901 to 1902, we see that the Lewises were founding members of the active social club which was the hub of early community amusements.

Three of the Lewises lived near this portion of the valley which has been earmarked for a walking park for future generations to appreciate. Bill Lewis had a log cabin in early years just west of the Quarry near the creek - we recall it still standing some 20 years ago. P.C. Lewis lived in what is now a red brick two storey house in full view of the Quarry escarpment. Norman Lewis, son of John Lewis, lived his entire life on the old Symons Valley farm, and only for his last year or two did he reside in a Senior Citizens' home in Calgary. Norman was one of the last threshermen to operate in the district.

With such a colourful, community-minded family, devoted to all worth-while causes for the wellbeing of their neighbours, we hope and anticipate that the walking trail through this historic area will be named "The Lewis Trail" in tribute to those respected old timers. For this we will be ever grateful.

Submitted by C. Redvers Perry, 1982

Conclusion

100 years ago the huge grazing leases were approved. While we actually learned little from their operation, this was the advent of a tremendous, vital industry whose product was required world wide. From ranching to mixed farming, and more recently a specialized type of agriculture, the Nose Creek district from Calgary to Crossfield has been most productive and prosperous. Industry and expansion of one type or other has removed thousands of acres from use, but that which remains continually proves itself as number one in agricultural production.

In tribute to the old timers and all those involved over the 100 years of farming and ranching, we recognize the name of the Lewis Trail in historic Symons Valley to mark agriculture in our district. At some time in the not too distant future a plaque will mark the walking trail for all to appreciate.

Submitted by C. Redvers Perry, 1982

BEDDINGTON, ALBERTA
Sunday, December 5, 1982
2:00 p.m.

ELEVENTH LOCAL
HISTORICAL RECOGNITION

**AGRICULTURE IN THE
NOSE CREEK AREA
1882 - 1982
and
PRESERVATION OF THE SANDSTONE
ESCARPMENT IN ITS NATURAL ORIGIN**

in conjunction with
Interdenominational Church Service
at
BEDDINGTON HALL

Sponsored By
NOSE CREEK HISTORICAL SOCIETY
in conjunction with
UNITED and ANGLICAN CHURCHES

Nose Hill — Peter Fidler Hudsons Bay employee at Rocky Mountain House. First mentioned the general area in 1792 on his southern travels — Sec. 9 - Last rancher Art Savill, P. Burns previously. Photo taken 1969. Nose Hill Spring to right centre (75 Ave. - 7th St. N.W.).

*This is a Historical Document. Please value it on the basis of posterity.
It is compliments of The Nose Creek Historical Society.*

28 Bill Northcott with the the first municipal spray unit using a 1940 surplus R.C.A.F. gas tank mounted on a Dodge truck.

Using a Hart Parr tractor to pull a three furrow plough. (May 1935)

Harvesting oats on the Perry farm, 1937. Clem Perry is riding the binder with a four horse team.

King Perry on a Hart Parr Tractor towing an Oliver Plough. (1935).

Leighton Perry mounted on a new 'D' Case and seeding with a John Deere 10 foot Van Brunt drill (circa 1940). This tractor was unique in that it possessed rubber front tires, enabling it to manoeuvre with greater ease.

The second one of its kind in the immediate Balzac district in 1951, this Massey Harris #21, powered by a Chrysler motor performs combining duties on the Perry farm. (Below) a 24" brush breaker clearing a patch of land at the White farm. Spring 1962.

Clem Perry on a new Frost & Wood binder, 1933. King Perry is serving as stooker.

A Model 'D' Case tractor using seed drill, seeder, discer and packer planting in spring.

Redvers Perry operating a model 510 combine harvester. 1967 Chevy truck handles the grain.

A 1987 50-foot flexicoil harrow and packer being pulled by a Case 2290.

Poultry provides a reliable source of food.

Chemical insecticide ready for use on a modern farm. (1985)

Balzac Seed Plant readying Century peas for delivery.

A typical chemical weed spraying operation.

Apples in Fall

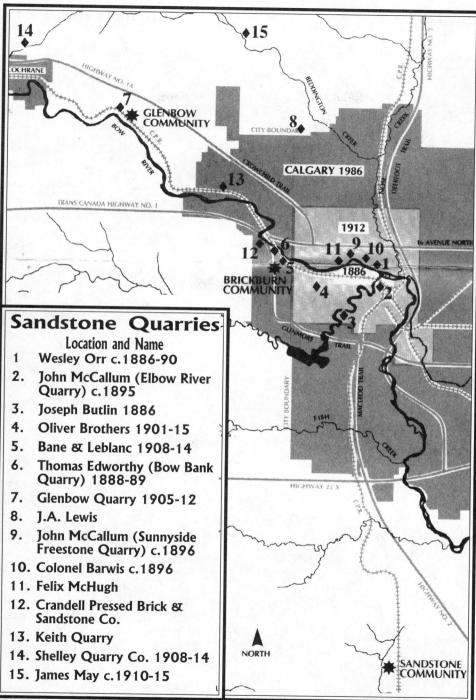

Sandstone Quarries

Location and Name

1. Wesley Orr c.1886-90
2. John McCallum (Elbow River Quarry) c.1895
3. Joseph Butlin 1886
4. Oliver Brothers 1901-15
5. Bane & Leblanc 1908-14
6. Thomas Edworthy (Bow Bank Quarry) 1888-89
7. Glenbow Quarry 1905-12
8. J.A. Lewis
9. John McCallum (Sunnyside Freestone Quarry) c.1896
10. Colonel Barwis c.1896
11. Felix McHugh
12. Crandell Pressed Brick & Sandstone Co.
13. Keith Quarry
14. Shelley Quarry Co. 1908-14
15. James May c.1910-15

*Will Pearce, Supt. of
Calgary Parks
Planning, examines a
sandstone fissure
June 6, 1994.*

Above: *This split-rock
formation is located at the
Bell L Ranch, Symons
Valley.*
Right: *"Big Chief Symon'
outcrop is being inspected
by Sarah Jane Gruetzner of
City Parks & Recreation
(June 6, 1994). In the
background is the Hanson
Farm (in the '20ies, the
Banderob place).*

THE SANDSTONE INDUSTRY
1886 – 1912

THIS BEATTY & SONS HORSE-
POWERED WINCH, USED TO
LOAD SANDSTONE IN THE
NOSE CREEK VALLEY QUARRIES
NORTHWEST OF HERE, WAS
RESTORED BY THE NOSE CREEK
HISTORICAL SOCIETY AND
PLACED HERE IN TRIBUTE TO
THE PIONEERS OF BEDDINGTON
AND BALZAC DISTRICTS.

DEDICATED 1980

Above: *Restored winch used in sandstone quarry on display at the
Beddington Co-op, 8220 Centre Street N.E.*

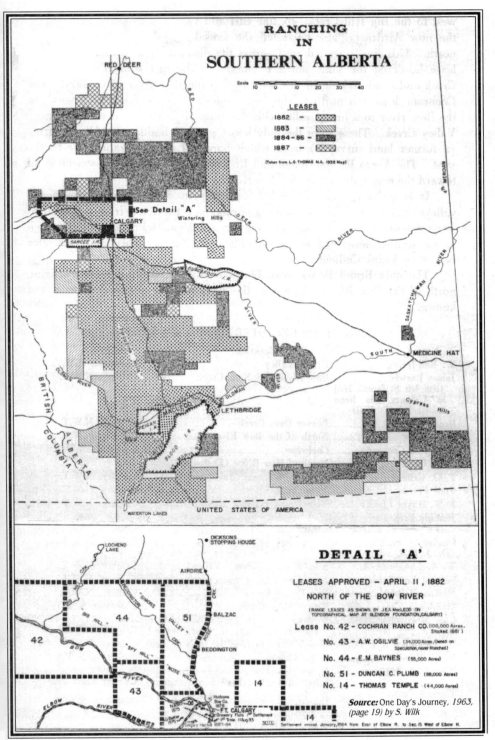

RANCHING
IN
SOUTHERN ALBERTA

Scale 10 0 10 20 30 40

LEASES

1882	—
1883	—
1884–86	—
1887	—

(Taken from L.G. THOMAS M.A. 1936 Map)

RED DEER

See Detail "A"

CALGARY

Wintering Hills

SARCEE I.R.

BOW RIVER

BLACKFOOT I.R.

MEDICINE HAT

Cypress Hills

BRITISH COLUMBIA

ALBERTA

PEIGAN I.R.

LETHBRIDGE

OLDMAN RIVER

MACLEOD

BLOOD I.R.

WATERTON LAKES

UNITED STATES OF AMERICA

DETAIL 'A'

LOCHEND LAKE

DICKSONS STOPPING HOUSE

AIRDRIE

BIG HILL

44

BALZAC

51

BEDDINGTON

"SPY HILL"

42

43

BOW RIVER

ELBOW RIVER

FT. CALGARY

14

14

LEASES APPROVED — APRIL 11, 1882

NORTH OF THE BOW RIVER

(RANGE LEASES AS SHOWN BY J.E.A. MacLEOD ON
TOPOGRAPHICAL MAP AT GLENBOW FOUNDATION, CALGARY)

Lease No. 42 – COCHRAN RANCH CO. 100,000 Acres. Stocked 1881

No. 43 – A.W. OGILVIE (34,000 Acres, Owned on Speculation, never Ranched)

No. 44 – E.M. BAYNES (55,000 Acres)

No. 51 – DUNCAN C. PLUMB (88,000 Acres)

No. 14 – THOMAS TEMPLE (44,000 Acres)

Source: One Day's Journey, *1963, (page 19) by S. Wilk*

NOTE: Settlement moved January, 1964 from East of Elbow R. to Sec. 15 West of Elbow R.

CHAPTER 17: ARRIVAL OF THE C.P.R. IN CALGARY
TWELFTH LOCAL HISTORICAL RECOGNITION: 1883-1983

The Approach to the Mountains, 1883

When William Cornelius Van Horne was hired as Canadian Pacific's general manager at the beginning of 1882, he announced that he would lay 500 miles of track before the end of the season. Many professional engineers scoffed at what was thought to be an idle boast made by an overly self-confident, upstart American railroader. Yet he accomplished his goal and by the end of the year, the track was 587 miles west of Winnipeg, a few miles east of what is now Maple Creek, Sask.

In mid-April 1883, construction resumed. The target for this year was the summit of the Continental Divide at Kicking Horse Pass, 370 miles away, a reduced objective contrasted to 1882 caused by the more difficult terrain once the prairies were left behind at Calgary. By the end of May, the railhead reached the South Saskatchewan River at what is now Medicine Hat, and a temporary wooden trestle was built across the river pending the completion of a permanent structure, so that construction could continue onward towards the mountains.

During June 1883, about 65 miles of track was put down, an average of better than 2½ miles per working day being maintained. On the 3rd of that month, 4.68 miles of track was laid in a single day, starting about two miles west of the present site of Brooks, Alta. Four days later, on July 7, this record was broken when 6.02 miles of iron was put down through what is now Lathom, Alta. Conscious of the fact that workers on the Union Pacific Railroad in the USA in the 1860s had established a record of ten miles in one day on similar construction, the contractors decided to make one last effort, before the construction left the prairies, to establish a new tracklaying record. The day selected was July 28, 1883, while the rails were being spiked down through what is now Strathmore. The day was hot (33 degrees C) and dry, but owing to what General Superintendent J.M. Egan described as a lack of organization—"a grand fizzle", to use his own words—the previous record was exceeded only by about one-third of a mile, and the advance for the day totalled 6.38 miles. On August 15, Calgary was reached.

Construction through the foothills along the valley of the Bow took much more time. It required until the end of November to reach the summit and the end of the season's work, in Kicking Horse Pass, 125 miles west of Calgary. Difficult and challenging terrain lay beyond the Pass, and nearly two years would be required before the unbroken band of iron was linked through to the Pacific.

The actual work of construction as far as Calgary was carried out by Langdon, Shepard & Company, a construction firm based in St. Paul Minnesota, which had signed a contract with Canadian Pacific on March 1, 1882. The contractor was under the immediate supervision of James Ross, Manager of Construction, who reported directly to Van Horne. As a tribute to the St. Paul [contractors, railway sidings] Nos. 18 and 19, were given the names Langdon and Shepard. West of Calgary, Ross acted as his general contractor. The men employed in construction were North Americans, part of a large pool of experienced railway workers recruited by labour agencies, who were regularly engaged in such work, season after season.

In accordance with train operating requirements of that time, divisional terminal yards and engine facilities were established at intervals of about 125 miles, thus determining railway terminal roles for what would become Medicine Hat, Gleichen and Canmore, where yards and roundhouses were built. Initially, Calgary was not a division point, but following the building of lines connecting it with Edmonton and Fort Macleod early in the 1890s, it was accorded this status and locomotives and crews ran through from Medicine Hat to Calgary instead of Gleichen.

Some months were required to ballast and level the track, construct stations, water tanks and other service facilities. During this period, the numbered sidings were given names by Van Horne. The line was opened for regular train service as follows:

Swift Current-Medicine Hat .... 151 miles, June 10, 1883
Medicine Hat-Calgary .... 179 miles, December 2, 1883
Calgary-Laggan .... 116 miles, December 2, 1883

The final stage in the story of transcontinental railway construction came in November, 1885, when the last rail was laid in Eagle Pass in the Columbian Mountains of British Columbia. Scheduled freight and passenger train service between the east and west coast of Canada was begun in July, 1886 with the inaugural run of the "Pacific Express", which left Montreal on June 28 and arrived at Port Moody on July 4 of that year. The 370 miles of main track constructed in 1883 were covered by this train in about 18 hours from the morning of July 2 to the morning of July 3, 1886.

By Omer Lavallee, Corporate Historian and Archivist, Canadian Pacific Limited

100 Years Across the Bow

There have been numerous excellent accounts written by first hand witnesses of thrilling episodes to do with the coming of the Canadian Pacific Railway across the prairies; little more can be added at this time. Those who desire a more detailed account of the arrival of the rails and the famous old steam engine "#147" on the memorable day of August 11th, 1883 at Calgary, need only to contact the Glenbow Archives, to which we are ever grateful, for a multitude of information. The linking by rail of the Atlantic Ocean to the Pacific Ocean will be one of the most memorable events in Canadian history for years to come.

While the spot where the tracks arrived in Calgary is not in the Nose Creek Historical Society's territory, it is just across the Bow River. So we paddle across the Bow just to nip a little history that made a tremendous impact on the development of the west, and indeed the Nose Creek area north of the Bow is no exception. The first farmers and ranchers arrived in our area of Nose Creek in 1883, and without question many of their families and belongings came west by C.P.R. Records reveal how Calgary simply broke out at the seams as the rails brought in tons of building materials, of farming and industrial effects, to build the west. Nearly everyone's family history makes reference to some interesting item involving the railroad, be it humourous or otherwise. Rail travel made a great impression. We acknowledge the lasting contribution of those who laboured so hard, enduring tremendous hardship, with maybe not the best wage for reward. Many of those who toiled were of foreign extraction, unable to converse in English, far from their homeland, and in some cases they lost limbs from accidents or even their lives. We salute their earnest efforts. As we journey by train, auto and the air, when deep in the Rocky Mountains, we ponder in utter amazement just what a tremendous feat it was. To the ability of those who plotted its course, blazed the trails of exploration and engineered the railroad through all its geographical and financial difficulties, today we pay the deepest thanks and respect. They laid the path for our pleasant way of life over the last 100 years; may the Good Lord bless us with its continued existence.

Submitted by C. Redvers Perry, 1983

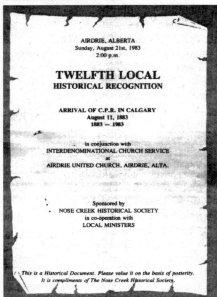

AIRDRIE, ALBERTA
Sunday, August 21st, 1983
2:00 p.m.

TWELFTH LOCAL
HISTORICAL RECOGNITION

ARRIVAL OF C.P.R. IN CALGARY
August 11, 1883
1883 — 1983

in conjunction with
INTERDENOMINATIONAL CHURCH SERVICE
at
AIRDRIE UNITED CHURCH, AIRDRIE, ALTA.

Sponsored by
NOSE CREEK HISTORICAL SOCIETY
in co-operation with
LOCAL MINISTERS

*This is a Historical Document. Please value it on the basis of posterity.
It is compliments of The Nose Creek Historical Society.*

Above: *Royal Train carrying King George VI and Princess Elizabeth on their 1939 visit to the Prairies.*
Below: *C.P.R. trans-Canada train heading for BC*
Bottom: *CPR passenger train, Calgary, 1889.*

C.P.R. passenger train, Calgary, 1889

1981

Above: *As the display at the Grain Academy, Calgary, indicates, over time, rails grew bigger and heavier to cope with the increasingly higher volume of traffic:-*

1. *1883—56lbs.*   5. *1931—130lbs*
2. *1897—80lbs.*   6. *1938—100lbs*
3. *1908—85lbs.*   7. *1966—115lbs*
4. *1921—100lbs.*   8. *1977—136lbs*

Left: *Tragedy occasionally mars an otherwise excellent system.*

Below: *This float at the Nose Creek Historical Society parade in Airdrie honored the arrival of CPR a 100 years ago.*

Bottom: *Crossfield's first railwaystation, built in 1904. It was destroyed by a fire in 1931.*

117

CHAPTER 18: THE 75th ANNIVERSARY OF AIRDRIE'S VILLAGE CHARTER
THIRTEENTH LOCAL HISTORICAL RECOGNITION: 1909-1984

Trails leading northward towards Fort Edmonton were in evidence some years previous to the establishment of Fort Calgary in 1875. They had deep ruts, clear evidence of heavy loads drawn by oxen and burly horses. Stories from these trails could be told, of hope, thrills, anticipation, hardships, disappointments, and most of all determination. In a few short years Calgary became a main hub for opening up the west for southern Alberta. The C.P.R.'s appearance in August 1883 was the torch of flame that got things in motion; from Atlantic to Pacific, all types of business and industry literally took off.

In the pre-railroad years, the first place of shelter and hospitality was one day's journey north of Calgary. It was known as the Dickson Stopping House and later called the Johnston Stevenson Stopping House. This was the site of the first local school classes, a mail service, and also occasional church services. The Stopping House continued in full swing until 1900, when a railroad siding was established at what was to be named Airdrie. A water tower was put up there to replenish the thirsty trains which had made their presence known for ten years; the rail link to Edmonton had been established in 1891.

As soon as the townsite was located things really took off. The Stevenson Stopping House became a farmsite, and all activities previously going on at that historic site now focussed on the new location of Airdrie. It rapidly grew in no uncertain terms as many settlers moved in from the British Isles, Eastern Canada, the American midwest, and Europe. Alberta's local history books show how many people moved into Western Canada, from 1900 to 1905 as an example. While there is not space to recount all events of Airdrie's rapid growth in the few years before its incorporation as a village in 1909, a few highlights are worthy of mention.

In 1901, A.E. Bowers built the first house and barn. It took only a few years for settlers to construct a post office, two stores, a lumberyard (which only this month in 1984, has ceased to exist), a grain grinding outfit, a hotel, some restaurants, three grocery stores, three blacksmith shops, a livery stable, a butcher shop, a drug store, a bakery, and the Royal Bank. All these structures were available for the advantage and enjoyment of the towns-people and the settlers in the surrounding countryside. Most welcome too was a grain elevator in 1904. It was small of course, compared to what was later constructed; in 1923 the Alberta Pacific Grain Company elevator, and in 1927 the National Grain elevator. What would a new town be without a newspaper? So in 1908, *The Airdrie News* appeared, published by J. Newhart - first edition on July 16, 1908.

With the rapid advance of Airdrie, application for village status was made to the provincial government. On September 10th, 1909, Alberta Order-in-Council #526/09 made Airdrie a Village; a step proudly accepted by the villagers as showing the future was theirs to determine.

History has never passed Airdrie by, in various distinctive ways. Airdrie Hotel served as a hospital in the 1918-1919 flu epidemic, during which many died. Airdrie's first medical doctor, Dr. W.F. Edwards, worked tirelessly under severe weather conditions and against tremendous odds to restore numerous hopeless cases to renewed health. Heritage Park, well known in south Calgary, contains some historic contributions from Airdrie, too. Flett's Blacksmith Shop and the residence of the Flett family have been beautifully restored and given a place of honour along the historic park's street. The Atlas Lumber office building is also nearby. Well do we recall the bustling activities in these early enterprises.

Schools progressively came into operation as the population increased. In fact, the first church built in 1903 was eventually used as a school up until the 1940s. The new United Church was constructed in 1922, and the older church was then used as a school. Education facilities in Airdrie have kept pace with the times, as some rock-hard decisions have to be made on many occasions.

118

The United Church built in 1922 is still in constant use; now enlarged and renovated, it has done great service. With Airdrie's 1984 population nearing 10,000, there are ten churches serving the various religious beliefs, sincere evidence of Canadian freedom of choice in religious affairs.

Airdrie has certainly kept pace with all sports and community activities. From its early beginnings, in keeping with times of prosperity or depression, it has done a commendable job. As of 1984 there are over 70 clubs and organizations serving all segments of society, from toddlers to old age pensioners. A credit to all involved.

In conclusion; Airdrie was originally an agriculturally based centre, then considered to be a long way from Calgary. All of its places of business served the farmer and rancher well. For example; five farm implement companies were in operation during the 1930s to 1950s; as of 1984 there are none. Farm hardwares and a service centre are all that now exist. Airdrie has changed to a residential community with no end of services to accommodate to a large population level. We have witnessed a vast change, we who walked the wooden sidewalks of Airdrie in the 1920s, to the modern shopping malls of today. We look back on the "Good Old Days", yes; and the "Not Too Good Old Days". Both ages have had their good points, indeed for my part I am glad the Good Lord granted me health and the ability to see and witness the span of nearly three score years and ten to appreciate it all - good, bad or indifferent.

Airdrie we wish you well. Think ahead, think positive and be cautious.
Submitted by C. Redvers Perry, 1984

Editors' Addition:
How Airdrie Got its Name

Airdrie, Alberta, was named by William MacKenzie, a contracting engineer, after a place in his native Scotland. The town of Airdrie is a few miles northeast of Glasgow. Historians have come up with several explanations for the name of the Scottish town:

...The interpretation with which the historians of the town are satisfied is that the true meaning of the word is "The King's Height". Chalmers, a British historian, in his work on "Ancient Caledonia," adopts this view and asserts that the rising ground upon which the modern town of Airdrie, Scotland, is built was the actual scene of the Battle of Arderyth, fought in the year 577 between the armies of Aeddan, King of Kintire, and Rydderich the Bountiful, King of Strathclwyd. However, even this view has been questioned by other scholars.

Wherever the Battle of Arderyth was fought, it was "an important decisive engagement" because it secured the independence of Strathclwyd as a kingdom for about 400 years. If we accept Chalmers' theory it is interesting to note that the name of the town had its beginnings in a fight for independence and freedom. Although scholars speculate and disagree on the origins of the name, at least we can be proud of the fact that the name "Airdrie" had its origins in antiquity.
By Stephen Wilk, from *One Day's Journey*, 1963

AIRDRIE, ALBERTA
Sunday, November 25th, 1984
2:00 p.m.

THIRTEENTH LOCAL
HISTORICAL RECOGNITION

75th ANNIVERSARY

COMMEMORATING AIRDRIE'S
VILLAGE CHARTER

SEPTEMBER 10th 1909 — 1984

in conjunction with
INTERDENOMINATIONAL CHURCH SERVICE
at
AIRDRIE UNITED CHURCH, AIRDRIE, ALTA.

Sponsored by
NOSE CREEK HISTORICAL SOCIETY
in co-operation with
LOCAL MINISTERS

*This is a Historical Document. Please value it on the basis of posterity.
It is compliments of The Nose Creek Historical Society.*

1

SPECIAL CITY COUNCIL

MEETING

**Wednesday, July 22, 1987
7:00 p.m.**

**Royal Canadian Legion Hall
Airdrie, Alberta, Canada**

2

AIRDRIE Alta

3

4

1   *From village to city.
pamphlet celebrates
the transition.*

2   *Notice of a special
council meeting to
read a proclamation
twinning two commu-
nities: Airdrie, Scot-
land and Airdrie, Al-
berta*

3   *Airdire in 1907. Nose
Creek is in the fore-
ground.*

4   *Airdire in 1984, with
some of the buildings
constructed in the
early part of the cen-
tury still in use.*

FOURTEENTH LOCAL HISTORICAL RECOGNITION: 1875-1930's

Hay is not the most romantic subject to honour, nor to write a story about for that matter, but just for a few lines let's look at this simple little topic.

As settlements and townsites and eventually great cities developed in North America, they were usually in locations where foodstuffs could be produced, unless a seaport or mining industry was the reason for settlement. Even then, in years gone by, trails had to be located to bring in food for the townsmen.

Here in the west where 75% of industry on the prairies was agriculture, horses and oxen were vital to all modes of travel and to the propulsion of farming implements. Our towns and cities depended on horse power to deliver goods, draw in fuel supplies and take businessmen to and from work, not forgetting the pleasant evening drives to social engagements. So here we are - horses galore but where are the hay and oats when winter snows blow and there's not even a chance to graze on tether at a nearby vacant lot? Well, this is where the farmer-rancher came into prominence. They needed hay, and he needed ready cash to buy many necessities for his newly acquired homestead. He arranged to get a mowing machine; a five foot cutter bar could soon mow a lot of prairie wool (the native type of grass). After it was cut and left standing for a few hours, he raked it with a 10 foot dump rake pulled, of course, by horses. The mower knife was sharpened with a grindstone, a round 18 inch stone propelled by two foot pedals rotating it over the mower blades to whet them. He and his family might stack upland or prairie hay by hand or by slide stacker and 14 foot wide hay sweep, for a winter's storage. On many occasions the hay was loaded on the 8 x 16 x 5 hay rack to go direct to the city consumer's hay loft, all forked on and off the rack by hand.

Haying was usually done in July and August. Usually two years' growth was quite acceptable, but the current year's green growth was most attractive in quality and pleasant odour. The term used by old timers was to "hit the hay trail" which meant off to town with a load of hay. We are paying tribute today with a plaque in memory of those respected old timers, to trails, the paths of travel taken to the hay's destination. Trails wandered for seemingly endless miles. Lines of least resistance, they avoided wet marshes, steep hills, rough rocky terrain, and tipsy valleys, and followed a nice gravel base or not too steep creek banks when fording a creek or river. Snowdrifts in the winter, or icy terrain which could occur after a Chinook or warm spell, also affected the line of trail. As one can see from all these conditions, it is no wonder that our hay trails on maps, or that can still be seen on open prairie areas, take on an aimless here, there and everywhere pattern. The goal was the haymarket - to weigh, sell, unload, eat a meal at one of the hospitable cafes, and get home before dark or storm.

The haymarket in Calgary, for those who did not have private deals previously arranged, was just opposite the Langevin Bridge on 4th Street East, just north of the Cecil Hotel along the river bank. I well recall the horses and wagons lined up there in the 1920s, and the city weigh scale. Visible hay trails over the prairies were still used in part up until 1930, but with road development, the use of tractor power and the operation of larger trucks, the hay trails went out of existence along with the pioneer hay haulers. Some of us nearing the three score years and ten bracket still had lots to do with upland prairie hay, but on the level of hauling it home to feed our own livestock. The same wandering prairie trails saw many a settler's wagon drawing oats to town for the horses who kept the city going, from the business executive's driving horse, to the horses drawing the grocer's and butcher's delivery rigs, and the local ambulance and fire brigade. Also not forgotten is the "end of the trail" undertaker's horse-drawn hearse, to carry one to one's last resting place in the Union cemetery on Calgary's south side. So from beginning to end the hay trail was Calgary's first "energy pipeline", and also served for a well worn path for the settlers and their families to go to town and shop for weekly provisions.

As I wander over the few pasture lands yet untouched in our district, the faint two-rut trails remind me of the great hope and confidence those hardy pioneers who were yet young and ambitious had in the western prairies. I often think "Oh! If those trails could talk - What secrets they hold". Like our respected old timers they fade away - but never to be forgotten.

Submitted by C. Redvers Perry, 1985

Editors' Addition:
Prairie Wool

Prairie wool was the name of the hay made from the original prairie grassland and surrounding hills. These upland grasses, as opposed to meadow or slough grasses, shared a common characteristic of maturing late in the summer and "curing on the stem" with high nutritional value. The name prairie wool came from the curly, sooly appearance of these grasses when they matured without disturbance. The rangeland grass fauna included several wheat grasses, June and Blue grasses, oat grasses and several species of fescue. One of the most sought after species was rough fescue, which cured with 6-8% protein and an energy level which easily sustained cattle and horses over the winter. The Nose Hill and many areas of the west Nose Creek district are still primarily native range and could produce prairie wool. The common practice of homesteaders or ranchers was to cut prairie wool every second year. In the early days, the main source of income was hauling prairie wool "hay" to the hay market. Pat Burns' packing plant or his Bow River Ranch (in present day Fish Creek Park) and later to the Calgary Stockyards.

A steady supply of live cattle was required for Burns Packing Plants in Calgary and Vancouver by the turn of the century, creating a demand for prairie wool in Calgary. C.J. Duggan partnered with Pat Burns to set up livestock feeder camps on the Nose Creek to hold cattle until the plants needed them. The home ranch was north of Crossfield, while other camps were on the Nose Creek south of Airdrie and on Nose Hill. Duggan would drive around the country contracting with homesteaders to put up hay on the open prairie. The hay had to be prairie wool. Stacks, put up with a buck sweep and stacker, were fenced with three wires and protected from prairie fires with a ploughed fire guard. After thirty days the stacks were measured and the hay paid for in cash at three to five dollars per ton. This was the grubstake for the winter for many homesteaders. In the winter the homesteaders or Duggan crews hauled the hay to the cow camps or to Calgary to the packing plant.

The "hay trail", as it was known, was the route taken by those hauling prairie wool along the Nose Creek Valley to Calgary. Hay racks on sleighs were loaded one day; early the nextmorning the horses were hooked up for the long trip to Calgary. In the early days a number of Balzac area families hauled hay on the "hay trail" on a regular basis, regardless of weather. Prairie wool hauled over the hay trail could fetch up to ten dollars per ton.

The "hay trail" changed significantly with the construction of roads, but the demand for prairie wool lasted into the 1960's. Charlie Church and Bert Kerslake ran big prairie wool haying crews in both branches of the Nose Creek Valley and with the Hawkwood Brothers on Nose Hill until that time. They shipped thousands of tons of prairie wool by truck to the packing plants, stockyards and Stampede Grounds in Calgary, as well as loading hundreds of box cars with hundred pound, wire-tied bales over the platform at Balzac and Beddington for shipment to many points in British Columbia.

Most of the prairie has now been broken up for crop or tame hay production, however, a lot of native range still exists in the west Nose Creek and Nose Hill areas. There are not many mowers left which can cut the tough prairie wool! The prairie wool has gone the way of the foot powered grindstone used by so many homesteaders to sharpen mower knives.

Submitted by Dr. R.B. Church, 1996

BALZAC, ALBERTA
Sunday, July 28th, 1985
2:00 p.m.

FOURTEENTH LOCAL
HISTORICAL RECONGNITION

THE HAY TRAIL
From 1875 to 1930's

in conjunction with
INTERDENOMINATIONAL CHURCH SERVICE
at
BALZAC UNITED CHURCH - BALZAC, ALBERTA

Sponsored by
NOSE CREEK HISTORICAL SOCIETY
in co-operation with
LOCAL MINISTERS

This is a Historical Document. Please value it on the basis of posterity. It is compliments of the Nose Creek Historical Society.

(Top, left) Nose Creek Historical Society prepared this historical document to recognize the importance of hay to early settlers. *(Top, right)* Arthur Savill mowing Prairie hay in Symons Valley, 1943. *(Above)* Raking hay.

(Above, left) A full load of hay heading for the slide.
(Above, right) Stacking Prairie wool hay using a mechanical slide and cage.
(Left & below left) Sweeping up the hay.
(below) Raking up in Prairie hay on the T.L. Perry farm, 1944

123

Above left: The loft serves as square hay storage space. The truck is a 1951 Ford. *(**Above right**)* A Massey Harris 55 stacking bales of hay at the White Farm, 1962. A baler and a 1950 Ford Mercury truck (all pictured) play an important role in the operation.

Haying on the Davy Place c. 1948 (above) and (right) baling the hay, 1946.

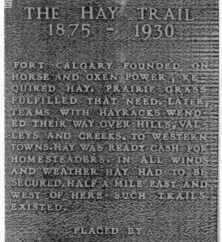

THE HAY TRAIL
1875 – 1930

FORT CALGARY FOUNDED ON
HORSE AND OXEN POWER, RE-
QUIRED HAY. PRAIRIE GRASS
FULFILLED THAT NEED. LATER,
TEAMS WITH HAYRACKS WEND-
ED THEIR WAY OVER HILLS, VAL-
LEYS AND CREEKS, TO WESTERN
TOWNS. HAY WAS READY CASH FOR
HOMESTEADERS. IN ALL WINDS
AND WEATHER HAY HAD TO BE
SECURED. HALF A MILE EAST AND
WEST OF HERE SUCH TRAILS
EXISTED.

PLACED BY

NOSE CREEK
HISTORICAL SOCIETY
JULY 1985

George Kimzie (above) with a load of baled hay at Crossfield and (below) a sweep load of hay ready to go on the stacker. The plaque on left honours the importance of hay in building the prairie provinces.

CHAPTER 20: TRIBUTE TO THE SURVEYORS

FIFTEENTH LOCAL HISTORICAL RECOGNITION: 1880-1905

The Hardy Surveyors

While surveyors were not the first white people to arrive in the western prairies, they certainly were a close second on deck, setting the development pattern in order. It was not long after the odd, lonely pioneer came over the open prairies with his covered wagon and the vital necessities, including family members, that the North-West Mounted Police arrived. The whiskey traders' activities, using unscrupulous trading practices to take unfair advantage of the true western pioneers, the Indians, had necessitated the Mounties' presence. When they had established law and order in a firm and acceptable manner, the western prairies were ready for ranchers and farmers to establish agricultural enterprises. As time went on past the turn of the century, settlers moved in rapidly and towns and villages were springing up everywhere, supplied by wagon trains which soon were overtaken by a series of railroad networks.

Before the main influx of settlers into the prairies, let our attention turn to the western part of Alberta and areas "North of the Bow". Two men who had a vital part in the surveys of our area were Montague Aldous, Dominion Land Surveyor [D.L.S.] and Dominion Topographical Surveyor [D.T.S.], and S.L. Brabazon, D.L.S. Records reveal that in the summer of 1880, M. Aldous surveyed the 5th Meridian from Stony Plain south through the Crossfield, Airdrie and Balzac areas, and on through to the International Boundary. Aldous made many references in his land evaluation reports to the land's qualities; it's remarkable how true they remain to this day, over one hundred years later. S.L. Brabazon was just one of several members of a family who were involved in Dominion Land Survey activities, later having been active in doing Alaska-British Columbia boundary surveys in 1905-06. In 1884, however, he was very much involved in the surveys of Townships 25 and 26, Range 1 and 2, West of the 5th Meridian. (This meridian is our present No.2 Highway from Calgary's airport to Crossfield.) Brabazon's assessment of land values or uses is also extremely accurate. He doubtless put no end of effort into describing the countryside so future purchasers would know the potential of what various properties would be capable of producing. There are some interesting copies of his reports of lands in the above described areas, which many of us live on or near - a remarkable assessment indeed, indicative of the intense interest those hardy men took and indeed the hardships they endured.

One could write endless accounts from the interesting material available on the surveyors of Western Canada. However, in limited spaces one must be brief. It is evident from photographs that a survey party comprised about eight hardy souls with a transit, rods, sixty-six foot chains, and plenty of ambition. Pack horses were used and two wheel carts, or at best a covered four wheeler wagon to carry supplies. In the line of duty, creeks and rivers had to be forded and marshy areas approached with poles to skip from one foothold to another, no doubt many times while wet up to the arm pits! Mountainous terrain was scaled in deep treed areas; if a natural object was in the way it had to be approached somehow. If the transit operator required a pole marker or a stake driven, there were no questions asked - "There it is - so there it must remain". In short, a survey is a permanent mark of property lines, numbered and professionally described, to be used by future generations as an acceptable legal property line.

M. Aldous surveyed the townsite for Edmonton, as indicated by the obituary account in 1946, when he died at age 96. Hard work and roughing it out certainly didn't affect his health and stamina! A native of Prince Edward Island who came west at age 24, he was deeply involved in locating the 4th Meridian (Saskatchewan's west border) and the 5th Meridian, our local Highway No.2 from Calgary to Edmonton. In one of his reports he praised the farmers and ranchers of the Calgary area for their respect for their adopted country. He apparently gave a glowing report on the beautiful agricultural land south of Calgary in a letter dated September 30, 1880.

S.L. Brabazon was a native of Quebec. His family was active in politics, but were also frequently mentioned in Dominion Land Surveys even away up in the Yukon, where there is a glacier named in honour of A.J. Brabazon. There appears to be no record of the conclusion of S.L. Brabazon's involvement with the Dominion Land Survey, or of his death.

It is with a great deal of respect and indeed in high tribute to the many surveyors and their devoted assistants who were involved with the arduous task of surveying miles of lonely terrain that we unveil this bronze plaque in their honour. Many other surveyors are noted to have worked in the 1880s: T.R. Hewson - 1883; C.E. LeRue - 1883; T. Fawcett - 1883; L. Gosselin - 1884; L.R. Ord - 1884; R.C. Philips - 1883; and W. Ogilvie - 1882. At this site, suitably situated on the western edge of the 5th Meridian and so named after the first house of lodging and stable for travellers' teams, the Dickson-Stevenson Stopping House, we sincerely hope that the generations to come appreciate the surveyors' contributions to Western Canada.

Submitted by C. Redvers Perry, 1986

Early Surveys of the Nose Creek Region

In June 1880, Montague Aldous, D.L.S., D.T.S., one of the first of the "Special Survey" surveyors, ran the Fifth Meridian from Stony Plain to the 49th parallel. The 5th Meridian, being 114 degrees of longitude west of Greenwich, England, is one of the three control meridians for the township system of land settlement in Alberta.

This part of Alberta was a surveyor's dream; flat, no bush to cut, few lakes or rivers to traverse. In a letter to Lindsay Russell, Surveyor General, Aldous wrote, "After crossing the Red Deer River we had a fine run of about 70 miles to the Bow River," and in his final report,"Southward from the 9th Baseline to Bow River is an open undulating plain entirely destitute of wood, the soil in the northern half of this section is of fair quality but gradually becomes light and gravelly as we approach the Bow River, the country is generally very dry, water rarely occurring except in several small brackish streams which flow through this section."

Despite the ease with which Aldous was able to survey this 70 mile section, he had considerable problems in the northern section where he encountered -50 degree [Farenheit] temperatures and was required to extend his lines across both Pigeon Lake and Gull Lake. In southern Alberta his lines ran into the Porcupine Hills, which caused him to divert his line several ranges eastward.

In closing on the International Boundary, Aldous was somewhat taken aback to find that in running the 5th Meridian some 300 miles from Stony Plain to the 49th parallel he had accumulated an error of 22.60 chains or 1500 feet. Reflecting on this error in his book *Vision of an Ordered Land*, Dr. J.G. MacGregor notes contributing factors that Aldous pointed out: the roughness of the terrain, which made it difficult to hold a chain horizontally while measuring steep inclines; and the high altitude of the district, which meant that there was a greater distance between two points as measured over the curve of the earth, than there would be between corresponding points at sea level.

Despite his error, which works out to a little over one foot in eleven hundred, Aldous' work was remarkable, considering the instruments available and the conditions under which he had to work.

Based on the framework Aldous and others established, the subdivision and settlement of Western Canada was to proceed in earnest. In 1883, 27,000,000 acres of land were surveyed into 1221 townships. This stands today as an unchallenged record of surveying and settlement planning. Supplemental to the survey of these 170,000 quarter sections or units of future settlement was a massive amount of land information pertaining to the soils, vegetation, topography, hydrography, forest cover and many other geographical attributes to assist the homesteader in choosing his future abode and to assist government and private agencies in managing this valuable resource, the land. In effect, these surveys created one of the largest and most comprehensive geographic information and management systems known to man.

But let us come back to Nose Creek. In June of 1884, three years after the 5th Meridian was established, Samuel Brabazon, D.L.S., was contracted to survey Townships 25 and 26 in Ranges 29, West of the Fourth Meridian and Ranges 1 and 2 West of the Fifth Meridian.

Sam Brabazon was from Portage du Fort, Quebec. He was the patriarch of the Brabazon survey dynasty who were destined to leave their marks in such diverse locales as the Canada-Alaska boundary, the Maritimes, the North West Rebellion and the House of Commons. Brabazon was somewhat more lucid in his description of the Nose Creek region than Aldous, since it was his specific responsibility to divide the territory for settlement. In his report to the Minister of the Interior regarding Township 25, Range 1 West of the Fifth Meridian he wrote:

> ...This township is all open prairie hevily (*sic*) rolling and hilly, particularly so in the SW portion where Nose Hill attains considerable altitude above Bow River. There are however, some parts of it suitable for cultivation - say 40 percent - and throughout, the soil is of the richest quality.
>
> An abundant supply of excellent water may be had from Nose Creek the two branches of which join in Section 14 forming a V in the township.
>
> The grass is very luxuriant and wild pea is found in many places - the township would suit admirably for grazing purposes the hills and coulees affording the best of shelter for stock.

In his field notes for the North boundary of Section 31 in Township 26, Range 2 West of the Fifth, is this delightful little passage: "Nose Creek is a beautiful clear stream about 4 feet wide and 2½ feet deep with gravelly bottom and runs through a deep ravine. Banks 250' high." I'm sure they omitted to state that they'd booked off for a few hours to catch a fresh cutthroat trout supper for the crew.

Handout distributed by the guest speaker, G.K. Allred, of the Alberta Land Surveyors' Association, at the interdenominational service on November 16, 1986.

"DEFINITIONS"

Regarded as one of the best survey systems in existance apparently this system was used in Minnesota and North Dakota, U.S.A. and bordering our Country it was reasonable to be contiguous. So with road allowances of 66 ft. being allowed in Canada there was very little change.

MERIDIAN LOCATIONS.   4th Saskatchewan's West Border.
                      5th From Waterton Lakes - Calgary - West of Edmonton.
                      6th Runs through Jasper on West side of Keg River Post.
TOWNSHIP - 6 Miles Long, 6 Miles Wide in Squares of 1 Mile each. Numbered from S.E. corner as 1 to S.W. corner as 6 and so on to 36 sections.

A TOWNSHIP EXAMPLE.

31	32	33	34	35	36
30	29	28	27	26	25
19	20	21	22	23	24
18	17	16	15	14	13
7	8	9	10	11	12
6	5	4	3	2	1

As an example the land location of Balzac would be described thus:

    South East 1/4
    Section 13
    Township 26
    Range 1

West of the 5th Meridian or #2 Highway as we know it.

Section is 640 acres.
1/4 Section is 160 acres.
Road Allowances every 2 miles North to South
every 1 mile East to West.

Townships number from 1 to 126 from U.S.A. Border, to Northern Alberta Boundary. Every 6 miles per Township in length. Ranges from Saskatchewans 4th Meridean to 5th Meridian. From 1 to 29 every 6 miles per Range in width, example.

CROSSFIELD, ALBERTA
Sunday, November 16th, 1986
2:00 p.m.

FIFTEENTH LOCAL
HISTORICAL RECOGNITION

TRIBUTE TO THE
SURVEYORS
From 1880 - 1905

In conjunction with
Interdenominational Church Service
at
Crossfield United Church, Crossfield, Alberta

Sponsored by
NOSE CREEK HISTORICAL SOCIETY
in co-operation with
Local Ministers

*This is a historical document. Please value it on the basis of posterity.
It is compliments of the Nose Creek Historical Society.*

(Left) Pamphlet honours and celebrates the invaluable work done by surveyors to help prevent chaos in granting land rights. *(Above)* Surveyor at work in Grande Prairie area, 1909. *(Below)* Living in extreme conditions, surveyors managed to get the job done. *(Bottom)* Dominion Land Surveyors near Peace River, Alberta, c. 1914-1915. J. Home Johnston, second from left, located the site of Fort Fork, an old fur trading post in 1927.

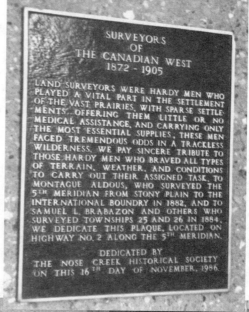

(Below) A plaque at the Dickson-Stevenson Stopping House, south of Crossfield was unveiled November 16, 1986. It honoured Montague Aldous who, in 1882, surveyed the Fifth Meridian from Stony Plain to the international boundary (Full text on right). Unveiling the plaque are, left to right, Joe Oneil, Rocky View Council, Pete Morison and Ken Allred *(Bottom)* Squatters like these pictured here had to be evicted as and when it was ascertained the land they settled on had already been set aside for purchase by other settlers.

CHAPTER 21: THE FUR TRADERS' TRAIL

SIXTEENTH LOCAL HISTORICAL RECOGNITION: 1887-1987

ALSO NAMING THE AIRDRIE-CROSSFIELD NEW ROAD "THE DICKSON-STEVENSON TRAIL"

The earliest fur trading [by Europeans] in what we now call the province of Alberta was up in the northeast corner. Huge Lake Athabasca was the location, and near its southwestern extremity in 1789, Roderick MacKenzie of the North West Company established a trading post named Fort Chipewyan. The Hudson's Bay Company had been established in 1670 and was well entrenched across the prairies to the Rocky Mountains and beyond, and in 1821 the two fur companies united. Apparently a Hudson's Bay Post still operates at "Fort Chip" today.

The fur trading industry flourished for countless years, giving employment to many settlers of new Canada, and a means of income for the native Indians and halfbreeds. Endless interesting facts could be recounted from the many historic accounts dealing with the romantic fur trade, but the space limitations of this brochure make it impossible to print.

When furs had been secured and prepared for processing at the final destination, the traders had the problem of arranging for transportation, as time of travel was an important factor. The great rivers and lakes of the prairies answered their need in early times, with canoes and river barges as the method of propulsion. As time went on the squeaky Red River cart and the huge cumbersome four wheeled bull wagons were used to transport goods, and furs were quite frequently their predominant cargo. The heavy four wheeler bull wagons, travelling in trains, were suitable on the hard prairie soils in the south, but in areas north of Olds (as we now know it), the terrain was bog-land and too marshy for them. The two wheeled Red River cart was able to make it to and fro between Fort Calgary and Fort Edmonton, relieving the embarrassment of the bull trains' failure to get through. Bull trains were a common conveyance from Fort Benton, Montana, to Fort Whoop-Up near Lethbridge, and on to Fort Calgary. They were slow and cumbersome but did carry heavy cargos.

The Calgary-Edmonton Trail had sparse traffic here and there before the 1880s; we know Rev. John McDougall used it coming from Edmonton in 1873, but he veered off to Morleyville, since Fort Calgary did not yet exist. It was in 1883 that the Calgary-Edmonton Trail entered its boom period. The C.P.R. arrived in Calgary that year, and materials went out from there by the trail for eight years. Used by every possible overland means of travel, it was spoken of as "the most travelled wagon trail in the Dominion." Stage coaches had regular schedules, with established rates for cargo and personal luggage. There were stopping houses along the way where food and lodging could be secured. The first stop north from Calgary, in our district, was the Dickson Stopping house - later taken over by the Stevensons, and in operation from the 1870s to 1900, when Airdrie was established. A stage coach trip was scheduled to leave Edmonton or Calgary on Monday, and hopefully arrive at its destination on Friday.

The life of a stage coach driver or freighter was a tough one. For the trip between Calgary and Edmonton, horses or oxen took from 5 to 10 days in good weather, and it could be 15 days for freighters in poorer conditions. The driver might sleep at a stopping house, or out under his wagon. He might get hot food at the various stopping houses, or a bite out of a bag on the cargo wagon. There were rivers to ford, prairie fire menaces, blizzards, and numerous other complications. These drivers and freighters were men of the frontier, adventurous and able to confront all problems which arose. Where they came from, or what their past consisted of, or where they eventually went, often remained a mystery.

Today we are paying tribute to the fur trading industry. It was 100 years ago, in 1887, that $75,000 worth of furs passed through our Nose Creek district on two wheeled carts drawn by single horses. These furs were going to be unloaded at the C.P.R. station in Calgary and shipped to eastern outlets. From all appearances the 1887 photo of this shipment was located on 9th Avenue and 3rd or 4th Street east near what many of us knew as the C.P.R. freight sheds. This apparently was one of the last major shipments by the famous Hudson's Bay Company, and it occurred during the eight boom years of the Calgary-Edmonton trail from 1883 to 1891. What a colourful age in our local history! One only has to view the deep ruts northeast of Balzac, near the Buttes Hills, to appreciate the tremendous volume of traffic that passed through. According to historical records, furs and pelts were gathered from points as far away as the Arctic Circle, brought to Fort Edmonton by various means; canoe or cart, and sorted over for the continuing journey to Fort Calgary. In earlier years furs had gone to Fort Benton by pack horses or carts. The railroad connecting east to west made the western prairies develop in no uncertain terms. Then in 1891, the "C and E" railroad came into existence, and it only took 12 hours for the first passenger train to make its way between Calgary and Edmonton. The stage coach service halted at once. Competition was the end.

So the old Calgary-Edmonton trail saw moderate travel by local settlers for a while. Old trails were upgraded with bridges, and eventually gravelled for the autos of the early 1900s. Then came the No. 2 Highway, with its cloverleafs, white marked lines, and unlimited speeds by motor vehicles of all sizes and descriptions.

We look back in great respect to those hardy young pioneers, adventurers, tough risk-takers in the true sense. The gradually vanishing deep rut trails and early gravelled auto roads are the only true mark of the exciting adventurous past of those who established our western heritage.

Submitted by C. Redvers Perry, 1987

Plaque

Shipment of Furs

In June, 1887, a shipment of furs valued at $75,000 passed this way en route to the railway line at Calgary. Packed in a caravan of almost two dozen creaking two-wheeled Red River carts, the furs had been gathered from Hudson's Bay Co. trading posts in the Far North and were destined for Eastern and European markets. This was one of the last big fur shipments to be sent overland from Edmonton. Within three years, the Calgary and Edmonton Railway was under construction, changing forever the dominent [sic] position of the fur trade in the north.

The Veil Used To Unveil the Bronze Plaque

This wolf hide was brought to Keg River Hudson's Bay post in January 1950 by the local Indian trappers of the area. It was purchased by Redvers Perry in its untanned condition, and tanned in Calgary.

The Dickson-Stevenson Trail

To the local people, this small portion of the Edmonton Trail was referred to as the Dickson-Stevenson Trail after the Dickson-Stevenson stopping house. These operators ran the first stopping house north of the Bow River, from 1879 to 1900. It proved to be a multipurposed dwelling. Not only did it provide overnight accommodation to travellers, but also it served as a school for local children, a post office, and occasionally a church service would be held there when a clergyman passed through.

The tales of this trail have been laid to rest - an epoch past; but to this era tribute long overdue has been realized. Today, Sunday October 25th, we are proud to participate at the 1987 Ribbon Cutting Ceremony, naming it officially "The Dickson-Stevenson Trail", linking the two Historical Settlements of Airdrie and Crossfield with an excellent road of communication.

Submitted by C. Redvers Perry, 1987

Editors' Additions:

Excerpts from "The Great Buffalo Migration"

[In 1939, Richard Brodrick recalled talking with some of the old buffalo hunters who had settled near Calgary, and who told him many stories about the tens of thousands of buffalo there used to be in the area]

...I was given the following information by Mr. George Emerson and other hunters.

Take Calgary on the East to where Geddes took up a homestead, to Shaganapi Point on the West, the Bow River on the North, to where Billie Scullen and Jim Owen took up land on the South. This area would measure over two thousand acres. These bottoms or flats were, during season, one mass of moving forms...

[*Brodrick goes on to describe where the main herd of buffalo would migrate*]

...When the buffalo started their trek in the Spring from Montana, they made a complete circle before returning to the U.S.A. After crossing the line into Canada, they grazed northeast to the Maple Creek flats resting there about ten days. Drifting north to the North Saskatchewan River the main herd crossed at a good ford where the town of Battleford was built, then grazed north to Beaver River. The small herd that did not cross at Battleford drifted west on the south side of the river until coming to a good ford opposite to where Fort Pitt was built, crossed there, grazed east until meeting up with the main herd. When the buffalo thought it was time to complete the circle they all turned at once as if on a pivot, then fed northwest to a line running due north from Fort Saskatchewan, then made another left turn, fed south to Buffalo Lake. Resting there about a week, they moved southwest to Wetaskiwin, making a stayover there two or three days, and drifted southwest to McPherson's Coulee, fed there a day or two, then south to the Big Bow river. The main herd kept west of Nose Creek fording the Big Bow where McPherson and Jim Barvis took up land. That would be the bottom west of the mouth of Nose Creek. They grazed up the Elbow River until coming to the bend from which the river derives its name. Fording at this point, they met up with the small herds that kept east of Nose Creek, and the Elbow River. Together they drifted south down Wilson Coulee to east of Okotoks, crossed Sheep Creek at the old ford near where McMillan kept a stopping place. Proceeding south they kept to Sheep Creek ridge, fording the Highwood River east of where Mr. Bedingfeld took up land in 1882, later known as the Round T Ranch. (The whiskey traders had a kind of fort in the brush a little to the east of the crossing. All that is left of it today is the stone the chimney was built with.) On south down Squaw Coulee, crossing Mosquito Creek at Mr. Drumheller's ranch, they grazed south to Bone Yard Coulee and Pine Coulee, via S---- Creek. The herds would feed around Bone Yard Coulee for seven or eight days; the main herd took to the high ground, south of Pine Coulee, then south to the Leavings, forded Willow Creek east of the Oxley Ranch buildings, grazed south to the Belly River, crossed the river near where Fort MacLeod was built, south to the Line, and so out of Western Canada...

From article by Richard N. Brodrick, 1939

Trails between the Forts: Fort Benton, Fort Whoop-Up, Fort Macleod, Fort Calgary, Fort Edmonton, Athabasca Landing

The Calgary-Edmonton Trail became the extension of the Whoop-Up Trail, and served the Nose Creek Valley; traders used this trail to bring staple goods to fur traders, missionaries and other early settlers. Interpretive centres at the three Fort Regional Museums, Forts Whoop-Up, Macleod and Calgary, offer a glimpse into life in southern Alberta in the 1870's. They encompass the history of the American-based whiskey and merchant trade, Blackfoot native culture, and the formative career of Canada's famed Mounted Police.

The Trail began in Montana at the former Missouri River port town of Fort Benton, 30 miles east of Great Falls. Fort Benton was situated at the place where the Missouri became too shallow for steamboats to travel further upstream, so the boats delivered goods which were then carried overland to the trading posts. It was from this port that the trade route into the British Possession now known as Alberta began. Fort Benton was a centre of transportation and trade in the west; its geographical position affected the development of both the American and Canadian West. The original American Fur Company post of Fort Benton was established in 1846.

From Fort Benton the Trail went north, crossing the International boundary at Sweetgrass, Montana and Coutts, Alberta. As the Whoop-Up Trail, it was the international highway of trade into southern Alberta from approximately 1867 to 1885. Along it, oxen or mule driven bull teams transported goods from Fort Benton to supply first the buffalo hide-whiskey trade, and later the outposts of the N.W.M.P. and the region's early communities.

Fort Hamilton was the official name of the site better known as Fort Whoop-Up; it was established in 1869 by Alfred B. Hamilton and John J. Healy, two Montana traders and adventurers. Fort Whoop-Up marked the birth of American commerce in the Blackfoot territory of Canada, as traders took the opportunity to profit from the buffalo robe trade. The traffic brought the Blackfoot people many manufactured items from eastern U.S. factories, such as cloth, sugar, guns, metal goods, blankets and beads. Traders also brought alcohol, which when mixed with a variety of other potent substances, could somewhat loosely be referred to as "whiskey". This so-called "trade liquor" had a devastating impact on the Blackfoot people. According to Gerald L. Berry:

...Most of the Indians would take it diluted, as long as it had some "kick" and was hot to the taste, so many weird concoctions passed for whiskey in the Indian trade. The Blackfoot liked their whiskey strong, and insisted that it must be potent enough to burn, hence the term "firewater".

Some of the Indian whiskey recipes were: 1 Gallon of high wine to 3 gallons of water; 1 quart of alcohol, 1 pound of rank black chewing tobacco, 1 handful of red peppers, 1 bottle of Jamaica ginger, 1 quart black molasses, water ad libitum, mixed well and boiled until all the strength was drawn from the tobacco and peppers; 1 keg of alcohol, Perry's Painkiller, Hostetter's Bitters, red ink, castile soap, Blackstrap chewing tobacco, water; alcohol, Florida water, Painkiller, tobacco and blue stone. There were instances of death recorded from drinking the final draught from the keg of some of these mixtures. The Indians went wild under the influence of alcohol, so the traders led a dangerous existence - they made their trade, collected, and barricaded the fort until the party was over.

Prices and grades in the whiskey trade were fairly stable. Robes were classified as follows in order of value: white, valued highly by the Indian for superstitious reasons; blue or silk, which had body color of a blue cast and long, fine silky hair; beaver, the color of beaver with fine wavy hair; black or black and tan, fairly common; and buckskin, the most common light tan shade. Two cups of whiskey bought an ordinary robe, two cups of whiskey and a blanket for a silk robe, four gallons of whiskey for a first grade buffalo pony, furs to the height of a gun to purchase the same...

The Nose Creek Valley connection to the whiskey trade appears in the name of Whiskey Coulee, which lies within the landmark McPherson's Coulee. This was a place where traders made their so-called "whiskey".

Five years of lawlessness came to an end in late 1874 with the arrival of the North West Mounted Police and their suppression of the fur trade. Fort Whoop-Up, however, continued its role as a centre of trade and social activity, and was used as the base of a ranch and as a Mounted Police post until 1888. Today the Fort Hamilton and Whoop-Up Interpretive Centre is located in Indian Battle Park. The Park is a natural river valley setting on the banks of the Oldman River, in the centre of the city of Lethbridge.

Thirty miles west of Lethbridge on Highway #3 lies the historic town of Fort Macleod, home of the Fort Museum of the North West Mounted Police. In response to the lawlessness and devastation surrounding the American liquor trade on its own western soil, the Canadian government formed the North West Mounted Police in 1873. The original police force marched west in the summer of 1874. They soon put an end to the whiskey trade and began building posts of their own.

The first of these posts was Fort Macleod. The I.G. Baker Company used the fort as a centre for its commercial activity in southern Alberta. The advent of ranching and the arrival of the railway gave an added boost to the growth of the settlement.

On Highway #2, 120 miles north of Fort Macleod, is the Stampede city of Calgary. The city had fairly humble beginnings, as one of the early N.W.M.P. posts, Fort Calgary. The fort was constructed by the I.G. Baker Company from Fort Benton in 1875. Although the actual fort operated for only a short time, it did provide a focal point around which a community could develop. Calgary grew with the arrival of the C.P.R. and quickly became a town. In 1894, Calgary was officially given city status, becoming the first settlement in Canada's North West Territories to gain this distinction. The site of the original fort is situated in the heart of Calgary, at the junction of the Bow and Elbow Rivers.

From Fort Calgary, the N.W.M.P. and other travellers could cross the Bow River and choose different directions; the Morley Trail ran west along the Bow River to the settlement of Morleyville. The Calgary-Edmonton Trail ran north to Fort Edmonton (or Edmonton House), a major fur trade centre built by the Hudson's Bay Company around 1795. This Trail passed a number of fine stopping houses, including the Dickson Stopping House, one day's journey north of Fort Calgary by horse-drawn vehicles. The slower ox trains took two days to get that far, with the first overnight stop having been near the Butte Hills (Sharp Hills) just south west of present day Balzac, Alberta.

From Fort Edmonton, the Trail extended yet further north to Athabasca Landing; there goods could be freighted out by water to serve settlements and fur trading posts throughout the northern territories. A long trail indeed, between the two ports; Fort Benton to Athabasca Landing.

From article by Bob Pearson, Coordinator, Fort Regional Museums, Alberta, 1996

134

AIRDRIE, ALBERTA
Sunday, October 25th, 1987
3:00 p.m.

SIXTEENTH LOCAL
HISTORICAL RECOGNITION
IN HONOR OF THE FUR TRADE
100 YEARS NORTH OF THE BOW
1887 - 1987
and
NAMEING THE AIRDRIE - CROSSFIELD NEW ROAD
"THE DICKSON—STEVENSON TRAIL."
In conjunction with
Interdenominational Church Service
at
Airdrie United Church, Airdrie, Alberta

Sponsored by
NOSE CREEK HISTORICAL SOCIETY
in co-operation with Local Ministers

Above: Bison graze peacefully. Where they once roamed in their thousands, these animals have relatively recently been re-introduced to the prairies.
Below: Buffalo Jump, Madden, Alta. Taken from a distance, this is one of the methods the Indians used to secure their food. A small herd of the animals was stampeded over the precipice and then butchered at leisure.

Twenty five Red River carts loaded with $75,000 worth of The Hudson's Bay Co. furs, CPR tracks 9th Ave - 4th St, Calgary June 1887

Above Left: A pile of buffalo bones ready to be turned into fertilizer awaits shipment at Langdon, Alberta, 1893. **Above Right** A typical fur press of the 1800's. This implement compressed the pelts into easily portable bales. Buffalo hides were bartered for blankets, beads, tobacco, gun powder, and food. **Below:** Crossfield Harness Shop. Cattle by-products, especially cowhide had a multitude of uses: saddles, boots, and harnesses.

CHAPTER 22: TRIBUTE TO LOCAL RURAL SCHOOLS
SEVENTEENTH LOCAL HISTORICAL RECOGNITION: 1896-1956

Time marches on! It won't be long before the little 22 x 32 foot school house of yesteryear will be but a faded item in history. So in this year, 1988, the Nose Creek Historical Society has the pleasure, with the co-operation of many old-timers of the district, to record valued memories of numerous local schools. According to records held at Red Deer, apparently the first school north of the Bow was built in 1887, in what is now Cronquist Drive and 60th Avenue, Red Deer, Alberta. The first school in our area was opened in 1886 and was known as Nose Creek School #433; on Sec.3, Tp.25 Rg.1 W-5 (North Calgary). The turn of the century saw an increased concern for education facilities, hence a number of school districts were set up from Calgary's northern boundary to the area north of Crossfield...that is, in the Nose Creek Historical Society's territory, drained by the Nose Creek.

It was no easy task to organize a school district. A good supply of water was essential, either dug or drilled. It had to be centrally located to accommodate the settlers it served, or else where the population density showed promise. Students in many cases came on horseback, so a barn had to be built to accommodate the horses. The schoolyard, two acres in most cases, had to be fenced, outside toilets constructed, and a coal and wood shed built, usually as a lean-to led off from the schoolhouse itself. Now we have the school and other facilities arranged for, where will the schoolteacher be staying? In most cases the teacher boarded at a nearby farm or ranch, with transportation to school either on foot or by horseback. Many varied and hilarious stories and amazing events were told of the schoolteachers' experiences. It was not unusual to spend the greater part of the morning stoking the coal and wood heating device to keep warm. Most schools were well maintained by local residents and the trustees who were quite responsible in seeing to the local educational needs. Summer holidays would see the barns cleaned out, the school renovated and painted, and the toilet repaired and maintained, all done in preparation for the September 1st school opening. The local school board arranged for coal and wood to be hauled in by team and wagon. It was an exciting time in the rural countryside when the teachers were engaged for the various schools. On many occasions the new arrival's stay in the district became a permanent one. Some lucky, available, young bachelor soon made an impression on the teacher, but only in the face of plenty of opposition from other eligible young men.

The following letter by Lois (Church) Perry expresses her view of the 1920-1930 era of school days:

I feel it was a privilege to have attended a one room prairie school, grades one to nine.

In Buttes School, through our dedicated teachers, we learned initiative and many sterling values.

Our teachers, as well as the pupils, had to contend with a cold classroom, as our Waterbury stove was temperamental and unpredictable!

Most students rode many miles to school. The zero temperatures of winter did not deter them. The teachers often boarded at our home, which was near the school.

During a blizzard the phones were out of order but the parents knew the children were safe in our home overnight. It was a fun time for the class to have a change of pace!

We enjoyed 'spelling matches' and Christmas concerts which were held in the school and as the memories flow back, I believe each, in his own way, learned encouragement, inspiration and guidance in Buttes School.

The Nose Creek Historical Society appreciates indeed all of the interesting local school histories printed here, contributed by many people. Without such co-operation the 'Little Red Schoolhouse' of yesteryear would be a faded memory.

Submitted by C. Redvers Perry, 1988

Abernethy School #2060

Abernethy School District No.2060 was established on October 23, 1909. Abernethy School was named after a town in Scotland and was located on the southwest quarter of Section 1-28-

2-W5. The first teacher was Carolynn Kidd, hired at $60 a month. The first trustees were Mr. Harrington, Jim Robertson, and Hector McKenzie. The secretary was Alec Ross. The school was closed in 1948 with Florence Landymore, who married Stan Price, as the last teacher. Some of the other teachers were: Miss Munroe, Miss Marbles, Miss Curly, Miss Lamont, Chris Robertson, Bessie Hargreaves, Anna Robertson, Bessie Snyder, Harold White, Don Matteson, Mrs. Sylvester, Jean Reid, who married Bob Nixdorf, Mrs. Chris Hanson, Betty Buck, Miss Anderson, Jennie Keegstra, and Irene Smith, who married Scotty Gellelli.

Ole Maylk and my Dad, Lloyd J. Smith, were trustees for several years. Anna Robertson boarded with my folks from April to June 1935, when Lloyd Smith bought Jim Robertson's ranch.

One horse I rode to Abernethy School was a thoroughbred I couldn't mount, as he went in circles, so Leonard Kininmonth came to my rescue. He twisted one of the horse's ears with one hand and gave me a boost with his other hand. Each day after school I ran to the barn to get my horse out first so I could have help mounting.
Submitted by Dorothy Tilleman, 1988

Airdrie School #918
Airdrie School started in 1904 and was located on the northeast quarter of Section 12-27-1-W5.

I entered my first year of school in 1918 in a one room building with twenty-four students and four grades. Some of the things I vividly remember are: the long horse barn at the back of the school yard; four very high swings, two for boys, the others for girls; the hand bell our Teacher (Miss Laundy) would ring so we would form two lines, girls in one and boys in the other, to march into the room and stand by our desks to repeat the Lord's Prayer; and the old hand pump that in winter would build up with ice, making it difficult to even fill a cup.

The school room had bare, oiled wooden floors with a "pot bellied" stove in the middle of the room; a blackboard covering one wall; the Teacher's desk and double desks for we pupils. Education in those days consisted mostly of reading, writing and arithmetic. Every Friday afternoon we looked forward to the "spelling bee", in which all children took part. School hours were nine to twelve noon and one to four P.M., with a ten minute recess morning and afternoon. Before being dismissed for the day, we stood to sing 'God Save Our King'.

I firmly believe if today's school system included a few minutes of patriotism and religion, there would be fewer problems among our young people. In closing, I might mention that the strap and other minor punishments were used when necessary, which were upheld by most parents, whose theory was - 'When in school the teacher is in control and when at home we, the parents are in control'.
Submitted by Heloise Lorimer, 1988

Beaver Dam School #1056
In 1904, people of the district requested the Department of Education at Regina to form a school district, which was established on July 8th. People could not agree as to where the boundaries or the site of the school should be. An inspector from Regina was sent to settle the question. He chose the site where the present building now stands on the southwest quarter of Section 30-28-2-W5. The Caldwell Brothers donated the land.

Frank Phillips and Mr. Walcott contracted to build the school. It cost about $500.00. It was 24 feet x 30 feet, and lumber was obtained from a sawmill west of Bottrel and Crossfield.

The second school was built in 1947. It was moved to south of Westbrook and is still in use as the Weedon Community Centre.

The third school building was built by Frank Phillips' son Phil Phillips. The school closed in the 1970s and it is now a private residence owned by Margaret Erlandson.
Submitted by Estelle Dodd and Edwin Rach, 1988

Beddington School #570
This school was located on the southwest quarter of Section 34-25-1-W5. Beddington

137

School district was formed in 1902 and the first board elected had John Barker as chairman and W.J. Church as secretary-treasurer. Tenders were called to build the school. Archie Bushfield and Joe Lewis were awarded the contract for the sum of $500.00. The school opened November 1, 1902 with 14 pupils, and our school district was #570.

Mr. Marshall was the first teacher and stayed two months. He was followed by Mr. Dobson, who stayed a year, but had no teaching certificate, thus no government grant. This was a severe blow to the finances of the school. The taxes were collected by the secretary-treasurer, and it was noted that George, Ken and Charlie Church rode many miles collecting for their Dad.

Over the years many board members served long and faithfully. The longest term was by Charlie Lewis; 1907 to 1941. Others that served long terms were Tom Pole, William Evans, Verna Pole, and Mary Bushfield.

The last annual meeting of the Beddington School was in January 1945, and it closed in June of that year. The children were then bussed to Dry Creek, and a year or so later the building was auctioned and sold to Evans Brothers, where it still stands tall and sturdy, as a shop. Just recently some of the blackboard was taken down from the wall and erected in the new Nose Creek Valley Museum.

Submitted by Doris Evans, 1988

Big Springs School #4237

Big Springs School was built in 1927, much later than many of the country schools. It was an attractive building nestled into the side of a wide green valley, on the northeast quarter of Section 32-26-2-W5. A set of windows looked out to the east, welcoming the morning sunshine. No outdoor "biffys" there, for indoor plumbing provided winter comfort.

The highlight of the winter was the Christmas concert. Practising for the concert began as early as November, as the performers knew they would be playing to a packed house.

The highlight of the summer was the picnic at the end of June. Again there was full attendance, as parents and students enjoyed the food and fellowship.

It was such a great community that most of the "School Marms" married one of the local bachelors and remained in the area.

The school was closed in 1946 and was later moved to Horse Creek.

Submitted by Margaret Morison, 1988

Buttes School #775

Buttes School started on December 31st 1902. It was located on the northwest quarter of Section 11-26-29-W4.

In September of 1921 I started riding a pony almost 4 miles to Buttes School. I had ridden very little before I ventured over the rough prairie trails. Badger holes were the real hazard and had to be avoided. I carried two lunches tucked away in my school bag slung over my shoulder, one for the pony, a cotton sugar sack with feed oats, and one for my own nourishment, consisting of sandwiches wrapped in newspaper. Our parents shunned the use of a saddle, as riding the pony bareback was safer.

Anytime I was early my first companion would be Bert Church, who was in Grade 8. Maybe Hugh, Margaret or Jock Cowan would share the rest of the journey. Josie Davy, a cousin who met a tragic fatal accident at the age of 9, would also join in.

The real challenge lay ahead. One dedicated teacher had thirty or more pupils from Grades 1 to 8. Today I realize that to attend a one room prairie school was a privilege and a blessing.

In my view, students became more resourceful and self sufficient; a thought that was often expressed by the late Premier William Aberhart. It was a common sight to witness older students helping younger ones in the lower grades; as well, they helped them dressing for home in the cold weather. The bigger children also helped them bridle and mount their ponies and would watch them as far as possible on their way home. The sense of co-operation and comradeship extended through all grade levels.

Of course, it was not always milk and honey. Differences were bound to occur but when the

138

chips were down a spirit of good will generally prevailed.

Asked to keep these memories short, I would suggest anyone interested in the heritage of our one room school system read *The Little White School House*, written by J. Charyk. I found his book to be informative as well as humorous.

I wish to pay special tribute to my first teacher, Miss. M. Rae, later Mrs. Charlie Church; also my second and third teachers, Helen Hamilton and her sister Eleanor Hamilton who later became Mrs. Ken Church.

Submitted by King Perry, 1988

Casa Loma School #3468

Casa Loma School was built in 1927 by Jim Elford on a two acre plot on the southwest quarter of Section 1-26-2-W5. This land was donated by Mr. F.R. Cathro.

Very appropriately the first teacher was Hilda Cathro, daughter of F.R. Cathro. During the time this school was in use, teachers to be remembered were: Ruth (Porter) Wigmore, Margaret (Murray) Johnson, Nellie Savill, Marjorie Tanner, Eileen Keyte, and Harry Sherk.

The first pupils were Margaret and Jack Murray, George and Kitty Fairweather, Buster Elliott, Tom Rance, and Cyril Woolliams.

The first school board consisted of the Secretary, F.R. Cathro and the Trustees, Billie Elliott, Tiny Marshall, and Colin Beaton. For many years Mrs. Beaton acted as Secretary-Treasurer. The last Secretary-Treasurer was Wesley Miller.

The name "Casa Loma" came from the Casa Loma Mansion "Castle on the Hill" which overlooked Mrs. Fanny Cathro's home in Toronto. Mr. Cathro also chose this name for his ranch name and the name of his purebred Black Angus cattle.

Many functions and entertainments were held there. The Christman Concerts were no doubt the highlight of the year. Other activities were dances, shadow dances, box socials, and leg auctions. In 1952, the pupils knitted a quilt for the Red Cross. The participants were: Elaine Woolliams, Helen Murray, Jerry Beaton, Cliff Davis, Duke Beaton, Bill and Vic Miller, Margaret and Bill Reynolds, Earl Brietzke, Frank Elliot, and Phoebe Anderson.

The grove of poplar and caragana trees were planted and maintained by Gus Brietzke.

The provincial government started to centralize the schools in the district and as a consequence the school was closed in 1947. The school board offered it for sale for a community hall. It was purchased by the Casa Loma Community Club and maintained for the use of all local community organizations, such as the Girl Guides, Boy Scouts, 4-H Clubs, and for showers, anniversaries or family parties.

In September of 1987 the school was sold to Mr. W. Sturm.

Submitted by Peggy Elliott, 1988

Columbia School #1731

In 1906 or 1907 a group of Americans, mostly friends, settled seven miles east of Airdrie, known as "Yankee Valley". Having young children, they built Columbia School with an enrollment of thirty pupils, ranging from beginners to teenagers. As Columbia was the only school for a while, pupils attended from outside the district. Its location was on the southeast quarter of Section 2-27-28-W4.

Our first teacher was Laura Coons. She was a splendid community worker as well as a good teacher. She helped organize a Sunday School. For many years church services were held in the school. To raise funds for a piano they held debates, and box and pie socials. There was a fine friendly feeling in the district. Space does not permit naming all the good teachers who taught in Columbia during the years, but Jack Oberholtzer was one with special ability.

The trustees who held office were Charles Ekstrom, Harry Woods, Paul Carpenter, and Alex Black.

When the pupils were bussed to Airdrie, Columbia School was closed. The building was not kept up, and sad to say this landmark was demolished recently.

Submitted by Bernice Shuttleworth, 1988

139

Conrich School

About 1955 the residents of Conrich and surrounding districts felt they needed a new school as the old one (Rockland) was old, cold and too small. Land was purchased from Dalton Ellis and the new school was built on the Conrich corner in 1956.

Enlargements and additions and classes were gradually added and then in 1961, Chestermere High School was built, taking grades 7 to 11 from Conrich. When Conrich was annexed to Calgary Rural in 1961, attendance was further depleted. The sale of acreages in the area again increased the attendance and in 1970 Conrich is again bursting at the seams, having over 240 pupils.

Submitted by Alice Hays, 1988

Crossfield School #752

Crossfield School District #752, on the northeast quarter of Section 26-28-1-W5, was incorporated in 1902. It was amalgamated with the Calgary Rural School Division No.41 in 1938. When Crossfield joined in 1943, their number became 7512. Surrounding schools gradually were closed.

The first school, originally one room, was located in the southwest part of town, with Miss Mallory (Mrs. Jack Grasley) as the teacher. Soon over sixty children, in all classes from beginners to those ready for high school, were in attendance. The building was moved near the present school site in 1907 and another room added. Due to rapid enrollment, Grade One had to be held over the Imperial Bank from 1908 until the four-room brick school, with science room, was completed in 1909, and a barn was built at the rear of the property. The brick school was replaced in 1954. The school offered High School education from 1932 on, except from 1962 to 1982 when the Seniors attended the George McDougall High School in Airdrie. In 1982, the William Murdoch High School opened its doors.

Fond memories include Bill Walker's remodelled buses and Jim Belshaw who was janitor for 43 years. Many will also remember the bank, where Miss Gesner (Mrs. Bill Laut) taught Grade One in 1909. It was later converted into a private dwelling. Recently our family, owners when it was demolished, donated the lumber to the museum in Airdrie where it was used for display buildings.

Submitted by Florence (Bigelow) Walker, 1988

Dry Creek School #855

This one room school was located on the northeast quarter of Section 22-26-1-W5 around 1905. While going through some of my father's material, I came across the minutes of the Dry Creek Literary Society. The minutes were dated June 14, 1906, and mentioned Miss Byrdy Marshall. I know from conversations with Dad and others that she was probably one of the first teachers.

Dry Creek School carried on until the fifties. The first school was replaced around 1930 and became St. Clement's Anglican Church at Balzac to the present day. The second school was moved and used at Beaupre, west of Cochrane. I believe it still is in existence, but not as a school.

I'm not going to list all the teachers that I may have known or heard of. The list would be too long. People who attended schools in the area during the thirties must remember the school inspector, Colonel MacGregor. As I recall, he was an imposing individual. To those of us who knew him, he was something to view with awe. Not often did anyone visit the school. We were drilled to rise by our desks and greet this great man with "Good morning, Inspector MacGregor" at the first sign of his entrance. The inspector wore a grey, well pressed pinstripe suit and drove a new car which we all viewed and admired at recess. No one dared touch it! I can still see Mr. MacGregor making his way to the front of the room. He had lost a leg in World War I, which left him with a swinging action when he moved. How impressive! The teacher had to be on her toes that day. This was her day of judgement. The students too were "random sampled". The inspector would ask someone to recite and before the verse was complete he would be ordered to "Sit down" and then on to the next. It was an earthly judgement day for us all!

For a short time Dry Creek School was divided in two in an attempt to provide schooling from Grade 1 through 12. On looking back, this was a valiant attempt to provide education for the community, but was not practical. Dry Creek, like so many other one room schools of the time, provided basic education. When one looks around at some of the students that attended there and see their endeavors, we can be justly proud!

Submitted by A. Leighton Perry, 1988

Eagle School District No.1637

The early pioneers wanted their children to have an education, therefore they got together, called a meeting and decided to build Eagle School. It was completed on May 13, 1907, on Section 26-26-2-W5. The pioneers originally wanted it called Eagle Nest School, as a bald headed eagle was always seen there, but it was called Eagle School. It burned down on November 29, 1936. An empty house was moved to the school grounds and used until a new one room school was built in October of 1937. Children were later bussed to bigger schools, and the land was sold in 1954.

The first teacher was Miss Yuill, a Scottish girl. These one room schools were not always the most comfortable. In the warm summer the windows and doors were opened for the "air conditioning" and in the winter a big heater provided the warmth. On some really cold days we all stood up periodically and would "run on the spot" to warm us up. Once in the 1930s a dust storm was so bad the school was forced to close as we couldn't see to do our work, it was so dark.

Grade VIII final high school entrance exams had to be written at Central High School in Calgary. This was discontinued when they realized it was too hard on country students competing with those from city schools.

The school was the centre of the district. Church services, christenings, sports days, dances and card parties were all held there. The younger children were always taken to these functions as no babysitters were used in those days. Some slept behind the piano and some on tops of desks pushed against the wall. The women brought lovely lunches and coffee was made in a big wash boiler. They had to carry water at first from a spring half a mile away. Later a well was drilled. Everyone always enjoyed these social events.

There are many fond memories for those who attended these one room schools.

Submitted by Joyce Butler, 1988

Elba School #2537

Elba School #2537, established on August 25, 1911, was built on the southwest corner of Earl Brown's land, Section 26-28-24-W4. The teachers boarded at the house on the property even after it was purchased by the Bills Family.

The usual school activities were organized. The frozen slough provided winter sports. A box social was held to raise money for the minister who held services every other Sunday.

The Fairview Hutterite Colony bought the Huser land. In the fall of 1943, their school age children attended Elba until they got their own school built.

After closure, the white schoolhouse, was moved to Beiseker and converted into a family home.

Submitted by Florence (Bigelow) Walker, 1988

Floral School #1570

Floral School #1570 district was established in 1906, with James McCool as secretary. It was located on land owned by Clarence Stafford; the southwest quarter of Section 6-29-28-W4. The first teacher was Miss Lutan. Some of the first students were from the Stafford, Ruddy, Thompson, and McCool families. The next generation included students from these same families, plus the Sackett, Wickerson, Elhard, and Bills families.

Two much loved teachers were Ken McRae, 1934-39, followed by Gladys McDonald. Ken

McRae became famous, or notorious, for his interpretation of Wilf Carter's "Strawberry Roan" as part of his Christmas Concerts.

Floral was closed in 1944 and became part of Calgary Rural School District #41. The last teacher was Beatrice McCrae. The building was purchased by Hall McCaskill, and moved to Crossfield for a workshop. Later it was demolished to make space for the Pete Knight Arena.

Submitted by Margaret (Wickerson) Mason, 1988

Glen Leven School District #2124

This school was named after a place in Scotland by Mrs. Fred Custead. It was located on the southeast quarter of Section 26-27-28-W4. It opened on February 8, 1910, and closed on June 30, 1955. The first teacher was Miss Allen, and the last was Mrs. Joan Kinniburgh, formerly Clandellon. In her farewell, she wrote: "Many of your parents and in some cases grandparents attended Glen Leven School - what better proof than this that rural schools have been a rung in the ladder of success in life."

Submitted by Kay Malyk, 1988

Glen Rock School #3436

Glen Rock was situated about four or five miles east of Airdrie on what is now known as the Irricana Road, on the southwest quarter of Section 17-27-28-W4. The original school burnt down in the early 1940s and a school known as Craigdhu was moved in to replace it. The Craigdhu School was built in 1926. Joan Clandellan was one of the teachers and later married Ted Kinniburgh, a farmer in the area. The Glen Rock School children later bussed to Airdrie, and a nice home was added to and built around the old Glen Rock School.

Submitted by Mrs. Alice Hays, 1988

Glenville School S.D. #1300

The Glenville School was built in 1905 with Mr. John Bishop of the district as contractor. It was located on the northeast quarter of Section 27-25-29-W4.

The first teacher was Elizabeth McDowell, a local girl who lived three miles west of the school. She rode horseback across country to school as there were no roads or fences.

The school became useful as a meeting place for social gatherings, dances, picnics, sports days and concerts. Church services were held in the school. These were under the direction of the Airdrie minister. Later a student minister filled the appointment. Services continued until 1914.

Mice were often a problem in the school, causing quite a flurry among pupils when seen scurrying across the floor. Hoping to rid the problem, the teacher put mouse seed around in the building. Seventeen of the little furry creatures chose the interior of the piano as their final resting place. As a result, school had to be closed for several days because of the terrible stench, while the building was cleaned and fumigated.

Glenville School was closed in 1956 and sometime later moved to be used in the Maryland School District in Calgary's southeast district.

Submitted by Marion Blair, 1988

Goldenrod School #1460

This school was located five miles west of Airdrie, on the southeast quarter of Section 18-27-1-W5. It started in 1906, with 23 pupils. The first teacher was John Seatter, hired at $50 per month. A tax was levied on the community at $10 per quarter section. The school was used on Sundays for church. The ladies raised the money for an organ with a Box Social.

Other teachers were: J.S. Irvine (1907), Miss Spencer, Mr. Fraser, Miss Hoskins, Mrs. V.E. Brown, Miss Ouderkirk (Mrs. Bert Fletcher), Miss Graves, Miss Cecilia Larue (1913), Miss Martha Knight, Miss Alberta Knight, Miss L.V. Shantz (1915), Roy Edwards, Miss Munroe (1921), Miss McLaren, Miss Laundry (1923), Miss McNeill (1926), Eva Hart, Miss Davis (1927), Miss Leisher (1928), Miss Simpson (5 years), Catherine Jenkins (Mrs.

Dale Wray; 2 years 1934-36), Roy Edwards (1936-38), Nellie Savill, Emily Marston (3 years). The last teacher was Eleanor May (Mrs. George Cooper). The school closed in June 1944 and the children were bussed into Airdrie. Goldenrod School was bought by Victor Watson and moved to his farm with some additions to serve as a seed cleaning plant.

Submitted by Allen Watson, 1988

Inverlea School #2239

Inverlea School #2239 was established on July 25, 1910, on land donated by W.D. Fraser. The school was named after a favorite spot he frequented in his youth, and was located six miles southwest of Crossfield, on the northwest quarter of Section 9-28-1-W5.

In 1943, Inverlea joined the Calgary School Division No. 41. The closing of Inverlea and other schools resulted in overcrowding at Crossfield. Inverlea School was then moved to town for use until the new pink-stuccoed school was built in 1954.

The School Division gave the Inverlea School to the Crossfield United Church and in 1957 it was moved and eventually renovated. It is appropriate that the school should end up as part of a church, as it was a regular preaching point in the earlier years.

Submitted by Florence (Bigelow) Walker, 1988

McPherson Coulee School #4143

This school was located on the northwest quarter of Section 26-27-1-W5 and was built in 1923. By this time there were enough families with school age children to make a new school district viable, so after due deliberation the school was built. Because of its proximity to McPherson Coulee, it received its name. There were two Clayton families, Blairs, DeWitts, Poles, Stevensons, Killams, and Endicotts whose children attended, myself being one of them. Shortly thereafter, children of other families joined the ranks in school, some of whom were Wrights, Camerons, and McCamblys, and others as well.

Our first teacher was Miss Bernice Black (presently Mrs. Bernice Shuttleworth), whom we loved and respected very much. She was followed by many other dedicated teachers who did their best under often trying circumstances to bring a really good education to the pupils.

We had our share of good times and bad times...wonderful Christmas concerts which have never been equalled, picnics, school dances, and school accidents. We, and by this I mean everyone, young and old, made our own fun and entertainment, took care of our own problems, cared for each other. We pupils made our way through the school grades and continued our education in one way or another, gradually taking on adult responsibilities and taking our place in society.

By 1944, the McPherson Coulee closed and pupils were bussed to Airdrie, thus began a new era in the Education System.

Note: McPherson was formerly the Mountain View School and moved to the coulee position after the original burnt down. Currently it is the Balzac United Church, moved down in 1944.

Submitted by Marion Bowen, 1988

Meadowside School #4216

Meadowside School #4216 was built in 1925, located seven miles east of Crossfield in the northwest corner of the Crockett land on Section 9-29-28-W4. It was a small square building with large east windows made up of many small panes, the newest design for country schools. The school furniture was up-to-date for those years. The teacher-pupil ratio was low - 10 pupils in 1928 and 13 in 1929. This low enrollment continued throughout the school's existence. It closed in 1944, and about 1954 it was moved to the present site of the Davies Community Centre.

Submitted by Pearl (Stauffer) Chalmers, 1988

Nose Creek School #433

I'm enclosing a short note of some of my memories during my teaching days at Nose Creek School. This was a two roomed school started on September 2, 1896, located on the southeast corner of Section 3-25-1-W5. I would say this was somewhere near the Edmonton Trail and McKnight intersection. Only one room used, for twenty-some pupils. The trustees were Mrs. Laycock Sr., Mr. Young, Secretary, and Mr. O. Short. It was a delightful school to teach in. I especially remember the year that Ellen Anderson, Sylvia Short, Robert Bennett, and John Wallace were in Grade 8. They worked so hard and all passed their Departmental Exams. I was so proud of them. Hugh Bennett, who lives east of the Airport, was one of those that attended, and he developed into a very pleasant writer. We all liked to sing, so one of our mothers, Mrs. Bennett, composed a ditty for us which we sang to the tune of "Neath the Shade of the Old Apple Tree":

> Neath the roof of the Nose Creek School,
> The teacher doesn't like us to fool,
> She wants us to work and never to shirk,
> Always remember the Rule.
> We must clean off our shoes and look neat,
> And always sit still in our seats,
> But whatever we do we must always be true
> Neath the roof of the Nose Creek School.

Submitted by Marguerite Wall, 1988

Oneil School #1176

Oneil School No. 1176, established on December 31, 1904, was named after J.H. Oneil. The large schoolhouse was built in 1905 on the southeast quarter of Section 12-28-29-W4. The school had hardwood floors with the teacher's desk on a raised platform, a telephone, and a furnace type stove with lengthy stove pipes. Later, Oneil became the only school to have indoor (chemical) plumbing, thanks to N.J. Wigle.

Pleasant memories include community socials and school activities such as the year-end picnic.

After closure, the school was bought by Mr. Taks Sr. in 1943, who tore it down and used the lumber on his farm. The barn was purchased by Win Landymore, and was moved to his farm where it is still in use.

Submitted by Alice (Oneil) Aldred, 1988

Pleasant Range School #1411

Pleasant Range School was located on two acres of land, one each from the northwest corner of 15-25-28-W4 and the southwest corner of 22-25-28-W4. The school land was donated by W.A. Jones and David Davidson. The school was built in 1907 by Olaf Odland, who hauled lumber from Calgary by team and wagon. To drill a well, they used a horse power sweep to supply power for the drilling rig. The circle worn by the horses' hooves became a place to play games for the school children for many years. Pleasant Range closed its doors in 1946. The children were bussed to Rockland. The old schoolhouse was eventually sold to Paul Nixdorff and moved away.

Submitted by Alice Hays, 1988.

Parkway School #4317

Parkway School No. 4317, located on the northwest corner of the northeast quarter of Section 10-26-28-W4, was opened in 1929 with Laura Ellis as the first teacher. The school continued in operation for twenty-two years before closing its doors.

Parkway was known for its Christmas concerts and school picnics! It was also a community centre with dances, card games, wedding parties, plays, meetings, and church services.

Parkway School is long gone but the community spirit lives on!

Submitted by Herb Jobson, 1988

144

Rockyview School #1000

Rockyview was a small one room school located on the Conrich road about two and one half miles east of Calgary, on the southeast quarter of Section 2-25-29-W4. It was built around 1904 and was in constant use until 1943. There were from nine to twenty-eight pupils in attendance, some of whom were transferred to Rockland in 1943. The first school bus (or car) was driven by T. Jensen. There were $1,000 of war bonds left, (from World War I) when the school closed. The Municipal District of Rockyview was named after Rockyview School, which was near the centre of the M.D. The school was also used to hold church services as many schools were.

Submitted by Alice Hays, 1988

Sunny Side School - Northwest Territories.

This school was built in 1899, not incorporated, and was located on the southwest quarter of Section 36-27-1-W5. The Sunny Side School was a private school situated near the first stopping house north of Calgary, halfway between the Collicut and Stevenson ranch buildings.

Emily Mason (Mrs. E.M. Clayton) was the first teacher, arriving on February 22, 1899. The school was about sixteen feet square, with homemade desks, built by Mr. Mackenzie. The pupils were the Collicut children, Georgia and Clarence; Mrs. Collicut's niece, Viola Martin; J. Stevenson's children, Bessie, Jack, and Louise. Wages were $15.00 a month and board.

Submitted by Marion Powlesland, 1988

Sunshine School #1773

Sunshine School #1773 was built in 1908 on a two acre plot on the southwest quarter of Section 31-29-1-W5, on the Blind Line, five miles west of Crossfield. The schoolroom, with four large windows on each side, was spacious, with a raised platform on one end for the piano and the teacher's desk. A big iron stove stood at the rear near the cloakroom door with a long line of stove pipes to the chimney in the front. This school room had a beautiful hardwood floor which was frequently used for community dances on Friday nights.

In 1951 Sunshine School closed its doors, when the district joined the Crossfield Consolidated S.D. In 1956 it was sold to Mr. Steve Bezjack of Madden where it continues to be used as a granary.

Submitted by Pearl (Stauffer) Chalmers, 1988

Westminster School #1848

Westminster School #1848 was built in 1908 and 1909 on the northeast corner of of the southeast quarter of Section 7-26-2-W5. It was contracted and built by Mr. J.C. Nelson; 20 feet wide and 30 feet long with a 10-foot ceiling, resting on a wood foundation. The cost of materials was around $300. It rested on the wood foundation until about 1920 or 1921, at which time it was jacked up and a cement foundation was put under it, with two cloak rooms about 16 feet by 20 feet being added. There were about seven pupils to start. Taxes started near $5.00 per quarter section, and doubled in 1911.

By 1921 or 1922 pupils had increased by about three times the number that had started. Many good times were had there over the years, with dances, concerts, box socials, and picnics.

Orchestras came and played from Airdrie, Beddington, and Calgary, and some were made up locally by the Lewises, Hopkinses, and Martinusens. Light was provided by coal oil lamps to start, then high-test gasoline lamps.

Submitted by Roy Teghtmeyer, 1988

Reference to School Histories

The above vignettes present a warm and nostalgic glimpse into the history of our schools. They were a place to learn, to play, and to worship; indeed, the hub of the community.

At the turn of the century parents viewed a sound education to be the cornerstone of their children's future, a belief parents and their communities have continued to foster to this day.

Submitted by Rosemary E. Church, Chairman Rocky View School Division, 1988

History of the Rocky View School Division No. 41

On January 3, 1939, by order of the Minister of Education, Calgary Rural School Division No. 41 was created, bringing into one administrative unit some seventy-six local school districts. The new School Division was divided into five subdivisions, each to be represented on the Divisional Board by an elected trustee. W.H. Evans was subsequently elected Chairman of the new Board, F.R. McVeigh was named Secretary-Treasurer, and Col. J.A. MacGregor appointed Superintendent of Schools.

The Division actually had its beginning when an early missionary, the Rev. George McDougall, established a school at Morley in 1875 and installed a medical doctor, Dr. George Verey, as the first teacher. It was two years later that the government of the North West Territories established Springbank School District No. 100. Other school districts were organized in rapid succession.

Since the creation of the Calgary School Division No. 41, the story has been one of continual growth. The number of teachers engaged by the Board has quadrupled until now there is a teaching staff of over 420. The only one-roomed schools that remain are located on three Hutterite Colonies. The pupil population has increased until in the school year 1986-87 it exceeded the 8,000 mark. In 1986-87 the Divisional Board is operating two senior high schools, two junior high schools, two junior-senior high schools, four elementary-junior high schools, eleven elementary schools, one junior vocational school and three one-room Hutterite Colony schools.

Cochrane School District No. 142 joined the Division in 1966 and in 1968 had sufficient students for it to be constituted as a sub-division. Consequently, another trustee was added to the Board bringing its membership up to six.

Very rapid growth in the Airdrie-Crossfield area resulted in the addition of another trustee in October 1981, bringing the Board's membership to seven.

Col. MacGregor completed his term as Superintendent in 1940 and was succeeded by G.L. Wilson (1941-52), G.J. Hollinshead (1953-60), W.S. Korek (1960-67), E.M. Erickson (1967-70), and J.C. Macdonell, who became the division's first locally appointed Superintendent in 1970. Following Mr. Macdonell's resignation in 1976, J.L. Sacher was appointed Superintendent and served until 1987. In February 1987, H.C. Parr was appointed as the eighth Superintendent of the Division. Mr. Evans served as Chairman of the Board of Trustees until 1942 and he has been followed by E.R. Baldwin, Col. H.C.A. Harvey, L. Akins, J.T. Cullen, R. Stanton, B.C. Church, J.H. Schmaltz, A.L. Perry, M.A. Gosling, A. Hodgson, and M.A. Gosling. E.D. Bottram was the second Secretary-Treasurer with O.P. Gosling succeeding him. Following Mr. Gosling's retirement in 1961, A.W. Burzloff was appointed and served until his retirement in 1979. In September 1979, D.H. Vizina was appointed as the division's fifth Secretary-Treasurer.

In 1977 the Calgary Rural School Division No. 41 changed its name to Rocky View School Division No. 41.

Rosemary Church was elected Chairman of the Board of Trustees at the organizational meeting in October 1987 and continues in that position at this present time.

Submitted by Rosemary E. Church, Chairman Rocky View School Division, 1988

146

Weedon School, north of Cochrane January, 1913 - moved to Heritage Park in Calgary, 1964.

This is a historical document. Please value it on the basis of posterity. It is compliments of the Nose Creek Historical Society.

The cover of the historical document (above) pays tribute to rural schools. Weedon School building (pictured), which used to be located north of Cochrane, was moved to Heritage Park, Calgary in 1964.

Sunshine School, 5 miles west of Crossfield. This structure was built in 1908 and closed in 1951.

Right: A pencil sketch by Peggy Orr of a typical school. Peggy was one of the editors of the book, **Prairie Sod and Golden Rod**. (The Crossfield Story).

Rodney School

Muriel Clayton the 1st school teacher in the Valley north of the Johnson-Stevenson Stopping house.

Miss Edith Mallory, later Mrs. Jack Grasley, was the first teacher at Crossfield.

Muriel Clayton's pencil sketch of the first school house—Sunnyside School, Airdrie—north of Fort Calgary.

Rocky View Division School Board. c. 1970 (l-r) Kathryn Beattie, Rev. Dr. Jack Collett, Norman Reddekopp, Clayton Edgelow, Al Burzloff, Delores Gardiner, Melfort Grosling, Jack Macdonell, Leighton Perry, and Bruce Booth.

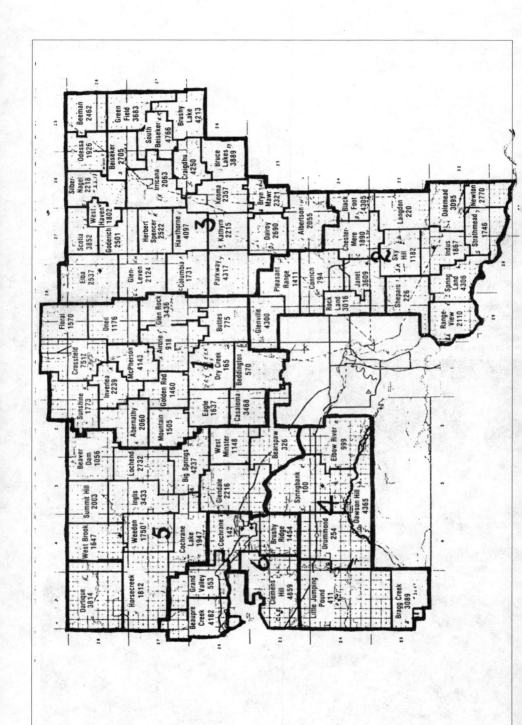

District	No.		District	No.
Beeman	2462			
Green Field	3683			
Odessa	1926			
Beiseker	2705			
South Beiseker			Brushy Lake	4213
Irricana	2063		Craigdhu	4250
Silber			Bruce Lakes	3889
Nagel	2218		Keoma	2357
West Haven	1802		Bryn Mawr	2321
Scotia	3852		Dalroy	2690
Godenich	2501		Albertson	2055
Herbert Spencer	2522		Black Foot	4305
Hawthorne	4097		Chester	
Kathyrn	2215		Mere	1890
Elba	2537		Langdon	220
Leven	2124		Sky Hill	1182
Glenview			Dalemead	3095
Columbia	1731		Newton	2770
Parkway	4317		Strathmead	1746
Pleasant Range	1411		Indus	1867
Conrich	794		Spring Land	4306
Glen Rock	3436		Rock Land	3016
Floral	1570		Janet	3609
Oneil	1176		Shepard	226
Airdrie	918		Range View	2110
Buttes	775		Bearspaw	326
Glenville	4300		Springbank	100
Crossfield	7512		Elbow River	999
McPherson	4143		Dawson Hill	4365
Dry Creek	165		Drummond	254
Beddington	570		Brushy Ridge	1454
Invertea	2239		West Minster	1148
Sunshine	1773		Casaloma	3468
Abernathy	2060		Little Jumping Pound	411
Golden Rod	1460		Clemens Hill	4859
Mountain	1505		Bragg Creek	3089
Eagle	1637			
Beaver Dam	1056			
Lochend	2732			
Big Springs	4237			
Glendale	2216			
Summit Hill	2003			
Inglis	3433			
Cochrane	142			
West Brook	1647			
Weedon	1750			
Cochrane Lake	1947			
Dartique	3814			
Horsecreek	1812			
Grand Valley	553			
Beaupre Creek	4182			

Rocky View School Division No. 41

Taken from the book *Acres and Empires*, R.M. 44 Rockyview.

148

CHAPTER 23: TRIBUTE TO LOCAL AND RURAL CHURCHES
EIGHTEENTH LOCAL HISTORICAL RECOGNITION: 1889-1989

Fort Calgary was established in 1875 and quickly developed into a town - but long before that, missionaries of various denominations had pioneered the west and brought the good influence of the Bible to the pioneers and natives of the prairies who were here during that time. With the town of Calgary in existence, there was little time to lose in getting a farming industry in production. John Glenn was noted as one of the first farmers, near what we now know as Glenmore Reservoir. North of Fort Calgary was the mixed farming district of Nose Creek and settlers soon were in operation providing vital food products. Families were established on the homesteads, and schools were given immediate consideration with church services, in some cases in advance of all other local needs. Records say early religious activities were held in the ranch homes, with layreaders conducting the service. This went on for only a short time, and in many cases the local schools were used for Sunday worship until a church was established. There was a great effort involved to organize a place of worship. Often a minister had to be arranged for from the city of Calgary. Weather had considerable influence as roads were anything but dependable. Someone had to go to the building to light the coal heater, clean the facilities, place chairs, sweep floors, and get all in order for the usual 3 o'clock service. Morning services were out as farmers had chores to do, and in winter months the place of worship had to have four hours heating in order to be comfortable.

A great deal of credit must be given to those nation builders of that time, who had such respect for the Bible and their particular faith that they organized the Sunday services, bringing the youngsters and elders to worship. We hope you appreciate the history which follows in this 18th historical recognition of the local churches' foundation over the past century.

Submitted by C. Redvers Perry, 1989

Airdrie's Fellowship Bible Chapel

Airdrie's Fellowship Bible Chapel was started in the fall of 1978 by Pastor Harv Trauter and his wife, Arlene. Services and Sunday School were held in the Airdrie Elementary School until the spring of 1980 when growth dictated a change. A triple Atco trailer was purchased and moved onto land leased for $1.00 per annum. By November 1, 1983, five years after Fellowship Bible Chapel opened its doors, we had outgrown the trailers. The Anglican Church generously shared facilities with us until the present church building was ready for occupancy on January 7, 1985.

In July 1988, Pastor Trauter went to another church in Edmonton, and in October Pastor Bill Ashbee and Bona Jean took over the ministry. This church, which began in 1978 with three families, now has 75 families.

Submitted by Marie Cole, 1988

A Brief History of Airdrie United Church

Before 1900, services of worship were often held in the Airdrie district by ministers of the Presbyterian and Methodist Churches, calling at ranch houses and stopping places. Beginning in 1901, the Rev. E.W. Wood came regularly from Carstairs to hold services in Airdrie itself; first in the Bowers' home, then in the railroad station waiting room and then in William Croxford's home. Upon Mr. Wood's untimely death in 1902, services were conducted temporarily by R.A. Whattam.

In November 1902, just 87 years ago, William G. Shaw, a student minister. became the first resident minister in Airdrie. Under his leadership the Airdrie Methodist congregation was formed and received its first members on July 1st, 1903. The charter members were: Mr. and Mrs. Thomas Fletcher, Mary Fletcher, William Croxford, Mary Croxford, Mrs. A. Bowers, Mr. and Mrs. E. Dodd, Edwin Dodd Jr., Mr. and Mrs. Johnson Stevenson, William G. Shaw, Allan Knudson, Mr. and Mrs. R.L. Hawkey, and Frank Hawkey.

A church was built when the Croxford house became too small to hold the congregation. The Rev. Thomas Powell, then Minister at Olds, dedicated the new building on July 18, 1903. Two months later the Airdrie "Mission" became an independent circuit, separate from the Carstairs "Mission".

Other events of interest include:

Spring of 1906: Shaver's Appointment was started, later to become Columbia Church.
January 8, 1922: Dedication of the present Airdrie United Church building.
June 10, 1925: Airdrie Methodist Church became Airdrie United Church, entering into union
November 15, 1964: Dedication of the Christian Education Centre.
October 19, 1965: Columbia congregation received in Airdrie as Columbia Church closes.

In January 1984, an addition was made to the old church which included two offices, a new narthex with cloak room and kitchen facilities, a nursery, and one extra large bathroom. The church now holds 350 people. In 1987 another story was added to the Christian Education building for extra class rooms, eight in number, which were greatly needed.

Submitted by Heloise Lorimer, 1989

Balzac United Church

In the early days church services were first held in homes, then in both Dry Creek and Butte Schools. Services were taken by student ministers, then by Airdrie ministers. The two schools joined to form the Balzac United Church. In 1929, the Balzac Hall was built and services were held there until 1945. A school from west of Airdrie was purchased and moved on December 15, 1944 to its present location. The Rev. Thomas Powell led the dedication service on Easter Sunday, April 16, 1945.

Mr. Rosenberger, the first Secretary-Treasurer, gave a report that the church was free of debt due to generous donations. Mr. Oliver Ingraham donated the piano, which is still in use today.

The first pianist was Mrs. Osia Rosenberger, then her daughter Mrs. W. Onia. Berenice Shuttleworth started as pianist in 1934 and has set a gold record, as she still plays the new organ Betty Lamb began a junior choir that sang at special occasions which we all enjoyed. Jean McElroy had a younger choir in 1974-75. An electric organ was purchased in 1973.

With many local volunteer teachers, the Sunday School has continued throughout the years with good attendance. Mrs. Rosenberger organized and also chaired the Ladies Aid Group for many years. This group has been very active in the community for years, and is now known as U.C.W. (United Church Women).

Not many of the original congregation are left, but many descendants of these pioneers and also newcomers continue to enjoy the fellowship of a small community church.

Submitted by Jack R. Osborne, 1989

Beddington United Church

Prior to 1900 church services were held in the home of Elizabeth and Joseph Lewis. The Lewis home was about one and three-quarter miles southwest of the present Beddington Hall. The Reverend Thomas Hutchinson was the first minister to come over the lonely prairie trails to conduct these early services.

Sometime after the Beddington School was built in 1902, church was held in the school, as the congregation was growing too large for the Lewis home.

In 1911 some ladies met at the home of Mrs. Barker and formed the first Ladies Aid. Plans for a church building was the main topic they discussed, which meant raising some money. The first event they held was a strawberry social, and the following year, 1912, the men of the congregation met and made plans to canvass the area for funds. This effort netted enough to begin building the church.

On February 23, 1913, Beddington Church was officially opened by the Reverend Dr. W. Shearer. The Reverend H.R. Davidson was installed as the first minister. Services continued for many years with dedicated ministers, Sunday school superintendents, organists and teachers. For most of these years we were associated with Pleasant Heights United Church. We were very fortunate to have their choir and young people help us out with the programs when we were raising funds to keep the church operating. Also, the Ladies Aid held chicken suppers, teas and three-act plays to help with the cost, as having a church in the community was most important.

In April 1963, Beddington Church celebrated its 50th Anniversary. On Friday night a supper and program of local talent was held at the hall with a capacity crowd. The following Sunday the Anniversary Church Service was held, with a full church of residents past and present attending.

The church remained open until February 1968 when it was officially closed. It was moved in April to its present site and was rededicated as Balzac United Church on September 29, 1968.

Submitted by Doris Evans, 1989

Church Beginnings in Eagle and Goldenrod

In the years before 1900 it was very difficult to bring the Bible message to the widely-scattered homes west of Airdrie. If a missionary or a minister made his way into the area, he usually held a worship service in one of the homes.

After the turn of the century, settlement increased as more people bought land. Services were held more frequently in the Goldenrod, Eagle, and Abernethy districts. These were still in the homes and were served by student ministers.

With the building of a school in each district, the school building usually served as the place of worship. During the 1930s services were held in the Goldenrod Community Hall. They were in the charge of students from the Calgary Bible Institute, and often included vacation Bible school for the children.

In 1946 a community non-denominational church was organized. Bible students form Calgary and Three Hills gave help. The minister from Crossfield Baptist Church preached on Sunday afternoons.

In 1953 this group bought the now vacant Eagle school house and moved it four miles south to a location on the Symons Valley road. In 1958 it became the Eagle Church of the Nazarene.

In 1962 it was decided to build a church in Airdrie and move there. Airdrie Church of the Nazarene was dedicated in the spring of 1963, and continues there.

Submitted by Margaret Morison, 1989

Columbia Church

Columbia United Church was located in the Yankee Valley district about seven miles east of Airdrie on the Yankee Valley Road.

It started about 1906 with services at the farm home of Mr. and Mrs. Sil Shaver, who had invited ministers to come out from Airdrie. Soon the Shaver Appointment was placed on the Methodist circuit. The congregation arrived in wagons, buggies, and on horseback.

When the Americans arrived with children of school age, the school was built, and in 1908 the Columbia Church was started in the school.

The Columbia United Church was an active part of this community for over fifty-five years, and closed in 1965.

Submitted by Herb Jobson, 1989

Crossfield Baptist Church

During the summer of 1930, special meetings were held in the U.F.A. Hall by the Rev. Morley Hall, pastor of Westbourne Baptist Church in Calgary. Interest grew, and so did the crowds. This prompted the beginning of the Crossfield Baptist Church. Charles McGrath, a young man from Ontario, was put in charge of this mission. Regular Sunday services were held in the Masonic Hall with about 40 interested people. On December 31, 1931, the church was organized with its first pastor, Charles McGrath; four deacons, Will Waldock, Hiram Warner, William Stauffer, and Roy Smith; and twenty-six charter members. They built the church on its present site at Limit Avenue and Strathcona Street, and held dedication services in June 1933. A parsonage was built in 1936.

Early pastors also held Sunday afternoon services at district schools, including Abernethy, West Hope, Summit Hill, and Eagle Hill. Through the years, as the membership increased and transportation methods improved, additions were made to the original buildings to better suit the members' needs.

Youth programs, held on Friday nights and open to all teens, have been a part of the church's

151

outreach, as have clubs for boys and girls which meet each week. Vacation Bible School has been held each summer for forty-four years. The active support program has sent out four pastors and seventeen young missionaries to home and foreign appointments.

In June 1981 the church celebrated its 50th anniversary of services to the community, which brought much joy to the congregation and praise to God for His faithfulness.

This is a list of the pastors through the years: Charles McGrath, 1931-33; Earle Phillips, 1934; Jack Pickford, 1935-40; David Milligan, 1940-45; Bill MacDonald, 1945-56; Glen Richardson, 1957-65; Don Rendle, 1965-69; Gerald Meller, 1969-74; Gordon Lean, 1975-81; David Peterson, 1982-84; and Glen Priebe, 1985-present.

Submitted by Pearl (Stauffer) Chalmers, 1989

Crossfield United Church

Before 1902 circuit-riding clergy served Crossfield and district, holding worship services in private homes and outlying schools.

In November 1902, Crossfield was added to the Carstairs Mission, under the care of a Methodist preacher stationed at Carstairs. Crossfield's first place of worship was the station - a boxcar without wheels. After McCool's new store was finished, services were held there, with the minister using the counter for his pulpit. Following this the church congregation used the first school, located in the southwest part of town, for its services.

When the congregation overflowed the school house, a church became necessary. In 1905 work commenced on the Methodist Church at the site of the present United Church (lot 18, block 2, plan 4504-1). At the same time land was secured and the foundation laid for the Presbyterian Church on what is now the Violet Hurt property, but this church was never built. The Presbyterians continued to hold their services in schools, and eventually in the new Methodist Church.

The Official Board of the Methodist Church planned to build a shell structure, that could be completed later, at a cost not exceeding $1,200. The committee's faith has to be commended, as not only was this the first year as a separate mission, but their bank balance was less than $100. The first recorded minutes, for November 10, 1905, show a financial balance of $92.15, which was a total from all preaching points: Crossfield, Beaver Dam, Jackson's Home, Rosebud, Stoney Creek, Tan-y-Bryn, Sunshine, Elba, Rodney, Inverlea, and Bottrel.

The homesteaders who were arriving had very little money, so volunteer labour had to be used as much as possible. They quarried and hauled stone for the foundation from jutting rock some three miles north of the village. A master carpenter and a master mason were hired, and the foundation was completed before freeze-up. This was indeed fortunate, as the winter of 1905-6 was extremely bad. One oldtimer who arrived in Crossfield during that period, Stuart Walker Sr., described March 1906 as one long continuous blizzard. He was often heard saying, "The lamb must have gotten frozen to death as March came in like a lion and went out like one too, that year."

In spite of the bad weather that winter, the interior of the church was completed, with an attractive plaster finish, making this the first plastered building in the community. Cash and pledges totalled $2,000, providing enough money for an organ and pulpit, but no pews.

The new church was dedicated on Easter Sunday, April 15, 1906. The congregation included adherents from several denominations, making the Crossfield Methodist Church a Co-operative Charge. In 1916 a local Union Church was formed, later becoming the Crossfield United Church.

Since 1925 there have been changes and additions to the original structure, made necessary by the growth of our church family. Some of these changes and additions include the balcony, the front entry, the kitchen/parlour, the front of the sanctuary, and the hall. Our hall was originally the Inverlea School, which was moved to Crossfield, and in 1957 was put on its present foundation. The Memorial Carillon was dedicated in 1969, and the room behind the balcony was finished in 1970. Chairs replaced the pews in 1976.

Over the past year a Building Planning Committee has been working on plans for a new building to carry on the traditions of Crossfield United Church, and to provide facilities for a new generation of expanded activities.

Over the years we have been served by thirty-five ministers. A list of their names has been prepared and is hanging in our sanctuary.

Submitted by Florence (Bigelow) Walker, 1989

History of Faith Community Baptist Church

Faith Community Baptist of Airdrie was born out of the vision and concern of Grace Baptist Church in Calgary for the rapidly growing community here. In 1981, after spending much time in prayer, Grace Baptist and the Central Alberta Church Extension Council of the North American Baptist Conference agreed to explore the possibilities. A home Bible Study was begun that soon led to the first public service of the church, in the Airdrie United Church Education Building on July 12, 1981. Harold Weiss accepted the call to become the first pastor of the church in October of that same year. The charter membership closed with 34 members on July 11, 1982, which marked the first anniversary of the church. Towards the end of 1983, the church had grown to the extent that the Church Education Building was no longer adequate. Thus, a warehouse type building was chosen on the east side of town to serve as the church's second location. In 1985, a Building Committee was struck and plans were made for a permanent building. The new building was completed in 1986 on a four-acre site located 1½ miles west of Highway 2 on Big Springs Road. It was dedicated on June 22 of that year. Harold Weiss resigned as pastor in April of 1988 and Lyle Buyer assumed responsibility as the church's second pastor in May of 1989.

Submitted by Faith Community Baptist Church, 1989

Lochend Church

Church services were held in private homes, at the homes of Mr. and Mrs. Joseph K. Laidlaw and Mr. and Mrs. King, prior to the building of the Lochend Church in 1908. The minister came out from Cochrane every two weeks.

The Lochend Church was built on two acres of land bought from the C.P.R., situated on the northeast quarter of Section 23-27-3-W5, on the south side of Lochend Lake, directly across the lake from the Lochend Post Office on the J.K. Laidlaw farm. It was an amalgamation of the Presbyterians and the Methodists and was called the Lochend United Church.

On January 19, 1909, the Lochend Church was dedicated by the Reverend Mr. McWilliams of Calgary, assisted by the Reverend Mr. Claxton of Cochrane. An Estey organ was purchased in 1914. For many decades Lochend was used as a church and a school, as well as for other community activities.

In 1972 the church was sold and moved some twenty-five miles northwest into the Grand Valley to be used as a residence. The original church/school grounds were sold in the early 1980s, and now a private home graces the site.

Submitted by Bobby and Sunni Turner, 1989

Lutheran Church of the Master - Airdrie

Lutheran Church of the Master was officially organized on May 3, 1980. The congregation was begun in 1978 through the initiative of Sharon Lutheran Church, Calgary, and has grown to encompass over 70 families. Currently meeting at the Bethany Care Centre, the congregation plans on being in its own facility by June 1991. Pastor Greg Mohr has served the congregation since 1983.

Submitted by Greg Mohr, 1989

Madden United Church

Madden United Church was built on the site donated by Mr. and Mrs. Nikolas King. The church was dedicated and opened for services on Sunday afternoon, February 1, 1942. This achievement was the fulfillment of a hope nurtured over the years by the congregation. Religious services had been held in this district since before the turn of the century, meeting in homes, in the Beaver Dam School, or in the Sampsonton Hall at various periods. Among the first monthly circuit-riders was the Rev. Dalgleish, and among the first worshippers were the Briggs, Ingham, Walsh, and Merton families. The Rev. Mr. Wood (Methodist) arrived in November 1902 to serve the Carstairs Mission, of which Beaver Dam was a rural appointment. Our Pastoral Charge was then served by

Presbyterian and Methodist clergy in alternating periods of two years each.

In 1916, we became a Union Church, co-ordinating the work of the Congregational, Presbyterian, and Methodist denominations. This congregation became part of the United Church of Canada at the time of Church Union, June 10, 1925.

Our present church home is somewhat larger than the original structure, with our present sanctuary, from the folding doors forward, having been added since then.

Madden, the name of one pioneer family, was applied to the community and Post Office, and subsequently to the church, with the coming of the railroad in 1929.

Submitted by Florence (Bigelow) Walker, 1989

St. Clement's Anglican Church - Balzac

Interdenominational church services commenced in this same little building when it was the newly built Dry Creek School. The first service was held on Sunday, January 29, 1905 at 3:00 p.m. It was a cooperative venture of Anglicans and Methodists chiefly, with all others welcome. Clem Perry was the layreader and had the valued assistance of Osia Rosenberger and William Northcott. It was not until 1928 that the original 1904 building was moved to Balzac to serve for Anglican services and as a parish hall, and a new school was established at Dry Creek. The building served for around a year as a church and social gathering hall until 1929, when the Balzac Community Hall was put into service. During the 1930's it was indeed a struggle to keep any institution in operation, the church being no exception; still, many devoted Anglicans attended the afternoon services.

Over the years creature comforts have been improved. Coal and wood stoves have been replaced by gas furnaces and the gas lamps by electricity; and now overhead fans have been installed for warm days. An electric organ, stained glass windows, comfortable pews, communion and altar appointments, and a reading desk have contributed to services over the years. The Rev. A.D. Currie, who resided in Crossfield, conducted services in Crossfield and Balzac from 1931 to 1944. Mrs. R.B. Marston of Airdrie faithfully played the organ during that time and for several more years. The organ was reputed to be the first one to arrive in Fort Calgary in 1882, one year prior to the railroad. This Bell Organ came by rail to Regina and by Red River cart to Calgary. It is now in the Glenbow Museum. A Sunday school room was added which had been an office building in Airdrie prior to its purchase and move to Balzac. Gratitude is extended to those devoted parishioners who've struggled to add every convenience to this historic building. We are indebted to so many who have passed on, and to those who presently give so freely of their time to keep the church a creditable house of worship for all who wish to attend. Services are currently held every Sunday at 9:30 a.m.

Submitted by the Perry Brothers, 1989

St. Francis of Assisi Anglican Church

The Anglican Church in Airdrie began as a mission parish of the Cathedral in Calgary. The first service was held on Easter Sunday 1979 at Edwards Elementary School. From there we became a mission parish of St. James, Calgary, and we moved to the Scout Hall for our services. Being a mission parish, we have had numerous priests and lay leaders to help us along with our faith. In the spring of 1982, Morse Goodman, then Bishop of Calgary, turned the sod at the site of our present church at 132 Alberta Street. St. Francis of Assisi was built by volunteer labour and our first service was held on October 2, 1982. Our full time priest, Jim Seagram, served from February 1984 to January 1988. Flo McDonald was our lay assistant until September 1989. Don Anderson was appointed as a part time priest beginning in the fall of 1988 and he is providing leadership until the present time.

St Francis Anglican Church, Airdrie, is one that is used to a lot of changes. We have learned much from all the people, past and present, and we are growing into a caring community.

Submitted by Jennifer Ingram, 1989

St. Francis Xavier ("St. Francis of Rome") Catholic Church

The first Catholic church services in the Crossfield area were held in the home of Mr. and Mrs. John Lennon. The first priest was Father Sultman, a big German man, well able to bear the hardships of the time. By 1907, it became evident that a private home could no longer accommodate the growing congregation. Accordingly, plans were made for the construction of a church to be built in town. Communications were made with the Bishop in Edmonton, as Calgary did not yet have anyone of that status.

The Crossfield Mission included some excellent carpenters, who gave freely of their time and substance. Construction was soon underway and the new church, "St. Francis of Rome", was dedicated by Bishop Legal on September 8, 1908. The church is located at 1138 Nanton Avenue in Crossfield.

Despite all the gratis assistance, the church carried a debt of $653.00 of the original mortgage of $1,000.00, This was paid off by the efforts of the Altar Society with their food booths at the Agricultural Fair.

A rectory eventually had been built at Carstairs, thus creating a parish with a resident priest.

Sunday services alternated between Crossfield and Carstairs. Church maintenance was provided by volunteer service. Families took turns with church cleaning, having a fire kindled, as well as keeping feed on hand for the priest's horse.

Since the priest was batching, he was grateful for an invitation to Sunday dinner, as well as donations of food to tide him over the week.

Names of some of the early parishioners appear on a legal document dated March 10, 1910. These include Peter McAnally, James Robertson, Bernard Madden, Peter Smyth, John Lennon, Eugene Mason, John Mason, and John Featherston. Descendants of some still live in the area.

One of the original oldtimers of the Carstairs Parish, later of Crossfield, Anna (Spalding) Mason, widow of Eugene Mason, died in her 101st year in September 1986.

After 55 years of services the church was in need of repairs. The only major improvement over the years had been the addition of the covered entry. Cost comparisons ruled in favour of building. Thanks to the efforts of the architect Mr. English and the building committee, headed by Father Clancy, "St. Francis Xavier Church" was constructed and was blessed by Bishop Carroll in 1963 and declared free of debt in autumn 1964.

The old building was sold and removed from the site directly east of the new church. It is still presently in use on an acreage three miles southwest of Crossfield.

Submitted by Catherine (Spalding) Harris, 1989

A Brief History of St. Paul's Catholic Church

We were a mission of Carstairs up until 1969, when six families, Champions, Harrises, Knittles, Martins, Schnells, and Sunderlands, got together to organize a parish. The United Church was our first home. Allowing us to hold mass in their church made for a good Christian relationship and many new friends.

Father F. McCarty O.M.I., was our first priest to celebrate mass in the United Church, but Father John Palardy was the first pastor of St. Paul's here in Airdrie and was followed by Father Eric Nelson, Father Edwin Kuefler, and then in 1979 by Father "Charlie" Brown.

A building/finance committee was formed and on September 5th, 1983, Father Pat Cramer, Vicar General of the Diocese of Calgary, blessed the ground and turned the soil for the construction of St. Paul's Church on Main Street.

A Parish Pastoral Council was formed. The following people exercised leadership in St. Paul's: Ernie Martin, Albert St. Pierre, Bernie Knittle, John Childrey, Paul Vogan, John Mulders, and Bill Kidby.

In 1981 the women were the first to get organized as a group; an organization not only to raise money but to help the spiritual, educational, and social growth of the women of the parish.

Through the efforts of Bernie Knittle in 1982, and with the help of Ernie Martin, the Knights of

Columbus were formed with Norm McNally as Grand Knight.

Sunday, March 18, 1984 was our first mass in our new church. Bishop Paul J. O'Byrne, with 13 priests, did the blessing and dedication of the church on April 27, 1984.

Our present priest is Father Ian McRae, formerly of Canmore. He now looks after a parish of 350 families here in 1989.

Submitted by Gloria Martin, 1989

The Crossfield Anglican Church of the Ascension

The Anglican Church of the Ascension was built in 1917. It would appear that services were first held in the Methodist church and in school houses.

There is very little on record re the parish at Crossfield. The following information was obtained from the archivist of the Diocese of Calgary.

The first recorded service was held June 18, 1911, under the Rev. Thorold-Eller. He used the text *I Corinthians 16:23*: "The grace of our Lord Jesus Christ be with you". Twelve adherents were in attendance and the collection amounted to 50 cents. The first baptisms recorded were the ten children of the Eagleson family on October 20, 1911.

In 1912 the services were linked with Airdrie, Buttes School, Crossfield, and Glen Leven.

The Crossfield congregation would grow, then fall off again, so it was a continual battle keep the little church open. For a short period during the forties only three faithful supporting families remained. Each served in many capacities, such as vestry man, warden, and lay reader. Tom Tredaway even had to be the organist when Vi Shephard was unavailable. Two young girls, Velma (Pogue) Van Maarion and Kathleen (Fitzpatrick) Shantz, also became quite adept at pumping music out of the old organ!

The Ladies of the Anglican Guild were very active down through the years and came to the rescue several times financially. In the early fifties, fourteen ladies regularly attended the meetings. Except for Jean Stevens, who resides at the Rocky View Lodge, most of these faithful members have moved away or are now deceased.

My mother, the late Emma Walker, had in her possession an excellent photograph of the Anglican Church and the old rectory. This snap has been recopied many times.

Clergy who served the parish in the earlier years were A. Thorold-Eller, 1911-13; George Hogbin, supply; J.P. Pringle, 1915-21; H. Clay, 1921-28; J.T. Adams-Cooper, 1928-30; and A.D. Currie, 1930-39. Several other clergymen, including Canon Morgan, the Rev. Mr. Musson, Jack Roe, and Harry Fairbridge, served Crossfield in more recent years along with short term supply people.

The Rev. D. Blackwell was the last rector, and services were discontinued after December 1967. The site was sold and the church was moved to the back of the lot and converted into a garage. A family presently lives in a new house that was built on the land where the church was formerly situated (1206 Hammond Avenue and Munson Street). The rectory is still in use and recently has been remodelled by the present owner, Victor Pearson.

Submitted by W.H. (Bill) Walker, 1989

The First Irricana Church of the Brethren

In the spring of 1910, a group of settlers that came into the area from the U.S.A. decided they would like to have a meeting place to hold church services in. In April of that year they planned a day; three families were to leave from the Weaver home and travel in a northwesterly direction while the Gumps and the Ebys would travel in a southeasterly direction, and wherever they met, they would put up a tent and have a church service. The site was just north of where the present church now stands, five miles west of Irricana and one mile south. After the service, plans were made to build a small church house. J.T. Miller donated five acres of land, which is now the present location. The building was 18' x 30' and the cost of the lumber was $125.00. Boards were placed over trestles for benches. With this crude arrangement and no roads, travelling done by horseback, grain wagons, and democrats, the church was organized. People were short of money, as the settlers were just getting started in farming. To help pay the expenses, they decided to charge a head tax of $2.50 per person, to be paid in two payments. They paid the janitor $7.00 for six months.

By the fall of 1917, one hundred and fourteen members were on the church roll. In August of 1918, they decided to build a larger church, which they finished and dedicated in 1919. Much of the work was done by church members. The cost was $8,405.00 and took fifteen years to pay all accounts. This church has been in service every Sunday for fifty-five years. At one time the church basement was used for pie socials and different programs, showers, and even wedding suppers. The U.C.W. did most of the interior decorating. In 1969, the Irricana Church of the Brethren united with the United Church of Canada. It is now known as the West Irricana United Church, serving three areas, Irricana, Kathryn, and Keoma.

A second Church of the Brethren was built in the Village of Irricana in 1940. Until 1930 both of these churches were serviced by local lay persons. It is my understanding there were only three Church of the Brethren churches in Canada, the origin having been in the U.S.A. There were two in Irricana and area, and one in Arrowood. After 1930 the American churches sent pastors from there to fill the pulpits in Canada, the congregation here to supply housing and wages. Many fine pastors came out and were well liked.

In 1962 the First Irricana Church and the Village Church found it necessary to meet as one group. Meetings are now being held at the West Church, now a United Church.

On April 19, 1985, the Irricana United Church was declared a Historical Site.

Submitted by Alice Hays, 1989

Young's Farm Vacation Bible School

Our Interdenominational School is operated under the Canadian Sunday School Mission. We held our first Vacation Bible School in 1963 after several years of planning and preparation. We developed from a smaller beginning to a registration of 281 in 1988. We are in an ideal situation, being about nine miles east of Highway Two, midway between Balzac and Airdrie with a circle of towns south, east, and north of us, beside all the farm and acreage people in this area. We provide for the spiritual and physical development of the children. Our prime objective is to bring the knowledge of Full Salvation through the Lord Jesus Christ to all we come in contact with, thus equipping them with strength for this life and acceptance with God in eternity. All children from those entering kindergarten to the end of Junior High are cordially welcomed to attend.

Submitted by Young's Farm (Ross or Alton Young), 1989

The Bell Organ

Little is known about just when the old Bell organ was manufactured. With its lifespan nearing 100 years, it has without question had numerous experiences, from its journey to the wild unconquered west to its solemn faithful duty in its work with the church. All that can be definitely established is written on its keyboard panel: W. Bell, Guelph, Canada.

Over the years old timers have handed down the story that the organ was one of the first in Calgary, with the belief that it arrived by ox-cart. However, there is no definite proof that it did arrive in such a manner, or in what year, or for whom. I quote from an account of the Diocese of Calgary: "The first service was held on the first Sunday in November 1883 in the old N.W.M. Police Barracks, the organ being brought in a wheel barrel from the home of Mr. S.W. Shaw." Archdeacon J.W. Tims apparently took the service. It may have been the Bell organ that was used in this service, as scholars generally agree that it came in the early 1880s.

Apparently it served in the Anglican Church until 1904; at this time the Cathedral Church of the Redeemer was constructed out of sandstone, the popular material used in the Sandstone City of the West in early years. In keeping with the handsome new building a new organ was installed and the old Bell organ was moved to the Parish Hall Sunday School rooms. In 1904 it was moved to the Nose Creek District to serve at Interdenominational Church Services. It remained in service until April 13, 1969, when it was taken to the Glenbow Museum in Calgary.

Submitted by C. Redvers Perry, 1989

NOSE CREEK VALLEY MUSEUM
AIRDRIE, ALBERTA
Sunday, November 19th, 1989
2:00 p.m.

EIGHTEENTH LOCAL
HISTORICAL RECOGNITION
IN TRIBUTE TO LOCAL AND RURAL CHURCH'S
1889 - 1989
In conjunction with
Interdenominational Church Service
at
Airdrie, Alberta

Sponsored by
NOSE CREEK HISTORICAL SOCIETY
In co-operation with Local Ministers and Assistants

The West Irricana United Church, previously Church Of The Brethren. Built in 1919. Joined
United Church of Canada in 1968. Located 14 miles east of Airdrie.

This is a historical document. Please value it on the basis of posterity.
It is compliments of the Nose Creek Historical Society.

Above: *This West Irricana United Church, previously Church of the Brethren, built in 1919, joined United Church of Canada in 1968.*

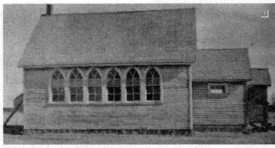

Airdrie's First church, built around 1903.

Above: *A fine example of practical use of resources. St. Clement's Anglican Church, foreground, used to be Dry Creek School in 1904. The church to the right was Beddington United—once located at Beddington Hall site, built in 1913—and relocated to Balzac in 1968. To the far right is United Church, which in its turn used to be the old Mountain View School. It was later moved to McPherson Coulee to replace the burned down McPherson School (circa 1940). It finally ended up in Balzac in 1944 to serve as the Balzac United Church.*

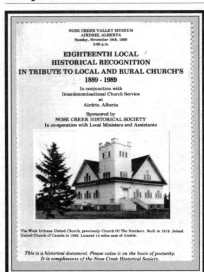

Above: *The old Crossfield United Church after the addition of the parlor in 1939.* **Right:** *The Crossfield United Church as we see it today, renovated in 1961.*

A typical pioneer Methodist Mission field. Horses were the common mode of travel.

This old Bell organ, one of the first in Calgary, arrived from Ontario by oxcart in the 1880's. (No one has been able to establish its year of manufacture). It served in the Anglican Church until 1904. It was then moved to the Nose Creek District to serve at Interdenominational Church Services. It remained in service until 1969 when it was taken to Glenbow Foundation, Calgary.

CHAPTER 24: TRIBUTE TO BLACKSMITHING

NINETEENTH LOCAL HISTORICAL RECOGNITION: 1902-1990

Fort Calgary was established in 1875 by the North-West Mounted Police; one must admit there would have to be a farrier or some type of a blacksmith to take care of shoeing horses and doing some iron work, so vital to carry on the many duties which just had to be attended to. Blacksmithing, one of the very earliest trades known to man, can be traced way back to the age when much softer metals than the iron we know of were moulded into tools to work the land or devices to do numerous tasks early man had to carry out. Brutal devices for use in times of war were also important to early civilizations. As time went on, various metals were blended to produce more durable material. To achieve these goals the early blacksmiths played the major role, and we acknowledge these people today, with gratitude for the part they endured in laying the basic foundations for developing the west.

The first blacksmiths in our area, according to the accounts received, were here as early as 1902 and were in operation well into the 1940s, when the local welders' shops became increasingly popular. Sharpening plow shares and shoeing saddle horses and work horses were the major occupations of the first blacksmiths in the west. Fitting wooden wheels with metal tires when the wooden wheels became aged was also a necessary work of their art. It was a hard, heavy, burdensome trade; it took plenty of heavy hitting at times, and a keen eye to know just where to swat and how hard. One would not have to enter the door of a blacksmith shop to find out whether or not it was in operation. The music of the heavy hammer and its "RAT-A-TAT-TAT" to the next skilful blow let everyone know for blocks around that business was in full swing. The odour of the special blacksmith coal was a special blend of its own, too; one can never forget what it was like to be one of the casual visitors or patrons of the village smithy. It is a pleasure today to pay our respects to those who have passed on from this special art of Blacksmithing, which contributed to the west's early foundations.

Submitted by C. Redvers Perry, 1990

Airdrie Blacksmiths

To gain good insight on the existence and workings of an old time blacksmith see Stephen Wilk's book *One Day's Journey*. Space rather limits us from quoting his excellent description. Of the early blacksmiths in Airdrie, it appears that W.D. Clark had a small shop on his farm located on the northeast quarter of Section 2-27-1-W5; it operated in the early years of the 1900's. A move to the new village of Airdrie showed promise, so he constructed a shop which would be located northwest of the present Airdrie Hotel. This building later became a service garage owned by E.C. Hegy.

Around the year 1908, Tom Flett and Son erected a blacksmith shop, about where the Department of Agriculture office is now located in what is known as the Provincial Building. This shop operated continuously with the Fletts hard on the hammer; brothers Lloyd and Thomas put in many long hours to serve the community.

"Scotty" Johnston also saw a good opportunity to serve the needs of the vigorous, far-flung community, meeting its requirements by moulding iron into whatever was desired. His shop was located just south and west of the current Airdrie United Church. For a brief period William "Scotty" McKay ran the Johnston Shop, but it served as a machinery shed for Mr. McCracken, the John Deere agent, for many years.

In 1930, Mac McHattie carried on blacksmithing once more in the same shop, but greener pastures in the hamlet of Balzac enticed McHattie to move south. There he served the district until 1946 when he dropped the hammer of smithing to start a fox farming enterprise.

To this day many of us recall the events and excitement that went on at the Airdrie shops. In fact, the Flett Brothers' shop and their two-storey home has a place of distinguished honour in Heritage Park, in south Calgary, where it is viewed by many tourists and Calgarians. A tribute in memory of the blacksmith trade across Western Canada is certainly long overdue.

Submitted by C. Redvers Perry, 1990

159

The Balzac Smithy

It was a much looked forward to adventure to annually ride my school pony to Balzac where the local blacksmith, Mr. McHattie, would prepare her for the coming winter roads. At that time little did I know that mine would be the privilege of sharing with you the exciting adventures of this stocky little man with the shy quiet manner and delightful Scottish brogue.

William "Mac" McHattie was born in 1880 in Near Forres, Scotland. At the age of twelve he began his blacksmith apprenticeship. During this five year course he spent the compulsory three months each year in the British Navy, thus having the opportunity to visit such points as France, the Mediterranean, and the South Seas.

In 1900, Mac arrived in New York where he worked a year in a blacksmith shop before going to Pittsburgh to be employed in the steelworks.

From then Mac combined his blacksmith trade with his love of travel and adventure. He visited Rio de Janeiro, then answered the call to pan for gold in the Yukon. Before returning to live in Rio de Janeiro for several years, he worked as a farrier for the great race horse, Dan Patch. Mac also talked about shoeing five hundred horses that were used in battles during the First World War, and how sad he felt that not a single animal returned.

During his lifetime he returned to his beloved Scotland five times. It was on one of these trips that he brought back his school days sweetheart, Miss Jessie Grigor. William and Jessie McHattie lived in Victoria for fifteen years. It was during this time that Mac operated blacksmith shops in both Vancouver and Victoria. Jessie's health deteriorated and required a drier climate. Mac sold his business and properties and moved to Eckville for twelve years, Airdrie for two and finally to Balzac. Many a plowshare was sharpened and tempered; many a school pony was fitted for shoes all by the expert hands of Mac McHattie during his years at Balzac.

In 1947, he joined E.P. Shuttleworth and remained there for the next twenty-seven years. During this time he became the much-loved "co-grandfather" to Sherrie, Dean, Chris, and Shannan Leinweber.

It was a very sad day when we all had to say a final good-bye in Mac's ninety-fourth year - August 14, 1974.

Submitted by Joy Leinweber, 1990

William George Turner, An Early Blacksmith

William G. Turner, an apprenticed blacksmith, came from Margate Village, Lutton, England to Calgary, then a frontier town, in 1905. He and his brother had their first blacksmith shop on 8th Avenue and 2nd Street SE, where the Queen's Hotel was and where the annex to the City Hall is at present.

In the early days he shod heavy horses for the local farmers, hay haulers, and milk haulers from the areas north and west of Calgary. Turner also sharpened plowshares and repaired wagon wheels, carriages, etc. He worked with wrought iron, building ornamental railings, fireplace screens, and the like.

Later on he specialized in working with show horses and jumping horses. After his retirement up to the late 1940's, many of his old customers in the show and jumping horse business, such as Eric Harvie, the Crosses, and Bill Herron, would pick him up to put the finishing touches on their prize horses.

William G. Turner passed away in July 1962 at the age of 85.

Submitted by Bobby and Sunni S. Turner, 1990

The Village Blacksmiths

In 1911 George S. Hope of the county of Cumberland in England, a descendant of many generations of blacksmiths, came to Cochrane and worked as a blacksmith at Morley, Alberta. Then he went shoeing horses at a coal mine five miles west of Cochrane.

After a time he worked in Cochrane for Christianson, the village blacksmith, where they were kept busy shoeing horses, welding farm machinery, and making branding irons. George S. Hope bought C.S. Christianson out in 1916. In 1919 he sold the blacksmith shop to George Bunney and in 1922 he bought it back; subsequently, in 1928, he sold it to Dave Murray.

Dave Murray, another Cochrane blacksmith, came to Calgary around 1908 from Dundee, Scotland. He first worked for Brewsters of Banff, who had one thousand horses at that time, and a day's work was shoeing twenty-five head of horses.

In 1928 Dave Murray purchased the Cochrane blacksmith shop from George S. Hope. Dave Murray was an excellent farrier, and he remained as Cochrane's smitty until 1955. He is also remembered for his colourful language in his blacksmith shop. He passed away in 1956, thus ending the era of blacksmithing in Cochrane.

Submitted by Bobby and Sunni S. Turner, 1990

Crossfield Smiths - Railway Street and Hammond Avenue

Dave Gallagher (1902-06) The first makeshift blacksmith shop in Crossfield was built in 1902 on Railway Street by Dave Gallagher, a C.P.R. section man.

Charles Webb (1906-07) Regular service was provided in 1906 when Charlie Webb took over. He emigrated from England to Ontario, where he took his apprenticeship, in the early 1890s. Employment in railway construction brought him eventually to Crossfield. The shop on Railway Street was very small, therefore he was able to purchase the site for a very reasonable price. The following year the Webb family vacated the shop for a homestead in the Cochrane district.

John Frew (1907-11) To fill the vacancy, Bob Arnott wrote to a village blacksmith friend in Scotland. John Frew arrived in Crossfield in 1908, and immediately interviewed Charlie Webb. A deal was made whereby Frew rented the blacksmith shop, and he went to work the next day. His first day's earnings amounted to $5.00, which was equivalent to the one pound a week he had been receiving in the old country. He was an excellent tradesman and his business boomed. The Frew family arrived that summer and was housed in a lean-to addition built alongside the shop. In 1911, John Frew sold his business, moved to Calgary, and started working for the city shoeing horses.

Alex Jessiman (1911-25) Alex Jessiman came from Scotland to Winnipeg where he learnt farriery. In 1911 he arrived in Crossfield, and bought the blacksmithing business from John Frew, who worked with him for a month to get him acquainted. Alex then proceeded to make his fortune! Instead he recalled just a lot of "damned hard work". In the fall he and his bride settled down in a house facing Osler Avenue and over the years they raised a family. The shop on Railway Street was small and inconvenient so Alex built his own place, kitty-corner across the back alley from their home. Jessiman's Blacksmith Shop was then located on the north side of Hammond Avenue, next to a machine agency building and a livery barn. They operated the business with a helper, Jack Fairburn.

On January 4, 1924, a fire broke out in the hotel in Crossfield and the main block of the village was completely wiped out. A second outbreak at 4:00 A.M. took the big barn, machine agency, and blacksmith shop across the street to the north. The blacksmith shop was replaced by Chris Asmussen as a financial speculation. In 1925, after rebuilding, Alex Jessiman's health was giving out, so he sold his business and went to the coast.

Charles Donald (1925-30) The business was now run in connection with the Massey Harris Agency. Charlie Donald's partner for a couple of years was a Mr. Clark. In the old 1925 directory, they are listed as having telephone #5. Otherwise, very little information is available about Mr. Clark. In 1929, Charlie obtained a new partner, James Sharp, who took over after they had been in business together for a year. Charlie Donald moved to Bottrell in 1930.

Jack (Jock) Fairburn continued as a hired helper until around 1929 when he moved to Madden and operated his own shop; Ed Corkill, who lived south of that hamlet, wanted to semi-retire.

James Sharp (1929-48) Mr. and Mrs. James Sharp and eight children moved to Crossfield in 1929. James Sharp sold his blacksmith shop in Bowden and entered into partnership with Charlie Donald, whose shop at this time still included the Massey Harris Agency. After Donald left in 1930, Walter Hurt, a welder, moved in with Sharp for one year, until each vacated the premises to go into business for themselves. In 1931, James Sharp built his own blacksmith shop which he continued to operate until his retirement in 1948. This shop, located on Smith Avenue, has been converted into a car garage by the present owners.

The Massey Harris Agency was transferred to Jim Williams at Crossfield's other blacksmith shop, located on Nanton Avenue.

Alfred Wittke (1934-43) After James Sharp moved from Hammond Avenue, the blacksmithing business was closed at this location for approximately four years, until Alfred Wittke took over. Chris Asmussen still owned the building. Alfred and Christine Wittke came to Crossfield in 1934. They rented a farm for 18 months before moving into town to rent and operate the blacksmith business on Hammond Avenue. Alfred Wittke renovated the back rooms of the shop into living quarters for his wife and five children; Ernest, Roy, Allen, Clara, and Annie. He ran a very prosperous business until he became ill with cancer and died on January 6, 1943. After his demise his widow moved to Medicine Hat where she lived for fifteen years before moving to Calgary.

Before 1940, Leonard Beddoes had purchased the property from Chris Asmussen. He eventually operated a business selling Case and Oliver machinery in the old blacksmith shop, which has since been demolished.

Submitted by Florence (Bigelow) Walker, 1990

Rettschlag's Blacksmith Shop

Crossfield's second blacksmith shop was located on Nanton Avenue on the property adjacent to the Bill Walker home.

Gus Rettschlag came to Crossfield in 1917 and purchased the blacksmith shop from Mr. Strong. While they were living in Crossfield, six children were born to the Rettschlags, and they lived in rooms at the back of the shop.

When a new bank was built in Crossfield on Main Street, Rettschlag got a chance to buy the old one. He had the building moved over with horses and placed just west of the blacksmith shop. It was a happy day when the family moved from the old cramped quarters into their new home! By this time the elder ones in the family were able to help their father, so Mrs. Rettschlag didn't have to assist so often with the blacksmithing. She was able to tend to the mansion in proper style.

In 1928 the blacksmith shop was sold and the next year the family moved to Calgary where Gus specialized in ornamental iron works. Mr. and Mrs. Rettschlag eventually had 13 children. Two sons who took up the blacksmithing trade, Albert and Ernest, built and donated the Crossfield Cemetery gates in 1950.

Jim Williams purchased the house and blacksmith shop from Rettschlag in 1928, and he became the first electric welder in Crossfield. He later took over the Massey Harris Agency from Charlie Donald, who was selling out his share in Crossfield's first blacksmith shop on Hammond Avenue.

Later, the Larsons bought the property from Jim Williams, and Mr. Larson also was a blacksmith and welder. Then in 1943, the place was sold to Bill Walker. Shortly after 1953, Bill built a larger shop which was far more suited to his needs for his telephone business. The blacksmith shop was torn down so that the east portion of the property could be sold. The lumber was stockpiled.

The blacksmith shop replica in the Nose Creek Valley Museum in Airdrie has been built out of the actual lumber from Rettschlag's Blacksmith Shop.

Submitted by Florence (Bigelow) Walker, 1990

The Yankee Valley Blacksmith

Alex D. Black learned the blacksmith trade as a young man in the late 1890's in a town called Huntingdon, near Montreal. After working in a couple of towns in the east, he came west in 1904, buying land east of Airdrie. He spent a couple of summers as the blacksmith on the Irrigation Ditch, where he had his first experience shoeing mules. During those early years he also worked with the Fletts in Airdrie.

After 1907, when settlers arrived in Yankee Valley, Alex Black was the blacksmith for the neighbourhood. He spent many hours shoeing neighbours' horses and sharpening plowshares. It was often a nerve wracking experience, as some of these horses were anything but well broken.

As his farming increased he stopped doing custom work, but continued doing his own blacksmith work.

Submitted by Alexa Church, 1990

A Blacksmith - From 1892-1947

My forge and hammer lie reclined,
My bellows too have lost their wind.
My fire extinct;
My forge decayed and in the dust
My vise is laid.
My coal is spent
My iron - gone.
My anvil broke;
My work is done.
So, farewell to a grant old art,
I need a rest.
—By William McHattie; Handed in by Joy Leinweber, 1990

Editors' Addition:

A Contract for Apprenticing for Blacksmith

In 1849, James Smith of River de Leile, Lower Canada, signed an indenture to become an apprentice to a blacksmith in Upper Canada named George Munro. James was 18 years old, so his guardian also signed the three-year contract. The terms of the indenture were strict, and written in archaic style:

> *...the said apprentice his Master faithfully shall serve, his secrets keep, his lawful*
> *commands everywhere gladly do; he shall do no damage to his master, nor see [it]*
> *done to others, but to his power shall let or forthwith give warning to his said master*
> *of the same; he shall not waste the goods of his said master, nor lend them unlaw-*
> *fully to give warning to his said master of the same; he shall not waste the goods of*
> *his said master, nor unlawfully to any; he shall not commit fornication nor contract*
> *matrimony within the said term; he shall not play cards, dice tables or any unlawful*
> *games, whereby he shall neither buy nor sell; he shall not haunt taverns or play*
> *houses, nor absent himself from his said master's service day or night unlawfully*
> *but in all things as a faithful apprentice he shall behave himself toward his said*
> *master and all his during the said term...*

The blacksmith also agreed to terms; he was to pay James five shillings, and:

> *...By acknowledging his said apprentice in the art of Blacksmith which he useth*
> *by the best means that he can, shall teach and instruct finding and providing unto*
> *the said apprentice sufficient meat, drink, lodging and all other necessities during*
> *the said term. And moreover the sum of five pounds per year during the term of*
> *years as apprentice for the true performance of all and every Covenant and Agree-*
> *ment...*

At the end of the three years, George Munro wrote:

> *...I hereby certify that the written James Smith has signed his indenture in full. I*
> *can plead that he has at all times conducted himself in an honest, sober attentive*
> *manner and is a good worker and a lad of good principles and scruples. I have no*
> *scruple in recommending him as [a] fit and proper member of any Christian society*
> *wherever his lot may be cast; I hereby do discharge him.*

It is possible that James Smith learned an extra skill during his apprenticeship; George Munro was also the local dentist!

Submitted by Dorothy Tilleman, 1996

NOSE CREEK VALLEY MUSEUM
AIRDRIE, ALBERTA
Sunday, August 19th, 1990
1:30 p.m.

NINETEENTH LOCAL
HISTORICAL RECOGNITION
IN TRIBUTE TO BLACKSMITHING
1902 - 1990

In conjunction with
Interdenominational Church Service
at
Airdrie, Alberta

Sponsored by
NOSE CREEK HISTORICAL SOCIETY

Mac McHatties Blacksmith Shop 1940 pieces located in Balzac where Suntropical Green Houses are today. Note the wheels in front to be refurbished with steel tires. Note the small hand car shed on C.P.R. right of way, and Balzac Hall in the distance.

This is a historical document. Please value it on the basis of posterity. It is compliments of the Nose Creek Historical Society.

Above: A wide variety of horse shoes **Left:** The blacksmith was pivotal in the drive to tame the West. The pamphlet on the left acknowledged that fact. **Below:** The Turner Blacksmith shop, Calgary, c.1900. **Bottom:** August 1990. Bobby Turner and son demonstrate the dying skill of horse-shoe making.

Above. Calgary International Stampede Blacksmith competition: here the world's best create horseshoes and vie for the $10,000 purse.

this is the world famous
OLD BLACKSMITH'S SHOP
MARRIAGE ROOM
GRETNA GREEN

(WORLD FAMOUS FOR RUNAWAY MARRIAGES)

The Orginal History of Gretna from Pennent's 'Tour of Scotland', 1780

At a little diftance from the bridge, ftop at the little village of *Gratna,* the refort of all amorous couples, whofe union the prudence of parents or guardians prohibits: here the young pair may be inftantly united by a fifherman, a joiner, or a blackfmith, who marry from two guineas a job, to a dram of whifky: but the price is generally adjufted by the information of the poftilions from *Carlisle,* who are in pay of one or other of the above worthies; but even the drivers, in cafe of neceffity, have been known to undertake the facerdotal office. If the purfuit of friends proves very hot; and there is not time for the ceremony, the frightened pair are advifed to flip into bed; are fhewn to the purfuers, who imagining that they are irrecoverably united, retire, and leave them to confummate their unfinifhed loves.

ANVIL WEDDING PERFORMED

CHAPTER 25: TRIBUTE TO LAYING OF CALGARY-EDMONTON RAILROAD
TWENTIETH LOCAL HISTORICAL RECOGNITION: 1891-1991

It is impossible to pin-point when humans first roamed the Canadian western prairies. From more recent records, if we can term 1792 as recent, Peter Fidler passed over this area, travelling from the Rocky Mountain House trading post. David Thompson can be recognized as the next white man who wandered through here on one of his many explorations in western Canada, on November 21, 1800. It was not until Fort Calgary and Fort Edmonton were active trading posts that communication between the two points came into existence. The first modes of travel were by heavy ox-carts, bearing loads of the vital necessities of life and returning with furs from the trapping industry. Stage coaches and two wheel carts for lighter loads, buggies and the reliable saddle horse for faster transportation were seen on the deep rutted trails and in the river fords and bog lands that were all so prevalent in early years. The stories of thrills, expectations, and excitement are endless, and no doubt there were tragedies too.

It was in 1890 that the first railroad project was started north of the Bow, which appears to be long ago to most of us. When one looks back into history one sees that steam power was first patented by James Watt of Scotland in 1769. We all recall the story of James Watt and the tea kettle! In 1804 Richard Trevithick of England built the first steam locomotive. In 1825 the first regular steam-operated railroad, owned by Stockton and Darlington, operated in England. From then on railroad travel seemed to rapidly progress around the world, and what a marvellous contribution to the betterment of mankind.

The "C and E" started in Calgary on July 21, 1890, and a spectacular project it turned out to be, with the completion date on July 27, 1891. The last spike for the Calgary and Edmonton railway was driven in Strathcona, on the south side of the North Saskatchewan River at Edmonton.

Stage coach travel came to an abrupt stop as soon as the railroad came into action; after all, who would ride a stage coach for five days when a train could take you the same distance in a matter of a few hours! So here we are on this date of October 20, 1991, with railway passenger service non-existent for the past ten years or so and air travel a mere 35 minutes, Calgary to Edmonton. How times have changed. To many of us some fond memories exist, and yes, memories of some tragedies too. On the brighter side, there was the welcome telephone call: "Coal is in", which meant the weigh freight had dropped off a carload of coal for local farmers to replenish their stove and furnace fuel. There was the delivery of farm machinery from steam tractor engines to mowing machines, and the movement of our grain and hay for export or city consumption. Early oil tankers were also on the weigh freights. Nothing could beat their firm commitment to be on schedule right to the minute; only a severe blizzard would cause a delay. There was Mail Service, Mail Order Service, Parcel Pick Up, and Parcel Movement Service; not to forget the opportunity to catch the train to Calgary or wherever for at least 90 years. This all adds up to a deal of appreciation for the "C and E" to 1903, and then the C.P.R. Yes, there were tragedies too. I well recall December 11, 1926; a two day raging blizzard; two freight trains in collision at Airdrie; there were human casualties; but most memorable to us was a sunny cold day after the blizzard, at Balzac on our way to the Buttes School. We heard heavy rifle fire some two miles or so south of Airdrie. It was the police shooting the poor bawling cattle who were painfully injured during the terrible collision. There were also human tragedies; in 1896, a young 16 year old boy was killed while trying to catch a ride just south of Balzac railroad crossing, as we now know it; Walsh was his name. Also recalled is Councillor P.C. Lewis phoning Dad to relate that Mr. Giffen, a well known Jewish cattle buyer, had been hit by a train south of Beddington Siding and killed. So here we are in 1991, and we quite frequently hear of tragic train accidents in spite of stringent regulations and warning lights.

A wealth of memories both humourous and tragic many of us hold; not forgetting the Dirty Thirties when the unemployed or loosely termed "Hobos" literally swarmed to catch a ride on the C.P.R., while others walked the rails stopping to beg for a bite to eat. Many of those same railroad roamers joined the Canadian forces to serve with distinction in World War II. "Memories - memories - dreams of long ago!"

Today we salute the Canadian Pacific Railway's 100 years of service.

Submitted by C. Redvers Perry, 1991

First Plaque

This plaque commemorates the inauguration of rail service between Calgary and Strathcona (South Edmonton). The first Calgary & Edmonton Railway Company train made the trip, with 22 stops to serve settlers along the route, on Sunday August 23, 1891. In 1898 the line was incorporated into the Canadian Pacific Railway System and, with construction of the High Level Bridge in 1913, downtown Edmonton and Calgary were linked by rail.

Second Plaque

Calgary & Edmonton Railway

The Calgary & Edmonton Railway received its charter in 1890 to build a railway from the CPR mainline at Calgary to a point "at or near" Edmonton. The first sod was turned on July 21 and the track reached Red Deer by the end of the year. On July 27, 1891, the last spike was driven at Strathcona. The rapid construction was due to the valiant efforts of surveyors, graders, and track layers, some receiving only $1.50 a day in wages. The Canadian Pacific Railway signed a lease to operate the new line and in 1903 it finally bought a controlling interest in the C&E organization.

Submitted by Jack Peach, 1991

Reliving history: The romance and sense of adventure that goes with steam travel is captured in the Stettler -Big Valley privately owned run.

NOSE CREEK VALLEY MUSEUM
AIRDRIE, ALBERTA.
Sunday, October 20th, 1991
1:00 p.m.

**TWENTIETH LOCAL
HISTORICAL RECOGNITION IN TRIBUTE
TO LAYING OF CALGARY - EDMONTON RAILROAD
1891 - 1991**

In conjuction with
Interdenominational Church Service
at Airdrie, Alberta

Sponsored by
NOSE CREEK HISTORICAL SOCIETY

"THIS PLAQUE COMMEMORATES THE INAUGURATION OF RAIL SERVICE BETWEEN CALGARY AND STRATHCONA (SOUTH EDMONTON). THE FIRST CALGARY & EDMONTON RAILWAY COMPANY TRAIN MADE THE TRIP, WITH 22 STOPS TO SERVE SETTLERS ALONG THE ROUTE, ON SUNDAY AUGUST 23, 1891. IN 1898 THE LINE WAS INCORPORATED INTO THE CANADIAN PACIFIC RAILWAY SYSTEM AND, WITH CONSTRUCTION OF THE HIGH LEVEL BRIDGE IN 1913, DOWNTOWN EDMONTON AND CALGARY WERE LINKED BY RAIL."

A salute to Canadian Pacific Railroads is the subject of the above pamphlet. It took only a few hours to cover the distance between Edmonton and Calgary. A stagecoach took five days.

Rail service between Calgary and Edmonton commenced in 1890 (right) with a sod turning ceremony. Within a year, the system was up and running.

Calgary & Edmonton Railway

The Calgary & Edmonton Railway Company received its charter in 1890 to build a railway from the CPR main line at Calgary to a point "at or near" Edmonton. The first sod was turned on July 21 and the track reached Red Deer by the end of the year. On July 27, 1891, the last spike was driven at Strathcona. The rapid construction was due to the valiant efforts of surveyors, graders, and track layers, some receiving only $1.50 a day in wages. The Canadian Pacific Railway signed a lease to operate the new line and in 1903 it finally bought a controlling interest in the C&E organization.

The venerable steam engine became officially obsolescent in 1955. The engines to the left and below are making their final run through Airdrie. and (below left) the Airdrie railway station in 1904.

CHAPTER 26: TRIBUTE TO LOCAL COMMUNITY HALLS
TWENTY-FIRST LOCAL HISTORICAL RECOGNITION

As far back as biblical times, there have always been places of assembly, where people have gathered to present their views or come together to celebrate a special occasion. The Nose Creek communities are no exception. We hear from old timers' stories that there were Sunday worship services at various homes; the neighbours came by horse and buggy over the old prairie trails, now faded and gone. One of the first local organizations was the Nose Creek Literary Society. This was a club of sorts that concentrated on amusements and competitions. Their activities included singing, recitations, debates, political discussions, and caring for the wellbeing of the members. They also showed concern for anyone who had problems and needed assistance. Over the years, the need for more organizations of one sort or another increased as the population expanded and more concerns gained prominence. The ordinary homes that had been meeting places became inadequate.

From 1904 onward, schools were built and were certainly used to the fullest extent. School was held during the week and a dance on the weekend, with a local church group using the building on occasion for Sunday worship. Problems of inadequate capacity in the schools soon were recognized, with the answer being community halls. In the Roaring Twenties many halls were constructed on the prairies. A "Go-Go" time it was. Money was plentiful. It was necessary to accommodate to the new age seen on the horizon. Some school houses were renovated and enlarged as halls, while in most cases a completely new community hall was started by volunteers with no end of enthusiasm. By today's standards the material and labour charge was dirt cheap, and volunteer labour was easy to secure and enthusiastically given. But the sad part was the 1929 economic crash, which left many community halls with a debt that in many instances took ten years to pay off before the community was able to celebrate the "burning of the mortgage".

However, today we see some grand community halls all over the prairies; every modern convenience, central heating, and accompanying sports grounds. Long gone are the coal stove or furnace, Delco light plants and outside rest room facilities, not forgetting the chilly basements for midnight snacks.

In our memories we recall the good times; three-act plays, Christmas concerts, dances with lively five-piece orchestras and the musicians all in appropriate dress uniforms. There were jam-packed political meetings, fall fairs, church bazaars, children's summer schools, church services, and on the sad side, local peoples' funeral services. Out on the hall grounds some lively baseball games took place, and the local hockey rink had its action too, in spite of the accumulated snow that had to be shovelled off. Oh yes, there were the "no-no's" too. While the evening entertainments were in full swing, some goings on were in progress behind the scenes. Spirits were not served, unlike today when licences allow drinks to be sold; any imbibing of spirits then had to be done off the premises, with the container stashed up the road in the badger bush or a certain gateway where hopefully no one would catch on. The authorities kept close watch, which led to some exciting times which many recall, and some which are seldom spoken of.

So today we pay tribute to the local community halls in Historic Nose Creek; "Memories, Memories" of tales and songs of Long Long Ago never to be forgotten.

Submitted by C. Redvers Perry, 1992

Golden Rod Hall
On January 6, 1927, a meeting was held at Golden Rod School to make plans to build a community hall. A hall board was appointed with Mr. Hoback as president, Bert Clayton as secretary, and a finance committee composed of Angus Robertson, Delbert Watters, and Milo Martinusen. The name was to be "Mountain View Hall".

The land for the hall was purchased from Mr. Kai Olsen for $30 on part of the southwest quarter of Section 17-27-2-W5. The bank account was augmented by holding dances in the Burr Barn, which became Colpitt Dairy Farm. It still stands three miles south on Symons Valley Road. Charles Kelly,

who also built the Burr Barn, accepted the hall contract for $3,600 with $100 more for extras. In 1941, the hall completed payment in full for the note, which was held by Fred Northcott. The board purchased a piano for $450, on terms of $50 cash and $50 every six months with interest at 8%.

In 1938, the Mountain View Ladies Club installed an electric plant. They continued to contribute by holding dances and making quilts.

In 1959, the name "Mountain View Hall" had to be changed to "Golden Rod Hall" due to the same name having been used in another district further north.

Many wonderful changes have been made since then; from gas lights to a power plant and lastly to Calgary Power; from furnaces of coal and wood to natural gas; and from outdoor "biffies" to flush toilets. At present this fully modern hall is proud to accommodate weddings, dances, and many meetings, including 4H activities.

It is an excellent example of cooperation and of a hard-working group of volunteers. Proud they may very well be!

Submitted by Arlene Olsen, 1992

Crossfield Community Hall

The Crossfield Community Hall stood secure and proud on Railway Street for 43 years and it served the district well. The building was originally the East Crossfield Community Hall and was moved to town around the middle of June, 1949. Therefore, the history of the hall's beginning starts six miles east of Crossfield on the Blind Line.

Construction of the East Crossfield Community Hall, which was promoted by the Junior U.F.A., commenced in 1925. The site chosen was the northeast corner of the northwest quarter of Section 28-28-28-W4. Generous donations were made not only by the people in the district, but by merchants in the village of Crossfield. Later, a bank loan of $3500 was needed for completion.

The structure measured 60' x 30' with a 12' x 8' entrance. The basement walls extended six feet into the ground and three feet above, allowing for the installation of several windows to light the lower floor. At first the basement floor was left unfinished except for the kitchen area and the ladies' powder room. On each side of the front entrance there were stairs leading to the basement. Also, at the rear of the hall were two separate stairways, one going downstairs and the other directly to the 24' x 12' stage. The main dance hall had an open-beam ceiling, built-in benches around the walls, and a fir dance floor. Lighting was supplied by a 32V Delco plant, and heating was provided by a very large coal-burning furnace. Cedar shingles were used on the roof and the exterior was finished with a cedar-lap siding, painted a buff colour. The plumbing consisted of two "out-houses" placed a discreet distance apart!

The cement for the basement floor was not poured until 1927 and at the same time cement gate posts were installed. One post still stands at the original site and the date 1927 is clearly visible. This date has caused some confusion among historians as it did not coincide with the date when the hall was built.

Ma Trainor's Orchestra supplied music for the opening of the East Crossfield Community Hall on February 16, 1926. The price of admission was $1.25 per couple, including supper.

The first executive consisted of 12 members, each taking turns to look after functions during a one-month period. For many years, the cost of admission was 50 cents for men with the ladies providing the lunch. The big events for many years were the Calico Ball held every March 17th, and dances held on July 1st, Armistice Day, and at Christmas. Music was provided mostly by local family orchestras such as Guy Gazely, Mac Ferguson, and Ken Borbridge.

About 1946, many in the district felt the hall could serve a better purpose if it was moved to town. Walter Hurt, Mayor of Crossfield, was instrumental in undertaking this project. He signed documents dated from February 17, 1947 to August 30, 1952 in regards to the actual moving of the hall to Crossfield (1949) and the later building of the extension (1952). The building was moved by Frizzell's of Red Deer at a fee of $1000.

The hall was placed on a full-size basement, and a large 20-foot front entrance with washrooms was built on at this time. A stairway led to the Scout Hall above this front entrance. Two gas furnaces and a modern electrical system were installed. When the new hardwood dance floor was laid, it was the talk of the whole area for miles around. The extension on the west side and an enlarged stage were not completed until 1952. An 80' x 30' lounge with carpet and furniture was added in 1975 on the north side, and the side windows were sealed as the building was stuccoed. The complete cost of this addition, including the stucco, was $25,500. More recently green asphalt shingles replaced the original cedar ones. The basement, complete with a modern kitchen, storerooms, tables and chairs, provided accommodation for banquets, bridal showers and meetings for many years.

A new Community Centre was built in Crossfield in 1991. Dar White's Fabulous Rock'n Roll Band played for the last dance in the Old Crossfield Community Hall on April 6, 1991. Stanley Walker, President of the Crossfield Bandits Hockey Club, reported that the price of the six-piece band was $1000, and tickets sold for $10 each. This cost included a late night buffet, but liquor drinks were $2 extra.

Crossfield's mayor, Ed Murray, "Locked the Doors" of the Old Crossfield Community Hall on May 1, 1991. The first dance in the New Crossfield & District Community Centre was held on May 4th, with the Grand Opening taking place a month later, on June 8, 1991.

There was much controversy over the future of the Old Hall. The final vote was close but the building got a last minute reprieve from the wrecker's ball and it was hoped it would be transformed into a heritage-type museum. The Crossfield & District Historical Society was formed in May 1992. But the dream never materialized. The struggle was lost, and the sturdy old building was demolished on July 6, 1992.

Submitted by Florence (Bigelow) Walker, 1992

Balzac Community Hall

The need for a community hall in the Balzac district became evident in 1928. Because the weather was mild, construction began with the digging of the basement that December. An intensive local campaign raised funds among farmers and businessmen. Volunteers performed most of the labour, with one main qualified carpenter, Nels Keddy, supervising.

The building was completed in June 1929 and a grand opening dance was held on July 5; the Premier, the Hon. J.E. Brownlee, officiated at the ribbon cutting ceremony. The original hall board consisted of George E. Church, A.E. Robinson, O.R. Ingraham, Ed Rosenberger, H.J. Jobson, E. Sireni, W.J. Davy, and J. Weir.

The hall has served the community well over the years, and has provided a meeting place for a great variety of activities, including everything from dances and box socials to political meetings and grand community turkey suppers. It even provided a location for the United Church to hold worship services from 1929 to 1945. It served also as a medical clinic in 1932 where tonsils and adenoids were removed en masse.

In 1977, major renovations and modernization took place when a large seating area, bathrooms, a modern kitchen, and a new entrance were added. Once again the labour was voluntary, under the excellent direction of master carpenter Doug Ekman. The hall board was very active and enthusiastic under the leadership of President Earl Northcott.

During the next few years, modern commercial appliances were installed in the kitchen with funds raised by the continuous efforts of the hall board, which catered for hundreds of functions.

In 1979, the 50th Anniversary of the hall was celebrated in a "Welcome back to Balzac" two-day extravaganza, which saw about 1500 people come and enjoy everything from welcoming teas and pancake breakfasts to bed races, barbecues, and a real old-time dance with Bill Lewis' Orchestra and with Don Burwash calling the square dances. There was a church service jointly attended by the Anglican and United Churches and tree plantings to honour pioneer families. A cairn was unveiled honouring Gus Gouin, 1879 mail carrier. The event culminated with more afternoon tea and visiting.

Today the Balzac Hall is still a place of action and is used extensively. More renovations have taken place and the basement of the old structure is completely modernized, providing a comfortable space for community meetings of all sorts.

The grounds also boast a well-used tennis court and an open air skating rink and club house, all of which are enjoyed by the youth of the community.

From 1929 to 1992 and still going strong! A proud and useful heritage, it is a credit to all the volunteers who have worked so tirelessly for their community.

Submitted by Ronnie Northcott, 1992

Beddington Halls (1922-1990)

The original Beddington Hall in 1922 was moved with teams of horses to the present site from the old Vestrum farm which is now part of Coventry Hills. It had first served as a store, then was bought by the Beddington U.F.A. and became a hall in which meetings, dances, and concerts were held. At

the new site it continued to be used by the community. Old timers talked about the floor that moved with the dancers and the odd sliver that penetrated a lady's foot through her satin slipper. However, all agreed that many good times were enjoyed there. The hall's final home was at Harry Pole's farm where it was used as a barn.

In 1928, the U.F.A. and U.F.W.A. decided a new building was needed that would be more spacious and comfortable. The U.F.A. canvassed the district and raised a total of $4,000. Nelson Kaiser was employed as head carpenter, and the men of the community pitched in as helpers, soon erecting a fine building with a balcony. This feature later proved to be more a liability than an asset, as you can guess where the kids wanted to congregate. The grand opening of the Beddington Community Hall was held in 1929.

In 1932 disaster struck; in the month of August, the hall burned to the ground after being hit by lightning. Only the chimney and foundation were left.

In 1933, after the insurance money had been turned over to the hall board, another hall was planned and built with many improvements. Once again the Beddington people rallied to the cause, donating $50 and "time" to help Nelson and Elmer Kaiser erect the new hall. This hall was larger, with a beautiful hardwood floor that the Kaisers and their helpers were very proud of, and many people have commented on its beauty.

Over the years many events and entertainments were held; I will list as many as possible: meetings of organizations, political meetings, July 1st Community Picnic, dances, box socials, variety concerts, three-act plays by local talent, fowl suppers, Christmas concerts, wedding banquets and parties, showers and even one wedding ceremony, farewell parties for the men and women who left to serve their country and a welcome home party for those who returned, the Country Fair and Auction to raise money for the Red Cross, the 50th Anniversary of Alberta celebration at which many residents received scrolls, a presentation of two community books-*The Nose Creek Story* and *My Neighbours and Yours*, the Beddington Church 50th Anniversary supper and concert, Farmers' Day barbecues and dances, the Old Timers' Reunion for many summers, and finally, the activities of the Nose Creek Community Club.

Throughout the years faithful hall boards worked hard to keep the hall open with no charge to the users until later, when rent was charged to cover the cost of power and heat. Many people who served on the hall board could be named, but rather than miss someone, we will just remember their dedication to the community as a whole.

The later years saw changing times due to the city's growth, the creation of small holdings, and the movement of many community people leaving the original farms. Thus in 1989 a decision was made to sell the hall, and it now belongs to the Professional Rodeo Cowboys Association. They have done extensive renovations, adding indoor plumbing and many improvements.

Today the money from the sale of the hall is invested and each year the interest is distributed to local groups, organizations, and individuals who qualify and need assistance. It is in reality a memorial fund to the people of the Beddington district and is being used for the good of a larger community.

June 20, 1992 will see the wind-up reunion in the form of a barbecue and dance. This will be the end of an era when the Community Hall, Church, and School stood on three acres of land donated to the community by Jack Barker. These were an important part of the lives of the people present and those that have gone before.

Submitted by Doris Evans, 1992

Casa Loma School and Community Centre

Casa Loma School was built in 1927 on two acres donated by F.R. Cathro. The name "Casa Loma" means "Castle on the Hill". It was used as a school for 20 years and was closed in 1947. During that period the school was the centre of community activities, including social and fund-raising functions. This was particularly true during the Second World War, when funds were required by numerous associations for the support of the war effort.

At the closing of the school, the site and buildings were bought by the Casa Loma Community Association. It was maintained and used as a community centre until 1987. Many functions were held at Casa Loma including annual Christmas concerts, novelty dances, plays, socials, wedding dances and anniversaries; and Brownies, Girl Guides, and Boy Scouts had free access for various functions for many years. It was also once used as a dormitory for a visiting group from the United States.

Maintenance and care were provided by the Casa Loma Community Association. These included yard work, regular cleaning, floor waxing, and on one occasion hand sanding of the hardwood floor which had been laid after the purchase of the property.

Use of the facility declined during the latter part of the 1980s and when the hall's expenses and care were not justified by its use anymore, the property was sold to W. Sturm for use as a private residence.

The site is still quite outstanding, surrounded by trees and hedges planted during the period when the children of Symons Valley took their early schooling there.

Casa Loma Community Association is still very active, operating without the use of the "School". Interest on the sale price of the property is used exclusively for the support of various charities. Annual social functions are held at the homes of various members and in neighbouring facilities.

Submitted by Bill Miller, 1992

Airdrie Hall

During the years 1903 and 1904 the late Luther Hawkey constructed a building on what is now First Avenue North, just east of Main Street. It was a two-storey building with a number of stores on the lower floor, while the second storey contained suites of rooms in which people lived. Also on that floor was a large room in which meetings, church services, and dances, etc., were held. It was known as the I.O.O.F. Hall (Independent Order of Odd Fellows), and was the only community hall in Airdrie at that time.

This hall was used until 1948, when a new hall was built, located on the west side of Main Street where the Airdrie Centre Building now stands. It was a steel Quonset-type building, in which the main floor was a large hall and was used for various meetings, dances and social events. It had a full-sized finished basement in which many suppers and meetings were held, and a smaller room which had been built over the entrance. Much of the work required to build the hall and do the finishing was done by people who volunteered their time and energy to the project.

This building served the community until 1977, when a new complex named the Town and Country Centre was completed. The new building was made up of a large hall and several smaller rooms, as well as a Curling Rink, the Public Library, a kitchen, and the Over-50 Club Room. The Town and Country Centre is located at 275 Jensen Drive NE, Airdrie, Alberta.

Submitted by Lorne Fowler, 1992

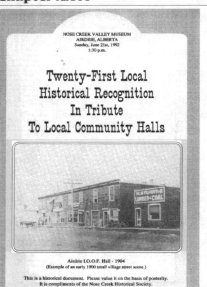

NOSE CREEK VALLEY MUSEUM
AIRDRIE, ALBERTA
Sunday, June 21st, 1992
1:30 p.m.

Twenty-First Local Historical Recognition In Tribute To Local Community Halls

Airdrie I.O.O.F. Hall - 1904
(Example of an early 1900 small village street scene.)

This is a historical document. Please value it on the basis of posterity.
It is compliments of the Nose Creek Historical Society.

ORDER OF SERVICE
Sunday, June 21st, 1992
Nose Creek Valley Museum, Airdrie, Alberta
Conducted by Rev. Dr. Stephen Wilk
Organist Lorne Fowler

PROCCESSIONAL
Words of Welcome - Mrs. Alice Hays, Pres. N.C.H.S.

"O CANADA"
INVOCATION PRAYER
Hymn #146 "The Churches One Foundation"

SCRIPTURE READING - Howard Pole
Hymn #391 "Amazing Grace"

PASTORAL PRAYER
LORD'S PRAYER

ADDRESS
Rev. Dr. Stephen Wilk
"The Vital part Community Halls Played in Rural Alberta"
Hymn #129 "Unto the Hills"

OFFERING
Ray Howden, Floyd Reynolds
Duet - Liz Bilben, Donna Audenaert

THANKS AND APPRECIATION
Pres. Alice Hays

COMMENTS BY AUDIENCE
Presentation of Historical Stock Show Document
to the Nose Creek Valley Museum - From Perry Family

GOD SAVE THE QUEEN

In paying tribute to local community halls, history acknowledges the contribution made by various segments of communities towards building this great nation. Despite the overwhelming odds, people still found time to thank and praise God for their good fortune.

Above: *Nose Creek Historical Society float honoring community halls at the Airdrie parade, 1992.* **(Below)** *Presidents over the years: (standing l-r) Joe Jaffery, Lois Habberfield, Bob Bilben, Doug Habberfield, Fred Bushfield, Harry Pole, Lloyd Farr, Don Evans, Cyril Woolliams. (Seated) Donald Burwash, Walter Bushfield, Buster Pieschel, Arnold Jones and Stanley Jones.*

CHAPTER 27: TRIBUTE TO PIONEER WOMEN
TWENTY-SECOND LOCAL HISTORICAL RECOGNITION

Prairie Women as Partners

Life on the prairies was hard in the early days, with just a few people inhabiting a huge, open country that made them feel small and lonely. The Indians had lived lightly on the land, in small groups that followed the buffalo herds and then joined in large seasonal gatherings to socialize and hold religious ceremonies. In contrast, the settlers stayed in one place and put down roots, and the early ones might see no one else for weeks or months. Perhaps they welcomed the hard work of setting up a farm, to help them forget about the loneliness. No doubt it was a great comfort to see neighbours arrive, and to begin meeting for church and to socialize. The individual couple or family, however, were the ones who built up each farm. Women and men each made their unique contribution to the success of the family.

Among the Indians, the first people to live in our area, the men did the hunting, which was often hard and dangerous work. The women were constantly busy, at home and while on the move. The missionary John McDougall described the work they did:

...Packing and unpacking dogs and horses, making camps, providing wood, making and mending moccasins and wearing apparel, cooking, cutting up, drying and pounding meat, rendering grease, chopping bones to get out the marrow fat, making pemmican, stretching, scraping and dressing buffalo hides to make robes or leather - a long tedious process, in which not only the brains of the worker were needed in order to excel, but also those of the dead animals as well - kept her going early and late. Besides all this the manufacturing of saddles, travois, tents and shagganappi also devolved upon the women; and yet, notwithstanding all this, they seemed, generally speaking, to be contented and happy, and with true feminine resource still found time to give to attire and adornment, and the practising of all those mysterious arts which have charmed and magnetized the other sex, doubtless through all the past of our race. No wonder these women and girls were at a premium, and cost all the way from a blanket up to a band of stolen horses! The more of them a man had, then the greater man was he...

The women who settled and farmed on the prairies usually worked as long and hard as the Indian women had done. They came seeking a better life, and with work and luck some found it here, though others ended up leaving to start again elsewhere. They came by train from Eastern Canada, by wagon from the United States, by ship and train from Europe, leaving behind their families and familiar landscapes for the empty, open prairies. The women came west with their husbands and their children, or sometimes as single women, who soon had their choice of hopeful bachelors.

Sometimes the woman's husband had come out first, so she had a house or at least a shack to live in when she arrived. Often the whole family came together and lived in a tent until they could build a sod house; it might be a couple of years before they could afford lumber for a frame house. If they were lucky, they would have a good well dug nearby; if not, they might have to haul water by wagon in barrels from the nearest creek or slough.

Some homesteaders brought farm implements along with them and were able right away to break land and prepare it for cropping. In other cases the family was short of cash, and the husband would have to go to work for other farmers, or in coal mines, or building the railway, to earn money for food, livestock and machinery. The wife would be left on her own, to look after the family and start the farm work herself.

Whether her husband was home or not, the wife had plenty to do. She would milk the cows and churn the butter; feed the poultry and gather the eggs, as well as killing, plucking and cooking chickens; look after the garden, digging, peeling and cooking potatoes; bake bread and pies; make preserves and jam; make soap so she could wash the dishes and do the laundry, after she'd hauled enough water in and heated it up; keep the house clean, which wasn't easy in a sod house; sew, knit and mend clothes; and feed her family, the threshing crew, the hired hands, and any visitors who dropped in. Often she would help with the field work as well, while her husband would help with the chores around the home.

Grant MacEwan has estimated that during threshing season, the farm woman would feed fifteen to twenty-five men at a time, and she commonly served a total of 400 to 500 meals in one threshing season. He has also described the unhappy experience of one threshing crew at the farm of a bachelor:

> ...Even the rough and ready teamsters were critical. One of them had the temerity to wash out the endless or 'perpetual' hand towel that had hung on the roller since the last threshing. Another undertook to empty the teapot and discovered, among the accumulation of time, one mouse. The engineer poured corn syrup on the table-top to serve as a fly trap in the hope of relieving the atmosphere of some of its wildlife. Eventually the gang worked long into the night, finishing by lantern light to avoid the necessity of eating another breakfast at Bachelor Hall. It was a costly affair for the farmer, considering the reckless manner in which the sheaves were heaved into the feeder that dark night and the inevitable loss of grain in the straw, but was a good lesson because, before the next thresh-ing, he had a wife...

If a pioneer woman was pregnant, she might be lucky enough to have a doctor available when she went into labour, or unlucky enough to have only her husband present; but often she would depend on her neighbours who had had children themselves. She would nurse the children when they were ill, teach them to read, write and figure until a school could be started nearby, and teach them how to work around the home.

It is no surprise that western women were instrumental in getting the vote for women and achieving other reforms in Canada. Although the laws of Canada said that they were not equal to men, the women who settled the prairies knew that they had been essential partners in building the farm and the nation.

Submitted by Valerie Jobson, 1993

Dedication to Pioneer Women

As we remember the sacrifices and legacy of love left by our mothers, grandmothers, and yes, even in some cases great-grandmothers, we should take some time to pause and reflect on the actual tasks that they performed each day. What I remember the most is that I never got the feeling that any of their hard work was begrudged; it was a labour of love for the family.

The early pioneer woman would usually begin her day between five and six in the morn-ing. She would have to rise early to start the fire on the coal and wood stove in order to prepare breakfast. While she was preparing breakfast, her husband and older children would go out and do the necessary morning chores. These would include such things as milking the cows, feeding the horses, and pumping water for the animals.

After the chores were done, the family would eat breakfast. The children would then go to school and our pioneer mother would continue her day. She would have her own projects and work to do all day long. A lot of her day revolved around the kitchen, as all the food had to be prepared from scratch. Sometimes it would even be necessary to make yeast from fermented potatoes in order to make bread. The mornings would be spent preparing for the noon-time meal, which was usually the biggest meal of the day on the farm. Also the heavier household jobs such as washing clothes would be performed in the morning.

In the springtime a lot of her time would be spent working in the garden and planting vegetables to put in the root cellar for the winter. The garden would be a continual source of work all through the summer, as it was necessary to weed and thin the plants. In the late summer she put a great deal of work into pickling and preparing preserves, as well as waxing some of the vegetables for winter storage.

Our pioneer mother usually had a few chickens that she kept and raised. The revenue from selling eggs and butter was usually considered to be her income. Our grandmother would travel by horse and buggy to take the children to school or to go to the Ladies Aid meeting. She would travel alone on shorter trips, but would be accompanied by her husband for longer excursions.

The pioneer woman's life revolved around her family and her home. The weekends would be time for relatives to visit and spend an evening playing cards or checkers, singing, making music, and visiting. People would make their own entertainment when visiting, not relying on mechanical forms of entertainment as they do now.

Sundays were usually spent attending church. Our pioneer mothers and grandmothers were generally referred to as God-fearing people. They had a practical and honest no-nonsense approach to living out their faith.

Submitted by Ann Hollands, 1993

Pioneer Women of the West

Much can be said with regard to the part pioneer women played in opening up the west, both here in Western Canada, and also in the western U.S.A. After all, both our nations were settled by those who immigrated to North America from similar origins. Those who came west by Red River cart or a common, heavy-duty covered wagon surely endured some terrific obstacles, which demanded no end of courage and stamina. There were no medical services, no schools, no churches or other sources for the meeting of a homemaker's every day needs; but when the railroad came to the west, these things became more accessible.

Rail service reached the town of Calgary in August 1883. In our Nose Creek District, most of the settlers arrived after 1883 and into the early 1900s. Sincere admiration is felt for all of them. Actually it was well into the 1920s before country living became an easier way of life. Having lived in the Nose Creek District since 1917, I have a few recollections of what the housewife's daily duties were, which may be of interest to my readers. As Ann Hollands states, an early rise at six o'clock in the morning was common. Light the fire in the cook stove if father hadn't done it already. A hearty breakfast for all: porridge, bacon and eggs, and toast made over the hot crimson coals. Children readied for school, wrapped well for a chilly ride some 3 and 3/4 miles to school. Daily chores, cleaning lamp chimneys, trimming the wicks and refilling with coal-oil or with gas if mantle-type gas lamps were used.

Monday was wash day: boilers placed on the stove to heat the water to wash; scrub board in action; and soapsuds galore. During the morning, wood and coal to be brought in by someone. Ashes from the cook stove and heater to be removed to the ashpile. Hungry men appear at noon; "Lunch ready?" After lunch, a time to converse around the table, then all at once a rise to duty. Washing to be finished and the house to dust; the old coal stove and the dusty labourers had the effect of making extra cleaning every day, with endless sweeping of floors. Tuesday was ironing day; irons were heated on the stove - supreme comfort on winter days, but excruciatingly hot in summer months! Wednesday; mending tears in clothing and darning socks. Thursday was butter churning day; producing some 80 pounds of butter, all cut into pounds and wrapped in butter paper with the words "CHOICE DAIRY BUTTER" stamped on the top surface. Friday was town day; butter and eggs were loaded on the democrat buggy, or in later years into the automobile, all to be traded for the groceries or clothing required. Amidst it all there was a large garden to take care of. The canning was a time-consuming operation, but pioneer women were more than proud of the shelves on row upon row of preserves, vegetables, meats, and British Columbia fruits in season.

Oh! I must not forget; in spite of all the heavy arduous work load, the Friday Night Dance at the local hall was a social attraction. Regardless of the workload, there was time for the hair curlers to be heated above the coal-oil lamp chimney, and for hair to be styled. After all, attraction was important, and she may just be the "Belle of the Ball" and be danced off her feet. Saturday was a happy day, chatting over all that was experienced at the dance the night before. The afternoon was a busy time as usual, preparing items to entertain the weekend guests. A ten-pound roast was not uncommon, along with pies and cakes. The well cooked roast would be served in various ways during the week, with a stew in prospect by Thursday.

It was quite common to see a neighbour lady walk a mile or more to pay an afternoon visit to a close acquaintance. Very often she would carry a bit of baking or another treat along with some fancy work to be busy with while passing an hour or two before hurrying back to get supper ready. We also recall the single horse and buggy or team and buggy. Ladies seldom drove an auto even if one was available.

There were the salesmen who called in: machinery agents; Watkins man; Rawleigh man; the fruit man, usually of Chinese origin travelling by auto van; Fuller Brush man; horse buyers; animal hide dealers; magazine sellers; all gave us something to think of and often stayed for dinner or afternoon tea. It was in 1912 that Nose Creek received phone service, with fourteen or more homes on the rural line. Many a time emergencies would be reported on the line and action taken in accordance. Oh Yes! There were pleasant social calls too, and the latest news of the community related over the line.

We must not forget those who milked the cows, fed the hogs, washed the eggs, and tended the sitting hens which the baby chicks came from. Turkeys, geese, and ducks all were raised for cash. Pioneer women were well aware of remedies for sickness, and seemed to have the answers for those flash illnesses. Oh! the curtains to be made, the floors to be scrubbed, and more tasks too numerous to mention. These brave ladies who made such endless efforts in the past sleep soundly in the wilderness areas where they are laid to rest. We will remember them—veterans of our past.

Submitted by C. Redvers Perry, 1993

Our Last Arrival by Bull Team

Thank you very much for your very kind letter. We are quite proud to have the honor of having our names recorded on your Map as being resident owners of N.W. ¼ Section 10, Township 26, Range 1, West of the 5th Meridian from October 1935 to 1952. My father, Wm.F. Foster, came to Alberta in the year 1882 from Swift Current, which at that time was the end of steel. He walked to Pincher Creek, spending two weeks enroute in a tent, sick with the measles, at what is now Medicine Hat, where he established himself in a little blacksmith shop. By trade he was a blacksmith.

In 1884 my mother, Mary D. Foster, came bringing my sister, four years old, and me, two years old, via Fort Benton by bull team to Fort Macleod, then from there to Medicine Hat. The part from Fort Benton to Fort Macleod took 16 days. My brother Charlie was born on June 24th, 1885. In the fall of 1885 we moved to Fort Macleod, where my father worked at black-smithing for Albert Keyes, who had a shop there.

At the age of 24 my mother died on April 24th, 1886, leaving my father at the age of 26 with us three babes, with no relatives nearer than Nova Scotia, from whence we had come. Two Metis ladies, sisters, helped with us children. One of them took my baby brother with a housekeeper. These were women arriving in the country with their husbands and families, glad to have the shelter of our home while their husbands established homes for them.

Finally when I was six years old my father found a couple who took my sister and me to board, and another to take charge of my brother. These ladies raised us. I finished high school in 1901 here in Calgary, and went to Normal School in Regina the same fall. Perhaps I have given you more than was necessary of my early history, but when I got started I had to finish the story.

Apologies! Anyway I hope it helps a little and I wish you every success in your project.
Submitted by Ruth L. Sandgathe, 1967

[Letter sent to C. Redvers Perry when the Nose Creek Historical Society was compiling the Nose Creek Map]

Sister Agnes Carroll

A site for a Holy Cross Hospital was chosen beyond the end of the tiny settlement of Calgary in 1892 and four sisters of St. Boniface, of the Order of Grey Nuns, were summoned from Montreal to staff it. The four women, led by Sister Agnes Carroll, arrived by train with $73.75 between them and faced the task of running a little two-storey building on the prairie that was the temporary hospital.

A small stove supplied heat, candles furnished the light, and water had to be hauled in buckets from a nearby well, with laundry water being bailed from the Elbow River close by the 24-foot square building.

Sister Agnes Carroll was a born organizer spurred by the necessity of acquiring larger facilities, for the settlement was growing at a breakneck speed as was the list of demands made upon the nursing Sisters.

Two of the women travelled back and forth on the train that ambled between Calgary and Edmonton, collecting donations from those along the route. They solicited larger bequests and gifts from Calgary townspeople, receiving one donation from a drama group that, under the direction of maverick lawyer P.J. Nolan, staged a benefit performance.

One coup in the fund raising campaign sparkplugged by Sister Agnes Carroll was a donation of 25,000 bricks from the Oblate Fathers, the bricks being sent from a brickyard operating in those days on Calgary church property.

From the date of her arrival in Calgary Sister Agnes Carroll was appointed Superior of the Sisters of Charity (Grey Nuns), a post she held until 1907. Under her guidance in 1892, during a smallpox epidemic, two of the Sisters staffed a tent hospital for five weeks in an isolated spot three miles from town. There was a diptheria epidemic in 1893 that created the need for a hastily improvised isolation ward. Sister Agnes Carroll in her dedicated way met the challenge by setting up an isolation ward on the unfinished top floor of the new three-storey Holy Cross Hospital.

In 1907, thanks in very great part to the example set by this unusual woman, the Holy Cross Hospital received certification as a nursing school, for by that time it was a highly respected and vital part of Calgary's services to humanity.
Submitted by Jack Peach, 1993

Twenty-Second Local Historical Recognition In Tribute To Pioneer Women Of The Western Prairies

Pioneer Wagon or Cart
(Appropriate to pre - 1883 era or before railroad came to Calgary)

This is an historical document. Please value it on the basis of posterity.
It is given with compliments of the Nose Creek Historical Society.

(Above, left) Harvesting potatoes, (above) a Sioux woman in tribal regalia, (left) Pioneer women were honoured in this 1993 pamphlet. (Below) The important role of churning butter was usually left to the womenfolk. (Bottom, left) At age 17 in 1933, horses were part of Violet Jobson's everyday life. (bottom right) Everyone pitched in when there was work to be done.

CHAPTER 28: TRIBUTE TO THE TELEPHONE ERA
TWENTY-THIRD LOCAL HISTORICAL RECOGNITION: 1912-1994

Communication! Far back in history, the only way messages were relayed to distant points was by runner, or later by pony express on land. Sea-going points of communication were connected by sailboats which were quite unpredictable. Amazing to everyone was the introduction of the telegraph in 1837 by the British physicist Charles Wheatstone. He is credited with the invention of the electro-magnet telegraph that relayed messages in code form; it was indeed the forerunner of modern communication. It was not until 1874 that Alexander Graham Bell invented the telephone, and he received the patent right in 1876. In 1884 the first telephone came to Alberta, with Edmonton having the honour. The first person to have a telephone in Calgary was none other than Colonel James Walker, whose long association with the N.W.M.P. will be remembered. He acquired the modern communication gadget in 1885, a mere ten years after his arrival in Calgary. By 1900 there were 150 telephones in Calgary, but not until 1903 was the first telephone directory printed for the use of subscribers, just two years before Alberta became a province in 1905. Alberta had the honour in 1906 to be the first in North America to build and operate its own lines.

As for the local telephone system, I quote a diary entry of the late C.W. Perry for Saturday, July 6, 1912: "Telephone men here about poles!"; again on Wednesday, September 18, 1912: "Telephone men here putting in poles."

The Calgary Public Library's History Division has a 1913 telephone book with numerous local phone numbers therein; it's interesting to see the early subscribers. So many interesting items could be mentioned in regards to telephones: batteries to energize their use, storms that made the exposed wires fail, grass fires that burnt poles off, waits for the lineman to arrive and fix a problem. There were from 15 to 20 subscribers to each line, with local rings to identify each household on the line; a long, or two shorts and a long, or one short and a long, or two shorts. A crank on the side of the telephone box was used to ring the desired code. Just use your imagination for a second or so - or a long ring - did it!! We also recall the emergency General Alarm - a long continuous ring which would signal all on the line to listen in; fire, accident, sickness, no doubt an appeal for help! Let's not forget the "rubber necks"! Though never admitting it, all were guilty, no doubt. The "rubber neck" was one who would lift the receiver and listen to a conversation, the latest scandal, or what the neighbours were doing. "Well!" "That's the talk of the country!" One would just not say anything that was not fit for everyone to know. Some conversations would go on and on, so a card was printed stating a limit of three minutes per conversation; however, it was seldom honoured! Over the years telephones have been constantly improved; fancy table models, answering devices, portables which can be used on a walk exercise or in an auto, tractor, or whatever. So today we make a long overdue report on the telephone, the most used item in the world for communication form 1876 to 1994, and all in an instant.

Quite a contrast now to when we used to lift the receiver with the words "Is the line busy?" Or ring Central and the operator would answer "Number please", upon which time you would ask for the number required. "Time marches on."

Submitted by C. Redvers Perry, 1994

The Airdrie Mutual Telephone Company

On February 9, 1934, a meeting of subscribers was held to discuss the sale of rural telephones to subscribers. Alberta Government Telephones (A.G.T.) proposed that a company be formed to acquire the property on the basis of $27.50 per subscriber.

On March 2, 1935, at a second meeting, it was proposed by H.P. Wright and seconded by R. Blair that the Airdrie Mutual Telephone Company (the Company) be organized. The following were elected as the original Board of Directors: G.A.C. Dougan, President; F. Northcott, Vice-President; H.P. Wright, Secretary; O.H. Woods, H.F. Benedix, A.P. Robertson, and R. Blair, Directors.

The directors subsequently canvassed the area designated and 59 subscribers agreed to become shareholders, with 14 more possible investors. On March 18, 1935, it was proposed that A.G.T. sell on the basis of 68 subscribers at $27.40 each, which offer was accepted by A.G.T. with a commitment to supply seven additional telephones and batteries at no cost.

On April 1, 1935, H.P. Wright was appointed Secretary-Manager, to be paid $35.00 to December 31, 1935, and $25.00 for the full year of 1936. Mrs. Inez Clayton was appointed Assistant Secretary to collect accounts and do the necessary clerical work.

Carl Armstrong was hired as the first trouble man and was expected to reset five poles per month as part of the jobs, with payment of 30 cents per pole for additional resets. The Company set its original rental rate at $1.50 per month, which continued until March 1945, when it raised the rental to $1.75. The original policy of the Company, as set by the directors, obliged a new subscriber who needed a new line to move any available used poles and wire to his location and to erect them according to the Company's requirements. The new subscriber would purchase a share for $27.40 and the Company would supply a phone, expending the balance above the cost of the phone toward erecting lines to connect with existing circuits. In several instances this policy resulted in new shareholders joining the Company.

From its inception until 1949 the Company utilized the services of part-time repairmen (Carl Armstrong, E.C. Hegy, Herb Shaw, and Harold Watters) and relied on volunteer work from shareholders to do some of the maintenance work. However, as time passed it became difficult to obtain volunteers for this work. The Company entered into an agreement with the Crossfield Mutual Telephone Company to share the services of Bill Walker, who eventually was able to do repair work for other telephone companies, converting his operations into a full-time business. This arrangement was very satisfactory, maintaining continuity from year to year, and Bill provided good service from the time he started working for the Company until it was dissolved. Also, the Company and Crossfield Mutual were able to save on costs by together purchasing new poles by the carload.

The minutes of board meetings show that the directors passed resolutions regarding the collection of rentals which indicates that there were problems in this area from time to time. At the 1936 annual meeting a resolution was passed that subscribers charge five cents for every call made by non-subscribers and turn these collections in to Central Office. There is no record that any money was actually collected in this manner. In 1942 a resolution was passed that one long ring would notify subscribers of an emergency or disaster. This no doubt was the precurser of the present 911 service.

As time passed, the Company had to face problems of increased business activity and excess use of the party lines by considering restrictions on use by homeowners. Through negotiations between the Company, A.G.T., and business, this problem was resolved to the general satisfaction of all parties; at the same time subscribers were notified that all phone calls should be restricted to ten minutes.

On reviewing the records of the Company, it is interesting to note the effects of inflation on the operation of a nonprofit company. The original rental was set at $1.50 per month in 1936, and by 1968 it was $2.75 per month. In 1937 E.C. Hegy was paid sixty cents per hour for trouble shooting, and by 1968 the wage rate was $3.25 per hour. The secretary-manager's salary, originally $25.00 per year, was $125.00 per year in 1969 . In light of what has occurred since then, however, even the above wages would appear to be very low. This is an indication that small mutual telephone companies provided a service to the community at minimal cost.

In 1961, A.G.T. advised the Company that the system was to be converted to dial telephones by June 3, 1962 and that 38 miles of new relief circuits would be needed to accommodate the new system.

Since this new undertaking required considerable expenditure and the Company was receiving more requests for new telephone installations, the share structure of the Company was revised to 200 shares with a value of $80.00 each, with the legal description of the land on the share. At the same time, new installations would now cost $240.00 which covered the cost of construction of three fifths of a mile plus the $80.00 for a share. As the Company had accumulated a reserve of funds, it accomplished the conversion without any financial difficulty.

Operations of the Company proceeded on the foregoing basis with only slight changes until October 16, 1969, when A.G.T. proposed that it take over operation of the area served by the Airdrie

Mutual Telephone Company. Effective June 4, 1972, AGT would dismantle all above ground installations, purchase all telephones for $7.50, and install underground cable to replace the Company's above ground material. This proposal was voted on on November 6, 1969, when it was decided to accept the proposal and dissolve the Company. After the takeover, A.G.T. set the rental at $4.75 per month, which was an increase of $2.00 per month.

After all material belonging to the Company was removed and stockpiled in Airdrie, it was disposed of by auction; subsequently the Company funds were paid out to shareholders on a pro rata basis. The books of the Company were officially closed on May 9, 1974, ending the forty-year life of the Company.

Special mention should be made of the contribution of Inez Clayton to the Company. Inez operated the telephone exchange for A.G.T. and in addition acted as Assistant Secretary Treasurer for the Company from 1935 to 1969. Inez was meticulous in collecting and accounting for the rentals of subscribers during this entire period, and her good humour and effectiveness was greatly appreciated by all directors, managers, and shareholders.

Thanks also to Margaret Carlson for providing excerpts from the minutes of the Company meetings, on which this commentary is based.

Submitted by Andrew Benedix, 1994

Balzac Mutual Telephone Company

The Balzac Mutual Telephone Company received its charter on April 1, 1936. There were 35 shares valued at $22.00 each. The monthly rental was $2.00. Over the years this rate varied from $1.50 per month to $2.50 per month.

Osia Rosenberger was president from 1936 until 1948. At that time Dave Girletz took the chair and remained in that position until 1958, when Earl James was elected. In 1965, Earl Northcott became president and continued to preside until the mutuals were taken over by Alberta Government Telephones.

Harold Bushfield acted as secretary and lineman from 1936 to 1956. Redvers Perry was secretary from 1956 to the end of June 1957 when Margaret Rush took the position, which she held until the company was dissolved in 1970.

Other linemen were Earl Northcott, 1956, and Bill Walker, 1967-1970. The company called work bees when there was a need for extra pole setting, or when the lines were downed.

At first the company had two lines but as demand for phones increased, it obtained two more lines in 1958 and one more in 1961. These new lines meant an increase in shares and their value had to be raised first to $44.00 and then to $100.00.

Before these new lines were brought in, there had been 19 subscribers on a line, which made using it rather difficult; notices were sent out asking that calls be limited to five minutes, but this was hard to regulate.

In 1967 we were informed by A.G.T. that they were planning to install four-party underground lines which were scheduled to be ready in 1970. A.G.T. had to get the consent of all the mutuals in the area.

The poles, wire and parts were collected at Gavin Scott's, and were sold by auction after the underground lines were in.

Submitted by Margaret Rush, 1994

The Beddington Mutual Telephone Company

The story you are about to read is true; some of the names have been changed to protect the guilty.

"Beddington" - it was a good name and we wouldn't have wished any other, although Beddington station was a mile beyond our west boundary. We served a strip of country seven miles long and two miles wide; three miles wide on the south where our lines crossed the tracks; and we served a dozen homes inside the Calgary City Limits. We had 52 subscribers, more or less, on four lines. The lines were identified as nineteen hundred, twenty hundred, twenty-one hundred, and twenty-two hundred. Sixty percent of our customers were permanent farmers, and the rest were acreage people constantly on the move.

Alberta Government Telephones, in the midst of the great depression, foresaw the demise of the rural lines and gave the farmers a gift of the poles, wire, and instruments. Thus was the formation of the many mutual telephone companies across Alberta. Shortly thereafter, at an annual meeting of the subscribers of Beddington Mutual, I was asked if I would be Secretary, of which my knowledge was nil. Mr. Ard, who had worked for the largest auditing firm in Toronto and came west to farm, offered to show me bookkeeping. How to deal with people? - I was on my own. The incentive to do this job had to be the challenge, it certainly wasn't the $25.00 a year salary they paid me. One man moved into the area and moved out leaving a five-dollar long-distance bill unpaid. This called for new rules; everyone must have a refundable forty dollars in the company. If rent was paid by June 30th, the amount was $18.00 for the calendar year; if paid after that date, the rent was $36.00 for the year. Needless to say, the mentioned five dollars was the only money every written off in my fifteen years as secretary.

Listening on the line

My mother, every fortnight, received *People's Friend*, a small publication from Scotland from which she clipped a recipe for wheat wine. She gave the recipe to Mr. Stillwell, a neighbour. His wheat, which sold be $.25 a bushel at the elevator now brought $32.00 bottled. One day the Stillwell phone rang and rang and others on the line wondered why and listened. Mr. Stillwell had been caught selling the stuff, had spent B & B courtesy the City of Calgary, and was now phoning his wife.

"Where are you?" Mrs. Stillwell asked of her husband. (He wouldn't say.) "The police are here looking for the damn thing, their car is stuck in the snow."

"Leave them there," replied Mr. Stillwell.

Soon my phone rang. "Have you a team in the barn?" asked Mrs. Stillwell. It was a long, cold trip over snowcrusted fields to pull the police out. It was old news to those on the line when the writeup in the *Morning Albertan* told the story that the police were unable to find Mr. Stillwell's still and he would be released. People were indignant if it was suggested they ever listened on the phone and exclaimed "Who me?"

Phone Privileges

Mrs. Seymour had five daughters, four living away from home. From her phone on the 1900 line, which had 18 other subscribers, she would phone her girls and monopolize most of every morning. The ruling was a five-minute limit, and many complaints came to me of how Mrs. Seymour and many others abused this privilege. I would pass on these complaints to the guilty and would get the same answer, *"Who me?."* I often thought how true the lines from Robert Burns *"If we could see ourselves as others see us, it would from many a blunder free us and foolish notion,"* and how applicable they were here.

A New Secretary

When Kit Gadeski, another subscriber, took over the books from me I recommended they pay her $100.00 a year. She stayed until the Alberta Government Telephones took the lines back and installed underground systems. We had a little money in the bank which we returned to the subscribers, but the best result was the acceptance of the Beddington Mutual Telephone Company books to be placed in the archives in Edmonton. Some day I will open that old book and look through the pages where so many names of good friends are written, except for one - the guy that got away with the five dollars.

Submitted by Hugh Bennett, 1994

Buttes Mutual Company

The Buttes Mutual, like other mutuals in the area, was formed by the farmers in the year 1936. The farmers bought shares to form the Company, paying in the neighbourhood of $30.00 per share. Rent per month for the phones started at about $1.50 and finally rose to about $2.00. John Kirby was the first secretary of the company. Mr. Ham, Bert Church, and J. Davy were directors at that time.

Thunderstorms, snow, and hoar frost always raised havoc with the telephone lines. One day the Seventeen Hundred line was out of order, and the lineman phoned to the farthest subscriber to ask if their phone was working. When the lady of the house answered, the lineman said, "This is the Telephone Company speaking. Is your husband home?" The lady replied "No, but come on down."

Another time there was a broken pole on one of the lines so the lineman went to replace it. While he was putting it in, a thunderstorm came up, so he had to sit in his vehicle until it quit raining. The lightning hit the new pole and broke it off, so the lineman had all kinds of elements to contend with.

Some of the first East Linemen were Jock Cowan, Wilber Ham, Rae Church, and the last was Bill Walker of Crossfield. The last secretary was Muffin Ekman, and the last president was Harry Kirby.

Submitted by Redvers Perry and Eleanor Meyer, 1994

Crossfield Mutual Telephone Company

The Bell Telephone Company brought service to Crossfield in 1905. James Sutherland was the local manager. A single pay phone connected up to the Calgary-Edmonton long distance toll line, was placed in Sutherland's Store on Railway Street.

The Alberta Government Telephone Company (A.G.T.) bought out the assets of the Bell Telephone Company in April 1908. They opened an exchange in Crossfield in 1909 and James Sutherland continued to be the agent. A.G.T. found it very expensive to reach the rural areas so only four county lines were built in 1910 and 1911. McPhee & Wicks Livery supplied transportation for the twenty workmen.

In 1911, Mr. Sutherland sold his hardware store to the Laut brothers. The telephone exchange was then moved to the McKay Building on Hammond Avenue along with the new post office facilities. Charlie McKay became the postmaster and took over the telephone agency. He moved away during the early years of World War I.

The agent was paid a salary from A.G.T., and in turn would hire the operators. The telephone operator was indeed a public servant, often working sixteen hours straight. The first telephone operator in Crossfield, in 1910, was 16-year-old Marie Anderson. When Marie left her position in 1917 to marry Wilson Stafford, the community gave her a gift of a horse and buggy in appreciation of her excellent service.

When Crossfield went to 24-hour service, A.G.T. decided that it was more convenient and economical to run an exchange from an agent's home. Jack Crocker was the agent from 1920 until he passed away in 1941. He and his family lived in a large house on the south side of Osler Avenue.

The next agent was Catherine Price, from 1941 to 1945. During her stay the telephone office was moved across the street to the vacated Rosebud Municipal brick building and AGT converted the back rooms into an apartment for the agent. Gerry McGill took over the position, followed by Goldie Lambert. Ruby Varndell served as the last agent from 1953 to 1974, when the dials system came in.

In the early days service to the farmers was indeed haphazard. Most made the choice to do without a telephone, although a few isolated families used the barb-wire fence transmission.

Farmer-owned companies started to form in 1914, and 15 years later there were 87 Mutuals in Alberta. One such company was the Crossfield and Sampsonton Mutual Farmers Telephone Company. Ephraim D. High was the secretary, and Daniel Fike a trouble man. This company had 17 subscribers on one line, number 7.

By the early 1930s the Crossfield area was covered by the Crossfield exchange, which consisted of a public pay station, 61 local phones, 130 rural AGT phones on 13 lines, and the Farmers' number 7 line.

In 1933, due to economic reasons, the government had a difficult time maintaining rural telephones. Therefore, A.G.T. gave the farmers the chance to run their own systems, with the assurance that A.G.T. would eventually resume ownership. It was felt the farmers could keep the rates lower as they could operate more economically. The Mutuals would pay A.G.T. a switching charge and pin space rental. In return the government sold out for about five percent of book value.

Co-operative companies formed rapidly, as they seemed to provide a workable alternative. Meetings were held with A.G.T. representatives, a board of directors was elected, and shares were sold on a payment plan. Times were really tough, but most farmers considered a telephone a necessity. Most Mutuals didn't go to the added expense of forming a limited company, so 20 years later a special committee had to be set up.

The Crossfield Mutual Telephone Company was incorporated in 1934. The one-line Sampsonton Company amalgamated with Crossfield Mutual, as their store had been moved and had been named Madden in 1931. Frank Laut was nominated President and William Murdoch Vice-President. Bill Murdoch held this position for 15 years, then took over the presidency for 25 years. He even acted as their lineman for a time. Tom Treadaway, Secretary for the Village of Crossfield, accepted the position of bookkeeper.

The Crossfield exchange rendered services as usual. The ordinary observer could notice no difference. Farmers took turns driving or walking the lines, but some members were not qualified, so a part-time lineman was hired.

In 1944, Tom Treadaway retired and Harry May took the books over until ill health forced him to resign. Then Jean Stevens looked after the Mutual books until the dial system came in.

The history of the mutual telephone companies in this area would not be complete without reference to Bill Walker of Crossfield. Back in 1947, it was William Murdoch, President of the Crossfield Mutual Telephone Company, who got him started as a lineman. Mr. Murdoch met him on a street in town and asked him if he could fix telephone lines. In May 1952, Florence Bigelow came to Crossfield to work in the telephone office. She married Bill Walker, the rural lineman, on September 10, 1953. They have been teased many times that Bill did his courting on company time. She left her position one year later to start a family, and to take over the books for her husband's company: W.H. Walker Telephone Construction. Bill Walker eventually ended up working for the Mutual Telephone Company for 25 years, from 1947 to 1972, followed by two years as a subcontractor. He worked at various jobs over a span of 60 years, and by far his favourite "occupation" was being a lineman.

When Bill Walker commenced employment with the Crossfield Mutual Telephone Company, William Murdoch, who lived west of town, was responsible for the west country including Madden. Many other excellent directors served on the board over the years. Two in particular who held lengthy terms were the late Fred Wilson, a director for 25 years in charge of the Dog Pound region, and the late Jim Scholefield, the representative for East Crossfield.

At first Bill Walker had a hard time climbing poles. Tommy Goodsir, A.G.T. Superintendent, spent two and a half days teaching him a lot about trouble-shooting. Bill hired Eddie Aldred and all summer they repaired lines in the Crossfield district. When Airdrie needed a telephone man, Bill took on that area, hired more crew, and made a full-time job of it. Gradually he took on other districts. Besides Crossfield and Airdrie, Bill was the lineman for Didsbury East, Carstairs East, Carstairs West, Greenwood, Freshfield, Buttes, Balzac, Beddington, and Symons Valley. After he formed his own company, he did subcontracting for A.G.T.

Bill travelled all over his fifty-square-mile district, untangling wires and replacing poles and phones. He was attacked by bees, and had the odd confrontation with vicious dogs, but he had no serious difficulties other than trouble-shooting in all kinds of weather; winter snowstorms, wind, sleet, hoarfrost; and in summer lightning and sharp hail stones sliced the wires. He never looked at the clock and he never worried about his pay cheque...he loved his job!

The wages paid by the Crossfield Mutual Telephone Company were quite low. The men were paid forty cents an hour, and Bill received seventy-five cents with a car allowance. Bill took the back end off one of his old school buses and added a flatdeck, so he could haul poles and rolls of wire.

As times improved, the wages were increased. For a trouble-shooting trip he was paid six dollars and fifty cents. Sometimes it was a half-hour job, other times it took three hours, depending on the weather and road conditions. Bill was then in a financial position to get better equipment and trucks.

Over the 27-year span that Bill worked for the Telephone Company, he hired 85 men, mostly local high school and university boys, and most of whom have advanced to good jobs. Bill also hired some older men who didn't climb poles. They sharpened tools and kept things tidy. His last employee, in 1974, was his eldest son Stuart, who subsequently went on to become a manager for A.G.T.

The government got involved when the complicated automatic phone service became a reality. The Alberta Mutual Telephone Companies Association was founded in 1951 to secure proper action for the farmers from the government and large corporations. The provincial Minister responsible for both A.G.T. and the Mutuals attended an annual meeting held in June each year. Crossfield was one of the four centres where these meetings were held; Bill Murdoch from Crossfield chaired them.

In 1964, before the underground lines went in, the Farmers' Union of Alberta (FUA) approached the Alberta Government about taking over the rural telephone system. The A.G.T. takeover started in 1965 and took over ten years to complete.

When the telephone wires were put underground the Mutual companies were dissolved. Bill Walker's company got the job of installing the new phones.

A.G.T. resumed ownership of the Crossfield Mutual Telephone Company on November 1, 1974.

After the automatic service came to Crossfield, the telephone office on Osler Avenue was closed. All calls were then channeled through an automatic switchboard located in a small building near Highway 2A. Telephone users could now dial any number on the Crossfield or Airdrie systems. Soon afterwards Carstairs and Calgary became part of our free-toll area.

The Mutual Company's agents and operators as a whole are missed. Bill and Florence will always treasure their mementos and memories of that happy period of their lives. Today they are grateful for a great telephone service and happy that progress didn't change the kind neighbourliness of the community of Crossfield.

Submitted by Florence (Bigelow) Walker, 1994

The Freshfield Mutual Telephone Company

The Freshfield Mutual Telephone Company was incorporated July 8, 1936. It was part of Alberta Government policy to transfer rural services to local co-operatives as an economic measure in the depression.

The first meeting to discuss the formation of a phone company was held with the following present: G. Bowman, J. Ralston, B. Johnston, A. Shuttleworth, Mrs. Polland, J. Sandilands, Al Griffith, E. Anderson, Mr. and Mrs. Cookman, Mr. and Mrs. B. Robinson, Mr. and Mrs S. Roberts, R. Stark, and J.L. Bull.

Art Shuttleworth suggested the name Freshfield be used, as there had been a post office of that name in the area.

The Company was started with the purchase of four lines for $831.85. B. Robinson was elected President, O. Ingraham Vice-President, and the Directors were E.C. Cookman, E. Anderson, J.L. Bull, and J. Ralston. Mrs. G. Robinson was Secretary.

The Company started with $1500.00 in capital, to be divided by 60 shares, each share to cost $25.00.

Mr. Cooper was the first repairman, but directors corrected the problems on their own lines whenever possible.

The secretary was paid 10 cents per name per month. L. Bull and B. Robinson used their own trucks to transport a ladder tall enough to reach the line, and were paid for their gas. Phone rent was $2.00 per month, with A.G.T. to receive $1.00 per month for the service.

The bills could be paid at the bank, but as some subscribers forgot to leave their names there, it was decided to have bills paid at the home of the secretary.

In 1939, H. Soderberg was hired to be the lineman, and he continued until 1949, when Mr. W. Mosier was hired.

In 1940, the Department of National Defence strung wires to Airdrie Airport, using Freshfield poles for which the Company was paid 10 cents per pole per month for $39.00 per year.

Subscribers were given a free phone for six months in 1943 due to the Company having a substantial bank balance. There was also a report at this time of "combine menace" with damage to the line paid for by the operator of the offending combine.

Twice bad storms put the lines down, in 1947 and again in 1951. The lines had to be rebuilt both times, necessitating a rate increase to $3.00 per month.

In 1957, because of the great distance from the east boundary, two of the western lines were transferred to the Beddington Mutual.

Mr. Mosier, in 1953, had to use a boat to repair line 21; as a result, that line was moved. The number of lines was increased from four to five in 1957, and in 1960, rent was increased to $4.50 per month and the number of shares increased from 60 to 80.

In 1963, because of an overlap with Airdrie, Freshfield's boundaries were moved two miles north. Mr. Mosier retired as lineman in 1965 and Sanford Sydness became our lineman. 1966 saw the rent decreased to $2.50 per month, and the beginning of integration with AGT.

In January 1967 a meeting of all Mutuals surrounding Calgary was held at the Co-op #3 auditorium. The mutual companies that attended were in favour of integration. In April 1967 a meeting was held at Chestermere Hall. Attending were representatives of Beddington, Chestermere, Conrich, Dalroy, Freshfield, and Shepard Mutuals, and all favoured integration.

Bill Walker became our lineman in January 1968 and continued in this capacity until the Freshfield Mutual Telephone Company was totally integrated with A.G.T. in November of 1972.

Between the years 1936-1972, Freshfield Mutual overcame many obstacles. During the depression years, subscribers helped each other and gave much time to keeping up lines. Through the war years materials were in short supply. There were few bad accounts, but some people tended to talk too long. However, the phone was a vital part of community life.

Submitted by Kathy Shuttleworth, 1994

Symons Valley Mutual Telephone Company

Symons Valley Mutual Telephone Company maintained and operated two lines in the community with a total of about 34 subscribers; 17 families per line. The unwritten rule was five minutes per call but of course this was a most difficult restriction when there was news to be shared and we were all guilty of exceeding our time. Each subscriber had their own signal comprised of long and short rings. Of course the telephone rang in each home on the same line, so if you wished to know what was new in the neighbourhood you only had to pick up your receiver to share in the news. This practice was commonly known as "rubbering," and I believe everybody at one time or another was guilty of participating in this pastime.

Mutual Telephone companies were operated by a Board of Directors. In 1960 and earlier, the Symons Valley directors were Jim Fairweather, Jack Murray, Gus Boehlke, Jack Evans, and Wesley Miller, who acted as Secretary-Treasurer until his passing in 1962. Millie Miller was asked to fill this position, and she held it until the mutual telephone company was again taken over by Alberta Government Telephones.

Early records of Symons Valley Mutual show that Charles Oldfield was the line repairman during the '30s and '40s, and I believe his charge for service was about thirty-five cents per hour. Following his retirement, Walter Mosier became lineman; he was succeeded by Bill Walker of Crossfield for the last several years of operation.

In 1960 or 61 the original wooden crank-style telephones were replaced with new models at a cost of $36.00 each. This was paid for by an assessment of $1.00 per month per subscriber, and our monthly charge was raised to $4.00 per month. This rate remained in effect until closure of the company.

Around 1965, telephone exchanges were enlarged and we were able to split into four lines with a maximum of ten subscribers per line. Also during this period many people were leaving the city for a country acreage, a new home, and a new lifestyle. They all required telephone service, which the mutual telephone companies simply could not provide. During the late sixties, Alberta Government Telephones negotiated with the mutual telephone companies to provide rural telephone service; this was effected in Symons Valley in 1969. Initially, we were offered a four-party line service. Private line service was also offered at a relatively low cost. This was later upgraded to private service with underground wiring for all rural telephone subscribers. Quite a monumental achievement in a relatively short period of telephone service in rural Alberta.

Submitted by Millie Miller, 1994

NOSECREEK VALLEY MUSEUM
AIRDRIE, ALBERTA
Sunday, June 26th, 1994
1:30 p.m.

Twenty-Third Local
Historical Recognition
In Tribute To
The Telephone Era
In The Western Prairies

Burwash Corner - 1971
One of the last telephone lines in the district.

This is an historical document. Please value it on the basis of posterity.
It is given with compliments of the Nose Creek Historical Society.

A 1907-style telephone commonly used in the Valley.

Brochure cover on the left acknowledges role of telephones in development of the West. (Above, right) An early phone mechanism used in Alberta. circa 1908.

*The very first switchboard in use in Alberta **(below, right)**. Manufactured around 1880, it was installed in the office of Major James Walker in 1886, a lumber merchant. It was replaced in 1887 when Bell Telephone system came to Calgary.*

***(Left)** A typical telephone switchboard operator's transmission board, brought in from Eastern Canada at the turn of the century. Pictures courtesy **Singing Wires—The Telephone in Alberta**, by Tony Cashman, 1972. See pps 37, 73, 51, and 174.*

CHAPTER 29: TRIBUTE TO PIONEER MEN
TWENTY-FOURTH LOCAL HISTORICAL RECOGNITION

Men of the Soil
During the pioneer days, the man of the family often came west alone, seeking good homestead land. Once he had filed, he lived in a tent while he built a shack on his claim, perhaps did some fencing and breaking, and then sent for his wife and children.

Single men coming west found women to be in short supply -- about three men for every available woman. Some bachelors had sweethearts back home, waiting to come west to be married, while others improved their homesteads and hoped they would find a bride among their neighbours or schoolteachers.

It was a harsh life for pioneer men. They were up before dawn, doing the chores before breakfast, and then toiling all day at the hundreds of tasks that needed doing on the farm. In the spring they tilled and seeded, and in the fall they worked from morning till night bringing in the harvest. In addition, there was new breaking to be done, fences built or mended, cattle to be tended, buildings constructed or repaired, machinery to be serviced, and goods to be hauled to market. Regardless of blazing sun or raging blizzards, the pioneer homesteaders had to be outside seeing to the needs of their farms and their livestock. They were truly "men of the soil."

Submitted by Hugh A. Dempsey, 1995

Men on the Lone Prairie
Stand up on Nose Hill, and you can see for miles across the prairies. The city of Calgary at your feet and the farms and communities to the north do not begin to fill up the landscape. Much of the land is crisscrossed by roads and highways, but the feeling of open prairie space is still there. You can imagine how it was before the city was there, before the farmhouses, fences, and roads were built.

The farms along Nose Creek north of Calgary were settled by homesteaders mostly after 1900. Before that, during the 1880s and 1890s, while Calgary grew from a small fort and tent town into a city, the surrounding land was leased out to ranchers; herds of cattle wandered over the fenceless grassland. Travellers passed through on the coach road or the railroad between Edmonton and Calgary; a few people lived in the area, but not many.

Before any of those people came, for thousands of years, there were no houses there but tepees, no roads but rough trails. Huge herds of buffalo wandered over the land; small groups of people slowly crossed the prairies as they followed the herds. The first people in this area were Indians, who travelled on foot in family bands. At times several bands would gather to hold a communal buffalo hunt. They developed strong traditions of generosity, sharing the proceeds of the hunt with everyone, and of equality, where men were not respected for their wealth, but for their wisdom and skills. Women were not treated as equals in making decisions, however, and men and women often did different kinds of work to help the band to survive. For instance, men were warriors and hunters, while women clothed, fed, and taught the children, and passed on their traditions.

Men did the dangerous work of stalking the fast, skittish buffalo, on foot and armed only with spears or arrows. They needed to cooperate to avoid stampeding a herd prematurely. Together the hunters would surround buffalo herds at watering places, lure them into corrals, or drive them off cliffs. "The prehistoric hunter showed a lot more savvy than the gun-toting cowboy," wrote author Gail Helgason, when describing how carefully they planned their strategy.

When horses arrived, the prairie Indian culture became a horse culture overnight. A man could ride a good horse up beside a running buffalo and shoot arrows or bullets into it, which was easier and more fun than hunting buffalo on foot, though still dangerous. Parties of Indian men now travelled further to attack their enemies and to steal these valuable horses, and a man with many horses was a rich man. When the buffalo vanished and settlement of the prairies pushed Indians onto reserves, their horse culture developed into a ranching and rodeo tradition which is still strong today.

Even with horses, travel was difficult for the early Canadian and European visitors and settlers on the prairies. Travellers could take weeks to cross a few hundred miles, over wild land with no roads but plenty of coulees, rocks, and wild animals. They might spend several days dismantling wagons to float them across a river, and some people drowned while crossing rivers. In winter, they ran the risk of freezing or starving to death before reaching their goal. They found safety in travelling in groups, and relied on the guidance and good will of more experienced people, often Indians or Metis.

The few early settlers in this spacious land felt vulnerable and lonely, and they developed a strong tradition of hospitality to strangers, welcoming any chance to socialize and learn the news. Gradually telegraph and railway lines were built, making travel and communication faster and easier. This was a great advance to men who had left friends and families in the east, and had been receiving mail just a few times a year.

A few early pioneers did bring their families out, but even some of them spent many lonely days away from home. John McDougall, the Methodist missionary, and James Macleod, the Northwest Mounted Police Commissioner and judge, both wrote long affectionate letters to their wives and children when their duties kept them out on the road for weeks. Macleod's letters are full of humour; he described a wagon trip with Indian Commissioner Edgar Dewdney in which Dewdney was tormented almost to madness by mosquitoes. Dewdney wore one hand-kerchief on his head and neck, and was constantly wiping his face with another one; meanwhile Macleod sat beside him at ease, simply slapping his neck once in a while.

Many of the immigrants who came out before 1900 were young men, some looking for an adventure, others thinking of their future prospects. They came out as fur traders, missionaries, mounted policemen, cowboys, teamsters, surveyors, railway workers, miners, and merchants. They may have been wild risk-takers at first, but as time went on, they felt the need to settle down. A few went home back east, but many found that the open spaces had soaked into their bones. By the hundreds, these men thought it over and decided to stay out west, taking up homesteads, starting farms, ranches, and other businesses, and working to build communities. A few married local women; many wrote or travelled back home to persuade their sweethearts to take the plunge, or to seek out young women who would be willing and able to make a new life in the west.

The people who settled this area after 1900 had the courage to come out in hope of a better life. Their way had been prepared by the earlier pioneers, who showed them it could be done, although it would not be easy. Much of the land was claimed for homestead, but it was never crowded, and men continued to work together and socialize when they could.

There was room on the prairies for all types of men; some were hermits by choice, but most were not. The loneliness they had to bear at times made human contact all the more precious. They relied on their families, helped their neighbours, and welcomed strangers to their homes. Down the years, from holding communal buffalo hunts, to fighting prairie fires, to joining farmers' cooperatives, prairie men have survived by cooperating. They started a tradition which we need to remember and to cherish today.
Submitted by Valerie Jobson, 1995

Grandfathers and Fathers

I grew up in a family of pioneering men. The one single thread that runs through the stories they told is all the hard work. I remember my grandpa telling how he had dug the basement of his house out with a shovel and a pickaxe. This was an incredible undertaking since the earth was solid rock. As I mainly remember, he seemed to think that this was just part of another week's work. I still at times visit that old house and marvel at the naturally solid rock walls that formed this basement. Our pioneering ancestors definitely were not afraid of hard work and difficult circumstances, including a harsh climate. How empty this land must have seemed when they first arrived, with its miles and miles of endlessly rolling prairies. But what we would call obstacles or hindrances only seemed to call forth from them even more courage, and a greater hope for a better future in this new country.

My grandpa's family arrived in the Calgary area in the early 1890s. He was one of a family of seven sons and one daughter. The first project for them was to build a house in the Bridgeland district. The lumber for this effort was obtained by floating the logs down the river from west of Cochrane. The completed structure was an attractive two storey house with a wrap-around veranda. In 1895, the brothers came out to the Balzac district to farm. My grandpa's brothers had a variety of careers as well, and it is interesting to learn what types of occupations dominated the scene in pioneering times. One brother ran the Minneapolis Moline dealership; another worked as a surveyor, an oilman, and a real estate agent. Another brother had a gravel pit by Turner Valley. One of his nephews was the Calgary Stampede announcer for over fifty years!

They started on the farm and then progressed into other areas of work. My grandpa was the only one who remained on the farm. The farm work was intense and took long hours to complete. I always think that the farm seems ten times larger on a horse than when I'm riding a tractor or a truck. All the work was done with horse-drawn machinery and the gentle black Percherons faithfully pulled and laboured long hours. The land was cultivated, ploughed, seeded, and harvested with horse power and long arduous days.

In 1906 my grandpa married my grandmother and took her to San Francisco for her honeymoon. There was a sense of chivalry amongst our forefathers. Grandpa kept a house in town for Grandma when the weather was bad. My uncle and dad were born in Calgary. Dad was born during the week of the first Stampede, a happy event which nevertheless provided a conflict of interest for a rodeo-loving father!

Our hats should be off to all the pioneering fathers and grandfathers and the love and willingness that they brought to their efforts to build a better life for themselves and us. When we look around and see our community and district we can truly say that their works have followed them.

Submitted by Ann Hollands, 1995

In Honor of Pioneer Men "North of the Bow"

Speaking of pioneers, one just can't imagine how our first settlers - the Indians - survived the profound weather changes and the erratic environment that is found from year to year in Alberta, and across Canada for that matter; floods droughts and severe cold. Our real pioneers were our Plains Indians. From tipi rings to buffalo jumps, there is evidence galore. A salute to these hardy pioneers who came from Asia many centuries ago!

Just imagine leaving one's home in the British Isles, Central Europe, Scandinavia, or China. There were so many who left by sailing ship, saying goodbye to Mother and Dad, sisters and brothers, not realizing they would never see them again.

Through the myriad of stories related by immigrants who came to Canada and the U.S.A., we discover a common bond; we are cousins in that we all immigrated from overseas countries of prominence.

Pioneer men arrived in the Canadian West, known then as the North West Territories, with Regina as its capital. Local administrations had to be set up. These were known as "local improvement districts" which eventually became municipal districts and counties. One cannot imagine that the services we now take for granted were once non-existent; services such as schools, community centres, and churches.

Roads, as they were first constructed, were aligned along the lines of least resistance, and followed the western wagon trails of early traders. As we speed along our hard-surfaced roadways, it is more than fascinating to look along the dips and turns of hills and valleys now all levelled to take a line of smooth travel. These are the marks of time, much of which can be credited to the efforts of frontiersmen who came here originally. The railroad entered Calgary from the east on August 11th, 1883, and our district, "North of the Bow" came into being.

According to Hugh Dempsey, "Men usually arrived in the west as singles, setting up a farm of sorts prior to the arrival of their wives and families. The luxury of train travel far outweighed the covered wagon and squeaky ox-carts." Our "Tribute to Pioneer Women" highlighted their tremendous contribution to opening the west. The needs of the children, the home preparations, sickness of various types; these problems were confronted daily. With the help and advice of the ladies the pioneer men met the challenges head on! It was not until the 1920s that the women even had the rightful privilege to vote! The men had the full responsibility to carry out district and provincial development. There is no doubt that on numerous occasions the advice of the so called "weaker" sex was acted upon with confidence and appreciation.

Looking back on the daily activities of a pioneer family farm, we notice from historical data that it was a "mixed farming" era, with huge cattle ranches in our local area. Mixed farming included milk cows, a flock of laying hens, turkeys, ducks, pigs, and sheep. The proximity of the Calgary markets for such produce made a difference, such was the case for all farms surrounding growing towns and cities at that time.

Farmers formed a lasting affection for the livestock; they were pets of sorts. "Come and see my animals" was a common form of invitation and always looked forward to. The happy arrival of the new colt underlined the dual purpose of horses in those days; they were prized for the pleasure they brought to the family as well as for their hard work. In the early years, many farmers were involved in hauling hay and grain to the cities by horse and wagon, plus the horse and buggy were a common form of transportation. Farmers supplied hay and oats for city dwellers' requirements. That in turn provided income and ready cash to spend for food and clothing. Time and again, we are reminded from old time diaries about a trip to Calgary with hay and oats to fuel the numerous modes of horse travel; lawyers' buggies, businessmen's carriages, delivery vans, fire engine services, and all sorts of other horse drawn vehicles right down to the undertaker's hearse on its solemn journey to the Union Cemetery, just south of what we now know as the Calgary Stampede Grounds.

The word "boredom" was never used on the homestead, as men and women had no end of daily duties to attend to. Outside the farm were plenty of opportunities to participate in school boards, municipal district councils, political parties, farm organizations, and church activities. Lots to do for both the young and the elderly. Telephones did not arrive until 1912-1913.

As we pay tribute to the "Pioneer Men of the Prairies", a good deal of credit is due to those hardy souls who came here from far away countries, those who worked hard to make Canada a nation we can be proud of. In World War I and World War II they all joined forces to keep Canada free and settle worldwide differences, hopefully forever. Many gave their lives, as did numerous pioneer men who in disastrous situations gave their all. They never had the opportunity to enjoy our current comfortable standard of living, a way of life we take for granted.

Time and again, as we turn on the electric light switch or turn on the natural gas to make a mean or heat our luxurious homes, many of us think back to the days of chopping wood to light the fire, carrying in coal, emptying ash cans, lighting the lamps after filling them with coal oil, and cleaning the chimneys.

So to those who came to Canada from various countries and stood firmly together to co-operate and make this new nation of Canada, a sincere tribute is in order.

Today we honour our pioneer men and women "North of the Bow".

Submitted by C. Redvers Perry, 1995

Editors' Addition:

Nose Creek Valley Man Honoured

William "Bill" Walker (pictured left) received a Canadian Citizenship citation in Ottawa on April 10, 1990, along with 24 other people. The Crossfield Town Council had nominated him for this honour to recognize his many achievements in the community.　　　Bill Walker was born in Cochrane on March 26, 1914 and raised near Madden on the family farm. In 1928, he moved to a farm near Crossfield and farmed for five years, then worked as a truck driver and manager of a service station from 1933 to 1947 , also driving and building school buses during the 1940's. From 1947 to 1972 he was the maintenance lineman for the local Mutual Telephone Company. He was a janitor for the Rocky View Lodge for eight years, then from 1980 to 1988 worked for a local fertilizer dealer, Redi-Go Services. In 1988, he retired but continued his many volunteer activities.

He was a volunteer firefighter from 1933 to the present, including Honorary Fire Chief; Councillor of Crossfield for a term; was active in the Crossfield Dramatic Society, the Odd Fellows, the Elks, the Legion, the Nose Creek Historical Society, and the Nose Creek Valley Museum Society; volunteer janitor of the United Church; Boy Scout leader for 12 years; and for decades he acted as the community's Santa Claus at local Christmas parties.

Certainly he deserves national recognition as an exemplary citizen!

Based on a profile by M.L. "Lorne" Kosack, Deputy Mayor of Crossfield, 1990.

CONCLUSION:

We have seen how sociological and historic factors such as the coming of the fur traders, explorers, missionaries and mounted police into Indian territory led to a peaceful transition into a new age. The development of transportation and other favourable conditions led to the arrival of ranchers, farmers and enterpreneurs, whose struggles to adapt to the prairie environment were the basis on which the pioneering community grew. Community developments such as schools, churches and co-operative activities emerged to meet the primary needs of community life. The various services and commercial enterprises grew out of the need for survival, as did political structures. Soon the enterpreneurial development of the Valley produced industrial and commerical expansion. Then the growth of population in the area accompanied by technical advances within the Valley ushered in the present. All of these factors formed the basis of the Nose Creek Valley's rural and urban characteristics which typify the changes taking place in this segment of Alberta's culture.

THE BALLAD OF THE COWBOY'S BRONC

They put his wild horse in the chute,
　　He screwed his saddle, down,
Then climbed upon the quivering beast,
　　The fight was really on.

The gate was opened wide you see
　　And horse and man were out
The wondering crowd did watch the fight,
　　Which one would win the bout?

The man did rake the horse with spurs
　　From mane to flank and more,
The horse did pound the dusty ground
　　With hooves both hind and fore.

The crowd was yelling on its feet
　　The rider "he will win",
Then that fool did wave his hat,
　　The girl, she caught his grin.

The horse, he sensed this show-off act
　　He bucked so straight and high
The cowboy lost his solid grip
　　And sailed out through the sky.

He came to earth with sounding thud
　　The, bronc had won the round
The man lay in a crumpled heap
　　Upon that dusty ground,

And this to you my bronco friends
　　Is but a warning heed,
Quit looking for that little gal,
　　And watch your bucking steed.

—by Wendy Vaughan

Sunday, June 25th, 1995

7:00p.m.

**Twenty-Fourth Local
Historical Recognition
In Tribute
To Pioneer Men Of The
Western Prairies**

(Below) An artist's concept of pioneer men threshing. This picture is part of a mural—by the late Georgia Jarvis—at the Grain Academy, Calgary.

Branding and vaccinating: a common sight on pioneer farm and ranch operations. This picture taken in 1962.

The
**Nose Creek
Historical Society
25th**

Anniversary of
Theme Celebrations
History Book Project

1996
Dedicated to preserving our
heritage and making history live.
[Incorporated 1969]

WE HAVE A STORY TO TELL...

Above left: Pamphlet detailing aims, purposes and ideals of the Nose Creek Historical Society. ***Top right***: The Book Project Committee at work. (left to right): C.R.Perry, local Historian; Floyd Reynolds, President; Leighton Perry, Chairman, Ways and Means Committee; Eleanor Meyer, Secretary; and Howard Pole. Treasurer. Also on the committee but pictured separately are (**above**) Rev. Dr. Stephen Wilk, B.Sc.Agr., (U of S); B.D. (UBC), D.Min. (San Francisco Theological Seminary), Chap II (Retired) R.C.N.V.R., President and Editor of the Alberta Northwest Conference Historical Society's Journal, Chaplain to the McDougall Stoney Mission Society as well as to Legion Branch 284, and Honorary Member of the Nose Creek Historical Society for almost forty years; (**right**) Valerie Jobson, B.Sc., Biology, B.A., M.A., History (U of C) is a researcher and historian. **Below,** The Nose Creek Historical Society float at an Airdrie Parade, July 1996.

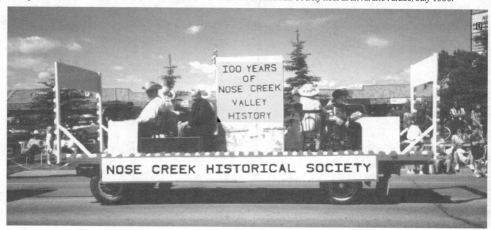

PART IV: URBAN CENTRES AND THE VALLEY
INTRODUCTION

Having presented various aspects of the historical settlement of the Nose Creek Valley, we now turn to the history of urban growth at Crossfield, Airdrie and Calgary.

The northern border of Nose Creek Valley passes through the town of Crossfield. Some of Crossfield's people and institutions have been described in other parts of this anthology under particular themes. We present here a history of the town of Crossfield written by Florence Bigelow Walker. It demonstrates a sense of the boosterism which was common to many prairie towns during the settlement era and is still strong in southern Alberta.

The City of Airdrie lies in the centre of the Valley. Ralph McCall, a longtime teacher and Deputy Mayor, wrote the story of Airdrie's development from a village into a town; he intended to complete the history of the city to the present, but his untimely death ended his writing career and left his manuscript unfinished. His beloved wife Marilyn, a volunteer librarian, knew the value of Ralph's work. She kindly consented to include his manuscript in this anthology and prepared it for publication. "Rambling with Ralph", as he called it, covers the history of Airdrie from 1964 to 1979.

A few pictures of Balzac are inserted between the urban centres; this reflects the position of the hamlet as a rural district caught between two growing cities and enjoying both good and ill effects from the proximity.

The City of Calgary continues to spread into the southern end of the Nose Creek Valley. As was shown in Part III, Calgary has been a strong influence in the area since its beginnings: as a police post and centre of trade, a crossroads for major transportation routes; a centre for ranching, farming, and lately the oil industry. Many histories of the city have been written, but its effect on surrounding rural areas has received little attention, and would reward further research and academic study.

We present a timeline showing events in the two cities of Calgary and Airdrie, and articles describing two areas in which Calgary has served the Nose Creek Valley well; in medical care and in higher education. The articles dealing with these topics briefly describe the institutions which have served residents in Calgary and surrounding districts. It should be noted that the native peoples had their own traditional medicine and educational methods long before doctors and teachers in the European tradition arrived, but it is beyond the scope of this book to describe them.

In 1892 the C & E Railway, which provided transportation between Calgary and Edmonton, had a policy of placing sidings or stations at 10 mile intervals. A siding which became identified as Crossfield was situated 29 miles from Calgary, with the service centre of Airdrie and the future flag station of Balzac in between. This siding, named for William Crossfield, the chief engineer with the C.P.R. surveyor crew, was the beginning of the town known today as Crossfield. It was located on the highest ground between Calgary and Edmonton, but unfortunately was surrounded by wetlands and sloughs.

The first stopping house in the area, opened in 1886 by John Dickson, was located seven miles south of Crossfield, near where the C.P.R. siding of Hemsdale was located. The stopping house was later taken over by Johnston Stevenson. The provincial government named its present rest area just south of the Crossfield turnoff on Highway 2 after these two gentlemen. The original site of the Dickson-Stevenson Stopping House is located west of this modern facility on Don Copley's land and was marked in 1975 by the Nose Creek Historical Society. The registration of Crossfield precluded any further growth around the Dickson-Stevenson stopping house area and Hemsdale ceased to exist. A stopping house in the Crossfield area was opened by Mrs. Hannington in 1890. It lay one mile west of the present townsite on the corner of the old Calgary-Edmonton Trail and the route going to Sampsonton, a hamlet now known as Madden. Mrs. Hannington's daughter Cora married Peter Patmore, who opened the first real estate office in Crossfield in 1904. In the meantime, the stopping house, which was known as Fairview Ranch, was sold in 1906 to Mr. Oldaker, who subsequently sold it to Amery and Sons. At the present time the original house and barn are still used as a farm site.

By 1902, commercial entreprises began to start up in Crossfield. J. Sutherland started a lumber and hardware business and Dave Gallagher, a C.P.R. section man, built a blacksmith shop. Over the next five years the bustling centre acquired a post office, two general stores, a barbershop, a grocery store, two livery barns, a meat market, a Chinese laundry, a real estate office, a drugstore, a bakeshop, a hotel, a C.P.R. station, a harness shop, a bank, a grain elevator, and a nearby creamery. Civilization had arrived when the community built its first school, a one room building located in the southwest part of town, and completed work on the Methodist Church; and when Dr. Bishop set up the first medical practice.

Crossfield was incorporated as a village on September 14, 1907, with Dr. George Bishop as Mayor and Donald McKay as the Secretary-Treasurer. This was fifteen years after it had first been registered. The original town of Crossfield comprised seven blocks and scattered acreages, and it continued to grow rapidly over a period of fifteen years. After Alberta became a province in 1905, the sidings along the C.P.R. railway lines were marked out by a developmental firm named Osler, Hammond & Nanton. This firm was made up of wealthy businessmen, lawyers and engineers working for or with the C.P.R. It can be noted that streets in Crossfield as well as several provincial towns such as Carstairs and Nanton carried the names of this firm. Other names often used were Chisholm, Munson, Ross, Smith and the prominent name of Grey.

Due to the growth in population a second bank, the Imperial, was opened and a Catholic Church was built. The school was moved to the north end of town and a second room added on. Then in 1909, a four room brick school was built on a location a little further north, on the present school site. Soon afterwards a confectionery and restaurant opened, followed by a farm implement agency and the first garage. Alex Gordon became the first owner of an automobile, an International Harvester. It was indeed the typical horseless carriage, running on high democrat wheels made of hard rubber, and driven by two chains, one on each wheel. The 1909 automobile which Horatius McPhee and Claxton Wicks used in their livery business was also a great attraction, especially when the passengers wore their long auto dusters.

In 1913, Robert Whitfield took over the printing office. After moving into the spacious Calgary Colonization Building on Railway Street, he published the *Crossfield Chronicle* regularly.

An Anglican Church was built in 1917 and the telephone exchange business progressed to twenty-four hour service. Following this period, the first of several devastating fires took place. The privately owned elevator built by Amery, Stooke and Gray (the Washington-Alberta Land Co.) burned down in 1919. Crossfield continued to prosper until January 4, 1924, when the main block of the business district was destroyed by fire. A second outbreak at 4 a.m. destroyed several other buildings.

Many old-timers have colourful personal stories to tell of this horrific event. Our own family's history is interwoven indirectly. A two-story building located on the south side of Hammond Avenue which over the years had housed the Imperial Bank, drugstore and grade one school room, escaped the fire that occurred in January. A blacksmith by the name of Gus Rettschlag had previously moved the building over to Nanton Avenue, placed it just west of his shop and converted it into a private dwelling. This property was sold to Bill Walker in 1943, ten years before we were married. Twenty years later, after our new home was finished, the old place was demolished and the lumber was donated to the Nose Creek Valley Museum in Airdrie, where it was used for display buildings.

Old timers while reminiscing always mention 1924, not only in reference to the January fire but also because the village was ravaged again in November by another fire of near equal ferocity. Some of the destroyed businesses were eventually replaced, while others never did get rebuilt. In spite of these terrible setbacks, Crossfield continued to grow. Several more grain elevators were constructed and additions to the existing ones completed. Two more garages were opened and a shoemaker moved to town. Unfortunately, over the years, Crossfield was damaged by bad fires on several other occasions.

The original townsite was classified as a regional centre, therefore the number of services provided by the local businesses was very high compared with what is offered today. The town was expected to provide all essential supplies as customers were unable to run into Calgary for a quick shopping trip. Road travel was difficult, and the cost of train fare was often too much for the average person. The town struggled to keep abreast of the times, installing electricity in 1928.

As an economic centre, Crossfield boasted a bank, post office, several stores as well as diverse other businesses. As an administrative centre the town had the municipal offices of the Rosebud Municipality (the previous name of the present Rocky View District), the telephone exchange, the fire hall, the town office and medical services by a doctor and a nursing home. There was also a town constable who operated a lock-up in the town office located above the fire hall which was located on Hammond Avenue. (The old fire hall was renovated into a private residence and is still in use.)

As a social centre, Crossfield was always first class. Even in the early days inhabitants of the village and the surrounding area enjoyed an active social life. There were dances and card parties held in school houses that dotted the countryside, sport days in summer and many excellent clubs and year round organizations. Some societies, such as the "Crossfield and District Oldtimers Association", which had its beginning in 1926, are still in existence today. Then there was the very popular "Dramatic Society". The town also had churches of the United (formerly Methodist), Catholic, Anglican and Baptist denominations, as well as a Masonic Hall, a pool hall, an undercover poker den, an outside skating rink, tennis courts and a dance hall. Then there was a hotel, a motel and several boarding houses.

Crossfield prospered with little change until the end of the Second World War. The roads and cars improved so that commuting to Calgary was much more practical. The original railway station which had been built in 1905 was burned down in an elevator fire in 1931. The later station, although it lacked the magnificence of the original, was run very efficiently. Travel of all kinds was now accepted and affordable. Crossfield remained a regional centre, but was starting to be affected by the urban growth of Calgary. New residential building took place with the town spreading west and northward, incorporating existing acreages, and expanding the present school sites. To the east, development was restricted by the C.P.R. railway tracks, and to the south by a sour gas well site. Expansion was also restricted on all sides but the north by extensive sloughs. These wetlands provided a sanctuary for game birds, grazing land for cattle and a place for the older children to have fun rafting, but were a big hindrance to future development. The only businesses to be established on the east side of the railway tracks were Joe Gilchrist's service station and a commercial enterprise pursued by Evertt Bills. In 1940, Bills' service station, cafe and motel complex was built in close proximity to the old Highway number 2, presently Highway 2A. The three motels were made out of renovated C.P.R. box cars. Later on, Bills moved a small house in from the country for Bill Walker, who was the first caretaker. Years later these buildings were converted into a facility for a fertilizer company.

After the war, the town's progress gradually started to falter. Business dropped off and many of the original companies closed their doors. This was mainly due to the rapid growth of Calgary and the invasion of modern transportation. Some local residents also tried to halt growth, fearing that Crossfield would lose its rural friendly character and become a bedroom community for Calgary. Two major undertakings took place during this period; water and sewer systems were installed in 1953 and natural gas came into use in 1956. These accomplishments rejuvenated the growth of the town substantially. The biggest impact on the surrounding rural area during this era was from oil and gas exploration. In the fall of 1967 the Amoco Gas Plant south of town was built and became a strong contributor to a stable economy. In the years since the plant went in, both company and community have grown together. But nothing could stop the inevitable; the front street of Crossfield was changing drastically.

In the mid 1970's, development occurred on a large scale. For the first time the town began to develop an industrial base in response to demand by investors. By this time, the surrounding sloughs had been largely drained, and a modern sewer system, installed in 1953, was running smoothly. The paving of the streets, in 1976, was another very expensive major undertaking, as Crossfield was built on boggy ground. An effort had to be made to get down to clay foundation and install a proper drainage system. Before this was achieved, the south entrance to the town had been moved twice. In the early days, the access road had crossed the tracks at the end of Nanton Avenue, connecting up to Elevator Road near the entrance to the stock yards. It was later moved south of Grey Avenue, but as the road was built on marshy ground, it too was subject to flooding. When the present Laut Avenue was built it became the southern town access with only minimal changes being made whenever it is upgraded. The warning lights at the railway crossing were set up later on. On the north side, the present route of Limit Avenue and the Madden Road location is unchanged since the founding of Crossfield in 1892.

Before further development could take place, the village had to ensure a plentiful supply of good water. On August 31, 1977, the village was connected to the Mountain View Regional Water System. Around 1980, nearly 400 acres of land was designated for residential development, with 10 acres for commercial use, 80 acres for industrial sites and 100 acres zoned for recreational and park use. This allowed the town to continue to grow during the 1980's and 1990's. During the following fifteen years, the rapid increase was seen especially in residential subdivisions, as commuters who worked in Calgary took advantage of the small town atmosphere of Crossfield. The Rocky View Senior Citizens Lodge which was built in 1964 became overcrowded, so ten rooms were added to the main lodge in 1983. A separate building which houses twenty-four apartments (Dr. Whillans Manor) was also created.

A great hindrance in Crossfield was the lack of recreational facilities. In more recent years a successful attempt has been made to rectify this problem. The town did have a curling rink and a nice hall, as the East Crossfield Community Hall had been moved to town in 1949 and renovated several times over the years. Then in 1977, the Pete Knight Arena was constructed; there activities such as hockey and figure skating take place in the wintertime and the very popular Farmers Market is held between May and October. This was followed by new schools with up-to-date gymnasiums, a multi-choice of restaurants, a modern library and the Golden Key Drop-In Centre for Seniors. The new ball diamonds and race track were direct results of the Big Country Summer Games which were held in Crossfield in 1989. All of this was topped in 1991 by a million dollar Community Centre.

The Pete Knight Rodeo Grounds are located near the camp grounds west of the industrial park. South of town, the new Collicutt Siding Golf Course, opened in 1995, is located on the former Kenley Jersey Farm (Stuart Walker Sr.'s old farmstead).

Of course as in all towns, many facilities fell by the wayside. Some of these closures may have retarded our town's growth, but on the other hand some can be chalked up to modernization. The R.C.M.P. barracks, for example, was moved to Airdrie permanently when they centralized their services in 1973, and the telephone office closed in 1974 when the automatic system became a reality. The high school was moved to Airdrie for twenty years, from 1962 to 1982, before it was eventually returned to Crossfield after the population surge.

Then there were dreams that never materialized, such as having our own Heritage Museum. It is very unlikely that this adventure will ever proceed even though it came close to reality on several occasions. When the C.P.R. decided to sell the old station in 1980, a feasibility study was done on the building. Although the station had only been built in 1931, it had become very dilapidated, so was considered not economical for use. Years later a second chance arose on May 1, 1991, when the old Crossfield Community Hall was closed after the new Centre opened. Some members of the Historical Society were involved for one year, in the controversy over turning the old Hall into a Museum. Their struggle was lost, and the sturdy old building was demolished on July 6, 1992.

Crossfield is now a small but substantial supply centre. The town can once again boast a variety of stores and services, bulk fuel and fertilizer facilities, a lumber yard, a machinery dealership, and garages, as well as a very active industrial enclosure. Many things have been done for the town without going into terrific debt to do it, such as the new sewage lagoon development and the more recent street improvement program. The proximity to Airdrie has become advantageous to our town, as we benefit from amenities they provide, without having to take on extra debt ourselves.

The Crossfield Fire Department can boast of a modern Fire Hall, trucks and the latest equipment. A far cry from the original acid and soda tanks mounted on wheels and pulled by hand. Bill Walker can vouch for this as he was a volunteer fireman for Crossfield for over 62 years.

On August 1, 1980, the Village was incorporated as a Town, as the population had then reached over 1000. Don Gatto was the Mayor when this historic day was reached. Crossfield's population continues to grow slowly but steadily, by about 50 people per year. In the 1980's when the town first instigated a long-range expansion plan, it was estimated that the present land site could accommodate up to 5600 people. The 1983 census showed a total of 1358 people living within the town's boundary. The figure had increased to 1800 by the year 1992. It is expected that Crossfield's population will be around 2000 when the next census is taken in May 1996. Thus, we still have plenty of room to grow.

In summary, land use in Crossfield has changed substantially over the years. Intended at first as simply a railway commercial centre, the town prospered with a large commercial base, but with little residential growth. The town went into decline during the 1930's, then showed a slight gradual improvement over the next forty years. During the 1970's an industrial park was established and started to draw in newcomers, and the residential development mushroomed.

Today, in spite of the small mercantile base, the process of decline has stopped. In the beginning Crossfield had a strong influence in the local area, but it is unlikely that the town will ever again experience the same degree of power. With its growing industrial centre and its ideal location near the busy Number 2 Highway, however, Crossfield could once again show a rapid growth pattern. Our future expansion depends on how well we promote our town.

Promotion of Crossfield has taken several forms. In 1974, the town sponsored a "Welcome to Crossfield" sign contest which ran province wide. After receiving several excellent designs, the council awarded first prize to Stuart Walker of Crossfield, a high school student. His design used the catchy phrase "Progress Through Friendship", which the town fathers later adopted as their trademark slogan. A large sign was erected and placed prominently at the northeast corner of Banta Park near the north entrance to the town, with smaller signs at the other two locations. The Chamber of Commerce used a design of the Crossfield sign on the letterhead of all correspondence in an effort to help the town council in their promotion strategy. Stuart received $15 and a certificate but what he valued was the honour of making a public statement for his town.

Crossfield celebrates its connection with Pete Knight, the rodeo champion. Pete Knight was raised on a farm east of Crossfield, having moved there with his parents when he was thirteen years old. His first competition was at Crossfield in 1917, and he went on to become a World Bucking Horse Champion. He won this title four times between 1924 and 1937, an honour never won by any other rider. Wilf Carter, the legendary cowboy singer and writer, made the names of the broncs Pete rode and the fact that he came from Crossfield famous.

To pay tribute to this famous, respected cowboy, Crossfield named its arena after him. When the Pete Knight Memorial Arena was officially opened on June 25, 1977, Babe Knight, Pete's widow, attended. She was the guest of honour and rode in an antique car at the head of the Pete Knight Days Parade. That evening Wilf Carter put on a concert with all profits going to the Arena.

Crossfield celebrated their 75th Anniversary in 1982 with a three day extravaganza! Hundreds of people attended the Homecoming Ceremonies and the excellent coverage by the media served as another opportunity to promote Crossfield. For the occasion, a Crossfield pin was designed by a local businessman, Alan Wilson. The pin featured Pete Knight on a bucking bronco with the slogan "Progress Through Friendship" in a semi-circle around the design. This pin, a large size version of the present-day Crossfield pin, became a sought after souvenir. The design was used as the model for the large sign used on the town float which was displayed in the parade, at the Homecoming, and in all subsequent parades held at the Annual Pete Knight Days, in June. This logo featuring Pete Knight and the slogan is also used on town trucks.

During the 1980's, the Economic Development Committee was formed to encourage and advertise Crossfield's achievements and prosperity. One of their excellent ideas was to run a town flag design contest involving the local schools. A grade three student named Darren Hinger, from the Crossfield Elementary School, won over the other 175 submissions. His simplistic drawing shows part of a red Maple Leaf flying against a green and yellow background representing grass and a farmer's field. A sheaf of wheat is superimposed on the Maple Leaf. In November 1988, the new flag was endorsed by the town council.

In 1994, it was decided to get a new town sign, one featuring Pete Knight on a bucking horse, which would be in harmony with the town's promotion theme. The old sign had served the town well for twenty years, so it was felt that the catchy phrase "Progress Through Friendship" would be used on the new sign as well. The slogan is very appropriate as Crossfield's progress can be credited mainly to its friendly atmosphere.

Friendliness and perseverance shaped the first community in 1892. The same characteristics are true today. The people who choose to live in Crossfield must be willing to participate and take advantage of all the activities and facilities that the town has to offer. Be enthusiastic, get involved and be a volunteer. Discover for yourselves that there isn't a better place in all Alberta to live.

Crossfield has had a fascinating past and all of the residents, including Johanna (Jo) Tennant, our first lady Mayor and myself, are looking to the bright and exciting future! Step into the past for a taste of small town life and journey into the future with us as we proudly demonstrate "Progress Through Friendship".

Submitted by Florence (Bigelow) Walker, 1996

Florence Walker has written many articles for the Nose Creek Historical Society. Her ideas for naming historic sites have also met with approval; she suggested the names for both the Dickson-Stevenson Rest Area and the Pete Knight Memorial Arena. She writes; "I have always been extremely interested in the history of Crossfield. I have gathered photographs, newspaper articles and souvenirs over the years. In 1990, David Hill, a Crossfield resident at the time, contacted me to look through my material. He was doing research for an article he was writing on Crossfield for a University Planning course. My thanks to David Hill for giving me his manuscript to help me in my summary of the history of Crossfield."

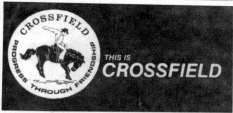

Legendary rodeo cowboy Pete Knight settled here as a young boy when his family discovered there wasn't a better place in all of central southern Alberta to raise a family. Everything is within walking distance but for those who occasionally hanker for 'the big city'. Calgary is less than an hour's drive away. Enjoy the fabulous mountain view and take advantage of all the activities and facilities geared to young families.

Step into the past for a taste of small town life and journey into the future with us as we proudly demonstrate -

"Progress through FRIENDSHIP"

A typical contemporary harvest scene.

Bales of straw for winter.

Amoco gas plant.

An aerial view of Airdrie (above and below).

Western Rock Bit Co. (above) manufactures vessels for storage of liquid petroleum gas products.

Pete Knight Memorial Arena.

Cowboys demonstrate their skills at the annual Crossfield Rodeo.

CHAPTER 32: "RAMBLING WITH RALPH"—THE STORY OF AIRDRIE

A Tribute to the Late Ralph McCall

Ralph McCall was born in Morrin, Alberta in 1925, but for most of his youth lived in Rumsey. He acquired part of his high school education at Eckville, and spent one year in the Signal Corps of the Canadian Army. In 1948 he graduated with a Bachelor of Education degree from the University of Alberta and began his teaching career in Acme, Alberta. He continued taking summer courses and in 1956 received his Master of Education degree. He was elected as the Calgary District Representative on the executive of the Alberta Teachers' Association from 1955-58 and in later years served as Professional Development Consultant. In 1958 he married Marilyn Gale, a fellow member of the Acme teaching staff and they eventually raised three children; Cheryl, Janet and Donald.

In 1963, the family moved to Red Deer where Ralph was on staff at the Red Deer Composite High School. A year later, they came to Airdrie and he taught for 21 years in George McDougall and Bert Church High Schools before retiring in 1985. In addition to his teaching duties, Ralph was active playing ball, curling and coaching volleyball, basketball and hockey. He sang in church choirs for at least 40 years.

When the Town of Airdrie came into being in 1974, Ralph served on the first planning commission. He was elected to Council in a by-election in 1976 and was chosen to serve as deputy mayor in 1977. His colleagues on council conferred this honour on him every year until his retirement in 1989.

In the following years he continued as a board member with the Nose Creek Valley Museum and enjoyed acting as museum guide for hundreds of touring children and seniors. In October 1992, Ralph was one of four Airdrians honoured with Canada's 125th Commemorative Medal for contribution to their community's well-being. He was also presented with an Integrity Award by the Rotary Club of Airdrie.

Always interested in history, Ralph was in the process of writing a book documenting the growth of Airdrie from a village to a city when he became ill with cancer and died in January 1995, with his book just half completed.

Submitted by Marilyn McCall, 1996

RAMBLING WITH RALPH

Section 1: Airdrie as a Village: 1964-1974

Early Airdrie

I moved to Airdrie in July of 1964. My previous knowledge of the village was limited. I was aware that many couples from Calgary visited the local hotel on weekends since mixed drinking by males and females was not permitted in cities. (This law came into effect in 1956 because alcohol related disturbances had increased. The law was abolished in 1967.) I also heard vague rumours that Airdrie had a race track in the middle of the village but it had disappeared by the time I arrived and Jensen Park now occupied the west end of the track.

In my teaching, before coming to Airdrie, I used Airdrie as an example of a location where the glacial ice from the Rockies and the ice sheet from Hudson Bay met. Evidence indicates that the ice sheet from Hudson Bay overran the mountain ice and moved several miles further west. Just to the northeast of Airdrie is a large erratic known as Split Rock. (In the early 1900's, Split Rock was a popular recreation area, but now few of the newcomers to Airdrie are even aware of its existence.) Geologists tell us that this rock came from the Jasper area and perhaps one may assume that its location marks the eastern limit of the ice sheet from the Rockies. If you should travel from Banff to Jasper, you may see, between the mountains, the snouts of glaciers which are remnants of the last great ice sheet that began melting about twelve thousand years ago. Apparently the melting of ice was completed in this area about eight thousand years ago.

Further proof of the ice age are the Sharp Hills or Buttes just a short distance southeast of Airdrie. You may see them on the east side of the road as you drive to Calgary. Pictures of these hills have

204

appeared in geology books as excellent examples of eskers which are made up of sand and gravel formed by streams under glacial ice. Some of my students have speculated that a giant dinosaur is buried under these hills, but other than their serpentine ridges there is no other scientific evidence to verify that theory.

In 1964 the transportation system in Airdrie was somewhat different from present day. We thought we were fortunate to have a four-lane undivided highway from Airdrie to Calgary. Today you can still see a portion of that highway, now called Edmonton Trail, which provides a north-south connection to Highway 2. If you think Edmonton Trail looks rather narrow for a main highway, consider the fact that as late as the 1950's much of the highway north was two-lane. (The Provincial Government let out the first contract for upgrading Highway 2 in 1924 and by 1938 it was hard surfaced.) As you can imagine, on weekends it was not uncommon to see lineups of cars two or three miles long travelling at 35 miles an hour. Highway 2 at that time went through all the small towns it could find, and you can still travel on parts of this highway which is now called Number 2A.

In 1964 the boundaries of Airdrie Village were Highway 2 on the east and the railway on the west. The boundary did skip west of the railway to include the grain elevators. The northern boundary was what is now Highway 567 and the southern boundary was just south of First Avenue South.

At that time there were four service stations serving Highway 2. Most of these service stations did a certain amount of garage work as well. On the east side of Highway 2 was an Esso station, as there is now, and on the west side of the Highway was a Shell station, a Texaco station (where the Turbo is now located), and Gordon Morris's Gulf service station and garage (now Petro Can) which remained in operation until 1980.

The only east to west road through Airdrie was First Avenue North. There was no North Overpass and people travelling from the east on Highway 567 had to turn south into Airdrie if they wished to proceed west. Big Springs Road from the east you might say terminated at Highway 2 although there was a dirt road, usually impassable in the spring, which continued on west. On one occasion a traveller had to go as far south as Balzac before he found a safe road to proceed west across Nose Creek.

Main Street was one block long between First Avenue North and Centre Avenue. There was a dirt trail which continued on south through pasture gates until it reached its destination - the village garbage dump or nuisance ground. Its present location would be on the east side of Main Street across from the Firehall. The trip to the dump could be a good nature study outing as you greeted the horses that came to meet you or you watched a family of foxes at play. On one occasion I observed a weasel making a successful kill of a gopher. Perhaps it is just nostalgia but I think a trip to the dump then was more interesting than driving down Main Street today.

Main Street North ended in a farmer's field. All the main roads were gravelled but none were paved. Even First Avenue North, once it crossed the tracks, was subject to flooding in the spring. After a few warm days in March, somewhere to the north, spring run-off waters would suddenly break loose and Nose Creek would rapidly become a few hundred feet wide. Water would come as far east as the present Main Street. A diversion of waters upstream and a straightening of the Nose Creek channel has probably alleviated the danger of flooding.

Early travellers were aware of high flood waters along Nose Creek. If you look along the base of the Sharp Hills (Buttes) as you travel south to Balzac you can see that the old Calgary to Edmonton Trail used by stage coaches was well above the spring flood plain. From the present highway the different coloured summer foliage indicates where the Trail was located. (Believe it or not in 1886 there was a stagecoach robbery near where Airdrie is today.) For stagecoaches it was a 'one day's journey' travelling from Fort Calgary to the Johnson-Stevenson Stopping House located just north of Airdrie. On the other hand, the slower bull trains could only travel half as fast and were forced to camp at the base of the buttes before continuing to the Stopping House.

The older homes today indicate the rather small populated area of Old Airdrie. In 1964 the only street of new houses was on 1st Avenue South from Smith Street to Allan Street. This was known as the Built-Rite home development on which construction began in 1959. Many of the original occupants still live there today. The Church of the Nazarene was built in this area in 1962.

Centre Avenue extended west of Main Street on a dirt road across a rather antiquated bridge to the railway station. To the north of the station was a scrap metal yard. (That area is now occupied by Airdrie Auto Dismantlers.) Also on the east side of the track near First Avenue North was a feed mill. On the west side of the track were a number of grain elevators. North of First Avenue North and west of the grain elevators was situated the Airdrie Golf and Country Club. This land was owned by Hugh Hamilton who had his real estate office located there for a short time. The course was never fully developed and its biggest drawback was that it was subject to flooding. The winter of 1969 was particularly cold with heavy snow. Airdrie was subject to wind chill readings of -70 degrees Fahrenheit. The next spring Nose Creek was in full flood and the golf course was covered by a huge lake. In later years the creek bed was straightened in the old golf course area as well as down stream in housing areas.

One block west of Main Street between Centre Avenue and 1st Avenue North was an older building containing two sheets of artificial curling ice. Directly to the east was an open air skating rink while to the south was a lumber yard that had seen better days. On the northwest side of Main Street was a small F.U.A. building and to the south was a Quonset hut which served as the community centre. (A picture of this building is hung on the wall of the Town and Country Centre.) Further south was a building jointly shared by the Fire Department and Calgary Power.

In the late 1960's Abe Klassen established a small Quonset hut on the west side of Main Street from which he did welding and manufactured iron works. The building remains there to this day although it now seems out of place. Abe's wife, Irene, ran a daycare nursery from her home on First Avenue South and later the couple built a new home and daycare centre northeast of Airdrie.

On the southeast corner of Centre Avenue and Main Street was a hotel (presently called "The Old Hotel") which photographs indicate was already there by 1907. To the north, on the east side of Main Street, the main buildings from south to north were Cooper's store, Jock's restaurant, Dusan's clothing store, Edward's barbershop and poolroom, and on the corner of First Avenue North and Main Street was a two storey building with the Bank of Nova Scotia on the bottom floor and living quarters above. In fact a number of businesses along Main Street had living quarters attached. Across the street on First Avenue was the new brick post office built in 1960, and just to the east was a two storey building with John Loveday's Jolly Shopper store on the bottom floor. Further east on First Avenue was Jim Lorimer's welding shop on the corner of Bowers Street. In the next block was the Airdrie United Church built in 1922 and beside it a Christian Education Building was in the process of being constructed. A block further East was the Airdrie Elementary and Junior High School providing accommodations for grades one to eight.

The only other major businesses in Airdrie were Tiger Torch on Centre Avenue owned by Frank Young (his propane heating torches are internationally known) and, on Edmonton Trail, a drive-in restaurant, a trailer court, E. Bowen's John Deere Agency, and Walter Moen's Massey-Ferguson Agency. Just off Edmonton Trail and west on First Avenue North was Bob Young's tire shop. On Edmonton Trail and north of Third Avenue North, Merv Stewart owned a large area of land and a maintenance building. The Stewart Equipment Company bought and sold large machinery across Canada and the United States with offices in many other urban centres. The business at times employed 40 or more people. (East on Yankee Valley Road, at the Airdrie Airport, ATCO employed 500 people. Jefferson Lake Petrochemicals to the north also employed a large number of people.)

On the north side of Third Avenue North and Virginia Street was the George McDougall High School where grades nine to twelve were taught. (The school was named after an early missionary who worked and died in this area.) The school commenced operations in 1962. Students were bussed from Calgary's boundary on the south, to Madden on the west, and Crossfield on the north. Many people of Crossfield were particularly unhappy to see the town lose its high school although Crossfield was a larger urban centre than Airdrie.

Airdrie - 1964-1974

This then was Airdrie in July of 1964. I considered myself fortunate that Calgary Rural School Division had a three bedroom bungalow teacherage on Centre Avenue that was available for me. They also owned the large two storey home just to the east which was built in 1920 by L. Van Sickle (father of Heloise Lorimer) a former store owner and Reeve of Airdrie. It was the first home I had seen with a dumb-waiter. The building was made into a duplex for a while but when so many teachers preferred living in Calgary, it was converted back to a single family home. To the west of my house was the home of Frank Young, the owner of Tiger Torch. His house was once the property of the legendary figure Dr. W.F. Edwards. Dr. Edwards served the Airdrie district from 1907 until his untimely death in 1940.

Just west of the Young home was a two storey house, a bit the worse for wear, that was built about 1900. It was originally a confectionery store, then a laundry, then a jewelry store. In 1932 it became an A.G.T. office and home for Ernie and Inez Clayton. Thereafter it was a residential building. Finally in 1970 Ernie and Gloria Martin had the building torn down and replaced by a new house.

Across the road from me was another of the very early homes in Airdrie and just to the east of it was the home of Ernie and Inez Clayton. They had moved there in 1941 and until 1962 Inez ran the switchboard exchange from this house on the corner of Centre Avenue and Smith Street. In 1962 the automatic switchboard came into use and local operators were no longer required.

I felt fortunate to live in such an area when many of these early pioneers and their families were still present in the district.

For the next ten years the land south of me was a large open area within village limits and south of that was Jensen's grain field. (On more than one occasion a helicopter landed in the open area behind my back yard and the pilot had coffee with his friend who lived next door to me.) At the south end of the field was a line of poplar trees a few of which can still be seen today. In the spring the children would be out in these open areas flying kites and it seemed to me that my yard, which had no fence, stretched all the way to Calgary.

Airdrie Council

When I arrived in Airdrie it was a village with a population of 678 according to the 1963 census. (In 1911 Airdrie had a population of 250 but after that the population hovered around 200 and as late as 1959 the population had only risen to 309) Until Airdrie became a town the mayor was selected by Council and referred to as "Reeve". The Reeve in 1964 was Bob Edwards and his councillors were William Peever and J. R. Johnson. Only three people served on Council until 1965, when five people were elected. The Councillors elected at that time were Bob Edwards, Pat Bennett, Gordon Morris, Walter Moen, and Hugh Hamilton. Bob Edwards remained as Reeve. Pat Bennett was the first woman elected to Council in Airdrie. Many people are probably not aware that she spent three years on Council before her husband Darrell became involved in politics.

Village Council held its regular meetings in the small F.U.A. building on Main Street. The Village Secretary in 1964 was Norman McCracken. In the summer of 1966 the Village opened a new civic centre on the south-west corner of First Avenue North and Bowers Street. The building provided office space, council chambers, a police station and a garage for maintenance vehicles and fire trucks. This was the first time that the R.C.M.P. were stationed in the Village.

In the 1968 election the Councillors elected were Bob Edwards, Walter Moen, Gordon Morris, Norman Mosley and Howard Stapley. Bob Edwards remained as Reeve until 1971 when Walter Moen was chosen. In the 1971 fall elections the Councillors elected were Darrell Bennett, Jim Dunne, Charles Campagne, Don Grisbrook and Norman Mosley. Darrell was selected as Reeve. It was during the term of this Council, in 1974, that Airdrie became a town.

Since the early sixties Norman McCracken had been Secretary-Treasurer of the Village of Airdrie. (Norm was born in Airdrie and his father, J.R. McCracken, had been Reeve at one time.) As the Village grew, his wife, Elaine, assisted him in the office. However, Norman's health deteriorated and thus in April of 1973 Dennis King was hired as Assistant-Secretary. It was hoped that he would learn the job over the next few months. Later in the year Norman died. McCracken Crescent is named in honour of the family.

A few months later Rita Cota was hired to assist in the office and some time after that Darlene Hilt and Joyce Hiebert were added to the office staff.

Airdrie Utilities

A water and sewage system came to Airdrie in 1959. A lagoon for the sewage was established west of the tracks. There were five wells within the Village to supply the water and a Tower was built to store water for emergency purposes. On a hot summer day the water pressure was almost non-existen Water rationing went into effect. Part of the reason for the lack of pressure in the six inch water lin was due to insufficient elevation of the Water Tower. (The western part of the Village had more pres sure since there is a 65 foot drop between the Tower location and the railway track.) In 1967 a new we was dug that recorded 25 gallons per minute thus producing almost as much as the other five put to gether. Shortly after that a seismic crew drilling in the ditch west of Airdrie struck a flowing well whic they found difficult to cap. Walter Moen felt this was the answer to our water supply and he persuade Council to drill on a location just south of First Avenue North and almost as far west as our present Cit boundary. On the fourth try the drillers hit a gusher that was pumped at a hundred gallons a minute fo a long period of time. It was later recorded as 50 gallons a minute. It appeared Airdrie had conquere the water problem.

The Village purchased two acres at that site from Lorne Fowler. Unfortunately the drilling of th new well affected his water supply and he was forced to drill a new well to a greater depth. Whe Airdrie went on Calgary City water, in March of 1976 (officially August, 1977), the level in the rur wells returned to its original depth.

An interesting aside of the well drilling story is the different versions of the final moments. Th story that I had heard at the time of the event was that the well was dry at night but in the morning th water had broken through. Other very reliable sources said that the drillers went to dinner and whe they returned the water had appeared. The two drillers, George Becker and Fred Portmann, have sin told me that they struck the water after dinner in the normal process of drilling. You can believe whic ever story you wish. Such is the basis of all good legends.

Perhaps this is the time to discuss divining or witching wells. In the aforementioned drilling the fir three holes had been properly witched with a forked willow branch. When a diviner walks over stream of underground water, the fork twists in his hand and dips downward. However in this case th first three wells were not satisfactory, so George Becker threw his Copenhagen "snoose" box over h shoulder and drilled where it landed. That was the successful well. Other instruments that have bee used in divining are a crowbar, chains, a rubber hose, and in one case a gentleman said his wire fram glasses twisted on his head when he walked over water. Another method is to hold a copper wire each hand and when they cross each other that is the place to drill. As you might guess some peop swear by their methods and others swear at them. But you can't beat success.

In 1972 a 500,000 gallon reservoir was built at what is now the south end of Fletcher's Park. Aft this there was little need for the much smaller and inefficient 40,000 gallon water Tower reservoir. I 1977 it was no longer used to store water. Today the Tower stands as a well known Airdrie landma

In the fall of 1974 the Nose Creek Historical Society placed a stone cairn near the Water Tower commemorate the hundredth anniversary of the R.C.M.P. (In 1874 the Force was known as the Nor West Mounted Police.) At that time the R.C.M.P. station was located just west of the Tower. The V lage Council responded in a letter to Redvers Perry of the Historical Society that the property where t Water Tower is located would not be sold for one hundred years. This seems to insure that the Wat Tower will remain standing.

In 1964 there was no garbage collection. Each household had a burning barrel and when it becar rather full the home owner hauled it to the garbage dump. However, there was a village bylaw whi forbade people burning garbage on Monday since that was traditionally wash day and people hung th laundry out on the clothesline to dry. It wasn't until 1966 that the village set up a regular garbage colle tion.

Natural gas and electricity in Airdrie were provided by private companies.

In the early part of 1971 an oil company drilled a well just off the dump road (now Main Street)

on what is now Tower Lane Mall property. They flared gas from a long pipe for a short time and then plugged the well. If we run short of gas, we haven't far to go to find more. There is also a large field of excellent quality coal lying in a deep underground vein stretching from Calgary to Crossfield. Perhaps sometime in the distant future this energy may be recovered by such means as coal gasification.

Public Works

By 1960 Airdrie had re-organized a fire brigade with a new fully equipped fire engine. The executive of the Fire Department consisted of both village and rural members and all fire fighters were volunteers. Since there were no paid employees, a number of local ladies, usually firemen's wives, answered the fire phones and sounded the siren. Heloise Lorimer and Ruth Fletcher were on standby night and day. In later years with younger members on the brigade there were complaints to the paper that a number of volunteers were creating a hazard by driving too fast to the fire hall when the siren sounded. All the roads were still gravelled and on a dry summer day a cloud of dust descended on the fire hall. Even in later years when I dealt with the fire department I felt they were a pretty "gung ho" bunch but we were thankful for their enthusiasm when they were asked to risk their lives fighting fires. If they needed additional water, especially in the rural areas, Bob Miller would supply a tanker truck to haul water free of charge.

In 1966 the Village purchased some land and extended Main Street for two blocks north. Lots were sold at $500 each for those who wished to build houses along the west side of the road. By 1970 a number of houses had been built. In November 1967 a 24 stall trailer park to accommodate semi-permanent residents was opened on the northern limits of the development, and by the end of the year it was fully occupied. An additional 24 stalls were provided in 1968. The private trailer park on Edmonton Trail closed down. In 1970 Highway 567 was extended west of the overpass and Main Street was extended northward to meet with 567. With traffic now able to use the north overpass, construction in the area quickly increased.

In 1967 as a Centennial Project, a beautification and tree planting program took place in the west end of the park and a wading pool was added. The area was named Knud Jensen Park in honour of a citizen who was on Village Council from 1943 to 1961. Half of that time he served as Reeve. His home, surrounded by a beautiful grove of trees and a big red barn, still stands on the northern edge of Old Airdrie. Knud died suddenly in 1965 but his wife Lily still plays a large part in community affairs and won the award for "Woman of the Year" in 1991.

In 1968 the outdoor skating rink was moved to Jensen Park and positioned where the Plainsmen Arena now stands. The next year a cinder block change building was erected at the west end of the open air community rink. (The building is now part of the Plainsmen Arena.) A dedication ceremony and ice carnival took place on Sunday February 8, 1970 with "Buckshot" of CFCN TV as the Master of Ceremonies.

The RCMP had been confined to rather tight quarters in the Airdrie Civic Centre since 1966. In 1971 the Village built a police station by the Tower. It was large enough for municipal police as well as the Highway Patrol.

In 1973 there were eight members of the RCMP stationed in Airdrie. Five patrolled the highway and three were on general patrol in the Town. That year Sergeant Bracewell and Corporal Buchanan were posted to Airdrie. Corporal Buchanan spent most of his time heading the highway patrol while Sergeant Bracewell was in charge of the detachment. Both men became leaders in the community. Laurie Bracewell was very concerned about social problems and worked hard in the field of preventive crime. His superiors were not always supportive of his actions. Laurie resigned from the RCMP in 1979 and left Airdrie for other employment. Herb Buchanan resigned from the RCMP in 1978 but fortunately for Airdrie he and his wife, Doris, remained in the community and continued to play a large part in community activities. Joe Paul of the RCMP and his wife Wendy came to Airdrie in 1975. They have continued to live in Airdrie since that time although Joe retired from the RCMP in 1994. Wendy acts as a Justice of the Peace, conducting occasional weddings.

On October 14, 1971 the Airdrie Library was formed. Nine groups and clubs agreed to provide financial backing with the Women's Community Club becoming the official supporting organization. In December Village Council passed a bylaw establishing a Municipal Library. A room 13 feet by 15 feet was provided in the new police station. (Perhaps this prompted people to return books on time.) The first Library Board included Joanne Baxter, Marilyn Mazza, Dick Clapperton, Marge La Marsh, and Charles Campagne and the first volunteer Librarian was Marg Jensen. A host of other volunteers assisted. Most of the original 2400 volumes were used books. In the fall of 1972 the library moved to larger quarters — a little white building by Gordon Morris's service station. There was a concrete floor and no plumbing but the extra space was appreciated.

Schools

I found George McDougall High School a welcome relief from what I considered overcrowded classrooms in Red Deer Composite. (On one occasion I had a list of 46 potential students at the beginning of a trimester). In Airdrie the classes were much smaller in number and since you had the student for the whole school year you could become acquainted personally and in many cases get to know the family as well. Not all teachers enjoy that personal touch, but I always felt it was to my advantage to become part of the community.

The principal of George McDougall at the time was Frank Morrell. He loved to joke with the staff before classes in the morning. He was fair with students, but firm as an administrator. However, on one occasion I saw him very irritated when loud electronic music was first introduced at school dances. He told the members of the orchestra to either turn it down or go home. He was ably assisted by Guy Doll who was also a no nonsense administrator. Perhaps the most strict teacher of them all was Mae Masters - a grade 9 teacher who demanded that the students give their best efforts, and their excellent marks on departmental exams proved they did. The oldest member of the staff was a kindly cigar smoking gentleman by the name of Ben Halbert. Ben could get riled though, for I remember one occasion when he came to the principal's office while I was there and complained to Frank about the actions of two boys in his class. Frank listened sympathetically and then suggested that Ben sit in the staff room for a while before returning to class. Ben sat in the big chair, lit up a cigar and blew smoke rings. That was the closest to "blowing off steam" that I ever witnessed. I think the best laugh Frank had was on "dress up" day when Ben and I went on stage as a couple. Ben was dressed as a Swiss youth in short pants and I was dressed as Little Miss Muffet on a pogo stick. Teachers can have a little fun too, you know.

Also on staff was Jean Roberts, wife of a former principal in Airdrie. Jean was a great community worker and choir leader. Nev Lyons came on staff the same year I did and has remained on high school staff until the present time.

Airdrie Elementary and Junior High had as its principal Norman Reddekopp. On his staff were a number of excellent teachers who had spent most of their professional years in this area and continued teaching in Airdrie until their retirement. These teachers were Bernice Shuttleworth, Lillian Edwards, Hilda Clapperton, Emily Duncan, and Myrtle Moen. Many of the graduates from this school still speak of how their lives were enriched by the dedication of these people.

When I arrived in Airdrie, the Chairman of the Board of Calgary Rural School Division No.41 was Bert Church who was a school trustee from 1951-1964. I had first met him many years previously when I represented a teacher for the Alberta Teachers' Association in a dismissal case. Although we had been on opposite sides of the table at that time, we found humour in the situation some years later when reviewing the circumstances. Bert Church was a capable dedicated leader and it was appropriate that the next high school built was named after him.

Mrs. Bert (Alexa) Church was president of the McDougall Home and School Association during the late 1960's. W.S. Korek was the Superintendent of Schools at that time.

In 1966 Guy Doll left George McDougall and Blaine Askew became the new vice-principal. Frank Morrell who had been principal of George McDougall since its opening in 1962 resigned in June of 1970. During those eight years Frank ran a very successful school. Classes were kept to a reasonable size and students' results on examinations were very good. The school excelled in divisional sports and it was expected that Airdrie would win at the track meet. The parent-teacher relationship was also very close. But changes were coming. Class numbers were increasing. In 1969 the semester system was introduced and also that year students were given credit for work on special projects. The young people were being allowed more freedom than ever before. Frank approved of some of these changes but I think he felt it was time to let younger hands do the guiding.

The new principal was Ron Dunglison, an Australian, who was a disciple of the new school of thought which gave the student much more freedom. Bob Lang who had already been on staff for a number of years became the new vice-principal. Bob belonged more to the old school of thought and thus became the disciplinarian. He gave some balance to the administrative team. In 1965 Leighton Perry became the Airdrie school trustee and later the Board Chairman. He remained on the Board for nine years, retiring in 1974.

In the Airdrie Elementary and Junior High, Norm Reddekopp was principal until 1970 when Alex Semenoff was hired for the position. Alex remained with the school until 1979. Both of these teachers were rewarded for their excellent work as administrators by being promoted to Head Office.

In September of 1970 my daughter, Cheryl, came home to announce that she was the captain of the newly-formed School Patrol Team. First Avenue North was probably the busiest road in Airdrie.

With the growth of the Village came the growth of school population. Crossfield's expansion and the increase in acreages in the rural area also added to the crowded conditions in Airdrie classrooms.

In 1967 an addition was made to the Airdrie Elementary and Junior High to accommodate the two grade 9 classes that had been in George McDougall. This proved to be a short term solution and in 1972 Edwards Elementary School was built.

The new school was named in honour of Airdrie's pioneer doctor—Dr. W.F. Edwards. It was also a tribute to the Edwards family. Dr. Edwards' sister, Nellie Pole, came to Airdrie in 1910 and was very active in the community. She was also well known for her contribution of awards - especially to education. (At age 85 she still drove her own car.) Roy Edwards, brother of Dr. Edwards, and his wife Lillian had both been school teachers in the district. (Lillian taught for 39 years and still managed to raise a family.) Their three children still lived in the Airdrie area at that time. They were Bob (former Reeve of Airdrie), Don, and Bernie (Morison). All of them played a very active part in community affairs.

The official opening ceremonies took place December 6, 1972. The principal at the time was Metro Dmetrichuk. The president of the Airdrie Home and School Association, Marilyn McCall, made a number of presentations.

During the period 1964-1974 teachers in the Edwards School and Airdrie Elementary-Junior High who served for a number of years were: Jim Black, Frances Neil, Marie Scott, Joan Bailey, Marilyn Dahl, Loreen Hamilton, Rhoda Schlender, Sally Ruttle, Vola Farquharson, Donna Patrick, Paul Krueger (his students knew how to do push-ups), Giselle Gerlitz, Al Kratz, Estelle Dodd, Lynn Jackson, Don Cooper and Ed Pluemeck. Another teacher at that time was Linda O'Neill, a graduate of George McDougall, who went on to become a school trustee. Also in 1974 Ray Bryden taught aeronautics and as a reward for top marks his students received one hour of flying instruction.

George McDougall teachers who served for a number of years were: Connie Allen, Vern Befus, Verne Friesen, Ethel Friesz (Mrs. Barnett), Bill Pauls, Vic Bonnet, Nancy Rush, Don Schultz, Larry Sorensen and Gabe Ziegler. Two excellent band masters were Dan Brown and George Kuperis both of whom stayed only a short while. We also had on staff Joe Forzani who at that time played with the Calgary Stampeders football team. He and his brothers Tom and John were outstanding football players. In the winter a number of the football players who lived in Calgary would play exhibition games with the Airdrie high school boys basketball team.

Spence Morris and Don Edwards were long-term school custodians. Arlene Wood has continued as teacher-aid and school librarian for many years. In George McDougall School, Shari Arnold and Marilea Perry were the secretaries.

In 1967, W.S. Korek was followed by E.M. Erickson as School Superintendent and in 1970, Jack MacDonell was hired for that position.

In 1973, the Rocky View Further Education Council was formed. In the first year all courses were held in Airdrie. On the Council from Airdrie were Betty Davis (Chairman),Dawne Dunglison, Marilyn McCall, Virginia McKinnon and Jim Davis. Although confined to a wheelchair, Betty Davis took an active part in community activities and her husband, Jim Davis, missing one arm, was still a competent Shop teacher. Jim wrote a book about the life of the famous Crossfield cowboy— Pete Knight.

The Railway

The first train passed through Airdrie August 23, 1891. The original line was known as the Calgary and Edmonton Railway. It was sold to the C.P.R. in 1903. Airdrie was a favourite stopping spot for the steam locomotives since a dam on Nose Creek provided a good supply of non-alkaline water. In the early 1950's there were four passenger trains a day each way.

The trip I remember best was riding the "Midnighter". You could board the train in Calgary any time after 10:00 p.m. and go to sleep in your berth. When you awoke in the morning the train was sitting on a side track by the station in Edmonton. After using the bathroom to wash and shave you would be ready to face a day's work when you left the train. Now that was comfort! I still think it is better than driving to and from airports and waiting for planes. The morning train could get you from downtown Calgary to downtown Edmonton in less than three hours.

By 1960 the old steam locomotives between Calgary and Edmonton were replaced by diesel engines. Later in the 1960's the passenger train with the locomotive was replaced by the Dayliner. Each unit was self-contained and could be driven from either end. There were usually two units on each train through Airdrie. It travelled at great speed — much too fast for level crossings. A number of times when I travelled to Edmonton we were involved in accidents — once four youths in a car were killed. The last station agent in Airdrie was John Schmal who has been an alderman in the City of Calgary for a number of years. The train did not normally stop in Airdrie so John had to issue a train order to stop for a passenger. John left Airdrie in 1968 and shortly after that the station was torn down. The Dayliner with its dwindling number of passengers made fewer and fewer trips. Its last run was September 5, 1985. (Bob McCaskill, originally a Crossfield boy and now a retired railroad engineer, provided me with much of this information.)

People and Events

In 1964 the postmaster was Gordon Bevan who was assisted by his wife Vera. (Gordon also found time to work on the Village Council as well as on the fire department.) After 21 years of postal service, he retired in 1978.

The first manager of the Bank of Nova Scotia that I remember was Al Lawther. He came to Airdrie in 1962. Al was very active in community affairs and a member of Village Council. In 1970 he gave up banking to become an accountant with Miller's Trucking. He was replaced by Bob Tronsgaard who stayed until 1974 when he left to go into the store business. In 1992 we had a neighbourhood reunion of people who lived in our area during the early seventies. Among those attending with their families were Bob and Evelyn Tronsgaard, Bob and May Bannerman, Bob and Bev Bailey, Wanda Klassen, Gordon and Vera Bevan and our family, the McCalls.

Fortunately for the office staff, the new civic centre built in 1966 was kitty-corner to the residence of Heloise Lorimer, who often sent over samples of some of her home baking. Mrs. Lorimer was the first child born in Airdrie. She and her husband Jim married in the early thirties and, because of a shortage of money, took seven years to build their house. There were no mortgages involved. Lorimer's garage was just across the road from the house. Jim operated the business for 50 years until his death in 1971. Heloise celebrated her 80th birthday in 1992 and extended an invitation to everyone to come to her 90th birthday. Her home is still a drop-in centre for friends who wish conversation, coffee, and pastry or home-made bread.

The school bus drivers were an important group of people in a small village. Believe it or not Heloise Lorimer drove the first school bus which in fact was an old Cadillac. Except for backing out of the garage with the door closed, she apparently did rather well. During my early years in Airdrie some of the drivers that I remember were Opal and Bob Edwards, Don Edwards, Gordon

Morris, Spence Morris and Ward and Ki Dryden. In 1969 Ward was preparing for the afternoon school bus trip when he had a heart attack and died.

I remember talking to John Loveday shortly after his friend's death, and he said he would have to get out of the store business or he would be next. John did an amazing amount of business from his small Jolly Shopper store and this resulted in extensive hours of work. On a Saturday there would be long lines of cardboard boxes, filled with groceries, standing along one side of the main aisle. These had been packed for people who phoned in their orders. That fall John rented the store to Louie Menagozza and in 1972 he sold his business to Stan Yee. (John served on the Village Council from 1953 to 1962 - the last four years as Reeve. He died in 1990.)

Another important person in the community was the news reporter who kept everyone informed in some detail about all the local activities. Most of these reporters were long time residents so no one moved in or out of town but that you would hear about it. When I came to Airdrie the correspondent for the *Rocky View Times* was Mrs. Mildred Drummond. Unfortunately in February of 1969 some friends arriving for an evening meeting found her dead in her home. The amiable Marge La Marsh became the next correspondent and she kept that position until 1978 when ill health forced her to resign. She died shortly afterwards. Margaret Kinniburgh, an old time resident, followed as correspondent but by this time the town was growing in size and the personal touch of the newspaper column was being eroded. However, Redvers Perry of Balzac has produced a personal rural column in the local paper I believe since newspapers were first invented, but Redvers says it was really just since 1957. He still writes material and has kept copies of his columns which are a series of local history books in themselves.

In October 1972, the *Tri-Neighbour Press* was published covering events in Airdrie, Cochrane, Crossfield and surrounding areas, but this venture did not prove to be successful.

When Airdrie became a town, there was a feeling in the community that we should have our own newspaper to cover local events in more detail. As a result, the Airdrie and District Peoples' Service Council published a monthly pamphlet style newsletter beginning in December of 1974. Called *The Community News*, it was published throughout 1975. Probably the need for the paper diminished when Andy Marshall began publishing the *Airdrie Echo* in November of that year. An interesting observation is that the acting editor of *The Community News*, Ellen Johnstone, later became a reporter for the new *Airdrie Echo*. Ellen was able to maintain a personal touch with people and events in the community.

Airdrie was fortunate in having a very well qualified music teacher. Mrs. Elizabeth Neil, who came to Airdrie in 1907, taught music until shortly before her death in 1975. One of her students was Lorne Fowler who has been the organist at the United Church for almost sixty years. Mrs. Neil's husband, Ken, at one time held the position of Village Secretary.

Villages often lack specialists but there is usually someone you can call on in time of need. If your furnace stopped working - night or day - you called Sid Howe, although farming was his regular occupation. I remember one summer afternoon when Marilyn was baking some cookies, there was a flash of blue light in the kitchen and the electric stove quit working. Sid arrived on the scene and found a wee mouse had contacted a bare wire. It apparently came in the door the kids had left open. The word must have got out to the mouse kingdom about the electrocution for ne'er a mouse has appeared in our house since that time.

If you wanted any carpentry work or painting done you called Jim Morris. He always took pride in his work and was sure to leave his workplace neat and tidy. Jim, who has never really retired, is still the United Church custodian.

An event of 1966 was the coming of Bill and Libby Bice to town. They were Texans but Bill's work brought them to many parts of the world. He was in charge of the construction of the Crossfield sulfur plant. I marvelled at their ability to adjust to a new community. The first Sunday they went to Church they walked to the back at the end of the service, shook hands with the minister, and then proceeded to shake hands and introduce themselves to everyone in the congregation. Within a short time they were heavily involved in church and community activities. Both sang in the senior choir and Libby organized a junior choir. (Bill said the greatest sight in the world was a breeze rippling across a wheat field on a sunny fall day in Alberta.) When they left in 1968, Bill had his construction company donate a building to the Boy Scouts to be used as a Scout Hall. This building was then moved to a location close to where the Anglican Church now stands.

Whenever I hear anyone say that it is hard to make acquaintances in a small town, I think of Bill and Libby. When I first came to Airdrie I was told it was difficult to get to know the old timers, but that is exactly the group Bill and Libby dealt with.

There were only two church buildings in the village between 1964 and 1974 - the United Church and the Church of the Nazarene.

The United Church minister I remember best was Norm Radway who arrived late for church one Sunday morning to announce that he was now the father of twin girls. In the summer of 1972 Norm and family were travelling in Ontario when their Volkswagon van broke down. As they were being towed away, Norm sat with the truck driver while his own family rode in the van behind. Fire broke out in the van and a passing motorist flagged down the tow truck driver who was unaware of the frantic commotion behind him. Fortunately no one was injured. Janice Radway, Debby Clayton and my daughter Cheryl were inseparable friends.

The minister I remember best from the Church of the Nazarene was Reverend Titterington.

The Catholic congregation met in George McDougall School in Airdrie as early as 1965. They were a mission of Carstairs. In 1969 they formed their own St. Paul's Catholic Church parish and began holding services in the United Church. The times of worship of the two churches did not clash and the congregations met for coffee and fellowship between the two services. Father McCarty told the story of the first mass in the church. At the moment when the congregation was supposed to kneel he looked down and the people had disappeared. The United Church had no 'kneelers'. Thereafter the motto "when in Rome do as the Romans do" was adopted and henceforth there was no more kneeling.

The three churches in town in 1971 began having a joint Christmas service. The participants I best remember through the years were choir leaders Jean McElroy and Linda Verhaege, and soloists Margaret Giles of the United Church and Barbara Bradley of the Church of the Nazarene. The best known duet singers were Bruce and Joyce Harris of the United Church and Bill and Pat Jeffray of the Catholic Church. Lorne Fowler, organist, and Karen Becker pianist were the best known accompanists.

The Airdrie Lions Club, chartered February 25, 1965, attempted to give the community something to celebrate by sponsoring a barbecue on Farmer's Day in 1966. The event was snowed/rained out. However, the next year was Canada's Centennial Year and the large parade and Sports' Day organized by the Lions was greeted by excellent weather. Cliff Tebb on a black horse led the parade and he was followed by two riders holding a banner proclaiming "Airdrie's Celebration" in large letters and underneath "1867 - 1967". (I mentioned Cliff Tebb on a black horse because in subsequent years he rode a palomino.) The Sports' Day was held in Jensen Park.

July 1 parades have continued ever since 1967 with Cliff Tebb and Allen Fletcher playing a prominent part in their organization. The Sports' Day was expanded to include Gymkana and an evening dance and in 1976 amateur rodeo joined the celebrations with the first one held at the Auction Mart grounds in east Airdrie. I remember coming home covered in dust. In 1968 the Calgary Stampede did not hold infield events on Sunday. That year Airdrie held a Sunday stampede and had a number of top riders participated, including Dean Oliver, six-time world champion calf roper. In later years the rodeo was held on the land where Towerlane Mall is now located and also on locations west of the tracks. It never found its present home west of town on the landfill site until 1981.

Celebrations on Centennial Day were marred somewhat when Torry Fletcher broke his arm while falling into the "dunk tank". To this day the injury still gives him trouble. However, Torry was always a man of action. Our next door neighbour, Alanna Hamilton, was having trouble with her saddle horse so Torry offered to break it in. Somehow the horse got its head down and bucking horse and rider came leaping through our garden while we stood on the back step in wonderment. Only in a small town can you see such action so close to home.

About that same time I was lying in bed on a peaceful Saturday morning when suddenly the quiet was broken by a loud "Moo". When I recovered my wits, I jumped up to look out the open window and came face to face with a cow. In fact there was a large herd of cattle in the yard next door. After a phone call to a local farmer the cattle were soon home from their urban visit. You know now why I put up a fence when I purchased my home.

Through the late 1960's and 1970's it was not uncommon to see the flying Claytons over Airdrie. Frank and his three sons Sterling, Brian, and Melvin were often seen spraying crops nearby. Actually they worked over much of the province. On one occasion Melvin had an accident with his plane but his worst discomfort occurred when ambulance personnel wrapped him in a woollen blanket to which he was allergic. Some of the aerial photos of Airdrie at this time were taken from Clayton planes.

Another flying group of the early 1970's was the Tom Conroy family. Tom purchased the Airdrie Airport in 1971 and he, his wife Gwen, son Tom, and daughter Beverly were all excellent pilots. It was a thrill, especially for World War II veterans, to see as many as four Harvards flying in formation on special occasions such as July 1. Their flying became the subject of a special television program. Unfortunately Tom Conroy died in a plane crash in 1979 but his family carried on the operation of the airport as well as the tradition of flying.

Charlie Campagne taught in the High School (after being vice-principal of the Junior High School for a period of time) and also served on Village Council. Charlie had a spirit of adventure. He built his own house when others thought he didn't have the necessary skills. Later he left teaching to go into real estate. At one time he promoted a large urban centre near Chestermere Lake although his plans never materialized.

I remember in the early seventies watching some boys in the stubble field to the south. I thought they were attempting to drown gophers when suddenly the stubble was ablaze. The fire trucks soon arrived to put out the fire. What I hadn't realized was that the boys had set fire to gasoline in an attempt to smoke out the gopher. Edwin Gibeau still carries the burn scars of that episode.

Another incident of those years involved my four-year-old son Donald (a Centennial baby) and Holly, the girl next door. One hot summer day they crawled into the toolbox in the back of her brother's truck. Down came the lid and the clasp and they were locked in. Fortunately the brother heard a noise and looked in the box before he drove away. The children were already suffering from heat exhaustion.

In 1971 Arne Nielsen moved his Shell Station business to the old Texaco Station (now the Turbo) that had been run by Frank Cool. He made major renovations including a new coffee shop. Emery ran this restaurant which was famous for "Grandma's" soup and banana cream pies. People would come out from Calgary to eat there. Arne set up an old gasoline pump for viewing purposes only, and also a "dog restroom" complete with fire hydrant.

Arne had quite a sense of humour and strange things often happened when he was around. (I am sure he couldn't have been directly involved.) One gentleman who had been into "the sauce" a bit heavily one night awoke the next morning to find a large number of fried chicken boxes in the back seat of his car. He was informed that he had purchased them on credit the night before to feed his friends. (Actually they came out of the garbage barrel.) He then proceeded to the local drive-in to pay his bill.

Another gentleman who lived along the Number 2 Highway north of Airdrie was complaining about how close the new highway was coming to his house. He returned home one day to find surveyor stakes running right past his front door. (These were put there by some of his 'friends'.)

Changes in the Downtown Area

During the latter part of the 1960's there were a number of changes in the downtown area. A fire burned out the buildings on Main Street where the Royal Bank now stands. The old A.E. Bowers building was part of that loss. Jock, who ran the restaurant on Main Street, was injured in a car crash while on his way to Calgary and his wife was killed. Dusan Multinovic purchased Jock's building, which was adjacent to his.

In l967, Calgary Power erected a new building on First Avenue North which today is Natily's Laundromat.

In 1970, Merv Stewart sold his Equipment Company building to the "Recon Centre". This new company held regular sales of used Chrysler vehicles.

Many people can remember the times when the Stewarts held an annual pre Calgary Stampede barbecue with guests coming from various places in Canada and the United States. In 1972 there were three bands providing entertainment for the 248 guests in attendance.

In June 1973, John Fowler started an automotive shop in the former Lorimer building.

Highway Construction

Perhaps one of the most important events in Airdrie's history was the construction of a six lane divided highway to Calgary. In l970 work on the northern overpass on Highway 567 began. It was at this time that Highway 567 was extended westward as far as Main Street. (Not until l974 was the gap in the highway westward completed.) The six lane No.2 Highway was diverted eastward to go around Airdrie so that traffic wouldn't have to slow down. (Previous to this time the speed limit on this highway was 60 miles per hour, but it was reduced to 40 miles per hour through Airdrie.) By l97l the Yankee Valley underpass and the Balzac overpass were completed. (The road east of the underpass is named Yankee Valley Road after early American settlers. The road west is called Big Springs Road as it leads to Big Springs Park further west.) Then in l972 Highway 2 which used to skirt the east side of the airport to 48th. Avenue (now known as McKnight Boulevard) was diverted north of the airport to descend the hill to Nose Creek. The road then followed Nose Creek Valley southward and this portion was later named the Deerfoot Trail. This highway change enabled people to travel from Airdrie to downtown Calgary in approximately 20 minutes. There is no doubt this new transportation corridor encouraged many people who worked in North Calgary to move to Airdrie.

It is remarkable how the new highway, paving, and storm sewers have changed surface water flows in Airdrie. A number of sloughs have completely disappeared. In the spring a large stream of water from the northeast used to flow across the school yards, follow along the north side of Second Avenue North, cross the area where the Treasury Branch now stands and continue on its way to Nose Creek. Some people claimed that they went fishing in that area during early spring floods. However, it may be just a fish story.

The Year 1972

The year l972 was of particular significance to me for that is the year I purchased my home. The Rocky View School Division decided to sell the two teacherages in Airdrie. It was not just by chance that I was the only one to bid on my home. Others were interested and undoubtedly would have bid more, but when they learned that I wished to retain the home I had lived in since l964, they withdrew from the competition. With neighbours like that, is it any wonder I have remained in Airdrie to this day?

I immediately went to work to landscape my yard, build a fence and a garage and do a considerable amount of cement work. The man in charge of the project was Ed Barkley. Ed is the miracle man who has just the one hand but can drive nails faster than the average person. He is also a great competitor in hockey and swimming.

Airdrie experienced record construction in l972. Main Street North began to take shape. New housing on the west side of the road filled in gaps and north of the trailer court Rocky View Industries began construction of a furniture manufacturing plant. This plant was a subsidiary of A.A DeFehr Manufacturing of Winnipeg. Frank DeFehr was the manager.

On the east side of Main Street developers started the construction of the ll,000 square foot Plaza I shopping centre. The official opening was October 7, 1972. Development also began on the area to the north for 60 new homes. (In l966 a Husky station was built on what today would be the south end of Plaza I.) Two early tenants in the shopping centre were Reuben Schaffer with his hardware store and Steve Diertens who operated a very successful bakery. On First Avenue North next to what was then Calgary Power, Bill Glass built an IDA drugstore. Bill had previously been established in Crossfield so when he came to Airdrie, he provided a room at the back of his store for the Crossfield doctor, Dr. McKenzie, to make visits to Airdrie. As far as I know, this was the first doctor service in Airdrie since the days of Dr. Edwards. In earlier days if someone was hurt at George McDougall School, the principal, Frank Morrell, would call Millie Stewart who had been a nurse.

West of George McDougall School, work commenced on the Edwards School. Across Highway 2, construction began on a new livestock auction centre which was situated on what is now the east side of East Lake Boulevard and just south of Highway 567. East Lake Boulevard had not yet been built. Supply Rite Transport now occupies the site.

It was in 1972 that the United Farmers of Alberta established a farm supply store in the area where it is still located today, along Edmonton Trail.

After Highway 2 had been diverted around Airdrie, there was left a small island of land between the main highway and Edmonton Trail. John Fowler attempted to operate the garage that had previously been owned by Wally Anderson, but the new highway resulted in a drastic loss of business.

John gave up the business in 1972. The building was used for other purposes for a short time but it stood vacant until 1976 when the owner gave the Fire Department permission to burn the "abandoned hulk". John was given the pleasure of throwing in the torch to begin the conflagration. (Al Gibeau has pictures of this event.) Imperial Oil owned the land and today the Airdrie Esso Self Serve stands on that location.

Meanwhile Hugh Hamilton acquired all the land to the south of Imperial Oil property. In 1972 he built his offices just to the north of the present McDonald's. A huge HAMILTON sign, used to attract passing motorists, left many strangers wondering if that was the name of the Village. Further to the south was the former Becker house. This home stood in the way of development so in 1973 the Fire Department was called in and in a short time the house ceased to exist. It had served to give the volunteer firemen some practice training.

The Year 1973

In 1973, Airdrie began its first major paving program. First Avenue North was paved from the track to Edmonton Trail. Main street was paved between First Avenue North and Centre Avenue. Centre Avenue was paved from Main Street to Edmonton Trail. The paving was debentured and home owners had the choice of paying a lump sum, the amount depending on the length of frontage, or paying over a period of 15 years. New sub-divisions were paved as they were developed and these paving costs became part of the price of the homes.

Airdrie and District Chamber of Commerce played a major role in the promotion of industrial development in Airdrie. People from all walks of life joined the Chamber - including farmers and teachers. On March 26, 1973 approximately 150 people attended a supper meeting in the basement of the Community Hall to listen to a speech by their M.L.A., Clarence Copithorne, Minister of Highways and Transportation. He announced that the Government of Alberta had purchased three quarter sections of land on the east side of Highway 2 between Secondary Road 567 on the north and what is now East Lake on the south, for two major projects. A Department of Highways and Transport Maintenance Branch was to be built employing an estimated 50 people. The second development was a fully modern regional Veterinary Laboratory. He also announced the completion in the near future of Secondary Road 567 from the west overpass to Secondary Road 772. This meant there would be a continuous road westward. Needless to say, there was great joy in the hearts of Airdrians that night. This road was completed in 1974.

During the year plans were made for zoning various types of industry that would be suitable for the Industrial Park. Meanwhile the Alberta Housing Corporation quietly purchased parcels of land to the south and east of Airdrie for housing purposes.

The Year 1974

On January 1, 1974, Airdrie annexed all the land east of Highway 2 that at present is part of the city of Airdrie and extended the western boundary along 8th Street West from Highway 567 to Big Springs Road. The Village was now contained within a two square mile area.

According to the 1973 census, Airdrie had a population of 1294. A population of 1000 qualifies a village to become a town. The Village Council applied to the province for that designation and on May 1, 1974 Airdrie was incorporated as a town.

In the ten years since I had arrived in Airdrie the population had grown from 616 to 1294—an increase of 578. In the next ten years it was to grow from 1294 to 10,264 —an increase of 8,970.

Section 2: Airdrie as a Town: 1974-1979

Growing Pains

Between 1955 and 1970 I had been heavily involved with Central Office activities of the Alberta Teachers' Association. Now after four years of relative peace and quiet, I was caught up by the air of excitement in Airdrie with all the proposed changes. When Leighton Perry suggested to me that I should join the new Municipal Planning Commission, I accepted his advice.

At a Council meeting of June 17, 1974, Dave DeFehr, Herb Buchanan, Dick Clapperton, Ralph McCall, and Bill Glass were appointed to the Commission to act as an advisory board to Council.

At this point I should explain that the Calgary Regional Planning Board consists of local government representatives from Calgary and the surrounding rural municipalities as well as individual towns and villages. Its job is to oversee planning, zoning and subdivision in its area and has the power to overrule local planning boards. The administrative staff of the Regional Planning Board helps all local governments in its jurisdiction who require assistance. A higher authority is the Alberta Planning Board.

The first major decision of the Airdrie Planning Board was perhaps its worst. Its members voted to approve the application for a Mushroom Farm in Airdrie. The area was designated "Agricultural" and there were no houses east of the highway at that time, but more research should have been done. Permitting composting outside was unforgivable. We were assured there would be little chance of any odour from the operation beyond the farm's property boundaries and any inquiries we made elsewhere did not seem to dispute that evidence. As far as I am aware, there were no objections from the Calgary Regional Planning Commission. It all goes to prove that none of us knew "beans" about growing mushrooms.

To understand what happened to Airdrie in 1974-75 one has to look at a bigger picture.

In 1973 an Arab-Israeli war occurred and the oil supply from the Middle East was in jeopardy. Oil prices tripled. While driving across the United States that year, I was concerned by reports that some gas stations were closed for lack of fuel and I wondered if this heralded the decline of the automobile era. Certainly it brought an end to the popularity of the large car.

What brought misery to the rest of Canada and other parts of the world brought prosperity to Alberta. Workers flocked here to get jobs in the oil industry and oil companies sometimes hired more people than they needed for fear there wouldn't be enough workers to go around. One of my former students told me she sat in an office for weeks trying to find something to do.

There seemed to be a shortage of everything. Between June 1973 and June 1974 there was an increase of 11.4% in inflation. Food prices increased 20%. I remember a butcher shaking his head and saying "No one will buy hamburger at a dollar a pound". The average price of a home in Calgary jumped from $30,000 to $40,000 in a very short space of time.

There was a shortage of housing accommodations in Calgary and people began to move outside the city to acreages or satellite towns where land costs were much lower. Calgary planners had asked for an annexation of land that would have doubled the size of the city but in October 1974 a plebiscite was held and voters turned down the proposal. This rejection encouraged the expansion of satellite towns.

The province and the Calgary Regional Planning Commission were in favour of satellite towns while Rod Sykes and Calgary City Council felt that these areas would siphon off property taxes and attract industrial firms while at the same time using City services without paying for them.

Calgary Regional Planning went public with a new proposed General Plan for Airdrie in the fall of 1974. The Plan pointed out that Airdrie had enough land for a population of 8,000 to 12,000 and suggested that housing should stay on the west side of Highway 2 and industrial land on the east. The southern half of the land on the east side was described as possible future urban. Industry in Airdrie should be of the "dry" type that does not require large quantities of water or produce large amounts of sewage. School facilities would be adequate for at least another year. An interesting observation was that of the 984 students attending Airdrie schools, 425 lived in town, and 559 came from Crossfield and rural areas.

The biggest problem for Airdrie was the water supply. The province announced studies for a pipeline from the Little Red Deer River to serve all the urban centres along Highway 2 as far south as Airdrie. Airdrie's water needs, however, were more immediate and thus a water line from the Bow River was proposed.

Meanwhile Calgary's City Planning Commission had a change of heart and endorsed higher density development in surrounding towns. Perhaps this was prompted by developers who were proposing to build new towns in rural areas. Abbey Glen proposed to build a town of up to 60,000 people at Beddington just two miles north of Calgary City limits. Calgary realized it was better to help direct growth instead of just opposing it.

In the fall of 1975, the Provincial Government decided to run a water line from near Baker Sanatorium on the Bow River to Airdrie. Farmers along the original proposed direct route wanted permission to tap into the line for their own use before they would grant land easements. The Provincial Government's answer was to divert the route several miles east and to follow the road allowances.

Now the size of the water line was in dispute. Bill Yurko, Minister of Environment, wanted a 12 inch line and Airdrie Council thought it should be 16 inches. The compromise was a 14 inch line. Some reports suggested it would provide enough water for 30,000 to 40,000 people. The truth proved to be that the line wouldn't provide adequate water for much more than 8,000. The water line was finally completed to Airdrie in March of 1976 but the official ceremonies did not take place until August of 1977 when the line from the Little Red Deer River to Crossfield was also officially recognized. Throughout 1976, Crossfield had to truck water from Airdrie to supplement its own supply. In both cases the Provincial Government owned the lines and sold water to the users.

Originally Airdrie had proposed using sewage lagoons which would be flushed twice a year into Nose Creek. When well known Calgary environmentalist Darwin Cronkhite heard about this he raised a "stink". (The first time I met Darwin was at Acme in the early 1960's when he came to investigate the death of thousands of Lapland Longspurs that became disoriented in a snowstorm on their spring migration north to the tundra.) Calgary Council soon concurred that it would rather have the sewage come through a pipe line than down Nose Creek. Calgary Mayor Rod Sykes assured the Town of Airdrie of "cooperation in every way" and to a large extent this has been the attitude of Calgary City Council since that time.

When Airdrie became a town it was pretty obvious that the outdoor skating rink was outmoded. A Building Committee was formed to represent the Airdrie and District Recreational Area, with three members each from the Town of Airdrie, the Recreational Society and the Agricultural Society. I became a member of the Agricultural Society. At the time Leighton Perry was Chairman and Marg Johns was Secretary. The Agricultural Society was formed not only to give advice but to qualify for a Provincial grant for the building of a new arena. The first controversy that arose was over the location of the arena. The Agricultural Society was in favour of the area where the Town and Country Building now stands. By a close vote, however, the majority of the Building Committee chose Jensen Park, since water and sewage was immediately available. The arena was built on the existing skating rink site utilizing the cinder block building already located there. The projected cost - $380,000. The arena was to be funded $50,000 from the Town of Airdrie, $50,000 from the Recreation Board, $180,000 from the Provincial Government and $100,000 from public canvas. The official opening was January 9, 1976. In May 1976, Bob Sloane, President of the Agricultural Society, presented a $25,000 cheque to Don Edwards, President of the Recreation Board. In spite of generous donations from the public, the Arena Fund had a $60,000 shortfall which was picked up by the Town of Airdrie and paid out of general revenues.

In return for supporting the Arena, the Agricultural Committee was promised two days a year for community use. Thereafter, the Airdrie Fall Fair, which began in 1966 in the Community Hall, now made use of the Arena. The Spring Trade Show used the other day allotted.

The next controversy was over parking. The original intent was to have parking on the west and east ends of the Arena. It was also proposed to remove eight trees on the south side of the Arena and provide angle parking. There was a petition opposing the removal of the trees and the paving of the southwest corner of the Park which was a well landscaped picnic area. It was then agreed by Council to develop a parking area on the north side of the Arena. By this time I was a member of Council and, needless to say, in support of the north side location. Throughout my term on Council, from time to time, I found myself involved in struggles to protect the Park from further encroachment.

Transportation

At one time in the 1970's serious proposals were put forward to provide facilities for high speed passenger trains between Calgary and Edmonton. Also there were proposals for commuter trains between Calgary and Airdrie. These dreams never came to fruition.

On November 1, 1975, Chuck Dahl began his own Satellite bus service between Calgary and Airdrie. He also catered to the charter and tour bus demand. All seemed to go well except for the odd clash with Council over parking a bus on a residential street.

Then in 1978 came the growth of the Big Springs Residential area on the east side of Town. The Rocky View School Division refused to provide school busses for this area although by law it had to make provision for transporting students living more than 1.5 miles from school. Chuck Dahl stepped into the breach, but administration of the venture proved to be too much. There were complaints about such items as costs and the type of bus required. The community was divided over the correct approach to the problem. The result was that in September 1979, Airdrie Council agreed in principle to establish a public transportation system. The *Echo* conducted a random survey and found 88% of the people questioned were in favour of a public bus system.

Deryl Kloster was put in charge of the Transit System. Two second hand busses were acquired and an 8.7 mile route was established. Busses would operate Monday to Friday. On December 12, 1979, Al Dickinson took the first bus out of the Town garage and his first passenger was 9 year old Miguel Gosano. Transit had a ridership of 504 the first day.

An unfortunate repercussion of the introduction of a public transportation system was the fact that Chuck Dahl pulled his busses out of Airdrie, also eliminating his commuter service to Calgary.

An interesting sidelight to the transportation problem is that as early as 1975 a delegation approached Council requesting the Town to consider a Dial-a-bus Service for the handicapped and the elderly.

Early Land Development

In the summer of 1975 the Calgary Regional Planning Commission gave approval in principle for an Industrial Park containing 107 industrial lots and four reserve parcels on a 349 acre site in northeast Airdrie. There was some concern about drainage into a body of water now referred to as East Lake. The problem was later solved by putting a storm basin on the edge of the Lake where excess water would be diverted through a storm sewer to empty into Nose Creek just east of the bridge near the present Museum location.

Meanwhile, Behrens Contractors in partnership with ATCO Central Limited proposed a housing subdivision in what has since become known as Airdrie Meadows. There was to be a total of 464 units on 75.5 acres. The area of each home was to be between 940 and 1400 square feet. Lots were to have frontages of 37-54 feet and depths of 105 feet. (Perhaps because I came from a small village I was always reluctant to vote for anything less than a 50 foot frontage.) Council, led by Deputy Mayor Jim Dunne, asked for underground services. Jim, who was the local manager of Calgary Power, insisted that people do not like power poles in the back lanes. (Alberta Government Telephones was already placing its cable underground.) Mr. Behrens pointed out that such services would add $400 to unit cost and this could make or break someone trying to manage a down payment. Council also imposed a levy of $1000 an acre on all land being developed to help defray the cost of recreational facilities. Problems in establishing a sewer system to Calgary held up development, but by the fall of 1976 scraping and topsoil preparation began. In the spring of 1977, Behrens sold his one-third interest in Airdrie Meadows to Engineered Homes. ATCO continued to hold a two-thirds financial interest. Shortly thereafter lots were put on sale and within six hours ATCO had orders for 110 family homes in Phase I and people were putting their names on lists for homes in a proposed Phase II. Houses sold for as little as $46,000.

ATCO first came to Airdrie in 1957 when the company set up a manufacturing plant at Airdrie Airport. Otto Steiner, a senior official with ATCO, was to play a large part in a number of projects. He was part owner of Woodside Golf Course Inc. when it was formed.

The most controversial development was proposed in the fall of 1975 when the Alberta Government announced that it would build a huge mobile home park in Airdrie east of Highway 2 and south of the Industrial Park. The project would provide room for 920 mobile homes on 206 acres of land. Phase I was to offer 420 lots plus a 5.5 acre school site and 28.5 acres of public park. Lots were to be sold to individual buyers.

The first hurdle to overcome was the rejection of the project by the Calgary Regional Planning Commission. The Commission stated that the proposal did not comply with Airdrie's General Plan which called for housing to be developed on the west side of the highway and expressed concern that such rapid expansion would overload the schools. The Rocky View School Division stated that it could not handle such a drastic school population increase. Even the Department of Environment said the separation by Highway 2 would create a "wrong side of the tracks" phenomenon.

However, Housing Minister Bill Yurko noted that the need for low cost housing was still there and Murray McCarger, an Alberta Housing Corporation spokesman, said he had 500 applications for the first 400 lots. The lots would range in price from $7500 to $9500. Mobile homes were expected to sell in a range from $15,500 to $30,000.

Pressure was put on Airdrie Council to appeal the Calgary Regional Planning Commission's decision to the Provincial Planning Board. A rumour, never officially confirmed, was that the $2 million in provincial government financing for a sewer line to Calgary would be cancelled if the mobile home project was rejected. This would stop further development on both sides of the highway. Airdrie Mayor, Darrell Bennett, said an appeal would immediately be made. The result was that the mobile home subdivision was approved. The Chairman of the Alberta Planning Board said he sympathized with the school board but other areas in the province in similar circumstances had managed to cope.

A few problems still remained. The Rocky View Planning Commission asked for legal access to the sewer system for all quarter sections along the route. Provincial officials pointed out that permitting people to tap into water and sewage lines would encourage the construction of an urban type sprawl along the lines. Another group of Balzac area farmers opposed the planned sewer system on the basis of lack of information. Their appeal was denied.

Finally at a meeting in Edmonton in September 1976 between the Town of Airdrie and representatives of the Provincial Government a number of outstanding matters were resolved. Mayor Darrell Bennett and Deputy Mayor Jim Dunne attended the meeting. They reached an agreement on financing the sewer line to Calgary, since all easements for the right-of-way had been secured. Housing construction could now begin. Also a key agreement for the financing of the Industrial Park was concluded with a forecast of development beginning in the spring of 1977. It was agreed that Airdrie would not insist on a vehicle overpass being built in the immediate future to join the two sides of town, but the town did require a pedestrian overpass. They also agreed that the Big Hill Springs Road intersection would be completed with an underpass.

The East Side housing development was at first called Belmont Estates. However, Council was later informed by a provincial official that Belmont was the name of a rehabilitation centre for alcoholics in Edmonton and he thought it best we change the name of the subdivision to Big Springs Estates.

Council

In the fall election of 1974, since Airdrie was now a town, the people voted directly for the mayor and six councillors. (The word "Reeve" was no longer used.) With that election Darrell Bennett became mayor, and the six councillors were Jim Dunne, Norm Mosley, Jake Dyck, Al Lawther, Phil Wallace and Reuben Schaffer.

Jake Dyck resigned from Council in the fall of 1975, and in January 1976 Norm Mosley handed in his resignation. This resulted in a by-election being held on March 17.

In those days there was no political campaign. You simply let your name stand for election, and the local press published your picture and a write-up concerning your background. Having served on the planning board since its inception, I was prepared for Council activities. In the March 17 by-election Rick Kunst, a Calgary city policeman, and I were elected and sworn in at a Council meeting on April 5. I was to remain on Council until October 1989.

In the subsequent election in October 1977, Jim Dunne and Al Lawther chose not to run. This was a loss to Council as Jim had been Deputy Mayor and was keenly aware of problems of land development, while Al Lawther, a former manager of the Bank of Nova Scotia, was very capable in financial matters.

In that election, Darrell Bennett was returned as Mayor and the Councillors were Phil Wallace, Barbara Lazerenko, Ellen Johnstone, Ron Davidson, Reuben Schaffer and Ralph McCall. This marked the first time two women were elected to Council. The representatives were a good cross section of the electorate. Phil Wallace was an accountant. Barbara Lazerenko ran a catering service and did an excellent job for the short time she was on Council. Ellen Johnstone was a newspaper reporter and certainly knew the concerns of people in general. (She told me that when she was not sure how to vote, she voted with her 'heart'.) Ron Davidson was general manager of a contracting firm and had a good knowledge of the business world. (He had also been a volunteer member of the Fire Department.) Reuben Schaffer owned the hardware store and knew the problems of the local business community. I, of course, was expected to act as liaison between Council and the schools.

The Deputy Mayor is elected each October by the members of Council. I was honoured by being chosen unanimously for that position for 1977-78 and for each year thereafter until 1989 when I no longer stood for election.

That fall Council attempted to divide Airdrie into a ward system with a Councillor in charge of each area. Provincial officials informed us it was not permitted.

Darrell Bennett received his schooling in Lougheed, Alberta and used to skip classes the odd afternoon to play pool with his close friend Don Mazankowski. The Principal may have objected at the time, but later Darrell married Pat, the Principal's daughter. Darrell and Don purchased their first car as a joint ownership deal. Mazankowski went on to own a car dealership and later became the right hand man to Prime Minister Brian Mulroney. Darrell went into the oil drilling business and after a period of time in Brazil, he returned to live in Airdrie. He was involved in a drilling company in Calgary and became President and General Manager. While I was on Council with him he always kept me informed of his absences. Besides travelling to Canadian destinations, he was a frequent visitor to South America, the Middle East and Africa. He also acted at times as a negotiator between other international firms and countries. He tells me he's as busy today as he's ever been - especially in Africa. He has logged millions of air miles in his career.

Obviously Airdrie was fortunate to have Darrell for Mayor during the town's period of rapid growth. He was a skilled negotiator who was well known by both business people and politicians. He used his skills on Council and sought a compromise that all members could accept.

In November 1978, Barb Lazarenko resigned from Council and moved to British Columbia. Phil Wallace resigned effective December 31, 1978. (This all occurred shortly after a major dispute with the Planning Board.) A by-election was set for February 21, 1979 for two positions on Council. At the close of nominations only Rick Jones had filed papers. Dale Nichol, Town Manager, then announced that nominations would be held open another two days. Terry Haggarty and Brenda Henderson (whose husband, Barry, became a Councillor in later years) were both nominated but

222

after a meeting between the two, Brenda withdrew her application. Therefore Rick Jones and Terry Haggarty were elected by acclamation. At that time Rick was President of the Community Association in Big Springs and Terry lived in Airdrie but taught school in Calgary.

Taxes - 1974-1979

Taxes in Airdrie during this five year period were probably close to average for the province rising from $300 to $550 for the average home owner. This included both municipal tax and school tax. You would think that an average increase of $30 a year would not provoke controversy, but not so. I remember that one gentleman who opposed tax increases would arrive in a state of inebriation. I always wanted to tell him he had his spending priorities wrong but I refrained from commenting. In general, however, the taxpayers were tolerant. Airdrie always kept potential business prospects aware that the Town had no business tax.

Perhaps the most unusual move in Alberta tax history was the Municipal Debt Reduction Program introduced by the Provincial Government in June of 1979. The Government felt it had an excess of oil money on hand and thus it provided each eligible municipality with $500 per each permanent resident. Primarily the grant was to help municipalities reduce debenture debt but municipalities that had no debt were permitted to start their own "heritage fund". Airdrie's total benefit was $2,125,633.20. This wiped out all Airdrie's debenture debt and left us with an unconditional grant of $166,231.06. Airdrie's population in 1979 was 3879 but by 1982 it had risen to 9981. Had the plan come into effect three years later Town treasury would have had an extra 3 million dollars. The Town of Brooks, which has not yet reached city status, had most of its population increase before 1979 and thus received $6,108,119.79. The Municipal District of Rocky View had very little debt and therefore was able to put its share of $8,256,956.00 into a "heritage fund" of its own. School Districts for some reason never received any money from this plan.

What provokes the most furore for any local government is not the normal tax increase but rather re-assessment time. Assessment must take place at least every seven years and Airdrie's turn was in 1975. A number of properties had obviously increased in value. A provincial assessor carried out the procedure which resulted in no increased revenue for the Town but did result in increased taxes for some, and lower taxes for others. Many of those with increased taxes let both Council and the press know of their predicament but seldom was anything heard from those with lower taxes. Municipal Councils always go through a good deal of turmoil dealing with this problem over which they have little control.

Fire Department

The Airdrie Volunteer Fire Department Board consisted of representatives from both the rural and urban areas. The chief difficulty was finding volunteers to fight fires during the day. Some use was made of Village staff and some high school students. It was not unusual to hear the fire siren and have a student, who was a volunteer fireman, suddenly leave his desk and be gone regardless of the circumstances.

A recurring problem for the fire fighters was their need for more equipment. I was appointed as Council representative to the fire department in 1977 and at the first meeting I attended I was confronted by a rather fiery Fire Chief, Mac McQuarrie. He had a long list of required equipment. Fortunately for me, Councillors accepted my recommendation for purchase without question. This was the beginning of the friendly relationship I had with the Fire Department throughout the years.

Fire Chiefs of that time were: 1970-74 - John Fletcher; 1974-76 - Art Stevenson; 1977 - Mac McQuarrie; 1978 - Art Stevenson for a short period until he moved away and then Bill Hawkes. Some of the volunteers I remember who fought fires for a considerable period of time in the 1970's were: Ron Davidson, Butch Davy, Dave Kernaghan, Albert Gibeau, Ken Bilben (now with Calgary Fire Department), Henry Tetz (who drove the Miller water tanker), Lorne Hart, Ray Saurette, Ray Bremner, Larry McGraw, and Jeff Cook.

One of the worst fires I remember was the one on Main Street in 1968. I was in John Loveday's "Jolly Shopper" when someone said there was smoke coming from a building south on Main Street. The Fire Department arrived and apparently put out the fire, but that night the blaze broke out again and burned out all the buildings from Centre Street and Main up to Jock's restaurant. That was the end of Cooper's store and locker and the former Bowers residence.

Late in 1977 the roof of the new Regional Agriculture Centre caught on fire. The combustible roofing had been built too close to the chimney stack. Airdrie fire equipment proved to be inadequate in the cold weather and the Calgary Fire Department was called to the rescue. Fortunately the damage was minimal.

Another major fire occurred on March 21, 1978 when the Airdrie Recon Centre, situated just south of the Town and Country Complex, burst into flames. I was supervising a few students in my upstairs classroom and we were able to view the catastrophe. We saw an explosion and then billowing smoke and fire. Two people were seriously burned in the shop area but office staff escaped by jumping out of second floor windows. A number of former students worked there and we were all concerned for their safety. Three fire fighting units from Calgary joined the Airdrie Fire Department at the blaze.

In August 1979, a spectacular fire next to the Airdrie Airport destroyed the Alberta Drywall Supply Plant. The building, which had been recently modernized, had originally been a World War II airplane hanger.

Another bad fire destroyed a house east of Airdrie in 1979. A good deal of controversy took place, including letters to the editor, concerning what was said and done during the response to the fire. One thing it did prove is that the rural area needed a numbering system for location purposes.

It was rather obvious in the late 1970's, with the increase in population in both the rural and urban areas, that the old system of administration and operation would have to change. I remember a rural pumper that had Coventry motors which made it necessary to send to England for new parts. John Horn who was a rural representative on the Fire Board was one of the few persons who knew how to make the repairs. Although they were a gallant group of volunteers - members of the Fire Board, firemen, ladies answering the fire phones, and Bob Miller providing trucks to haul water to the fire free of charge - the system still had to be modernized.

In 1977, Airdrie had only nine active and three inactive firemen who were trained and available. At least 20 were needed. Also, full time firemen were becoming a must. More and better equipment was required. In 1978, the Airdrie Fire Department received a new fire truck built to its specifications. I remember Chief Stevenson stopping by my home for me to admire the new purchase. Meanwhile the Rural Fire Area was redrawn with its border extending into the country four miles north, one mile south of the Big Springs Road, twelve miles west and eleven miles east of Airdrie. Calgary and Airdrie signed a mutual aid agreement so that Airdrie would respond into Calgary's Fire Department area as far south as the Balzac Road. In return Calgary would answer with assistance to Airdrie when required. These responses would be at no cost to the recipient. Airdrie also signed similar agreements with other fire departments in Crossfield and Beiseker. These agreements became effective January 1, 1979.

The main purchase by the Airdrie Fire Department in 1979 was the Hurst Power Jaws - better known as the Jaws of Life. I remember watching firemen as they practised cutting their way into old cars provided by Lorne Hart who was in the auto dismantlers business. By 1979, the number of volunteers increased to more than twenty.

The Fire Department has always been well known for becoming involved in community activities and bringing information about their department to the schools. Perhaps their most famous venture was the annual Christmas Eve delivery of candy canes door to door. Santa rode on a fire truck and the elves delivered the canes to the homes. The project, which began before 1975, received television coverage across Canada in later years.

The one venture that proved to be too much for the Fire Department was the building of a Scout Hall in Fletcher Park. (The old Scout Hall that had been located just north of the present Anglican Church site was gutted by fire in 1975.) Throughout 1976, firemen sponsored a number of activities to raise money for the endeavour and building began. It proved to be too big a project for volunteers; finally Airdrie Council took over the financing and completed the project using funds from the sale of the land on which the old Scout Hall had sat. Mayor Bennett cut the ribbon for the official opening December 4, 1977. The Scouts, Cubs and Beavers had found a home.

Before leaving the Fire Department I should mention the sirens in town. The fire siren, located on a post behind the Town Office, was sounded by the fire phone ladies when a fire call was phoned in. It was also heard at 7 p.m. Monday night to announce fire drill.

In addition there was a Civil Defence siren which apparently was to be sounded in case of an enemy missile attack. (This was a carry-over from the Cold War of the 1950's.) One day this siren began to wail and no one knew how to turn it off. Airdrie's Town Manager phoned Civil Defence in Calgary but no one there knew anything about the siren nor did they know where Airdrie was. Members of Calgary Power eventually cut the wires. Council then sent a letter asking that the siren be removed. If our side didn't know where Airdrie was, the enemy wouldn't likely know either.

Town Employees

The Town Foreman in charge of outside workers had been Jesse Baker, but he was replaced later in the 1970's by Walter Moen, a former mayor of the Village. The custom was for the foreman to attend each meeting and give Council a blow by blow description of what had occurred since the last report. This part of the agenda took up a good deal of time and as the town got busier the foreman no longer reported to Council. As late as 1978 there were only four other outside workers - John Fletcher, Dave Kernaghan, Hans Brombeis and Butch Davy. Knobby Clark also worked for the Village but his job was to supervise the arena.

By the fall of 1977 it became obvious that Airdrie could not continue to use Underwood and McLellan as Town engineers since there was a conflict of interest when local developers used them as well. Brisbin and Gates both of whom had worked for Underwood and McLellan saw their opportunity to set up their own engineering consultant service which would cater to towns and villages in the surrounding area. Airdrie Council accepted their proposal and they remained consultants to Airdrie throughout the Town's rapid growth stage.

In 1978 Airdrie Council ran afoul of the rules of the federal government's Anti-Inflation Board. The government allowed no more than an 8% increase in wages. When we explained to them that help was scarce and we were still much below Calgary city wages, we were forgiven.

The rapid expansion of Airdrie led to the replacement of Airdrie's Town Administrator, Dennis King, in August 1978. Dennis had been a loyal employee who had given unstintingly of his time. However, Council felt an administrator who had experience with larger urban centres was required.

Just previous to the departure of Dennis King, Ralph Waldo had been hired as Development Officer and Building Inspector. He had spent four years as Inspector for the Alberta Housing Corporation. Then in July, June Byatt joined the Airdrie town staff as Office Manager. She accepted the responsibilities of Town Manager between the departure of Dennis King and the arrival of Dale Nichol. In September Daryl Kloster was appointed as the Director of Social Services. Daryl had a Master's Degree in Social Work and had worked in that field for a number of years in Calgary. He must have believed in the future of Airdrie for he was already a resident of Airdrie Meadows. In October Dale Nichol was chosen to be Town Manager. Dale had previous experience in municipal affairs in other urban centres as well as in social service work in Calgary. In April 1979, Knobby Clark died of a heart attack while attending to the Arena and shortly after that Sterling Clayton, who was working there at the time, was appointed Arena Manager. That year Doc Jones became the new Town Foreman. With all these new appointments Airdrie was preparing for its rapid growth.

Town Projects

Community Centre

In March 1976, Les Olsen, President of the Airdrie Curling Club, met with Council to discuss the need for new facilities. He said the existing rink was too small to handle projected populations and the building was not worth renovating. Soil tests indicated that a new building on that site might present problems. He said his committee recommended as a new site the seven acre parcel of community reserve just north of George McDougall High School. Council pointed out to him that the

Calgary Regional Planning Commission insisted that access points and future road patterns would have to be resolved first before the land could be utilized. It was felt that these objections could be overcome. Not only did Council agree to the location but members suggested that a new community hall and a multi-purpose facility should also be built on that site. This would reduce construction costs, and in addition the facility would become eligible for a 50% capital grant instead of the 35% grant available for single purpose buildings.

Nothing seemed to occur during the summer and the Curling Club became resigned to another winter in the old building. They did, however, buy the necessary steel structure for a new building at a very reasonable price from an urban centre that had purchased it and then changed its mind about building.

That fall ATCO came forward with a proposal that seemed impossible to refuse. They would purchase Town land where the old skating rink and curling rink were located as well as the Community Hall land. The estimated value of the these parcels was $350,000, money which could be used in the building of a new community complex. In addition it was thought that the Unifarm building on the north end of Main Street would sell for approximately $80,000 and perhaps some of that might be donated towards the new structure. ATCO offered to build the new community centre on the land north of George McDougall School for an estimated $700,000 with a promise of occupancy by the fall of 1977. The old community hall and curling rink would not be removed until the new structure was completed. The sale of the land and government grants should assure that little if any of the cost would have to come out of taxes.

A Complex Planning Board was established with Erling Olsen and Bert Carlson representing the Hall Board; Kathy Northcott and Les Olsen representing the Curling Club; Lambert Farr and Willard Wray representing the Over 50 Club; and Mayor Darrell Bennett and Reuben Schaffer representing Town Council. In December, Marilyn McCall, spokesperson for the Library Board, asked that space be provided in the complex for the Library since their present facility of 650 square feet was severely cramped. At a later meeting Council agreed to the addition of 1500 square feet for the Library and Marilyn then became a member of the Complex Planning Board.

Otto Steiner of ATCO took a very personal interest in the construction of the Complex and in October 1977 he turned the keys to the new Town and Country Centre over to Mayor Darrell Bennett two weeks ahead of schedule. This seemed like a miracle since so many other projects took so long to evolve.

After changes to the original plan, the final cost of the building and the necessary contents, including the kitchen equipment, was $840,000. Funds came from the sale of Town owned land, the $1,000 an acre recreation levy on new development, Provincial Government recreation and culture grants, a $40,000 cheque presented by President Ray Howden of Unifarm and donations from various individuals, companies and community organizations.

The main access to the building was a temporary gravelled road that ran from Third Avenue North northward along the east boundary of George McDougall School land. Access was also provided from the west as the new subdivision in that area completed its road system.

One cannot deal with the Town and Country Centre without mentioning the first custodians, Paul and Shirley Rabel. Paul was permitted to move a mobile home to a location near the southeast corner of the complex. With the help of their four boys and their families, they looked after the curling rink as well as the maintenance of the building. Paul and Shirley retired early in 1993 and their home was moved from the site in June of that year.

Enlarging Town Hall

By February of 1978, consultant Ken Brisbin suggested the Town should explore the possibility of providing more space for the expanding number of staff. Council decided to renovate the present building and add offices in the garage area on the south end. Outside staff would have to find a new home. Meanwhile all equipment and records were moved to the curling lounge in the Town and Country Centre. (All of this confusion happened in the summer of 1978 with its hectic staff changes.) By late September the workers moved back to the new town offices although some renovations on the building still continued.

226

New Fire Hall and Maintenance Building

The next problem was to provide a home for outside workers. The location chosen was the west side of Main Street across from the old Dump which was owned by the Town. (The Dump location has since proved to be a good parking area for staff.) The land for the new building was purchased from ATCO. Council then made agreements with Dwayne Bray who owned the land on the east side of Main Street and ATCO who owned the land on the west side to pay for the extension of Main Street as far as the new Maintenance Building site.

A dispute arose with the Airdrie Planning Commission and the *Echo* on one hand and Council on the other. The main objection was that the Town did not get a development permit for their proposed building. (Government projects are not required to do so if they own the land.) Andy Marshall, who was both a member of the Planning Commission and the publisher of the *Echo*, also felt that the location was wrong and the materials used in the building not appropriate. In fact Council did use the material that was at one time purchased by the Curling Association at a very good price. Actually the steel material had suffered no harm and it proved to be a cost effective way of building. Later the building was enlarged to house maintenance workers on the south end and firemen and paramedics on the north.

New Water Reservoir

Council was not through with its projects for 1978. The 500,000 gallon water reservoir near Fletcher's Park was inadequate (especially in case of fire) and further water storage was required. In February 1978, Ken Brisbin, engineering consultant, recommended that a water storage reservoir and pump station be constructed in the area which is just east of the present Nose Creek Valley Museum. The Town of Airdrie owned that land. Council chose a two million gallon reservoir rather than one half that size. The cost of the second million gallon storage was less than half the cost of the first. It was suggested that further storage would be required before Airdrie's population reached 15,000.

New Garbage Dump

By 1976 the Department of Environment began enforcing the rules about burning of garbage in urban areas. (In earlier years residential burning barrels were common in both Calgary and Airdrie. They did not become illegal in Airdrie until June 1981.) In 1976 the Town of Airdrie received official notice that burning at the sanitary landfill must cease. The problem was that the landfill was nearly full and only by a system of burning could it continue to operate. The Town was seeking a new landfill site but finding one that satisfied all the requirements and was acceptable to the nearby residents was a difficult undertaking. Somehow fires still continued at the Town Dump. When Council inquired who lit them, no one seemed to know. Finally in January 1977 the Department of Environment fined the Town $1500, but this was rather a light penalty considering the amount of garbage that would have had to be transferred elsewhere. In July, Airdrie officially closed its dump and permission was sought to use the Municipal Dump near Crossfield. Carmen Clark, who had previously collected garbage for Airdrie, had his contract renewed under the new conditions. Problems arose at the Crossfield landfill because of the large amount of refuse being hauled in by Airdrie developers. Finally after a number of meetings and hearings the new Airdrie sanitary landfill site, located five miles west of Town, opened on January 22, 1979. Permission was granted to burn dry materials - mainly from developers - since not to do so would have greatly shortened the life of the site. The cost of the land was $160,000 and the development of the site cost an equal amount.

Boards and Committees

Police Commission

In November 1972, Airdrie Council passed a bylaw establishing a voluntary Police Commission. The first members of the new commission were Alex Dyball, Spence Morris, Fred Cawthorpe, Reuben Schaffer and Barb Lazerenko. Alex Dyball was chosen as chairman. The job of the Commission was to maintain a liaison between the police and community but they were not to get involved in actual police operations.

They made many recommendations concerning traffic flow and traffic bylaws. In 1978 the Commission recommended traffic lights at the corners of First Avenue North and Main Street but the 4-way stop is still there. Eventually they received approval for parallel parking instead of angle parking on Main Street. A 4-way stop was also installed at the corner of Centre Avenue and Main Street. Perhaps the most difficult traffic problem was convincing people to use parking lots instead of parking on Main Street.

Preventive Social Services

Connie Allen, acting as a high school counsellor, was certainly aware of social problems in the community. She often met with welfare officers such as the one I remember - Mr. Cooper. From this developed meetings with other people interested in social problems. In April 1978, Airdrie Town Council appointed seven members to a Preventive Social Service Board (now known as Social Planning Board). The members appointed were Connie Allen as Chairperson, Bernice O'Neil, Laurie Bracewell, George Shenton, Mel Vance, Bob Hunter and Barb Lazarenko. (George Shenton and his wife provided a home for a large number of foster children throughout the years.) In October 1978, Deryl Kloster began his career in Airdrie as Director of Preventive Social Services (P.S.S.).

The job of P.S.S. was to promote and assist community service programs such as Boy Scouts, Girl Guides, the Boys and Girls Club and adult groups dealing with the tensions and strains of society.

The Provincial Government provided 80% of the funding and the local government 20%. Allocation of funds was the responsibility of the local P.S.S. Board.

In 1979, Daryl Kloster was appointed as Assistant Municipal Administrator and Laurie Hashizume was appointed as Assistant Director of P.S.S.

An offshoot of the P.S.S. was the formation of the Airdrie Information Centre in May of 1979. The old brick post office building on the corner of First Avenue North and Main Street was purchased by the Town and it soon became a hot bed of activity. It also provided meeting rooms for other community groups. Irene Carlson became the first full time staff person in the Centre. During the summer Andi Bartnek headed a group which introduced the first Airdrie Guide Book. Another group (160 people in all) produced a 23 page questionnaire dealing with 908 topics. There was excellent participation by the citizens and this generated a good deal of enthusiasm among the populace, City Staff and Council which lasted for a number of years. This was especially true as new Town projects came on stream as a result of the recommendations.

Planning Board

In the fall of 1976 Steve Allen became a member of the Planning Commission and in 1977 he became the Chairman. He suggested that the Board should adopt a more active role and deal with a large number of planning issues rather than just reviewing development applications and making recommendations to Council. Council gave his proposal its blessing. One of the major differences that soon appeared was the Planning Board's belief that population should be restricted to an increase of 1000 persons a year while Council felt that was a reasonable objective but would be difficult to enforce without discouraging new development in Airdrie. Besides, a greater population would help to share the cost of the expensive infrastructure such as water and sewage. This issue had little to do with what eventually occurred, however.

The new Planning Board received some assistance in April of 1979 when a Department of Building and Development was formed with Brenda Beck as Director. Darlene Hilts was appointed as her assistant. Bill Hawkes became a member of the Department with the designation: Building Inspector.

The members on the new Planning Board who were to remain on that Board for a number of years were Reg Hashizume as Chairman, Peggy Graham and Peter Schonekess. Reg, of course, was a lawyer, Peggy had taken university courses related to planning, and Peter was a Provincial Environmental official. All of these members had qualifications very valuable to a Planning Board.

Also in 1979, a Development Appeal Board was formed so that any decision of the Local Planning Board could be appealed to a higher authority.

There were 732 building permits in 1979 with a total value in excess of 29 million. Airdrie was on the move.

Recreation Board

Previous to 1979, recreational and cultural facilities were run by individual boards while parks and sport fields were operated directly by the Town. The Airdrie and District Recreational Board, which mainly looked after the Plainsman Arena, also gave some financial assistance to the Balzac and Goldenrod Halls. In April 1979, John Graham was hired by the Town to head a newly formed Parks and Recreation Department. In the same year a Recreation Master Plan was prepared to provide guidelines for future developments. Agreements for joint use of facilities were made with the Rocky View Municipality and the Rocky View School Division. The two main issues that had to be dealt with were the joint use of school buildings and school use of Town facilities. Authorities such as the Town and Country Centre and the Library Board kept their separate identities.

When one group is replaced by another there is usually a feeling of alienation by the original group. In the early days the rural people had often been the driving force behind promoting recreational events. As Airdrie's new Recreation Department began operating facilities in a more professional manner, many of the rural old timers had the feeling they were being left out.

This feeling was apparent in the negotiation of a new recreational agreement between Airdrie and Rocky View. Airdrie wanted to claim ownership of facilities while giving access to rural residents in return for a payment from their municipality. At the time the rural municipality contributed $20,000 a year to the Airdrie Parks and Recreation operating budget of over $201,000. Airdrie wanted a higher contribution from the rural municipality, and also an extra two Town members on the Recreation Board which would give the Town representatives a majority. Many rural people felt that they had put so much into the building of some of the earlier facilities that they should not be asked for a greater increase in funding. Some of them also felt that they should be part owners of the facilities. Finally after several months of negotiations an agreement was signed on November 2, 1979. It provided for Town ownership of facilities, a majority of Town members on the Board, an increase in revenue from the rural, and a guarantee that rural persons "will continue to be able to use recreation facilities on the same terms as Town residents". This feeling of alienation by some of the rural population continued to appear in a number of rural-urban disputes that occurred in various joint projects in the ensuing years.

A large source of revenue for recreational purposes, as mentioned before, was the $1,000 an acre that Airdrie levied on all new land development. The original levy was imposed in 1976 and in 1979 this sum was raised to $2,000 an acre.

Airdrie Library

The Library moved into its new quarters of 1500 square feet in the Town and Country Centre in 1977. However, it still depended on a large number of volunteers to keep the operation going. In 1979, the expansion of the Town and Country Centre gave the Library another 450 square feet. By this time the work and organization had become too much for volunteers and so Nellie Jackson was hired to be the first paid librarian. Volunteers were still used but the Librarian gave more stability to the organization. In the fall of 1979 the Library Board gave serious consideration to joining the Marigold Regional Library System. Since a number of the patrons came from the rural areas, and the M.D. of Rocky View was not interested in joining, the final decision was that Airdrie could probably operate better outside Marigold.

Churches

Throughout the 1975-79 period Bob Hunter remained as the United Church minister. The choir members were pleasantly surprised to find that Bob was an accomplished organist and pianist. In addition to his church work, he was very active in the field of social services. Renovations took place inside the United Church, and outside, new landscaping, new sidewalks, and a paved parking lot improved the facilities.

In 1976, Pastor Dick Titterington supervised the building of an addition to the Church of the Nazarene on Smith Street. The sanctuary expanded, doubling the seating capacity from 100 to 200. Other rooms were added as well.

The Catholic Church continued holding services in the United Church. Father Palardy was here

229

for a number of years. Late in the 1970's the Catholic Church acquired a small acreage along the Edmonton Trail where the R.C.M.P. station now stands. In 1979, Father Charlie Brown arrived in Airdrie - probably with the thought in mind that he would have his parishioners build their own church. In no time it seemed Father Charlie Brown knew everyone and everyone knew him. No one would ever forget his name. On more than one occasion when I was walking to school he stopped his car and offered me a ride.

Airdrie Fellowship Bible Chapel started in the fall of 1978 in the Airdrie Elementary School. Pastor Harvey Trauter and his wife Arlene remained in Airdrie for a number of years.

Land Developers

Big Hill Springs and Edgewater Estates

As mentioned earlier, Alberta Housing Corporation (A.H.C.) purchased land in east Airdrie in 1973. Shortly after that, A.H.C. bought the land, west of Highway 2, that lies south of Airdrie Meadows subdivision and north of the Summerhill subdivision. This area was eventually named Edgewater Estates.

Development did not occur as rapidly as anticipated. Because of the water and sewage problems previously mentioned, A.H.C. didn't get approval for development of Big Hill Springs Estates until October 1976. Unfortunately the developer had nothing but trouble. Cement workers went on strike and the weather didn't cooperate, but the main problem seemed to be the lack of overall supervision on the site. Stick built homes take time to complete, but mobile homes provided by different companies could move in so quickly that a building inspector couldn't keep up with them. In addition some people who had been waiting a long time were desperate to move in and they received permission to do so before development work was completed. Phase I began in the north and the first home owners to move into the area were Mr. and Mrs J. Ouellete who arrived in December 1977. In a letter to the *Echo* they described the general chaos. Private contractors, each doing his own thing, were getting in each other's way, natural gas didn't arrive until a month and a half late, and frozen water lines meant long periods of time without water.

It seemed Town Council had to deal with a new problem in Big Springs Estates at every meeting. Council was reluctant to get too involved in some problems where costs to the Town were involved since the whole project was the responsibility of A.H.C. This resulted in a good deal of bickering between A.H.C. and Town Council. In retrospect, Council probably should have hired a building inspector earlier than it did and not have relied on A.H.C. to supervise the project.

Two questions arose - should home owners be permitted to add stick built structures to their mobile homes; and should modular homes be allowed in the development? Both requests were eventually accepted.

In June 1978, A.H.C. started stripping its land for Phase II to the south of Phase I. The Corporation had no permit as yet. I remember our town engineer, Ken Brisbin, informing me of that fact on a Saturday morning and since neither the mayor nor other Council members were available at the time, we proceeded to put a stop order on the work. The Monday night Council meeting was a fiery one. Mayor Bennett expressed himself rather forcefully that night. Council felt A.H.C. should clean up the mess in Phase I before it started Phase II. Ken Sheddon of A.H.C. pointed out that withdrawing from the stripping contract would involve considerable extra cost and several men would be out of a job. After A.H.C. promised to spend additional money to correct errors in Phase I and to keep Council better informed in the future, Council agreed to permit the development of Phase II to continue.

This latest furore over Big Springs Estates prompted the Heritage Fund Committee to visit Airdrie. Members included in the delegation were Housing Minister Tom Chambers, Fred Kidd, M.L.A., Gordon Taylor and opposition leaders Bob Clark of the Social Credit Party, and Grant Notley of the New Democratic Party. At a public meeting at the Town and Country Centre, Mayor Bennett pointed out that in spite of inclement weather and a cement strike, Airdrie Meadows was much further along than was Big Hill Springs Estates. Rick Jones, spokesman for the mobile home owners, pointed out problems with roads, water mains and school bussing. One home owner, Henry Funk, "brought down the house" when he suggested that the weather excuses of A.H.C. were a "snow job".

On October 27, the first newcomer to the southern half of Phase I was Herman Dyck. Mr. Dyck was a former contractor himself and knew how to locate and install homes. His relative, Henry Funk, moved in a few days later. They became long time residents.

In November the Big Springs residents met at the Agriculture Building to form a Community Association. The officers selected became well known in the community for a number of years - Rick Jones, President; Al Hughson, Vice-President; Larry Stowards, Treasurer; Debbie Cunningham, Secretary; and Glen Lyth and Della Hughson, Recreation.

The only road into Big Springs Estates during the early period of development came from Highway 567 on the north and paralleled Highway 2 as far south as the present day twin arena. It then made a slow curve eastward to what is now Big Hill Circle. Following this road to the southeast corner, it turned directly south to meet Yankee Valley Road just west of the mushroom plant. By late 1978 the northern half of East Lake Boulevard was graded and paved and this became the new entrance to Big Springs Estates. The old entrance road eventually disappeared at both the north and south ends but just lately has reappeared in the northern half as a one-way road leading to the north overpass. A pedestrian overpass across Highway 2 was completed in 1978 to link the mobile home subdivision with the west side of Airdrie.

In January 1979, C.H.A.P. (Co-operative Housing Action Program) introduced a new concept in the building of homes. Participants were responsible for the building of their own homes and had to take courses two nights a week for 15 weeks to deal with the types of problems that would occur. The stick built homes were to cost not more than $52,000 including both the house and the land. Some owners did make provisions for additions later. To qualify for the program owners had to have a yearly salary of $19,500 or less. Many home owners did much of the work themselves and shared their expertise with others. One participant who built a very nice home showed me his costs which were less than that of some of the mobile homes. Town Council was indeed pleased with this new program.

Alberta Housing initially sold 80 lots in the south-east area of Phase II of Big Springs Estates for C.H.A.P. homes. Also, they provided 276 lots in the new A.H.C. subdivision on the west side of Highway 2 which became known as Edgewater Estates. C.H.A.P. homes were under the sponsorship of the Department of Public Works which provided excellent supervision of their development. There was an obvious rivalry between Public Works and A.H.C., which was a Crown corporation. On one occasion a large C.H.A.P. sign was placed directly in front of an A.H.C. sign. By the fall of 1979 the building of C.H.A.P. homes was well advanced and there was a large number of families on a waiting list. In February 1980, the family of Nels and Cindy Seerup was the first to move into a C.H.A.P. home.

Borger Land

Borger Investments outbid Alberta Housing Corporation for a forty acre parcel of land situated in the middle of the Big Springs Estates Development. They received permission from the town to postpone development since they didn't think they could compete with the low priced homes of A.H.C. No development was started on that land until 1994.

Airdrie Meadows

As mentioned earlier ATCO Central Limited in 1975 had proposed building homes in Airdrie Meadows but it wasn't until the fall of 1976, when Airdrie was assured of an adequate water and sewage system, that developers were given the go ahead. By the fall of 1977 approximately 70 families had moved into the subdivision and by the spring of 1979 Airdrie Meadows had a population of 1160.

Summerhill

In the spring of 1976, the Alberta Nurseries properties owned by Ted Lord were sold to Kentron Homes of Calgary. Cirrus became the land developer. By the summer of 1977, a plan was developed on the 148 acre site for homes to accommodate 3000 people with building to begin in 1978. The first phase of 21 acres took in the northern section of the land between the railway tracks and Nose Creek and included a site for a small shopping centre. By late 1978, some homes were already occupied. Cirrus had done an excellent job of paving the residential roads as well as the Main Street section but there was no road north through the Edgewater Estates. Main Street on the north was just recently paved but only as far as the fire hall. Residents of Summerhill had to find a circuitous way to get to downtown Airdrie. Not until September of 1979 was Main Street completed and paved. By this time Cirrus was already planning a Phase III which included 200 more homes.

Ridgegate

In February 1977, Nu-West applied to the Town of Airdrie for reclassification of two quarters of land in the south-west. Since much of this area was along Nose Creek or lower lying lands, Alberta Environment was called in for assistance. To my surprise the representative sent to speak to Council was Tom Slater, a former student of mine. A number of environmental changes had to be made. The original Nu-West spokesman was Richard DeWitt, a member of a long time Airdrie District family. Since the land lay on both sides of the C.P.R. tracks, Nu-West engineers presented a plan that called for a pedestrian and service underpass to go under the tracks to connect the two developments, but to date only the land on the east side of the tracks has been developed. In August 1978, Council gave permission to Nu-West to develop Ridgegate subdivision which covered about 19 acres and was to provide about 41 building lots. The grand opening of Ridgegate took place in the spring of 1980.

Meadowbrook

Early in 1977 Wimpey Western Ltd., one of Britain's largest developers, bought land in East Airdrie formerly known as the Katie Cook quarter and proposed building homes on that site for approximately 3,115 people. Airdrie Planning Commission initially rejected the plan as "far too premature" since there were enough housing projects already underway. However, Council did approve an outline plan in June of that year. By 1979 work on Phase I of the Meadowbrook Subdivision had begun for 156 homes. In July the first families began moving in. The price of a three bedroom bungalow home of approximately 950 square feet was $60,000. Six other construction companies were also involved in the Meadowbrook Development.

Jensen Estates

As mentioned before, houses were built along the west side of Main Street when it was extended two blocks north to meet with the new road now called Highway 567. In the early 1970's houses were built along Hawkey, McCracken, and Farr Crescents. Finally in March 1978, a consortium of small builders under the title Marketplace proposed to build 105 homes, including some duplexes and a 16 unit apartment, on the Jensen land adjacent to the Town and Country Centre. Residents of that area had a number of objections to the development, the need for wider roads being the main item of contention. In July Council gave the go ahead to the builders and by September 1979 the residents moved into Jensen Estates. This occurred about the same time as the completion of the addition to the Town and Country Centre and provided the Centre with a road system to the west.

Thorburn

By 1977, Qualico had purchased a quarter section from Helen Chitwood. However, it wasn't until August of 1979 that Phase I, which became known as the Thorburn Subdivision, was approved by Council for development. It was noted at the time that this area would cater to high quality homes.

Henderwood

In June 1977, Henderwood Industries, supported by the landowner, proposed that the Town of Airdrie annex the quarter section west of Main Street and north of Highway 567. Subsequently the 152 acre area was annexed to the Town effective January 1, 1978. Henderwood wanted the 65 acres nearest to the track to be classified Industrial so that they could develop a number of industries. They would require a spur line from the C.P.R. railroad.

The Planning Board approved the classification of the 65 acres as high density so that development might take place. Council, however, decided to reclassify the whole quarter although no one had expressed the desire to build on anything other than the industrial part of the land. When the Calgary Regional Planning Board met to consider reclassifying the Henderwood and Qualico quarters they were presented with a letter from Steve Allen, chairman of the Airdrie Planning Board, personally opposing Airdrie Council's bid for reclassification of Henderwood. In addition there was a letter from Andy Marshall, also a member of the Airdrie Planning Board, who personally opposed the reclassification of the Qualico quarter on the grounds that it was premature. Needless to say, this proved to be very embarrassing to Airdrie Council although their request for reclassification was approved. As mentioned before, this was probably the main factor when none of the five remaining Planning Board members were re-appointed to the Board the following November. The irony of it all is that as the result of a downturn in the economy, Henderwood never did develop the 65 acres, other than removing a bit of top soil, and it has again been classified as agricultural land. The Qualico quarter that Andy was concerned about had no houses built on it until the 1980's.

Industrial Park

Although our M.L.A., Clarence Copithorne, announced in 1973 that the Alberta Government would assist Airdrie in establishing an industrial park, for a number of years there was a great deal of talk and little action. By 1976 there were 30 or more positive applications from various industries and this prompted a move toward development. The park contained 350 acres. Phase I consisted of 57 acres mainly located along the north end of East Lake Boulevard. Tenders for development were awarded in the fall of 1977 with Alberta Housing front-ending the costs. The Town of Airdrie was responsible for promoting and marketing the lots.

The first sale in March of 1978 was for 2 lots purchased by Indel Limited of Montreal, manufacturers of window frames. Lots sold for approximately $50,000 an acre which was well below the costs of lots in Calgary. In April, Mouillierat Holdings Ltd., received approval to construct a body repair shop on its site in the Park. Leo moved into his shop November 1, 1978 although he was six weeks without a phone. This second business in the Park is still there today with the same owner.

By the end of 1978, 21 of the 39 lots in Phase I had been sold and options had been taken on five lots in the second part of Phase I which mainly borders on Highway 2. This land would not be ready for occupancy for some months since development did not begin until the fall of 1979. Needless to say Council waited impatiently for more action.

In January 1979, the Recon Centre, based in Mississauga, Ontario, opened its 9600 square foot building. The company had its original location on the west side of town but the structure had burned down the previous March. This area is now a housing development.

On August 7, 1979 Propak Systems, employing 150 people, moved to Airdrie from Calgary. The official opening was October 19. Their main item of production was a gas plant system which they would deliver and install any place in the world. At the time of their official opening, they were already expanding their fabrication plant. Rod McPike, Construction Manager at the time, was to play a prominent part in the community in the ensuing years.

Par Auto Parts, with John Fowler as Service Manager, also had its official opening in October. The Provincial Steel Buildings Ltd., Ionel Electric and a manufacturer of wooden trusses were already in operation and the pipe coating and sandblasting business in the Roy Mackenzie building was about to begin.

Both Westinghouse Canada and the Tortilla factory were in the preparation stages.

Education

The growth of Airdrie meant nothing but trouble for Calgary Rural School Division No. 41. (In 1976 Calgary School Division changed its name to Rocky View School Division No. 41.) The Provincial Government was putting the squeeze on building funds and other grants just as the population surrounding Calgary was increasing rapidly. Trustees of the School Division declared that they would not accept any new pupils from the mobile home parks in Airdrie unless more grants and money for school construction was forthcoming. There was the feeling that mobile homes would not sufficiently increase the tax base. In the fall elections of 1974, Gerald Hurt from Crossfield became the new trustee and did his best to deal with Airdrie's problems.

In spite of the controversy about school budget cuts, the Provincial Government in 1976 did approve an addition to Edwards School consisting of eight classrooms, a lunch study room and an addition to the gymnasium.

Four cabinet ministers including Julian Koziak, Minister of Education, visited Airdrie in the fall of 1976. Acting as a private citizen, I voiced some of the grievances that had been expressed to me by teachers, trustees, and parents. I urged the government to pay grants promptly to alleviate school board borrowing; I requested special assistance for school boards in rapid growth areas; I asked that the Provincial Government continue to shoulder a large share of the bussing costs and that school board tax increases not be subject to plebiscite. (Plebiscites were not held for municipal government tax increases.) Some of these changes actually did come to pass.

School Division No. 41 did lose out on a plebiscite and as a result fees for riding the bus were imposed. However, there was so much parental resistance that the bus fee proposal was abandoned.

One statement by politicians that I always abhor is; "cutbacks will not affect the quality of service". In all my years as a politician I never made that statement, for I felt it was an insult to the intelligence of the public.

In the midst of the furore over plebiscites and bus fees, J.L. Sacher became the new Superintendent of Schools effective September 1, 1976. Having come from the fast growing urban centre of Fort McMurray, he was aware of growth problems. He came under heavy attack almost immediately, but to his credit, within the year he had smoothed a number of ruffled feathers. One of his first actions was to cut back on the number of deputy-superintendents.

The new Muriel Clayton School officially opened on September 20, 1979. Muriel had been the first teacher at the Sunnyside School located near the Dickson Stopping House. That school had opened on February 22, 1899 with nine students. Muriel Clayton had 14 children of her own and a good number of them were at the official opening. One of her sons, Dick Clayton, was presented with an award by Bill Jeffray, school trustee, for suggesting the name for the new school. Norman Reddekopp, Deputy-Superintendent and former Airdrie school principal, was chairman for the evening and Jerry Sacher, School Superintendent, gave the keynote address.

The first principal of Muriel Clayton School was Alex Seminoff who had a staff of fifteen teachers. However, on September 1 when school opened 370 children were registered and two more teachers and one teacher's aide had to be hired. The school was designed to add portables if necessary.

By October 1979, the Rocky View School Division gave approval for a new elementary school in Big Spring Estates which was later to become known as the R.J. Hawkey School. Plans were also going ahead for a new high school in Edgewater Estates, but that school never materialized. The developer of Edgewater Estates used a good deal of clay fill to level an area on the west side of Main Street as a location for a high school, but after much discussion with Council, the School Board decided there was insufficient room and the noise of trains would interfere with classroom instruction. Today the Catholic Church stands on that site.

Other teachers who taught at George McDougall High School but who have not as yet been mentioned are: Alex Biletski (a former hockey linesman from Flin Flon), Mrs. Geppert, Don Laerd, John Brown (librarian), Velma McKay (she and Larry Sorensen were former students of mine at Acme), Nancy Roberts (a former George McDougall graduate), Jane Singer-Laing, Bill Robson (a Korean War veteran), Susan Summers and Miss MacDonald. Ray Bryden, Paul Krueger, and Don Patrick came over from the Junior High School. Mrs. Russell was the school secretary.

Not everything was serious business for I remember in the spring of 1976 the Airdrie Grade 9 class was raising money for an Alberta tour. Brian Gancheff, a relatively new teacher at the time, and I offered to put on a skit as our contribution to a program. Brian, dressed as an American chef, carried a ball glove and intermittently tossed a ball in the air and caught it. I dressed as a French chef and announced that I was from "Pari" and was visiting my good friend Redvers "Pari" who lived on an estate near the French hamlet of Balzac. In the midst of nonsensical conversation, Brian and I prepared a chip dip consisting of everything imaginable including a number of undesirable ingredients. When we were through, we offered potato chips and our dip to the audience but they refused to taste our concoction. When we merrily ate the dip the audience realized that we had secretly exchanged our brew for a chip dip previously prepared. Brian has become a little more sedate in recent years as principal of R.J. Hawkey School.

234

People and Events
The Year 1975
Airdrie's official population for 1975 was 1383. In spite of all the talk of expansion in that year, the population actually dropped for a short time. Part of the reason for this is that the acreages east of the highway were moved out to make way for the Big Springs housing project. The lack of a water and sewage system from Calgary was the main reason for the lull in the storm. Council was beset with all sorts of proposals that were just waiting to get off the drawing board.

One building constructed in 1975 was the Highway Maintenance Repair Shop and Storage Depot. It was completed close to the proposed date but the construction of the Veterinary Laboratory was delayed.

In June 1975, Great Plains Mushrooms began operation.

In the downtown area the Bank of Nova Scotia constructed a new bank around the old one. The large open area at the front of the present bank is where the old two storey building once stood. The official opening was November 27.

In 1975, Fred Kidd became our new M.L.A. That same year the Airdrie Over 50 Club was incorporated under the Alberta Societies Act. Actually an Over 60 Club began in 1968 with meetings held in The George McDougall Library. Later the age limit was lowered to 50 in order to attract more members. In 1970 a Board of Directors was elected with Jack Sutcliffe chosen as president. Meetings continued to be held in the school until the opening of the Town and Country Centre. The official grand opening of all community facilities in the Centre was November 16, 1977.

In 1975 the three largest congregations were The United Church, the Nazarene Church and the Catholic Church. The church leaders at the time were the Rev. Bob Hunter, United; Pastor Dick Titteringham, Nazarene; and Father Palardy, Catholic.
The Year 1976
In 1975 the three largest congregations were: the United Church, the Nazarene Church, and the Roman Catholic Church. The Church leaders at the time were: the Rev. Bob Hunter, United; Pastor Dick Titteringham, Nazarene; and Father Pallardy, Catholic.

Early in January Dr. Melvin J. Vance opened a chiropractic office in Airdrie. He is still practising here and has contributed a great deal to community affairs to this day.

In this same month the Plainsman Arena was officially opened and by March the waterline from Calgary was completed. This was also the month I was first elected to Council.

The official opening of the Treasury Branch was on June 18 with Bill Yizek as the first manager. Previously, for a few months the Treasury Branch worked out of a trailer on the opposite side of the street to its present location. The rest of the Provincial Building, consisting of the Courthouse and Liquor Store, was officially opened in August.

In July the Airdrie Lions Club erected the Big A sign near the North Entrance to Airdrie. It listed all the names of the various organizations in town.

Also in July, Stan Mitchell officially opened his Buyers Drug Mart Store. Stan had purchased the drugstore from John Wong who bought it from the original owner, Bill Glass.

In August A.G.T. opened its new telephone exchange on Allan Street. Airdrie was now introduced to the "touch tone" calling system. Customers now had to dial all seven digits whereas previously only the last 4 numbers were required for local calls.

Also in August, Dusan's Clothing Store marked its 26th anniversary. Dusan and his wife Maya lived in the back of the building and raised six sons and one daughter. All the children went on to take post-secondary education. This was also the year the first "for sale" sign went up in the store window.

In September the Nazarene Church officially opened the new addition which consisted of a Sanctuary providing accommodation for 200 people.

In October Mr. and Mrs Reuben Schaffer moved their Link Hardware business from Plaza I Shopping Centre to their new building on Main Street. The old Rocky View Gas Co-op building had come down to make way for the new store. Terry Treleaven, Reuben's son-in-law, joined him as a partner in the business. The store became a family affair with Elsie and Reuben, Carol and Terry all on staff. The official opening was held on December 3 and 4.

Also in October Cliff Ayers, driver for Greyhound Bus Lines, received an award in recognition of his 20 years of driving without an accident - in all 1,300,000 accident free miles. Some time after that Cliff retired and offered to drive a handi-bus. I was in the Town Office when a city clerk asked him if he had any previous driving experience.

In November Robin Burwash, a George McDougall student, was named High School Amateur Rodeo Champion. He and a fellow schoolmate, Jim Dunn, went on to win several championship events in bareback riding, including the $50,000 ride at the Calgary Stampede. I remember when the two of them would practise riding on a mechanical device at noon hour. Their fellow students worked the machine as fast as they could to try to throw them.

In December the Town bought the new dump site approximately 5 miles west of Airdrie.

The Year 1977

By census time the population of Airdrie had risen to 1442 - an increase of 34 people from the past year. This was the last of the small increases.

In January, Hugh Hamilton asked Council for permission to subdivide his five acres of land on the east side of Edmonton Trail. He proposed building a drive-in restaurant on one site. (This site eventually became the home of the Doubletree.)

In the same month Dick Buchanan opened his Air-Alta insurance office in Plaza I.

In February, Earthland Developers proposed to build a shopping centre just west of Edmonton Trail and along the north side of First Avenue South. By December the shopping plaza was open with a steak house, a laundromat, a grocery store and a clothing store as occupants. An interesting side light was that a local person, Ginny McKinnon, after a lengthy battle with Council received permission to establish her Airdrie's Country Wearhouse in the plaza. The new laws prohibited anything other than highway commercial businesses in that area but she proved she had made her application before these by-laws had come into effect.

Early in the year the Planning Commission recommended that no high density apartment building be allowed in the residential part of Old Airdrie. This meant that an Engineered Home application to build an apartment just west of the Horsemen store on Third Avenue North and Allen Street should have been rejected. In spite of much protest by nearby home owners, a 17 suite apartment was permitted and the building was largely completed by the end of the year.

In February, the owner of Buyer's Drug Mart on First Avenue North proposed that another building similar in design and size to his own be built just to the west of his store. This building was completed later in the year.

Early in April Council announced a tree planting program as well as the construction of a foot path along the east side of Main Street between Flett and Jensen Drives. There was some discussion about a linear park along Nose Creek but it was to be seventeen years before that became a reality.

On the 20th of April, the Toronto Dominion Bank moved into the south end of a newly built shopping centre located on the west side of Main Street just north of the Treasury Branch. Gary McGregor was the manager. In July, Sam Nanjee and Amin Panju held a grand opening of their Mayfair Food Store situated in the north end of the small shopping centre. Dave Kinniburgh, formerly of Dave's Meat Market, operated the meat counter.

On April 23-24, the Airdrie District Agricultural Society and the Seed Fair Committee sponsored an Agricultural Fair and Seed Show in the Plainsmen Arena. They had excellent attendance. This show had formerly been held at the Stampede Grounds in Calgary.

In May, Lincoln Developments proposed a 60-unit town house development near the railway tracks on the parcel of land west of First Street West between the extension of Centre Avenue and First Avenue North. Since then a number of proposals for the use of the land have been made but by 1994 the land was still vacant.

In June, NORDCO Developers got the go ahead for a 132 apartment development east of Highway 2 and just north of the cemetery. These 10 acres were the former Grochmal land.

In July, Alberta Government Telephones built a 6 foot tunnel under Highway 2 for its utility services. Council agreed to assist with the costs in return for the right to send storm sewer and water lines through the tunnel.

Also, Rocky View Industries began an extension to their furniture factory. (This building burned down in the years since this script was written.)

Late in July a number of businesses moved into the basement of Airdrie Hardware on Main Street. For the first time, *The Echo* found ample room to publish the paper. Other businesses on the lower level were Mildred's Fashions, Shirley Hay's barber shop, and A.E. Lepage Melton Real Estate Office. Don Yantz, who previously owned the pool room and barber shop across the street, was now a real estate agent for Lepage.

During the summer, Council dealt with the sale of the Auction Mart on Highway 567. Since the Industrial Park was not yet approved and East Lake Boulevard did not yet exist, a number of problems arose. Negotiations were necessary for the sharing of costs for future storm sewers, sanitary sewers, water lines and road development. Mayor Bennett was a shareholder in the company and had to withdraw from discussion. Matters were later resolved and the 31 acres of land were divided into six lots and sold.

On August 31, Fred Kidd, M.L.A., officially opened the new water system from Calgary. Actually, Airdrie had been receiving water from the city since March of 1976.

In September, the Town hired Ken Brisbin as its engineering consultant. Also, that month they hired Butch Davy to work with the Town Crew. Butch was fresh out of high school and already an experienced fire fighter. He is still employed by the City and has been with the Paramedic Unit since its inception.

In the fall, ATCO unveiled a plan for a Town Centre building and pressure was put on cleanup crews to remove the old curling rink and the Community Hall. The curling rink had been built in 1945 and the first dance in the Community Hall held on July 1, 1948. On October 9, 1977, the Hall hosted its final program including an open house honouring those people who had been involved in Hall activities throughout the years.

I remember being vehemently opposed to the first plan ATCO presented for the new Town Centre for I felt the parking provided was totally inadequate. In subsequent negotiations a 45 stall parking lot was provided west of the building. It took time to convince drivers to use the parking lot, but as traffic increased they had no other alternative. Today the lot is well used.

Also in the fall, the construction of a new post office began on the corner of First Avenue North and First Street West, the former curling rink site. One thing Town Council learned was that the Federal Government did not have to follow Town planning bylaws.

Greg Blair, manager of the Bank of Nova Scotia since 1974, announced in October that he was leaving Airdrie. His last official function as President of the Airdrie District Chamber of Commerce was to chair the candidate forum for the upcoming election of Council. His replacement as bank manager was Peter Clark. Peter later became a member of Town Council.

Also in October the Kitchen Building on the corner of Main Street and Centre Avenue was completed. Located in this building, the Royal Bank had its official opening October 11. Randy Parsons was the manager. The Frontier Tack and Togs store owned by the Kitchens opened about the same time. The last tenant to move into the building was Brad O'Neil who, in November, opened a men's wear store. The entrance faced on Centre Avenue just behind the Royal Bank.

On October 14, 1977, the British Airways Concord jet flew low over Airdrie. We had been prepared for the event and my son, Don, and I sat on the garage roof watching with our binoculars. It was a beautiful sight to see as the huge plane came in for a landing at Calgary International Airport.

In November ATCO purchased about 80 acres of land just west of Main Street and south of Centre Avenue. Part of this area was to become the home of Tower Lane Mall.

I remember being involved in the December 2nd official ceremonies for the opening of the Regional Agricultural Centre with its 12 laboratories devoted to animal and bird diseases and food processing. This Veterinary Laboratory, as it was referred to in 1973, was finally completed.

On December 4, Mayor Bennett officially opened the new Scout Hall at the north end of Fletcher Park.

Also in December, the Planning Commission approved a 41-unit motel on land occupied at the

237

time by Hugh Hamilton's Horsemen store on Third Avenue North. Coincidentally, the name of the motel company was Horseman Development Ltd.

Before the end of December, the first family moved into Big Springs Estates.

The Year 1978

Airdrie began to develop quickly in 1978 and at census time in June the population was 2265 an increase of 823 persons. There were 1138 students in Airdrie schools.

The year began with Airdrie hiring its first full time dog catcher. The drilling of gas and oil wells around Airdrie became an issue early in the year. Fortunately for the town, none of the producing wells were close enough to be a threat to the urban population.

In February the Don Edwards family, and all of Airdrie, suffered a deep tragedy in the death of Mrs. Laura Edwards. She was among the victims in a commercial plane crash at Cranbrook, British Columbia. Television showed among the wreckage the book entitled "Act of God" which she had borrowed from the library. Laura had been involved in a church study of death a short time before and the Minister, Bob Hunter, was able to use many of her thoughts in his delivery of a most touching and comforting funeral service.

Also in February, a Boys and Girls Club was proposed for Airdrie. Fred Cawthorpe was an original promoter of the idea and he continued to give a great deal of his time for a number of years to this group.

In this month Airdrie's new Police Commission held its first meeting. It is interesting to note that Fred Cawthorpe was a member of this group as well.

John Fowler received permission from the Planning Commission to remove the old Lorimer garage and replace it with a new office building.

In March, Hugh Hamilton moved his Horseman Western Store on Third Avenue North to make way for the new motel. The log cabin style store was eventually relocated on the north shore of East Lake. It became the home for Cubs and Scouts.

That spring, Council gave approval to any company that wished to install Cable T.V. lines. About the same time, A.G.T. announced that they would install 4 plug-in phone jacks to any home free of charge.

In the spring of 1978 the streets in East Airdrie became a sea of mud as a result of all the construction and the road to the cemetery became impassable. Later this road was paved but it was still difficult to locate the entrance to the cemetery. I remember once having to ride in the lead car of a funeral procession to direct the driver to his destination.

In the down town area the new building just west of the drug store on First Avenue North now housed Hungry Herbies Restaurant and Hawarth's Shoe Store. Hawarth's son ran the store and the father, Ernest Hawarth, had his veterinary office in the back of the building. Ernest remained a lead singer for a number of years in the choir of the Calgary Opera.

New tenants in the commercial centre north of the Treasury Branch were a lawyer, a travel agency and Air Alta Insurance. Dick Buchanan moved his office from Plaza I to this new location and has remained there to the present time.

There were now 2 doctors and a chiropractor in town.

In April approximately 6,000 people attended the Annual Farm and Trade Fair. By this time Dick Buchanan had established himself as a public address announcer and is still active at that job to this day.

In July Engineered Homes announced a proposal to build a 36 unit apartment plus 2 clusters of townhouses with 28 units in each cluster. The 5.2 acre land parcel on which these units were to be built was bounded by Second Avenue South, Allan Street, and Edmonton Trail.

The new post office officially opened August 8 with Betty Upham as post mistress.

Also in August Brad O'Neil. representing the Chamber of Commerce, received $10,000 from Council to upgrade Main Street. The plan called for the street to be lined with trees, flower pots, benches and trash receptacles placed on a new brick sidewalk. The Devonian Foundation promised to put up two-thirds of the cost if the Town contributed the other third. It eventually took 2 or 3 years to complete the project.

This was the summer of many changes in the operation of the Town including the hiring of a new

238

Town Manager.

On September 8, the Fowler Commercial Building on First Avenue North and Bowers Street officially opened. The five tenants were A.E. Lepage Real Estate, Mildred's Fashions, Sears and Children's Choice, Dr. Ho, Optometrist, and Peter Koop, Accountant. Peter has remained at this location since that time although, when he first came to Airdrie in 1976, he had his office on Main Street just north of Dusan's.

On October 4 the Horseman Motel was officially opened. The well known Calgary lawyer and politician, Peter Petrasuk, was present as a director in the company.

Across the street on the east side of Edmonton Trail and some distance south, Hugh Hamilton and Andy Yau's restaurant was nearing completion. Originally it was to be called the Buckboard Inn, but it became the Doubletree Restaurant instead.

Also in October crews were busy preparing for a November 1st opening of the ATCO Town Centre Building on Main Street. Among the first tenants were One Hour Drycleaning, Radio Shack, Ardelles Beauty Salon, Maryanne's Beauty Salon, Airdrie Meat Market, and the office of Dr. Ho, Dentist. Dr. Ho's office remains in the building to this day.

Meanwhile in October a Lions Tree Planting crew consisting of Ted Lord and Gordon Delair planted trees along the boundary of the Town and Country Centre. Also, the Town of Airdrie created two new tot lots and provided them with equipment. One lot was located in the north end of Fletcher Park and the other north of Flett Drive. The lot to the north is on land that has been set aside to widen Highway 567 but Council decided that this area might as well be put to good use in the meantime.

In October Council received a proposal from Calgary Masonry Holdings Ltd. to build a concrete block plant west of the railroad and just south of Highway 567.

Also in October Connie Osterman won the Conservative nomination for the Three Hills provincial constituency.

As the year came to a close, Main Street was completed as far south as the Fire Hall.

One cannot leave 1978 without mentioning that a building to house Rocky View School Division and Rocky View Municipality was finally completed August 1 in Calgary after much controversy.

Another observation is that John Groarke, a well known Calgary journalist, joined the staff of *The Echo* in 1978.

The Year 1979

The June census showed that Airdrie had gained in population the past year by 1614 persons for a total population of 3879. The average age of an Airdrian was 23.3 years.

January began with a battle over rezoning in the older part of town. Old time landowners on the south side of Centre Avenue between Allen Street and Virginia Street learned that this area had been zoned for possible apartment building. They insisted that the land be down zoned to its original single family home classification. In the early 1970's vacant land south of Centre Avenue between Albert and Smith Street had been zoned for fourplexes and duplexes. Those people wishing to buy older homes on Centre Avenue and replace them with apartments were thwarted in their efforts and the land classification went back to single family homes.

Reg Hihn arrived in Airdrie in December of 1978. He purchased the drug store from Stan Mitchell and in January 1979 opened his Centre West Drug Store on the First Avenue North Site. Reg quickly took part in community activities and was President of the Jaycees when they had their Charter Night in October of that year.

Reg Hashizume was another resident who arrived in Airdrie in the latter part of 1978 and in the first part of 1979 he established his own law office. He also was a Charter Member of the Jaycees.

In January Springtree Village, situated near the east end of the walkway across Number 2 Highway, began leasing rooms. Also in January, Terry Haggarty and Richard Jones joined Council.

In February Earthland Developers approached Council to help them find some commercial land for a proposed shopping Centre. Thereupon Council negotiated with Alberta Housing for 12 acres of land situated on the north end of Big Hill Springs Estates. After much negotiation, Council paid $500,000 for the 12 acres and they sold 3.685 acres to Earthland Developers for $400,000. The remaining 8 acres eventually became the site for The Airdrie & District Recreation Complex.

That spring Council decided that a swimming pool would not be built on the west side of Highway 2 as originally proposed but would instead be erected near the south end of East Lake. ATCO won the bid of $1.185 million to build the pool which wouldn't be completed until 1980.

In the Provincial election in March, Connie Osterman became our new Conservative M.L.A.

In June a Hire A Student Office was opened in Airdrie for the first time and my daughter, Janet, was hired to be Manager. I had opposed her application since Council had a representative on the Committee, but was overruled by both Janet and the Committee. Henceforth my family never applied for anything that appeared to be a Town summer job. Instead all three siblings became proficient in the restaurant business during their high school careers. One thing I learned from this experience is the importance of tipping for good service. Donald didn't get involved in tipping, but he did receive a sizeable scholarship from McDonald's for his years of work with that establishment.

In June Airdrie Restaurants Ltd. submitted a proposal to the Planning Commission for a family restaurant to be built on the land just south of the Airdrie Hardware building on Main Street.

Late in the spring the building of two new hotels was proposed for Airdrie. One hotel was to be built just east of George McDougall School and the other to be located south on Edmonton Trail. There were petitions against the building of both hotels, but the one near the school site became the most contentious proposal. I was on the Development Appeal Board at the time and had to excuse myself from voting since I was a teacher at the school. The selling of liquor so close to the school became the main issue and the final outcome in November was that the Alberta Liquor Control Board refused a liquor licence for that site. The other proposed hotel became the Driftwood Inn. In December permission was granted to add a third floor to the Inn. The manager of the Driftwood Inn was Vern Scheid who had operated Airdrie's original hotel on Main Street for a number of years. Vern had at one time run for Village Council and later sat on the Planning Board for a few years.

Hugh Hamilton approached Council to annex two quarter sections on the south-east edge of Airdrie. His primary aim was to build a golf course. Hugh had once had his own golf course west of the tracks, but he has tried to establish one so many times since, that I am sure when his ship comes in there will be a golf course on it.

As summer approached I became heavily involved in two Council issues. First I wanted to have a 4 way stop installed at Centre and Main since Main Street South would soon be completed. Secondly I wanted the Town to stop dumping clay fill in the slough at Fletcher Park. There were a number of birds and animals making their homes there for the summer and I felt no further work should be done until fall. For a number of years Ron Davidson used to "rib" me about saving the black terns.

In August the Doubletree Restaurant opened its lounge with Valda Harris, a local singer, providing the entertainment.

Also in August Cablevision began installing lines with the hope that most homes could be provided with service by the middle of December.

By September the extension on the north end of the Town and Country Centre was almost completed. It provided for 4 new sheets of curling ice, a lounge, a larger library, a larger Over 50 Club and additional washrooms. Also the parking lot was partially paved.

An interesting story lay behind the new curling rocks required for the four new sheets of ice. The rocks were to be in Airdrie by fall for the official opening of the addition. In June Janet Skog, a director of the Curling Club, was visiting her former home in Scotland when she decided to pay a call to the factory in Ayrshire where the curling rocks were to be made. She inquired about the rocks but they hadn't started work on them yet. They thought the rocks were to go down the road a short way by lorry to Airdrie, Scotland. Instead, because of their weight, the rocks were to go by ship to Vancouver and then on to Airdrie. Some scrambling took place and the result of it all was that some rocks that were supposed to go to Portland, Oregon ended up in Airdrie, Alberta on time for the opening of the four new sheets of ice.

The fall became a very active time. Barney's Kentucky Fried Chicken opened in December as well as a number of businesses in the Industrial Park. Muriel Clayton School was officially opened and Allen Wood apartments welcomed their first renters.

Connie Osterman was honoured by being appointed Party Whip in her first year in office.

Dan Johnson, a well qualified writer, became a reporter for *The Echo*.

Although the Chairman of P.S.S. was supposed to be from the Town, George Shenton, from the Rural, was felt to be best qualified for that position.

In September, angle parking was banned in the down town area.

Already Council was talking about the need for a new water line from Calgary.

Nose Creek was to be re-aligned with 2 vehicular bridges and a pedestrian crossing to be constructed.

In November, ATCO gave details of their plan to build the shopping centre now known as Towerlane Mall and in December, Airdrie's public bussing system began.

Dick Buchanan became Airdrie's Santa Claus for the year. This was the beginning of a new career.

Submitted by Marilyn McCall, 1996

Ralph McCall: Devoted Teacher and Community Leader

Ralph McCall at opening of BMX track in Airdrie and (below) teaching at Bert Church High School in 1984.

Airdrie City Council, 1996: Back row-, left to right, Alderman Richard Siemens, Alderman Stan Softley, Deputy Mayor Murray Buchanan, Alderman Rey Rawlins. Front row, left to right, Alderman Linda Bruce, Mayor Dan O'Neil, Alderman Alan Warnock.

Airdrie's early beginnings; Nose Creek bridge in the foreground.

Reunion of Airdrie teachers, Class of 1967: Back row, left to right. Roberta Davies, Guy Dahl, Blaine Askew, Jean McElroy, Pearl Chalmers, Norm Reddekopp, Frances Hunt, Bob Lang, Ralph McCall, Neville Lyons, Ben Halbert, Gabe Ziegler.
Front row, left to right. Ina Baxter, Marion Blair, Bernice Shuttleworth, Mae Masters, Marjorie Stiles, Myrtle Moen, Lillian Edwards, Hilda Clapperton.

In Honour of Ralph McCall

Above: Ralph McCall welcoming the Olympic Team Torch runners in 1988.
Above right: Ralph McCall at opening of Towerline Mall, Airdrie, 1982
Right: Ralph McCall, hanging flags for the 1988 Winter Olympics.
Below left: Surrounded by contestants in a local beauty contest, Ralph McCall, as Deputy Mayor (holding banner) poses with Peter Cartwright (Economic Development Officer), while on a promotional trip to Taiwan.
Below right: Still in Taiwan, Ralph McCall and Peter Cartwright meet with government officials.

Above left: Presenting a flag of Airdrie city to Taiwanese officials.
Above right: Naming a room after the late Ralph McCall at the Airdrie Public Library, April 1996.
Left: Back row, left to right, Ralph McCall, Allan Warnock, Terry Haggerty, Brian Gillespie. Front row, left to right, Lorna Jones, Ron Davidson, (Mayor) and Elaine McCracken.
Below: Back row, left to right. Bob Lang, Ralph McCall, Verne Befus, Gabe Ziegler, Larry Sorensen, Verne Friesen, Neville Lyons, Don Shultz, Mel Esler, Ron Dunglison (Principal). Front row, left to right. Jean McElroy, J.A. Gajdos, Sherry Arnold, A.A. Jansen, Connie Allan, C.E. Friesz, J. Hall, Nancy Rush. (Picture taken circa 1970).

1. Historic town office, originally a U.F.A. hardware store, became a Massey Harris dealership, was later moved to Balzac and attached to St. Clement's Church and later used as a Sunday school.
2. The Curling Rink: usually the centre of community winter activity.
3. The old curling rink in the town centre.
4. Main entrance of the community hall, west side of the main street.
5. Historic W.R. Jenkins Grocery store serving the Valley.
6. Side view of the community hall, Airdrie Town Centre.
7. From left: Corner of J.J. Stewart Hardware, Les Farr's office, became Duson's Store, Bowers' Store and finally Jock's Chinese Cafe.
8. Les Farr's Garage with the south side of the Community Hall in the background.
9. North side of Jim Lorimer's Garage. It became part of John Fowler's property and was later demolished.
10. Jim Lorimer's garage served the Valley for many years.
11. A typical pioneer home. This one belongs to the Croxfords and is located east of present-day Airdrie Feed Service.

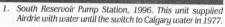

1. *South Reservoir Pump Station, 1996. This unit supplied Airdrie with water until the switch to Calgary water in 1977.*

2. *R.C.M.P. station, built in 1971, is now a Daycare Centre (1996).*

3. *Plainsman Arena, Airdrie, March 1996.*

4. *Former Post Office, erected in 1960. It later became an Information Centre and is presently vacant.*

5. *Meadowbrook School, Airdrie. March 1996.*

6. *R.J. Hawkey Elementary School, 1996.*

7. *Muriel Clayton School, Airdrie, 1996.*

8. *A.E. Bauer Elementary School, Airdrie. 1996.*

9. *Edwards Elementary, left; George McDougall High School, center; Airdrie Middle School, right.*

10. *The fire station, Airdrie. Built in 1978.*

Flooding in Nose Creek. This picture was taken looking east. Old Airdrie is in the background.

The Airdrie Golf and Country Club under water.

Winter of 1986. And seven days later: the effects of a Chinook on an Airdrie backyard

Unusually heavy snow at the George McDougall school.

Airdrie volunteer fire department battling a fire at the original Scout Hall.

A Chinook cloud overhangs the valley. In the foreground is the Scout Hall, which has since been replaced by the Airdrie Fire Hall.

Spring flooding: a common sight in the Nose Creek Valley. (1969).

The start of Airdrie Meadows development, 1977: a S.W. view.

Airdrie's second library.

Nose Creek turns into a torrent and swamps the Airdrie bridge.

Airdrie Historic Community Hall. The tiny building to the right is the F.U.A. building, and at the brick structure at the extreme right is the Government of Alberta (Treasury Branch).

Tower Lane Mall, constructed in 1982, was officially opened by Ralph McCall, town councillor.

Airdrie Centennial Parade, 1967. Cliff Tebb is riding the lead horse.

Building boom in Airdrie: The Plainsman Arena undergoes construction.

Airdrie's old lumber yard, now located in the Heritage Park in Calgary.

CHAPTER 33: MILESTONES IN THE GROWTH OF TWO CITIES IN THE NOSE CREEK VALLEY: CALGARY AND AIRDRIE
Compiled by Stephen Wilk

Pre-1870 Aboriginal peoples camped along the rivers and valleys in the foothills of the Western Canadian Rockies. The confluence of the Bow and Elbow rivers, with the Nose Creek drainage basin emptying into the Bow nearby, was a popular camping spot. The Nose Creek Valley and McPherson's Coulee provided excellent hunting and winter shelter. Fur traders, explorers, and missionaries came to trade and settle in the region.

1871-72 The Dominion Lands Act was passed, making it possible for homesteaders to obtain quarter sections of land in Western Canada, which allowed settlement in the Nose Creek Valley.

1873 George McDougall and his son John established, among the Stoneys, the first Methodist mission in southern Alberta at Morleyville. They often visited the native and non-native people in the region under discussion.

1874 The North West Mounted Police came west and started to eliminate the whiskey trade.

1875 Fort Calgary was built as a N.W.M.P. post. A Roman Catholic mission was founded in the present day Mission District. Stores were built by I.G. Baker and Company of Fort Benton, Montana and the Hudson's Bay Company. Calgary's first hospital was a N.W.M.P. infirmary which served both the police and settlers from 1875 to 1880.

1877 Treaty Seven was signed at Blackfoot Crossing by the tribes in southern Alberta, paving the way for immigrants to settle the land.

1881 The Cochrane Ranch was established and became a symbol of the ranching era.

1883 Canadian Pacific Railway arrived in Calgary, causing it to grow quickly. *Calgary Herald* began to be published.

1884 The town of Calgary was incorporated on November 17, with a population of 4000.

1885 Calgary School District N.W.T. #19 was created.

1886 The *Calgary Tribune* began publishing and was renamed *The Albertan* in 1899. The Dickson-Stevenson Stopping House was built 35 km north of Calgary.

1887 The town of Calgary received electrical power from the Calgary Lighting Company. The first telephones were installed.

1889 The first Calgary street lighting was installed

1890 Mrs. Hannington opened a stopping house on the Calgary-Edmonton trail near Crossfield. Calgary's first General Hospital was established in a rented home.

1891 The Calgary-Edmonton Railway was completed and Airdrie station house built. Beddington, Balzac, Airdrie and Crossfield were designated as railway stops. The Grey Nuns founded the Holy Cross hospital.

1893 Calgary's first opera house, built by William Hull, opened.

1899 The first school teacher north of Calgary, at the first stopping house, was Muriel Clayton (nee Mason), starting on February 22, at a private school called Sunny Side School, N.W.T.

1900 Airdrie Post Office opened.

1901 The first house in Airdrie was built by Arthur E. Bowers, on his first homestead.

1904 Airdrie's first bank was opened by the Union Bank of Canada.

1905 The Province of Alberta was created, with Edmonton as the capital.

1906 The Calgary Normal School, a teachers' college, started classes in Central School, preparing teachers to work in rural schools, such as the many schools serving the Nose Creek Valley.

1907 Dr. W.F. Edwards began to serve the Valley; he was based in Airdrie (1907-1940).

1909 Airdrie was incorporated as a village with a population of about 250, 31 houses and 2 schools.

1911	Mount Royal College was inaugurated as a Methodist institution.
1912	The first Calgary Exhibition and Stampede was born from the vision of Guy Weadick and the financial backing of "The Big Four"; Pat Burns, A.E. Cross, George Lane, and A.J. McLean. This started a long tradition of showing Nose Creek Valley's best agricultural achievements at the Stampede. Classes began in Calgary College, a private university, in the newly opened public library. The proposed City of Lackner, with a steel factory, was started in the Beddington district 10 miles north of downtown Calgary, but the real estate "boom" went "bust", and the project was abandoned.
1914	Large oil deposits were discovered in Turner Valley, establishing Calgary's position as Canada's oil capital. (A wildcat oil well in the Nose Creek Valley was discovered in July 1956 on the Smith ranch at the head of McPherson's Coulee; it is still producing.)
1914-18	World War I involved people from Nose Creek Valley.
1916	Provincial Institue of Technology began classes in Colonel Walker School. Airdrie's first grain elevator was built.
1918-19	The worldwide Spanish influenza epidemic; Dr. Edwards, Nurse Margaret Kinniburgh and many local people helped nurse the sick in an Airdrie hotel turned emergency hospital. All public meetings were banned in Calgary to limit the spread of the deadly disease.
1921	Airdrie's first newspaper, *The Airdrie Recorder*, began publishing.
1922	The Provincial Institute of Technology was moved to a newly constructed permanent building on the North Hill of Calgary; students included some from Nose Creek Valley.
1923	The Calgary Exhibition and Stampede became an annual event.
1928	Airdrie had its first electricity.
1929	The Great Depression lasted for ten years, including worldwide economic depression and prolonged drought in North America. The Valley did not suffer as much crop failure as other parts of western Canada, due to its favoured climate and geographic location. Unemployment was rampant in Canada. Many men "rode the rods" from town to town looking for work and relief. In the Renfrew district of Calgary the "municipal flying field" became the Calgary Municipal Airport. Rooftops were used to indicate the direction of the airport landing field.
1936	The discovery of crude oil at Turner Valley affirmed Calgary's status as Canada's oil capital.
1939	World War II started, and lasted until 1945. Calgary continued to expand into the Valley, as the municipal airport was moved to the present McCall Airfield and named after Fred McCall, a WWI pilot credited with having brought aviation to Calgary.
1940	Airdrie Airport was established by the British Commonwealth Air Training Plan, four miles southeast of Airdrie on the road to Yankee Valley. It covered 640 acres and was bought by Gordon Bowers in 1948 and by Ron Southern of Alberta Trailer Company in 1957.
1945	Calgary Normal School became a branch of the Faculty of Education of the University of Alberta; it later became the University of Calgary.
1955	The Province of Alberta celebrated its 50th Anniversary as a province by building the Southern Alberta Jubilee Auditorium in Calgary, providing cultural enrichment to southern Alberta.
1958	The sod was turned for construction on the present University of Calgary campus; the first buildings were completed in 1960.
1959	The Airdrie Water Tower was built, called "Horton Watersphere"; it is presently used as a landmark.
1964	Calgary's Heritage Park opened, with the Airdrie Flett Blacksmith shop in its collection of pioneer buildings from all over Alberta.
1966	The University of Calgary became autonomous from the University of Alberta.
1967	Canada was 100 years old as a nation. The Husky Tower was built in Calgary and is now called the Calgary Tower, a landmark visible to many parts of Nose Creek Valley. Many oil and gas, banking and commercial buildings were also constructed.
1974	Airdrie, with a population of 3879, incorporated as a Town.

1977	The original site of Fort Calgary, rehabilitated as a Calgary Centennial project, opened as an interpretive centre.
1980	The Beddington Homecoming was held, and the 75th Anniversary of Alberta as a province was celebrated.
1985	Airdrie incorporated as a city, with a population of 10,631.
1988	The City of Calgary hosted the Olympic Winter Games. The City of Airdrie welcomed the relay team carrying the Olympic torch to Calgary.
1994	Calgary celebrated its 100th Anniversary as a City.
1995	The Nose Creek Historical Society launched this History Book Project.
1996	Airdrie's population is projected to be approximately 16,400. The 25th Anniversary of the Nose Creek Historical Society's annual interdenominational services celebrating historical themes by completing this anthology, *100 Years of Nose Creek Valley History*.

Statistical Information

Compiled by Stephen Wilk

Year	Calgary population	Airdrie population
1884	506	
1891	3,876	
1894	4,000	
1901		31
1906	11,967	
1909		250
1931	81,636	
1948	104,718	
1951	127,057	
1956	179,711	
1959		309
1963		678
1974		3,879
1978	505,673	
1980		8,265
1985		10,631
1994		14,506
1996	767,059	16,374 (projected)

Valley Weather Facts

Reproduced from a City of Airdrie promotional brochure, 1996

Average Temperature	July +16.9/January -9.6degrees Celsius
Sun (average)	2,394 hours/year; daily average, 6.34 hours
Rain	30.03 cm. per year
Snow	13.54 cm. per year
Wind Speed	16.90 km./hr. or 10.6 mph
Wind Direction	20.6% of time from the N.W.
Climate	Classed as *cold temperate*

Chapter XXXIV

The Hamlet of Balzac

Balzac, the second hamlet north of Calgary on the Canadian Pacific Calgary-Edmonton line, received its name in 1891 at the hands of the railway officials. An engineer, who was fond of the famous French novelist, Honore de Balzac, who lived from 1799 to 1850, was responsible for the actual suggestion which led to the naming of Balzac.

July 1st Airdrie Annual Parade: Balzac float paying tribute to agriculture.

Present-day Balzac centre. Left to right: elevators, churches, store, and hall.

Above & below: Eighth annual Tribute to the mail service and celebration of the 50th Anniversary of Balzac Hall.

Loading up grain cars at Balzac, blue cars belong to the Alberta Government, orange, 'Trudeau' cars, as they were referred to, were owned by the Federal Government.

CHAPTER 35: THE HISTORY OF MEDICAL CARE FOR CALGARY AND THE NOSE CREEK VALLEY

Early Beginnings

Earlier chapters of this anthology have noted that traditionally native tribes gathered at the confluence of the Bow and the Elbow Rivers close to where the Nose Creek flows into the Bow River. By 1873, George and John McDougall, missionaries from Pigeon Lake, Fort Victoria and Fort Edmonton, brought Dr. George Verey with them to southern Alberta to help establish the Morleyville Mission. Dr. Verey was probably the first medical practitioner in the area, except for the native healers who had been around for centuries. There was little permanent settlement in the Calgary area until 1875, when a detachment of the Northwest Mounted Police built a fort where the Elbow met the Bow. When they built Fort Calgary the detachment also established an infirmary, with the encouragement of Dr. Richard Barrington Nevitt, the N.W.M.P. surgeon from Fort Macleod. At that time Dr. Nevitt, an artist as well as a surgeon, spent considerable time with the Stoney tribe in the Foothills at Morleyville Mission some 40 miles west of the fort and throughout the territories. In 1881, Calgary had a permanent population of approximately 25, with the remaining population scattered across a vast territory; serious medical needs could be met only by long and arduous trips.

On April 4, 1883, the *Macleod Gazette* reported "the new hospital [at Fort Calgary] is now open, comfortable, large and well lighted, and one of the best in the country". This infirmary although small, served the Northwest Mounted Police and the early settlers in what was Calgary's first hospital. The first civilian practitioner, Dr. Andrew Henderson, arrived in Calgary soon after the hospital opened. Later in the same year, the Canadian Pacific Railway reached Calgary, bringing with it two famous early physicians, Dr. Nevill James Lindsay, and Dr. Robert George Brett.

The Calgary General Hospitals

By 1890, Calgary residents of the city became distressed by several incidents of men or women dying alone and uncared for, and they started the Calgary General Hospital at 933-7th Ave. S.W. This was a rented house which served eight patients. The hospital was moved to 12th Avenue within a few years and by 1895, a 25 to 35 bed hospital was opened, which much later became an isolation hospital, for patients with contagious diseases. By 1910, with the population growing to 50,000, a third and final facility was opened on the present site, north of the Bow River in northeast Calgary. This new General Hospital could accommodate up to 200 patients in its early days, and much later it became a full serviced complete hospital for that area.

More recently, in 1986, the Peter Lougheed General Hospital was built as a further extension of the city's hospitals. Among others, it serves many patients from the Nose Creek Valley.

Holy Cross Hospital

In 1887, Roman Catholic Bishop Grandin invited the Montreal-based Sisters of Charity to found a hospital in Calgary. Four "Grey Nuns" arrived in Calgary on January 30, 1891, and started the hospital in a 24 foot square house. This temporary facility accommodated 35 patients. The Holy Cross Hospital grew into a major facility on the Elbow River, providing care to Calgarians until it was closed in 1996.

Medical Clinics

In early times, physicians joined in consortiums to share resources in a series of clinics, as a way to deal with the rigors of rural and urban practice. This was due to lack of funds and access to hospital equipment; hospitals gave privileges only to a limited number of doctors. Since some physicians in these clinics also used the hospitals, the clinics tended to become associated with the medical services of the hospitals over the years, becoming part of the health care delivery system for the city and the surrounding area. The first practitioners of note to provide this type of practice were Drs. N.J. Lindsay, G.D. Lafferty, and Harry Goodsir Mackid.

The Grace Hospital

The Salvation Army opened a small home and hospital to serve unmarried mothers in 1910, and it has provided medical services for families and women for many years. In recent times they developed a hospice program which continues today. Other parts of the Salvation Army Grace Hospital were closed in 1996, and some facilities such as the Women Centre transferred to the Foothills Hospital.

The Colonel Belcher Hospital

The Colonel Belcher Hospital grew out of the need to serve the medical needs of military and militia veterans after World War I. Its first location was in the Ogden Hotel prior to moving to the Morse Warehouse on 8th Avenue S.W. In 1926, it moved two doors east to another warehouse, the Blow building. The new premises on 12th Avenue and 4th Street S.W. were opened by the Department of Pensions and National Health in December of 1943. The facility handled 376 veterans at its peak time during World War II. Many veterans from the Nose Creek Valley and Calgary area have been served, and continue to be served, by the Belcher Hospital which is now being run by the Regional Health Authority.

Alberta Children's Hospital

A hospital for crippled children was opened by the Junior Red Cross Society in 1922 in a rented house located at 522-18th Avenue S.W. This home, called the Brickburn House, accommodated 35 children with mainly orthopaedic problems. In 1929, the hospital moved to the three story building on Royal Avenue S.W., with an increased capacity of 50 persons. A third 128 bed Children's Hospital was opened on the present site in 1952. By 1958, the hospital had been taken over by the Children's Hospital Society and its role was widened to serve all types of paediatric needs. In 1981, the present hospital was dedicated as a comprehensive child health centre to serve the population of southern Alberta. It remains the only children's specialty hospital within the province.

Baker Memorial Sanatorium

The Baker Memorial Sanatorium opened on the north side of the Bow River Calgary in 1920 for the treatment of tuberculosis victims in Alberta. By 1952 it was serving only southern Alberta. Since medical advances caused a marked decrease in tuberculosis cases, in the 1960's the Sanatorium became a residential facility for the mentally handicapped. The Sanatorium officially closed in 1981 and was changed to the Baker Centre for the mentally handicapped. In 1987, this too closed and the building became a Family and Social Services Facility.

Foothills Hospital

In 1959, the provincial government authorized the building of the Foothills Provincial General Hospital to become a university training hospital. This was in association with the developing University of Calgary. Construction began in 1962 but was somewhat prolonged, reaching completion on May 30, 1966. Over the years additional parts were added to the hospital, such as a nursing residential facility, a south tower for offices and residential accommodations, and a special services building which included the Provincial Laboratories and the Tom Baker Cancer Centre. The Foothills remains a full service hospital for the northwest part of the city of Calgary and surrounding area.

Rocky View General Hospital

The Rocky View General Hospital (Highwood Building) opened in 1986 and was dedicated to the treatment of patients primarily in the southern sector of the city. This hospital was developed to meet the exploding population of Calgary and is a part of the district hospital group; Holy Cross, Belcher and Rocky View—all under the aegis of the Regional Hospital Authority.

Nose Creek Valley

The Nose Creek Valley's pioneering physician, Dr. W.F. Edwards, resided in Airdrie and served the valley area from 1907 to 1940, when he died prematurely. Dr. George Bischoff served the Crossfield area from 1906 to 1918, transferring to Calgary in later years. Both surgeons spent many a trip by horse and buggy between these communities north of Calgary. Dr. Edwards and Nurse Margaret Kinniburgh assisted in the 1918 influenza epidemic, taking care of the medical needs of many farmers and ranchers and villagers of the valley. After his death, the population drove to Calgary for their medical needs.

Other doctors working in the valley were Dr. W.G. Fowler, who served Irricana and moved to Acme around 1918; Dr. T.G. Richie, who began his practice in Cochrane in 1904; and Dr. George Bishop who served Crossfield from 1904 to 1914.

Submitted by Gerald McDougall and Stephen Wilk, 1996

Gerald M. McDougall M.D. F.R.C.P.C. is a Professor in the Faculty of Medicine at the University of Calgary

Dr. George Bishop served out of Crossfield from 1904-1914.
Dr. Edwards (right) served from Airdrie from 1907 to 1940.

Dr. W.J. Fowler served out of Irricana moved to Acme around 1918.
Dr. T. G.G. Richie served from Cochrane in 1904.
(See **One Day's Journey,** by S.Wilk, 1963 pps 132 ff)

Peter Lougheed General Hospital.

Alberta Childrens' Hospital

Foothills Medical Centre.

Holy Cross Hospital.

Rockyview General Hospital.

The Calgary General Hospital.

Grace Hospital.

Colonel Belcher Hospital.

CHAPTER 36: HIGHER EDUCATION SERVES THE VALLEY
The University of Alberta and the University of Calgary

After Alberta became a province, with control over education, it needed to establish a Normal School to train teachers. This facility was the first post-secondary institution to influence the district. The Alberta Normal School began operations in Calgary in 1905, changing its name to the Calgary Normal School after similar schools started in Camrose and Edmonton. It continued as the primary post-secondary institution in the Calgary area until it was absorbed by the University of Alberta's Faculty of Education in 1945, sharing accommodations with the Technical Institute from 1922 to 1960.

The Calgary Normal School gradually lengthened its programme from four to eight months, and included both recent high school graduates and university graduates in its student body; it also prepared teachers for elementary secondary, rural, town and city schools. Many of the teachers in the Nose Creek Valley schools described in Chapter 22 of this book were trained at these Normal Schools.

Provincial control and uncertain finances due to the changing economy meant that the institution wrestled with pressures to overcome teacher shortages, a centralized curriculum and fluctuating enrolments. The staff were innovative, however, and helped introduce Progressive Education (the Enterprise Method) to Alberta schools in the 1930's. The Normal School made short summer school courses available, encouraged independent study by the 1930's, and established special programmes for rural teachers, including practice teaching in rural schools. Textbooks written by these teachers were used in Alberta schools.

An interesting part of the Normal School experience was the "lits" class, with literary exercises. Held on Friday afternoons, these exercises allowed each class or group of thirty or so students to develop skits, produce musical reviews, and present poetry or prose readings. All of these helped student teachers hone the skills needed to create future productions of events such as the Christmas pageant, a mainstay of school life in rural areas.

The student body at this time was overwhelmingly rural; for example, in 1928 only 71 of 349 students came from Calgary. As well three quarters of them were women. An examination of yearbooks of the period suggests that a number of the students came from the Nose Creek Valley district. The yearbook for 1924-25 recorded the favourite pastime of Melva Benedix; making biscuits. In 1926-27 Bertha Baker from Beddington, Alice Martineau of Airdrie, and Dorothy Ingham of Crossfield were said to have ambitions to ride a Chrysler roadster, dramatic interests, and to have studied interior designing. Through the years others from the district attended Calgary Normal School, including Alberta Spitzmesser in 1929-30, Mae Carlson, Catherine Jenkins and Gladys Tebbs in 1930-31, John Oberholtzer and George Cooper in 1931-32. Even Symons Valley, Balzac and Yankee Valley sent students to Normal School. The existing yearbooks for 1911 to 1945 identify at least 36 people from the area. This does not include some who went to Calgary for their Grade 12 and are listed as coming from Calgary, nor others who may have lived on the edge of the area but whose post office box was outside the Nose Creek Valley.

Long before the University of Alberta took over teacher training and officially established its campus in Calgary, there had been attempts to establish university level classes in Calgary. In 1907, the provincial government chose Edmonton as the site of the University of Alberta. This led to an angry reaction in Calgary, already smarting from the loss of the capital; a group of businessmen supported by some university-educated residents of the area attempted to establish and maintain a private university. Calgary College existed from 1912 to 1915, when it collapsed partly due to the war and partly because some courses were not necessarily of university level. In the 1920's some of the same people lobbied for the establishment of a junior college which would offer first and second year courses. This too was unsuccessful, though the university did give Educational Psychology courses on weekends for a couple of years.

When the University of Alberta set up a Faculty of Education campus in Calgary in 1945, demands for local university education increased. In 1947, Arts and Science classes as well as Music and Physical Education began to be added to the faculty's programme, thus allowing education students to study for two years in Calgary. The Faculty of Arts and Science was officially created in 1951, resulting in friction between the two faculties over content and methods of courses and the role of summer school. Until the late 1950's and early 1960's, most education students were women from rural areas, while Arts and Science classes were overwhelmingly filled with men from Calgary.

Business classes began in 1953, and the addition of Engineering courses solidified the increasing diversification of the university campus. In the meantime the name was changed to the University of Alberta at Calgary. As a result of pressure from professors, students and a citizens' committee, demands for autonomy increased, especially after 1960. In that year, the university moved to its present site, ending the shared accommodation with the Technical Institute.

In 1966, the university became fully autonomous as the University of Calgary. As its growth accelerated, new programmes and faculties such as Management, Law, Medicine, Nursing and Environmental Studies were established. It has been said that the most important people on University campuses are the students, for without them and their choices, spurred in part by the economy, the university would not hire new professors or establish new programmes.

The University of Calgary has a tradition of drawing from the immediate region. Yearbooks include a number of students from the Nose Creek Valley. A cursory glance at yearbooks from 1945 to 1966 show at least 26 people from Airdrie, Crossfield and Balzac, with names such as McIvor, Church and Clapperton. Since 1966 the numbers have grown, and as the Nose Creek Valley has increased in population other graduates have settled in the area. The Alumni Association suggests the numbers of University of Calgary graduates in the Nose Creek Valley are in the hundreds.

It must not be forgotten, however, that the University of Alberta served for fifty years or more as the sole provincial university. As a consequence, it has a long tradition of drawing on rural students, which continues. For those in specialized faculties such as Agriculture, Medicine, Pharmacy and Dentistry, this university became the locus for studies. Among the recent Nose Creek Valley names attending are Shuttleworth, Ralston, Jones, Hanson and Church.

Not only were students affected by the University of Alberta but the population of the region as a whole felt its impact. Some early textbooks were written by faculty members such as Broadus and Hardy. An integral part of the influence was the university's growing reputation for practical and scientific research. This was reflected in the fact that the university's president, Henry Marshall Tory, drew from University of Alberta scientists when establishing the Alberta Research Council and later the National Research Council. Much of the university's research benefited farmers in the Nose Creek Valley and elsewhere.

The Faculty of Agriculture, for example, was one of the first faculties established, in 1910. Before the Second World War, this Faculty had established programmes in plant breeding, animal nutrition, general ecology and soil testing: staff kept in close touch with farmers and farm organizations in the province. Later, programmes dealing with genetics and veterinary science were added. From this Faculty came many of the District Agricultural Representatives. By 1918, the Faculty of Agriculture began to teach Home Economics, which later became an independent school until its recent absorption as a result of economic stringency. Many of the District Home Economists who served Alberta were educated in this programme. Students from rural areas were influenced by Farm Week on the campus, which was sponsored by the United Farm Women, among others. After the Second World War this tradition continued. Indeed, the growth in enrolment led to expansion in a number of facilities due to crowded conditions. The Faculty of Agriculture added new buildings in 1954, enlarging on a previous expansion of 1930.

Another important part of the University of Alberta mission to the people of Alberta was through its continuing education or extension programme, initially located within the Faculty of Arts and Science but later a separate division and faculty. President Tory saw this as a fundamental tool to demonstrate that the university belonged to the whole province. University professors and staff such as E.A. Corbett toured the province giving talks and presentations. Former President Walter Johns has suggested that when the Director, Dr. Ottewell, was promoted to Registrar in 1928, he had worn out seven Ford cars; Johns surmised that there were few students at the university whose communities Ottewell had not visited at some time. It should be noted that the University of Calgary has continued this strong emphasis on extension, continuing education and distance education. Indeed, Andrew Doucette, the first director of the Calgary campus of the University of Alberta, gave a great many speeches throughout the region to promote the fledgling campus as the university for the area. CKUA radio was established in 1927 as an integral part of university extension; programmes such as *Question Box*, *Homemakers' Hour* and *Music Hour* as well as organ recitals became familiar to Albertans.

Olds College of Agriculture

The province wrestled with the problem of agricultural education. In 1911, a demonstration farm was located at Olds. At about the same time the Board of Agricultural Education under H.M. Tory decided agricultural education should not be confined to the University of Alberta but should include three schools of Agriculture elsewhere, including one at Olds. The graduates of these schools were able to get some credit for their two years if they decided to attend the university. The first buildings at Olds were constructed in 1912, and with federal funding, classes began. During the 1930's, the federal government passed the Dominion Youth Training Programme Act, which allowed farm boys among others to get further education. Later the agriculture programme at Olds expanded to include Home Economics. A survey in 1959 noted the limitations of the programmes with the decline in farm jobs, and as a result of this and changes in provincial post-secondary education policy, Olds College became a community college with expanded programmes. By 1969, its offerings included classes in Agricultural Technology, Horticulture, Fashion, Irrigation, and commercial and academic studies. One programme which has affected the Nose Creek Valley has been Animal Technology, as many assistants and technicians in veterinary clinics have been trained at Olds. A survey in 1968 suggested that about half the students at Olds came from the immediate area, including the Nose Creek Valley.

Southern Alberta Institute of Technology

Another institution which has served the Nose Creek Valley is the Institute of Technology (Tech), now the Southern Alberta Institute of Technology (SAIT). The failure of Calgary College in 1915 led to a provincial inquiry on post-secondary education. Headed by the President of the University of Toronto, the Commission recommended that Alberta keep one provincial university and start a provincial institute of technology. Hence, in 1916, the Provincial Institute of Technology was established at Calgary. The first classes were held at Colonel Walker School in east Calgary.

By 1919, 300 students were crowded into classrooms in four locations. Programmes included metal working, electrical, coal mining and commercial classes. Again federal aid was involved. In 1922, the Tech moved to Heritage Hall, on the present site of the Southern Alberta Institute of Technology. There it shared facilities with the Normal School except during World War II, and the fledgling university campus. Indeed, from 1947 until 1962, the Faculty of Education had a Industrial Teacher education programme using links to the Tech.

The Tech, one of the first in Canada, initially taught trades. Enrolment grew rapidly in the 1920's to almost 900 full-time students, so that enrolment had to be restricted for some courses. Evening and correspondence courses also flourished, and by the 1930's aeronautics courses had been added. The 1930's was a time of struggle, yet the institution survived and student life continued. Unemployment fuelled demand and the Tech participated in the Dominion Youth Training Programme, and arts and handicrafts became part of the campus.

After World War II, the campus took back facilities that had been loaned to the Armed Forces, and by 1956 over 5500 students had enrolled for classes. In the years following, increased funding allowed the Tech, renamed Southern Alberta Institute of Technology in 1960, to shift from a trade school to a polytechnic institute. With the rapid post-war changes in the economy, and federal initiatives under Prime Minister Diefenbaker and his successors, other programmes such as petroleum technology, health technology, business, broadcasting, tourism and library technology developed as the campus grew rapidly and more students enrolled. By 1980, 39,000 full-time and part-time students were registered. As well, the institution struggled for autonomy, succeeding in 1984.

The people of Nose Creek district have been influenced by the Tech. Through its programmes have come many of the local tradespeople, from carpenters, sheet metal workers, plumbers and electricians who build and service residences, to automotive specialists servicing vehicles, to laboratory technicians helping to keep people healthy.

Other Educational Influences

Finally, the Nose Creek area was influenced by the nursing schools at the General, Holy Cross, and Foothills Hospitals, and by the business colleges of Calgary.

In brief, the Nose Creek Valley has been served by the post-secondary institutions of Calgary, Olds and even Edmonton through the programmes which have attracted students from the valley. As well, it should not be forgotten that many of the specialists and professionals who have located in the valley or serve people from the area were trained at these institutions, and these residents continue to enhance the quality of life in their professional and voluntary endeavours.

Submitted by Dr. Robert MacDonald, University of Calgary, 1996

Nose Creek and Mount Royal College

The Nose Creek Valley, with its fertile land, was most attractive to settlers seeking homesteads in the early years of this century. Many of the settlers just north of Calgary came from the United States. While making arrangements to stake out their claim it was necessary for them to spend some time in Calgary. A great many of them made contact with Central Methodist Church, which was located in the heart of downtown Calgary, having been established by the pioneer Methodist Missionary, the Rev. John McDougall. In July 1903, the Rev. George Kerby came from Toronto to be the minister of this growing congregation. A large number of the would-be homesteaders became acquainted with this dynamic young clergyman, a relationship which lasted for many years.

At the urging of the now Rev. Dr. George W. Kerby, the Canadian Methodist Church agreed to establish one of its church related schools in Calgary, a decision that received the approval of the Alberta Government. In July 1912, Kerby resigned from Central Methodist Church to become the first principal of the new school called Mount Royal College.

Kerby planned for this new college to become not only an educational centre but also a cultural Mecca for a fast growing city. In addition to the academic programme, he also established the Conservatory of Music and Speech Arts, designed to bring much needed culture to Calgary.

The opening of Mount Royal College was greeted with enthusiasm by rural residents, including the homesteaders in the Nose Creek area. Now they were able to send their children to a residential school where there was excellent supervision and in addition, they had a centre for piano and other music lessons. From the very beginning, they have given Mount Royal College loyal support.

In the early years the College had an elementary school which was widely supported by some parents who otherwise would have had to look to Eastern Canada for a place to send their youngsters. The rural school district, however, was making its appearance. After a few years the elementary section of Mount Royal was eliminated because of the increasing availability of rural and urban elementary schools. Then the secondary school became the ever-growing part of Mount Royal until the rural high schools were organized. Mount Royal was the first high school in Calgary to introduce the semester system, which attracted many students. This was followed by an affiliation with the University of Alberta to bring much needed University courses to the Calgary area. Through all the changes caused by a developing city and district, the rural areas including Nose Creek offered loyal support to the College. The Conservatory of Music and Speech Arts continued to serve the area effectively.

Not only did the district support Mount Royal College by sending their children as students to the various departments, they also helped provide it with solid financial support. It was necessary for the College to seek help for its various building expansions. The old original building on the northwest corner of 11th Street and 7th Avenue became too small for the growing enterprise. In 1948, the Kerby Memorial Building and the G.D. Stanley Gymnasium were built on the south side of 7th Avenue. Both structures were opened free of debt because of the generous donations from supporters in Calgary and rural areas.

Howard P. Wright and his family moved into the area west of Airdrie after making a lasting contact with Central United Church and Dr. Kerby. He was an outstanding farmer and an expert in seed grains. The University of Alberta recognized his accomplishments by awarding him an Honorary Doctor of Law Degree. Dr. Wright, when he retired and moved into Calgary, established a relationship with Central United Church and took a great interest in Mount Royal College. He was a member of the College's Board of Governors and on the retirement of Chief Justice C.J. Ford, became its Chairman. He guided the College in its transition from a church-related institution to a Junior College of the Province of Alberta. Despite failing health he watched the construction of the new buildings in Lincoln Park. The Wright Theatre in the College is named in his honour.

It would be a well-nigh impossible task to list the names of those from the Nose Creek District who have supported Mount Royal over these many years. The alumni list is filled with names that evoke many memories. From Cochrane, the Edge family appears. In the Beddington area the Pole family is prominent. The Balzac area makes one recall the Perry family that today leads the fight to stop the insidious Calgary urban sprawl which threatens to absorb irreplacable and fertile farm land. The Airdrie district yields such names as Brookmeyer, Dahl, Ferns and Giesbrecht. As the children of the early settlers grew up and married, some of them continued the farming tradition. They moved to other communities but carried the Mount Royal tradition with them. Thus from the Irricana area such names as Butters, Hendrix and Lintick appear.

Submitted by Dr. W. Jack Collett, former Principal of Mount Royal College, 1996

Dissatisfaction at the University of Calgary's status vis a vis University of Alberta was dramatically illustrated in this attempt to paint out the word 'Branch.' Officials suspected local students of perpetrating this bit of nocturnal editing.

CONCLUSION TO PART IV

Over 100 years, growing from a vast prairie region to a growing rural, agrarian economy, the Nose Creek Valley has experienced benefits and problems from its proximity to a growing and burgeoning metropolitan city. Although rural forces have always been and still are significant to our understanding of the Valley's history, one cannot ignore the effects of urbanization upon the community under study. We have seen how medical services and higher education have served the Valley as these institutions expanded to meet growing needs.

The agricultural economy and tradition is still strong in the Valley, however, and the following chapters describe some of the many businesses and organizations which have served the people of the Nose Creek Valley.

Proposed site of the Uof A, Calgary, 1956.

Construction begins, 1960.

MacEwan Hall, 1972.

Aerial view of the University of Calgary campus. (1987)

Above: the main building opened its doors in 1922. (Below, left), an aerial view of the campus, photographed in 1966. (Below, right), the Mechanics' Class, like all other courses offered at S.A.I.T., is thorough and comprehensive.

The Alberta College of Art—an independent body, 1984.

The John Ware Building.

(Above) The Aeronautical Engineering Department enjoyed tremendous growth after World War II. Third-year courses, along with an Aeronautical Engineering program, were offered.
(Below, left), the library has the proper ambience for study. (Below, right), A field trip of sorts: S.A.I.T.'s Surveyor students map out the campus.

261

Hon. Lt. Col. Rev. George W. Kerby,
B.A., D.D.L.L.B.

Downtown Campus.

Old Mount Royal College, 1912

HISTORICAL MILESTONES

1910	College opens in downtown Calgary under sponsorship of Methodist Church
1925	Becomes a secondary school of the United Church of Canada
1931	Junior College affiliated with the University of Alberta
1966	Becomes a public institution under the Colleges Act of the Province of Alberta
1972	Main campus relocates to southwest Lincoln Park
1985	The first in a series of satellite downtown campuses opens
1989	Completion of $73 million facility expansion project
1989	Mount Royal Court student residence, a $12 million Olympic legacy, opens
1989	Expansion of two-year University Transfer programs in Arts and Science
1990	City Centre Campus, a new downtown facility, opens
1993	The Foundation launches $15-million Capital Campaign
1994	The Small Business Training Centre opens at City Centre Campus
1995	The College introduces two applied-degree programs

Lincoln Park Campus. Expansion is nearing completion, 1972

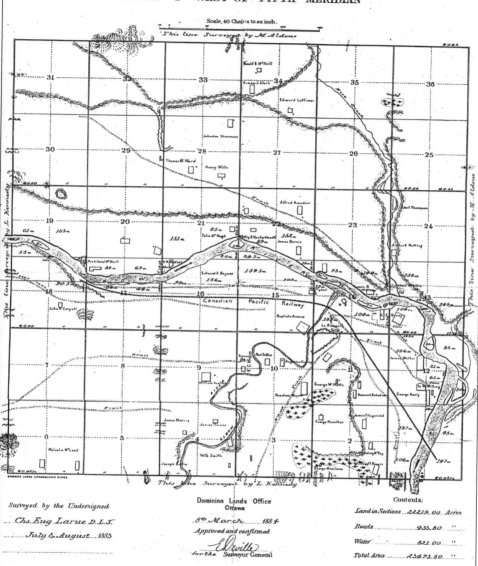

PLAN OF
TOWNSHIP Nº 24
RANGE 1 WEST OF FIFTH MERIDIAN

Scale, 40 Chains to an inch.

This line Surveyed by M. Aldous

During the summer of 1883, while the CPR tracks were being laid into Calgary, the area was surveyed for the Dominion government by C.E. Larue. Settlers at that time included several ex-Mounted Policemen (ie. Denny, Walker, Butlin, Barwis, Van Courtlandt), former Metis buffalo hunters (ie. Faillan, Anouse, Mayett, McGillis), and recent arrivals. At the confluence of the rivers were the NWMP fort and Hudson's Bay Co. post, while up the Elbow was the R.C. mission. In the winter of 1883-84, squatters established a tent town on the east side of the Elbow along the railway tracks but in the spring of 1884 the CPR laid out the official town of Calgary on Section 15.

Adapted from the Glenbow Library Map #1, 1981

Calgary, 1883

Historical Growth of the City of Calgary
1884-1976

ANNEXATION MAP

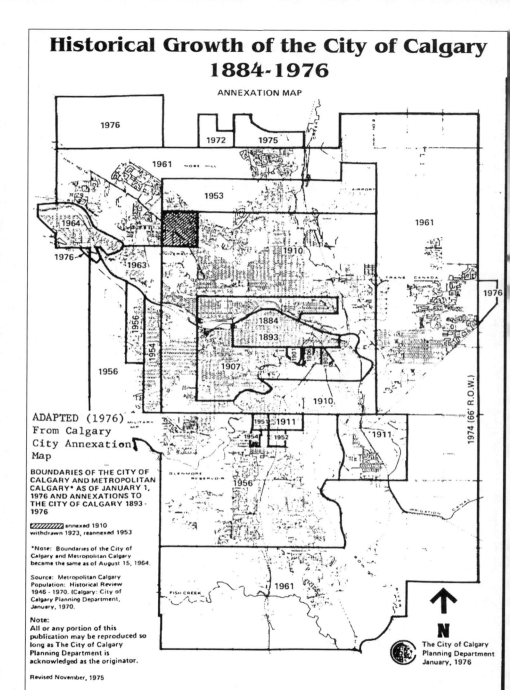

ADAPTED (1976)
From Calgary
City Annexation
Map

BOUNDARIES OF THE CITY OF
CALGARY AND METROPOLITAN
CALGARY* AS OF JANUARY 1,
1976 AND ANNEXATIONS TO
THE CITY OF CALGARY 1893 -
1976

▨▨▨▨ annexed 1910
withdrawn 1923, reannexed 1953

*Note: Boundaries of the City of
Calgary and Metropolitan Calgary
became the same as of August 15, 1964.

Source: Metropolitan Calgary
Population: Historical Review
1946 - 1970. (Calgary: City of
Calgary Planning Department,
January, 1970.

Note:
All or any portion of this
publication may be reproduced so
long as The City of Calgary
Planning Department is
acknowledged as the originator.

Revised November, 1975

N

The City of Calgary
Planning Department
January, 1976

ANNEXATION MAP CITY OF CALGARY

From Stephen Wilk's Doctoral Dissertation, 1978, page 61 — San Francisco Theological Seminary

City of Calgary: History of Annexation

(from page 21, 1996 Municipal Handbook, the City of Calgary Planning and Building Department,)

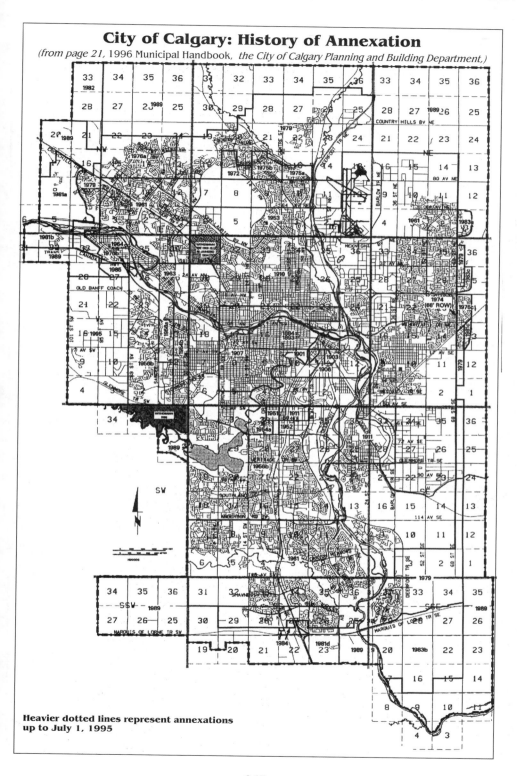

Heavier dotted lines represent annexations
up to July 1, 1995

265

DESCRIPTION OF CALGARY'S OFFICIAL CREST

The design for The City of Calgary's crest was chosen through a contest held by the Calgary Herald and adopted officially by City Council as the basis for its Corporate Seal in March 1902 By-law 4671. The winning design was submitted by J.C. Wilson of Calgary and A.C. Racey of Montreal.

The upper third of the shield depicts the Rocky Mountains, and Calgary's proximity to them. The lower two-thirds bears the red Cross of St. George, on which the Canadian Maple Leaf is mounted. Within the Maple Leaf is a bull buffalo, the former master of our region. Supporting the shield are a horse and steer. They represent the original wealth on which our city was built.

The crest above the shield contains a mural crown (a symbol of loyalty) and a sun setting in the west.

Below the shield are the Leek of Wales, the Rose of England, the Thistle of Scotland and the Shamrock of Ireland. They signify the ancestry of the majority of our early settlers.

The scroll contains our motto Onward and the dates of incorporation as a town (1884) and as a city (1894).

Under the scroll are the Union Jack, which signifies our relationship with the British Commonwealth of Nations, and the Canadian Ensign, which for many years was our country's Flag.

In the original design, the date shown for the incorporation as a town was 1882. This date was supplied in error at the time the design competition was held.

City Council officially changed the date in the design in 1975.

From 1902 to 1984, the official crest existed in black and white only. In 1984, Alderman Larry Gilchrist asked the Public Information Department to develop the city Crest in full color by using the original concept approved by Council in 1902 (By-law 66M84).

DESCRIPTION OF CALGARY'S OFFICIAL FLAG

The design for The City of Calgary's official flag was chosen through a competition conducted by the Centennial of Incorporation Committee. It was adopted officially by City Council on October 3, 1983. The winning design was submitted by Yvonne Fritz and Gwin Clarke of Calgary.

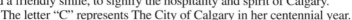

The design of the flag, incorporating the white Stetson and the letter "C", symbolizes a harmony between The City of Calgary and the hospitality and spirit of her people.

The Stetson has been worn with pride by Calgarians since Calgary's date of incorporation as a town (1884) and as a city (1894). For the past 35 years, the white Stetson has represented the key to our great city. It has been given to people from around the world, with a warm handshake and a friendly smile, to signify the hospitality and spirit of Calgary.

The letter "C" represents The City of Calgary in her centennial year.

Historically, this letter has signified the character, change, culture and charm that has become synonymous with the Calgary community.

The official colours of red and white were chosen to show vividly the liveliness of our city's development. The scarlet of the Northwest Mounted Police uniform is reflected in the brilliance of the red and white colours seen on the playing fields.

This combination of colours illustrates the zest of Calgary's hospitality and spirit.

SONG FOR CALGARY

Following a national contest held in 1986, "Neighbours of the World", an original tune composed and written by Barry Bowman and Tom Loney, was selected as the song for Calgary.

THE CITY'S FLORAL EMBLEM

Calgary's official floral emblem, the Red Pasque Flower *(Anemone Pulsatilla Rubra)* was adopted by City Council on July 2, 1991.

The Red Pasque Flower was chosen because of its close resemblance to the Prairie Crocus which grows wild in the Calgary area. Unlike the Prairie Crocus, the Red Pasque Flower has been hybridized and can be grown by local gardeners. The bright red flowers can be seen in early spring.

CALGARY MAYORS

1884-1886	George Murdoch	1910-1912	John W. Mitchell
1886-1888	George C. King	1912-1914	H.A. Sinnott
1888-1889	A.E. Shelton	1914-1918	Michael C. Costello
1889-1890	D.W. Marsh	1918-1919	Robert C. Marshall
1890-1891	J.D. Lafferty	191 9-1922	Samuel H. Adams
1891-1892	James Reilly	1922-1926	George H. Webster
1892-1894	Alexander Lucas	1926-1929	Fred E. Osborne
1894-1895	Wesley F. Orr	1929-1944	Andrew Davison
1895-1896	Alexander McBride	1944-1949	James C. Watson
1896-1897	Wesley F. Orr	1949-1959	Donald H. Mackay
1897-1898	Arthur L. Cameron	1959-1963	Harry W. Hays
1895-1899	James Reilly	1963-1965	J.W. Grant MacEwan
1899-1900	W.H. Cushing	1965-1969	John C. Leslie
1900-1901	James S. Mackie	1969-1977	Rodney Sykes
1901-1903	Thomas Underwood	1977-1980	Ross P. Alger
1903-1904	Silas A. Ramsay	1980-1989	Ralph Klein
1904-1906	John Emerson	1989	Don A. Hartman
1906-1908	Arthur L. Cameron	1989-	Al Duerr
1908-1910	R.R. Jamieson		

The Weather In Calgary

SUMMARY OF METEOROLOGICAL OBSERVATIONS AT CALGARY, ALBERTA
Data Supplied by Atmospheric Environment Services – Calgary Weather Office

	Jan.	Feb.	Mar.	Apr.	May	Jun.	Jul.	Aug.	Sept.	Oct.	Nov.	Dec.	Year
Normal Data 1961-1990													
Daily Max. Temp. C	-3.6	-0.5	3.3	10.6	16.4	20.6	23.2	22.7	17.4	12.6	2.9	-2.3	10.3
Daily Min. Temp. C	-15.7	-12.3	-8.4	-2.4	3.0	7.4	9.5	8.6	3.8	-1.2	-9.0	-14.4	-2.6
Daily Mean Temp. C	-9.6	-6.3	-2.5	4.1	9.7	14.0	16.4	15.7	10.6	5.7	-3.0	-8.3	3.9
Rainfall (mm)	0.2	0.2	1.5	9.2	43.9	76.7	69.9	48.7	42.7	6.4	0.6	0.1	300.3
Snowfall (cm)	18.0	14.9	18.7	20.4	10.2	0.3	0.0	0.0	6.4	11.5	16.0	19.0	135.4
No. of Days with Measurable Precip.	9	8	9	8	11	13	12	10	9	6	7	8	111.0
Average Sunshine Hrs.	113.8	136.8	174.0	214.8	256.0	285.5	320.1	284.8	201.8	179.0	125.4	102.5	2394.6
Average Wind Speed (km/h)	16	15	16	17	18	17	15	14	15	15	15	16	16
Prevailing Wind Direction	W	S	S	N	NW	NW	NW	NW	S	S	S	W	N
Extreme Data 1881-1990													
Extreme Max. Temp. C	16.5	18.9	22.8	29.4	32.4	35.0	36.1	35.6	33.3	29.4	22.8	19.4	
Day/Year of Record	10/1987	12/1934	30/1906	29/1926	30/1986	26/1926	25/1933	03/1914	01/1967	02/1943	04/1975	05/1939	
Extreme Min. Temp. C	-44.4	-45.0	-37.2	-30.0	-16.7	-3.3	-0.6	-2.2	-13.3	-25.7	-35.0	-42.8	
Day/Year of Record	31/1893	04/1893	09/1951	02/1954	01/1954	08/1904	05/1884	30/1886	24/1926	31/1984	30/1893	17/1924	
Greatest 24 hr. Rainfall (mm)	7.6	6.4	23.4	37.1	65.0	79.2	95.3	80.8	92.6	45.7	5.6	6.4	
Day/Year of Record	07/1902	26/1885	23/1910	30/1912	01/1902	01/1932	15/1927	25/1945	12/1985	01/1915	11/1948	03/1885	
Greatest 24 hr. Snowfall (cm)	25.4	27.7	24.1	45.7	48.4	24.9	0.3	6.1	22.9	29.7	35.6	21.8	
Day/Year of Record	03/1913	10/1951	13/1889	21/1932	06/1981	06/1951	23/1918	25/1900	19/1895	04/1914	13/1914	11/1889	
Extreme Wind Speed (km/h)	84	89	85	105	90	82	82	97	84	90	84	100	
Prevailing Direction	N	NW	NW	N	NW	NW	NW	N	NW	W	W	N	

267

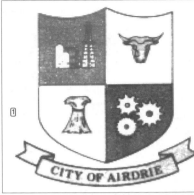

City of Airdrie Crest

Upper left—natural resources: oil and gas industry

Upper right—Agriculture livestock: beef industries

Lower left—Agriculture: crop, grain farming

Lower right—Manufacturing: processing

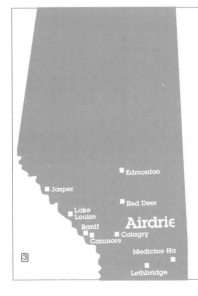

*(Above) Rock View School Division #41 (1996) administers the public schools in Airdrie and the Valley, north of Calgary. (Below) Statistical data courtesy **Lifestyle**, the City of Airdrie Lifestyle Profile.*

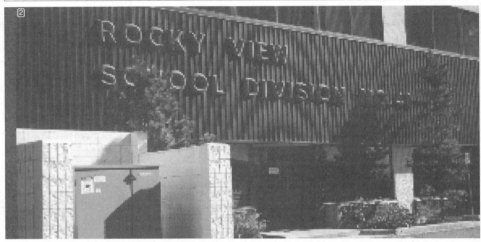

Driving Distance from Airdrie to:

Location	Distance
Calgary City Limits	10 km
Calgary International Airport	18 km
Downtown Calgary	30 km
Red Deer	112 km
Edmonton	261 km
Canmore	136 km
Banff	159 km
Lake Louise	209 km
Lethbridge	259 km
Medicine Hat	323 km
United States Border (south)	367 km

PART V: WORKING AND SOCIALIZING IN THE VALLEY

Introduction

In the first four parts of this anthology we presented a broad overview of the history of the Nose Creek Valley and how it is being preserved. We have seen how its geological and topographical features have influenced the Valley's development; how the native people wandered, following the buffalo herds before anyone else came; how the arrival of European explorers, fur traders, missionaries, and mounties ushered in the age of ranching and farming. We have looked at a variety of themes influencing the growth and evolution of settled life in the region. The effects of urbanization have been described, showing how the cities of Calgary and Airdrie encouraged continued intensive development along the Nose Creek Valley corridor north of the Bow River.

We now turn to descriptions of enterprises and organizations within the Nose Creek Valley. For such a large area, we can only give a few examples of the kinds of group activities that take place in the Valley; a description of all of the families and businesses would fill several more books. Here we present stories of the business of agriculture: family farms and ranches; grain growing and marketing; raising livestock, genetics, and meat packing; dairying. We have a sampling of other industries, some of them family enterprises, others large companies which still take part in community life; they range from aviation to horticulture to newspaper publishing, oil and gas to leather and fur. Another common type of enterprise in the Valley is the co-operative, large or small. Finally there are the organizations which serve all walks of life, providing entertainment, education, service to charities, and a chance to socialize.

CHAPTER 37: FAMILIES AND FARMS

Introduction

The pioneers who settled the Nose Creek Valley came mostly from Eastern Canada, the United States, and Europe. Although the bulk of European settlers were from Great Britain, others immigrated from Scandinavia, Germany, and Central Europe. Each group brought its cultural survival skills and knowledge of farm practices. The members of each ethnic group contributed to and enriched the developing communities. This chapter gives only a few examples of the hardiness and entrepreneurial skills of those who ventured into the Valley to make a new start of life's journey. The succeeding generations learned from their ancestors how to enrich the quality of life. Here we focus on some settlers, and their descendants, of Scandinavian and British origins. We see how important family and community were to the settlers, whose own extended families were far away.

The Hansen Pioneer Farm

My father Hans Andreas (Andrew) Hansen served in the Danish cavalry during World War I. He attended "folkschool" after his discharge, and in 1920 he emigrated to New York and worked on farms near West Winfield. In March 1922, he came to Calgary and the first summer he worked on farms in the Beddington area near the Beddington Hall. I cannot recall whom he worked for, but he did mention knowing some of the Pole families. He then worked on farms in the Goldenrod area west of Airdrie. I recall him telling about working on threshing crews using a steam tractor, and hauling the straw to fire the tractor's boiler. Later he rented a quarter section from the Claytons and although I am not sure about which land it was, I found a reference to the northwest quarter of Section 26-27-11-W5 in his notes, although I always thought he lived further west. During this period he also worked on Frank Collicut's ranch. He told stories about tending to the cattle as part of a work crew, living in bunkhouses and eating in cookhouses. He liked horses and working with animals. A photo showing him in a cowboy outfit was probably taken at a booth at the Calgary Stampede during this period.

Dad returned to Denmark for a visit early in 1926. His brother Aage and my mother

Jenny Larsen arrived in Airdrie during the summer of that year. Mom lived with and worked for William Pole's family after her arrival. Apparently she even did field work such as sweeping hay. In March of 1927, my parents were married and bought the east half of Section 2-27-29-W4. There was a house circa 1911, and one other small building located near the middle of the south quarter, overlooking a coulee with a small creek which drained into Nose Creek. In 1928 Dad hired a carpenter (Mr. Hermansen?) to help build two barns, one for his horses and the other for his cows. I believe that he was also helped by the Olorenshaws. In 1929 a hailstorm ruined the crops, and the Depression hit. During the following difficult years, Dad also worked on the reconstruction of the Calgary to Edmonton highway when the route was straightened. He had a four horse team with a fresno, and I think he supplied a second team of horses. He also built up a herd of over 20 dairy cows, and we usually had two hired farmhands to help in the field and with milking the cows. Mom made butter and sold it and eggs in Airdrie to private customers and I believe to Van Sickle's store. She used a horse ("Bullet") and a buggy to make her deliveries, and on occasion I would go along with her. A photo taken beside one of the glacial erratic stones near the farm shows Mom with her rig. Even though times were difficult in the 1930's, Dad continued to improve the farm. In 1934 when he was renting the C. Gump quarter, later Everett Bennett's place, he purchased a new Massey Harris binder. He planted trees for a shelterbelt in 1935, even though another hailstorm destroyed part of his crop. In 1935 he also acquired his first car, a 1926 Model T, bartered from a neighbour for a load of grain. In 1936, due to the drought, the crop was so poor that the grain was too short to be tied into bundles. Lou Switzer designed a "header" box to replace the knotter on the binder to collect the heads of grain and helped to convert the binder. In 1936 and 1937, with assistance from the P.F.R.A., he built a dam across the creek to hold water year round for the cattle, using a horse drawn walking plow, a slip and a fresno. A new house and garage were constructed in 1948.

Sometime not too long after Dad purchased the farm, my uncle Aage Hansen purchased the N.W. quarter of the same section (sometimes known as the Thorburn quarter). The remaining S.W. quarter was owned by Robert Burns, who operated a slaughter house there until 1936. About 1934 or 1935, Dad helped Aage to build two structures. They used a slip and fresno to excavate two large "trenches". They had taken two wagons and teams out towards Water Valley to the forest reserve to get some logs which they used for shoring up the walls and supporting the roof which then was mostly covered with sod. They also built shelves to support compost racks which were subsequently used to grow mushrooms. Aage would clean out neighbouring farmers' horse barns to get material for the mushroom compost. It is a strange coincidence that in later years Money's Mushroom Factory was established on almost the same site. Although Aage did produce some mushrooms for sale, the project did not ever get really established, as my grandfather passed away in 1938 and Aage went back to Denmark to tend to the estate. He got trapped in Denmark by World War II and never came back to Canada.

Dad, Mom and Aage were some of a number of Danish and Scandinavian farmers in the Airdrie district, and even though times were difficult, they enjoyed a good social life. Several families would get together to celebrate Christmas, New Year's, Easter, and especially birthdays and wedding anniversaries. These events were celebrated in the Danish manner with Danish cooking, playing games, singing and dancing. The large Danish gatherings gradually became less frequent during the wartime, as the children grew up and made new friends. The children or grandchildren of some of these families still farm on the same land but most of their farms have now been sold or subdivided, since many of the original farmers retired or their descendants moved away from the district. I was away from our farm during the winter of 1946/47 and moved to Calgary in the fall of 1948 and gradually lost touch with many of these families.

Most of the Danish and Norwegian families came to the Airdrie district following World

War I up until the early 1930's. I believe that they made a significant contribution to the community of Airdrie. They tried many agricultural innovations, such as my Uncle Aage's attempt at mushroom growing. I also recall that Halvar Kolstad grew many acres of potatoes during the early 1930's. I remember that we tried to raise ducks, guinea fowl, and turkeys at various times. Dad was a strong proponent of the cooperative movement and supported the U.F.A. organization and the Alberta Wheat Pool. He believed that there was a right way to farm and conduct his business even when it was not the most economical thing to do. The history of Airdrie as told in the book *One Day's Journey* by Stephen Wilk does not tell much about these Scandinavians. This may be due to the fact that most of the early settlers were of British origin and outnumbered the smaller ethnic groups. Perhaps it was due to their reluctance to submit stories of their part in the growth of the Airdrie district. I know that most of the Danes learned and spoke English except among themselves, and I know that Dad insisted that we speak English at home. However, I regret that I didn't learn more of the Danish language. I hope that the contributions to the Nose Creek area by the Scandinavian farmers and also of other farmers of various ethnic origins will be acknowledged.

Submitted by Charlie Hansen, 1996

The Jensen Family

This is the story of another Scandinavian family who played a significant role in the settlement of Airdrie and district. Having been pioneers and owning some of the land in the city centre, it was appropriate that Jensen Park in Airdrie was named after a member of this Danish family.

In 1930, Soren and Maren Jensen immigrated to Alberta from Denmark, with their three children, Knud, Karsten, and myself. We came and stayed with Soren Pedersen of Petersen Florists in north Calgary. As a note, I believe the Pedersens started their operation in their back yard, and it blossomed into what is now known as Golden Acre Nurseries.

The Jensens worked as a hired man and housekeeper for A. Knudsen, on a farm in Airdrie which we now own. Mr. Knudsen lost the farm back to Louis Petrie of Petrie Wholesalers. A young fellow by the name of Henderson bought it, but also ran into hard luck and lost it back to Petrie as well. Mr. Petrie offered it to Dad, who at that time could not begin to afford it, but Mr. Petrie was willing to take a chance on it.

Knud Jensen, the eldest child, returned to Denmark and married Lilly Sorensen, and later they came back to the Doc Edwards farm. They lived there until Knud passed away at age 49 in 1965, and Lilly still resides there. They raised a family of two, Spens and Lydia.

Karsten married Mary Reid from Airdrie. They lived on the Bert Hayden farm and raised four kids, Kathleen, Jerry, Frank and Kristine. Karsten died at age 53 as a result of a motor vehicle accident in Calgary in 1971.

During the war years, the boys had joined the army, and I stayed home and helped the folks with the farm and drove a milk truck. My husband-to-be also stayed home to help his folks farm and operated a local pound, a place in the community to put stray animals, mostly horses. If their owners could not be found by advertising, they would be auctioned off.

I married Robbie Davy in 1946 and we dairied for six years at the Croxford farm in Airdrie, where the Airdrie Feed Mill is presently located. The Croxford house was the first to be built in Airdrie. We had three boys; Danny and Soren were born in Airdrie, and Mark (Butch) was born after we moved to the home farm. We moved there when Dad passed away in 1955, and farmed until Robbie passed away in 1988. I remained on the farm for another six years and then moved to Woodside in Airdrie. Our boys have continued with the Davy farm.

Submitted by Margit (Jensen) Davy, 1996

271

Above: The Hansen ladies help with gathering up the hay.

Above: Hans "Andrew" Hansen in full cowboy regalia at the Calgary Stampede.

Above: A pioneer-style house overlooks a coulee that feeds Nose Creek. (1927).

Above: On her way to Airdrie to sell her butter and eggs, Mrs. Hansen pauses by an erratic rock.

Right: Harvesting crops with a horse-drawn thresher. (circa 1934).

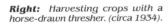

The Hansens inspect the year's crop. A 1930-model A two-horse team mows prairie grass for hay. car is in the background.

Above: An aerial view of the Hansen Farm in the 1950's. Airdrie and Nose Creek Valley are in the background.

Above and right: A family gathering in the thirties.

Above: A picnic at Big Hill Springs in 1934.

Above: Picking Saskatoon Berries at the McPherson's Coulee.

273

The McKinnon Farm and Ranching Story Northeast of Airdrie

Pioneer Lachlin McKinnon arrived in Alberta from Ontario, on March 10, 1886. He worked as a ranch hand until starting the LK Ranch, south of Dalemead on the Bow River, in 1895. He raised cattle, horses and got into extensive farming. As the family of thirteen children became involved, more land was purchased at Dalemead. In 1921, he purchased the XL Ranch at Bassano.

The XL Ranching and Farming Co. Ltd. bought eight and three-quarter sections of land east of Airdrie from Simon Wheal in 1929. Arthur, a son of Lachlin, moved there on April 10, settling on the SW 1/4 of 18-27-28-W4. Brother Edwin followed in 1935 to 32-27-28-W4. That year the land was split between Art, Ed and Fred (a younger brother who was an oil man). Beef cattle, draft and saddle horses and farming were the main enterprises.

Ed and Harriet had no children. Art and June raised Dan, Ian and Stephen. In 1958 Running M Ranches Ltd. was formed with Art, Ed, Fred, Dan, Ian and nephew Don Stewart as shareholders. Cattle feeding became another enterprise. In 1958 we started performance testing the cow herd and crossbreeding. The following spring we started using artificial insemination. This continued until 1976.

In 1966 Art, Dan and Ian bought 3 and 3/4 sections and all of the cow herd from Running M Ranches. Three Cross Cattle Syndicate was formed and in 1981 incorporated as Three Cross Cattle Ltd. Ed and Don sold to the Brigan family from Beiseker and retired to Calgary. Ian sold his land to Ben Thorlakson and moved to BC for a while, eventually settling on a ranch near Lousana. In 1966 Art, June and Stephen moved to Calgary and continued active at the farm. Art became involved with his brother Don in Farm and Ranch Management Ltd. He passed away in 1983 and Stephen in 1984. June is presently active in Calgary.

I married Donna Gieck, whom I met through 4-H. We have three children. Upon completion of high school they sought further education at Olds, Calgary and Edmonton. Each spent time working abroad in New Zealand, Japan, South Africa and England. Brenda married Bryan Giesbrecht. They have two children, Marlon and Rebecca, and carried on the farming tradition. Scott married Pam Brown from Strathmore. They have two boys, Wynn and Max. Todd married Michelle Durand from the Camrose area.

In 1975 we joined Beefbooster Cattle. This organization produces and markets beef cattle seedstock in five provinces and the US. Three Cross provides the feeding and testing facilities for over 1600 bull calves each year. We also feed commercial calves and run a 290 head research cow herd.

As did many of the farmer/ranchers from the Nose Creek Valley, Donna and I moved to Airdrie in 1991. I still go to the farm most days. Scott and Todd and their families live on the farm and are active in the daily operations of Three Cross.

Submitted by Dan McKinnon, 1996

An aerial view of the McKinnon Farm/Ranch feedlot

Cattle feeding on swathes created by combine harvester.

Commercial cattle are cross bred to maximize hybrid vigour

An overall view of the McKinnon Farm/Ranch

Above: Cattle feeding. Below: A calf getting its dinner

A Brief History of Church Ranches

Prior to the settlement of western Canada, buffalo grazed, coyotes roamed and the Stoney and Blackfoot Indians traversed the land on and around Church Ranches. In 1880, the Dominion of Canada leased the land to the legendary Cochrane Ranche and the some of the first cattle herds of Alberta grazed on these lands. In 1901, the lease ended and the title of this section (one square mile) was given to the Canadian Pacific Railway.

For the next 40 years, various settlers, living only in sod or log dwellings, attempted to purchase the title of the section from the CPR. Due to many setbacks, however, these settlers were never able to complete the payments required to obtain title.

Finally in 1941, Henry Teghtmeyer, a farmer in the Bearspaw area, purchased the section for his cattle operation and the land title was transferred from the C.P.R. for $7 an acre.

Teghtmeyer built the first permanent house and barn on the section in 1942. The buildings are still in use on the southwest corner of Church Ranches. He then sold the land to his son Carl, who together with his wife ran the cattle operation for 20 years. Today, Carl 90 years old, resides in Cochrane.

In 1968, Stan and Frances Church bought the section and moved into the old house. From this base, they started a purebred Simmental cattle business, importing the Simmental cattle from Switzerland. They added new barns and corrals and in 1974 built a new house just west of the original home.

Church Simmental Ranches grew to be one of the largest Simmental cattle seedstock operations in Canada.

Now, in the mid 1990's this land has evolved one step further....Church Ranches, a community of secluded properties with nature at one hand and all the conveniences of city living at the other....A very long way from being the home and range of the buffalo and those who followed the majestic herds.

Submitted by Stan Church, 1996

Premium Water Supply

Rocky View Water Co-op is Alberta's largest rural water treatment and distribution co-operative. It services 775 members in Bearspaw, Symons Valley and Balzac, including Church Ranches. At capacity, the Co-op can service over 2,000.

The Water Co-op selectively pumps water from the Bow River only when the river water quality is at its optimum to ensure premium quality water for its members.

Storage in the Co-op's large reservoir gives this incoming water a chance to settle which further increases its quality. An on-site treatment plant operates under strict Alberta Environment regulated standards. Testing is done daily. Water is distributed at a constant pressure (6 gpm at 100+ psi) backed up by a standby emergency power source.

From Church Ranches Information Booklet, 1996

A community of secluded country properties

The hawk, a bird of prey, soars over the Nose Creek Valley.

The Church Ranch grew to be one of the largest Simmental Cattle seedstock operation in Canada.

278

Families Near Balzac

The eastern side of the Nose Creek Valley and beyond, with its flatter terrain and warmer climate, tended to have a larger emphasis on grain growing, particularly after 1910 when the early maturing Marquis wheat strain was perfected. Marquis wheat was ripe enough to harvest before it could freeze, and it was resistant to insect pests. Still, most farmers engaged in mixed farming, raising livestock as well as crops. Because they used workhorses, they often bred their own horses and as was the general custom in western Canada, good quality stallions were brought around to visit the farms to improve the stock. The farmers needed to be jacks-of-all-trades, and they did other kinds of work when time permitted; Art Shuttleworth was a hail insurance adjuster; Grant Shuttleworth fixed engines and equipment; H.J. Jobson was an auctioneer. As well as taking part in co-operatives, the local farmers also shared their ideas and knowledge of the complexities of farming, talking at length after church and at social gatherings.

I remember sitting around talking with a group of classmates at Kathyrn School around 1970; we realized that when we included connections by marriage, we were all related to each other. Most of us lived on farms, and usually they had been settled by our grandparents and passed on to our parents. The farming community was strong and stable partly because of this kind of interrelationship.

When Edie Woolliams published *My Neighbours and Yours*, she wrote that new arrivals in the district would be warned "Don't talk about anyone in the community, they are probably relatives." Her Nose Creek Tree showed some of the relationships but was incomplete because the page did not have room to show how every family was kin to every other one.

Part of the reason for the many connections was that the settlers often had large families. In 1902, Henry and Mary Jane Ralston came to Balzac with six children, and each of them married and farmed in the Balzac district; Edith married Hugh Cooper, whose farm was north of Balzac; George married Ada Church and stayed on the original family farm; Annie married Herbert J. Jobson, Henry married Alice Oldfield, Jimmy married Bea Northcott, Ethel married Grant Shuttleworth, and all four of them farmed several miles east of Balzac, raising crops and livestock, as most people in the district did.

Another large family was the James Jones family, which brought nine children to settle east of Balzac in 1903. There are still several Jones families farming in the area; some of them have been raising fine Herefords for many years. We used to joke that my family, with its Ralston connections, were related to everyone around except the Joneses; then in 1977, George Ralston married Polly Jones. They had gone to school together as children and had each been married and widowed. George and Polly were age 82 and 81 at the time of their marriage, and they continued to go dancing and travelling for years; they had about 13 years together before George died.

The "family farm" may sound like a cliche nowadays, but the fact was that it often took the whole family to keep the farm going, as well as a hired man or two. Even when children grew up and moved to farms of their own, they continued to help each other out. A 1922 picture of a threshing crew on the H.J. Jobson farm includes H.J. Jobson, his brothers-in-law Jimmy and George Ralston, and his hired man, Syl Webster, as well as several other men. The family farm tradition continues today; for instance Art, Ted and Grant Shuttleworth came to Balzac with their mother in 1919 and farmed

279

together as Shuttleworth Brothers, growing wheat and running a threshing crew as well as raising cattle and horses. After Art died in 1967, Ted and Grant developed their own operations. Ted's daughter Joyce worked with him, breeding purebred Arabian horses, and has carried on. Grant Senior's son Grant Junior runs Charworth Farms with his family, which is growing; they raise high quality Charolais cattle and grow hay and crops ranging from flax to wheat to canola. Lloyd Ralston carried on his father Jimmy's farm, and Lloyd's daughter Brenda became a District Agriculturist; Henry's son Robin Ralston kept farming until he retired to Calgary. George Cooper carried on his father's farm, and his children Ann Hollands and John Cooper now have their own operations, with John growing crops and Ann raising livestock. Herbert H. Jobson carried on his father's farm till retirement; his son Brian lives on the farm but works for the M.D., while Maureen and Valerie live and work in Calgary. Many other families have had some children working with their parents and continuing to farm, while the other children took up careers and families elsewhere, such as the Pieschels, Joneses, Andersons...and the list goes on and on.

Another kind of family immigration to western Canada has been chain migration. When Hazel Mills of Prince Edward Island came to work as a nurse in Calgary, it was partly because her uncle Bill Mills lived in the city; he was a carpenter who came to Calgary before the First World War. After Hazel married Herb Jobson and settled east of Balzac, some of her relatives began to come on holiday visits. In the boom years of the 1960's and 1970's, many nieces and nephews came west to work and were welcomed by Hazel and Herb, who acted as parents to them. Some eventually went back east, but four of the girls did settle in western Canada and raise families, three of them in Calgary. In just the past couple of years, the next generation in P.E.I. has begun to move out here, settling in Calgary where they have quite a few relatives now, or passing through on their way to work in British Columbia.

With the changing times and the growth of Calgary and districts, the old Balzac farming community has seen many new people settle in the area. The community welcomes those who have arrived over the past two or three decades; but it also remembers and celebrates the closeness of the pioneer families in this area.

Submitted by Valerie Jobson, 1996

Calves take a dinner break.

Saddle-back transportation: Violet Jobson & horse Trig.

Milk cans ready for transport to town on a horse-drawn cart.

Grandpa Herbert J. Jobson and the family Clydesdale.

A six-horse outfit engages in Springtime drill seeding.

An eight-horse team helps relocate a granary.

Tractors slowly took over farm chores from horses.

Workers take a break from threshing on the Jobson farm.

A vintage binder at work during the Fall season.

A Model T Ford changed the lives of many pioneer families.

A NOSE CREEK TREE

Andrew ADAMS (Senior)

Section 16, Township 26, Range 1, West of 5th

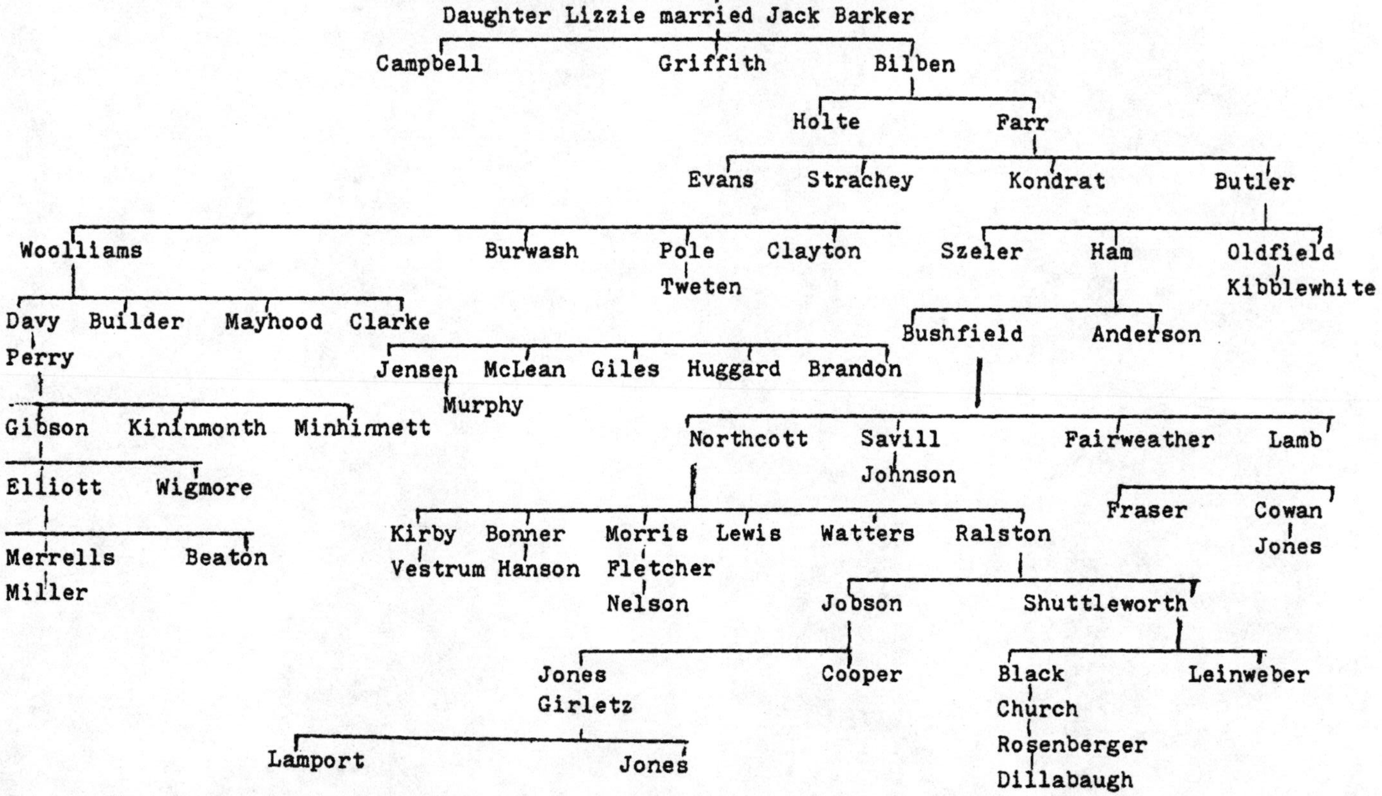

Daughter Lizzie married Jack Barker

Campbell

Griffith

BiIben

Holte

Farr

Butler

Oldfield

Kibblewhite

Evans

Strachey

Kondrat

Szeler

Ham

Anderson

Bushfield

Pole

Clayton

Tweten

Burwash

Northcott

Savill

Johnson

Fairweather

Lamb

Jensen

McLean

Giles

Huggard

Brandon

Murphy

Kirby

Bonner

Morris

Lewis

Watters

Ralston

Cowan

Jones

Fraser

Shuttleworth

Leinweber

Black

Church

Rosenberger

Dillabaugh

Vestrum

Hanson

Fletcher

Nelson

Jobson

Cooper

Jones

Girletz

Jones

Woolliams

Davy

Builder

Mayhood

Clarke

Perry

Gibson

Kininmonth

Minhinnett

Elliott

Wigmore

Merrells

Beaton

Miller

Lamport

282

Reproduced (with permission) from Edith Woolliams', 1982 publication, "My Neighbours and Yours."

AUCTION SALE

OF
FARM STOCK - MACHINERY

Having Been Favoured With Instructions From:

Mr. A. J. LOEWEN, of Simon's Valley

I WILL SELL THE UNDERMENTIONED AT HIS FARM, SEC. 22-26-2-W.5, LOCATED 16 MILES FROM CALGARY ON SIMON'S VALLEY ROAD, and 1 MILE WEST OF EAGLE SCHOOL, OR 2 MILES NORTH AND 8 MILES WEST OF BALZAC, ON

TUESDAY, NOV. 2nd, 1948

Commencing At 11.00 A.M. Sharp

38 Head Cattle:

6 MILCH COWS, Fresh and Coming In.
8 RANGE COWS. --- 8 CALVES.
6 HEAD OF YEARLING STEERS.
9 HEAD OF YEARLING HEIFERS.
1 REG. HEREFORD BULL.
(The above Cattle are in good condition).

HARNESS:-- 8 Sets of Good Farm Harness.

69 Hogs:

8 YORKSHIRE SOWS --- 1 BOAR.
60 YOUNG PIGS, 4 Wks. to 5 Months Old.

8 Head Horses:

1 SADDLE PONY.
1 SIX-YEAR-OLD, Green Broke.
2 BAY TEAMS, quiet & good workers; 1400 lbs.
1 BLACK TEAM, quiet & good workers; 1400 lbs.

Implements: International #10 Hammer Mill, almost new; Fairbanks - Morse 2-h.p. Pump Engine, almost new; 1 Cutting Box; Grain Loader; Int. Horse Binder; 2-Bot. Plow; 8-Ft. Cockshutt Tiller, in good shape; 20-Run Double Disc Oliver Drill; 1 12-Ft. Int. Horse Rake; J. Deere 20-Run Tractor Drill Double Disc, (almost new); J. Deere Mower; 10-Ft. Land Packer; J. Deere 8-Ft. Binder, in good condition; 10-Ft. Cockshutt Rod Weeder; 21-ft. Wood Harrow; J. Deere 1½-h.p. Engine; 2 Pump Jacks; 2 Water Troughs; 25 x 42 Goodison Threshing Machine (in good condition); 3 Wagons with Racks; 1 Sleigh with Rack; 1 Wagon with Box; New J. Deere Duckfoot Cultivator on Rubber; 1941 Model "D" J. Deere Tractor, on New Rubber (recently overhauled); Oliver 3-Bot. Tractor Plow;

J. Deere Manure Spreader; Gas Pump; Fanning Mill; 6-Volt Wind charger; Forge; Anvil; Post Drill; Electric Fencer; Crowbar; Post Hole Digger; Forks, Shovels; Woodworker's Bench; Taps & Dies; Brace & Bits; Carpenter's Tools; Tamarac Fence Posts; Barb Wire; Fence Rails; Slip Scraper; Grain Hopper; 2 Stacks of Alfalfa Hay (10 & 4 Tons); 1 Stack of Prairie Hay, etc., etc.

Household Effects: Stove; Table; Chairs; Radio and Garden Tools. Quantity of Bricks. Cream Cans; Dishes; Table Cream Separator; Firewood, etc., etc.

NOTE: The above listing is a good one, and everything will be sold without reserve, as Mr. Loewen has sold his farm and is moving away. Don't miss this sale!

TERMS CASH (Lunch Provided) **NO RESERVE**

A. J. Loewen, Owner, R.R. 4, Calgary, Ph. 91-1325

H. J. JOBSON, - Auctioneer

1401 - 4A ST. N.W., CALGARY (License No. 119-48-49) TELEPHONE H 4227

Examiner Press Ltd., Calgary.

Courtesy, Leonard Esler

283

Certified Copy of Pedigree Recorded in the Canadian Belgian Stud Book

POMP 3894

SIRE	DAM
SIRE: Holmswood, Jacob 1523	**DAM:** Daisy 2207
SIRE OF SIRE: Romanus 48 (52138) (imp)	**SIRE OF DAM:** Ambassador 950 (9626)
DAM OF SIRE: Belle Patte (imp) 489	**DAM OF DAM:** Mignonne de Questenne 841

THE BELGIAN STALLION **POMP 3894**, BLACK WITH STAR, HAS BEEN EXAMINED BY AN INSPECTOR OF STALLIONS AND BEEN FOUND TO BE FREE FROM HEREDITARY UNSOUNDNESS, AND OF GOOD TYPE AND CONFORMATION, AND IS ALLOWED TO STAND FOR PUBLIC SERVICE IN THE PROVINCE OF ALBERTA.

Signed W. N. CHANT,
Minister of Agriculture.

POMP 3894, carries a Life Certificate to travel in Alberta, and will stand for Public Service on the following Farms, during 1936

MONDAY NOON— J. ANDERSON, DELACOUR.	**MONDAY NIGHT—** H. J. JOBSON, BALZAC.
TUESDAY NOON— G. F. REICHERT, BALZAC.	**TUESDAY NIGHT—** GEORGE JONES, BALZAC.
WEDNESDAY NOON— TOM GRAY, BALZAC.	**WEDNESDAY NIGHT—** C. S. ARBOGAST, BALZAC.
THURSDAY NOON— BUSTER JOHNSON, CONRICH.	**THURSDAY NIGHT—** WATSON BROS., CONRICH.
FRIDAY NOON— ARTHUR HODGSON, FOREST LAWN	**FRIDAY NIGHT—** J. ARCHIBALD, CONRICH.
SATURDAY NOON— E. W. JOHNSON, CONRICH.	**SATURDAY NIGHT—** TALLY CLEVELAND, DELACOUR.

TERMS:—TWO DOLLARS CASH AT TIME OF SERVICE, AND EIGHT DOLLARS WHEN MARE PROVES TO BE IN FOAL. ALL MARES ACCEPTED AT OWNER'S RISK

JOCK McKENZIE, Calgary,
Groom

HARDY E. SALTER, Calgary,
Stallion Owner

TAGGED TROPHY

As the rancher stood gassing up his truck
At his local service station
A truck full of beaming hunters stopped
And one asked without hesitation,
"Would you be kind enough to look
In back at our cow moose perhaps?
We don't know why upon her feet
Are nailed these iron straps!

by Wendy Vaughan

284

CHAPTER 38: GRAIN AND GRAIN MARKETING

Bussey Seed Farms Ltd.

The growing of seed in Airdrie's Yankee Valley district first began in the early spring of 1943 with the seeding of James Bussey's first Pedigreed crop. Some of the early varieties were Red Bobs Wheat, OAC21 Barley, and Bison Flax. Montcalm Barley won the World Malting Barley Championship in 1947 for James. He has gone on to win many awards, including the prestigious Robertson Associate title in 1994. The name Bussey Seed Farms Ltd. was incorporated in 1989 by James' son Gordon Bussey, and the business continues to offer fine pedigreed seed to make agricultural production more profitable for customers across Canada and the U.S.A., as well as locally. In 1982, Gordon was chosen as one of Canada's Outstanding Young Farmers, and he has produced pedigreed seed for 25 years. The business still operates from the farmstead established by James' Dad, Lewis Bussey.

Submitted by Bussey Seed Farms, 1996

Balzac Seed Cleaning Plant Limited

The first organizational meeting of the seed cleaning plant was held on August 14, 1955. Fred Bell was elected chairman and Jim Huggard was elected secretary. This meeting was called to create a provisional Board of directors; Al Brown, J.M. Fairweather, Cecil Anderson, Lionel Perry, G. Randal, Earl Harwood, G. Barker, L. Beddoes, and Fred Bell were elected. They set shares at $25 apiece, and cleaning rates at 6 cents per bushel. They met many times in the next year to find out how to go about building and operating a seed plant. Zones were set with a person from each zone nominated for the board of directors. They were Leonard Beddoes, Zone 1; Glen Morison, Zone 2; Lionel Perry, Zone 3; J. Huggard, Zone 4; J.M. Fairweather, Zone 5; G. Barker, Zone 6. The other directors elected Lionel Perry as president.

Cliff Rush was hired as the first manager in October 1956, at $2700 per year. He was a local farmer who had been travelling about the country with his grinding and seed cleaning outfits, and he operated the seed plant until September 1960. Walter Goebel was then hired, and operated the plant until 1978. Brian McCallister succeeded him as manager until 1980, when Joe Walisser took over.

There have been numerous directors over the years; George DeWitt, Jack Evans, Stan Jones, Fred Bell, Hume Porteous, Al Philips, Don Bateman, John Church, A. Bell, and Ray Howden. The current directors are Eric Newman, Allen Holmes, Ralph Pole, Dennis Wearmouth, Doug Hardy, and Marvin Fowler.

The Grand Opening was held on December 12, 1956. George Fairweather was the first farmer to unload his truck that day after the ceremonial ribbon cutting by R.N. Putnam, the Deputy Minister of Agriculture. At that time there were 15 seed cleaning plants operating in Alberta.

Submitted by Joe Walisser, 1996

The First Establishment for Grain Marketing in Balzac

The railroad passed through Balzac (not then given its name) in 1891. Grain for the most part went to Calgary by team and waggon. It was not until a company named Strong and Dowler, with Mr. Moore as its first manager, began to buy grain locally that any amount of grain was moved. Prior to that, grain was shovelled from waggon to C.P.R. boxcars by hand. Strong and Dowler introduced a flight type grain loader, powered by a three horsepower John Deere single cylinder engine. Local farmer Mac McTeir was the operator. What a labour-saver that was, and it enthused a lot of customers.

In 1923 the Alberta Pacific Grain Company established a modern elevator at Balzac. I well recall the single cylinder Fairbanks Morris engine with the power shaft running into the main elevator with its pop! pop! pop! echoing up the Balzac Valley. Horses were used to haul the grain waggons, hence a manure pile was close-by, from the nervous horses that

*Bussey Seed Farms has won many awards for fine pedigreed seed. Gordon Bussey, **below**, has been chosen as one of Canada's Outstanding Young Farmers.*

entered the strange new structure. Among his other duties, the manager had the task of cleaning up the droppings.

Early elevator managers were Mr. Russell, A.W. Pratt, Harvey Hanson, Bert Antonio, Allan (Buck) Moore, and Don Brodie. Hank Neubauer was the last manager, prior to the elevator being demolished in 1990.

Submitted by C. Redvers Perry, 1996

Alberta Wheat Pool in the Nose Creek Area

This summary is written to reflect on the history of sixteen grain delivery points located in the general area of Nose Creek. The Bow River constitutes the south boundary as far east as Bennett Siding and north to include Irricana. The west boundary extends approximately to Nier. The sixteen delivery points described or mentioned in some way are all located on either the Canadian Pacific or Canadian National railways. Alberta Wheat Pool owned and operated an elevator or elevators at all of them for some period since 1923.

The elevator points included are: Airdrie, Balzac, Bennett, Conrich, Crossfield, Dalemead, Dalroy, Delacour, Indus, Irricana, Kathyrn, Keoma, Langdon, Lyalta, Norfolk and Shepard. The area includes parts of three delegate districts, the boundaries of which have occasionally changed. The general interests of the farmer-delegates have centred on service to members and marketing philosophy cum policy for wheat, feed grain and oilseeds.

It was early fall in 1923 with harvest in prospect that determination to have an elevator system of 'our own' became an issue demanding immediate action. The big meeting in Calgary had been held, the *Calgary Herald* editorials cried for farmer action, believing that government would not be decisive unless grain growers in Alberta immediately created a new system of marketing their product.

1923

1923 was just five years after the "Great War"; Western Canada had been through a short but serious depression which began with demobilization in 1919. After the war, reunion babies were being born in impressive numbers. All available and suitable farm land in the area was already under the plow and growing crops, mostly wheat and some barley, in this section of the province.

The Manitoba Grain Act had been in place for several years and Canadian law already forbade the railways to engage directly in the buying, selling, exporting or otherwise dealing in wheat. Yet there was general dissatisfaction with the line elevator companies. Henry Wise Wood of Carstairs had attended the meeting at which Aaron Sapiro spoke; he is reported to have stood at the end, knocked the ashes from his pipe, and asked the large assembly: "Now where do we go from here?"

The resulting plan was to organize a sign-up of grain producers who would wish to be members of a company owned and controlled by farmers. The rule would be "one man one vote", and the objective would be to achieve a sign-up of half or more of all grain growers in the province BEFORE HARVEST IN 1923. It amounted to a two-week sign-up all over the province.

Most townships on the prairies had about 72 farms operating. The campaigners were assigned between sixteen and twenty calls and expected to call back as necessary in order to fulfil their mission. It was a case of "saddle up and take to the road" and work 'til dusk if the job is to be done before harvest ties up everyone. In my father's case, he hitched up his driving team (we would not have an automobile for another thirteen years), and used his buggy to see the neighbours and strangers on his list. The request was for a commitment from each farmer to consign all his or her wheat during the five year contract to Alberta Wheat Pool. Fifty percent of the wheat acreage in Alberta in 1923 was calculated to be just over 2.8 million acres. In fourteen days the sign-up had achieved a total of over 2.5 million acres.

In Alberta the United Grain Growers and Alberta Pacific Elevator Co. agreed to handle Pool grain during the five year contract period. Progress in Saskatchewan at this date did not match the Alberta achievement, but the Alberta committee determined to proceed re gardless of the situation in Saskatchewan or Manitoba. Late in October the infant corpora tion began operations. Money was short, owned and leased space was scarce, but wheat was being delivered wherever a contract could be put in operation.

The Problem of Country Space

Two trains of thought governed the new management and board of directors. It was soon known that certain entire line elevator companies would be willing to sell all Alberta located elevators to the Pool, at a negotiated price. It was assumed that individual elevators would be available for purchase from several small, mostly family owned companies. The desire to proceed down this road was considered less useful to grain growers than the idea of signing handling agreements with various country elevator owner-operators. Naturally, the failure to provide an outlet close to several communities in which the recent sign-up had been quite successful was a serious problem in the fall of 1923 and throughout 1924.

Airdrie was an early Alberta Wheat Pool delivery point, as was Crossfield, Irricana and Keoma. By 1930 all sixteen of the points mentioned earlier in this article had a Pool eleva tor. A typical facility had a storage capacity of 40,000 bushels, though the house at Irricana was a 29,000 bushel capacity unit; and Shepard was awaiting completion of its new elevator. Evidently a country elevator, once obtained was considered adequate for quite a few years. A survey of the sixteen points mentioned shows that relatively little change had taken place in any of the Nose Hill Creek area country elevators operated by the Pool. An increase of 1,000 bushels in capacity can probably be explained as bin modification or the like.

Our community of elevators continued to be stable for another ten years, judging by the descriptions of licensed elevators published by the Canadian Grain Commission for the crop year 1940-41. The exception is Crossfield, where storage capacity now stood at 69,000 bushels.

The Thundering Thirties

Crops harvested in both 1927 and 1928 throughout western Canada were about one third larger than previous harvests. As the major receiver of wheat in Alberta, the Pool system found itself in possession of more wheat than seemed likely to be demanded by the interna tional market. Comparatively high wheat prices had stimulated production of several years leading up to the surge on the Canadian prairies. On the 1928 crop an initial payment amounted to 85 cents per bushel. An interim additional payment was made by the Pool in early and mid 1929.

The stock market crash of 1929 created a financial panic. Stock prices fell drastically, bankruptcies abounded and trading arrangements throughout the world were threatened improperly cancelled and abused in the short term. The quotations for wheat fell radically a orders were cancelled, shipments were suspended and loans were called in by lending insti tutions everywhere. These actions were not all precipitous, as traders tried to buoy up the markets and financial interests bought futures in many commodities, expecting a resurgence in the economy. It was to be a long time coming.

The year 1929 ended with the Pool in possession of over half the wheat which had been delivered to the system. The price of wheat had descended to around $1.35 per bushel, and as the 1930's came along, would fall again and again. Argentine wheat, of good quality, was offered on the world market for twenty cents less than 'whatever Canadian agencies' were asking. Rural Alberta, along with the rest of western Canada, slumped as the facts of the situation were realized.

It should be mentioned here that south-eastern Alberta had undergone its time of agony caused by drought, earlier than that now to be experienced in Saskatchewan. The migration from homesteads from Pincher Creek through Suffield and north toward Bindloss and Buffalo had occurred in the drought period of the late 1920's. Still, the great daily dust storms blew black and relentlessly through the years of the 1930's, now forcing abandonment of virtually all of Alberta farm areas to be classified as Special Areas 1, 2, 3 and 4. Much of that area lies beyond the districts mentioned at the beginning of this article as do such stations as Sunnynook, Dorothy, and Sheerness.

Being an elevator agent in the depression was not very exciting. Cars to cooper were few and shipments were rare. It was a time to play cribbage or bridge with the fellows who were just as idle most days, so they tended to gather at one house and amuse themselves, keeping an eye out for a wagon or a truck coming along the access road. Wheat prices were a disaster though yields in many cases were very discouraging, and grasshoppers were a plague sent to make a farmer cry. Naturally, no one petitioned for additional elevator space in those years: the world had a glut of wheat, the trading nations had built trade tariffs to discourage foreign commodities from entering each country. Japan had occupied Manchuria and Italy had conquered Ethiopia before the wretched decade ended.

War Declared and Food Becomes Strategic

Not long after war was declared in 1939, the food produced by Canadian farmers was recognized as essential to the survival of Britain. The slogans became "Bacon for Britain" and "Wheat For British Babies". Canada began to assess two vital ingredients in the equations, rail capacity to seaboard and sea transport across the Atlantic. Both were seen to be deficient but the wheat surplus existing in western Canada was surely going to be a blessing. The carryover of wheat in 1939 amounted to 280 million bushels.

One evident result of the renewed demand and need for constant supply during these years was an increase in country storage. By 1950, the record shows substantial increase in elevator capacity at all the sixteen points mentioned earlier in this piece. Airdrie, Crossfield, Keoma, Irricana and Indus had expanded their capacity through purchases, additions to existing structures and attached annexes. More will be said about annexes later.

The increased export of wheat was accomplished while production and export of beef and pork expanded markedly. Annual wheat exports rose by an average of one-third annually during the war years. Beef exports averaged an increase of about 50% and pork exports almost doubled by 1944 from the long time average. All parts of Canada shared in the war effort, an important segment of which was "enough nourishing, appetizing food" for Britain until the allied invasion of Europe, and then to many countries in need of sustenance, especially The Netherlands.

Annexes

A government of Canada subsidy to elevator companies, intended to encourage the construction of temporary grain storage bins attached to existing elevators, resulted in a very large number of annexes. These structures came with one of three names: balloon, Loxstave or cribbed. The wartime annexes were usually built much like a rectangular shed, using 2 by 6 inch timber. Called balloon annexes, they may have had an auger to transfer the grain from the annex, but many had no such fancy equipment installed and the elevator operator soon learned to store only long term keeping wheat in such a building. When the day came for the annex to be emptied and the grain shipped out, it was a matter of hiring an auger or even worse, shovelling the thing empty. Clearly it was priority number one to put only dry grain of a grade unlikely to be called for by the market. Failing that, the best course of action was to be on vacation when the order to ship came in.

The Loxstave annex, an 8 sided building of much smaller dimension than the balloon annex, was fairly common on elevator row. Many Loxstave models held only about 6,000 bushels when full. A round annex, made of plywood and maintained by metal bands around the structure was less common.

The cribbed annex was usually built attached to the existing elevator, and to the same height as the elevator. Cribbed annexes usually had one or more augers to facilitate removal or conditioning of the grain. Some cribbed annexes would hold as much as 60,000 bushels and were clearly intended to be semi-permanent structures.

As it turned out, the balloon annexes gave a new meaning to the word "temporary", still serving as storage bins up to twenty years after they were built. At some delivery points the row of elevators with balloons attached made an almost continuous building, built in wartime and ignoring fire and safety rules because they were "only temporary".

One more annex should be mentioned. It is the concrete structure at Airdrie. It was an experiment conducted by the Alberta Pool, encouraged by the Canadian Grain Commission. It has a storage capacity of 84,000 bushels and consists of 21 bins.

The Transportation Crisis in Peacetime

Canada's two major railways had not built cars designed for carrying grain for many years. Capacity was inadequate for the job of moving larger than ever amounts of export grain to seaport in the 1960's. Canada had developed the Asian market and had broadened the variety of special grains to an extent that stock on demand was becoming a necessity. Japan had a policy of ordering grain from Canada on a weekly basis. Inter-country contracts with countries such as China were becoming important. Emphasis was on prompt delivery, our railway capacity was declared inadequate. The federal and provincial governments had an additional fleet of hopper bottomed grain cars built and provided to CPR and CNR.

However, the pressure on the system to reduce its size and let thousands of miles of rail line be abandoned (mostly carrying only grain) was growing. The Federal Government was listening and a series of studies and committees were commissioned to evaluate the various suggested courses of action. Names such as The Grains Group, Canadian Congress on Agriculture, Emmett Hall Study, Snavely Report, Gilson Report and others were topics of everyday discussion.

Alberta Pool played an active part in all the negotiations and examination of data, history and proposed action. The Pool insisted that the full costs of any reconstruction, reconfiguration and abandonment should not be imposed on the producer of grain in western Canada. Fully fifteen months before the Gilson report was filed, it was evident that a number of branch lines would disappear, a large number of elevator points would probably wither and a considerable construction expense would be imposed on grain elevator operators, especially Alberta Pool in Alberta and B.C.

Branch lines on both railways have been abandoned. Entire lines of elevator points no longer have a delivery point close by. Faced with longer hauls the farmer has tended to buy bigger equipment with which to transport his grain. Alberta Pool has anticipated this to mean a need for large scales in elevators, long railway sidings at large elevator points and a system geared to stock on demand.

The governing system of Alberta Pool has always emphasized the decisions of the delegate body. The once a year annual meeting has become two shorter meetings, with more immediate agenda items to deal with. While the Board of Directors and spokespersons have often been best known and more available than sub-district delegates, there has never been any question about which body has and will determine Pool policy. It will be the job of the delegate body, meeting to discuss and debate, who will pass or defeat the motions which must guide Alberta Pool until the next meeting of the delegates.

The Nose Creek area, with the sixteen delivery points previously mentioned, happens to be located near a main line of the CPR. The railway early applied to abandon the line west of Crossfield. Everyone is aware of the abandonment of the line from Stettler to Munson. Not so many will recognize the loss the rail line to Gem and to Dorothy. None of these lines happen to lie in the area we are discussing, but the rail lines mentioned are close enough to be recognized by readers.

Directors

The general area we have covered in this article has provided three directors, if we extend the boundary to include Carstairs. O. Keith Rosenberger of Balzac was a member of the Board of Directors from 1960 until his death while still in office in 1974. Ray C. Bell of Carstairs became a Director in July, 1953 and occupied that office until December, 1961. Patrick J. Durnin of Kathyrn became a Director in December 1987 and left the Board in 1990.

In summary, Henry Wise Wood was Chairman of the Board from 1923 until 1937. Keith Rosenberger was a Board member from 1961 until 1974; he farmed at Balzac. Pat Durnin was a member of the Board from 1987 to 1989; he farmed at Kathyrn. Ray C. Bell of Carstairs was elected to the Board from 1954 and remained in that capacity until 1960.

The list of Wheat Pool delegates who served long or shorter terms, who farmed in the area we are reviewing is as follows:

Name	Address	Years as delegate
Wood, Henry Wise	Carstairs	One year prior to election to Board
Huggard, F.G.	Kathyrn	1929 - 1930
Greig, J.C.	Balzac	1930 - 1941
McKinnon, Ed.A.	Airdrie	1942 - 1944
Rosenberger, O.K.	Balzac	1945 - 1960
Bell, Ray C.	Carstairs	1940 - 1941
		1945 - 1952
Reumiller, A.	Keoma	1950 - 1951
Colwell, Chas. O	Dalemead	1945 - 1948
		1951 - 1952
Wood, Ray	Carstairs	1953 - 1955
Evenis, Rudolph	Dalemead	1953 - 1955
		1960
Clayton, C.S.	Airdrie	1956 - 1974
Barker, W. Gordon	Calgary	1961 - 1962
Matheson, Allan D.	Balzac	1963 - 1964
Bricker, Arthur G.	R.R. 5, Calgary	1961
		1964 - 1967
Brander, John	Langdon	1968 - 1974
Winkler, Daryl J.	Calgary	1995 - present
Steward, Harold J.	Dalemead	1974 - 1979
Riddle, Jack C.	Carstairs	1975 - 1980
Fowler, Alvin	Airdrie	1976 - 1983
Duhn, Robert	Delacour	1979 - 1986
		1991 - present
Bird, Lionel	Carstairs	1981 - present
Durnin, Patrick	Kathyrn	1983 - 1986
Clayton, Barrie	Calgary	1990 - 1991

Managers

The list of governing managers, general managers, chief executive officers or perhaps another title is not long. Chester M. Elliott was engaged as Manager of Alberta Wheat Pool - October 15, 1923. He died in office in October 1924. C.M. Hall was appointed General Manager in August 1926. A recurrence of symptoms caused by an old injury forced Mr. Hall to retire in 1928. R.D. Purdy (Rush) was appointed General Manager. He would occupy that position until 1953. He died in office at a time when Alberta Wheat Pool was soundly established as an exemplary, progressive business. In June 1953, A.T. (Bert) Baker was appointed General Manager. At that time he was a member of the Alberta Pool Board of

Directors, and resigned from the Board to accept the job as Manager. He retired in 1969. J. Wallace Madill succeeded Bert Baker as General Manager, the title was later amended to Chief Executive Officer. Garry Dewar replaced Madill as Acting General Manager, September 1989. That appointment terminated in May 1990, but Garry Dewar was appointed Chief Executive Officer in April 1992; he retired in April 1995. Meanwhile Don Heasman was hired as Chief Executive Officer in June 1990. His tenure ended in April 1992. The present appointment was made in January 1995 when Gordon Cummings was hired. His title is Chief Executive Officer.

The Federal Grain Purchase

The Canadian grain handling industry had gradually concentrated itself from a large variety of elevator owners, including several family units with one to six elevators, to a fairly consistent system of six large companies operating in Alberta. They were: United Grain Growers, Federal Grain Ltd., Parrish and Heimbecker, Cargill Grain Canada Ltd., Pioneer Grain Co. Ltd., and Alberta Wheat Pool.

Federal was an amalgamation of several long-time line elevator companies, operating throughout western Canada. The new company was called Federal. It included such former grain handlers as Midland Pacific, Alberta Pacific, Bawlf, Searle, McCabe and others. In the early 1970's, the Board of Directors of Federal Grain began to ponder the question whether the last expenditure needed to update the country and terminal elevator operations was the best investment they, as shareholders, could make. By 1971, they had decided to 'try the waters' and see what offers they might get for the extensive system. A year later a deal was struck with the three Pool organizations, to take over the assets of Federal, with separate deals in each of Alberta, Saskatchewan and Manitoba, depending on the physical assets and type of operation being carried on regionally.

It was a huge step for Alberta Pool to undertake but the prospect of a considerable portion of the Canada's system becoming inactive and eventually abandoned was something which the Pool's delegate body saw as catastrophic. Alberta Pool took over all Federal assets located in Alberta plus a large part of the Federal terminal at Vancouver. The purchase left several elevator companies competing for market share. The main ones in Alberta are United Grain Growers, Pioneer Grain, Cargill Ltd., Parrish and Heimbecker, and Ellison.

While a majority of the former Federal staff were offered employment with Alberta Pool, some chose cash settlement and/or early retirement. Producers who had a long-time association with a certain elevator manager, who was no longer available to handle the farmer's grain, resented the takeover. However, many others, some located at delivery points where they had long awaited a Pool elevator, welcomed the change. The opportunity to make another Vancouver grain terminal efficient, with assured supply and a chance to become specialized was especially beneficial.

Returning to the sixteen elevator points often mentioned in this piece, Lyalta became an important delivery station again, as a large modern elevator (slope bin construction) was opened. The system was making adjustments however, and by 1974 there were no longer Pool elevators working at Bennett, Delacour or Keoma. Langdon and Norfolk had also joined this list, as had Dalroy.

It is interesting to notice from which owners some of the Pool's early elevators were purchased. A few prior to 1928, with the delivery point in brackets, were: Alberta Pacific (Lavoy, Vegreville): Liberty (Mannville): West Canadian Flour (Equity): Brooks Elevator Co. (Stettler): Home Grain (Shouldice): Fraser (New Norway): Lake of the Woods (Milo): and Pioneer (Blackie, Carmangay).

Elevators had been acquired by Alberta Wheat Pool by 1926 at sixty six points. They were Bawlf, Berwyn, Brant, Castor, Carstairs, Coaldale, Dalemead, Daysland, Dowling, Ensing, Esther, Fleet, Galahad, Glenwood, Hemaruka, High River, Hillspring, Hussar, Kathyrn, Killam, Kirkaldy, Leo, Marwayne, Naco, Namaka, Ohaton, Okotoks, Ponoka,

Pultenay, Rockyford, Scollard, Strathmore, Streamstown, Strome, Sunnynook, Tudor, Twining, Warden, Watts, Welling, Woodhouse and Woolford. Elevators are located at seventeen of these points today.

Years of Service

Trails in the Sunset, a book which marked the sixtieth anniversary of the Alberta Pool, included a list of Pool staff members who had been awarded gold watches after twenty five years of service with Alberta Pool. Over five hundred names were listed there in 1983. The majority were names of elevator managers, though many on the list were construction, maintenance staff, grain graders, employees from the grain terminal, accounting staff, travelling superintendents and all forms of job description. What they had in common was a loyalty to the grain producers of Alberta and a faith in the organization which employed them. Amongst the twenty-five-year names were forty-five persons who had been on staff for at least forty years.

Presidents

We have all read about presidents of various corporations who make a career out of travelling to prestigious gatherings and making remarks about the economy in hopes of gaining a headline in the newspaper. Presidents of Alberta Pool have a different code of behaviour. To begin with, they must be genuine farmers in their own right, and are expected to continue to operate the farm while in office. They are also required to provide themselves with a dwelling in Calgary, where the Pool maintains its head office.

They are expected to be at work on a day to day basis throughout the year, the only exception being a three week absence between board meetings and harvest. Presidents of Alberta Pool are always appointed to a number of provincial, national and international agriculture related bodies. Pool first vice-presidents are also expected to make their residence in Calgary and to serve on a daily basis at a desk in headquarters, or perhaps be in attendance at one of many meetings, conferences or jurisdictional bodies to which they have been appointed. Indeed the second vice-president is also appointed to a good many committees, boards and enquiries and is expected to be in a position to represent the Board and the membership at such policy making gatherings. The second vice-president is not required to live in Calgary, however.

Nine men have occupied the chair as president of Alberta Pool. Henry Wise Wood of Carstairs was the first, serving from 1923 to 1937. Lew Hutchison served as president from 1937 to 1941. He farmed at Duhamel. George Bennett of Mannville was president from 1941 to 1943. Ben Plumer of Bassano was president from 1943 until 1957. Gordon Harrold's term extended from 1957 to 1978, and he farmed at Lamont. Allan Macpherson served as president from 1978 to 1987, farming at Delia. Douglas Livingstone of Vermilion was president from 1987 to 1990. Ray Schmitt of Milk River succeeded to the president's chair, his term 1990 to 1993. Alex Graham became president of Alberta Pool in 1993; he farms at Spirit River.

Submitted by A.W. Beattie, 1996

Allan W. Beattie ws raised on a farm in the Swalwell, Alberta, area. He spent four years in the R.C.A.F.; attended the University of Alberta and earned a BSc. in Agriculture. He served as district Agriculturalist for 20 years and then went on to become Public Relations Officer for 18 years for the Alberta Wheat Pool until his retirement.

Nose Creek Valley grain is shipped to the Alberta Wheat Pool Terminal, Vancouver terminal facilities (above and left) whence it finds its way all over the world. Alberta Wheat Pool is the largest in the port of Vancouver, with a storage capacity of 283,000 tonnes. It is situated on the south shore of Vancouver's Burrard's Inlet. The terminal has handled from 2.9 to 3.7 million tonnes annually during the past five years and set a terminal record in 1986/87.

***WHEAT POOL BOARD OF DIRECTORS**, 1996. Since Alberta Wheat Pool is owned by the farmers, appropriately, all the Directors are involved in farming. (Sitting, from left) A.L. Aasen, N.D. Silver, Second Vice President; T.A. Graham, President; J.F. Pearson, First Vice President; G.A. Groeneveld.(Standing) A.L. Pidruchney, B.G. Lindeman, D. Nanninga, A.L Oberg.*

Balzac (left) and Airdrie (right) grain elevator. Crossfield Wheat Pool grain elevator. (below).

Left: The upgrading and addition of new fertilizing equipment at many Pool locations has expanded the range of products and services available to customers.

Right: The new Legacy Junction Terminal (near Camrose) is Alberta Pool's fastest and largest facility. It is strategically located to handle future grain flow patterns and production trends.

The Grain Academy is provided for the benefit of all who care to learn the story and value of food. It is located in the Round-up Centre at the Calgary Exhibition and Stampede Grounds.
The Academy is open throughout the year for both the general public and school groups. Grains are the direct source of more than half of our food needs.
The Grain Academy has been demonstrated as practical, and an effective way to teach people of all ages about the industry which made the opening of Western Canada possible

Below: *Curators Wayne Lawson (standing, second from the left) and Jerry Hall (standing, right) with official Japanese Agricultural mission.*

CHAPTER 39: THE GENETICS INDUSTRY

Introduction

Nose Creek Valley has many breeders of fine livestock, so the development of local genetics companies was a logical next step.

Alta Genetics Inc.: Western Breeders Service History

Western Breeders Service, located west of Balzac, opened for business in 1969. The brain-child of Douglas G. Blair, Rodney James, Gordon Delair and the late Earl James, Western Breeders started producing and marketing bovine semen from the newly imported European breeds of beef cattle. These four individuals are to be credited with having the foresight to anticipate the increasing demand for improvement to livestock genetics. Western Breeders also offered a custom semen collection service for private breeders to collect and distribute semen from their own sire line-up.

The original site, that had been part of Earl James' ranch, still houses the Western Breeders division of the now expanded company, Alta Genetics Inc. The company's product line has expanded from the original beef semen collection and sales, to embryo collection and transfer, Holstein sire proving, an elite Holstein milking herd, live cattle sales to world markets, as well as research and development of genetic improvement in livestock. Facilities have been built in Conrich, Bearspaw and Crossfield to advance the growth of the company, which now boasts sales of over $40 million annually. Douglas G. Blair, one of the original founders, remains President and C.E.O. to date with the company successfully operating four divisions worldwide, Western Breeders in Balzac, Altagen in Bearspaw (northwest of Calgary), Landmark in the USA and AltaPon in the Netherlands.

Many of the staff presently live or were raised in the Balzac, Airdrie and Crossfield areas and have been a part of the Western Breeders legend since its inception in the late 1960's. Alta Genetics Inc. (Western Breeders division) is proud of its growth in the international marketplace and credits its success to the people connection of rural Alberta as well as the top rated product line developed from great Canadian genetics available in this area of Alberta.

Submitted by Western Breeders, 1996

World Wide Reputation of Nose Creek Livestock

The Nose Creek Valley has been home to a large number of outstanding purebred livestock establishments ever since the turn of the century. Although the herds known for their excellent horse, dairy and beef cattle breeding stock are too numerous to list, some names such as Black, Bushfield, Church, Collicutt, Colpitts, Dollar, Fowler, Hanson, Hole, Hunter, Jones, Mathews, McKinnon, Watson, and Wright figure prominently in establishing the Nose Creek Valley's reputation for quality livestock. The quality of the livestock genetics, the excellent cattlemen and the climate of the area all contributed to the international reputation of the cattle, sheep, hogs and horses. The Calgary Spring Bull Sale and the Calgary Exhibition and Stampede earned their worldwide reputation for livestock as the showplace for local herds. Hereford and Angus breeding stock were exported to the USA and overseas. In 1967, Agriculture Minister Harry Hays opened the door for importation of continental beef breeds into Canada. Some of the first importations were held in farm quarantine around Calgary. The American demand for Charolais, Simmental, Limousin and other cattle genetics resulted in the establishment of artificial insemination studs such as Western Breeders at Balzac, BCAI at Conrich, Prairie Breeders at Priddis, and ABS at Primez Creek. In 1971, the entrepreneurial zeal of two dentists, David Dyrholm and Ted Mitenko; the Animal Clinic Partners; Brian Edge, Ed Moss, Murray Jacobson and Wayne Burwash; legal counsel, Stan Church; and reproductive geneticist, Bob Church, resulted in the formation of Alberta Livestock Transplants (ALT) as the first commercial company devoted to embryo transfer to increase the number of offspring from elite donor cows. ALT was a world leader in innovative genetic and reproductive technologies. The group was the first to produce "super litters" of calves from various breeds. For some years ALT recipient cows carrying exotic embryos were featured at fancy auctions in Western Canada and the United States. ALT was the first embryo transfer group to develop non-surgical donor-embryo recovery and transfer, as well as the ability to freeze embryos for storage and export around the world. ALT was among the first groups to split embryos to produce identical twins and later to utilize technology developed by Steen Willadsen to "clone" calves. ALT became a public company as Alta Genetics Inc (AGI) which later merged with Western Breeders to become one of the world's top sources of beef and dairy cattle, as well as goat genetics. Since 1971, ALT and more recently AGI have had an ongoing research and training association with the Faculty of Medicine, at the University of Calgary in the area of molecular genetics and reproductive technologies. This has resulted in the development of DNA markers for sexing embryos and for genetic defect testing by the Animal Genetics Laboratory.

Every ninety seconds a calf is born in one of some forty plus countries around the world which started life as semen or an embryo at Alta Genetics, probably collected from the excellent donor cows or bulls raised by today's Nose Creek Seed Stock Producers - known the world over for their abilities as stockmen and for the quality of their cattle.

Submitted by Dr. R.B. Church, 1996

Bob Church grew up on a ranch near Calgary, Alberta, and received National recognition for 4-H youth activities. He graduated from Olds College, earned a BSc and MSc in Animal Genetics at the University of Alberta, and received his PhD in Animal Genetics from the University of Edinburgh, Scotland. He also studied in Sweden and has taught at universities in Seattle, Colorado, Russia and Australia. His association with the University of Calgary started in 1967; he was the founding Head of the Department of Medical Biochemistry, Associate Dean (Research) in the Faculty of Medicine, and is now Professor Emeritus in that faculty. He has published many papers on genetics, and has been a consultant on medical technologies, biotechnology, embryo manipulation and livestock management businesses world-wide. He was inducted into the Canadian Agriculture Hall of Fame and the Alberta Order of Excellence, and was named Chief Black Eagle by the Treaty Seven tribes. He is a Past President of the Calgary Exhibition and Stampede, and has served on the boards of numerous businesses and scientific organizations. Bob is President of Church Livestock Consultants Ltd. He and his wife Gina own and operate Lochend Luing Ranch in the foothills west of Airdrie, Alberta, where he does his own cowboying! As an educator, medical scientist, cattleman and entrepreneur, Bob has been called a "Renaissance Man" for recognizing opportunities for the application of new technologies in the development of new products and services in response to customer demand.

Olds Agricultural College, 1939, educated a lot of Valley residents.

Peartone JACKPOT ET (EX-Extra)

A Mark CJ Gilbrook GRAND ET (VG-Extra)

Loubel VOLCANO ET-Red (VG)

Duregal Astre STARBUCK ET (EX-Extra)

Top selling Charolais sire, SKYLITER

Popular Angus sire, PINE TAR

Elite Simmental sire, FERDINAND

Don Blair, pictured with 'Duregal Astre Starbuck', one of Alta Genetics' top rated sires. Astre has progeny in 44 countries throughout the world.

The AI facility in Balzac houses administration, distribution, and marketing staff. In addition it has the capacity for over 130 custom collection bulls at a time.

The I.B.R. negative facility at Conrich accommodates over 150 proven and young sires for Alta Genetics' domestic and international semen sales.

Breeders from all over the world look to AltaGen's ET centre in Calgary for top genetics and training.

Veterinarians from as far away as Brazil come here to learn the techniques of successful embryo transfer.

Semen is shipped in liquid nitrogen containers pictured (left), alongside an artificial insemination supply kit.

Western Breeders has its own fleet of trucks to make deliveries direct to the farmer's yard.

Daughter of Astre

Eric Baker (2)
   Chairman of the Board
   President, Almiria Capital Corp.

Douglas Blair (1,2)
   President, C.E.O.,
   Alta Genetics Inc.

Donald Dufault
   Executive Vice President, C.F.O.,
   Alta Genetics Inc.

Robert Mee (1)
   Vice President, Almiria Capital Corp.

Terrence Mitenko
   Vice President, Alta Genetics Inc.

Robert Francis (1)
   President,
   Agriteam Canada Consulting Ltd.

Edward McNally
   President, Big Rock Brewery Ltd.

Stanley Church (2)
   Partner, Beaumont Church,
   Barristers & Solicitors

Clarke Nelson (3)
   Businessman

(1) = Member of the audit committee
(2) = Member of the executive
        compensation committee
(3) = Effective March 2, 1995

The facility is located between Airdrie and Balzac.
Tel: (403) 226-0666
or
Fax: (403) 226-4259
Visitors are welcome!

Original site of Western Breeders' livestock plant at Balzac. (Inset) Western Breeders delivery truck.

Western Breeders' livestock plant at Balzac as it is now.

Western Breeders' staff in 1978 and as it is now, 1996 (below).

CHAPTER 40: LIVESTOCK AND MEATPACKING

Introduction

Ever since day one Alberta farms and ranches produced more beef and milk products than they could absorb and they needed to seek outside markets. The livestock industry had its roots in the golden age of ranching and has continued to the present. The second world war especially created a demand for meat, which encouraged more farmers to raise cattle, sheep and pigs.

In the past, Herefords were especially popular in the Nose Creek Valley district, and Angus and Shorthorn cattle were common; in recent decades a number of newer European breeds have become established, such as Charolais and Simmentals; a similar process has gone on with sheep and hogs. We present a few sketches of the livestock industry, travelling "from the pasture to the plate".

A Typical Ranch in the McPherson Coulee

The history of McPherson Coulee, its topography, geology, archaeology, and its suitability for ranching and farming, have all been covered in *One Day's Journey* and other historical writings. However, a typical ranch within the coulee borders was the Frank Collicut ranch, owned by Jim Robertson, a pioneer who came out from Scotland in the 1880s. He was born in Scotland in 1849 and came to western Canada as did many Scots to make a new beginning. In 1880, he was placed in charge of the first purebred Aberdeen Angus bulls to be shipped to the Cochrane Ranche. He moved to a homestead in the northwestern end of McPherson's Coulee southwest of Crossfield and lived in a sod house until a better home could be built. He was one of the first ranchers in the area to register his cattle and horse brands in 1894. Like many of the neighbouring ranchers, he sent his children Angus, Christine, Margaret and Anne for their early education to Abernethy School.

The Twin Nier Lakes, draining into Nose Creek, lie 6 miles west and 1½ miles south of Crossfield and 7 miles west and 5 miles northwest of Airdrie. The ranch occupied the entire east lake near the Nier elevators.

This pioneering ranch was sold in 1935 to Lloyd James Smith who had successfully ranched on the Rosebud Creek since 1912, and owned 600 head of cattle by 1917. As did many farmers and ranchers in the horse era, he farmed with eight horses on a three bottom plough and six horses on a 14-foot drill and a four horse binder. He bought a new Model T Ford in 1917 for $550.00

In those days there were thousands of acres of open range where he ran his horses and cattle. He also had 200 head of Clydesdale horses, which he raised and green broke, selling them to farmers. (His great-grandson, Josh Tilleman, owns a team of black Clydesdale fillies which he bought with his earnings working for farmers by age 16 and shows at the Calgary Stampede.)

As settlers moved in and bought up the land, rangeland became scarce, so in 1935, since he needed more land for his 350 cows, Lloyd Smith bought the Jim Robertson Ranch on the McPherson Coulee with the Nier land and springs. These run down the McPherson Coulee and empty into the Nose Creek by Airdrie. The Frank Collicutt Ranch bordered Lloyd's land to the east on the McPherson Coulee.

Only 300 acres had been broke on the 4½ sections so Dad first hired Doug MacDonald with his Rumely to break 50 acres and Lawrence Stone broke another 50 acres. Lloyd had a 15-30 International tractor and a 30 Caterpillar and brush cutter that he used to clear brush, in all clearing and farming 1200 acres.

In those days not many cattlemen knew how to feed baby beef heifers, so often fed them too heavy feed and burned them up. Lloyd Smith introduced finished market heifers at the Calgary market. His heifers brought as much at market as steers at this time. Some selected quotes depict the constant quality of his cattle:

- May 18, 1944, *Market Report* Alberta Stock Yards, Calgary Alberta-- "Again we sold 19 heifers for Mr. Lloyd Smith at the top notch price of $12 per cwt."

- *Calgary Herald*, June 7, 1945-- "We had another load of Baby Beef for Mr. Lloyd Smith, which averaged 945 pound and made the top of $13 per cwt."

- Starte & Treanor-- "According to old timers around the yards we are supposed to have put an all time high on the heifer market this week. On Tuesday, we sold 32 head of baby beef heifers for Mr. Lloyd Smith & Sons. Heifers average 840 lbs. and sold to the Union Packing Co. for $16.25. We understand that this price was never known in the history of the Calgary yards. $16 topped the best steers for the week."

- *Calgary Herald*, June 11, 1949-- Crossfield Farmer Top Calgary Market with Load of Choice Baby Beef. "When Lloyd J. Smith and Son Neale of Crossfield shipped this load of 32 head of baby beef to Burns & Co. this week, *they topped the market* bringing 23 cents per pound. Average weight was 865 pounds.

- Calgary, Alberta, May 18, 1950-- "We sold a load of top baby beef steers and heifers mixed for Lloyd Smith, Crossfield on Wed. of this week at 28 cents per lb."

Lloyd Smith had a herd of Angus cattle when he moved to the Jim Robertson Ranch, then crossed them with Hereford bulls, producing a bigger beef animal than the regular purebreds of that day. Jack Daines of the Innisfail Market told Dorothy Tilleman they topped the market with a pen of steers at $1.47 per lb. for over 600 lb calves.

Lloyd Smith was a School Trustee for 12 years for Abernethy School. His five children--Donald, Neale, Dorothy, Jean, and Eunice rode horse back to this school. Four of his children took up farming nearby. The youngest, Eunice Welsh, is a musician and nurse and her husband is a plumber.

Lloyd Smith was known for his honesty, friendliness, being a good neighbour, and having great faith in God. He always kept his fences in good repair between all his neighbours. He lived on the Ranch and had a keen interest in the cattle until his death in 1982 at the age of 88. His son, Neale Smith, was in partnership with him, and carries on ranching.

Submitted by Dorothy Tilleman, 1996
Dorothy Tilleman is Lloyd Smith's daughter.

*Katchen Bros. packing plant, Calgary stockyards, c. 1936. The greatly enlarged business later became Calgary Packers and was sold to Canada Packers in 1954. Further information on the pioneer Jewish experience is available from the book, **Land of Promise**, published by the Jewish Historical Society, 1997. Picture courtesy, **Discovery**, The Journal of the Jewish Historical Society of Southern Alberta. Vol 7, #1, Winter 1997.*

Lloyd and Esther Smith's Ranch, 1935-1982. Now owned by Neale & Eileen Smith. Neale ranched and farmed with his parents Lloyd & Esther Smith. Note Nier Lakes are situated on the extreme west end of the McPherson Coulee and located on Lloyd and Esther Smith's Ranch.

Brightly painted Nier Elevator located near Nier Twin Lakes (pictured above) has been featured on TV after **Hockey Night in Canada** for years.

Lloyd J. Smith on his best roping horse, **Sox.**

Lloyd and Neale Smith's steers just after a Fall 1979 auction where steers fetched 23¢/lb and calves, $1.05/lb.

303

Neale and Eileen and their personal airplane.

July 1956: Neale Smith at the controls of one of the first self-propelled swathers. The oilwell in the background is still producing today, 25 years later.

(Above, left) Neale with a deer he bagged and (above right) Eileen displaying the geese he brought down.

(Above) Neale with the self-unloading wagon he built. Jean and Dorothy threshing (Below)

(Above) Neale and Eileen combine harvesting. (Below) A threshing outfit. A 1928 Chev one-ton truck and steel-wheeled tractor complete the picture.

Lloyd with caterpillar and brush cutter

Branding the hard way—1937.

1937 Cattle round-up crew. Dorothy, Donald, and Lloyd Smith, Lloyd Snider, and Ole Malyk.

Don Smith using a Caterpillar to run a combine harvester.

Two case binders being towed by a tractor, 1940.

1944 branding crew. Pig barn in the background.

og pig barn and pole corrals, 1935.

Dorothy on Bawldy, Jean on Shetland Pony, Buster.

The Breton Spotted Cattle Story

This is a brief history of an uniquely coloured cattle herd often seen along Highway 56? west of Airdrie or Highway 616 west of Breton, Alberta.

The story begins in August 1963, with the auction sale purchase of a day-old heifer calf a Thorsby by my parents, Les and Emilie Raines. They are now deceased, but at that time they lived one mile east of the Breton Plots at Breton, Alberta.

The unique colour of this calf, now known as N8C-206U, may be what saved her place i history; she was dappled like a Dalmation dog. Added to this, the spotting was symmetrical the left side was a mirror image of the right side, and when viewed in the field, her colou appeared to be blue spotted. Her actual genetic history was unknown, but she was assumed to be mostly Shorthorn with a touch of Holstein. She developed into a big cow, weighing just over a ton in good pasture condition.

When I saw 206U's first calf by an Old Hermitage Black Angus bull, I persuaded my parents to retain him as a bull, not only because of his dam's colour pattern, but also because he had 1990's beef qualities in the 1960's.

In 1971, we added a stylish growthy son of Canadian Colossal, one of the greats o Canadian Black Angus cattle, who added size, conformation and growth rate, and retained the colour pattern. (About one Angus bull in four will produce spotting when crossed on a spotted cow.)

In 1973, my wife Jean and I purchased my parents' complete cattle herd, most of which were blue spotted; moved them to Airdrie, and commenced performance testing them agains our Angus x Hereford commercial cow herd, which was bred to a Charolais bull.

During the 1970's, the spotted cattle matched the three-way cross herd for total pounds o beef produced, and soon displayed their advantage as a maternal type. Our selection criteria may have influenced this result:

1. Heifers and bulls must breed as yearlings
2. Heifers must calve and mother-up, unassisted
3. Cows must wean a calf indexing 90% or better, without creep, and breed back
4. No milking (we leave that to the dairy men)
5. Any foot trimming is done just behind the ears
6. Cattle must be foragers, with an easy fleshing ability
7. Cows with lifetime production of 6,000 pounds of calf weaned (adjusted to 200 days are the source of long term replacements

During the 1970's and 1980's, we attempted to reproduce spotted cattle through use o many external breeds, all progeny proven, using artificial insemination and multiple breed combinations, all to no avail; after 30 years every spotted animal (about 100) in the herd i: traceable to the original cow, N8C-206U.

The Breton Spots marginally outperform the best of Black Angus at all levels of produc tion, although they are predominantly of Black Angus blood lines. These marginal benefit may accrue from extensive use of yearling bulls and heifers, accurate pedigrees and records progeny-proven bulls by A.I. (artificial insemination), performance testing and rigid culling

Why would anyone go to this much trouble?

1. An interest in livestock breeding and performance since before coming to Airdrie i 1954.
2. The undesirable type of purebred Angus in the 1960's, with which I was well ac quainted as a licensed A.I. technician.
3. The first cross calf in 1965 was truly one of nature's wonders and had a colour conus a well.
4. The unknown—why do we get spotted calves only from certain Angus blood lines and not from other British breeds?

Jean and I may not have enough time or energy left to answer Point 4, but DNA technol ogy may supply the answer. Nevertheless, it has been a challenge with many frustrations which are soon forgotten come spring when 20 to 30 spotted calves go romping across the field.

The nucleus is here for an economically viable beef breed with super-maternal characteristics and a unique colour. Will this project make Canadian Breed Status? Only time will tell.

Submitted by Chuck and Jean Raines, 1996

Lamport Polled Herefords and Zoo

When travelling northwest of Balzac you will come to Lamport's Polled Herefords, started in the early 1940's by Dave and Anna Gerlitz.

Also of interest is a bird collection of some 250 birds. Brad Lamport has an assortment of a dozen or more different kinds of pigeons, several types of pheasants, as well as different types of geese, ducks and chickens. Along with this collection are a small flock of pygmy goats. Brad has won quite a number of trophies and ribbons with his birds.

Visitors are most welcome to stop in and view his small zoo.

Submitted by C. Redvers Perry, 1996

nion Packing Co. Ltd., Nose Creek, 1919. The plant was built by Jewish cattlemen Henry Belkin and Joe ukatsky; A.H. Mayland became a partner in 1920. The much-expanded plant was sold to Swift Canadian in 946. Courtesy Discovery, The Journal of the Jewish Historical Society of Southern Alberta, Vol7, #1.

A herd of Breton Spotted cattle along Hwy 567, east of Breton in the Pigeon Lake area.

Chuck & Jean Raines produce world-famous Breton Spotted cattle (above and below).

Raising Sheep in the Valley

Aerial view of the Fowler Farm and Sheep Ranch

Chester Fowler: 65 Years of Success

Regarded by some as a pioneer of sorts, the legacy of his name is sure to be a part of the sheep world for generations to come. Amidst all the awards and accolades reflecting his success, Chester Fowler modestly displays ribbons, photos and articles documenting one man's 65 years in the business.

Although his life and times are neatly presented in artifacts and awards, Chester displays them modestly, shrugging off the achievement and his 65 years of hard work and determination.

"Oh I don't know," he says. "I don't think it needs to be mentioned," he comments on his long years in the business.

With his humble beginnings of the purchase of his two Oxford ewes back in November, 1930, Chester has devoted primarily 65 years of his life to raising, breeding and selling sheep.

Not born into the business, his interest in sheep, though undetermined, has always been prevalent. When he purchased his first two Oxford ewes, Chester was only a kid. His earlier experience in the business was very practical and hands-on.

"I bought my first sheep when I was 14 years old," says Fowler. "I was still going to school and plain and simple I liked sheep."

"I learned a lot from hanging around guys born into the business. Old shepherds like 'Jock' Stephens taught me a lot."

Through the years Chester and his flock travelled from show and sale and back again, building a name for himself one show at a time. When asked to estimate the number of sales he has attended over the years, Chester chuckles "Oh - I have no idea. Back when we travelled by train we'd take in about five sales a summer. To know every sale we've attended...I have no idea."

After adding Southdown, Hampshires and North Country Cheviots to his flock, it was in 1947 that Chester made his first purchase of six Suffolk ewes and two or three Suffolk rams. From 1947 to 1966, Chester continued to build his Suffolk flock which during the late 40's

309

and early 50's was in great demand.

Extensive exhibiting gave Chester and his flock exposure and recognition through the years. A great recognition came in the form of an award in 1962. Chester was rewarded for 25 consecutive years of showing his sheep at the Calgary Stampede and Exhibition. As well, he is a lifetime member of the CSBA and he has received the Alberta Good Shepherd Award from the Alberta Sheep Breeders Association. Again he's modest when explaining the awards. "Well, they had to give it to someone."

Quick in downplaying praise, Chester is just as quick at giving credit to others around him. He credits much of his success to his wife Rilla and his four great children who have helped maintain and show his quality flock. Rilla is just as quick at displaying their awards and achievements, evidently very proud of her husband.

"Chester is a very well respected man, with or without the sheep." she says.

Looking back over the past six and a half decades, many memorable moments are remembered. But a different excitement is added when Chester recalls a special acquisition. "One of the most exciting days," he exclaims, "was bidding for the Kilannan 067N. It was definitely a highlight of the business."

What Chester is referring to is a very notable acquisition - the purchase of the Kilannan 067N back at the All Canada Sheep Classic in 1982. He recalls bidding and eventually purchasing the sheep for $9,000. That purchase was a recognized buy for the Fowlers, a purchase that increased the quality of their flock.

The Fowlers repeatedly give credit for their success to Peggy and Gordon Newman, stating they have been instrumental in their continued success, especially over the past ten years. Chester says they have helped enormously with the showing and sale of his flock of sheep.

"Gordon and Peggy Newman have done a lot for us. If it hadn't been for their help and support, we wouldn't be where we are today."

And today the Fowler farm, located just outside Airdrie, Alberta, is home to Chester, Rilla and approximately 70 head of sheep. For Chester, he has no plan of giving up the sheep.

"I like looking after my sheep," he says. "It's a reason to get up in the morning. In the winter it gets me out and moving. I have no intention of slowing down any time soon."

This is apparently so, with Chester and Rilla attending the Fourth Annual World Sheep and Wool Congress in Britain. Fowlers have attended three of the four congresses, with Chester increasing his knowledge and improving on his flock with each passing year.

And with advancements comes new opportunities to be explored. And it seems the Fowlers have explored many other avenues.

From attending shows and sales from Quebec to the Top of the Rockies in Colorado, Chester has also sold his sheep to Mexico for breeding stock as well as consigning sheep to Brazil. In addition he has bred to prominent stock such as Kilannan 067N, McTaggart WC and Ashton 33R.

Despite all the accomplishments achieved in one lifetime it seems Chester has held to the truth and honesty that have made him honorable.

"I have lived a pretty good life. Some ups and downs - more ups than downs," he says. "But in this business quality is what people want. It's what they demand. I hope that's what people think when they hear my name."

With 65 years under his belt and a lifetime of "more ups than downs", it's safe to say that Chester would have been a success regardless of his career choice.

"Now Chester would never say this." says Rilla, "but his greatest quality is his ability to accept adversity and still go on."

With the respect and quality that is synonymous with his name, the Fowler flock is sure to go on for years to come.

by Joanne Schmidt, in *Sheep Canada*, Summer 1995

Above, left) C.W. Fowler poses with a high-priced sheep purchased from Kilannan Farms, Ontario.
Above, right) One of the many awards received by the Fowlers.
Below) 1985 winning Grand Championship Suffolk Ram. Chester and Rilla Fowler and Tina Young.

(Above) Chester and Rilla receiving the Reid Trophy at the P.N.E. 1984. (Right) Grand Champion Suffolk Ewe at the 1991 Canadian Western Agribition, Regina, Sask.

Competitors at the Calgary Exhibition and Stampede.

(Above) A selection of the hundreds of ribbons won by the Fowlers.
(Below) Chester Fowler and Carl Ham with another prize-winningSuffolk sheep

(L to r, above) Rilla Fowler, Marilyn and Peggy Newman preparing their entries at the Ontario Sheep Exhibition Markham, Ontario.
(Below) The Fowlers displaying Suffolks at the 1985 Pacific National Exhibition, Vancouver, BC.

Winter lambing (above). Suffolk ram, Ashton, at 1 year and 3 months. (Right).

(Above and above right). Sorting on the Fowler Farm.
(Right) Loading sheep into a double decker transport for show and sale, Markham, Ontario.
(Below) Sheep feeding.
(Below, right) Relaxing after a long trip.

(Above) S.W. Shaw Woollen mill, circa 1908.
(Below) A typical Merino Sheep Ranching enterprise, Mitford, Alberta, in the late 1880's. {The town of Mitford used to be located west of Cochrane and no longer exists}.

Pat Burns and the Beginning of the Meat Packing Industry

The Nose Creek Valley livestock growers benefited from their proximity to Calgary with its entrepreneurs, such as Pat Burns. Max Foran has described Burns' importance to the livestock industry:

...[*At the turn of the century*] Calgary remained primarily a shipping point for livestock. Exports of dead meat to eastern markets were negligible. Inadequate refrigeration and reasonable freight rates on livestock shipments combined to create local and regional markets for Calgary's dressed meat products. The healthy nature of these markets stimulated Calgary's economy and gave rise to the city's first *bona fide* millionaire, Pat Burns. More than anyone else, Burns gave substance to the city's role as the centre of the livestock industry. While other meatworks and associated businesses existed in Calgary before and after his arrival in 1890, Burns was the only person able to provide operations large enough to promote Calgary on a national scale. Burns' comment in 1912 that he had "made Calgary" was not without some foundation.

Burns' legendary rags-to-riches story claims that he walked most of the way from his homestead in Minnedosa to Winnipeg in 1886. He was unprepossessing, chubby and uneducated, but had an excellent eye for cattle and opportunity. He came west in the 1880's with the railway construction crews of Mackenzie and Mann and filled beef contracts in Saskatchewan before reaching Calgary in 1890. From a small slaughterhouse in east Calgary, he supplied beef to construction workers on the Calgary-to-Edmonton line. In the next decade he opened the British Columbia market, floated cattle down the Yukon and simultaneously met local demands for beef. By 1899, Burns had expanded beyond the distributing and marketing business and had entered the beef-packing industry. His Pacific trade in that year was estimated at $1.5 million. Extensive facilities were built in Calgary, his head office. In 1902, Burns began experimenting with summer deliveries of frozen dressed meats and in July shipped 400 head of dressed cattle wrapped in cotton and burlap to Vancouver. By 1905, Burns' meat enterprises had made Calgary the headquarters of a western Canadian beef-packing industry.

Burns' success depended on his willingness to gamble on regional markets. He had been so confident of the British Columbia market that, in 1897, he offered to buy every available head in southern Alberta. In 1902, he began to put a stranglehold on the western Canadian market by acquiring the holdings of William Roper Hull, also of Calgary and owner of extensive abattoir facilities and several retail outlets in Alberta and British Columbia. Burns attempted to control all phases of production from owning his own breeding herds to selling the finished table product. The *Herald* referred to Burns' organization in 1899 as "the most efficient distributing plant on the continent of America in the hands of an individual or firm"...

Extract from *Calgary: An Illustrated History* by Max Foran, 1978

Balzac Meat Processing

This business was started in 1976 by Spencer Hays. It was brought into being because of the severe drop in cattle prices. The only way to get a better market for them was to butcher and sell sides of beef. There was a large market for other farmers to do the same, therefore we opened a provincially-inspected plant.

Balzac Meat Processing does custom kill, cutting, wrapping and freezing of beef, sheep and hogs. It expanded in 1982 to do curing, smoking and sausage-making. At this time a new addition was built to allow for processing of wild game also.

Balzac Meat Processing now has a retail counter as well that serves a large surrounding area of Balzac, Airdrie and Calgary.

Submitted by Spencer Hays, 1996

Premier Meats Ltd.

Premier Meats Ltd. and the meat packing industry as a whole developed because of the original pioneers of our country who chose to take on the first challenge of sustaining themselves. They included the pioneer ranchers of the Nose Creek Valley, which has been producing cattle as one of its major agricultural based enterprises for over one hundred years. Originally animals were slaughtered on the farms and ranches. Soon the local abattoirs were established and the first slaughter/packing houses began to emerge. By the very early 1900's the supply of livestock outnumbered the local demand. Cattle moved east to the Montreal market and to Britain during the war years. Markets expanded south to the U.S.A.

To understand the beginnings of this fine industry, the contributions of people such as Patrick Burns, the formation of the Calgary Stockyards and the evolution of the Calgary Livestock Exchange must all be taken into account, with the early slaughter and packing companies, Katchen Bros., Union Packing and Calgary Packers. in addition to Burns Foods Ltd., Canada Packers and Lakeside Packers. Today the playing field has come under the control of two mega-players, Cargill and I.B.P. [Iowa Beef Processors]. Smaller Alberta companies exist and do well if they stick to niche markets and maintain a strong service commitment to the customer. They achieve sustained growth by forming alliances with related distribution and trading companies. Other important factors are the methods of packaging and consistency of quality developed by the industry to ensure the safest and highest quality gets to the hands of the end user.

Premier Meats Ltd is a pioneer in the food service industry as it pertains to portion control beef, pork, veal and lamb products to the restaurant industry both domestically and on offshore markets. The present owners, E.J. "Gene" Chiakowski (President) and Robert M. Porter (Vice President), both began their careers with Burns Foods Ltd in the late sixties. By 1976, they had established Premier Meats Ltd in Calgary, Alberta, based on the realization that the food service industry was highly specialized. It could not be housed in a production facility that relies on high volumes, large numbers and the mentality that goes with them. Today the major players in the industry have accepted this fact; they maintain separate entities which cater to the needs of the hotel and restaurateur. There is still room in these niche markets for the small entrepreneurial company such as Premier Meats.

Premier Meats provides the following products for the domestic and off shore market: Rib Eye Steak, New York Steak, Top Sirloin Steak, Beef Tenderloin Steak, and fancy meats such as Beef Tongue, Outside Skirts and Hanging Tenders. These products are packaged with modern advanced packaging to protect the integrity of the product and follow strict government standards. Premier Meats Ltd. is a member of the Meat Export Federation.

As the demand for fine beef and the refinement of safe handling and packaging continues so will the agri-business. Alberta must continue to pursue and develop its export business in order to further the economic viability of this industry. Also, the whole spectrum of activities of this industry needs to attract and nurture the young people. It must develop and educate them so they will keep a genuine and positive interest in the value of this industry. That is the challenge of the 21st Century.

Submitted by Eugene J. Chiakowski and Stephen Wilk, 1996

Spencer Hays inspecting sides of beef prior to dispatch.

Andrew Mevters processes a bison for family consumption.

Professional meat cutters (Above and below, right) reduce the meat to manageable portions.

Bacon being smoked.

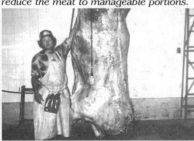

(Above) Andy Mevters prepares to cut up a beef carcass. (Below) Spencer Hays indicates the choicest cuts.

(Above) Terri Gartner looks after the wide range of meat products Balzac Meats is famous for.

Gene Chiakowski overlooks a beef processing procedure.

E. J. 'Gene' Chiakowski, company President, and Robert M. Porter (Vice President) keep in constant touch with the international market.

Quality checks form an integral part of the export market.

A computer controls the portion sizes.

The boning line: where top quality has priority.

The latest technology is used to ensure optimum standards of cleanliness are maintained.

High tech—computer portioning, the human touch—skin packaging, and precision—meat slicing— all make for a quality product.

Ceremony held at the Bow Valley Ranch, Midnapore, Alberta, July 7, 1943, to honour the Burns family for supplying the native Indians with meat over the years. Left to right, standing: Judas Hunter, Dan Wildman, Chief David Bearspaw, Michael John Burns (Chief Proud Eagle), Patrick John Peter Burns, Chief Enos Hunter, Tom Powderface. (Seated, left to right): Nat Hunter (later Chief Nat Hunter), M.B. Peacock, Norman K. Luxton, Banff, Alberta, Alma Catherine Pallesen Burns, Jack Hunter, Johnnie Bearspaw.

Wayne Colbourne, Scotty Horne, and Kirk Thompson pose for a postcard promoting Alberta Beef.

CHAPTER 41: THE DAIRY INDUSTRY

Introduction

In the early days of settlement, milking cows was a ready income source for pioneer survival. Milk was sold around the town of Calgary which provided the townspeople with milk, cream, butter and cheese. Distribution was somewhat primitive in that most milk was peddled from milk cans from the farm areas surrounding Calgary. The further out from town the farmer lived, the more difficult it was to provide milk for the requirements of the growing population.

Farmers further out stored their cream and butter in root cellars and ice houses. Store keepers would trade dry goods and staples for fresh cream and butter. Rancid cream and milk supplies would be fed to the hogs on the farm.

The first cheese factory was built at Springbank in 1888 by Ebenezer Healy. As Calgary allowed milk cows in town, excess milk products were sent to the cheese factory until 1896 when the factory had to close because there was no steady market. It then later turned into a barn.

There were several cheese factories in the area around Calgary, and in the early 1890's, D.M. Ratcliffe pioneered a farm and a creamery at Big Hills Springs whose cold stream provided a ready cooling and churning from the force of the stream turning a water wheel.

Near Crossfield, George Becker established a large dairy farm and creamery in the early 1900's, however a fire destroyed the creamery which was never replaced.

When the cheese factories closed the farmers then depended on their milk products to be picked up for a fee and transported to factories in Calgary. A bottling plant was set up by the Laycock family in the Bridgeland area near the mouth of the Nose Creek Valley. This plant was later sold to the Carlyle Dairy. In 1917, Thom Hodgson formed the Union Dairy in partnership with the Carlyle family of Chestermere. This company later was absorbed into the Alpha Milk Company System.

As was typical of the mixed farming in Nose Creek Valley, family farms in the Bearspaw and Glendale districts west of Calgary separated cream from milk and fed the skim milk to the pigs. Then again, purebred Holstein dairy farms operated by Pete Pallesen situated at the Spy Hill jail, shipped milk and dairy products to Calgary and soon the Campbell and Griffin and the Carlyle Dairy became part of the Union Milk Company.

By the 1920's trucking routes were established to deliver fresh milk to the city dairies, but some farmers from the Nose Creek Valley hand delivered their fluid milk, while others used the service of the train by having milk cans shipped to Calgary.

Jim Colpitts operated two dairy farms specializing in Holstein cattle and started "Model Dairies" in 1930 to market his produce. His first plant was on his Springbank cattle ranch and later moved to the Calgary location. By 1934 he constructed a new dairy building and Model Dairies became the second largest distribution in Calgary by 1960. In 1965 it was sold to Palm Dairies. Many Nose Creek Valley farmers were happy to make good use of this outlet for their dairy produce. Another example, the Church family in the Balzac district developed their homestead milking into a major dairy operation. George Church was a prime mover in establishing the Co-op Milk Company in 1929. He became President of the Co-operative and a member of the Central Alberta Dairy Pool.

Let us turn to four examples of the significance of the Dairy and Creamery enterprises which affected the growth and development of other industries. We will also see how family connections from ranching spread into almost every area of farm and industrial development to meet the demand of modernization.

1. The Pallesen Family's Dairy enterprise and;
2. Carlyle Unimilk Enterprise
3. The Colpitts' Model Dairies
4. The Foothills Creamery Enterprise.

The Pallesen Family, Pioneer Dairy Entrepreneurs

The dairy manufacturing industry took root from the Nose Creek valley and surrounding districts when the Pallesen family arrived from Denmark. Niels Peter Pallesen, R. af Dbg. was born on 17th May, 1873 at Nisset, Denmark near the city of Silkeborg, the eldest of ten children of Mette Katrine Pallesen (1847 - 1918) and Niels Pallesen (1846 - 1938) of which eight emigrated to Calgary between 1899 to 1911. His father an army veteran was president of the local dairy co-operative. The Pallesen family of Nisset are of the Evangelical Lutheran tradition. Agricultural co-operatives were first established in Denmark in 1882. Niels Peter Pallesen served in the 29th Battalion of the Royal Danish Army and after discharge emigrated to Calgary, N.W.T. in April of 1899.

The Northwest Territories Creamery

Shortly after his arrival in Canada, he entered the service of the Dominion Department of Agriculture and received an appointment from Dr. Christian P. Marker (1869 - 1949), then Dominion Dairy Commissioner, to manage the Dominion Cold Storage Warehouse in Calgary located in the Brewery Flats (Inglewood)) district. The plant, one of the most modern west of Montreal, had been built in 1895. In 1901, he became the first official cream grader in the Northwest Territories. During that year, the Northwest Territories Creamery was established at the site of the warehouse and acquired mechanical refrigeration equipment at a cost of approximately $12,000.00. This application had compressors using ammonia for cooling, replacing the need to harvest and store ice from nearby sources such as the Bow River. This was the first continuous creamery operation established in the Calgary area. He continued to manage the warehouse and creamery, which in February of 1906 became the Provincial Cold Storage Warehouse and creamery under the control of the new provincial government.

Central Creameries and the Pallesen Dairy

The evolution of the dairy manufacturing industry continued when in May of 1910 Mr. Pallesen struck out on his own and established the Pallesen Dairy at 602, 11th Street S.W., with the Nose Creek Valley as a primary source. This plant was managed by William Smith and was amalgamated with the Calgary Central Creamery in 1916. In the first year of operation the 11th Avenue plant had 86 shippers and produced 46,220 lbs of butter. The firm with four employees was the first dairy manufacturer in the province to have a policy of paying cash for all shipments of cream. Farmers responded well to this business strategy, they needed cash to meet their expenses. This resulted in keen competition between Central Creameries Limited and the Edmonton City Dairy.

In 1912, Mr. Pallesen established the Calgary Central Creamery, owned by his firm Central Creameries Ltd. with a new plant at 602 - 612 - 3rd Avenue S.W. The facility was equipped with mechanical refrigeration and an icemaking plant with Wm. Smith as plant manager. His business quickly expanded and he began to manufacture cheese and distribute milk. Butter, wrapped with labelled paper, "Our Own Brand" and "Danish Breakfast", was distributed into the Alberta and British Columbia markets. In 1913, the plant reached 400,000 pounds of production of butter in the first six months and secured awards at exhibitions from Toronto to Victoria. At the beginning of the First World War, a staff of about sixty was employed by the firm and a herd of seventy-five horses were kept at the Spy Hill Stock and Dairy Farm in the Bearspaw district for rotation on the Calgary delivery routes. Production reached 770,000 pounds, making it the second largest butter producer in the province with a 14.3% market share. Production was increased to 1,219,000 pounds in 1915, with supplies coming from as far north as Camrose. In 1916, the Camrose Central Creamery was built and the Olds Central Butter and Cheese Factory on Railway Avenue East. During this period the fourth plant, the Eckville Central Creamery was opened at the S.E. corner of the town. In 1918, Central Creameries Limited continued as the second largest producer in the province, with the Nose Creek valley milkshed playing a major role.

On 1st March, 1918, an amalgamation of the four largest producers in the Calgary area took place and Mr. Pallesen became a managing partner of Central Creameries Limited. This was a response to the "Economic Chain", a marketing strategy developed by Dr. Marker to bring together the major dairy manufacturers. The partnership included the Carlyle Dairy Company of James Weldon Carlyle and Thomas M. Carlyle (1880 - 1945), a firm established by their late father in 1911; Hays & Company established in 1915 owned by the late Dr. Thomas E. Hays (1876 - 1968) of Carstairs, father of the late Senator Harry William Hays, P.C. (1909 - 1982); and the Co-operative Dairy of Calgary.

In 1920, the Central Creameries Limited plant in Calgary reported a production peak of 1,500,000 pounds of butter. In 1922, Central Creameries Limited purchased four branch plants from the D. Morkeberg Creamery Co. based out of Markerville, excluding the Markerville Creamery itself now a Provincial Historic Site. The Markerville Creamery was a co-operative of thirty-six shareholders first formed as the Tindastoll Butter and Cheese Association in 1899. The D. Morkeberg Creamery Co. later became the Independent Creameries in central Alberta, with the Honourable Dan Morkeberg, R. af Dbg, M.L.A. (1870 - 1959) and other dairy pioneers Wm. Morris and Wm. Haines Jackson as partners. In 1923, Central Creameries Limited and the Edmonton City Dairy exported quality grade butter to the United Kingdom via the Panama Canal. Some of the cream supplies from the Nose Creek Valley were thus reaching the British market as quality grade butter. Butter production reached 3,016,000 lbs in 1923, representing 16.7% of the Provincial Creamery production.. By 1924-25, Central Creameries Limited operated out of twenty locations with creamery plants located at Calgary, Olds, Eckville, Camrose, Red Deer, Innisfail, Lacombe, Bowden, Youngstown, Rocky Mountain House, Rimbey, Delburne, Okotoks, Carstairs and Alsask, Saskatchewan; buying stations at Sylvan Lake, Sundre and Bentley; and distribution warehouses in Vancouver and Victoria. In December of 1927, Mr. Pallesen sold his business interests and Central Creameries Limited amalgamated with Carlyle's Union Milk Company. After he passed away in 1933 his widow the following year obtained a Calgary dairy licence and established the Spy Hill Dairy. The name was changed to the Pallesen Dairy in 1935 with the creamery located at 336 - 14th Street N.W., purchasing supplies from the Calgary area, including the Nose Creek Valley. This creamery was sold to Palm Dairies Limited in 1945, a division of Burns & Company, and continued to trade under the Pallesen surname until 1949. Burns & Company which first entered the dairy manufacturing industry in 1923, sold Palm Dairies Limited in 1978. This inheritor of the efforts of the early dairy manufacturing pioneers trades products under the name of Beatrice.

Annie and Niels Peter Pallesen Dairy Farm at Spy Hill

The late Niels Peter Pallesen, R. af Dbg. was a member of the Canadian Food Commission during the First World War, Alberta Representative on the National Dairy Council, and a founding director of the Alberta Dairymen's Association in 1919, serving two terms as president in 1922 and 1923. He served as Danish Consul in Calgary between 1918 to 1928, representing both the Danish and Icelandic governments. His Majesty King Christian X of Denmark (1870 - 1947) awarded him the Order of Dannebrog (Danish Flag) on 26th June, 1928. Danish pioneers had settled in the communities of Standard, Dalum, Tilley, Spruce

View and Dickson. He joined the Calgary Exhibition and Stampede Board in 1917 as a director and was second vice-president from 1926 to 1932. Mr. Pallesen was married by the Reverend Dr. James Chalmers Herdman then Superintendent of Presbyterian Missions, on 19th December, 1902 to Annie K. Ostrom (1882 - 1952). She emigrated from Norway with a sister, Bertha Ostrom (Norgaard) and settled in Wetaskiwin in 1898, where their uncle Thorstein T. Belsheim had established a blacksmith shop on Pearce Street. A second sister, Sigrid Ostrom (Bakken) arrived in 1909. Annie K. Ostrom moved to Calgary in 1900, and was employed by the Peter A. Prince household at 240 - 4th Avenue S.W. The Prince residence now stands in Heritage Park. Annie and Niels Peter Pallesen kept homes at the Heart's Delight Ranch located on Section 27 of the Spy Hill Stock and Dairy Farm, 630 - 3rd Avenue S.W., and 707 Prospect Avenue S.W. built in 1912 and demolished in 1986. Mrs. Pallesen, Sr. retired to Calgary in 1950, purchasing her residence at 3042 - 2nd Avenue S.W. from the late F.S. Mannix. The late Judge William Sellar, O.C. (1910 - 1968) handled her business and legal affairs. The Annie Pallesen House was donated in her memory by her family as part of the Providence Creche Society established in 1943 for disadvantaged children. The family horse and cattle brands first registered in 1907 are mounted at the Nose Creek Valley Museum, the Western Heritage Centre and the Ranchmen's Club in Calgary.

The Spy Hill Stock and Dairy Farm

The Spy Hill Stock and Dairy Farm, established in 1909 by Niels Peter Pallesen later to comprise 3,840 acres in the Bearspaw district, was a primary supplier to Central Creameries Limited until 1920, converted to a grain growing operation for a few years, then reverted to a dairy operation in about 1930. The poplar trees planted in 1910 on the northern perimeter of the farm were standing as late as 1996. Sections 25, 26 and 27, comprising part of the E.N. Baines lease granted on 11th August, 1882 were purchased from John J. Young (1867 - 1923). Young had moved to Calgary in 1894 and purchased the Calgary Herald. The Spy Hill, rising to an elevation of 4,200 feet at the Pallesen holding, is one of five sites in Alberta with this name. It is reputed to have been an early signalling post for the First Nations, and was visited by the Palliser Expedition on 6th August of 1858, as noted in Sir James Hector's (1834 - 1907) diary. The first buildings were completed in 1910 at the base of the hill and a herd of pure-bred cattle brought in from Ontario in 1912. A major residence on Section 27 known as the "Heart's Delight Ranch" was constructed and completed in about 1920, and destroyed by fire in the summer of 1932. His Royal Highness Prince Erik of Denmark (1890 - 1950) stayed as a guest during his extended visit to Alberta between 1922-24, and receptions were held for the "originals" of the 1912 Calgary Stampede on 24th August, 1927, and for visiting members of the Danish-Norwegian Journalists Association during July of 1928. Farm managers included Peter Jensen (1881 - 1960) between 1912 to 1920, and Christian Christensen (1885 - 1964) between 1924 to 1950. Mr. Jensen settled in Canada in 1907, worked on railway tunnel construction near Field, B.C., thereafter joined Central Creameries Limited in 1910. He returned to Denmark in early 1912 to marry and received a telegram from Mr. Pallesen to return early in order to take over as foreman at the farm. He arrived at the farm on 1st April, 1912 having cancelled his honeymoon holiday on the ill-fated "RMS (Royal Mail Ship) Titanic." The Great Flu of 1918-1919 left many on the farm stricken, and Dr. R.B. Francis came by horseback to treat the ill. The farm became self-sufficient in the 1930's with considerable credit due to the Chinese cook, Mr. Sing Chew who served meals over the years from a double tier revolving table. The farm, comprising 2,560 acres, was sold to George Stryker of Manyberries in October of 1950 and the pure-bred cattle herd was sold to Carmen Ellis of Hubalta. The Provincial Government bought the farm in 1956, and the site, now at 11333 - 85th Street N. W., is the location of storage facilities for the University of Calgary, a radio repeater station operated by Alberta Public Works, and the Calgary Wildlife Rehabilitation Unit. Instruments are used by the university atop the hill for measurements related to geology and geophysics. An experimental farm for genetic research at the former farm site is managed by the Department of Animal Sciences of the Faculty of Medicine of the university. The site includes four correctional institutions with the first completed in 1958 on Section 27.

The Annie and Niels Peter Pallesen Family Benefits Valley Residents

Every pioneer and contemporary farm and ranch in the valley benefited from the enterprises developed by the extended family. Their activities included the dairy manufacturing industry, meat packing, road building, road building equipment and the sale of steel grain bins, culverts, snow fence and other products for farming and ranching. Annie and Niels Peter Pallesen had five children. Their son N. Daniel Pallesen (1903 - 1971) received his B.Sc. degree from the Ontario Institute of Agriculture and he was employed by Burns & Co. moving to Toronto in 1939. The Pallesen's eldest daughter, Alma Catherine (1905 - 1958) married Michael John Burns, M.B.E. (1883 - 1953) of Calgary on 7th November, 1934 in New York City. A nursing graduate, she served as president of the Alberta Region of the Victorian Order of Nurses. Michael John Burns was the eldest of five children of Thomas Burns (1848 - 1912) who came to Calgary in 1906 and settled at 1036 - 8th Avenue S. E. in the Inglewood district. The house built in 1886 is Calgary's oldest private residence. Thomas Burns was the eldest brother of the late of the Senator Patrick Burns, K.C.G. (1856 - 1937) who settled in Calgary in 1890. Michael John Burns following his education at St. Boniface College, joined P. Burns & Company in September of 1901, became general manager in 1916, president in 1934, Honorary Chief Proud Eagle of the Stoney Nation on 7th July, 1943, was awarded an M.B.E. from the King's Honour List in June of 1946, and retired as Chairman of the Board of Burns & Co. in 1950. The firm thereafter was headed by R. Dinning, J. Howard Kelly, Alec Hill, Arthur J.E. Child and Ronald Jackson, and sold to Maple Leaf Foods in 1996. Alma and Michael John Burns made their homes at the Bow Valley Ranch, Midnapore, and a company owned residence at 930 Prospect Avenue S.W. The Bow Valley Ranch was purchased by Senator Burns from William Roper Hull in 1902 who built the heritage residence in 1896 still standing on the property. Alma and Michael John Burns hosted the English singer Gracie Fields (1898 - 1979), the Danish opera tenor Lauritz Melchoir (1890 - 1973) and Lady Florence Eaton (1881 - 1970) of Toronto during their years of residence at the Bow Valley Ranch. The Pallesen's second daughter, Selma Marie (1912 - 1976) married Lt. Commander Durward George Withrow (1903 - 1971) in 1939 who served in the U.S. Navy, and was a mining engineering graduate and businessman. They made their homes in El Paso, Texas and Laguna Beach, California.

The Pallesen's second son, the late Norman P. Pallesen (1914 - 1994) married Florence Dora Evelyn Mannix of Calgary on 21st August, 1933 by a ceremony officiated by Monsignor John S. Smith, P.A. (1878 - 1966). She was a daughter of the late Mr. Frederick Stephen Mannix (1881 - 1951), a fifth generation Western Canadian, and Mrs. Byryid Helen Mannix (1890 - 1931). Byryid Helen Mannix who married F.S. Mannix in Edmonton on 9th January 1907, was a daughter of William Fitzpatrick who commenced to homestead in the Stony Plain district in 1892. Mr. Mannix born on the family farm near Stonewall, Manitoba, started contracting in 1898, moved to Edmonton in 1905, and to Calgary in 1914 where the family settled in the Bankview, Victoria Park, Mission, Mount Royal and Roxborough districts the years to follow. He was engaged in numerous unincorporated joint construction ventures from British Columbia to Quebec until he established Mannix Co. Limited in 1936, based out of Calgary. He also farmed and ranched, owning the Thumb Hill Ranch near Dorothy, Alberta from 1912 to 1918 and a grain farm in the Rockyford district, where he kept horses for construction projects. Mannix sold his ranch in 1918 to Alex Nesbitt. Nesbitt had worked for George Lane (1856 - 1925) on the Bar-U Ranch, and formed the XL Ranch south of Bassano in partnership with Charlie McKinnon. The Bar-U Ranch itself was purchased by P. Burns Ranches Limited in 1927 and sold in 1950. The Mannix grain farm was sold to John Ambrose Wise of the Rockyford district. Mr. Mannix was a long standing friend of the late Alex Gillespie, a rancher and feedlot owner.

F.S. Mannix was a son of George Charles Mannix (1845 - 1934), a veteran of the Fenian Raids Campaign of 1865-66, who served with the Second Battalion of the Quebec Rifles of the Red River Expedition of 1869-70 of which James Farquharson Macleod, C.M.G. (1836 - 1894) was Brigade Major. G.E. Mannix emigrated from Cork, Ireland in 1862 to Quebec City. He filed for a homestead near Stonewall, Manitoba through the Military Bounty Land Script in 1871 where the family settled until 1904. He married Frances Bunn Mannix (1849 - 1918) on 25th November, 1872, at a ceremony officiated by Anglican Archbishop Robert Mackray, First Anglican Primate of All Canada. Mrs. Frances Bunn Mannix born at the Red River Settlement was a descendent of the Cree Nation, the La Force family of New France (Quebec), and of the Bunn, Campbell and Sinclair families, members of the Hudson's Bay Co. and Northwest Co. which settled in Upper Canada in 1771, and Rupert's Land in 1782. Several family members are buried in St. John's Anglican Cemetery, Winnipeg and Schooner's Creek Cemetery, York Factory. The mother of Frances Mannix, Magdalene Campbell Bunn (1822 - 1908) was born at Fort Dunvegan.

F.S. Mannix was succeeded by his son, the late Frederick Charles Mannix, O.C., LL.D. (1913 - 1995) when the family firm was reorganised in 1943. F.C. Mannix was a past president of the Canadian Council of Christians and Jews, a past Governor of Hockey Canada, a co-founder of the Canada West Foundation, a laureate of the Canadian Business Hall of Fame and an officer of the Order of Canada. The firm now trades under the name of the Loram Corporation with business operations in Canada, the United States and abroad. Senior executives included the late Everett W. Costello, Q.C. whose family settled in Calgary in 1883, and he married Florence Ballachey of High River. Others included the late Robert Alphonso Kramer, K.C.G., the late Senator Stanley Charles Waters and the Honourable Edgar Peter Lougheed. The Carthy Foundation established by the late F.C. Mannix, donated the Carthy Organ which stands in the Calgary Centre for the Performing Arts.

Norman P. Pallesen graduated from the Agricultural College of the University of Manitoba in 1936 and was president (1947 - 1971) of Ferguson Supply (Alberta) Limited, the province's oldest established construction equipment dealer (1913 - 1988). The firm which became a group of three companies with five branches, represented the Euclid-Terex Division of the General Motors Corporation, the Dominion Road Machinery Co. which manufactured the Champion line of motor graders and the Industrial Division of the J.I. Case Corporation. The Calgary branch at 610 - 9th Avenue S.W. was moved in 1954 to the Manchester district and the Centennial Parkade stands on the former downtown branch site. The firm in the mid-1960's invented, manufactured and distributed both on the domestic and foreign markets the "Twin-Hitch" used between motor scrapers. Mr. Pallesen served as chairman of the Providence Creche Society was also a partner with Rosco Metal Products (Alberta) Limited later Westeel-Rosco which manufactured steel culverts and grain bins used throughout Alberta. The Pallesen's youngest daughter, Kathleen Helen (1918 - 1969) married Andrew Jeffery Shirriff of Toronto, who was with Shirriff Foods Limited, a food processing firm established by his grandfather.

Two grandchildren of Annie and Niels Peter Pallesen settled in Calgary. Patrick J.P. Burns (1936 - 1975), a great-nephew of Senator Patrick Burns was a graduate of Strathcona School for Boys, St. Mary's Senior High School, Trinity College School, Port Hope, Ontario, and earned a B.Comm. degree from the University of Alberta. He was chairman of the Burns Foundation Limited, first established in 1925, which sold the Bow Valley Ranch in 1973 to the Provincial Government now comprising part of Fish Creek Provincial Park. He served as a member of the Board of Governor's of Mount Royal College and a board member of the Providence Creche Society. The Burns family in Calgary is remembered at many sites and the Burns Memorial Fund. The late Mrs. Patricia Eleanor McCaffery (nee Pallesen (1935 - 1994), an honours graduate of the University of British Columbia married Michael Thomas McCaffery, Q.C. (1932 - 1994) in 1958. He was a son of Calgary lawyer Joseph Patrick McCaffery (1896 - 1962) a law graduate of Osgoode Hall, a grandson of Thomas McCaffery a Calgary pioneer contractor and Joseph Antoine Aldous Beaupre (1873 - 1965) and a great-grandson of Victor Joseph Beaupre, a former Deputy Minister of Public Works in the Norquay government in Manitoba, and a railway contractor, who settled with his family in Gleichen in 1883.

The Extended Pallesen Family Serves the Valley

The Pallesen name became synonymous with early dairying in the Calgary and the Forest Lawn, Chestermere Lake, Conrich, Rocky View, Nose Creek and Bearspaw districts. Niels Peter Pallesen established the "Home Farm" in 1904, the site now at the S.E. intersection of McKnight Boulevard and Barlow Trail N.W. near the present Calgary International Airport. This was the focal point for his four brothers and three sisters when they arrived from Denmark between 1902 to 1911.

Thomas Pallesen (1878 - 1953) arrived in April of 1902 and joined the "Home Farm" when it was established in 1904. The farm was dissolved in 1913 and he took over the operation going into partnership with his brother-in-law Cecil Christiansen, expanding the operation to 2,000 acres including land in the Conrich district. He was an early member of the Alberta Wheat Pool established in 1923, married Christa Christiansen (1893 - 1968) in 1914 and they had two sons. The late Stanley George Pallesen (1915 - 1995), a partner of Gienow Sash & Door Limited, was the only private citizen nominated in the 1994 Calgary "Century of Spirit" campaign as a philanthropist. He was instrumental in the establishment of Camp Jubilee for the Girl Guides of Canada at Cochrane and is remembered at the site by Pallesen House. Dr. Leonard Carl Pallesen of Chestermere Lake, former Deputy Superintendent of the Calgary Public School Board, served as Mayor of Chestermere Lake for eight years.

Martin Pallesen (1878 - 1938), a twin brother of Thomas Pallesen arrived in April of 1902 and joined the "Home Farm" in 1904, and was employed as shipping manager of Central Creameries Limited between 1912 to 1918. The former Martin Pallesen farm established in 1918 is now located at the intersection of 90th Avenue N.E. and McKnight Boulevard. His home at 626 - 3rd Avenue S.W. purchased in 1912 and sold in 1918, was built by Peter Dewar in 1907. Known as the "Cottage Hospital", it was transplanted to Heritage Park in 1979. Martin Pallesen married Jensine Larsen in 1911, a member of the Hans Larsen family which settled to homestead in the Ponoka district in 1895. Jensine and Martin Pallesen had three children; Florence Marie Blight, Violet Clowes and Albert Pallesen (1918 - 1994).

Berg F. Pallesen (1886 - 1950) arrived in February of 1906 and was employed at the

"Home Farm" and commenced to purchase land in 1909 for his own farm. The former Berg Pallesen farm stands at the intersection of what is now 16th Avenue N.E. and the Barlow Trail, the site of the first family reunion in 1915. Berg Pallesen married Hilda Odlund (1898 - 1932) on 25th September, 1919, the daughter of Olaf Odlund (1863 - 1932) who arrived in Canada in 1899 and in 1901 commenced to homestead in the Rocky View district. Hilda and Berg Pallesen had three children; Thelma Katrine Neumeyer (1920 - 1990), Evelyn Hilda Irene McGurk and Helen Eileen Olsen (1927 - 1995).

Otto W. Pallesen (1889 - 1955) arrived in February of 1906 and joined the "Home Farm". After the farming partnership dissolved in 1913, he farmed briefly in the Rocky View district and then moved to the Hesketh district about 1920 where he farmed until his passing. Otto W. Pallesen married Norma Soley (1892 - 1971) on 17th May, 1917 who was born in Calgary on 8th August, 1892. Norma Soley Pallesen was a daughter of Sigvart Jorgenson Soley (1860 - 1929) and Anna Marie Ness Soley (1858 - 1906). Mr. Soley arrived in Calgary on 6th June, 1886 with the Eau Claire Lumber Company. The extended O.W. Pallesen family branch by marriage shares common descendants with the Kubinic family, owners of the Joan of Arc Ranch in the Ghost Pine district, and the Spady ranching families of the Alliance - Castor districts which first settled in Stony Plain in 1898. Norma and Otto W. Pallesen had five children; Otto Ralph Pallesen (1918 - 1977), Douglas Norman Pallesen, Helen Poppitt, Clifford Hugh Pallesen and Sybil Poxon.

Elizabeth Matilda Pallesen (1891 - 1994) arrived in Calgary from Denmark in 1908. She married Kristen Anton Andersen (1885 - 1960) on 18th August, 1911, and they later farmed 480 acres which now comprises part of the district of Forest Lawn. They had two children; Gladys Evelyn Rayburn and Lawrence Anton Andersen (1919 - 1978). The family by marriage and common descendants are related to the late Millward Valentine Anderson who founded Anderson Plumbing and Heating in the early 1900's. A second sister, Nielsine Marie Pallesen (1883 - 1910) arrived in April of 1910 and passed away after only three months in Canada.

Maren Anine Mikkelsen (1881 - 1965) arrived in April of 1911 with her husband Anton Mikkelsen (1872 - 1921) and their four children. Anton Mikkelsen a veteran of the Royal Danish Army, served in the Canadian Army during the First World War, and after his discharge, farmed in the Balzac district. He passed away in 1921 of war related injuries and his widow carried on with the farm. Their son Henry Mikkelsen of Westview Farms of Langdon married Isobel Carlyle in 1942, a daughter of the late Charlie Carlyle and Ethel Brown Carlyle. Mrs. Ethel Carlyle was a daughter of Robert Brown who settled to farm in the Chestermere Lake district in 1902. Charlie Carlyle a graduate of the Ontario Institute of Agriculture arrived in Calgary in 1904 and was a member of the Carlyle pioneer family. His cousins included Calgary dairy manufacturing pioneers James Weldon Carlyle and Thomas M. Carlyle of the Union Milk Company. His brother, the late Professor William Carlyle, was appointed manager in 1919 of the EP Ranch near Longview, Alberta, owned by His Royal Highness (H.R.H). Prince Edward of Wales (1894 - 1972). Professor's Carlyle's daughter, Helen Carlyle married Charlie Yule, general manager of the Calgary Exhibition and Stampede Board between 1941 to 1950. Maren Anine and Anton Mikkelsen had eight children; Rasmus Peter Mikkelsen (1903 - 1975), Niels Peter Mikkelsen (1905 - 1975), Henry Mikkelsen, Ingeborg Katrina Lynge, Thomas F. Mikkelsen (1911 - 1990), Marie Jensen (1913 - 1995), Katrina English and Gordon Mikkelsen (1920 - 1985). Two sisters of the first Pallesen generation remained in Denmark; Nielsine Katrine Indelukke (1895 - 1959) and Johanne Kristine Vesterkov (1876 - 1965). The extended Pallesen family, interwoven with the community tree by marriage with other pioneer families has enjoyed a long association with the Nose Creek Valley and surrounding districts in an array of ventures over the years, which first originated with the establishment and management of Calgary's first continuous creamery. Fond memories of the kindness and generosity received from other pioneer families remain in the extended Pallesen family to the present.

Submitted by Peter J.M. Pallesen, 1996

Peter J.M. Pallesen, M.Ed., M.Sc., a grandson of Niels Peter Pallesen and Frederick Stephen Mannix, is a graduate of Strathcona School for Boys, Mount Royal College, the Universities of Calgary and Portland, studied at the University of Salzburg and Harvard University and served with the Royal Canadian Mounted Police.

Model Dairies

James Colpitts emigrated to Alberta from New Brunswick in 1921 and started up a registered silver fox operation near the Elbow river west of Calgary. With pelts selling for over $200 and a good trade in the sale of breeding stock, his enterprise rapidly expanded to include a dairy at the Springbank location and a milk processing plant in Calgary (Model Dairies). Then in 1924, he purchased an additional farm west of Balzac. Previously owned by a Dr. Burr, it was good land for growing grain and had a single barn in the farmstead beside the Symons Valley road. He developed the farm as a dairy and built two additional barns to house a herd of 150 cows that were milked by hand three times a day. In summer their milk could be trucked into Calgary but during the winter it was necessary to resort to a horse drawn sled to haul milk through snow drifts to a streetcar terminal at the north end of Calgary.

For the first 15 years Arthur Steeves, from New Brunswick, supervised this operation. During that time the landbase was expanded by the purchase of an additional half section on the west side from the Bowmans and a full section on the east from the Barretts. Then in July of 1941 James Colpitts died, leaving both dairy farms and Model Dairies to his only son Stewart, who was 20 years old at the time.

At Symons Valley, Arthur Steeves retired and was succeed by Harry Colpitts as manager for the next ten years. In the mid 1950's Harry retired and was replaced by Hammond Watts who moved out from Model Dairies in Calgary. With the assistance of his wife Kathy, Hammond modernized the dairy operation and upgraded the farming equipment. By the time Model Dairies was sold to Palm Dairies in 1965, the Colpitts dairy herd was the largest in Alberta. For another ten years they continued to ship milk to Palm but Hammond's interest in purebred cattle was shifting to a type that were not milked by humans. In the early 1970's he bought 10 registered Hereford cows from Jim Hole and these were the seed stock of a beef herd that would later grow to 175 cows.

After the Symons Valley dairy herd was dispersed in 1975, Hammond concentrated on developing his beef ranching enterprise and eventually his cattle achieved considerable success at various shows and sales. Having managed the Symons Valley Ranch for some 40 years, Hammond Watts retired in 1994. His legacy is an excellent cow herd, a modern grain operation and a well kept farmstead with three large white barns on the west side of the Symons Valley road.

Submitted by Joe Zink, Manager

A Historic Sketch of the Foothills Creamery in Calgary

Owned and operated by Albertans, Foothills Creamery has been producing dairy products to meet government standards in Calgary since 1969. Besides its plant at 4207 - 16th Street S.E., the Creamery now has a warehouse in Edmonton at 9350 - 48th Street, serving Alberta and beyond. The Creamery is an active member of the Alberta Dairymen's Association, the Alberta Food Processors Association, the Calgary Food Executive and the National Dairy Council.

The Foothills Creamery originated in 1969 when the Swift Canadian Company, whose corporate headquarters were in the U.S.A., decided to close down this the last of their Canadian dairy operations. Swift had operated this plant on 10th Avenue S.E. in Calgary for 50 years.

There had been a growing trend toward reducing the number of creameries in Alberta over the years for a variety of reasons, namely the trend to vertical integration (or centralization), mixed farmers going out of business, unfavourable market conditions and government policies. According to provincial government statistics, the number of creameries in Alberta fell from 99 in 1925 to 80 in 1965. In 1996, there are only three creameries left: The Dairy World in Red Deer; Paint Earth in Castor; and Foothills Creamery in Calgary.

In spite of these trends, three former employees of the Swift Canadian Company took the risk of starting out on their own to form the Foothills Creamery Limited. These enterprising men saw a need to continue the creamery business in Calgary to serve Western Canada. They were offered an opportunity to purchase some of Swift's equipment and permission to continue to take delivery from some 500 dairy producers. Many of these producers were in the Nose Creek Valley area.

The three former Swift employees who started the new Creamery were: George Heidebrecht, a buttermaker, formerly from Tofield, with six years of public relations and experience with the company; Don Bayrack, formerly of Olds, had also worked there as an experienced buttermaker for three years; and Ken Farr, a farmer in the Nose Creek Valley west of Balzac, who had been with the firm's office staff for four years. In 1976, Barry Northfield became a partner when he bought out George Heidebrecht, and Brian MacPhail bought out Ken Farr in 1990.

Foothills Creamery took delivery of the raw products in cream cans and tank trucks and continues to do so at the present time. The area covered was from Water Valley to the west, Oyen to the east, Stavely to the south and Olds to the north.

In the photographs showing the pioneering technologies of producing dairy products, we see how the more modern technologies (with computerized abilities) began to be put into practice. These revolutionary changes have increased our capacity for producing a variety of dairy products to meet consumer tastes and demands. All of these advances in production have provided the Nose Creek Valley's growing and diversified rural and urban populations with a multitude of products produced by today's Creamery. Foothills Creamery products include a variety of styles, tastes and flavours of butter, ice cream, frozen yogurt, ice cream cones, and food service butter products such as patties and mini-cups. These are produced in large and small quantities for domestic and commercial kitchen and bakery use.

Submitted by Don Bayrack, President of Foothills Creamery, and Stephen Wilk, 1996

Snuff

Did you ever see a cowboy
With a bulging lower lip,
That didn't have a circle
On the pocket of his hip.

by Wendy Vaughan

(l-r, upper deck) Spy Hill Stock and Dairy Farm—Central Creameries Limited, Calgary Plant. (l-r, lower deck) Staff of Central Creameries Limited, Calgary Plant, churn room. (1913).

An aerial view of the plant.

Niels Peter Pallesen. c. 1920.

Pallesen family reunion at the Berg Pallesen farm in the Nose Creek Valley, 1915. Left to right, back row, Elizabeth Mathilda Andersen, Gladys Andersen (infant), K.A. Andersen, Berg F. Pallesen, Otto W. Pallesen, Anton Mikkelsen, Maren Anine Mikkelsen, children, Ingeborg, Peter, Rasmus, Henry, Thomas and Mary Mikkelsen.
Left to right front row: Jensine & Martin Pallesen, Florence Pallesen (child), Annie Ostrom Pallesen, N. Peter Pallesen, children, Norman, Niels Daniel, Alma, and Selma, Thomas & Christa Pallesen.

Dairy herd at the Colpitts farm.

The Colpitts Ranch, above, also owned Model Dairy, located on 17th Avenue and 2nd Street, southwest, Calgary.

A general view of the Colpitts barns. (1996)

Milk cooling and bottling equipment.

Milk pasteurizing vats.

A 3-barrel freezer manufactures ice-cream on a continuous basis.

Ice-cream mix undergoing pasteurization in a vat designed for the purpose.

Butter is packed and prepared for dispatch.

Andy Gunton testing with a high temperature short time (HTST) plate pasteurizer.

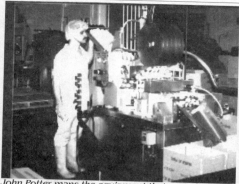

John Potter mans the equipment that manufactures individualized butter containers for restaurants.

Milk powder has to be stored in dry conditions.

Khang Nhan readies butter for packaging.

Ice-cream is stored in cold rooms prior to shipping out.

Refrigerated trucks (above and below) ensure the goods are delivered in peak condition..

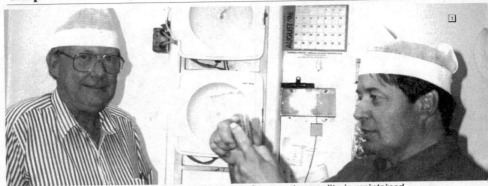

(left to right) Partners Barry Northfield and Don Bayrack ensure top quality is maintained.

Valley dairy farms keep the creamery supplied.

Foothills Creamery uses locally grown wheat flour in the manufacture of ice-cream cones to go with the ice-cream the plant manufactures.

Brian MacPhail, Production Manager, receives the 199 Award for Best Quality Butter in Western Canada fro Bill Boer, President of the Alberta Dairy Associatio Processing Section.

CHAPTER 42: INDUSTRY
Introduction

We present here an interesting mix of a few of the many businesses in the Nose Creek Valley which serve local needs and more widespread markets. It will be noted that, like the farms, many of these are local family-based businesses. Even the large companies, however, contribute to the welfare of the community in which they are based.

The Conroy Family

Thomas W. Conroy and M. Gwen Conroy (nee Eisnor) were born and raised in southern Saskatchewan. In 1950 they moved to Calgary where their children Thomas and Beverly were born. Gwen convinced Tom that they should learn to fly as a Centennial project in 1967. From that time on they owned and flew various aircraft in the business as contractors of service and bulk stations for major oil companies across western Canada. In 1969, they became members of the Airdrie community. They purchased the property on which the Airdrie Airport is situated - the east half of Section 35 and west half of Section 36-26-29-

Tom Senior, Gwen, Tom, and Bev.

W4. The airport was originally constructed by the Government of Canada in the early 1940's, as an auxiliary airfield to Calgary for the British Commonwealth Air Training Plan. It operated as a Service Flight Training School (SFTS) during the 1940's and early 1950's.

The Airdrie Airport has always been a place for aviation enthusiasts to meet. Tom Senior's mom, Evelyn May Sinclair, resided at the airport for many years and was fondly known as Granny to all who came and went. She would always have tea and goodies available for anyone who kept their aircraft there or dropped in for a visit. The Conroy and Ayles families still welcome many community organizations, schools, remote control aircraft clubs and aviators to the airport.

It was always Tom Senior's dream to own and fly four aircraft in a family formation. In 1977 this dream was realized, when the family took to the skies in the Harvard aircraft (also known as the Yellow Peril). The Harvard is a two place, single engine, low wing airplane used extensively in some 50 countries around the world, in their training plans during World War II and afterward. The family, Tom Senior, Gwen, Tom, and Bev flew at numerous community events and airshows around the country. They were featured in a CFCN television documentary entitled "The Flight of the Conroys".

Tom Senior was killed in an aircraft accident at Irricana, Alberta in 1979. Gwen Conroy resides in Airdrie with her family living close by. Tom and his wife Catherine Anderson and their children Chrystal and Justin live in Airdrie, while Beverly and her husband Dean Ayles and their children Christopher and Jennifer live a short distance to the east. Gwen, Tom, Cathy, Dean and Bev all hold current pilot licenses and enjoy the flying legacy passed on by Tom Sr. The four plane family formation was reactivated for the 1994 Remembrance Day services in Crossfield, Airdrie and Calgary. You will still see (and hear) an occasional Harvard or two soaring over the Airdrie countryside.

Submitted by M. Gwen Conroy, 1996

*Above left: October 1975: Airdrie Airport, an aerial view of "the country club of the air" was owned by Tom Conroy. The airport was built during World War II as an elementary flying school. **Right**: A 1945 photograph of aircraft maintenance in progress.*

*Above: Airdrie 1945 a hive of activity with the training of aircrews. **Right top**: A flight of Dakotas line up for a training mission. **Right**: Ambulance personnel prepare for any contingency. **Below**: Royal Canadian Airforce ground crew proudly work by the motto: "We fix 'em, you fly 'em."*

338

Above and below) A wartime airfield on the Prairie (3 miles east of Airdrie) has served many purposes over the
he years.

intage aircraft flying in formation at a local airshow.

Tall Taylor Publishing in Irricana

The first issue of the *Five Village Weekly*, now known as the *Irricana/Crossfield Rockyview Five Village Weekly* was published November 6th, 1975.

It was a 6-page edition on white bond paper for which Gladys sold the advertising, daughter Susan did the paste-up, and son Lorne and Paul Boisvert did the printing. The first advertiser was the Schmaltz car dealership in Beiseker. The first writer for the newspaper was long-time area resident, Enyde Black.

Over the 20 years that the newspaper business has been in Irricana many local people have been involved in its publications which now include the *Carstairs Courier* and the *Wheel & Deal*. Among those families who have made their mark on the newspapers are the Howden/Hawkins (3 generations) and the Miner/Gabruck (3 generations). Among those individuals who contributed during the first 10 years and helped get the company going are numerous country correspondents including the late Winnie Clark, Catherine Williams, the late Greta Vorgaard, Sarah Rau, Doreen Study, Dorothy Brand, and Redvers Perry. Two of these people still write for the *Rocky View Five Village Weekly*.

There are countless others who have been involved in the newspaper business in Irricana over the years, most of whom live within a radius of ten miles.

Headquarters for the newspaper business is on Irricana's main street in a building formerly known as Pat Patterson's Garage. It is probably the oldest building still in use in the village.

Submitted by Gladys Taylor, 1996

Balzac Garden Centre and Botanical Gardens

The Balzac Garden Centre, previously called Suntropicals Garden Centre, started in 197 in a small greenhouse in Bowness, Calgary. During the building boom of the 1970's and early 1980's, we supplied and maintained indoor tropical plants in offices, malls and commercial atriums throughout Western Canada. The business was started by Bob and Donna Stuart and has remained a family-run business since that time.

It was apparent that the commercial indoor landscaping boom was not going to last forever, and so we began to look for a location to build a larger greenhouse. We planned to widen our business base by beginning to produce our own bedding plants.

After much looking and deliberation, in the spring of 1981 we chose the site in "Beautiful Downtown Balzac" to build our new greenhouse. Since that time we have engaged in the production of indoor tropical plants, bedding plants, geraniums, perennials, poinsettias, herbs and other varieties of plant material. We have developed a successful Garden Centre that is open year round with the support of the local community as well as Calgary and Airdrie.

In 1994 we opened our Botanical Display Rock Garden and Water Feature. We did this in order to test plant material for suitability and hardiness to our particular area. It also provides a place for people to see many different kinds of perennials and trees and shrubs in full bloom so that they can see what they would like to try in their own gardens. We have had many wedding pictures taken among the flowers and waterfalls. The gardens also attract visitors from many areas who see our sign on the highway or hear about them from other people.

We have found the Balzac area to be supportive and friendly and we have not regretted our decision to locate in this growing and thriving community.

Submitted by Management; Bob Stuart, 1996

Lawland Gardens

In July 1970, Gerald and Joanne Law purchased a quarter section north of Calgary. The intention was to move to the farm from Calgary and provide a better environment to raise their children. They raised a few plants to be sold to supplement the farm income and called the farm Lawland Gardens.

They built a new home during the summer of 1973 and the Law family - Gerald, Joanne, and children Laura, Sheldon, Shelley, and Corinne became rural residents. All four children attended schools in Airdrie.

The tree growing expanded quickly, and by 1975 off-farm employment was discontinued, in order to concentrate time and effort on the nursery business.

As well as field-grown nursery stock, many trees, shrubs and evergreens are now grown in containers utilizing a drip irrigation and fertilizer injection system. "Pot-in-pot" growing of trees is being implemented. Lawland Gardens now offers over 100 varieties of trees and shrubs as well as perennials and garden supplies.

Lawland Gardens is proud and happy to have served the gardening public during the past quarter century. Many uncertainties lie ahead, but we are confidant we will meet the new challenges. Quality trees and shrubs and gardening supplies await the gardening enthusiast.

Submitted by Gerald Law, 1996

The Mushroom Growing Process

Our process begins with Filling day, where approximately 300 yards of nutrient-enriched compost is hauled down from our compost wharf in Crossfield. The compost is then run through the trayline, and fed into 590 6' x 4' growing trays, which are placed into two phase 2 rooms, and pasteurized over a period of six days. On the seventh day, the growing trays are removed, spawned, supplemented, fed into 388 growing trays, and placed into a steam-heated, A/C cooled spawn room for a period of 12 to 13 days. On the 14th day the trays are removed from the spawn room and cased with a soil mixture of peat moss, calcium carbonate, and poultry grit, and then are placed into two production rooms. Our production rooms are steam-heated, A/C cooled, and contain approximately 8700 square feet for growing areas. Air flow is controlled by an over pressure ventilation system and rooms are monitored and controlled for CO_2 levels, relative humidity, and air and bed temperatures. Approximately 19 later days later, the first break mushrooms appear and are picked off over a period of 3 to 4 days. Following this break, the beds are watered for approximately 3 to 4 days, and the second break mushrooms appear, and are picked off once again over a similar time frame. We grow three breaks of mushrooms per growing room, and generally yield around 5.2 pounds of mushrooms per square foot. The time span that the growing trays are in the production rooms to completion is approximately 38 days.

We employ 32 pickers, and the mushrooms are picked by hand and sorted for grade, quality and size. The mushrooms are then shipped to our packing room where the mushrooms are packaged and sent fresh to local stores, wholesalers, and canneries.

At crop completion, the production room is sealed and steam-heated to 150 degrees to ensure a proper "kill". The trays are then dumped outside, and the spent compost is sold to local loam companies, landscapers and home gardeners and then the process repeats itself.

Submitted by Money's Mushrooms Ltd., 1996

Carmen Valstar and Gloria May (above and below) tend to the everyday chores that ensure optimum quality.

Denise Smith checks on the progress of tropical cacti.   *1981: 4 suntropical units under construction.*

Planting season in 1980.

Growing lot for potted trees and perennial greenhouse.

Shrubs and evergreens are cultivated in this place.

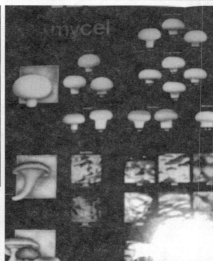

Processing mushrooms for market requires dedication and expertise.

344

Soil Preparation

Growing mushrooms in layers ensures optimum use of space.

Packaging mushrooms for market.

ATCO Ltd.

[*The early history of ATCO is given in One Day's Journey. It started out as Alberta Trailer Company in 1946-47, producing utility and house trailers in a plant in Calgary. In 1956, a tremendous explosion destroyed the plant and the company needed to find new quarters quickly in order to fill a major contract. The company moved to the air field southeast of Airdrie, and grew into a large plant over the next decade.*]

In the fall of 1965, ATCO Industries Ltd., as it was then officially named, commenced moving its industrial manufacturing facilities from Airdrie to Lincoln Park, Calgary. The ATCO Housing Division plant that manufactured residential housing remained in operation at the original site east of Airdrie until 1967.

Prior to 1965, the Head Office of the Company had been moved to 1243 - 48th Avenue N.E. (now McKnight Boulevard), Calgary, thereby continuing the Company's presence in the northern segment of Calgary. Currently, ATCO Travel, a division of the ATCO Group, and Frontec Corporation, a project office of a subsidiary, maintain offices in the building. The World Headquarters of the ATCO Group of Companies moved to the Canadian Western Natural Gas Centre, 909 - 11th Avenue S.W., Calgary, in May 1984.

Demonstrating its continuing interest in the thriving community of Airdrie, soon to be a city, the subsidiary ATCO Development jointly developed Towerlane Mall with its partner Easton Development. The mall officially opened on August 11, 1982. The ATCO Group retained its interest in the mall until April 1, 1996.

Canadian Western Natural Gas Company Limited, another subsidiary, provides natural gas service to the residents and businesses of Airdrie.

Over the years, ATCO Ltd. (ATCO) has maintained its world leadership in the manufacture of transportable housing; in addition, however, it has evolved into a management holding company with many facets and diversified subsidiaries.

Of particular significance to the growth, evolution and diversification of the Company was the acquisition of control in 1980 of Canadian Utilities Limited and all of its subsidiaries from International Utilities of Philadelphia, U.S.A.

ATCO, through its subsidiaries, provided work-force housing for numerous major domestic and international construction projects: Syncrude, Fort McMurray; Aleyeska Pipeline, Alaska; Jubail and Yanbu projects, Kingdom of Saudi Arabia; to name but a few.

Latterly, the Group has been utilizing its Alberta based electric generation expertise. Its subsidiary CU Power International Ltd. developed with partners, and solely operates the environmentally acceptable gas fired combined cycle 1000 megawatt Barking Power generating plant which was officially commissioned October 19, 1995 in London, England. In May 1996, this subsidiary completed financial close of a gas fired 180 megawatt cogeneration plant at Adelaide, Australia. The construction and operation in 1998 of this plant will be led by the company, which continues to pursue other international cogeneration opportunities, particularly in the United Kingdom.

As reported to shareholders in the ATCO Ltd. 1995 Annual Report, this Calgary based Corporation now has assets exceeding $4.3 billion with three operating groups employing more than 5,500 persons. R.D. Southern continues to control it by virtue of his control of Sentgraf Enterprises Ltd. which owns 77% of the Corporation's voting shares.

The Operating Groups:

Canadian Utilities Limited

Canadian Utilities' subsidiaries include Alberta Power Limited (electric power generation, transmission and distribution); Canadian Western Natural Gas Company Limited and Northwestern Utilities Limited (natural gas production, transmission and distribution); CU Power International Ltd. (international independent power generation and transmission projects); CU Gas Limited (gas gathering, transmission, processing and storage); CU Water Limited (water transmission and distribution).

Frontec Corporation

Frontec provides management, operation and maintenance and technical services in the defense, transportation and industrial sectors.

ATCO Structures Inc.

ATCO Structures manufactures, sells and leases industrial workforce housing to over 75 countries around the world from factories in Calgary, Canada and Budapest, Hungary. ATCO Noise Management, a division of ATCO Structures, designs and constructs buildings and acoustic barriers to reduce noise emissions from industrial facilities.

Submitted by Desmond P. Wood, 1996

Desmond P. Wood was an Officer of ATCO until he retired; he is now ATCO's historian

From early beginnings to a world-wide enterprise: ATCO Alberta Trailer Company, under the astute leadership of Ron Southern, has vaulted from a modest beginnings at 805-3rd Street N.E., Calgary in 1946-47 to the the Airdrie airport. The company continued its rapid growth, compelling it to move to even bigger premises in Calgary. Picture of horse jumping at left, taken at the Calgary International Airport, serves two purposes: it promotes Calgary's Spruce Meadows, with its international reputation, as well as an appropriate company metaphor.

—Editor.

Photos copurtesy of the Nose Creek Historical Society.

R.D. Southern, *Chairman & Chief Executive Officer, ATCO Ltd. & Canadian Utilities Limited, and co-founder with this father, S.D. Southern, of Alberta Trailer Hire in 1947 in Alberta.*

Right, inset: *Main manufacturing facility in Airdrie, Alberta until 1964, when it was moved to ATCO Industrial Park in southwest Calgary.*

Right: *Over the years, ATCO has been involved in many industries, including the housing and development industry in Alberta. ATCO built and managed the CU Centre building in Edmonton is headquarters for Canadian Utilities Limited, Alberta Power Limited and Northwestern Utilities Limited, all ATCO Group companies.*

This picture, inset: *ATCO Industries provided modular housing for scientific research teams at the South Pole in Antarctica.*

This picture: *Typical of the type of strong industrial housing required in the oilfields of Alberta, ATCO designed, manufactured and installed drill camps and wellsites in various remote locations. ATCO Drilling, now Akita Drilling, was active in the western Canadian oilpatch until the early 1990's.*

Above: *Frontec Logistics, one of ATCO's principal subsidiaries, won the contract to manage the sites of the North Warning System in northern Canada and the U.S.*
Left: *ATCO's diverse industrial activities include the development and construction of acoustic noise control buildings, such as these buildings in northern New York state, which house industrial generators.*

Left: Today, ATCO's portfolio consists of such new companies as CU Gas Limited, which is involved in natural gas gathering, processing, production, transmission, supply, storage and hub services.

Below: The 1000 megawatt electric power generating station, Barking Power, was officially opened in London, England in October, 1995 and reflects one of the future directions of the ATCO Group of companies.

Amoco Canada's East Crossfield Gas Plant

In the middle of this century, construction began in Canada on some of the world's great pipelines. Completion of three large natural gas pipelines from Alberta to Ontario, the Pacific Northwest, and California led to almost explosive growth in demand for western Canadian gas. Amoco Canada's East Crossfield gas plant has a long and proud place among suppliers of that demand.

The East Crossfield plant is 40 kilometres north of Calgary, west of Highway 2 and close to the town of Crossfield. Since going on stream more than 30 years ago, the plant has been an important part of the regional economy in the Nose Creek area. In 1995 alone, Amoco contributed over $1 million to the local economy through municipal taxes.

The facility was built in two parts. The Elkton plant was constructed in 1964 to process sweet gas from the Elkton formation, discovered in the mid-1950's. Initial production from the plant was 35 million cubic feet per day. Since then, additional gas pools have been connected to the plant. The volume of sweet gas from those fields processed at East Crossfield has totalled 150 billion cubic feet.

Surrounding the area was the East Crossfield sour gas field. Although the gas is "sour" meaning it contains a sulphur compound known as hydrogen sulphide ($H2S$), this field became increasingly attractive throughout the 1960's as sulphur prices rose and gas demand continued to grow. Sulphur is used to manufacture fertilizer, plastics, and pharmaceuticals, for example, so demand for this commodity has grown fairly steadily in the second half of this century.

To help meet the demand, Amoco (then known as Pan American) added the D-1 sulphur plant to the facility in 1968. When first built, East Crossfield was the third largest sulphur recovery facility in North America. Amoco has always operated the plant and is the major owner. The company has 16 partners.

The facility's original design was for throughput of 110 million cubic feet per day. Throughput peaked at 117 million cubic feet per day in 1972, and 1995 volumes averaged 50 million cubic feet per day. In addition to half a trillion cubic feet of sales gas, cumulative production since the plant went on stream has included 11.3 million tonnes of sulphur and 786 thousand barrels of condensate.

According to plant foreman Donnie Chalmers, who has worked at East Crossfield since 1968, having to process gas with a high sulphur content has always provided challenges for the plant. Those challenges intensified in the early 1970's, when the provincial government established air quality standards that stood among the toughest in the world.

The plant began a $6 million clean-up program for gas emissions in 1975. The project aimed to increase sulphur recovery and reduce sulphur dioxide emissions by 90 tonnes a day.

Amoco developed a process known as the Cold Bed Absorption (CBA) system. CBA uses a process known among chemists as the Claus reaction at low temperatures to convert hydrogen sulphide and sulphur dioxide to elemental sulphur. The novel regeneration system made it possible for East Crossfield to increase its sulphur recovery from 95.5 per cent to 98 per cent. This was the first time Amoco's Cold Bed Process was used commercially. Since then, it has been adapted worldwide.

According to Chalmers, throughout the plant's history good community relations have always been a priority. This process benefits from the fact that many plant employees are residents of the Crossfield community, many of them contributing as volunteers to social, athletic and other organizations. Since the 1970's, Amoco has participated in Crossfield's handicapped fish derby, sponsored by Alberta Fish and Game. Every June, about a hundred people of all ages - all challenged in some way - fish for trout in a pond located on plant property.

The plant also contributes to the Crossfield community by supporting infrastructure projects; for example, Amoco was a contributor to the local community hall, arena, and golf course.

Since the plant is only three kilometres from the town, in 1977 employees decided to improve its look. A beautification program included planting 250 trees and shrubs in front of the facility to hide piping and equipment in the storage area. In the early 1990's the plant's groundskeeper, retired plant operator Norm Mosely, won prizes in a local competition for the best commercial lawn.

To increase understanding about its operations, Amoco tries to educate the public whenever possible. This frequently takes the form of tours of the plant by students and other groups. In 1980, nearly 30 elementary and secondary school teachers from across Canada toured the plant as part of a seminar on energy and the environment. Amoco was an active participant in the month-long seminar, sponsored by an Edmonton-based private group called Society, Environment and Energy Development Studies Foundation (SEEDS).

Funded by both government and companies in Canadian energy industries, SEEDS has been effective in helping educate Canadians about energy and the environment. In fact, the organization has developed school curricula that are widely used in Canadian schools systems, and have been adapted for use as far away as New Zealand.

Like other Amoco facilities, East Crossfield has developed partnerships with local schools. In addition, employees help with school sports days, science fairs and other activities. The plant has also frequently hired students in work experience positions.

Like other large gas plants, East Crossfield regularly improves on its techniques and equipment, to operate the plant as efficiently and safely as possible. To keep the sour gas plant running at full potential, Amoco installed $15 million worth of field compression equipment in 1982. Four compressors were able to increase well pressure, pushing the gas through the pipe line, to the plant, and into a sales gas pipeline. Installing this equipment helped ensure that the mature plant could improve field production.

Employees are always looking for new ways to prevent accidents and protect East Crossfield from hazardous situations. In 1978, the company installed a $1.5 million safety surveillance system for the D-1 gas field. If a sour gas leak were detected, the affected facilities would automatically shut down.

Experimental equipment greatly aided East Crossfield in 1983 when an odour was being emitted from the plant. After close investigation, the rotten-egg smell was traced to H2S coming from the plant's new sulphur forming unit. Plant engineers designed a piece of equipment called a sulphur degasser to help determine what would need to be done to control the problem. They then turned the experimental unit into a full-scale degasser. Since being installed in August 1984, the plant has been able to remove almost all the hydrogen sulphide from the sulphur produced.

East Crossfield employees have made tremendous improvements to plant operations. In 1993, the plant went a record 84 days without excess sulphur dioxide emissions from its stack. In that year, employees reduced the number of stack emissions exceeding acceptable levels to 25 from more than 300 in 1988.

By mid-1996, however, this record has been eclipsed by a large margin. More than six months went by without a single stack incident, and as this book went into production that record continued to grow. Even more importantly, plant staff had worked for more than one million hours without a single lost-time accident. That record, too, grows by the hour.

After all of the gas was depleted from the Elkton sour gas formation in 1993, the plant turned the reservoir into a natural gas storage facility. A year later, that facility was expanded to capacity of 400 million cubic feet. According to Donnie Chalmers, it made good business sense to make use of the facility. It also kept jobs in the Crossfield area.

Today, the plant is running at 50% capacity. The number of employees has dropped from more than 90 in the early 1970's to about 35 now. At 1995 rates of production, the plant should remain in operation for at least five years. And if history is a measure of things to come, new technologies and ideas from people at the plant will increase extraction of reserves from the gas field around East Crossfield. With luck and good management, the plant could continue operating even longer still.

Submitted by Donnie Chalmers, Amoco Canada, 1996

Left: Elston plant in 1964 and the D-1 plant in 1993.

Above: Sulphur production is growing by leaps and bounds as demand grows.
Above left (inset): ph tests on run off water are periodically carried out in accordance with government regulations. These checks are designed to prevent contamination of surrounding areas.
Above right (inset): Water samples undergo purity tests.
Left: Checking voltage on an off-pump controller.
Below: Adjusting a pump-off controller at Pembina F-23

Balzac Gas Plant

The Balzac Gas Plant serves an area ranging from north of Airdrie to south of Chestermere Lake, and from east of Irricana to the #2 Highway on the west. It processes sour gas to produce natural gas, sulphur, propane, butane, and liquid hydrocarbon.

The Petrogas Processing Ltd. Balzac Gas Plant was built in 1961 to serve the needs of the energy and sulphur markets. The original well, called the Kathyrn wildcat, had been discovered by Mobil in 1954. Jefferson Lake Petrochemicals of Canada started its new drilling program in 1956 and discovered additional Crossfield sour gas wells and, in 1957, the Elktor field.

Since there were two reservoirs in the area, it was feasible to build a plant to process the gas. Petrogas Processing Ltd. was formed of all 28 operating interests in the field to produce and process the gas.

Construction started and was completed in 1961. The plant was officially opened by Premier E.C. Manning on May 1st, 1962. Most of the 700 guests for this event arrived by a special train that ran from downtown Calgary over the new spur line. "They disembarked onto a platform of pure yellow sulphur, laid especially for the occasion." Guests received small bricks of sulphur which some kept for many years.

In 1965, Canadian Occidental Petroleum Company took over Jefferson Lake Petrochemicals and has continued as operator of the plant to the present. It dissolved Petrogas Processing in 1995 and operated the plant as a joint venture with its partners.

The plant has had several expansions over the years: the LPG unit in 1965; for gas treating and sulphur recovery in 1967; inlet pressure being added in 1971-1974; the sulfreen unit to meet environmental requirements in 1975; and sales gas compression in 1982. The gradual turndown of the plant started in 1987 and continues. It is expected that the gas will last for another 15-20 years (unless more is found) and then the plant will be sold and torn down and the site cleaned up.

The Balzac Gas Plant has shipped sulphur all over the world, and it supplies much of the propane for Calgary's market. It had processed a total of 57,876,997.9 thousand cubic metres of gas as of late 1995.

Compiled from information supplied by Canadian Occidental Petroleum, 1996

A common sight in the Valley: one of the original wildcat oil well near Nier Lakes. Photo taken 1989, courtesy Dorothy Tilleman.

354

Modern technology is extensively used in the gas and oil industry.

Balzac gas plant: pipes gas to places as far away as California. The sulfur by-products are shipped all over the world.

Above, below and bottom left: Sulphur being hauled out by rail.

A typical oil and gas drilling rig in the Valley. Photo taken from the Alfred Bilben farm, 2.5 miles NW of Balzac, 1988

Neil Perry on a pipeline inspection tour, 1961.

New Central Control System
In 1987 a decision was made
modernize and centralize the tu
outdated control rooms.
Petrogas project personnel pose f
pictures in front of the new contr
screens shortly before its commissionir
Left to right are: Todd Jorgensen-Nels
(Plant Draftsman), Larry Hanson (Pla
Engineer, Control System Proje
Manager), Gilles Collin plant electri
instrumentation Supervisor, Contr
System Project Instrumentati
Coordinator), Al Woods plant Maintenan
Superintendent), Don Gabruck (Pla
Operations Superintendent), and Bill To
(Plant Process Superintendent, Contr
System Project Operations Coordinato

Ground breaking ceremonies for the new control room building,
September 30, 1988. Left to right are: Dan Richer, Don Gabruck,
Gilles Collin, Bill Kreft, Bob Orthlieb (digging), Vic Zaleschuk, Rick
Jensen, John McKay, Larry Hanson.

Close up view of the new control scree.

Old treater control room shortly before decommissioning. Most of
the instruments seen in the picture were installed when the plant
was built in 1961. Operating are Wayne Butler (front), Larry Fox
(middle), and Russ Foose (rear).

Cliff Hawkey (Plant Shift Superviso
inspects the electronic equipment whi
is the basis of the new control system.

356

The Leather and Fur Industry

The Nose Creek Valley was a source of fur bearing animals prior to its intensive settlement at the turn of the century. Beaver, coyotes, weasel, muskrats, foxes. lynx, rabbits, and buffalo provided the native peoples and early settlers with a ready source of fur and leather. Buffalo robes and furs helped to keep them warm and safe against the winter elements. Native peoples used buffalo hides to make tepees, and for many other domestic uses. Buffalo hides were used for industrial belts in eastern Canada. Fort Benton was a major shipping point: one historian estimates that from 1832 to 1884, 1,178,500 robes were shipped east from Fort Benton.

As cattle were introduced to the area, early ranchers and farmers would sell their beef hides to agents who would come around and buy the raw hides and ship them to local tanneries or to Winnipeg for tanning. The leather then was used to make harness and saddles.

Several tanneries in Calgary served the Nose Creek Valley. At the turn of the century, Edward Ferdinand operated the Calgary Tannery at 230 3rd Avenue East. His plant tanned all kinds of furs, robes and rugs made to order; he also specialized in repairs. Another historic furrier, Simpson and Lee, was situated on Centre Street.

In 1901, Eneas McCormick established a company with W.J. Riley, and by 1906, Riley & McCormick Limited was located at 111 8th Avenue West in Calgary. They were manufacturers of and wholesale dealers in harness, saddles, leather, saddlery hardware, fancy leather goods, gloves, mitts, purses, and Mexican carved leather goods. This firm went bankrupt in 1983, and Eneas' grandchildren, Carolyn and Brian, resurrected the company as an outlet on 7th Avenue and 1st Street S.W. It became known as "The Store With a Horse at the Door".

Another tannery operated by Mr. Briggs started in 1908 in the Burnsland district and closed down in the late 1970's. During the 1950's this firm was called Briggs Furriers and Fur Dressers.

Some of the other furriers in Calgary, mentioned in the *Henderson's Directory* for 1911, were August Kraft, situated on 1st Street East, MacKay and Dippie at 218 8th Avenue West, I. Pasternack at #8, 218a 8th Avenue East, and Van Veen Andre Co. at 1036 6th Avenue West.

By 1945 the *Henderson's* listings included Cecil C. Charlebois at 1416 1st Street West and Kraft the Furrier, Kraft Building, 22 8th Avenue West.

In 1950, Briggs Furriers and Fur Dressers had an office and factory in the Burnsland district, Charlebois had moved to 1309 1st Street S.W., and Robert Garbutt Ltd. was at 706 Centre Street.

1960 saw the following listings: Renfrew Furs Ltd. on 7th Avenue S.W.; Swears & Wells (Canada) Ltd., the successors to Kraft the Furrier, at 222 8th Avenue S.W.; Joe Verig and Furriers Ltd. at 507 17th Avenue S.W.; and Yeagers Furs Ltd., successors to Robert Garbutt Ltd., on 706 Centre Street East.

Fur dealers and furriers in 1991 were listed as Benzing Furs (1981) Ltd. on 1st Street S.W., Charlebois Furs Ltd. at 1506 4th Street S.W., David Fur Factory Inc. on 17th Avenue S.W., Renfrew Furs at 108 7th Avenue S.W., and John Vozniuk and Sons Furriers at 2133 33rd Avenue S.W.

The present Benzing-Charlebois Furs Ltd. is an amalgamation of two separate fur companies. One was Cecil C. Charlebois Furrier Co. Ltd., whose owner worked for the Hudson's Bay Company until 1938 when he established his shop. Charlebois retired in 1977 and sold out to Eric Donoghue and Wolfgang Kunze, both of Calgary. In the same year, Karl Benzing, the great-grandson of the founder of Benzing Furs of Germany came to Calgary and established Benzing Furs Co. Ltd. Due to ill health, he sold his firm to Harold Kohrs and Grant Ritchie, who operated the enterprise for ten years, then sold it to Eric Donoghue and Grant Ritchie. They formed the present Benzing-Charlebois Furs Ltd., situated at 1506 4th Street S.W.

Of special interest is the fact that most people think the hog is the most efficient of all animals. Eric Donoghue states, however, that when the mink is brought into the equation you really see efficiency! The mink is fed on a high protein diet of fish and waste products of other animals. They need this high protein to get a lustrous coat. After pelting, the carcass is given to the rendering plants to make into products such as mink oil and cosmetics which use mink oil.

Mink coats are made from their pelts, but none of the trimmings are thrown away. Indeed, entire coats can be made from the tails alone. Likewise, entire mink coats can be made from the leg areas and paws. This type of efficiency produces no waste and nothing injurious to the environment.

During the 1920's a number of fur farms were established around Calgary. M.D. Carlyle Harry Berry and W. Pollock, and others ran fox farms. The Colpitts Fox Ranch in the Springbank area became world renowned for its excellent pelt, produced from mutant foxes bred there. Fresh horse meat and gophers were fed to the animals.

By the 1930's the demand for fox fur had diminished and the fox farms went out of business. The last fox farmer left at Chestermere Lake was R.F. Carlyle, who shut down in 1943, followed in 1950 by the Colpitts operation at Springbank. Many smaller mink and chinchilla farms lasted a short time only.

Fur farming in Canada is now a highly scientific enterprise, as in other countries such as Sweden and Russia, where climates require extra protection form the cold. In Canada there are approximately 10,000 fur farms yielding about 120,000 silver fox pelts every year.

Submitted by Stephen Wilk and Eric Donoghue, 1996

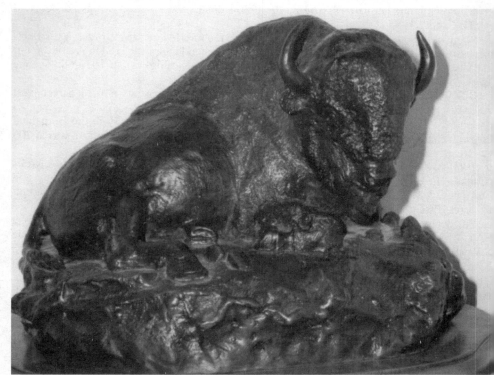

Food, fur, leather and other utilities: the buffalo came to symbolize all these. This sculpture, by O.D. Begg, Studio West, is #15 of 20 originals. (It was presented to Stephen Wilk, this book's editor, by Renfrew United Church on the occasion of his retirement in 1988.)

ENTREPRENEUR OF THE YEAR

Honouring those individuals and companies whose ingenuity, hard work, and innovation have created successful and growing business ventures, this Certificate Of Nomination is presented to:

Eric Donoghue

Benzing Charlebois Furs

Prairies Region Program Director

ERNST & YOUNG   McCarthy Tétrault   Bank of Montreal
NESBITT BURNS   McCarthy Tétrault   AIR CANADA

Business

Grant Ritchie, Vice President and Eric Donoghue, President of Benzing Charlebois Furs in Calgary. **Left:** a tribute to excellence.

Above: Canadian-made fur coats. **Right:** Shonna Truong (left) and Anna Bodzgon finish the furs at Charlebois Benzing Furs, Calgary.

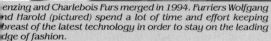

Benzing and Charlebois Furs merged in 1994. Furriers Wolfgang and Harold (pictured) spend a lot of time and effort keeping abreast of the latest technology in order to stay on the leading edge of fashion.

Fur storage vault.

Riley & McCormick Leather & Harness Shop opened in Calgary in 1901 and in Lethbridge in 1905. Brian Guichon (below) is committed to maintaining the company's high standrds that made it so famous for so long.

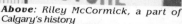

Above: Riley McCormick, a part of Calgary's history

Above: The cowboy depended heavily on leather products to function.

Below left: Canoeing used to be the main means of transporting leather and fur goods.
Below right: The leather boot was the most common part of the accoutrement of the pioneers.

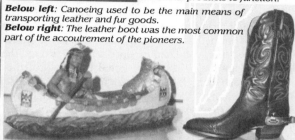

Above left:Riley & McCormick's pioneered the use of suede and sheepshin in protection against the Valley's winters. Above right: Kathy Elliott and store owner, Brian Guichon (right) inspect a new consignment.

Left:The various and varied use of leather. Above: Leather by-products on the horse attest to the the versatility of leather. Right: it protects you from the vicious winters, too.

CHAPTER 43: CO-OPERATIVES

Introduction

Life on the prairies has always been a matter of working and playing together; the Indians joining together for their buffalo hunts, and sharing the meat with everyone; the ranchers working together on roundups; the early settlers helping each other to build homes, schools and churches. The need for group action in the first decades of the 20th Century produced the United Farmers of Alberta. The U.F.A.'s political arm formed the Provincial Government from 1921 to 1935, and its social and economic influence on rural Alberta continued long after the political party had disappeared.

Co-operatives of all sizes were started to handle various economic needs. They ranged from the local beef ring, a group of farmers who would take turns butchering a cow and sharing cuts with all members, to large retail operations such as the Calgary Co-op, to establishing rural electrical and gas systems. We present the stories of some of the co-ops.

The Balzac Trading Company

The oldest business in the Balzac district is the Balzac Trading Co-operative Association of the United Farmers of Alberta. *The Nose Creek Story* relates that the Buttes local of the U.F.A. was formed in 1914 at a meeting of local farmers held in the Buttes School. Later they decided to expand and in April of 1920 formed the Balzac Trading Company (as it is commonly known). The provisional Directors of the Board were W.J. Church, George Coggan, Jack Greig, P.M. Ham, Clem Perry, Osia Rosenberger and Emil Sireni; when the Board was elected, George Barker and Herbert J. Jobson replaced Greig and Perry. As recorded in earlier histories such as *One Day's Journey*, the primary purpose of the little co-op was to purchase commonly needed items such as coal, fence posts, lumber and twine at wholesale prices. They also owned the post office and store along with weigh scales, a coal shed, a fuel shed and a stable.

Their next step was to expand into the insurance business and at a meeting held on March 17, 1922, they approved the expenditure of $3.00 for an agent's license to sell fire, auto, hail and accident coverage; the same license costs $75.00 today.

Over the years the need for and availability of these products changed dramatically. The Co-op sold the store and post office in 1958 and the last lots in 1965, and it dumped coal in 1971. The Board's meeting minutes indicate coal was discontinued because only two boxcar loads had been handled in 1970 and the old coal shed which had been repaired numerous times needed fixing again. This left the insurance business, which is still operating as of mid 1996, although on a reduced scale. The minutes do not say when they stopped selling hail and accident insurance, but when Saskatchewan Mutual went out of the auto insurance business in 1991 the Trading Company suffered. Many shareholders prefer to have one agency handle all their business, or their auto insurer/broker requires the property policy as well. This has left the Co-op with only 32 of its 112 shareholders still doing business with it, making its future uncertain.

The current officers of the Co-op are Arnold Jones, President (Director since 1972); John Church, Vice-President (Director since 1965); Rosemary Church, Secretary-Treasurer and Agent (since 1973) and Directors Wayne Ham, Bill Lamport, Earl Northcott, Chuck Raines and Max Smith.

This is a very brief history of an organization that was founded by the pioneer farmers of the area and one that has operated successfully for some 82 years; from 1914 to 1996.

Submitted by John Church, 1996

All About Light and Heat

We take it for granted nowadays, flick a switch, twist a dial, and there it is. In my lifetime what changes I have seen.

As a small child I remember having coal oil lamps and candles as a source of light. Along

C.R. Perry keeps his 1947 Minneapolis Moline, Model 7, tractor warm using a 'Tiger Torch' manufactured by Frank Young of Airdrie.

about four o'clock in the afternoon my mother would check lamps for coal oil supply and trim wicks if necessary. Then came the Coleman gas lamp. Fuel pressurized by a little hand pump built into the fuel tank would supply fuel to the mantles. They were two little cotton bags, which , when they were burned to a white cinder produced a white light. They were considered somewhat dangerous and made an annoying hissing sound. Aladdin produced a mantle lamp that was silent; it brought fuel to the mantle by a wick and produced a brilliant white light.

Enter electricity. First came the generators powered either by gas engine or wind power. These units not only provided light at the touch of a switch, but power to produce heat for a toaster, if you didn't use it too frequently! The ultimate answer to our needs of course was the Rural Electrification of our community in the early 1950's.

Set the thermostat and there it is, heat to the exact temperature you and your family desire. It was not always so. My first recollections were of my father chopping wood on top of the old "Home Comfort" cook stove. As I lay in bed in the morning, I could tell his mood by the way he chopped the wood in the kitchen.

Two "Quebec" heaters warmed the rest of the house somewhat, if they were tended constantly with coal. Ashes were removed and pipes cleaned annually or when it was necessary, if the things were to work.

Next came the gravity furnace in the centre of the basement, a monstrous contraption,

363

built with larger pipes to conduct heat to every room. What an improvement. This used large quantities of coal. A coal bin had to be provided in the basement, with its resulting dust percolating through the house.

Then came the oil furnace and space heaters. These devices burned diesel oil, stinky stuff it was, but at least you didn't have to shovel it and there were no ashes to haul out.

The forced air furnace of today is quiet, compact and clean. It is there at the turn of the thermostat. Natural gas fuelled, it does its duty virtually unnoticed.

Over time, I believe the greatest innovation in heating fuel was introduced to our area by Frank Young. I well recall Frank demonstrating a gas stove fuelled by a bottled gas under high pressure. This fuel burned completely clean and was virtually odourless in combustion. I am speaking of propane gas. At first it was offered in hundred-pound metal bottles. As time went by, large thousand-gallon pressure vessels were observed in town and on farms around the community. Frank Young ran a garage in Airdrie, but was an entrepreneur. He told me he came to Airdrie from Medicine Hat with eleven dollars in his "ass pocket", as he put it!

Frank's real contribution was the "Tiger Torch". This invention was a comparatively simple device. It consisted of a twenty-five pound bottle of propane, ten feet of high pressure hose and a suitable burner. These things were and still are made in Airdrie and have supplied instant heat all over, where portable heat is required. In the early years we didn't have an instant heat source to warm engines, thaw pipes, warm newborn animals, etc. Frank provided the means. The use of this device is endless; its use is worldwide.

Submitted by Leighton Perry, 1996

Airdrie Rural Electrification Association (R.E.A.)

In 1893, Eau Claire Lumber Company built the first hydro plant in southern Alberta, just below the company's sawmill on the Bow River in Calgary. The farms and ranches around Calgary, however, made their electricity from the wind, not water. They used wind-chargers on windmills to pump water from wells and to provide light at night. If the wind was not blowing that night, they could always use candles or coal oil lanterns.

Calgary Power built a power line north to Olds and beyond in 1926. Villages and towns along the line had sub-stations installed; a transformer sub-station a few miles south of Airdrie acted as a hub for energy moving from the Ghost River or Bearspaw dams north along the powerline, or east to Irricana, Beiseker and Rockyford. The village of Airdrie began to receive electricity in 1928. It was more than 20 years, however, before Calgary Power could sell power to the farmers. They did not really need it, and, going through the Depression of the 1930's and rationing during World War II, they had better uses for their limited cash.

Calgary Power set up the Farm Electric Services Ltd., a subsidiary company which constructed and operated farmer-owned lines within reach of Calgary Power's lines. Through it, Calgary Power offered engineering expertise to rural electrification associations at a low cost. On March 23, 1948, the West Airdrie Rural Electrification Association was formed, with Victor Watson as President, and R.V. Clayton as Secretary. Five Directors were also elected.

On October 1, 1949, 60 farms started using electrical energy. This improved safety in the homes, with little danger of fire, as there had been from exploding or overturned lanterns or lamps. In 1962, Airdrie R.E.A. had 113 members using electricity, which was 100% of occupied farmsteads; Balzac had 118, Irricana 104, and Crossfield 282 for a total of 607 power users on farms within 30 miles of Airdrie.

Summarized from Stephen Wilk, *One Day's Journey*, 1963

Balzac Rural Electrification Association (R.E.A.)

In May 1949, a group of farmers and rural residents held an organizational meeting at the Beddington Hall to form the Balzac Rural Electrification Association. This was done so they could gain access to electrical power. They agreed to collect $100.00 from each member as a token of good faith, and to map and canvass the district before September 1, 1949.

On November 30, 1959, George Wall moved they join a Union (R.E.A.); this was seconded by Grant Shuttleworth Senior and carried. In December of that year the City of Calgary proposed to annex some of the Association's power lines, just east of the Calgary Airport. On August 2, 1961, the Directors discussed selling the lines serving the residents at Jefferson Lake to Calgary Power.

On February 26, 1967, in several instances, permission was granted to A.G.T. to use R.E.A. power poles for its telephone lines.

On September 17, 1969, Grant Shuttleworth Senior moved, seconded by M.I. Griffith, that a presentation be given to Cyril Woolliams, as he was the last retiring member of the original Board of Directors. All Directors agreed to give presentations to Lionel Perry, Dulcie Perry, and Grant Shuttleworth Senior at the upcoming Annual Meeting on March 26, 1973.

In 1981 the Balzac Rural Electrification Association was sold to TransAlta Utilities (formerly Calgary Power); at that time there were 183 customers. Today the Balzac rural area has 180 accounts and West Airdrie has 229 customers.

Submitted by Margaret King, from the minutes of the Balzac Rural Electrical Association, 1996

Airdrie Rural Fire Association

In the late fall of 1961 and the early months of 1962, the farmers of Airdrie and district got together to form some means of fire protection. Our first Board of Directors was elected on May 7, 1962. They were: Cliff Clayton as President, Allan Fletcher as Vice President, Dick Clapperton as Secretary and Les Olsen as Treasurer. Directors were Ray Howden, James Bussey, Bob Dewitt, Pete Morison, Walter Moen, Redvers Perry, and Dick Clayton.

When it was decided to finance it with a one-mill tax rate in the M.D. of Rocky View, some of our good farmers, mostly to the south, got up a petition to kill our project. Our good old Airdrie FUA Local No. 1001 gave us their support in sponsoring our organization, by giving financial assistance to buy our first fire truck. (FUA stands for Farmers Union of Alberta, which existed before Unifarm got organized.)

The Airdrie Rural Fire Protection Association area was north from Calgary city limits to four miles north of Airdrie, and 12 miles east of Airdrie, also 12 miles west of Airdrie. The last Board of Directors is as follows: John Harn as President, Ray Howden as Vice President, Ross Giles as Secretary John Fowler as Treasurer, and James Bussey, Ron Schnell, Len Kininmonth as Directors.

In January 1967, Ray Howden and Bruce Clayton went to Toronto to drive home our new Ford fire truck. On December 29, 1977, we also bought a new 4x4 truck for the volunteer fire crew. The fire trucks were installed with mobile radio units.

Our Fire Protection Association was in demand for fighting fires for 18 years. James Bussey and Ray Howden were with the Board for this length of time. The Board of Directors disbanded our Association in November 1980.

Submitted by Ray Howden, 1996

Circle Eight Co-op

On Monday night December 13th, 1983, members of Circle Eight Equipment Co-op met at Milano's Restaurant in Beddington Square. The purpose of the meeting was to wind up the affairs of the co-op. It had been decided almost two years before to close down after more than twenty years of operation.

The concept of a co-op purchasing farm machinery and then renting it to its members at cost was the "brain child" of Harry Pole. He related to us how he had been wakened in the night by what turned out to be a bright idea. Hopefully his wife Gertie was not disturbed from her slumber! Well I remember Harry expounding on his theory, usually at the next

Unifarm meeting.

A meeting of all farmers in the immediate area was called to try and measure interest, but it was soon discovered that due to diversity of interests, age and affluence this approach was not practical. Undaunted, Harry gathered the most likely converts and a meeting was convened at Gordon Farr's on March 21st, 1961. At this meeting, since there were eight of us sitting around his living room that evening all "Gung ho" to follow Harry, Mr. Farr suggested we call our venture "Circle Eight Equipment". Walter Bushfield, being somewhat sceptical, was soon to nickname us "Crazy Eights".

The first year or two we had numerous meetings and were required to invest just over $600.00 each. As the business grew due to rental to non-members at a modest profit, we soon discovered we were better to borrow money for expansion instead of using our own. Our machinery inventory expanded and in order to gain co-op status two new members were acquired.

Fred Bushfield kindly consented to rent out, repair, and store our equipment in return for free rent for his own use. This worked for a while but it was soon apparent that this was too much to ask of one member, let alone the wear and tear on his wife, Faye! The equipment was then divided among the members. Each was required to rent out and maintain a certain item. This worked reasonably well. Besides certain specialty hand tools, we owned a post pounder, two large manure spreaders, a four-yard dirt mover, a heavy 22-foot disc, a fertilizer spreader, a calf cradle, a cow chute, a high pressure washer, a rock picker, and other pieces that I have neglected to list.

The rental arrangement had certain rules laid out, but much of it depended on trust and common sense. For example, if you rented the disc for a day's work, it was assumed that a day was approximately 10 operating hours. If it rained while you had the disc in your possession, you were not required to return it immediately but could keep it until your work could be completed. The time used was an honour decision. People who rented our equipment and had no mechanical knowledge were avoided the second time around; also in that category were those considered abusive. By their acts we knew them!

Members could relate many stories of how equipment would disappear from their yard only to reappear a few days later. Someone had decided to rent it! Once in a while someone would return a piece of equipment that was damaged and not tell the renter. He received the "high eyebrow" at the next encounter. It was not much fun lying under a dripping manure spreader doing a repair due to someone else's carelessness, or welding a post pounder someone had damaged and returned without saying a word.

At one point an attempt was made to get into bulk purchasing. Apparently the savings gained were hardly worth the trouble. One would have thought that acreage and smaller land owners would be our best customers. While this was true to some extent, many times we found larger operators would rent equipment simply because, on the basis of economics, they could see the advantage of renting a piece of equipment instead of tying their money up. The rental fee would be a direct deduction as an expense for income tax purposes.

I am sure our co-op could not have survived had we not had an excellent bookkeeper and financial advisor. I speak of Howard Pole. Howard had the ability to calculate what rental rates should be, where to invest surplus funds, and how to handle taxation to advantage. The original eight members were Harry Pole, Howard Pole, Fred Bushfield, Gordon Farr, Jack Young, Redvers Perry, Lorne Dunn and yours truly Leighton Perry.

Over the years membership for one reason or other had changed somewhat. At our dinner meeting the following members were present: Harry Pole, Howard Pole, Fred Bushfield, Lorne Dunn, Stan Jones, Arnold Jones, Gary Hanson, Roy Bushfield, Emory Jackson and Leighton Perry.

The co-op had developed as a way for farmers in the expanding stage to take advantage of new equipment becoming available. Many of the items were of the variety one would use for a short period once or twice a year. As farms became bigger, some co-op members entered partnerships with their sons and other members retired. It appeared the easiest way to divide the assets was to sell out. All our equipment was auctioned at Teske's Auction.

There is still a good reason to have a co-op of this nature in a farming community. All you need is a few people who get along together and some imagination. It may be interesting to note that not only did we provide a community service, but we multiplied our original investment six times in twenty years!

Submitted by Leighton Perry, 1996

Rural Gas Distribution Systems

We see here the development of rural gas service from the point of view of the provincial government

...By the early 1970's forward-looking farm and rural organizations such as Unifarm and the Alberta Association of Municipal Districts and Counties were suggesting that the Alberta Government undertake some form of policy to provide rural gas service. To implement such a policy would require substantial financial assistance because population is sparse in most of the province. Moreover, during the 1960's, a number of local gas systems developed adjacent to natural gas transmission pipelines; these local systems would force additional costs onto overall rural gas system design.

From a rural Alberta perspective, two basic problems were identified. Natural gas was not generally available to Alberta farmers. Moreover, future energy cost increase scenarios for oil-based fuels, propane and electricity were higher than for the largely unavailable natural gas alternative...

...Why should availability of natural gas be denied farmers in the province when, as citizens, they already partly owned the resource and since the majority of Alberta gas was being marketed outside the province? The author has had the interesting experience of being asked such a question while standing in a farmer's yard looking at a nearby producing gas well. The query came from the farmer, who was unable to obtain natural gas service.

In late 1972 the Alberta Government decided to proceed with development of a rural natural gas distribution system. Rural development opportunities were believed to be enhanced by expanding the availability of natural gas to rural users. The rural gas system became a new way to harness Alberta's substantial energy potential...

...the rural gas system is low pressure plastic pipe connected throughout local franchise areas. These areas are space-filling (that is, areas butt on one another) so all farms, hamlets, villages, etc. have the opportunity to choose natural gas as a fuel. In addition to residential and farmstead uses, irrigation pumping, grain drying, agricultural processing (e.g. alfalfa dehydration and pelleting) and rural industrial operations (e.g., kilns drying lumber) are uses made of natural gas supplied by the rural gas system...

...The Provincial Government quickly concluded in favor of a rural co-operative approach...for the following reasons:

1. rural people were familiar with this approach, based on their experience with rural electric systems;

2. representation from rural organizations in Alberta assured public acceptance and confidence in the approach;

3. rights-of-way would be more readily obtainable and less costly.

Each of these reasons is more important than superficial consideration might suggest. As later comments will reveal, sign up percentages (including "up front" financial commitments and rights-of-way permission), timeliness, and seasonality are crucial to the success of a rural gas construction program. Public confidence is a vital consideration...

...In a small number of areas, county (local municipal government) administration undertook the local gas system development...

...The overwhelming majority of franchise areas, however, were organized as rural co-operatives. Local initiative, combined with Government support and advice, was harnessed to establish local Boards of Directors reflecting geographic representation. The boards selected franchise names (usually noting regional identification such as Rocky View Gas Co-op near Calgary) and established sign up committees...

...Construction is nearly three-quarters complete. Service has been provided to about 60,000 new users (covering over 180,000 rural people); so far, the rural gas development system has installed over 63,000 kilometers of mostly polyethylene plastic pipe...The crucial requirement is *continuity* of fuel supply...

Extracts from "The Development of Rural Gas Distribution Systems in Alberta" by Allan A. Warrack, University of Alberta, 1981

Allan A. Warrack, Professor in the Department of Rural Economy and Economics, University of Alberta, was the Minister of Utilities and Telephones for Alberta from 1975 to 1979.

History of Rockyview Gas Co-op Ltd.

An organizational meeting to establish a natural gas co-op was held in the Beiseker Memorial Hall on November 29, 1973. Steve Beaudoin, Field Representative of the Alberta Department of Telephones and Utilities, outlined some government policies on natural gas co-ops and gave cost estimates. Peter Vang, of the Co-op Activities division of the Department of Agriculture, described the procedure for forming a cooperative organization.

Melvin Heinzlmeir moved and Fred Lyczewski seconded, that a natural gas co-op be established; this was carried. Other decisions made were that the co-op be named Rockyview Gas Co-op, and that the provisional board have 17 members.

The following people were nominated to the provisional board: for Crossfield, Mervin Fox and Eldon Stafford; for Airdrie, R.V. Clayton and Dan McKinnon; for Keoma, John Geier, Martin Geier and Harold Randall; for Acme, Allister Groundwater and Don Miller; for Irricana, Les Kent and Harold Knight; for Beiseker, Melvin Heinzlmeir, Joe Bosch and Ralph Wegener; for Dalroy, Ned Williams; and for Symons Valley, Allan Frazer. The rest of the board was to be filled at future meetings. Mervin Fox was elected as President of the Provisional Board, and Melvin Heinzlmeir as Secretary.

With the emergence of dozens of new gas co-ops, there was a shortage of plastic pipe. Rockyview Co-op was fortunate to be a little behind some of the others in getting started and the Board made the decision to buy Dupont pipe. Many other gas co-ops purchased a pipe made from an inferior resin which did not stand up. It had to be replaced at a tremendous cost both financially and in public relations.

In early 1974, sign-up meetings were held throughout the franchise area and letters were placed in each mailbox in the franchise area. Contracts, utility right-of-ways and lien notes were collected in such volume that it became necessary to rent office space in Airdrie, in the old Les Farr Garage building across the street from the Bank of Nova Scotia. The office was opened in mid August with Margaret Doherty as our first secretary. Ed Murray started as Manager on the first of October.

Burroughs Engineering was chosen to design the system and Swift Current Construction won the contract to plough in the pipe. Burroughs was succeeded by D&S Rural Services Ltd. A separate contract for surveying was signed with Tronnes Surveys Limited.

By August, 1975, and after lots of work by the staff and the Board, the plows began to break ground for the first gas lines northwest of Crossfield. The sign-up meetings had produced over 550 members, and by Christmas several of them were burning natural gas. Rockyview experienced very few problems building the system and our customers were happy to be burning natural gas.

·   By the end of 1976 nearly 450 customers were users and many a hectic day had been spent by staff and directors pitching in to help wherever needed. With the big job finished and with a bit more time, the Board began plans for a new office and shop which would be a adequate facility from which to operate a co-op which had grown to 650 consumers. A search for a suitable location was ended when a lot was purchased in Crossfield and construction was started in the first week of August and completed by the first week in October 1977 at a cost of $36,000.00 plus $15,000.00 for the lot.

The selling price for natural gas has fluctuated from a low of $1.00 in December 1975 to a high of $3.05 in September 1982, which was due to the Federal Sales Tax.

The size of the Board decreased from 17 directors to 13, then to 11 while the number of members continues to steadily increase.

Our auditor has been Ken Heywood of the firm Burrington & Heywood, based in Red Deer. This firm also audits five other gas co-ops.

Rockyview Gas Co-op has been a member of the Federation of Alberta Gas Co-ops since our Co-op's inception. The Federation is an association of gas co-ops and other small gas utilities, and it lobbies the government on items that are in the best interest of our members.

Submitted by Rockyview Gas Co-op, 1996

The History of the Calgary Co-operatives

Sarah Savill was Calgary Co-operative Association Member Number 1. She learned to support co-operation while growing up in England:

Sarah Savill, the No.1 Co-operator

...where modern co-ops got their start through the determined efforts of 28 weavers who decided that co-operation just had to be better for the common worker than competition. She used to tell her own four children that her family had been well dressed in England because they belonged to the co-op and took their patronage refunds in the form of bolts of cloth. Patronage refunds had to be taken in kind then; money wasn't refunded. So Sarah Savill's parents chose to clothe their family with the aid of the co-op dividends. No wonder Sarah was always positively disposed toward co-ops!...

In 1908, Sarah's husband Walter moved to a homestead in the Nose Creek area near Calgary, hoping thereby to cure his tuberculosis. Sarah followed a year later with their three children, a trip they never forgot; they had to be rescued from a sinking ship, then their train hit three cows and a calf in Northern Ontario, and two passengers were killed. The C.P.R. refused to let Mrs. Savill wire her husband to say they had been delayed:

...The train people just didn't want the public to know they'd had another accident. Those were the days when Bob Edwards took great delight in trumpeting across the front page of his famous *Eye Opener* . . . The CPR DIDN'T Have a Crash Today!

Walter Savill could only wait at this end, wondering what in the world had happened.

When finally the family turned up, a neighbor piled them all onto his hayrack and drove them out to the family home. It was a two storey shack and a bit of a shock for the family. The bottom floor of the house served as a granary - it was full of grain - and the upper part, which could only be reached by an exterior staircase, contained the living quarters.

Sarah Savill had been a milliner's assistant in England; Walter, a draftsman and engineer. This life was a far cry from home for them. The first cow they bought had no teeth. They were the proverbial British greenhorns. However, a living had to be made and they did it. Walter went out on threshing crews and ploughing jobs. Sarah learned to make butter and sell it; she learned to sell whatever she could, as a matter of fact -eggs, garden produce, mushrooms...

Walter died in 1918 and Sarah continued to farm with her children Arthur, Ernest and Nellie, while Mary became a teacher. The family's dairy operation prospered, so:

> ...in 1956 when the new co-op was out looking for money, Sarah Savill quickly bought $1,000 worth of shares and Arthur Savill another $1,000 worth. They became Calgary Co-op members No. 1 and 2 respectively.
>
> Sarah Savill died in 1963 at the age of 89 years. Her youngest daughter Nellie has her number now.
>
> Arthur Savill lives in Red Deer but he still retains No. 2 and uses it on his frequent trips to the city. Ernest Savill and Mary Bushfield also live in Calgary and are faithful Co-op members.
>
> At the opening of No. 10 store, the Beddington Heights store, Nellie Savill cut the ribbon and dedicated a great chunk of rock standing at the entrance to the shopping centre. It was one of the rocks that her mother and dad learned to work around on that first homestead in the Nose Creek area.

From *A History of the Calgary Co-op* by Rob and Nancy Millar, 1982

Calgary Co-operatives

From day one, Balzac has always been an integral part of Calgary Co-op. Back in the first formative year, Keith Rosenberger brought all the advantages of his co-operative background to the creating and building of Calgary Co-op. Keith spent 20 years on the board, mostly as First Vice-President, until his death in 1975.

Another Balzac person of importance was Bert Church. Bert spent two years on the Board. I wish I could have a list of the Balzac people who have been employees during the past forty years.

Sarah Savill from Beddington, our #1 Co-operator, came from a co-op background in England. She was given the #1 membership because she had the faith to put in $1000 for shares in the fledgling store. This was at a time when the early visionaries were knocking on doors, receiving $25 and $50 in shares from both rural and city people.

The United Farmers of Alberta gave the project a boost when they agreed that U.F.A. members could transfer their equity to the new venture. By September 1956, there were 232 urban transfers, 178 rural transfers and 387 new members.

It was enough, the board decided. Store #1 was opened November 15, 1956. Doug Symons reports:

> ...We waited behind the counter there, eight or ten clerks serving one after the other. We would write everything down. If you wanted a can of jam or a can of peanut butter, that was all written down and then we had to take around a basket and pick it all up for the customer...

If you had to wait, there were chairs in front of the counter for sitting and visiting with your neighbours.

From this friendly informal store where you became friends with the clerks, grew the Co-operative which became the largest Co-op in North America. In 1996 we have 15 stores.

Why were we successful? It is hard to define but perhaps the pride and joy of the members in their own store, perhaps their feeling that their Board and staff cared and perhaps the basic honesty of Co-ops all helped.

From day one, service was uppermost in the minds of Board, Management and Staff. We had cheerful carry-out boys and girls who were loved, particularly by the housewife with children. We had postal service. We had restaurants, chequeing privileges, service for seniors and shut-ins, supervised kiddie korrals for the children while Mom and Dad shopped and lastly, we had the patronage refund.

The very first year, the Board decided to pay out the patronage refund. Three percent was paid and the 308 members at the first annual meeting went home happy.

Store #1 downtown soon became too small. By 1959 membership had grown to 4,350. With much trepidation, Board member Dwight Ellis called out $101,000 at an auction for the land on which stands Store #2. In 1960 that was a lot of money. Debentures were issued to members for 7½% (2½% above Government bonds and roughly 1½% above prime bank rates). It was oversubscribed by the time construction began on July 1, 1960.

In 1962, new land was bought for Store #3, dubbed "Gordon's Folly" by a hesitant Board. Propelled by Chairman Gordon Barker's enthusiasm and belief in the future, Store #3 was soon running in the black.

1962 was also the year of excitement due to the talk of international unions. The employees' decision was to do their own organizing and the "Calco" Club was formed to serve both as a fully certified bargaining unit and as a social club.

The Co-op continued to flourish. New stores were built roughly every two years. In 1980 the Beddington Store was opened and once again Balzac played a large part. Rob and Nancy Millar wrote, in *A History of the Calgary Co-op*; "Nellie Savill, now member #1, unveiled a chunk of rock that had come from her folks' original farm in the Beddington area, now to stand outside this ultra modern centre as a reminder of the way we were, or how far we've come." The sandstone quarry winch described in Chapter 14 of this book was set up by the Calgary Co-op and the Nose Creek Historical Society at the southwest corner of the Beddington Heights Co-op, beside the ancient buffalo rubbing rock from the Savill farm.

Among its many projects, Calgary Co-op has supported the Credit Unions, the Co-operative Insurance, the Federated Co-operative, Co-op Taxi, the Co-operative Union of Canada, the International Co-operative Alliance and the Northland Bank.

It has also been active in too many local charities to mention; but a word should be said about over two million dollars raised for charity by the Co-op book exchange and recycling projects.

And now to modern times following the great upheaval of 1993, with supermarkets competing intensely for the retail trade. One of the large competitors issued an alternative to their staff; either accept a drastic cut in wages or they would pull out of Calgary. Their union agreed, and then followed drastic cutting of prices in competition with food giants, Cosco, Superstore and of course Calgary Co-op. Under new Chairman Bruno Friesen and new CEO Gene Syvenky there were many changes, and many pay-outs were offered to former employees. However, the Co-op has continued to thrive, still pays a patronage dividend and opened Store #15 in 1995. Since 1992 the Co-op has refunded about $40 million to its members.

Submitted by Mary and Gordon Barker, 1996

Mary (Dixon) Barker has always supported Gordon's co-operative endeavours, and has been active in 4-H, Home and School, church, Women of Unifarm, and Calgary Co-op. She has contributed to histories of communities, Central United Church, and the Calgary Co-op.

Gordon Barker was one of the Founders of Calgary Co-op and was President and Chairman of the Board from 1955 to 1987. He was also a director of Western Co-operative Fertilizer, the Co-operative Union of Canada, and the International Co-operative Alliance. He has served on boards of other organizations: Alberta Wheat Pool, Alberta Co-operative Council, Co-op Taxi, Co-op Travel, Calgary Better Business Bureau and Northland Bank. He has served on boards of the Heritage Park Society, the Salvation Army, the Parks Foundation and has been active with the Balzac Seed Cleaning Co-operative and 4-H.

Keith Rosenberger

The Millars' book A History of the Calgary Co-op *includes a tribute to Keith Rosenberger:*

It is not exactly surprising that Keith Rosenberger became a co-operator. In the early 1900's, his folks homesteaded in the Balzac area, an area that just seemed to naturally look for co-operative solutions. If there were fence posts to be bought, or groceries or gas, the residents figured out a way to buy them together in order to get a better price and better service. Co-operation was like breathing in the Balzac area, and still is in many ways.

On top of that, Keith Rosenberger married Lois Church whose father, uncles and aunts were all active in the co-operative movement. Her father, George Church, became the president of the United Farmers of Alberta.

Anyway, Keith Rosenberger chose the Calgary Co-op as one of his co-operative interests and served first on the provisional board and then on the regular board of directors until 1975. When he was honoured for his long and faithful service at the 1975 annual meeting, he told the joke about the minister who came along and found a little boy crying over a dead dog. "You shouldn't cry," the minister said. "I just buried my best friend and I'm not crying."

The boy looked up and said, "But you didn't raise him from a pup."

The Calgary Co-op had been very much a pup when it all started on very unsteady legs back in 1956.

Directors in the early days were much closer to the day-by-day action of the Co-op stores. One evening, a distraught woman phoned the Rosenberger home to tell Keith that her groceries had been left in the Macleod Trail store, and would he please unlock the store because she needed her groceries.

He couldn't do that, but he did get on the phone and keep phoning until he found someone who could rescue the late groceries.

Keith Rosenberger died the same year he retired from the Co-op board. His loyalty and hard work with co-op organizations earned him an honoured place among co-operators.

From *A History of the Calgary Co-op* by Rob and Nancy Millar, 1982

Circle 8 Windup Dinner

(Back row, left to right): Leighton Perry, Emory Jackson, Garry Hanson, Stanley Jones, Lorne Dunn. (Front row, left to right): Howard Pole, Arnold Jones, Fred Bushfield, Roy Bushfield, Harry Pole.

Gordon and Mary Barker, prime movers of the Cooperative movement which serves the Valley.

The Beddington Heights Coop provides both the Valley and city with a wide range of services—from groceries (above) through insurance to auto centres (below).

CO-OP AUTO CENTRE

Board of Directors, 1973. *(Clockwise, left to right): Ed Kott, Cecil Birch, Bruno Friesen, Barbara MacDougall Keith Rosenberger, Gordon Barker, Elaine Shaw (Secretary), John Suits (General Manager), Everett McGregor Jim McKnight and Allan Gibson.*

Board of Directors, 1995

(Back row, left to right): F. Jim Williams (First Vice Chairman), Sheila Johnston, Dick Schuler, Wilf Philips, Alice Brown, Al Fromm (Corporate Secretary)
(Front row, left to right): Gene Syvenky (Chief Executive Officer), Bruno Friesen (Chairman), Martha McDonagh Rick Smith (Second Vice Chairman).

CHAPTER 44: ORGANIZATIONS

Introduction

In view of the fact that the military service of people from the Valley during both World Wars has been covered in local histories already published, it was felt that an update should include this brief reflection on the Canadian Legion, who strive to keep the memories of those who fought and died in these conflicts for the freedom later generations sometimes take for granted.

Many other service clubs play a significant role in the community. The purpose of other organizations is to entertain, allowing people to relax or be active in pleasant company. Again, keep in mind that there were many more we could have mentioned such as the Nose Creek Community Club, and all sorts of curling clubs and other sports associations.

The Royal Canadian Legion Serves Valley Veterans

After World War I several groups serving veterans amalgamated to form the Great War Veteran's Association in 1917. By 1926 the Canadian Legion of the British Empire Service League continued the movement to support veterans and their families. The organization as we know it today grew out of the need, before and after World War II, to help re-establish war veterans and their families, and to advise them of the pension benefits available through the federal government. Some veterans were helped to take up land in places such as the Nose Creek Valley, while others were assisted with grants to take further vocational or professional education.

The organization was re-named the Royal Canadian Legion in 1960. It became one of the foremost non-governmental agencies working for the well-being of Canadians in virtually every community across the country. The three branches described in the articles following have supported Nose Creek Valley communities by donating to a wide variety of charitable organizations, and have also responded to situations of special need. The Legion is well known as Canada's pre-eminent non-profit veterans' support organization, and is also active in many other areas, benefitting society in general.

The Legion is the largest of the many veterans' associations in Canada, with a membership of some 580,000. It is a non-profit, dues-supported, fraternal organization with 1,750 branches in Canada, 34 in the United States, and three in Germany. It receives no financial assistance from any outside agency and membership is open to all Canadian veterans as well as serving and former members of the Canadian armed forces and their dependents.

The Royal Canadian Legion has assumed responsibility for perpetuating the tradition of Remembrance Day in Canada. Each year the Legion organizes and runs the National Poppy Remembrance Campaign to remind Canadians of the tremendous debt we owe to the 114,000 men and women who gave their lives in the defence of Canada during the two world wars and the Korean War. Contributions made during the campaign are used to assist needy veterans, ex-service members and their families.

The Legion's purpose and objective is to perpetuate the memory and deeds of the Fallen and those who die in the future; to ensure that proper attention shall be paid to the welfare of all who served and the maintenance and comfort of those who require special treatment, particularly the disabled, sick, aged and needy, and to promote the welfare of their dependents.

The Legion encourages, promotes, and engages in or supports all forms of national, provincial, municipal and community service as well as any charitable or philanthropic purpose. It will engage in those activities which will be to the credit and benefit of the Canadian Community.

Three Legion branches in the Nose Creek Valley have been described in following articles to underline the need for continuing the interpretation of federal war veterans policy to the men and women serving in the defence of Canada and peacekeeping in the world. Crossfield, Airdrie and Calgary's Chapelhow Branch were organized to support veterans in this area. All three of them have supported many charitable organizations in the Valley and continue to do so.

Of interest is the fact that Nose Creek runs through the City of Airdrie and North Calgary, passing within a very few feet of the Chapelhow Branch. Chapelhow Branch began its activities in the Renfrew District of Calgary, in which airmen were trained as pilots at what was Calgary's original municipal airport. Many of the World War II veterans recall having trained at the Airdrie and Calgary training bases.

Submitted by Stephen Wilk, 1996

A Brief History of the Chapelhow Branch #284 of the Royal Canadian Legion

December 5th, 1974 was a memorable night at the Renfrew Community Association hall. Branch No. 284 received its Charter. The presentation of the Charter was made to the first elected President of the Branch, the late Comrade Bob Gilson, by the Provincial President at that time, Comrade Jack Chapman During the Presentation Ceremony the late Comrade Tom Cuffling presented the Branch with the Poppy Flag, "Lest We Forget"; it still hangs proudly in the Branch.

It was in May 1974 that the formation of a Legion Branch was discussed The officers of the Renfrew Community Association were kind enough to le members of the Branch have their monthly meetings in the hall. On August 4th 1974, the first General Meeting of Branch No.284 was held. The membership had the numbers required to apply for a Charter.

The Chapelhow Branch...how did the Branch acquire that name? Two very fine people, Iris and Dick Chapelhow, Provincial Command Officers at tha time, offered words of wisdom and assistance to the Branch and its Ladies Auxiliary and were helpful in many ways. To honour them Provincial Comman was approached with the request to use the name "Chapelhow Branch". Witl the consent of Command and of Dick and Iris, the Branch was allowed to use the name.

For six years the Branch operated a Saturday night bingo in conjunction witl the Renfrew Boys and Girls Club. With the help of a number of volunteers, including the Ladies Auxiliary operating the canteen, Branch No. 284 was able to add a little more to its bank account.

In January 1983, the Branch moved to the corner of Edmonton Trail and 38tl Avenue N.E. Once again the volunteers went to work; painters, carpenters, an the Ladies' Auxiliary completed the renovations. The Branch was now able to operate.

Late in 1985, a decision was made to purchase land for a new building at 60 38th Avenue N.E. In 1987, the work of clearing the land and constructing th new home of Chapelhow Branch No.284 commenced. The Nose Creek run along the eastern boundary of the property.

On May 1st, 1988, the Rev. Dr. Stephen Wilk, as Branch Chaplain, conducte the Official Dedication of the present building. The cenotaph was dedicated o November 5th, 1988. Remembrance Day Ceremonies were held there to com memorate the World Wars of 1914-1918 and 1939-1945, and the Korean Actior

1950-1953.

The Branch has supported countless charitable organizations over the years and continues to do so; the list would cover several pages.

Submitted by Stephen Wilk, 1996

Crossfield Branch #113 of the Canadian Legion

The minutes of meetings for this Branch date back to March 27, 1931, when a special meeting was called to elect Clarence Crockett as Secretary. I. Lewis was the President at that time. The Branch bylaws were approved by Command on October 17, 1979. Our meetings are held on the second Monday of the month in the Arts and Crafts Room of Crossfield Community Hall.

In March 1981, the Crossfield Branch celebrated its 50th Anniversary with Provincial Chairman Bud Blackwell in attendance. A plaque of the Past Presidents was presented to Bert Sharp, and is now displayed in the Community Hall.

The 60th anniversary in 1991 was celebrated at the Community Hall. Bud Blackwell, now President of N.W.T. Command, attended once again, along with Zone President Wilf Japp. At this time Mike Budd was the President of the Branch, Diane Budd was the Secretary, and Jack Simmons was the First Vice President.

Submitted by Margaret King, 1996

The History of the Airdrie Branch #288 Royal Canadian Legion

The Airdrie Branch #288 was conceived in March 1983, when a few veterans decided Airdrie was in need of a Branch of the Royal Canadian Legion. A recruiting drive was undertaken for additional veterans to obtain the necessary number of Ordinary members (50) in order that an application could be made to the Dominion Command of the Legion, through the Provincial Command, for a Charter to establish a branch in Airdrie.

The first meeting was held in the Over 50 Club in the Town and Country Centre, and meetings continued there until 67 veterans (Ordinary members) had signed up. It was during these meetings that the Branch's first Executive was nominated and elected. The election resulted in Kelly Davy being named as President, Bill Hawkes as First Vice President, Jack Potter as Second Vice President, Pat Crumley as Third Vice President, Linda Peterson as Secretary, and Evelyn Dye as Treasurer.

On August 23rd, 1983 the Charter was granted by Dominion Command in Ottawa, On November 7th, 1983 the Charter was presented to President Kelly Davy at a ceremony in the Town and Country Centre. Approximately 350 people attended on this occasion. We were now officially a Branch of the Royal Canadian Legion known as the Airdrie Branch #288.

The first location for the Branch was in the Court Jester building on the east side of Airdrie in the Industrial Park. From there we moved to the Curling Lounge in the Town and Country Centre, then to the old R.C.M.P. detachment building, and finally to our present location.

While in the Court Jester building, the Branch established a Building Committee whose responsibility was to obtain permanent quarters for the Branch. The committee accomplished this by holding many meetings and negotiations with developers until one developer agreed to build a building for the Branch.

It was also while we were in the Court Jester building that the Ladies' Auxiliary started. During one of their meetings the Auxiliary nominated and elected their first Executive: Norma Morgan as President, Phyllis Brooks as Vice President, Audrey Sluggett as Secretary, Diane Lavallee as Treasurer, Robina Morris as Sergeant-at-Arms, and Angie Eagleson, Marlene Nault, Debbie Baron and

Linda Fraser as Executive Members. They applied for their Charter, which was issued on March 15th, 1984 and was presented to President Norma Morgan at the Town and Country Centre on October 9th, 1984.

On March 1st, 1986, the Airdrie Branch made its final move from the old R.C.M.P. detachment on First Avenue N.E. to its present location at 508 3rd Avenue S.E. The Branch then began to grow and prosper and on January 1st, 1992, Airdrie Branch #288 became the owner of the land and building in which it is presently located.

The aims and objectives of the Royal Canadian Legion is to provide assistance to veterans and their families in a time of need, and to work for seniors and youth groups and for the betterment of the community in general. The Airdrie Legion is proud of its accomplishments in these areas by donating in excess of six hundred thousand dollars ($600,000.00), to the aforementioned since it began in 1983. Some of these donations follow: half the cost of a new handibus to the C.R.A.B. Society in 1985 and the full cost of a new larger bus to the same group in 1988; the building of a cenotaph in what was to be called Veterans Memorial Park near the Town and Country Centre; a bursary for an honours student graduating from one of the high schools; an artificial leg for a Calgary teenager so he could compete in the downhill skiing in the Special Olympics for the handicapped; several electric and conventional wheel chairs loaned or donated to people in need; help to establish and sponsor an Army Cadet Unit in Airdrie; help for numerous youth groups in the areas of swimming, hockey and baseball; and the list of those who have benefitted from the generosity of the Airdrie Legion goes on and on.

My hope is that if and when the economy ever takes a lengthy downward turn the Airdrie Legion Branch #288 can weather the storm and continue serving those in need within the community.

Submitted by C.J. (Kelly) Davy, Charter President of Branch #288, 1996

A World War II shopwindow promoting the sale of Victory Bonds.

Crossfield Royal Canadian Legion, Branch #113, January 1993. Back row: Frank Northcott (Sergeant at Arms), Redvers Perry (Service Officer), Diane Budd (Secretary-Treasurer), Jon Skelly (2nd Vice President), and Ed Snyder (Sports Officer). Front row: Jack Simmons (1st Vice President), Bob Kellier (Chaplain), Clarence Crockett (Executive Committee Chairman and Life Member), Bert Sharp (Installing Officer), and Mike Budd (President).This branch was formed in 1931.

This cenotaph memorializes men from the Crossfield district who gave their lives in the 1914-18 war. Below: Remembrance Day November 1991. Bill Walker lays a wreath on behalf of the Nose Creek Historical Society.

Remembrance Day, 1994. Janelle Perry lays a wreath for World War I vets of Balzac. She's accompanied by Bill Walker.

LEST WE FORGET

Above: Royal Canadian Legion #288, Airdrie Branch.

Above: Airdrie Cenotaph.

Above: Airdrie Remembrance Day ceremony.

Above: Royal Canadian Legion #284, Chapelhow Branch.

Above: James Robinson plaque, located on Hunts Coulee, Secondary Highway 567 and Sunshine Road.

Chapelhow Executive. Top row: Glynn Thomas, Len Strandlund, Bert Arnold, Paul Preece, Sharon Portigal, Tom Stott, Marilyn Dunne, Lois Allen. Front row: Eric Stewart, Derrick Campbell, Brian Cooper, Peter Boast, Al Paskall (President), W.C. (Swede) Phillips, John Portigal, George Preston. Not in the picture: Eastman Dundas and Rev. Dr. Stephen Wilk (Chaplain).

Beddington Ladies Community Club

Our club came into existence after the United Farm Women of Alberta local and Beddington United Church Women groups ceased to be. The farm women were becoming more provincial in focus and our ladies were more interested in local affairs and the closure of the church. During the war years the two groups had met together and conducted two meetings; most of our endeavours were local so there existed a common bond.

After our organization became official in the late 1950's or about 1960, we carried on many of the programs of the two previous groups. For one of these programs we made baby layettes to go to the Grace Hospital, so that unwed mothers would have some clothes and blankets for their new babies. We sent young people to Young People's Week at Edmonton originally, and later to Gold Eye Lake. Today we make donations to the Students' Award Night at two schools in Airdrie. We helped our local Hall Board maintain the Beddington Hall for a number of years. We played a part in the 50th Anniversary of Alberta, the Beddington Church's 50th Anniversary, the launching of the *Nose Creek Story* and Edie Woolliams' book *My Neighbours and Yours*, and other historical occasions. For a number of years our funds were raised by catering to weddings and 4-H banquets, which was hard work, as the hall had no conveniences.

Another project that we carried on for many years started when the retired people from Beddington moved to Calgary. They formed a group called the "Cal Bees" under the leadership of W.H. Evans. The group met in their Calgary homes, and quite a large number attended, as many people who had originally lived at Beddington wanted to be a part of it. Someone suggested they would like to come out to Beddington and put on a program. Mr. Evans made the arrangements and it soon became an annual event with our group providing a meal, and the "Cal Bees" doing the entertainment. This was an enjoyable evening and it led to the seniors in our surrounding area being invited to join the Cal Bees, as the group's numbers were declining. We continued holding this event for many years, but it made for two hectic days in the heat of the summer. One day was spent cleaning the big hall inside and out, then the next day preparing the food. The people of the area enjoyed this get-together, as it was a chance to visit and renew acquaintance.

In 1980 our Beddington Ladies group, with help from the hall board, celebrated "Come Back to Beddington", which entailed writing invitations, making many phone calls, and sending notices to the papers in order to have as many people return as we could possibly contact. The special occasion turned out very well and left a great memory. At this time the hall board raised money by having a barbecue and dance in June, so our group helped with the meal by cooking roasts, etc.

Today the Beddington Ladies are not very active, with about eight or nine attending, but we have a short meeting once a month and a long visit. Sometimes we meet for a meal or take in a play in the area instead of having a meeting, which makes a change. We continue to support Awards Nights; we sponsor the Balzac-Beddington Cancer Drive with our members and original club members doing the canvassing; we send cards to the sick and bereaved, also on special birthday and anniversary occasions. We also give gifts and money to the Lioness Christmas Hamper Fund. Our membership extends from Beddington to Airdrie and Redvers Perry teasingly refers to our group as the Bedd Ladies. I am not sure we like this new title, but we are the last of the old Beddington organizations that touched so many people in the past.

Submitted by Doris Evans, Beddington Ladies Club, 1996

The Casa Loma Community Association

In 1935, the ladies of the Casa Loma district formed an association with Mrs

Billie Elliott as Chairman and Hilda (Cathro) Anderson as Secretary-Treasurer. The purpose of the Association was to knit for the Red Cross and promote friendship and good will throughout our neighbourhood. We did this over a cup of tea or coffee, served by our hostess, and many friendships have grown through all these years.

Meetings are held on the last Wednesday of each month except December. The executive now consists of a President, Secretary and Treasurer.

In 1947 the Association bought the school, as teaching there had ceased, and we wanted to use the school as a community hall.

We made money for our community commitments by having special teas, home baking sales, shadow dances, masquerades, box socials, and by catering. The Association sponsored the Brownies Pack and paid for the well and wellhouse for the Charles Butler Park. Members attended one-day trips, wiener roasts, family picnics, and tours of important buildings.

After we sold the school in September 1976, we invested the money, with 80% of the interest going to local charities and 20% used for community interests. As we grow older there is less business, so our meetings are slowly turning into a social afternoon.

Submitted by Peggy Elliott, 1996

A Brief Historic Sketch of the Ranchmen's Club

The Ranchmen's Club has stood over the years as a symbol of the major historic role ranching has played and still plays in the development of Western Canada. The Calgary club has its roots in the Golden Age of Ranching. This was when the vast western region of the North-West Territory was opening to the ranchers and entrepreneurs seeking to take advantage of the lush grasslands and ready water supply for the raising of livestock. The valleys and coulees of the eastern slopes of the foothills of the Rockies provided ready shelter for wintering cattle, horses and sheep. This was true of the regions surrounding Calgary and of the Nose Creek Valley.

The pioneer ranchers brought with them their traditions and customs. Hence the Ranchmen's Club was a natural development built on the British tradition of gentlemen gathering for time out and relaxation from the regions of pioneer ranching. The Club was a place for ranchmen to meet for the exchange of ideas, entertainment and cultural activity.

Further to the scenario in which the Ranchmen's Club was born, it was at the height of peace, prosperity, stability and security during Queen Victoria's reign. The nine founders formed the club in May 1891. Herbert Samson, rancher; H. Harford, rancher; A.E. Cross, rancher; J.P.J. Jephson, barrister; H.B. Alexander, rancher; A.D. Braithwaite, banker; T.S.C. Lee, rancher; D.H. Andrews, rancher; and D.H. MacPherson, rancher. This was the end of Sir John A. Macdonald's remarkable career in forging the development of Western Canada. He died the month following the formation of the Club. The population of the town of Calgary, according to the census of Western Canada, was 3,876 the following year.

The C.P.R. was completed in November 1885, bringing with it increasing numbers of settlers and travel by rail from East to West started the boom years of ranching. Prior to this milestone, only prairie trails wound north to Edmonton and south to Fort Macleod with horses and bull trains as the only means of transportation.

The establishing of the provinces of Alberta and Saskatchewan were some fifteen years away and few bureaucratic controls were evident, such as taxes, etc. Hence life was free and easy and Club life was very informal.

An ordinance of incorporation of the Club was passed by the first Session of the second Legislative Assembly of the N.W.T., sitting at Regina in 1891-92.

The first general meeting of the club was held in a leased room over Mariaggi's

Restaurant on Stephen Avenue on May 5, 1891 with fourteen members present. This meeting adapted the Montreal St. James Club constitution and by-laws with some modifications. The restaurant provided food and refreshments to the Club's upper room by dumb-waiter.

New premises were acquired on the purchase of property on McIntyre (now Seventh) Avenue where a new Club House facility was built. The Club did not move again until July 1914. A new clubhouse was built on the present property on 13th Avenue southwest.

The Club's traditions have endured two world wars, long years of depression, radical social change and, in 1981, a total restoration of its premises.

The walls of the Club are lined with Alberta's history - historical letters, brands, paintings by members of the Group of Seven, Nicholas de Grandmaison's entire collection of Impressionistic paintings of famous Alberta ranches, as well as our own pictures of members and past presidents.

The Club boasts nine private meeting/dining rooms for groups from two to 144. These rooms are available to Club members and guests for functions ranging from business meetings and cocktail parties to receptions and gourmet banquets.

Members enjoy a number of activities, many of which date back to the early days of the Club. Bridge leagues, Slash - an English style game of snooker (billiards), festive family buffets, Henry Smith golf tournaments, Stampede barbecues, black tie dinners with prominent speakers, oyster nights, and lobster buffets are just some of the organized activities. Three regulation-size billiard tables complement the Club's dining facilities.

The Ranchmen's Club members enjoy reciprocal rights with other Clubs around the world.

Of interest is the fact that the Ranchmen's Club voted to admit women as full voting members on Wednesday, February 17th, 1993. Its membership has grown over the years to approximately 600 in 1996.

Submitted by Patrick J. McCann F.P.C.M., General Manager, Ranchmen's Club and Stephen Wilk, 1996

Airdrie Lions and Lioness Clubs

The Airdrie Lions Club was chartered on February 25, 1965 with 38 members. Calgary North Hill was the sponsoring Lions Club. The 285 guests at the charter presentation banquet paid $5.00 per couple for tickets and could buy three drinks for $1.00.

Membership ranged from a high of 55 to a low of 23. This club has donated awards to 4-H, schools, Scouts, sports, and other community organizations. Members have planted trees and built fences and outhouses. The club was instrumental in starting the rodeo grounds west of the city, and it paid for the corrals and bleachers.

In 1967 the club organized a parade and kids' games to celebrate Centennial Year. This event has expanded into the four day Professional Rodeo and Parade held on each July 1st long weekend.

To raise funds, the Lions Club has held raffles for cars and other prizes, catered to weddings and barbecues, sold Olympic Torch pins and candles, and collected batteries, and run many other projects. The club sponsors Blood Donor clinics, pays medical expenses, and sponsors teachers to Drug Awareness and Life Skills programs. We have also held diabetes screening and chest X-ray clinics. Over $400,000 has been raised and distributed since the club's inception.

The Airdrie Lions sponsored a Lioness Club in 1977. At that time women couldn't belong to Lions clubs. The Lioness Club's main project is providing more than 125 large Christmas food hampers each year. They also raise money in several ways and help fund community needs.

Both clubs are very active and seeking new members.

Submitted by Danny and Donna McKinnon, 1996

Nose Creek Light Horse Association

The NCLHA was formed in April of 1971. Its membership was made up of approximately 30 people who, young and old alike, had a common interest in horses. Members lived as far east as Doug Jones, east of Balzac, to the Blacks, living on the western edge of Symons Valley, to the Waters family at Airdrie, and the Burwashes to the south, on the city limits of Calgary. Monthly meetings were held where various plans would be made for information meetings, playdays, riding clinics, trail rides and excursions.

The winter month's activities usually included guest speakers and potluck suppers, horse films and information meetings, and field trips to indoor riding arenas to observe local trainers in action. We had the benefit of knowledge from many well known horsemen in the Calgary area: Bob Echlin, Bill Collins, Bill Renard, Gina McDougall, Roger Heinz, Dr. Wayne Burwash, and Jim Rogers, to name a few.

In fine weather "playdays" were held at different members' farms, where 20 to 30 horses and riders would converge to participate in an afternoon of gymkhana-type events. Barrel Racing, Flag Picking, Pole Bending, Musical Tires, and just "horsing around" filled in the day. We also had trial rides at Elkana Ranch at Bragg Creek, and at the Bates Ranch northwest of Cochrane. As a fund raiser one year we raffled a yearling filly donated to the club by Elmer Lamb. Wes Shaw of Airdrie was the lucky winner. Our club colours were Royal Blue and Yellow, and each club member had a tie and white shirt for our annual appearance in the Airdrie July 1st Parade.

The club dissolved in 1974, but not before numerous people had contributed to many memories of fun and camaraderie among members of the Nose Creek Light Horse Association.

Submitted by Janet (Perry) Warner, 1996

Airdrie Lions, 1968. (Back row): Harry Kirby, Bill Morison, Don Giesbrecht, Robbie Davy, Bruce Harris, Al Lawther, Leighton Perry, Stuart Morison, Jim Reid, Welding Kolstad, Allan Fletcher.
(Middle row): Wes Bennett, Walter Bushfield, Stan Bishop, Bab Hunter, Howard Verbeurgt, Redvers Perry, Cliff Tebb, Hugh Hamilton, Lloyd Malyk.
(Front row): Joe Clayton, Buzz Kline, Ralph Northcott, Lloyd Clark, Dan McKinnon, Ray Bragg, Jim Dunne, Arne Neilson, Leonard Farr, Ian McKinnon.

THE WOLVES' DEN

W. F. Cochrane, 1893

E. J. Swan, 1893

In 1892 A. E. Cross established the Calgary Brewing & Malting Co. This was the first brewery in the North West Territories, and at that time Calgary faced a crucial building situation. The brewery plant was located in east Calgary and Ernest Cross, for lack of anything better, had a nearby boxcar converted into a clubhouse.

The car was comfortably furnished and had a number of interesting trophies hanging on its walls. One was the mask of a large timber wolf and the Calgary men who met there from time to time adopted for themselves the name ' A Pack of Western Wolves'.

It was then the custom to convey visitors on a tour of important local sites and this usually consisted of a visit to a nearby ranch and a trip to the new brewery for rest and refreshment.

Some of these hospitable young men were also the organizers of the Ranchmen's Club which had been officially incorporated under:-
"An Ordinance to Incorporate the Ranchmen's Club of the Town of Calgary of the North West Territories, 1891".

C. H. Hall and R.R.
Bruce, 1894

A.E. Cross, 1893

W (CPR) Hull, 1893

The new Club building (main picture) is located on 13th Avenue S.W., Calgary. Thw original club building (inset) was on what is now 7th Avenue S.W., Calgary

FOUNDERS OF
the
RANCHMEN'S CLUB
~ 1890

D.H.Andrews (Andrews & McKenzie)	IL	Horses RT T	H. Samson (Samson & MacNaghten)	✗ Ⴗ	Horses .LT T Cattle LT R
Duncan H.McPherson (High River Horse Ranch)	Ⴗ	Horses LT Rp. LT T	H. Harford (Samson & Harford)	✗Y ✗Y	Horses LT T Cattle LT R
T.S.C. Lee (Lee & Metcalfe)	⫪	Horses LT S Cattle LT R	A.E.Cross	a 7	Cattle LT R Horses LT S
	V5	Cattle LT R	J.P.J. Jephson		Barrister
H.B.Alexander	••	Cattle Both Hips	A.D.Braithwaite		Banker
		Horses LT S			

CHAPTER 45: YOUTH ORGANIZATIONS

Introduction

There have been many organizations and activities for youth in the Nose Creek Valley; all kinds of sports in school and between schools, Girl Guides, Boy Scouts, church choirs, music lessons, and 4-H. This chapter can only touch on a few of the countless organizations which provided education and enjoyment for youth. Balzac especially seems to have been a centre for 4-H clubs, with members coming from a large area.

One of the advantages of having a relative in the 4-H Beef Club during the 1960's was that they had the calf show at the Calgary Stampede; for three days the club members and their parents would divide their time between grooming the calves and enjoying the Stampede events; the younger brothers and sisters spent all day on the midway rides or trying to win prizes.

"First Balzac" Wolf Cub Pack

In 1967 it was decided that Balzac needed a club for young boys. Phyllis Tocher, Madeline Holmes and Marge Jones, all mothers of young sons, organized the "1st Balzac" Wolf Cub Pack, and Dot Perry became the Secretary-Treasurer. We were very pleased to have nineteen boys register the first year. The next five years were very busy - projects to earn badges, bottle drives, newspaper drives, etc., to raise money; "Cuborees" in summer, camping in the spring, "Father & Son" banquets and skating parties in the winter, entertaining at the Balzac Christmas Concerts, to name a few activities. The weekly meetings were held at the Balzac Hall until 1972 when the pack disbanded.

Submitted by C. Redvers Perry, 1996

Junior and 4-H Clubs in the Nose Creek Valley Museum Area

Some of the earliest Junior Clubs in this area were Conrich Grain, Simons Valley Calf, and Balzac Beef, which is likely the longest continuously run club to date in the area. It was organized in the mid 1930's with Art Bushfield as leader. In 1954 the club won the coveted Provincial Efficiency Award.

An Airdrie Junior Grain Club with about 22 members was organized in 1937-38 by Howard Wright, Master Farmer. In 1938 Cliff Tebb and Dick Clayton represented Alberta at the Royal Winter Fair at Toronto. There they competed in grain judging against club representatives from all over Canada.

Many Junior Clubs disbanded during World War II, as so many members enlisted in the Armed Services. After the war Junior Clubs were reorganized, and new ones with many different projects were organized for both boys and girls. About this time the 4-H Movement replaced the Junior Boys and Girls Clubs of Canada. In 1949 an Airdrie Beef Club was organized with Ed McKinnon as Leader.

When the 4-H Display was made at the Nose Creek Valley Museum, it represented Clubs in the Airdrie, Crossfield, Madden, Cochrane, Balzac, Keoma, Irricana, and Kathyrn districts.

We believe that the 4-H Clubs are the most worthwhile rural organizations for young people, teaching Cooperation, Social Skills, Public Speaking, Parliamentary Procedures, and Good Citizenship. As their Pledge says:

I Pledge
My Head to clearer thinking
My Heart to greater loyalty
My Hands to larger service
My Health to better living
For my Club, my Community, and my Country.

Submitted by Richard and Alma Clayton, 1996

Fred Bell on 4-H in the Valley: 1952-1959
Fred Bell worked with a number of 4-H Clubs around Calgary, including some in the Nose Creek Valley.

Airdrie Beef Club
The Airdrie 4-H Beef Club was centered in a mixed farming area where livestock and grain were found on almost every farm. The majority of farms were substantial in size. The farm of the original Leader, Mr. E.A. McKinnon, was more than two sections in size. He had a beautiful home with well planned and planted grounds. His old wooden granaries had been replaced by steel storage bins of large capacity including an elevator leg. He had a large feedlot with a capacity of 1000 or more cattle which he filled twice a year. His feeding, watering and weighing equipment were planned for convenience. Aside from what Club Members would learn in meetings, to see and study this farm management setup was an education in itself. Mr. McKinnon was a Leader with a 'vision'. While his club was handled with a very high degree of efficiency, Mr. McKinnon's goal was not in winning the prize this year as it was in what will these members be doing twenty years from now. He was strict and demanded attention; he wanted carefully prepared, but reliable, records. He was a business-man and taught business-like procedure. He knew how a meeting should be conducted. He was a good speaker who could say what he wanted to say in a manner that people could understand and he taught his club members to speak...

...Handicapped members were welcome. He said they needed help and with them he had the patience of Job and he saw to it that other Club Members respected them. I remember one retarded member that received a wonderful life in the Club. Another feature of this Club was that the Club Members were taught to think of others who were less fortunate. Every year the club raised funds for some charity...

...This Club did not capture as many high awards as some but it certainly ranked high, in my opinion, and Mr. McKinnon rates very high as a Leader and his leadership is being carried along by members that he has trained...

Balzac Beef and Grain Clubs
The Balzac 4-H Beef Club is one of the oldest in the Province being organized in 1938 and was an unusual one in that while the majority of clubs have a few outstanding members, some good members and a few not so good or just low markers, Balzac had some outstand-ing members and the remainder were good members. They did not have the low markers. I was told that a couple of Members were warned to improve their marks if they were to be members of the team. The older members spent considerable time helping the newcomers achieve the Club's goals.

The Balzac Clubs were unusual in at least two respects. The Balzac Wheat Club was one of the first ten wheat clubs in the province. It was organized jointly by Morrin Seed Growers Association, Red Deer Board of Trade and with the Alberta Wheat Pool providing the seed and part of the prize money in 1928. This was before the Alberta Department of Agriculture took over Grain Club work. Several people have told me that "someone" has a complete record of the achievements of the Balzac Grain Club, but I have been unable to locate that "someone." Mr. B.C. Church was Secretary of that club in 1932. His sons Robert and Gordon were officers of the same Club from 1951 to 1955. Both clubs had been operating for years when I came to Calgary in 1952. Mr. Harold Bushfield was Leader and Ted Campbell Assistant Leader of the Grain Club and Mr. A.J. Bushfield was Leader of the Beef Club. Both were outstanding Clubs and won many prizes and awards.

Extracts from *My Fifteen Years with 4-H Clubs: 1944-1959*, by N. Fred Bell, circa 1976
In 1944, Fred Bell was appointed District Agriculturist (D.A.) at Drumheller and, as part of his duties, was involved in 4-H Clubs in the region. When he transferred to the Calgary region in 1952, he continued his involvement with 4-H there, including clubs at Airdrie, Balzac, Bearspaw, Chestermere, Cochrane, Irricana, and Springbank.

The Bert Church Family Experience in 4-H

The Calf and Grain Clubs were in existence many years ago as Bert [Church] belonged to the Grain Club when it started. Robert started in the Beef Club in 1949 and had the Champion Hereford calf. The first year for Gordon, he had the Grand Champion and Robert the Reserve Champion calf. This was a great incentive to continue but just about then Mr. Fred Bell was appointed D.A. The members were awakened to the total concepts of a 4-H Club. They learned business procedure in their meetings which would have put most adult meetings to shame. Their reports were kept properly and marked. A standard of proficiency was kept and aimed for. However, Mr. Bell didn't stop with just that, he felt there were many other spheres for the club to develop in, and they took part in public speaking, a marvellous training for them, in Church services, entertainment and bonspiels. Mr. Bell expected 4-H club members to do their best and that meant every member in the Club had to do his best too; consequently the Balzac Clubs were known throughout Alberta and Canada as they were consistently represented on teams to Toronto and Montana. As a result we have some very close friends we still keep in contact with in Quebec, Ontario and Manitoba. The Balzac Clubs were very ably handled by their Leaders all the time our family was in 4-H - Art Bushfield for the Beef Club and Harold Bushfield, Ted Campbell and Keith Rosenberger in the Grain Club.

Mr. Bell was more than just a D.A. The personal interest he took in each member had far reaching results. Our boys and girl were very much aware of his efforts and his faith, in them, and drive, behind them, which directed them to their present success, in no small measure, and we are most grateful.

I feel this is the sign of a great leader - the ability to see the good in the youth and be able to bring it out in the right direction. All credit to you, Mr. Bell.

Letter from Mrs. Bertram C. (Alexa) Church, printed in *My Fifteen Years with 4-H Clubs: 1944-1959*, by N. Fred Bell, circa 1976

As the clergyman serving at Airdrie, Balzac and Columbia from 1958 to 1962, and since I am an agricultural graduate, Fred Bell had me meet with the 4-H clubs in the area to give lectures on setting goals and objectives in improving the members' quality of life. He also worked with me to have 4-H members participate in leading church services on 4-H Agricultural Sunday each spring season. - Stephen Wilk, 1996

Balzac 4-H Beef Club

The Balzac 4-H Beef Club is one of the longest running beef clubs in Alberta, being 62 years old. Originally known as the Balzac Junior Feeding Club, it has had more than 300 members from about 125 families, often with involving two generations, and sometimes three.

Art Bushfield was the epitome of the dedicated 4-H leader, and led the club for 25 years. The Bushfield family continues to donate the trophy for Club Champion Calf in his memory. Since then, club leaders have included Dwaine Jones, Ron Hanson, Alan Bushfield, Harold Evans, Buster Pieschel, Art and Lois Griffith, Gordon and Rosemary Church, Don and Trudy Evans, Bob and Norma Bilben, Laurel Pole, and Shirley Johnston. Several of these leaders are alumni of the Balzac Beef Club.

The members keep busy throughout the year with judging events, public speaking, camps and, of course, feeding and halter-breaking their project cattle.

On the long weekend in May, we band together with the Airdrie and Crossfield-Madden Clubs for our Tri-Club Achievement Day. Each club shows individually for club awards, and at the end of the day the champions compete against each other for the Tri-Club Awards.

The 4-H On Parade Show and Sale is held on the first weekend in June at Stampede park in Calgary. This is a district show, and the calves are shown in weight classes instead of clubs. The show has gradually moved forward, as years ago it was held at the old Calgary Stockyards in October.

Even though the farming community continues to shrink in this area due to urban development, the Balzac 4-H Beef Club continues its enthusiastic existence through the dedication of the members, parents, leaders and community supporters.

Submitted by Norma Bilben, 1996

Balzac Thunderboltz 4-H Light Horse Club

The Balzac Thunderboltz 4-H Light Horse Club was formed in 1992 to serve 4-H members in the Balzac area. The club began with some 15 members and now has nearly 30. Our club follows the 4-H guidelines of public speaking, record book keeping and community service, with the common interest of horsemanship to draw us all together. We meet at the Balzac Hall in the fall and winter, and begin riding lessons in the spring, just east of Balzac at the Bar 25 Arena operated by Lionel and Edna Jackson. Each year members put their riding skills to work at 4-H On Parade and come home with many awards. One of our major fundraisers is the Christmas Tea and Craft Sale at the Balzac Hall in November. We use money earned to help the members of the club pay for their riding lessons.

Submitted by Karen Bannike, 1996

Balzac 4-H Clothing Club

The Balzac 4-H Clothing Club was organized in 1960, welcoming members from Symons Valley, Beddington, Balzac and Airdrie districts. Eileen Woolliams was the club leader, with assistants Agnes Bonner, Isabel Vestrum and Ruby Builder. The original enrollment was 22 girls, which levelled off to approximately 12 as some members became aware the projects were not suited to everyone's taste and ability. In 1965 Millie Miller became leader, with assistance from Muffin Ekman, Bobby Evans and Irene Johnston. We continued through 1970, when the population of eligible girls dropped.

The principal project of the Clothing Club was to master sewing methods with an increasing degree of difficulty in procedure, and to use and study fabrics. Also included was wardrobe planning, accessories, makeup and general good grooming. Our secondary project was Public Speaking, always an interesting exercise, and many of our girls did very well at several levels.

The year's work culminated in Achievement Night, when all projects were displayed, modelled and judged. The girls provided a short program of entertainment and served tea to the attending public. After a suitable interval, the Annual Banquet and Dance was held, and awards were presented. Senior girls emcee'd all activities and the entire membership was involved in planning and executing functions, which also included fund raising, social special events.

We believe joining 4-H was a most worthwhile experience for the girls, providing them an opportunity to participate in a wide variety of projects, and to make the best presentation. While the girls worked hard to complete projects, we also have some good memories of the satisfaction and enjoyment of participating in the group and accepting personal responsibility to achieve our goals.

Submitted by Millie Miller, 1996

Balzac 4-H Field Crops Club - 1966-1972

The Balzac 4-H Field Crops Club was organized on February 25, 1966 with Dave Church as leader and an adult committee consisting of Walter Bushfield, Bill Butler, Earl James, Leighton Perry, Cliff Rush, and Ivor Sjostrom. The club's executive were Dale Sutcliffe as President, Lorne Sutcliffe as Vice-President, Donna Barkley as Secretary, Phil Perry as Treasurer, and Charles Butler as Club Reporter. The new club had 14 members.

The club met regularly throughout the year and held their Achievement Day in conjunction with the Nose Creek Fall Fair. The summer tour of all the members' plots was a very interesting and educational event, not only for the members, but for all their families as well.

The club tried to promote projects related to rural agriculture and grain farming in particular. They sold S.M.V. signs and highway safety flares, assisted in sponsoring a Tractor Rodeo at the Stampede Grounds, and supported the Calgary Stampede Junior Seed Fair with numerous entries. Members of the club succeeded in winning many major awards at this show, as well as at the Lethbridge Seed Fair. One of the members, Bob Anderson, received national recognition at

392

the Toronto Royal Winter Fair by winning the Junior World Wheat Championship, and in 1972 his brother Don Anderson won the Reserve World Barley Championship.

The club set up displays of their projects and work at the Junior Seed Fairs, held at the Calgary Stampede grounds during the Spring Bull Sale. It also joined with the Crossfield Crops Club in participating in the first Youth Achievement Fair in Flare Square during Stampede Week.

In July 1970, the club lost its leader, when Dave Church was killed in a welding accident on his farm. The club as well as the whole community were deeply saddened by the loss of this hard-working, well-liked young man. Harold Anderson took over the leadership of the club until it was forced by lack of members to close in 1972.

Submitted by Harold Anderson, 1996

Balzac 4-H Dairy Club

The Balzac Dairy Club was organized in 1955. Lucille Geekie canvassed the Balzac district and Jim and Lucille Geekie held the organizational meeting in their kitchen in October, 1955. Over 30 members and 30 to 40 parents attended.

There were several highlights for the club. Stewart Geekie had the 1956 Champion Yearling at the Provincial Heifer Show at Red Deer. In 1959, the Balzac Dairy Club won the stall award over all clubs at the Calgary Regional 4-H Show, and it won several more stall awards over the years. In 1962, Stewart Geekie was a provincial delegate to the National 4-H Club week in Toronto.

Some of the Club Leaders were Jack Hays, Jim Geekie, Elvira (Dolly) Schumaker, Albert Anderson, Gavin Scott, Earl Northcott, Barbara Barkley, Nick VanderZowen, Harold Gerlitz, and Jerry Hanson.

Families that were in the Club from 1955 to 1972 included: McCarthy, Barkley, Bilben, Geekie, Hays, Northcott, VanRingen, Hanson, Burwash, Jones, Bonner, Nixon, Losam, Steenhart, Sherman, Wallis, VanderZowen, Davy, Coyne, Gray, Havinga, Leeper, Scott, Schumaker, Cyfra, Gerlitz, Cox, Kirby, Schmidt, Henderson, Rush, Neufeld, Gilberg.

The Calgary Regional 4-H Dairy Show was the highlight of the year. The wonderful camaraderie among the families involved in the Balzac 4-H Dairy Club created lifetime memories and friends.

There were many hours of work and preparation for days before the show. Our reward was winning the stall competition many times. Spotless white flannelette blankets with BALZAC DAIRY CLUB neatly embroidered on each one were ready to place over the back of each animal. On show day every member wore white pants, and long-sleeved white shirts with the 4-H emblem attached. After the show, mothers would rush home with the soiled whites to wash, bleach, and iron them to perfection. They had to be ready the following day for the annual 4-H midday banquet sponsored by the Calgary Stampede Board.

Several members of our 4-H Dairy Club excelled at Public Speaking and Judging Competitions. Many of the members today are still involved with 4-H programs, either personally or through their children.

From 1967 to 1972, the club received a lot of support from a dairywoman east of the Calgary Airport, Margaret Gunn. She had one of the finest herds of Jersey cows in the district. Her trophies and cash awards were much appreciated by the Balzac Dairy club.

The 4-H club was terminated in 1972 due to the closure of dairy farms in the Balzac area; most farmers bound raising beef cattle took less work.

Compiled by Stewart Geekie and Gavin Scott, 1996

The 1954 Balzac 4-H Beef Club, Provincial Efficiency winners. Bottom L to R: *Joyce Hunt, Wilma Jones, Bruce Bailey, Arlene Jones, Richard Bailey, Beverley Church, Florence Bushfield.* Standing L. to R: *Mr. W. J. (Grandpa) Church, age 91, Honorary President, Ronald Jones, Douglas Jones, Dwaine Jones, Gordon Jones, David Church, Robert Church, Ronald Hanson, Gordon Church, Ronald Bailey, Mr. A. J. Bushfield, Leader.*

Source: *My Fifteen Years with 4-H Clubs by N. Fred Bell, circa 1970-1972.*

SCORE CARD FOR BALZAC BEEF CALF CLUB 1953

	Attendance at Meetings	Participation in Club Activities	Feeding Record	Judging	Placing at Show	TOTAL POINTS	Placing in Club
Possible Score	100	100	100	100	100	500	
Douglas Jones	100	96	91	87	100	474	1
Robert Church	100	96	93	92	90	471	2
Gordon Church	100	95	97	88	90	470	3
Dwaine Jones	100	90	92	93	80	455	4
Ron Hanson	100	96	87	82	90	455	5
Beverly Church	100	83	92	90	90	454	6
Art Griffith	100	92	96	86	80	454	7
Arlene Jones	100	90	92	90	80	452	8
David Church	100	88	87	80	90	445	9
Flo Bushfield	100	87	88	87	80	442	10
Gordon Jones	100	81	87	88	80	436	11
Wilma Jones	100	79	92	82	80	433	12
Richard Bailey	100	71	92	89	80	432	13
Ron Bailey	100	80	93	88	65	426	14
Joyce Hunt	100	80	87	84	65	416	15
Bruce Bailey	100	72	90	85	65	412	16
Ron Jones	100	81	89	75	65	410	17
Robert Northcott	100	76	79	82	65	402	18

The score for calves was based on the following values:

Grand Champion of Show - 100
Reserve Champion - 95
Special Grade - 90
Choice - 80
Good - 65
Acceptable - 50

The Balzac Club raised their score considerably after 1953 when for several years no calves in the Calgary District 4-H Show were graded below CHOICE.

This picture was taken at the 1956 Balzac 4-H Dairy Club Awards Banquet. Pictured left to right are: Lucille Geekie (Organizer of the Club in the 1st year) Stewart Geekie, Jean Geekie, Harvey Northcott and Jack Hays (Club Leader).

My fifteen years with 4-H clubs

1944 - 1959

N. FRED BELL

Above: N.F. Bell receives recognition for long service to the 4-H and other Alberta Youth.
Left: The cover of the book he wrote on his experiences with the club in the Drumheller district including the Nose Creek Valley.

Groomed and ready for the show in Calgary (Below) Achievement Day, 1964

Chapter 46: Historic Reflections—The Calgary Exhibition & Stampede

The Stampede, in legend and otherwise, is more than the chuckwagon races, the rodeo, and the grandstand show. Stampede visitors, whether from Calgary, out of town from the Nose Creek Valley region and elsewhere in Alberta, or visitor/tourists, are attracted by events such as the thoroughbred races, the rock and popular music stars performing in the sports arenas, the commercial exhibits, the Indian Village, and the midway rides and booths. As well the celebration has stretched to two weekends, covering ten days, and increasingly the "Sneak-a-Peak", held the Thursday night before the Friday morning parade and official opening, has become seen as part of the Stampede celebration. In addition, over the years some portions have disappeared or become less significant, while others have grown.

Given the location of the grounds and the growth in popularity, the Board of Directors has faced difficulties in making decisions regarding the Stampede's operation and future, and some of these decisions and visions have naturally generated controversies.

The Heritage of the Nose Creek Valley and other regions in Southern Alberta has been influenced by the Stampede. One example is that through the efforts of pioneer missionary Rev. John McDougall and others, the Indian tribes of Southern Alberta have participated from the first Stampede. Another is that the Stampede has become a symbol of a significant part of the Calgary and area lifestyle.

The volunteers over the years who sustained the implementation and organization have reinforced the volunteer spirit in Calgary and region. As well, the farm and ranch way of life has been popularized through the celebration. Moreover, the event and all it entails become part of the summer activities of resident and visitor alike.

Besides providing the farmers, ranchers, and their families with an opportunity to exhibit their animals, produce, and handicrafts, many leaders from the Valley area were elected to the Stampede Board. Seven of them were presidents over the years and many were life members. Included were: Dr. Frank Collicutt, George Church, Peter Pallesen (Sr.), Dr. Howard Wright, Chas Yule, Don Young, Bert Baker, Eleanor Bailey, M.A. Booke, Jack Brown, W.H. Copithorne, A.E. Cross, J.B. Cross, Don Cross, George Edworthy, W.H. Fowler, Neil Harvey, Harry Hays, Charles Kennedy, Tom Laycock, Howard MacDonald, Ed, Fred, Angus and Keith McKinnon, Don and Rob Matthews, Dr. Bob Church, and Marshall Copithorne. Those and others were volunteers and they helped keep the Valley area interests integrated into the event.

Some Valley participants, of cowboy and rodeo fame, were trophy winners. These were: Pete Knight, Robin Burwash, Jim Dunne, Harvey Northcott, Wilf Gerlitz, Dick Havens, Archie Craig, Clem Gardner, and Walley Livingston. Then again, outstanding early exhibitors from the Valley in various categories were: (**Beef Cattle**) Frank Collicutt, Charles Jones, Jim Hale, Don Matthews, The Booke Bros., Chas Yule, Art, Fred and Ray Bushfield.

(**Horse**) Andrew Dollar, George Church, Hardy Salter, Bill Reinard and Earl James.

(**Dairy Cattle**) A.D. Black, Peter Pallesen (Sr.), Joe Laycock and Jim Colpitts.

(**Sheep**) Chester Fowler.

(**Hogs**) Alex Webster, Carmen Kinniburgh, and George Andrews.

(**Hay & Seeds**) Vic Watson, Jim Bussey and Howard Wright.

The above added to the Stampede events of interest to Valley residents and beyond. Besides the agricultural displays, exhibited farm machinery and modern technology, commercial exhibits, and the horse racing not only attracted the adults but the midway has always attracted the youth.

In examining yearly attendance to the Stampede, it was difficult to know exactly how many were visitors from outside the city, and therefore it was hard to calculate what portion came from the Valley area or how many were tourists.

Although the above historical sketch gives a broad background of the Exhibition and Stampede, as a whole, Nose Creek Valley has played a significant role in the evolution of this annual event and continues to do so.

Submitted by Stephen Wilk, 1996

The Growth of a Legend

Calgary has packed a lot of living and a lot of changing into an existence that is a mere 100 years young. And as the city has grown and changed so has its major attraction, the Calgary Exhibition and Stampede, which began as a small agricultural fair and developed into an event that has become the Greatest Outdoor Show on Earth.

Beginnings 1886 - 1912

For a city that became known as Cowtown and for a celebration that is famous for events such as steer wrestling and bull riding, the Calgary Stampede owes its existence to a horse.

The name of the horse in question has long since passed into history but the strange events surrounding its claim to fame are the stuff of legend.

The idea of an agricultural exhibition was born in the early 1880's in Calgary when Major James Walker became president of the Agricultural Society.

But Walker's idea needed land - and in 1886 he seized a chance to acquire it during a visit to Calgary by a federal cabinet minister, A.M. Burgess, who was on a tour of area farms.

Unfortunately for Burgess he was thrown from his horse, breaking his collar bone. Walker saw his chance. He immediately came to Burgess's aid and insisted he return to Walker's house to recuperate.

With Burgess a captive audience, his host bombarded him with requests for the sale of federal land to stage an agricultural show - in fact Walker knew of the very spot along the Elbow River. Already in Walker's debt, Burgess returned to Ottawa and pushed through the sale of 94 acres of land for a cost of $2.50 an acre.

The Calgary Exhibition was born. However the first show in 1886 was hardly a raging success. Gale-force winds coupled with a lack of entries put a damper on the two-day show. Nevertheless, 500 people attended and it was decided to continue the Exhibition on a yearly basis.

Yet it wasn't until 1908 that the show finally took off.

Calgary got to stage the Dominion Exhibition, a government funded promotion which moved from city to city each year.

It meant major money for new buildings and to subsidize exhibitors. It ran for a week and the West had never seen its like before - included in the sights was a hydrogen balloon which crashed into the grandstands. But unlike the balloon, the Calgary Exhibition had taken off for good.

Ride 'Em Cowboy 1912 - 1923

The Exhibition had remained a purely agricultural affair since its inception but in 1912 the arrival of a charismatic cowboy in Calgary was to sow the seeds of the future Stampede.

Guy Weadick, a U.S. trick roper with a gift for promotion, saw the chance to turn Calgary into a major attraction through the staging of a wild west rodeo.

He managed to persuade four area businessmen, George Lane, Pat Burns, A.E. Cross, and A.J. McLean, to back his ambitious plan to the tune of $100,000 and Weadick's rodeo was off and running.

It opened September 2, 1912, and was a spectacle the West had never seen before kicked off with a never-to-be-forgotten parade through Calgary.

It was a week of excitement and fun, topped off for the mainly local crowd when a Blood Indian named Tom Three Persons won the bronc riding competition against the U.S. and Mexican challengers.

But it wasn't enough to make rodeo an annual event. It wasn't until 1923, with admission numbers slipping at the Exhibition, that the fateful decision was taken to combine the agricultural fair with the rodeo. Finally, the Calgary Exhibition and Stampede was born.

Yahoo 1923 - 1929

The 1923 Stampede became a worldwide affair. Weadick was back and he promoted the event as no other had ever been promoted. Notices were sent around the world and the best cowboys of the time turned up to compete.

And among the popular rodeo events was placed a makeshift new competition called chuckwagon racing which would soon become one of the unique features of the Stampede.

The festival was an unqualified success, bringing in a profit of $27,000 and allowing Major George Webster to announce on the final night that the Stampede was to become an annual event.

Such early status allowed the Stampede to ask for and receive the blessing of the professional rodeo cowboys, who included the event on their yearly calendar.

No longer would Weadick have to beg the best cowboys to come north. Now they wanted to come. In 1924, 300 cowboys took part and the numbers grew each year.

So did the Stampede's popularity. By 1929 attendance figures had swelled to the amazing figure of 258,469 and there looked no end to the future heights the Stampede would scale. But trouble was on the horizon.

Depression and War 1930 - 1944

The worldwide depression caught the Stampede in its vice-like grip as it did the rest of the globe.

And in an agricultural community like the West that grip could be deadly.

The first effects were seen in the attendance at the 1930 Stampede when the numbers through the gate dropped by 50,000 from the year before.

With hundreds of thousands unemployed the Stampede decided to act. Management came up with a plan to fill the seats. There were lots of empty seats in the big, new concrete grandstand and each day a whole block of seats was set aside for the registered unemployed and their families.

It was public relations masterstroke and it paid dividends years later when those same people got working again, for they came back as cash customers with their interest in the Stampede intact.

But the bad times couldn't last forever and with the outbreak of the Second World War the tide turned. By 1940 men were joining up and industry was making a comeback. There was money again and the attendance in that year proved it - jumping to 244,849.

The Good Times Roll 1945 - 1969

The good times were back with a vengeance at Stampede Park. A booming, Post-War economy in which wages were rising coupled with the removal of wartime restrictions on travel and spending fuelled a boomtime atmosphere. The new highways were thick with motor cars and tourists and what better destination for a summer vacation that the Calgary Stampede.

Alberta itself was going through a major upswing. The discovery of oil at Leduc, followed by about a dozen similar finds, transformed Calgary into the oil capital of Canada.

Between 1949 - 1957 the population almost doubled to 180,000, many of the newcomers moving from the U.S.

It gave the Stampede a ready made audience. These newcomers were already familiar with the rodeo and they embraced the Canadian version. They also brought something unique, a love for outdoor, portable barbecues. Soon Stampede Week in Calgary became a great excuse for a giant week-long barbecue as friends, neighbours and companies put on special Stampede breakfasts - a tradition that has only grown with time.

In 1950 the Stampede Corral was built at a cost of $1,400,000 and at the time it was the finest hockey arena in the West.

That was followed in the same decade by the Big Four Building, new horse barns, increased parking space and a livestock pavilion.

Spectators also got a chance to get into the act by winning big. Starting with the Kinsmen's car raffle in 1952, lotteries became a staple in the Stampede, quickly expanding into dream homes and pots of gold.

It was a time when the Stampede Board scoured North America for personalities to open the show, people such as Walt Disney, Bing Crosby, Gordie Howe, Earl Mountbatten of Burma, Senator Robert Kennedy and Bob Hope.

It had finally become the Greatest Outdoor Show on Earth.

Moving With The Times - 1969 - 1994

There was one major problem. The Stampede was running out of room. Every year there were more attraction. In 1969 a casino was opened in the Big Four building, by 1969 the Young Canadians came into their own performing in the evening Grandstand Show, in 1974 a new grandstand was built.

But it still wasn't enough and congestion was becoming a major problem. The relaxation of the Lord's Day Act allowed the Stampede to run through the Sundays and a city council decision to allow some expansion together gave some relief to the congestion problem.

Yet still the numbers continued to climb until in 1976 the attendance finally broke through that elusive one million barrier.

By now, thanks to the power of TV, the Stampede had become a major worldwide attraction and its rodeo finals a top class sporting event.

In 1982 the Stampede offered the cowboys a massive total purse of $500,000. It established the Calgary rodeo as one of the top events on the Continent.

Meanwhile two other events were slowly taking shape that would combine to make the 1980's the most dramatic decade in the Stampede's history.

After much wrangling and deal-making the Flames were brought to Calgary in 1980 and construction began on a state-of-the-art hockey arena on Stampede Park.

It would be called the Saddledome and The Calgary Flames had their proud debut in 1983 after moving from their temporary home in the nearby Corral. About the same time as the Flames were being courted in Atlanta, a group of ambitious Calgarians went after an even bigger fish, the 1988 Olympic Winter Games.

Sceptics laughed but the impossible dream was realized and the city and Stampede got ready for a celebration like no other.

And that's how it turned out. The Games were an unbelievable success and the spin off later that summer was the largest ever attendance in the Stampede's history - 1,213,646 people crowded through the turnstiles.

It was an amazing success and one that the Stampede plans to build on.

Horizon 2000 was a visionary document that outlined the long range plan The Calgary Stampede that will see Stampede Park meet the demands and anticipated needs of tourist while eventually developing the eastern section of the downtown core.

Horizon 2000 endeavours to set the framework for the Calgary Exhibition and Stampede for the year 2006. At that time the population of Calgary is forecasted to be over 1.0 million people with visitors to the Stampede estimated to reach 1.7 million.

Article by Chris Nelson, 1994. Courtesy: *Calgary Stampede 1996.*

Above: Guy Weadick and Calgary Stampede brands placed in the Ranchmen's Club in Calgary by the Historical Committee of the Calgary Exhibition and Stampede Board and the Florence Mannix-Pallesen family. Weadick brand, c. 1923; Stampede brand. c. 1975.
Below: a wide-angled shot of participants in the 1912 Calgary Stampede. This event drew people like Pancho Villa and a host of other notables.

Above: *Chuckwagon race.*
Below: *Stampede City: a view from 'Scotsman's Hill', North West of the Saddledome, 1996.*
Bottom: *The Stampede grounds.*

A Profile of Guy Weadick

In 1912, a brash young American vaudevillian named Guy Weadick arrived in Calgary and changed the face of the city forever. In a few days, he had convinced four leading Calgarians to put up $100,000 for the most spectacular frontier days celebration the country had seen. His vision ignited the city and set the stage for the "Greatest Outdoor Show on Earth."

Born in Rochester, New York, in 1885, Weadick was a trick roper who, along with his wife and partner Florence LaDue, had travelled the Wild West and vaudelville circuit in North America and Europe. In Calgary he found the perfect setting for a grand celebration of the cowboy way of life. The first Stampede was held in September 1912 and set the pace for Stampedes to come.

Weadick was invited back to Calgary in 1919 to stage a popular Victory Stampede. He returned in 1923 and from then on, the Calgary Exhibition and Stampede was an annual event, attracting top competitors and visitors from around the world.

Guy and Florence established one of the first dude ranches in southern Alberta, and Guy went on to produce western films, and write regular magazine columns celebrating the rodeo and cowboy way of life.

Guy Weadick was an outstanding promoter of the Calgary Stampede and all that it stood for. He attracted the attention of the world to Calgary and was instrumental in promoting women in rodeo, establishing chuckwagon races as a thrilling new event, and securing top prizes for the competitors.

Guy Weadick left the Stampede in 1932, but returned as special guest of honour in 1952. He died in 1953 and is buried with Florence in High River.

Submitted by Donna Livingston, 1996

Norman & Florence Mannix Pallesen enjoy a horseback ride while honeymooning on the Guy Weadick Ranch, 1936.

Interviews on the Life of Guy Weadick

1. According to Donna Livingston, author of the recently published **Cowboy Spirit, Guy Weadick and the Calgary Stampede** (Douglas & McIntyre, 1996), Guy Weadick was a key figure in bringing the sense of the cowboy off the range and into popular imagination. In summarizing his career, she says, "He arrived in Calgary at a key period in our history and reminded us of the importance of celebrating our western roots. He is best known for establishing the Calgary Stampede, but his influence was much wider than that. He was a writer, a dude ranch operator, a film producer, and a wester promoter par excellence. Through his enthusiasm and wide-ranging vision, visitors come from around the world to celebrate the cowboy spirit in Calgary."

2. Between the age of 6 to 9 years, Tommy Bews of Longview, a close neighbour over the years, was impressed by Guy Weadick's typical western cowboy uniform, big cowboy hat and fancy riding boots with four rows of stitching at the top. He lived in a well built, meticulously kept log house. Guy loved to drop in and visit and would spend many hours story telling about his experiences being a cowboy out on the range and at the Rodeo (Stampedes). He told of his putting on Wild West shows in the U.S.A., England and parts of Europe. He came to Alberta to see if he could produce a show and this is how the Calgary Stampede was started.

3. Tommy's sister Lenora McLean of High River as a youth remembers Guy as a colorful handsome gentleman, was good with horses. His wife Florence was not only a champion roper but also was a marvelous business woman, while he was a promoter. His guest ranch in the Highwood was one of the most well equipped in Canada. He ran cattle and had saddles made at Riley & McCormack harness and saddle shop to fit every size and shape of the riders. The guest ranch was a popular place where Royalty and Dignitaries were entertained. He always had good advice for the young people. Guy's motto for them was "Do your best at whatever you undertake". In summary both Tommy and Lenora affirmed that Guy and his wife Florence were excellent neighbours.

Submitted by Stephen Wilk, 1996

Relaxing on the porch of the Guy Weadick guest cabin are (left to right) Florence Mannix Pallesen wearing custom made cowboy boots, Eddie Duncan, an oilfield supplier, and two other guests. 1936. Above: Guy Weadick in a pensive mood.

Left: Guy Weadick in 1934 and *(below)* on a Calgary street in 1912. ***Bottom left to right.*** At the Guy Weadick ranch: Francis and Eddie Duncan, Norman Pallesen, Florence (née Mannix) Pallesen and a ranch hand. September 1936.

Pallesen, Burns, and Mannix Family Brands

In 1996 the Niels Peter Pallesen family branch together with the Historical Committee of the Calgary Exhibition and Stampede Board was instrumental in the placement of the brand of the late Guy Weadick (1885 - 1953) of Longview, Alberta the "originator" of the Calgary Stampede in 1912 and the brand of the Calgary Exhibition and Stampede Board itself for placement on a brand wall of the Ranchmen's Club in Calgary. N. Peter Pallesen (1873 - 1933) eldest of the Pallesen Bros. served as a director and second vice-president of the Calgary Exhibition and Stampede between 1917 to 1932.

The 1907 brand registered by the late N. Peter Pallesen (1873-1933) was placed on the historic brand wall of the Ranchmen's Club on 28th March, 1995. The 1907 brand was in application to the Pallesen Bros. 'Home Farm" partnership which they commenced in 1904 and was later the holding of the late Mr. Thomas Pallesen. This brand is symbolic of seven branches of the Pallesen family comprised of the five Pallesen brothers together with their two brothers-in-law that had an association with the 'Home Farm' between 1904 to 1913. A portion of the 'Home Farm' can still be viewed at the SE intersection of McKnight Boulevard and Barlow Trail near the Calgary International Airport. The 1915 Peter Pallesen 'MF' brand was in application to the Spy Hill Stock and Dairy Farm in the Bearspaw district, the 1915 Martin Pallesen '2D' brand was in application to his farm now at the intersection of McKnight Boulevard and 90th Avenue NE, the 1915 Otto Pallesen 'OD' brand was in application to his earliest ventures in the livestock industry followed by the establishment in 1920 of an operation near Hesketh, Alberta and the Berg Pallesen 'PF' brand is in application to his former holding now at the intersection of Barlow Trail and 16th Avenue NE. The family tradition continued with the Svend R. Pallesen '4P' brand for his former operation near Sundre, Alberta, the Shane Pallesen 'SP' brand for his Hereford cattle operation near Strathmore, Alberta, the 'X3' brand of Henry Mikkelsen now the brand of D. Wayne Mikkelsen of Westview Farms, Langdon, Alberta and the 'OP' brand from the original holding of Otto Pallesen of Hesketh, Alberta and later that of Douglas N. Pallesen. This brand is now used by Wendy (niece of Douglas N. Pallesen) and Michael Kubinec who are proprietors of the Joan of Arch Ranch near Trochu, Alberta being a Hereford cattle operation first established in 1905

N. Peter Pallesen (1907)
Pallesen Bros.

N. Peter Pallesen (1915)
Spy Hill Stock and Dairy
Farm, Bearspaw District

Martin Pallesen (1915)
Nose Creek Valley
(McKnight Boulevard)

Otto W. Pallesen (1915)
Rocky View District

Berg F. Pallesen (1915)
Nose Creek Valley
(Barlow Trail)

Otto W. Pallesen
Douglas N. Pallesen
Wendy Pallesen Kubinec
Hesketh, Alberta

Svend W. Pallesen (1972)
Sundre, Alberta

Aside from the Pallesen brand placed at the Ranchmen's Club, the five Pallesen Bros. brands are inscribed on the brand wall of the Nose Creek Valley Museum, Airdrie, Alberta. The Nose Creek Valley has a long association with the extended Pallesen family in both the farming sector and dairy manufacturing industry given the five farming operations of the Andersen, Mikkelsen, and Pallesen families in the Nose Creek Valley, one in the Bearspaw districts and one in the Hesketh district. Two of the Pallesen brands are inscribed on the ground marker at the N. Peter Pallesen family plot in Burnsland Cemetery. Inscriptions of the Burns family Bar U and NL from the Bar U and Bow Valley ranches are also inscribed on the ground marker. All of the brands are inscribed on the brand wall of the Western Heritage Centre, Cochrane, Alberta thus representing all eight branches of the Pallesen family.

Information in connection to more currently registered brands can be obtained from the Office of the Brand Recorder, Alberta Agriculture, P.O. Box 600, Stettler, Alberta, T0C 2L0 - telephone: (403)742-7570. Brand information can also be obtained from the Bert Shepard Memorial Library which is part of the Western Heritage Centre, Cochrane, Alberta, the Glenbow Museum Archives and the Provincial Archives, Edmonton, Alberta.

1. THE BURNS FAMILY BRANDS

Michael John Burns became General Manager of Burns & Co. in 1916 which owned P. Burns Ranches Limited at the time. Michael John Burns was a nephew and business successor of Senator Patrick Burns. Senator Burns acquired the Bow Valley Ranch near Midnapore in 1902 from William Roper Hull and in 1928 it became part of P. Burns Ranches Limited. The holding was sold in 1973 to the Government of the Province of Alberta later to form part of Fish Creek Provincial Park. The Bow Valley Ranch was the home of Michael John Burns and Alma Catherine Burns (nee Pallesen) after the passing of Senator Burns in 1937. Mrs. Alma Burns was the eldest daughter of Annie and N. Peter Pallesen. In 1927 the largest holding in the Burns network of ranches, the Bar-U Ranch established in 1891 was acquired by P. Burns Ranches Limited and later sold in 1950. The Bar-U Ranch was owned by ranching pioneer George Lane (1856-1925) who acquired this holding in 1905. Two horse brands were registered to P. Burns Ranches Limited as late as 1975. This would be in connection to the Priddis, Alberta holding owned by the late Patrick John Peter Burns (1936-1975). Two of the four Burns family brands comprise part of the 'Big Four' in connection to the establishment of the Calgary Exhibition and Stampede in 1912.

2. THE MANNIX FAMILY BRANDS

The Mannix family is best known for their wide activities in the general construction industry but otherwise is rooted in the cattle industry. This family branch is related through Mrs. Florence Dora Evelyn Pallesen (nee Mannix) of Calgary a daughter of the late construction pioneer Frederick Stephen Mannix (1881-1951) and a daughter-in-law of N. Peter Pallesen. The Mannix family association in the cattle industry commenced with the establishment of the Mannix farm near Stonewall, Manitoba in 1871 by George Charles Mannix (1845-1934) father of Frederick Stephen Mannix. The first Mannix family ranch in Alberta was the Thumb Hill Ranch near Dorothy, Alberta owned by Mr. Mannix, Sr. between 1912 to 1918. He acquired the Baxter-Reid brands first registered to the Thumb Hill Ranch in 1905. He continued with another operation between 1918 until the early 1930's in the Rockyford area and continued to register the L6 brand. His son the late Frederick Charles Mannix (1913-1995) continued with operations in the Fish Creek Dewinton, Millarville, Medicine Hat and Bindloss districts. A further Mannix family ranching operation is located in the Nanton, Alberta district.

Submitted by Peter J.M. Pallesen, 1997

Chapter 47

Historic Interpretive Centres

1. Fort Calgary Historic Park—Calgary

Fort Calgary Historic
Park Interpretive Centre

2. Western Heritage Centre—Cochrane

THE WESTERN
HERITAGE
CENTRE

*An Interactive Ranch &
Rodeo   Intrepretive
Centre*

3. Western Stock Growers Association Calgary

Celebrating 100 years of the Western Stock Growers Association

1. Fort Calgary Historical Park, Calgary, Alberta

In 1875, amid a sea of scarlet jackets and thundering hooves, 'F' Troop of the North West Mounted Police, led by Colonel J.F. Macleod, crossed the Bow River and built Fort Calgary. Sent from Ottawa, the troop was to impose law and order and stop the whisky trade which was devastating to First Nations communities.

The Mounties' occupation of the outpost ended in 1914, but their legacy lives on as the City of Calgary continues to rise behind the fort— where it all began.

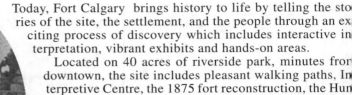

Today, Fort Calgary brings history to life by telling the stories of the site, the settlement, and the people through an exciting process of discovery which includes interactive interpretation, vibrant exhibits and hands-on areas.

Located on 40 acres of riverside park, minutes from downtown, the site includes pleasant walking paths, Interpretive Centre, the 1875 fort reconstruction, the Hunt House Historic Site and the Deane House Historic Site & Restaurant.

Images of the past

Located at the junction of the Bow Elbow Rivers th original Fort was completed in two months. In 188 the stockade was torn down and additional barracks wer added. Destroyed by fire in 1887 these barracks wer replaced the following year with an impressive two stor structure which remained until 1914.

Colonel J.F. Macleod

The arrival of the Canadian Pacific Railway in 188 prompted the original townsite to expand west across th Elbow River and huddle around the new station. The settlement of Fort Calgary, spurred by the arrival of the railway, offi cially became the City of Calgary in 1894. Streetcars and the first Stampede soo followed. In 1914 the site was sold to Grand Trunk Pacific Railway and the building were demolished.

In 1975, as part of Calgary's Centennial celebrations, Fort Calgary's 40 acres o riverside park were reclaimed from decades of light industrial use and returned to th citizens of Calgary. Fort Calgary is a designated national and provincial site.

Vision for the future

The Fort Calgary Preservation Society's mission is to preserve, interpret and pro mote the early history of the Mounted Police at Fort Calgary and of the Calgary area and to communicate Calgary's early cultural heritage and diversity to residents an visitors through the delivery of dynamic and interactive programs, services and ex hibits, thereby facilitating an enjoyable experience.

Volunteer and member support ensures this mission is met through the preservatio and continual development of new exhibits and programs at Fort Calgary Histori Park.

For hours of operation and admission rates phone (403) 290-1875.

THE DEANE HOUSE

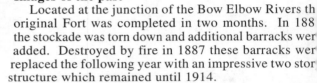

The Deane House, originally the home of Captain Richard Burton Deane, Superintendent of Fort Calgary, was built in 1906 at a cost of $6,200. In 1929 the house was physically moved across the Elbow River, a feat so remarkable it was profiled in a 1930 issue of Popular Mechanics Magazine.

Captain Deane who resided in the house from 1906-1914 was an avid gardener who developed the much admired gardens and lawn which surrounded his home. Today, the beautiful gardens have been recreated and are developed and maintained by community volunteers.

Since 1914 the house has seen duty as a railway agents home, boarding house, artists studio and restaurant.

Today, the house performs several functions. In addition to its restaurant and catering operation, the house is also an on-site location for educational-based school programs and home to Friday Night Mystery From History Dinner Theatre.

For information & reservations call (403) 269-7747

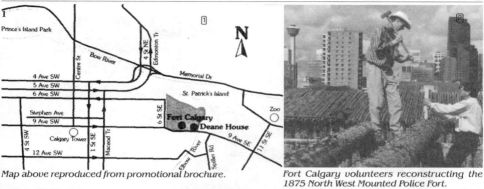

Map above reproduced from promotional brochure.

Fort Calgary volunteers reconstructing the 1875 North West Mounted Police Fort.

The Fort Calgary gift shop was inspired by the 1884 Hudson's Bay Company store at Calgary.

The reconstructed Fort Calgary will be complete and furnished by 2000.

Fort Calgary volunteer carpenters and blacksmiths demonstrate their skills daily on 1870-1900 reproduction tools.

The Fort Calgary Interpretive Centre features exhibits on the North West Mounted Police and the history of the Calgary area up to the 1930's.

'Fort Calgary in Summer,' 1875. Painted by N.W.M.P. Assistant Surgeon, R.B. Nevitt.   —Glenbow Archives

2. Western Heritage Centre, Cochrane, Alberta

THE WESTERN HERITAGE CENTRE
An Interactive Ranch & Rodeo Interpretive Centre

FACTS ABOUT THE CENTRE

The 87,000 sq. ft. Western Heritage Centre is the first major attraction in Canada dedicated to the livestock industry and the sport of rodeo.

The $15,000,000 Centre was founded by The Stockmen's Memorial Foundation and The Canadian Rodeo Historical Association.

This magnificent ranch style facility offers a number of exciting entertainment opportunities:

★ Dozens of exciting hands-on interactive exhibits that explore the past, present and future of farming, ranching, and rodeo.

★ First class dining in a 250 seat restaurant overlooking the historic Cochrane Ranche and the Rockies.

★ The Canadian Rodeo Hall of Fame and the Bert Sheppard Stockmen's Library and Archives.

★ A 209 seat multi-functional theatre.

★ The Horsemen's Art Gallery.

HOW TO TRACK US DOWN

Only 15 minutes west of Calgary, Alberta. 1/2 km north of Cochrane on Hwy 22. For more information call (403) 932-3514, fax (403) 932-3515, or visit us at our web site at www.whcs.com. ⍟

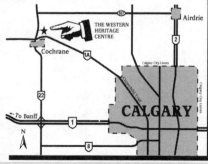

TACK AND LEATHER SHOP

DAIRY CATTLE EXHIBIT

THE EXHIBITS HALL

VETERINARIAN EXHIBIT

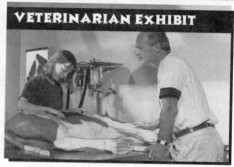

HOW DOES THAT COW WORK?

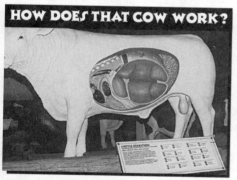

THE CO-OPERATORS THEATRE

THE DINING ROOM

CALF TYING

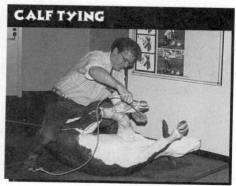

3. Western Stock Growers Association, Calgary, Alberta

Over 100 years of the Cattle Industry in the West

In 1996, the Western Stock Growers Association celebrated 100 years of speaking out on behalf of cattle ranching in the West. The Association grew out of several smaller associations and was formed in 1896. In 1864, the McDougall family had brought cattle from Fort Garry to Fort Edmonton; it was part of this herd that was brought south when David and John McDougall established the Methodist mission at Morleyville in 1873, bringing cattle into southern Alberta. This was twenty-three years before the establishment of the Association.

As described by historian J. Ernest Nix "a caravan was put together and on October 22, to settle at Morleyville on the Bow River." Nix says "It must have been an impressive entourage: John and ten carts, a 'double waggon,' and some loose horses and cows, and to manage there were himself, his wife driving a team, her eldest daughter Flora in the saddle driving the loose stock, and three native helpers or outriders. David had an additional ten carts, and two white men and several English and French mixed-blood families, these last with eight carts, making a total of twenty-two vehicles, thirty-five persons, and stock." These cattle provided milk and meat to sustain the natives and missionaries near the Old Bow Fort, a former trading post.

John McDougall in his reflections on *"Opening The Great West"*, Glenbow-Alberta Institute Calgary, 1970, pg 26-27, describes the basis of stock growing in Southern Alberta as follows: "During the autumn and just prior to my last trip, the first large bunch of cattle for stock-raising purposes came into the country. These were brought over the mountains from the Columbia Lakes by John Shaw. The band consisted of some 700 head and his intention was to drive them right on to Edmonton, However on my advice he left his cattle on the Bow and rode on first to see the Edmonton country for himself. Having done this he very gratefully came back and wintered beside us at Morley. These cattle, with the few I had brought out from Fort Garry in 1873 and some Kenneth McKenzie brought to Morley in 1874, laid the foundation of the stock-raising business since grown to such splendid proportions in southern Alberta."

In 1996 the Western Stock Growers Association celebrated the long history of cattle driven to the west. Over 1300 riders, 1500 horses and mules, 103 wagons and 2000 longhorned head of cattle gathered at Buffalo, Alberta to begin a six day drive across the Canadian Forces Base, Suffield, Alberta to Medicine Hat. Cowboys and Cowgirls from all over Southern Alberta including Nose Creek Valley area, under the leadership of Tom Butterfield, experienced the rigors and the beauty of prairie landscape as they made their way through Box Springs Coulee and Medicine Hat where they paraded through the city to the Stampede grounds. A steer was auctioned off as a way to partly pay for the trip. Numerous cattle and horses went astray during the historic cattle drive.

Many from Nose Creek Valley area were enthusiastic participants in this centennial event. Some of them were; Ron and Wayne Hanson, Murray Jones, Russ Fletcher, Barry and Earl Scott, Jim and Pat Simpson, Miles Fox, Blain Havens, Harvey Buckley, Bobby and Sunni Turner, Joe and Patty Bowhay, Harold Gerlitz, Buster McCullough, Calgary; Joyce McElroy, Calgary, and many others. This event became known as "The Great Centennial Cattle Drive" (1896-1996).

Submitted by Stephen Wilk with photos courtesy of Morris Flewwelling, Red Deer, Alberta, 1996.

CONCLUSION

We have presented some examples of our rich heritage of agriculture, business and industry, services and community development; each plays its part in of the dynamics of rural and urban life in the Nose Creek Valley. We now turn to local histories which have been written about the area.

Top and above: *The Cattle Drive begins.* ***Right:*** *Paul Gatty, Past President of W.S.G.A., drives this wagon.* ***Below:*** *The herd at the ranch south of Buffalo, Alberta, moves out.*

PART VI: REVIEWS OF BOOKS ABOUT THE NOSE CREEK VALLEY

INTRODUCTION

We have presented a plethora of articles describing various facets of the history of the Nose Creek Valley. Now we provide a look at the underpinnings of this anthology. The published and unpublished works reviewed here give detailed pictures of aspects of the Valley's history and people. We describe how some of this Nose Creek Valley literature came to be produced.

CHAPTER 48: *THE NOSE CREEK STORY*

How the Book Came to Be

About 1950 the first thought of a local history took place at a meeting of the U.F.W.A. [United FarmWomen of Alberta] at Beddington.

One of the members as part of the regular meeting had told her family story of how they had left England in the early 1900's to settle in Alberta. From this interesting story came the idea of a story or history of Beddington and its old-time residents. For some time no further action was taken although very often discussions took place as to its possibilities.

Finally a committee of Mrs. Sandgathe, Mrs. Hugh Bushfield and W.H. Evans was appointed

and assigned specific duties in gathering a History of Beddington. Later Mrs. R.J. Pole was included on the committee. So much interest was displayed by residents further afield than the actual confines of Beddington that three other persons, Mrs. N. Beaton, Mrs. F. Campbell and C.R. Perry, were added to the committee.

At a meeting of this enlarged committee it was decided to call the book "The Nose Creek Story." This stems from the fact that in the early days of settlement the whole district from Calgary north to Airdrie and including Symons Valley, Beddington, Buttes and Balzac was known as "Nose Creek," after the two branches of Nose Creek which flow through it and join the Bow River in East Calgary...

This book was launched December 14, 1960.

From the Introduction to *The Nose Creek Story*, 1961

Foreword to the Early History of Nose Creek

This is a brief history of a pioneer Alberta community, and is an attempt to preserve for future residents the names and dates of those early pioneers, and of the development, struggles and changes which have taken place over the years.

The name of Beddington was given to the railway siding by the C.P.R. on the building of the Calgary-Edmonton branch. For some years before the railway came, some hardy early settlers were sparsely scattered through the district north of Calgary then known as Nose Creek. This was in the years of 1880 to 1887. Even before these dates missionaries and traders were known to have been here. George McDougall, father of the Rev. J. McDougall, a well-known early missionary, was lost and frozen to death on a buffalo hunt in the Beddington district.

With the coming of the railway and arrival of settlers, especially after 1900, many changes were seen. The open prairie grass lands were gradually fenced. The prairie trails which we travelled leisurely by wagon or democrat are now graded and some are gravelled roads over which the milk trucks speed daily to Calgary. The three-ton truck takes the farm produce and grain which were formerly hauled by hayrack and wagon. The once-familiar drives of cattle to the stockyards by the farmer and his neighbours down the dusty trails on horseback are now speeded in by the farmer's own truck or by big cattle liners. Land, a few acres at a time, was broken and, with some fears but a lot of hope, was seeded to grain.

...The use of gasoline-powered machinery has tremendously increased the output of farm products, so that more is grown on fewer farms in 1958 than in the whole of Beddington Municipality in 1900. The colorful cowboy and rancher has almost disappeared.

The threshing machine, which through the years used such fuel as straw, coal or gasoline, and a very large crew of men and horses, has now almost entirely been replaced by the farmer's own combine. The high-powered automobile has taken the place of the saddle horse and buggy.

On the land which was once the farm homes of some of our earliest settlers, the Parsons and the Youngs - 1883 - now stands the airport, from which huge planes take off several times per day for distant world places. Edmonton is now only one hour's travel time away, Toronto just six hours away.

The old coal-oil lamps and lanterns have disappeared from homes and barns and have been replaced by electric lights. The small unpainted houses are replaced very largely by fairly modern houses where electric power is used to lighten the labour of the housewife. The problem of keeping meats, milk and butter and many other foodstuffs is taken care of by refrigeration or deep-freezes.

The old-timer who used to make trips by team to the "Bush," some twenty-five miles northwest, for firewood and fence posts, a three day trip, now uses propane gas for cooking and heating. So as in all things, improvement and progress take over, and "Time Marches On." Television and movies take care of the entertainment side of our lives.

Even the "everlasting hills" are changing in the search for gravel to be used in the building of the City of Calgary and on rural roads. Big machines are tearing them down.

The big Nose Hill, which for centuries has appeared to stand silent and inscrutable, brooding over the rolling 800 miles of prairies to the east is changing. The southern slope of Nose Hill is now a part of the City of Calgary, covered with modern homes, lawns and streets. It is expected that in the near future residences will reach the top.

Only the two branches of Nose Creek, as ever, roll on in their usual way to join the "brimming river."

One other important thing has remained unchanged, namely the great spirit of congenial friendliness which in those early days prevailed. This has continued on and on through the years making Beddington a place we are proud to call "Home."

Beddington, in the very early days, covered a much larger area than at the present time. Its southern boundary was the city limits of Calgary and it extended north to a few miles south of Airdrie, embracing what are now the district of North Calgary, Symons Valley, Casa Loma, Dry Creek and Balzac.

The early settlers, drawn from Eastern Canada, the U.S.A., the British Isles and many European countries, had one common denominator, viz. the age-old urge of man to acquire land, better his condition of life, and to establish homes.

Western Canada, with its rolling prairie lands and fertile foothills, where the Government would give 160 acres of homestead land and the C.P.R. would sell lands from $3.00 to $5.00 per acre, was the answer to that urge. As a result, Beddington gradually became settled from 1885 on. We find that almost immediately our early settlers took time to provide and establish the social facilities so necessary to any community.

Church services were started in the homes, then came the schools, later followed by Literary Societies. Then came the Farm Men and Farm Women's organizations, the Ladies Aid, the community hall, all of which are described in the following pages.

To these early pioneers this history is affectionately dedicated.

By W.H. Evans, October, 1958; from *The Nose Creek Story*, 1961

CHAPTER 49: THE REDVERS PERRY SCRAPBOOK COLLECTION

Local Historian, C. Redvers Perry compiled a series of scrapbooks detailing over 30 years of Nose Creek events. Redvers wrote this about his collection:

On January 14th, 1957, at a meeting of the Nose Creek Farmers Union of Alberta, held at the home of Mr. and Mrs. Raymond Bushfield, I was nominated by Raymond Bushfield to write the district news for a period of one year. Little did I realize one year would last so long! To the following newspapers I extend my appreciation for printing the news column regardless of the tight editing quite noticeable in some issues. The news outlets are as follows from 1957 to the present time 1989. ROCKY VIEW TIMES AND MARKET EXAMINER; THE AIRDRIE ECHO; THE CALGARY HERALD; THE AIRDRIE ADVANCE; THE ROCKY VIEW TIMES; TRI-NEIGHBOR PRESS, AIRDRIE; THE CALGARY SUN; ALBERTA WHEAT POOL BUDGET, GRAINNEWS; and the most recent ROCKY VIEW 5 VILLAGE WEEKLY OF IRRICANA. Thanks to all.

Those weekly accounts of events and happenings in the area "NORTH OF THE BOW",

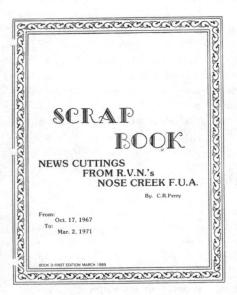

SCRAP BOOK

NEWS CUTTINGS
FROM R.V.N.'s
NOSE CREEK F.U.A.

By. C.R.Perry

From:
    Oct. 17, 1967
To:
    Mar. 2, 1971

BOOK D FIRST EDITION MARCH 1989

is unprofessional, and folksy with some faded print, misprinted names, left out words, etc., etc. This family scrapbook is a variety of news cuttings chiefly of local events from October 17, 1967 to March 23, 1971. We hope you enjoy reading over the events of yesteryear, and no doubt will relate happenings that are of value to your memories. If sufficient interest is shown it will encourage the printing of the next series which is up to date at the time of writing, April 1989.

Hopefully you will be patient when reading this book, and able to reminisce. My pleasure will be in knowing it will provide the future generations of the happy community life style we enjoyed in this open agricultural country side. May it continue to be left this way, for others to enjoy.

By C. Redvers Perry; Preface to one Scrapbook, 1989

Introduction to Each Scrapbook

The Nose Creek area, nestled against the northern outskirts of Calgary, is a rural district within sight of the shopping centres, sky scrapers, and pollution of the big city. Yet Nose Creek, Beddington, and Balzac have retained their rural focus. A person may shop in Calgary in the afternoon and attend a Farmer Union meeting in the evening. Children may join with city friends to go downtown on Saturday but join a country picnic on the following day.

Nose Creek has been able to find that fine balance to maintain a rural life in the shadow of a metropolis. Some of their concerns are common to any country district, but they have the added problems of city people dumping their garbage along their roads; weekend hunters ignoring signs and shooting at just about anything that moves; city revellers leaving their broken bottles strewn about; and hungry speculators who would like to turn rich farming land into new subdivisions.

Redvers Perry has seen all this happening and, since 1957 he has recorded it in fine detail. As the local historian and correspondent for district newspapers, he has written about the commonplace and the unique. And, like any good writer, he has dutifully clipped each story and each column and pasted them in a scrapbook. When one book was full, he started on another. Now, his nine scrapbooks form a unique look at the Nose Hill area for a period of more than 30 years.

Mr. Perry has written for the *North Hill News, Five Village Weekly* in Irricana, *Airdrie Echo, Rocky View Times, Tri-Neighbor Press*, and others. Sometimes the news was about a wedding. Other times dealt with the comings and goings of local residents or their children. And sometimes he simply wrote an interesting little tid-bit about the weather, the crops, or the community.

For example, on one occasion he reflected on the numbers of mice in the area. "Cats, poison, and traps can deal quite effectively with mice on the farm building site," he observed, "but in the field or the 'mice hatchery' we must leave it to nature. Hawks, owls, gulls and eagles are constant workers in our fight against mice... So beware of the 'trigger happy' who drives along the road and picks off our helpers after a hard day's work on our behalf."

Another time he noted that four meadowlarks were still in the district in February. "They live and twitter around the barnyard and take shelter by the cattle feed bunks." However, he reported sadly that one already had fallen victim to "foul play."

As people visited Mr. Perry, they poured over his scrapbooks, remembering little incidents or recalling families who had left the district. Many wished they could sit down and read the whole collection. Now, Mr. Perry has taken a step in trying to oblige all those interested people by taking the first scrapbook and reproducing a limited number of copies for sale. If the interest remains strong, he will follow with Scrapbook No. 2, and continue to publish all nine books as long as there is a reasonable demand. Each set will be punched so they will fit neatly into a binder.

Some pages are faded, because of poor newsprint. Others contain typographical errors, but that's the way they were. Sometimes a bit of scotch tape or glue has added to the discoloration. But the news is there, and the stories are there, just as they once appeared in the local papers. So read, and enjoy.

By Hugh A. Dempsey; in each of the Scrapbooks.

Redvers Perry and his collection: representing two generations of pioneer history.

CHAPTER 50: A HISTORY OF CROSSFIELD AND DISTRICT: *PRAIRIE SOD AND GOLDENROD*

Foreword from the Book:

The tumult of change has ever created a fascinating story. The pages of this book contain the stories of how some 400 families changed a way of life to adapt to a new land, whether it be hostile or benign. It relates the physical struggle and mental conflict experienced while trying to match ambition with reality. There were heroes and villains, fortune seekers and idealists, and countless ordinary men, women and children.

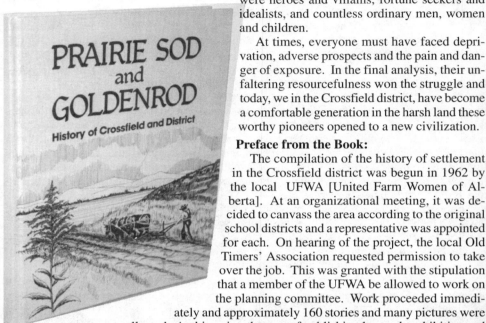

At times, everyone must have faced deprivation, adverse prospects and the pain and danger of exposure. In the final analysis, their unfaltering resourcefulness won the struggle and today, we in the Crossfield district, have become a comfortable generation in the harsh land these worthy pioneers opened to a new civilization.

Preface from the Book:

The compilation of the history of settlement in the Crossfield district was begun in 1962 by the local UFWA [United Farm Women of Alberta]. At an organizational meeting, it was decided to canvass the area according to the original school districts and a representative was appointed for each. On hearing of the project, the local Old Timers' Association requested permission to take over the job. This was granted with the stipulation that a member of the UFWA be allowed to work on the planning committee. Work proceeded immediately and approximately 160 stories and many pictures were collected. At this point, the cost of publishing loomed prohibitive and the venture was abandoned. The material was packed in a box and kept intact for many years.

In 1976, a group of local, interested pensioners decided that Crossfield should publish a history book. The stored material was read and found to contain much valuable information which at this time, would be impossible to obtain. It was decided to make use of this and update the coverage to 1930 instead of 1920 as was originally planned.

Many of these family stories appear as they were written in 1963-64. Some families, still in the district, have requested bringing their stories up to date. This has created some discrepancies as other stories have been terminated at 1930. However, circumstances must always alter cases, and we have conscientiously endeavoured to consider all submissions with due fairness.

Prairie Sod and Goldenrod; published by the Crossfield History Committee, 1977; Printed by Friesen Printers, Altona, Manitoba

CHAPTER 51: THESES AND BOOKS BY STEPHEN WILK

A Bachelor of Divinity Historical Thesis entitled "The United Church of Canada in the Airdrie District"

The following is a synopsis of a historical and sociological study of the United Church of Canada in the Airdrie district. This was a thesis submitted in partial fulfilment for the degree of Bachelor of Divinity [Equivalent now to Master of Divinity, M.Div.] in Union College of  British Columbia, August 1965 (230 pages unpublished). Copies are available at U.B.C. and at St. Stephen's College Edmonton and a microfilm copy at the Glenbow Foundation Library, Calgary, Alberta.

This is a study of a socio-religious organization and how it took root and grew in the Airdrie District, one of Alberta's pioneering communities. We have seen how the environment changed that organization and how the church changed its environment.

The story began with the struggles in the development of the Methodist mission first to the Indians then to the white man. The Methodists were the first Protestant missionaries to come to Alberta. The Presbyterians followed the settlers into the area. In the struggle, white man helped establish law and order, introduced education, and established a church which at first was not accepted by the Indian, but with various adaptations soon captured a dominant role in the establishment of the Indian. The church assisted the Indian through the whole process of settlement of white man.

The vigorous missionary work, educating and preaching of the Rev. Robert Terrill Rundle followed by the robust leadership of the Rev. George and the Rev. John McDougall made a deep seated impression on the life of those to whom they came to minister. They established a church which later became the primary root of the United Church of Canada in the Airdrie district.

In the early phase of development, aid in the form of leadership, money and men was arriving from outside the area under discussion. Even when the Methodist mission was able to be largely self supporting, it was part of a base for further missionary activity reaching other parts of Alberta and the world.

In reaching the Indians, Methodism gave them the opportunity to embrace Christianity. While they did not whole-heartedly accept the new faith, the Indians were prepared by the work of the Methodist church for a comparatively peaceful change from their ancient way of life and religious customs. The white man brought with him such revolutionary changes as industrialization and technological advancements. This revolution did not come without hardship and struggle.

For the benefit of the Indians themselves, Methodists, with a tradition of opposition to the liquor traffic, tried to stir the conscience of Canadians, generally, and of this geographical area in particular. Conscience was roused at first, but eventually it lapsed and efforts from time to time had to be renewed. In later years the United Church continued this opposition in order that there be some control in the use and influence of alcoholic beverages.

To help the Indian for the more complicated life which was to envelop him, education in agriculture, animal husbandry, and academic opportunity were provided in schools at Morley and Red Deer. This helped the Indian to adjust to the advance of settlement when, for example, agricultural developments changed the nature of his livelihood from hunting to farming and ranching.

There were a host of social problems in the early phase of church development to which the Methodist and later the Presbyterian churches addressed themselves. Denominational rivalry, mainly with the Roman Catholic Church, was prevalent in the early phases of establishment of the Church. This was due to divergent theologies competing for the loyalty of the Indian and settler. However, these tensions were overcome in the gigantic task of taming the frontier. Another social problem was the whiskey trade leading to the lowering of moral standards. To these problems the Methodist church led in the movement to have the government send in the North West Mounted Police. Methodists were also instrumental in bringing about the signing of Peace Treaty No. 7 with the Indians and assisted in putting down the Rebellion of 1884-85. There was also a problem of knitting the new founded missions on the frontier with the parent body. However, strong ties were established by the support of the Hudson's Bay Company and the Wesleyan Conference. There was also an increase in communications between church courts of eastern Canada with the west which helped to bridge the gap between the east and west.

Preachers came with the white man during the 1880's and 90's. The lonely life of the rancher, railwayman and farmer who settled in the Airdrie district, was brightened by the visit of the "saddle-bag" preacher, even when at first there may have been simply laughter at the awkwardness of the greenhorn. Both Methodists and Presbyterians followed almost the same pattern of using student ministers during the summer months when it was easier to get around and these men were available.

The Churches recognized how isolated people or ranchers were, so sent students out for the summer months. They were called "sky-pilots" by the settlers. At first the churches did not realize the necessity for sending their best, and they were told it would be better to send none, if not their best. They were given quiet horses which they rode from ranch to ranch, holding services in homes and bunkhouses. Most proved themselves worthy.

Those who were fitted for the life on the frontier remained to see the country fill with people as ranchers became farmers. It was during the Ranching period that the Methodist and Presbyterian churches established their church organization in Airdrie and throughout the province. The Methodist Church had distinct advantage in that it used lay preachers as the main source of manpower. The Presbyterians, on the other hand, were slower to become established due to lack of manpower and did not have as many followers in the Airdrie district. With the work of Methodists like the Rev. John McDougall and the Rev. James Woodsworth, together with a series of ministers who served at the Central Methodist and surrounding rural churches, the spiritual needs of the early settlers at Airdrie were met. Pioneer Presbyterians such as the Rev. James Robertson, the Rev. Andrew Browning Baird, the Rev. Angus Robertson, and the Rev. J.C. Herdman ushered the Presbyterian church into Alberta and to the Airdrie district. These men and other pioneer preachers carried the church over into the next and most expansive stage of development. In this phase the church went out into the country, with, or on ahead of the steel. It was their hope to modify the life of the community, and turn it into channels of right and decency.

Although there was some denominational rivalry in some parts of the early establishment of the Church, the Airdrie district was relatively free of cleavage. Co-operation rather than division was the key-note of settlement. However, because of numerical strength as well as ardent lay and ministerial leadership Methodism was kept the predominant influence. Thus the Methodist Church of Canada drew its heritage.

The mission to the Homesteaders was typified by parallel development of both church and school together with community organization. It was particularly during this period that the Methodist Church, even more than the Presbyterian Church, in the Airdrie district assisted the settlers in re-adjusting to this environment. The church provided the homesteader with a centre of focus in which his highest hopes and aspirations were expressed. It also provided him with a social centre as well as worship centre. The church tried its very best to keep the moral and spiritual tone of the community at a very high level. To this end the homesteader was given considerable assistance.

Ethnic and social class distinctions did not hinder the church from progressing. The Airdrie community was made up largely of people of British origin. Language barriers and racial conflicts were hardly known to affect the life of the Church. Other ethnic groups immigrating to Airdrie were readily accepted.

Both Presbyterians and Methodists assisted in every way possible to help the settlers adjust to the new surroundings. In the face of the hazards of frontier community such as, prairie fires, lack of finances and a multitude of obstacles to which he had to re-adjust, the homesteader found refuge in the worship services which were first held in homes. Then the schoolhouses soon became the neighbourhood worship centre. There was a growing inter-dependence between the community and the church. It was the spirit of the time to share in mutual concerns and co-operate in establishing the pioneering community. The church was considered to be a necessary community enterprise and came in for a good deal of inter-denominational support.

The Methodists, even more than the Presbyterians, gave visibility to the Church in the Airdrie district. While the church was attempting to change its environment, the community was at work changing the church. Starting out with all the trappings of the Canadian or British Methodist organization, the church found that people on the frontier could not, or would not support those features such as prayer-meetings and class-organization on which much of the almost sectarian drive early Methodism depended. Even the forms of early evangelism underwent a radical change and took on a more formal approach during the United Church period of development.

Two World Wars had a profound effect on the church. Young men, potential leaders, were taken from church at a time when they were needed to carry the church farther in its development. Furthermore, the experiences of the wars brought many changes in social and religious attitude to church life at Airdrie. What amounted to church control or domination over community social affairs soon changed as a variety of secular organizations competed for the loyalty and support of the young people in the church. No longer was the church building the centre of community activity. In later years the church began to lose its hold on the community when such organizations as the Home and School, Community Club took a large measure of focus from the church.

Methodism made a major contribution in the Airdrie church development as it was in the "lead". It provided the ground-work for the movement toward the union of the major de-nominations. Such features as co-operation by superintendents, a committee to control com-petition, and actual unions came about, forced by the exigencies of frontier life which saw that no denominational bickering should be allowed to stand in the way of the development of the church in the community. It was common for people of various faiths to fraternize. Methodists and Presbyterians used the same church building for worship at Airdrie before union. Hence, when formal union came in 1925, it was merely a matter of form with a minimum of debate and argument at Airdrie. The spirit of unity which prevailed in the early beginnings of the church continued through the years.

The Methodist organizational arrangement at Airdrie was evolved over the years and although never perfect, it did "work". When union came about there was no major problem in adapting the polity of the United Church of Canada. The strong leadership of laymen in the Methodist Church government tended to carry over into the United Church.

There were three main roots which came into union to form the United Church of Canada at Airdrie. Congregationalism played only a minor role in the United Church while Methodism and Presbyterianism were the most influential. This was due to the fact that these two groups were in the majority. And of these two, Methodism by far out-weighed Presbyterianism in continuing influence on the faith and practice of the United Church at Airdrie. This was mainly evidenced in the vigorous leadership of the laymen who carried on the background training and influence of the fore-fathers. Strong Class leadership in the Church School and mid-week activities, interest in Stewardship programs, and participation in church government were the main features of this influence.

Church services in farm and ranch homes were soon given up in favour of gathering in school houses which were in many cases the focal point of socio-religious activity in the pioneer community. These too, in time, were abandoned due mainly to socio-economic factors which modified the church to suit the needs of the community. Larger school units and centralization created a trend toward consolidation of church worship. Ease of mobility and increased interaction between rural and urban society were major factors contributing to these changes. Through these sociological changes there were many conflicts and antipathies which caused the church to lose ground in some quarters, but it gained in other areas of influence, especially in its ministry to young people.

The Methodist and later the United Church failed in meeting their ideals, yet they did succeed in creating a better atmosphere for young people so far as home and the establishment of tradition were concerned. This was most evident in war and post-war years when disintegration of family life had become apparent. The Epworth League of the Methodist Church and later the Mid-Week activities in the United Church did succeed in developing an active Christian Education program. The effects of the emphasis on the training of the young provided leadership in both church and the secular community. Many outstanding leaders were nurtured in these church youth activities. The stress on Christian Education of the young, altered the emphasis of the church from worship as being the most important aspect of Christian life to an almost secular emphasis on education. Even this emphasis underwent a change to include the need for family education as the recent New Curriculum of the United Church stressed.

Both the Methodist and United Churches were interested in the moral education of their young. Many of the early missionaries gave strong leadership in promoting better education. There was a continuing interest on the part of both ministers and laymen in Temperance education. Besides this concern they took an active part in the leadership of the unpopular cause of prohibition and the prevention of further liquor outlets.

The boom-recession pattern which characterised Alberta's economic life while having negative effects such as poverty, tended to have an integrating rather than disintegrating affect on church life. Depression and hardship brought about increased inter-dependence between families. The church brought to the situation the idealism necessary to give perspective. The church as an institution in the face of poverty, war, disease and the physical elements of environment, changed to a more humanitarian emphasis. It preached more readily the Social Gospel. Such services as the Red Cross, Medical Assistance, Welfare and the general promotion of the Agrarian Revolution [the shift from a homestead-productive economy to highly mechanized, large-scale commercial farming], were some expressions of the change to a more social emphasis that came about in the church. The influence of the church in the Agrarian Revolt [the entry of farmers into the political arena to change the economy and, ultimately, society] is hard to assess. However, both the Methodist and United Church members took part in the establishment of the Progressive Party and the United Farmers of Alberta Government and the short-lived Progressive Party, as well as such groups as the Farmers' Union of Alberta [F.U.A], and the Farm Women of Alberta [F.W.A.], Cooperatives, and other agricultural movements. The influence of the church although indirect, could be seen later in that services of worship were held in conjunction with these movements.

In conclusion we leave this study with the realization that over a century of continuous Christian endeavour has been expanded in the Airdrie district. It is difficult to determine the nature and extent of the influence of the church on the countless hundreds to whom it ministered. However, it is certain that without the leadership and influence of its predecessors the United Church of Canada would not have been the dominant influence in that district, nor would it have given expression to the faith of its forefathers.

Submitted by Stephen Wilk, 1996

Pioneers of the Faith

As the above study was pursued it became apparent after classifying the research material into themes, that there was enough material to begin publishing the themes. The first softcover book, *Pioneers of the Faith*, was produced in 1962, with the assistance of Frank Hawkey. 500 copies were published by the Airdrie United Church. Primarily this book is a thumb-nails sketch and overview of the beginning and growth of the Protestant faith north of the Bow River.

Tom Primrose in his column "Rural Round Up" commented on the book in the March 11, 1962 edition of the *Calgary Albertan*. He wrote: "Primarily the little book is a story of the beginnings and growth of the Protestant faith north of the Bow River. But it evolves into much more than a statistical recording of the growth of the church. Churches and faiths in Western Canada were founded and established by pioneers and their simple beliefs and practices of unselfish neighbourliness. Any story of growth of a pioneer church is the story of the pioneers themselves and the community they created."

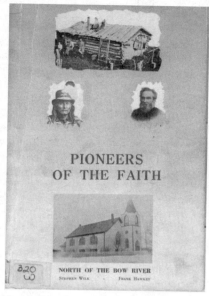

The Story of the Book *One Day's Journey*

A second book, *One Day's Journey,* was published in 1963 and 1500 copies were printed. The inspiration for this book grew out of the fact that for anniversary services at Airdrie, Columbia and Balzac United Churches, a variety of pioneer voices were recorded and played

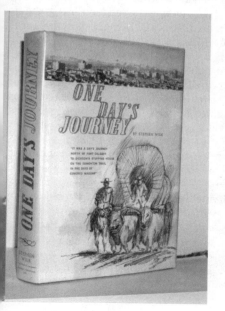

to the congregations. The enthusiasm of the audiences led me to suggest that we sponsor a display of pioneer artifacts in the Balzac Hall.. We called the event "Show and Tell." The variety of relics and photographs in the exhibit of pioneer artifacts inspired us all.

This experience reminded us that in order to obtain first-hand information from pioneers it was necessary to launch into a wider project. I was working on a Bachelor of Divinity (equivalent to a Master of Divinity degree). I began to gather historic information and classify it into topics and chapters. It soon became evident that there was not only enough data to write the thesis, which was accepted and the degree granted by Union College at University of British Columbia, but there was enough material in the file connected with the church growth in the area, that I persuaded the Board of Stewards to publish 500 copies of *Pioneers of the Faith*; these vanished rapidly. When examining the remainder of the chapters in a box of files, it became clear that there was enough data to write the book *One Day's Journey*; the title refers to the time it took to travel north from Fort Calgary to Dickson's Stopping House in the days of the covered wagon. The book covered an area of 900 square miles north of the Bow River. I was assisted by many of the Nose Creek Historical Society members and supporters and the Airdrie Community Improvement Association, who undertook to financially back the first printing of 1500 copies of the book. Needless to say this was a mammoth task, but with the typing skills of Phyllis Bosomworth and Helen Chitwood the manuscripts were made ready for the final editing. Pat Clayton headed up the indexing project with Nellie Pole, and Lillian and Laura Edwards assisting. Many others were encouraging and helpful in bringing this book to fruition. It was said by the *Calgary Herald* to be the first hardcover book printed in the City of Calgary. Previously, books were sent out to other centres to be printed. The book was published in 1963.

Of note is the fact that some forty pioneers were interviewed, and a good portion of them died before the book was published. An example of the urgency to record the reflections of the pioneers can be seen in that Muriel Clayton (nee Mason), the first school teacher north of Fort Calgary, was able to validate the chapter on Education three weeks prior to her passing. Then Dr. Ed Wright was able to validate the agricultural data, while Dr. Frank Collicut supported the documentation of the ranching period and George Church and A.D. Black confirmed the reality of the settlement era information. All these pioneers passed away before or shortly after the book was published.

Around one thousand photographs were submitted for the book project, of which only two hundred could be used. The remainder, together with the artifacts and the pioneer voices recorded on tapes, are preserved by the Glenbow Archives in Calgary under the catalogue listing "Stephen Wilk Papers".

Once the book was ready for distribution a program committee with Dick Clayton as chairman, Redvers Perry, Jack Osborne, and others began to develop the a book launching event.

The program committee wanted to haul a stagecoach load of books from Fort Calgary to Airdrie to re-enact the "One Day's Journey" trip. They looked all over Southern Alberta for a team of horses that were in shape to pull a load. There were plenty of horses on dude ranches and so on, but none were up to the task. The Glenbow Foundation had given us permission to use the old stage coach from the museum to no avail. The next best thing was to ask the Pioneer Auto Association of the city to drive out a load of books. This they happily did on behalf of the sponsoring committee.

The historic lesson which can be learned from the above episode is that when the horse was brought into the west, soon the buffalo disappeared...then when the tractor took over agricultural duties from the horse the work horses disappeared...now modern technology has taken over and we can cover the distances alluded to in "One Day's Journey" in a few minutes or seconds.

By popular request, plans are underway to publish a second edition of *One Day's Journey*. We are told it is one of the most commonly referenced books in the Calgary Central Library , especially by schoolchildren, senior citizens and researchers.

Submitted by Stephen Wilk, 1996

"A Critical Analysis of Metropolitan Mission Strategies for the Calgary Presbytery of the United Church of Canada"

Stephen Wilk's Dissertation for the degree Doctor of Ministry (D. Min), San Francisco Theological Seminary, was completed in 1978. It was a study of the Calgary Presbytery from a historic perspective, analyzing mission strategies in order to understand the dynamics of United Church organization from Biblical, theological, sociological and practical perspectives. Historically the Nose Creek Valley was part of the Calgary Presbytery of the United Church.

HISTORICAL

PROGRAM

Above, left: Bob Edwards, Mayor of Airdrie, greets guests. **Above right**: Howard Wright, chairman for the evening and Gladys Martinusen at the piano.

Above: the cover of the program reflects the old and the new.
RightA section of the audience at the book launching. Members of the Pioneer Auto Club of Alberta were also in attendance.

A contemporary dance formed part of the Roaring 20's skit held as part of the launching ceremony.

Joan Baxter, accompanied by Mrs. Neil on the piano, does a solo.

Clem Perry makes a presentation to a troupe of Indian dancers.

Stephen Wilk presents a copy of his book, **One Day's Journey**, to Phyllis Bosomworth in recognition of the contribution she and Helen Chitwood (not in picture) made to the book.

425

Above, left: Calgary Herald, dateline November 23, 1963. Rev. Stephen Wilk and Economy Bookbinder Vice President, Bob Mackie, check copies of book, One Day's Journey, scheduled for dispatch to prominent Canadians. The history book is believed to be the first to be bound in Calgary.
Above, right: Memories of bygone days are stirred by a pioneer skit. **Below**: Stoney Indians perform a ritual chicken dance.

Left: The Editor of the book receives a specially bound edition of the book along with other presents as a token of appreciation. **Above:** Hugh Dempsey receives a copy of the book on behalf of the Glenbow Foundation.

CHAPTER 52: *MY NEIGHBOURS AND YOURS*: PUTTING A HUMAN FACE ON HISTORY

My Neighbours and Yours, by Edith M. Woolliams, is a collection of articles which she had published in various newspapers, most of them based on interviews with oldtimers in the area. It is full of fascinating stories which add human faces and feelings to the plain historical facts. As Edie wrote in her foreword:

...When talking to newcomers and children they often think all the settling was done hereabouts hundreds of years ago and that there are no pioneers left.

At community gatherings it is a pleasure to see the delight in old friends and neighbours greeting each other, hearing them reminisce, listening as they tell of their families and the way it is and was.

While the community of the Municipality of Rocky View was still recognizable as it was or years, where many people still know folks throughout its seventeen thousand square miles, neighbours really, I thought I would attempt a little different way of securing some of their experiences in a friendly visit...

My Neighbours and Yours by Edith M. Woolliams 1916-1985

Clack, Clack, Clack. We remember that sound ever so well, resonating each day and late into the evening, in the old bedroom designated for our Mum's writing.

It is difficult to specify exactly when Edith Woolliams' writing career began; rather, it

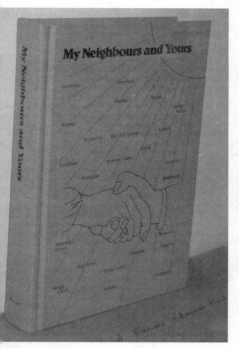

was something that she just always did. From poetry and other writing contests as a child growing up in small towns; to a long-awaited University teaching course and then teaching at Westbrook and Ogden schools; to a book on the history of the Calgary Girl Guides entitled *Boots, Tents, and Miniskirts*; to a weekly column in the Airdrie and area newspaper; to radio broadcasts and magazine articles; finally to a culmination of all her hard work: a book of her own.

Mum wanted to leave something for the next generation by writing about the rich heritage of this community. As she stated, "I enjoy writing, and pioneers should be recognized before they're all forgotten." For most of the pioneers she interviewed, it was the first time their story had been told, as often they did not realize the significance of their own lives. The profiles that did evolve are a legacy for everyone who sees the past disappearing, the landscape changing, faces fading away.

We wonder how she managed to gather everything together, as we now too have our own families and struggle to find time to do all the necessary chores and activities, let one pursue our own careers. But when we see the smiling face of a grandchild who looks so much like his or her ancestors, yet who never knew them, we realize the value of these works.

My Neighbours and Yours was unique among the many pioneer books launched. Edie, as she was often called, financed the publishing of the book herself, for her goal was not one of

427

monetary profit. Instead, she sacrificed her time, talents and money to record history for generations to come. Her book had its traditional launch on December 12th, 1982 at the Beddington Hall. Entertainment and addresses of congratulations preceded the auctioning of the first book. It was purchased by Henry Ole, a long-time resident of the area, who graciously bid $132.50.

An enormous amount of time and energy was required to initially record all of the memories on tapes, (which are now located in the Glenbow Museum Archives in Calgary), get photographs and finally transform the words into stories. Over six years, all the family became involved, whether driving, proof-reading, or designing the front cover, which incidently symbolizes rays of sunshine radiating out from the hands of pioneers, based on a photograph of Mr. and Mrs. J. Evans. (See illustration of book cover.) Edith's husband of over 29 years, Harold, passed on in 1984. Our dad had always worked with her, quietly beside her.

It is only now, some 14 years after the completion of this momentous task, and 11 years after the passing of our mother, that we can pick up a copy and sit down and enjoy reading all of the heritage that is now held so tangibly in our hands. And still, when the house is quiet, and the children are sleeping, we can hear the clacking of the typewriter keys, long into the night. Her legacy is with us always.

Books can be purchased by contacting either of Edith's daughters, Susan Brezinski or Sharon Woolliams.

Submitted by Susan Brezinski and Sharon Woolliams, 1996

*Edith Woolliams (second from left, partially hidden), author of **My Neighbours and Yours**, was one of the newspaper writers honoured in 1981.*

bove left: *Harold and Edith Woolliams with daughters Sharon and Susan*
bove right: *At the launching of **My Neighbours and Yours**, Grant, Sharon, Anita and Susan.*

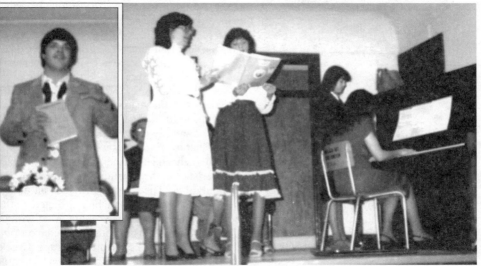

Above: *At the launching of My Neighbours and Yours, the choral group comprising Beatrice & Gerrit Vanden Dool, Doris and Theresa Butler.*
Inset*: Murray Jones auctions book #1.*

Harold and Edith Woolliams are honoured at the Book Launching, December 12, 1982, Beddington Hall.

429

CHAPTER 53: *ACRES AND EMPIRES*—HISTORY OF A MUNICIPAL DISTRICT

This is a history of the Municipal District of Rocky View #44 published by the Rocky View Municipal Council. Tracey Read was commissioned to research and write this 394-page history book, and it was dedicated on October 16, 1983.

In her foreword, Tracey Read reminds us that a century prior to the launching of this edition, C.P.R. tracks reached "the rough collection of tents and frame buildings that was

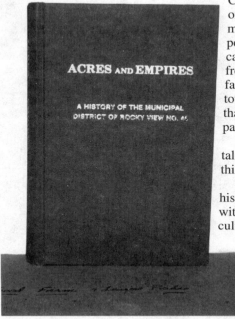

Calgary" and that this event ushered in the era of settlement which made possible the development of the municipality, which had reached a population of 16,000 by 1983. She also indicates the scope of this books historic coverage from settlement of the land, breaking of the land farming and ranching, to the developments of towns and the city of Calgary, the centre of focus that made the district around which the municipality was formed.

The typographical, geographical, environmental and aesthetic features of the area covered by this history are outlined in her own literary style.

The book encompasses the various stages of historical development. The first chapter deals with the pre-settlement period, including native culture before the Hudson's Bay Company received a charter for the area in 1670. It also points out that early traders and explorers helped to forge the Canadian West and make settlement possible in the Calgary area.

Chapter Two deals with immigration and settlement and describes the variety and characteristics of the squatters, ranchers and early settlers who formed the basis of the region's population. The chapter provides an understanding of the immigration and settlement policies and challenges which affected settlement. We also see the impact of European civilization upon this pioneering region with its multicultural and ethnic mosaic, portrayed with substantive illustrations. The chapter outlines the evolution of service centres such as Balzac, Beiseker, Bottrel, Bragg Creek, Chestermere Lake, Cochrane, Crossfield, Dalemead, Dalroy, Delacour, Indus, Irricana, Kathyrn, Keoma, Langdon, Madden, Mitford, Sampsontown, Shepard, and the several sidings of the railroad. All of these sustained the rural and agricultural economy.

The ranching period is outlined in Chapter Three, which depicts the challenges to development of the many pioneer ranches. It describes the various styles and methods of ranching, giving the reader an appreciation of ranch life with all its vicissitudes.

Farming as a way of life is reflected upon in Chapter Four. Here Read gives us an appreciation of farming from early homesteading to the present. We see how methods of farming changed in response to technological advances, and how farmers formed co-operatives in order to deal with the economic realities and challenges of marketing their produce. This chapter gives a thumbnail sketch of various farm adaptations developed to cope with the challenges of farming, including irrigation, which played a major role in enhancing production.

Rural lifestyles are portrayed in Chapter Five, entitled "Hearths and Homes". Here we are given an appreciation of architectural styles and designs of pioneers' homes and barns examples such as sod shacks, log homes, and modern wood-frame homes are illustrated

Utilities such as telephones, electricity, a water supply, and ice for refrigeration are among the features of lifestyle described.

Chapter Six tells of the common sorrows and challenges such as weather uncertainties, destructive forces of wind, blizzards, hail, wars, and the various coping mechanisms employed by farmers and ranchers as they faced those elements of nature and human nature.

"The Development of Community Life" in Chapter Seven deals with many organizations, and the role of men and women in social interactions in the neighbourhoods, a saliant feature of community cohesiveness. Schools and churches played a significant role in family and community development. This chapter also places emphasis on the importance of social life and the place of inter-cultural activities on the neighbourhood lifestyle. The spectrum of events such as dances, parties, rodeos, and community gatherings helped to keep the community knit together. Support systems such as medical and public health services and other municipal-supported services were important to fostering healthy community life.

Finally, Chapter Eight outlines the development of the Municipal Government, its evolution, services, responsibilities, administration of government policy, building and maintenance of roads, land use planning and supervision, and handling of a variety of municipal issues are outlined.

In all, this book is a comprehensive history of one of Alberta's municipalities in a dynamic part of the province and provides the student of history, researchers and public generally with important perspectives in understanding of the heritage of our province. This book helps to preserve important information for generations to follow.

Submitted by Stephen Wilk, 1996

SW view of the present M. D. of Rocky View No.44 administrative building. It stands on the eastern slope of the Nose Creek drainage basin. The Nose Creek waters continues southward to join the Bow River in Calgary City Center. (For a history of the growth and development of M. D. of Rocky View No. 44 see pages 345-354, **Acres and Empires** by Tracey Read 1983).

CHAPTER 54: *FURTHER READING ON NOSE HILL*

1.   *A POPULAR GUIDE*: Edited by Beryl Hallworth

The "Natural Areas Group" is part of the Calgary Field Naturalists' Society (C.F.N.S.) It was formed in 1972 to explore the natural areas of Calgary and collect data on plants birds, insects, mammals, etc., with a view to publishing our observations. The Group was organized by Dr. Charley Bird, and he was enthusiastically supported by members of the

CFNS. Two books were published, one in 1973 and one in 1974, entitled *Natural Areas o, Calgary*. The 1973 book had three editors. In 1975, on Calgary's Centenary, we published a different type of book, with all of our data in simplified form and illustrated. *Calgary's Natura Areas: A Popular Guide*, edited by Peter Sherrington, was very popular. In 1981 we published a comprehensive account of most of Calgary's natural areas; there were now fourteen areas instead of the five counted in 1973. This book was edited by Harold Pinel.   •

In 1985 Wayne Girich suggested that we should write a book on Nose Hill, another "Popula Guide". About twenty people were involved, and Mary Dover wrote the Foreword. The book's format followed that of our previous books; it began with an Introduction, followed by an article "A Geological View of Nose Hill" by Dex Allen, with illustrations by Elizabeth Allen. There were sections showing geological changes across the Bow Valley, from Broadcast Hill to Nose Hill and a separate diagram showing how the Cordilleran Icesheet from the west and the Laurentian Icesheet from the east converged on Nose Hill.

This was followed by an article on "Archaeology and History of Nose Hill and Nose Creek" by Beryl Hallworth, with several references and suggestions for Further Reading listed at the end of the chapter. *One Day's Journey* by Stephen Wilk was one of these.

Gordon Kerr wrote on "Habitats", dealing with aspen groves, ferns, mushrooms, lichens and mosses, with an Illustrated Glossary to explain botanical terms. Peter Allen, a graphic artist, prepared the drawings for publication. "The Flowering Plants other than Grasses" were described by Beryl Hallworth and Gordon Kerr. This chapter was illustrated by Elizabeth Allen, as was "Grasses", written by Linda Cole and Cathy Osborne. "Mushrooms o Nose Hill" were described by Bob Danielson of the University of Calgary's Mycolog, Department; again "Liz" drew the illustrations.

The chapters on "Lichens" and "Mosses" were written by Max Capen, and Harold Pine of the Inglewood Bird Sanctuary wrote on "Skippers and Butterflies". Elizabeth Allen also illustrated the latter chapter; we were very grateful for all the work she put in!

Don Stiles wrote a detailed account of the Birds of Nose Hill, describing the residents winter visitors, summer visitors, and migrants. We were very lucky to have the illustration executed by Peter Karsten, Director of the Calgary Zoo, now retired.

The final chapter, about "Mammals", was by Herta Przeczek. Eighteen kinds of mammals have been observed on Nose Hill; one of them, the lynx, has only been seen once Again, we were lucky to have drawings by Peter Karsten.

Wayne Eirich was our talented photographer - he photographed the Prairie Crocus on th cover (a good selling point!) and 12 of the coloured photographs at the back of the book. Two pictures, the Buffalo Rubbing Stone and the Tipi Ring, were provided by Dave Elphinstone, another talented photographer. The book includes a large map of Nose Hill.

Jim Posey was the Design Editor, and the general layout of the book owes much to him. He suggested we have the little "icons" at the head of every chapter; these are tiny drawings to illustrate the subject, eg, an Indian arrowhead for the Archaeology and History chapter, a bird's head for the chapter on birds, and so on. We were glad to have the friendly cooperation of our typesetter, Eileen Eckert.

The Natural Areas Group meets on the fourth Wednesday of every month at our home in University Heights. Laura Oakander is now one of our strongest supporters; she has sold about 1000 Nose Hill books! Don Stiles is our Chairman and gives up a great deal of his time keeping up with news of the various natural areas in Calgary. Some, like the Douglas Fir Trail, Tom Campbell's Hill, and the Elbow Valley Trail, now have their own groups looking after them, but we keep in touch with these groups who are "carrying on the good work." The "Friends of Nose Hill" are a strong group, and work very hard in their efforts to protect the natural areas of the hill.

After our Natural Areas Group had been writing the chapters of the Nose Hill book for about 3½ years, it was ready to be published. By good fortune, the Calgary Field Naturalists' Society published the book in 1988 - just when the future of Nose Hill was being hotly discussed. A political Task Force of six people had been set up with members from Edmonton and Calgary. It seemed that after nearly 18 years of fighting for a Nose Hill Park, there was a chance that it might be achieved. The Task Force worked very hard to reach a settlement with the developers, and to everyone's surprise, managed to obtain $13 million from the Alberta Government and $13 million from Calgary City Council, so that the land on the hill could be bought outright. It was a wonderful moment when we heard the news!

The fact that our book was published at this crucial time was sheer chance, but it undoubtedly had an impact, and we were all very thrilled when Nose Hill Park became a reality. When we started lobbying for the Park in 1972, the entire hill was owned by developers, just waiting to move in!

Our book has sold very well, and can be obtained from most bookstores. Laura Oakander supplies the stores in Northeast Calgary, and I also have many copies for sale. The book has already been reprinted twice, so we are all happy about that.

Redvers Perry of Balzac, a leading member of the Nose Creek Historical Association, was a great help to me when I was writing the chapter "Archaeology and History of Nose Hill and Nose Creek". He gave me many historical articles that he had written, which are acknowledged under the heading of Further Reading.

Nose Hill Park is the largest urban park in Canada - this is not generally realized. It is a lovely natural area, 300 feet above the city of Calgary, in view of the Rocky Mountains. There are aspen groves, south-facing slopes with lovely wildflowers including the Prairie Crocus, and prairie grasslands with many coulees. There are many birds, and interesting mammals add variety to the wildlife. Calgarians are very lucky to be able to enjoy Nose Hill Park.

Submitted by Beryl Hallworth, 1996

2. *Exploring Nose Hill: A Hands-On Field Guide.* **By Jill Kirker and Diana Kary**

This brand new field guide is aimed at helping elementary school children to explore scientific and historical aspects of Nose Hill Park, with an emphasis on environmental concerns. The guide describes the plants, wildlife, and geology of the park, using many helpful illustrations and maps. It discusses issues in park management, including the effects of people in the past and present.

The six habitats of the park include previously cultivated grasslands, with plant species that were originally introduced by settlers, and an abandoned gravel quarry. The more natural habitats are the native fescue grassland, the shrubs in coulees and ravines, aspen groves, and wetlands. Characteristic plants and animals tend to be found in each habitat.

The field guide describes walking tours of six areas on the hill which include environmental and historical themes. There are visits to tipi rings and other sites used by native peoples who lived in the area for some 8000 years before Europeans came. Visitors can note stone piles made by settlers clearing land, or imagine what it would be like to live in a tipi on Nose Hill.

This excellent book will help to teach children how people change and affect their environment, as well how the environment has changed and affected the history of people in the area.

Submitted by Valerie Jobson, 1996

"Nose Hill Park: Book delves into history of grassland sanctuary"

Exploring Nose Hill Park should be as easy as 1-2-3. And now, thanks to the work of two local supporters, it can be.

Jill Kirker and Diana Kary have just completed Exploring Nose Hill, a hands-on field guide to the sprawling urban park located at the north end of the city.

The book has been distributed to all Calgary elementary schools as a curriculum guide for teachers to take classes on field trips to the park. Study topics in the guide range from prairie conservation through to resource management and endangered species.

The guide covers all aspects of the park from its wildlife to plant life. It even takes time to explain several of the issues surrounding the park. "Nose Hill has so many issues surrounding it these days," said Kirker. "Some feel the park is for them. Others feel the park is for the wildlife; while some feel it should be shared."

Their book is geared for school-aged children, with six walking tours forming the basis of the book. There are sections on natural history, wildlife, plantlife, winter in the park, pond activities and park management. "We worried about it becoming too voluminous," said Kirker. "But it has paid off, because it's so comprehensive."

The guide explains in detail how a teacher can plan a field trip into the park, what is needed and how much time should be allocated. Each trip comes with activities that can be completed at home or in the classroom.

"For the teachers who are comfortable with an outdoor trip, this will allow them to do it themselves," said Kirker, who along with Kary are members of the Grassroots N.W. Environmental Awareness Society. "It's far cheaper than other field trips out of town."

Kirker says many people don't think of Nose Hill Park when they think of ecosystems and wildlife, yet the park is home to a wealth of natural resources. "Nose Hill is one of the largest reserves of native fescue grassland left," explained Kirker. "We are fortunate the city has left the land as a natural area park."

"Alberta Education has updated its curriculum this year to include more science," said Kary. "We gave a session at the annual Calgary Board of Education's teacher symposium and the teachers were climbing over the tables to get their hands on the book."

The park's animal life is illustrated throughout the book by local artist Nancy Hansen.

The book is also extremely up-to-date. The new dog leash laws which were recently implemented in the park are also explained in a section. A glossary of terms is included in the back to help explain difficult terminology to young people.

The book is stocked at Calgary Public Library branches for the public to read. The book was made possible through grants from the Alberta Eco-Trust, Bare Bones Publishing, Friends of the Environment Foundation and Grassroots N.W. Environment Awareness Society.

Article by Sasha Nagy in *Calgary Herald Neighbours*, 1996

CONCLUSION TO PART VI

The historical books and theses described here help to build a composite picture of the people who have worked to preserve their history for generations to come. The variety of interests and viewpoints demonstrate that no single presentation of historical data can give a definitive and complete picture of a large area's history. Together, however, a variety of historical writings can start to build a comprehensive picture of the history of an area, as the works described above do for the Nose Creek Valley.

CONCLUSION TO THIS ANTHOLOGY

The *Gage Canadian Dictionary* defines "anthology" as "A collection of poems or prose selections from various authors and it is derived from Latin and Greek; *anthos* means "flower", and *legein* means "to gather". In this book, our flowerbed is a collection of historical vignettes arranged into a pattern of variegated blooms, which reflects the story of *One Hundred Years of Nose Creek Valley History.*

The stories were written mainly by descendants of pioneers and persons involved in the present-day life of the Nose Creek Valley region. They have provided firsthand experience as well as reflections on the dynamic growth and development of a significant area of Alberta and Canada's heritage and culture.

At the outset we have seen how a small group of dedicated and highly motivated citizens recorded, marked, preserved and celebrated their historical roots. The Nose Creek Historical and Museum Societies supplied the driving force to preserve their history and make it live.

The Nose Creek geological corridor was formed over thousands of years by the last Ice Age and its meltwaters. This resulted in the valley's unique topographical and geographical features which attracted the native peoples, following the buffalo herds, for at least 8000 years, as well as the recently arrived fur traders, ranchers and settlers.

Part Three contains a variety of themes depicting many historical, sociological and socioeconomic elements, which combine to tell the story of pioneer days and early settlement life in the Nose Creek Valley. The historic importance of these developments were appreciated by those who helped form the present-day matrix of the region, and by their children.

Changes in rural and urban lifestyle patterns, with attendant technological advancement radically altered the face of the Valley. Industrialization, provision of goods and services, social and religious needs, together with modernization all played a role in forming present-day society in the Valley. The population growth of two cities had a profound effect on the area surrounding them. These growth trends have created tensions between rural and urban societies and their lifestyles, presenting a challenge to the historic sense of community and identity.

Varied and changing features of community life and economic development are reflected upon in Part Five. It describes many support systems which helped early pioneers and later farmers and ranchers to cope with the challenge of surviving in the natural and economic environment of the Valley. The vignettes show the reader the interplay between people and institutions which helped to create a sense of community and local identity.

Several books, theses, and collections of papers and artifacts have made important contributions in recording and preserving the Valley's history for present and future generations. To assist researchers and all those interested in pursuing further studies of the Nose Creek Valley and nearby districts, we have reviewed a number of major sources of information, as well as endnotes and a bibliography.

In the final analysis, we hope that this anthology will help present and future inhabitants of the Valley to retain their sense of identity and community, and will allow amateur and academic researchers to develop an in depth understanding of the Valley, its history and its people.

Photo Credits

CODE:
AB = Anniversary Bulletin
ABM = Alberta Beef Magazine
ACC = Alberta Cattle Commission
ACCVBS = Artists Concept Courtesy Virginia Boulay Studios
ACN = Amoco Canada News
AD = Advertisement
AV = Aerial View
AWP = Alberta Wheat Pool
B = Brochure
BCF = Benzing Charlebois Furs
BLT = Bottom Left
BRT = Bottom Right
BT = Bottom
CAAR = Co-op Association Annual Report
CB = Centennial Brochure
CCH = Calgary Co-op History
CE = Canadian Encyclopedia
CELB = Celebration Brochure
COB = Canadian Oxy Brochure
CR = Centre
CRN = Canadian Rodeo News
CRT = Centre Right
CSB = Calgary Stampede Brochure
DT = Delivery Truck
ED ARROL = The Late

FC = Foothills Creamery
FCF = First Choice Furrier
FCHP = Fort Calgary Historic Park
FVW = Five Village Weekly
GA = Glenbow Archives
GAM = Grain Academy Mural
GL = Glenbow Library
GM = Glenbow Museum
GEORGIA JARVIS = The Late
GR&PS = Golden Rod & Prairie Sod
GTBS = Gretna Green Tourist Brochure Scotland
IN = Insert
JHS = Jewish Historic Society
LLT = Lower Left
LM = Luxton Museum
LRT = Lower Right
LRT = Lower Right
LT = Left
LTBM = Left Bottom Middle
LTTPM = Left Top Middle
MC = Mayhood Collection
MLT = Middle Left
MRT = Middle Right
MSMS = McDougall Stoney Mission   Society
NA = Glenbow Library
NADP = Northern Alberta Dairy Pool

NCHS = Nose Creek Historical Society
CVM = Nose Creek Valley Museum
n.d. = No Date
ODJ = One Day's Journal
OMCPD = Original Mural Calgary Postal Depot
PAC = Public Archives of Canada
PAOA = Provincial Archives of Alberta
PC = Private Collectors
pg = Page
PMT = Premier Meats Technology
POF = Pioneers of the Faith
PSR = Postal Service Report
RCL = Royal Canadian Legion
RMBR = Rino M. Basso Ranch
RT = Right
R&M = Riley & McCormick
SAIT = Southern Alberta Institute of Technology
SAL = Stockmen's Association Library
TIS = Top Insert
TLT = Top Left
TP = Top
TPR = Top Right
WBS = Western Brokers Service
WHC = Western Heritage Centre
WSGA = Western Stock Growers Association

PG	PHOTO	PHOTO CREDIT	YEAR TAKEN	PG	PHOTO	PHOTO CREDIT	YEAR TAKEN
PART I	CHAPTER				5	F. Walker	1992
5	1	F.Walker	1994			CHAPTER 2	
	2	F. Walker	1974	20	1	City of Airdrie	1996
	3	Alice Hays	1992	21	1-3	C.R. Perry	1988
	4	C.R. Perry	1985		4	NCVM	1986
6	1-10	NCHS	n.d.	22	1-2	NCVM	n.d.
7	1	F. Walker	1992		3	Nick Visser	1996
	2	F. Walker	1991		4	NCVM	1988
	3-5	F. Walker	1992		5	NCHS	1996
	6	F. Walker	1991	23	1-2	NCHS	1996
8	1	F. Walker	1995		3	F. Walker	1992
	2-3	NCHS	1996		4-5	NCHS	1996
	4-5	F. Walker	1992	24	1	L. Perry	1982
9	1	C.R. Perry	1975		2	NCVM	1989
	2-3	F. Walker	1974		3	NCVM	1992
	4	C.R. Perry	1976		4-5	NCVM	1989
10	1	C.R. Perry	1988		6	Gwen Copley	1988
	2	C.R. Perry	1981	25	1	Julian Fell	n.d.
	3	C.R. Perry	1979	26	1	Julian Fell	n.d.
	4	C.R. Perry	n.d.	27	1-3	NCHS	1996
11	1	Ed Arrol	1974	28	1-3	NCHS	1996
	2	C.R. Perry	1974	29	1	FVW Vol.14 No.40	1988
	3	C.R. Perry	1977			CHAPTER 3	
12	1	L. Perry	1967	30	1	NCHS	1996
	2	F. Walker	1976	33	1-8	Rino Basso	1996
	3-4	Ed Arrol	1974		PART II	CHAPTER 4	
13	1	C.R. Perry	1968	38	1	Desmond Allan	1996
	2	C.R. Perry	1974	39			
	3-4	C.R. Perry	1968	40	1	ELizabeth Allen	1996
14	1	F. Walker	1996			CHAPTER 5	
	2-3	F. Walker	1992	44	1	Indians of Alta. By Hugh Dempsey	1979
	4	NCHS	1996				

PG	PHOTO	PHOTO CREDIT	YEAR TAKEN
45	1	NA 1654-1	1886
	2	NA 790-1	1880's
	3	E. NIX	1880's
	4	NA 973-8	1890
	5	NA 3412-2	1881
	6	PAC	1848
	7	NA 1700-156	1926
	8	NA 249-78	1874
	9	Hugh Dempsey	n.d.
46	10	NA 13-1-63	1884
	11	NA 896-1	c.1886
	12	Hugh Dempsey	n.d.
	13	GA Curtis Plate 642	1926
47	1	LM ODJ	n.d.
PART III		**CHAPTER 6**	
51	1	Ranchmen's Club	
		Donald S. Harvey	
		Peter Saunders	1996
52	1	Rino Basso	1996
	2	Calgary Sun	
		Jim Wells	1994
54	1-2	Ranchmen's Club	
		Donald S. Harvey	
		Peter Saunders	1996
55	1-3	WSGA Tamie Dyck	1996
	4	ABM	n.d.
	5	C.R. Perry	1961
60	1	CSB	1996
	2	CB	1974
	3	PS&GR	c.1930
	4	Stampede Brochure	1996
	5	GAM Georgia Jarvis	1996
61	1	Can. Rodeo News	c.1978
	2	Stampede Flier	c.1995
	3	PS&GR pg 323	n.d.
	4	Stampede Flier	c.1995
62	1	MC PC	1906
	2	Ranchmen's Club	1890
	3	NCHS	1996
	4-6	Ann Hollands	1996
		CHAPTER 9	
67	1	Ed Arrol	1975
	2	POF	1962
	3	NCHS	1996
	4	PS&GR pg 15	
68	1-5	Ed Arrol	1975
71	1	L. Perry	1996
	2	Boyd Waddell #68712-D	1979
		CHAPTER 10	
72	1-6	MSMS Historic Booklet #1	1996
		CHAPTER 11	
76	1	CB	1977
	2	C.R. Perry	1973
	3	NA - 40	1877
	4	F. Walker	1985
		CHAPTER 12	
83	1-2	Glenbow Library	n.d.
	3	C. Hansen	1929
	4	ODJ	
		Allan F. McQuarrie	1962
	5	C. Hansen	1935
	6	ODJ	
		Allan F. McQuarrie	1962
84	1	L. Perry	n.d.
	2	Marilyn McCall	c.1971
	3	Ed Arrol	1975
	4	C.R. Perry	1941
	5	Browarny Photo Graphics Ltd.	1995
	6	C.R. Perry	1943
	7	C.R. Perry	1988
		CHAPTER 13	
91	1	Ed Arrol	1976
	2-3	NCHS	1996
	4	NCHS	1987
	5	C.R. Perry	1987
92	1-2	NCHS	1979
93	1-2	NCHS	1996
	3	PSR	1995
	4	NCHS	1996
94	1	NCHS OMCPD	1996
97	1	CE By Hurtig	1985
98	1-6	NCHS	1996
99	1-8	Glenbow Archives	n.d.
101	1	NCHS	1996
102	1	C.R. Perry	1962
	2	C.R. Perry	1938
	3	NA 1162-3	c.1891
		CHAPTER 15	
103	1	C.R. Perry	1962
	2	C.R. Perry	1975
	3	F. Walker	1987
	4	F. Walker	1992
	5	C.R. Perry	1992
	6	Computer Image	1996
104	1	POF Map pg110	1962
105	1	NA 1274-12	
	2	NA 2769-1	
	3	NA 98-11	
	4	NA 354-32	
	5	NA 614-32	
	6	NA 789-107	
	7	NA 235-2	
	8	NA 354-12	
		CHAPTER 16	
108	1	CB	1982
109	1	C.R. Perry	1940
	2-3	C.R. Perry	1935
	4	C.R. Perry	1951
	5	C.R. Perry	1962
	6	C.R. Perry	1933
	7	C.R. Perry	1940
	8	C.R. Perry	1935
110	1	C.R. Perry	1946
	2	C.R. Perry	1972
	3	C.R. Perry	1985
	4-6	C.R. Perry	1988
	7	C.R. Perry	1985
	8	C.R. Perry	1987
111	1	City of Calgary	1996
112	1	C.R. Perry	1994
	2	C.R. Perry	n.d.
	3	C.R. Perry	1994

PG	PHOTO	PHOTO CREDIT	YEAR TAKEN
	4-6	NCHS	1996
113	1	ODJ pg 19	
		CHAPTER 17	
116	1	C.R. Perry	1939
	2	C.R. Perry	1936
	3	Ranchmen's Club	
		Peter Saunders	1889
117	1	NCHS Grain Academy	1996
	2	C.R. Perry	1981
	3	F. Walker	1983
	4	GR&PS pg 312	c.1904
		CHAPTER 18	
120	1	CELB	1985
	2	Airdrie Brochure	1987
	3	CELB	1907
	4	Airdrie Echo	1984
		CHAPTER 19	
123	1	CELB	1985
	2	Dorothy Tilleman	n.d.
	3	CELB	1985
	4-5	Dorothy Tilleman	n.d.
	6-7	CELB	1985
124	1	C.R. Perry	1951
	2	C.R. Perry	1961
	3	C.R. Perry	1948
	4	C.R. Perry	1946
	5	NCHS	1996
	6-7	Dorothy Tilleman	n.d.
		CHAPTER 20	
127	1	CELB	1986
128	1	NA 483-4	1909
	2	NA 1259-18	c.1907
	3	NA 2812-3	c.1914
129	1	Rino Basso #60	1996
	2	F. Walker	1986
	3	POF	c.1872
		CHAPTER 21	
134	1	Rino Basso	1996
135	1	NA 5315-1	n.d.
	2	NA 2848-1	
		Hugh Dempsey	1973
	3	NA 237-7	c.1893
	4	NA 664-1	c.1880
	5	NC 29-43	n.d.
		CHAPTER 22	
147	1	F. Walker	c.1908
	2	ODJ	c.1899
	3	PS&GR pg 336	c.1903
	4	PS&GR pg 341	1976
	5	ODJ pg 304f	
		Mrs. M. Sampson	c.1904
	6	F. Walker	c.1970
		CHAPTER 23	
158	1	POF pg 47	c.1903
	2	Rino Basso #19	1996
	3	CELB	c.1906
	4	F. Walker	1980
	5	POF pg 82	c.1913
	6	CELB	1969
		CHAPTER 24	
164	1	NCHS	
		Wm. Machattie	1990
	2	CELB	1990

PG	PHOTO	PHOTO CREDIT	YEAR TAKEN
	3	F. Walker	1990
165	1	CSB	1996
	2	GGTBS	1996
		CHAPTER 25	
167	1	F. Walker	1991
168	1	NA 3320-8	1890
	2-4	CELB	1991
		CHAPTER 26	
170	1	Arlene Olson	1992
	2	F. Walker	1992
171	1	Mrs. Northcott	1992
172	1	Doris Evans	1992
173	1	Bill Miller	1992
	2	Lorne Fowler	1992
174	1	F. Walker	1992
	2	C.R. Perry	1987
		CHAPTER 27	
180	1	NA 1367-74	n.d.
	2	NA 935-1	n.d.
	3	NC 43-12	n.d.
	4	NA 2083-6	n.d.
	5	Len Esler	1933
		CHAPTER 28	
189	1-4	Tony Cashman	1972
		CHAPTER 29	
193	1	F. Walker	1990
195	1	C.R. Perry	1962
	2-6	NCHS GAM	
		Georgia Jarvis	
		CHAPTER 30	
196	1	NCHS	1996
	2	Hunts Photography	
		CalgaryB8:386-2	1978
	3	David Ching	
		Photo Calgary	
	4	L. Perry	1996
PART IV		**CHAPTER 31**	
203	1	Crossfield Brochure 1996	
		CHAPTER 32	
241	1-2	Marilyn McCall	1984
242	1	City of Airdrie	1996
	2	NCHS	c.1907
	3	Marilyn McCall	c.1970
243	1	Marilyn McCall	1988
	2	Marilyn McCall	1982
	3-6	Marilyn McCall	1988
	7	Marilyn McCall	1996
	8	Marilyn McCall	c.1985
	9	Marilyn McCall	c.1987
244	1-10	Marilyn McCall	n.d.
	11	Margit Davy	1946
245	1-10	Marilyn McCall	1996
246	1-2	Marilyn McCall	n.d.
	3-4	Marilyn McCall	1986
	5-6	Marilyn McCall	1975
	7	Marilyn McCall	n.d.
	8	Marilyn McCall	1969
247	1	Marilyn McCall	1977
	2-4	Marilyn McCall	n.d.
	5	Marilyn McCall	1982
	6	Marilyn McCall	1967
	7-8	Marilyn McCall	n.d.

PG	PHOTO	PHOTO CREDIT	YEAR TAKEN
		CHAPTER 34	
	1-2	2511-2 C.R. Perry	1979
	3	C.R. Perry	n.d.
	4	Ed Arrol	1979
	5	C.R. Perry	1981
	6-7	F. Walker	1979
		CHAPTER 35	
254	1	Mrs. N.B. Pole	c.1907
	2-9	Hospital Brochure	
		CHAPTER 36	
259	1	Jean F. Tener University Archives	1991
260	1	Jean R. Tener University Archives	1956
	2	Jean F. Tener University Archives	1960
	3	Jean F. Tener University Archives	1972
	4	Jean F. Tener University Archives	1987
261	1	PAOA 81.149/274	1922
	2	SAIT 75th History pg 28	1966
	3	SAIT Archives	c.1945
	4	SAIT 75th History pg 43	1984
	5	SAIT 75th History pg 56	1985
	6	SAIT 75th History pg 22	1956
	7	PAOA 81.149/131	n.d.
	8	PAOA 81.149/80	1920
262	1	MRC	n.d.
	2	MRC	c.1960
	3	NA 2448-1	n.d.
	4	MRC N87-33-18	1972
263	1	Map - GL	1883
264	1	Map - S. Wilk 1978	1884-1976
265	1	Map - City of Calgary	1995
266	1	City of Calgary	n.d.
	1	City of Calgary	1996
26	3	City of Airdrie	1996
PART V			
272	7	C. Hansen P.C.	c. 1921-42
273	5	C. Hansen P.C.	c. 1921-42
275	3	D. McKinnon P.C.	c. 1995
276	3	D. McKinnon P.C.	c. 1995
278	1	A.C.C.V.B.S.	1995
	4	Stan Church P.C.	1986
280	LT	Jobson Family P.C.	n.d.
	RT	Jobson Family P.C.	c. 1933
281	8	Jobson Family P.C.	n.d.
282	1	Woolliams, Edith "MY NEIGHBORS & YOURS" pg. 425	1982
283	1	Leonard Esler P.C.	1948
284	1	GA M2382BR/C212A	1936
		CHAPTER 38	
286	2	Gordon Bussey P.C.	n.d.
294	3	A.W.P. Brochure	n.d.
295	TP 3	A.W.P. Brochure	n.d.
295	BT 2	A.W.P. Brochure	n.d.
296	TP 1	GA Calgary	n.d.
296	BT 1	GA Calgary	n.d.
		CHAPTER 39	
298	1	Redvers Perry P.C.	1939
299	16	Brochure W.B.S.	c. 1995
300	IN1	DT W.B.S.	A1980
300	2	AV W.B.S.	n.d.
300	3	AV W.B.S.	n.d.
300	4	Staff W.B.S.	1978
300	5	Staff W.B.S.	1994
		CHAPTER 40	
302	1	J.H.S.	c. 1936
303	TP 1	D. Tilleman P.C.	c. 1982
303	LT 1	D. Tilleman P.C.	n.d.
303	CR 1	D. Tilleman P.C.	n.d.
303	RT 1	D. Tilleman P.C.	1879
304	8	D. Tilleman P.C.	n.d.
305	8	D. Tilleman P.C.	c. 1935-44
307	1	J.H.S.	1919
308	4	C. Raines P.C.	c. 1994
309	1	C. Fowler P.C.	n.d.
311	3	C. Fowler P.C.	n.d.
312	7	C. Fowler P.C.	n.d.
313	7	C. FOWLER P.C.	n.d.
314	TP 1	Ranchmen's Club	c. 1908
314	BT 1	Ranchmen's Club	Late 1800's
317	TLT1	Alice Hays P.C.	1996
317	1	Left 2,3,4 & Rt OF 4 Balzac Meats P.C.	n.d.
318	TP6	N.C.H.S.	1996
318	BT3	PMT AD.	c. 1996
319	TP1	P.J.M. Palleson P.C.	1942
319	BT1	ALta Cattle Com.	1988
330	TP1	P.J.M. Palleson P.C.	c. 1913
330	BT1	P.J.M. Palleson P.C.	n.d.
331	TP1	P.J.M. Palleson P.C.	c. 1920
331	BT1	P.J.M. Palleson P.C.	1915
332	TP1	Cobpitts Ranch P.C.	c. 1939
332	CR1	RMB P.C	1996
332	BT1	RMB P.C.	1996
		CHAPTER 41	
333	2	N.A.D.P.	n.d.
334	4	N.C.H.S.	1996
335	6	N.C.H.S.	1996
336	4	N.C.H.S.	1996
336	LRT1	FC P.C.	1996
		CHAPTER 42	
337	1	Conroy Family P.C. CH. 1165-1	n.d.
338	TP1	Conroy Family P.C.	1975
338	1	2nd Left Conroy Family P.C.	1945
338	1	3rd Right Conroy Family P.C.	1945
338	1	4th Right Conroy Family P.C.	1945
338	BT1	Conroy Family P.C.	1945
339	1	Conroy Family P.C.	n.d.
339	1	Conroy Family P.C.	n.d.
339	CR1	O.D.J. pg. 385	c. 1956
339	BLT1	Conroy Family P.C.	1991
339	BRT1	Conroy Family P.C.	1979
342	7	N.C.H.S.	1996
343	3	Lawland Gardens	c. 1980
344	8	N.C.H.S.	1996
345	3	N.C.H.S.	1996
347	4	N.C.H.S.	1996
348	5	A.T.C.O.	n.d.
349	2	A.T.C.O.	n.d.
350	2	A.T.C.O.	n.d. 1964

PG	PHOTO	PHOTO CREDIT	YEAR TAKEN
353	RT1	Amoc	1993
353	CR1	Amoc	n.d.
353	CRT1	Amoc	n.d.
353	1	Lt & RtT ACN	1977
354	1	D. Tilleman	1989
355	IN1	COB	n.d.
355	TP	COB	n.d.
355	1	Redvers Perry	1973
355	1	Redvers Perry	1973
355	1	Redvers Perry	1973
355	1	Redvers Perry	1988
355	1	Redvers Perry	1961
356	1-6	Petrogas Brochure	n.d.
358	BT1	S. Wilk P.C.	1988
359	LT1	E.Donoghue P.C.	1996
359	RT 1	FCF	1996
359	5	BCF	1996
360	TP	R&M	1905
360	BT	N.C.H.S.	1996
361	1-9	N.C.H.S.	1996
361	BRT1	Jobson Family P.C.	1918
CHAPTER 43			
363	TP 1	Leighton Perry P.C.	n.d.
369	1	CCH	1981
372	BT 1	Leighton Perry P.C.	1982
373	1-3	N.C.H.S.	1996
374	TP 1	J.P. Photos	1973
374	BT 1	CAAR	1995
CHAPTER 44			
378	BT !	RCL	n.d.
379	ALL 1	F.B. Walker	c. 1940
379	ALL1	F.B. Walker	1993
379	ALL 1	F.B. Walker	1941
379	ALL 1	F.B. Walker	1994
379	ALL 1	F.B. Walker	1991
380	TP 1	Airdrie Legion	n.d.
380	CR 1	Airdrie Legion	n.d.
380	BT 1	Airdrie Legion	n.d.
381	TP 1	Chapelhow Legion	1988
381	LT1	Chapelhow Legion	1993
381	RT1	R.M. Basso	1996
381	BT 1	Chapelhow Legion	1996
385	BT 1	Airdrie Lions Club	1968
386	1-6	Ranchmen's Club	c. 1894
387	1-3	Ranchmen's Club	1953
388	1	Ranchmen's Club	1975
CHAPTER 45			
394	TP 1	4H Club History	1959
395	TLF2	4H Club History	1959

PG	PHOTO	PHOTO CREDIT	YEAR TAKEN
395	TRT1	Balzac 4H Club	1956
395	CRT1	Balzac 4H Club	1964
395	BT1	Balzac 4H Club	1964
CHAPTER 46			
400	TLT1	Ranchmen's Club	c. 1912
400	TRT1	Ranchmen's Club	1996
400	3	Ranchmen's Club	1912
401	1- 3	N.C.H.S.	1996
402	1	P.J.M. Pallesen P.C.	1936
403	MRT1	Calgary Stampede	1994
403	BT 1	P.J.M. Pallesen P.C.	1936
404	TLT1	Calgary Stampede	1934
404	TRT1	Calgary Stampede	c. 1912
404	BT 1	P.J.M. Pallesen P.C.	1936
405	1- 7	SAL	1997
406	1- 8	SAL	1997
CHAPTER 47			
408	TLT1	FCHP	1996
408	LT1	NA"354-1"	n.d.
408	BRT1	NA"3668-27	n.d.
409	1	F.C.H.P. Brochure	1996
409	TPR	Don Molyneaux	1996
409	LTTM	Wendy Aitkens	1996
409	LTBM	Wendy Aitkens	1996
409	RTTM	Don Molyneaux	1996
409	RTBM	Wendy Aitkens	1996
409	1	GA 64.8 Nevitt R.B.	1876
410	4	WHC	1997
411	8	WHC	1997
413	4	M. Flewwellen, Red Deer	1996
PART VI			**CHAPTER 48**
414	1	NCHS	1960
			CHAPTER 49
416	1	NCHS	1996
417	1	Redvers Perry P.C.	1996
			CHAPTER 50
418	1	NCHS	1996
			CHAPTER 51
419	1	NCHS	1996
424	2	NCHS	1996
425	8	S. Wilk P.C.	1996
426	5	S. Wilk P.C.	1996
			CHAPTER 52
427	1	NCHS	1996
429	6	Susan Brezinski P.C.	1996
			CHAPTER 53
430	1	NCHS	1996
431	1	NCHS	1996
	CHAPTER 54		
432	1	NCHS	1996

Museums Related to the Themes within This Book

Source: Directory of Alberta Museums; Alberta Museums Association

✛ **Aerospace Museum**
Hangar 10, 64 McTavish Place N.E., Calgary, Alberta

✛ **Alberta Government Telephones (AGT),**
Vista 33 Museum & View Gallery
33 Floor, 10020-100 St., Edmonton, Alberta

✛ **Alberta Science Centre Centennial Planetarium,**
701-11 St. S.W., Calgary, Alberta

✛ **Alberta Police Service Museum & Archives,**
316-7 Ave. S.E., Calgary, Alberta

✛ **Calgary Zoo, Botanical Gardens & Prehistoric Park,**
1300 Zoo Road N.E., Calgary, Alberta

✛ **City of Calgary Archives**
Main Floor Administration Bldg,
313-7 Ave. S.E., Calgary, Alberta

✛ **Energeum,**
640-5 Ave. S.W., Calgary, Alberta

✛ **Fort Calgary Historic Park,**
750-9 Ave. S.E., Calgary, Alberta

✛ **Glenbow Museum,**
130-9 Ave. S.E., Calgary, Alberta

✛ **Grain Academy (Alberta Wheat Pool)**
Plus 15 Level,
Roundup Centre, Stampede Park, Calgary, Alberta

✛ **Heritage Park Historical Village,**
1900 Heritage Drive S.W., Calgary, Alberta

✛ **Locomotive & Railway Historical Society of Western Canada,**
#4104, 2120 Southland Dr. S.W., Calgary, Alberta

✛ **Museum of the Regiments CFB Calgary,**
4520 Crowchild Trail S.W., Calgary, Alberta

✛ **Nose Creek Valley Museum,**
1701 Main St. South, Airdrie, Alberta

✛ **Petro-Canada Exhibition Gallery**
Petro-Canada Centre, 3 Floor Atrium
150-6 Ave. S.W., Calgary, Alberta

✛ **Sarcee People Museum,**
3700 Anderson Road S.W., Calgary, Alberta

✛ **Stockmens Memorial Foundation,**
(Located in the Western Heritage Centre) Cochrane, Alberta

✛ **The Western Heritage Centre,**
105 River Ave., Cochrane, Alberta

Following is a list of People who contributed articles to this anthology

Alberta Land Surveyors' Association
Aldred, Alice (Oneil)
Allen, Elizabeth
Allen, Desmond
Anderson, Harold
Bannike, Karen
Barker, Gordon
Barker, Mary
Bayrack, Don
Beattie, A.W.
Bedford, Judy
Benedix, Andrew
Bennett, Hugh
Berry, Gerald L.
Bilben, Norma
Blair, Marion
Bowen, Marion
Brezinski, Susan
Brisco Riding Club
Bushfield, Walter
Bussey Seed Farms
Butler, Joyce
Butler, Doris
Canadian Occidental Petroleum
Chalmers, Donnie
Chalmers, Pearl (Stauffer)
Chiakowski, Eugene J.
Church, Alexa
Church, Stan
Church, Dr. R.B.
Church, Rosemary E.
Church, John
Church, Janie
Clayton, Richard
Clayton, Alma
Clayton, Dick
Cole, Marie
Collett, Rev. Dr. W. John
Conroy, M. Gwen
Copley, Don
Copley, Karen
Creasser, Jim

Davy, Margit (Jensen)
Davy, C.J. (Kelly)
Dempsey, Hugh A.
Dodd, Estelle
Donoghue, Eric
Drohan, Paul (article)
Edwards, Lillian
Elliot, Peggy
Evans, W.H.
Evan, Doris
Faith Community Baptist Church
Fowler, Lorne
Gablehouse, Brian
Geekie, Stewart
Giles, Margaret
Hallworth, Beryl
Hansen, Charlie
Harris, Catherine (Spalding)
Hays, Alice
Hays, Spencer
Heritage Advisory Board, City of Calgary
Hickley, Mary
Hollands, Ann
Howden, Ray
Ingram, Jennifer
Jobson, Herb
Jobson, Valerie
King, Margaret
Law, Gerald
Leinweber, Joy
Lorimer, Heloise
Malyk, Kay
Martin, Gloria
Mason, Margaret (Wickerson)
Mayhood, S.E. courtesy of Cyril Woolliams
McCall, Marilyn
McCall, Ralph
McCann, Patrick J.
McDougall, Gerald
McHattie, William
McKinnon, Donna
McKinnon, Dan

McKinnon, Dan
Meyer, Eleanor
Miller, Millie
Miller, Bill
Mohr, Greg
Money's Mushrooms Ltd.
Morison, Margaret
Northcott, Ronnie
Northcott, Earl
Olsen, Arlene
Osborne, Jack R.
Pallesen, Peter J.M.
Peach, Jack
Pearson, Bob
Perry, King
Perry, Lois (Church)
Perry, C. Redvers
Perry, A. Leighton
Powlesland, Marion
Rach, Edwin
Raines, Jean
Raines, Chuck
Reynolds, Floyd
Reynolds, Nan

Rush, Margaret
Sandgathe, Ruth L.
Scott, Gavin
Shuttleworth, Kathy
Shuttleworth, Bernice
Stuart, Bob
Taylor, Gladys
Teghtmeyer, Roy
Tilleman, Dorothy
Turner, Sunni S.
Turner, Bobby
Walisser, Joe
Walker, W.H. (Bill)
Walker, Florence (Bigelow)
Wall, Marguerite
Warner, Janet (Perry)
Watson, Allen
Western Breeders
Wilk, Rev. Dr. Stephen,
Wood, Desmond P.
Woolliams, Sharon
Young, Alton
Young, Ross
Zink, Joe

Corporate Supporters and Gifts-In-Kind For The Book Project

Airdrie Echo
Airdrie Lions Club
Alberta Beef Magazine Ltd.
Alberta Cattle Commission
Alberta Historical Resources Foundation
Alberta Museums Association
Alberta N.W. Converence (United Church of Canada) Historical Society
Alberta Wheat Pool
Alderman Bow Hawksworth (Calgary City Ward 4)
Alderman John Schmal (Calgary City Ward 3)
Alpha Graphics Ltd. Imaging Centre
Amaco Canada Petroleum Company Ltd.
ATCO Ltd. & Canadian Utilities Limited (Ron Southern)
A-Zee Printing Ltd. (Calgary)
Balzac Garden Centre

Balzac Meat Processing
Balzac Seed Cleaning Plant
Basso, Rino M. Senior Preservation Advisor Alberta Community Development
Bedford, Judy (Planning Advisor) Historic Site Service Alberta Community Development
Bussey Seeds Farm
Calgary Co-Operative Association Ltd.
Calgary Furriers Benzing Charlebois Ltd.
Calgary Herald
Calgary Sun
Calgary Stampede (Saddle Bag) Network
Calgary Exhibition and Stampede Board
Canadian Occidental Petroleum Ltd.
Canadian Rodeo News
Chinook Country Historical Society
Church Ranches Ltd. (Stanley M. Church)
City Council of Airdrie

City of Calgary
Click Photo Design Incorporated (Peter Saunders)
Devonian Foundation (Donald S. Harvey)
Foothill's Creamery Ltd.
Fort Calgary Historical Park (museum)
Fort Calgary Museum
Fort Regional Museums Co-ordinator (Bob Pearson)
Geo-Syl Enterprises Incorporated
Glenbow Museum (Library and Archives)
Grain Academy (Calgary)
Haley, Carol M.L.A. (Three Hills-Airdrie)
Hansen, Charlie and Family
Hastings, Earl A. The Honorable
Historical Society of Alberta
Kanter & Meckelborg (Drs. of Optometry)
Lab Calgary The (Harvey Mitchell)
Lawland Gardens (Balzac)
MACH II Stock Exchange
The Calgary Western Stock Grower's Association (Calgary)
MacDonald, Dr. Robert J. (Arctic Institute of North America)
McClellan, Shirley Minister (Alberta Community Development)
McDougall Stoney Mission Society
McKinnon (Three Cross Cattle Ltd.)

Moneys Mushroom Great Plains Div. (Airdrie)
Municipal District of Rocky View #44
Nose Creek Valley Museum (Airdrie)
Pallesen, Florence (Mannix)
Pallesen, Peter J.M.
Premier Meats Ltd. (Calgary)
Provincial Museum Library & Book Store
Ranchman's Club (Calgary)
Riley & McCormick Pioneer Western Stores
Rocky View School Division #41
Royal Canadian Legion #288 (Airdrie)
Royal Canadian Legion #284 Chapelhow Branch (Calgary)
Royal Canadian Legion #113 (Crossfield)
Sheep Canada (B&L Publishing) Bert Hancock
Southern Alberta Institute of Technology
Stockmans Memorial Foundation, The (Cochrane)
Tall-Taylor Publishing Ltd. "Rockyview Five Village Weekly" (Irricana)
University of Calgary Archives
Western Breeders Service (Alberta Genetics)
Western Heritage Centre (Cochrane)

Individual Supporters Of The Book Project

Alexander Donald T. & Barbara
Anderson Albert & Evelyn
Anderson Walter & Edith
Becler Demmos & Karen
Benedix Andrew
Bishop Gordon & Shirley
Blair Mrs. Marion
Brewer Deanna
Budgeon Grace
Bushfield Walter & Lucille
Bussey James & Jessie
Church John & Barbara
Church Rae & Peggy
Clark Mrs. Annie
Clayton Alan & Kitty

McCall Mrs Marilyn
McCreary Brian & Dorothy
Meadors Bill & Lois
Meyer Mrs. Eleanor
Meyer Lavern
Miller Bill & Millie
Morison Pete & Bernie
Morris Jim & Lillian
Murdoch Frank
Murdoch Mrs. Grace
Nixon Carroll & Nancy
Northcott Earl & Ronnie
Northcott Mrs. Kathy
Norton Don & Carol
Osborne Jack

Clayton Patricia
Collier Bob & Betty
Copley Don & Karen
Crockett Clarence & Henrietta
Cullen Carol
Davy Mrs. Margit
Edwards Mrs. Opal
Fowler Chester & Rilla
Fowler Lorne
Fraser Miss May
Giles Ross & Margaret
Haase G.R.
Hansen Charlie & Ruth
Hanson Ron & Rene
Hays Mrs. Alice
Holmes Allan & Bea
Hobson Brian & Melanie
Jones Mrs. D. Viola
Kirby Mrs Ellen
Kirby Miss Irene
Lamb Elmer & Betty
Lawson William H. & Erma
Lorimer B.W. (Buzz)
Lubbers Warner & Myrna
Marston Robert & Jean
Marston Roland B.
Massie M. Dale & Beth
Mayhood R.B.

Osterman Joe & Connie
Padzun Jack & Mrs.
Perry J. Kingsley
Perry Leighton & Mary
Perry Redvers & Dorothy
Phillips Al
Pole Mrs. Gerdie
Powlesland Bert & Marion
Raines Chuck & Jean
Reid Mrs. Margaret
Reid Ken & Terrie
Reynolds Floyd & Nan
Snyder Ed & Ruby
Stewart Mrs. Helen
Switzer George
Tilleman Earl & Dorothy
Turner Bobby & Sunni
Tweten Len & Vi
Vanderheide Mrs. Evelyn
Vincent Gordon & Ingrid
Watters Harold & Bernice
Wearmouth Hugh & Vernice
Wigle Harry
Wilk Dr. Rev. Stephen & Reta

Nose Creek Historical Society: Members Over the Years

Alexander Don
Anderson Albert
Anderson Edith
Anderson Evelyn
Anderson Walter
Andvers Arlene
Armstrong George
Armstrong Mary
Barker Mabel
Barr Sylvia
Barr Gordon
Beard Eileen
Beaton Eileen
Beaton Myrl
Beaton Neil
Beattie Kay
Bell Walter
Bell Pearl
Bell Brigetta
Bennett Everett
Bennett Dorothy
Bennett Virginia

Besler Adele
Besler Irvin
Bilben Alfred
Bilben Walter
Blair Gordon
Blair Marion
Blomme Douglas
Bowen Edge
Bowen Marion
Bowhay Agnes
Brewer Deanna
Buchanan Dick
Budgeon Grace
Burnett Pat
Burwash Don
Burwash Vi
Buschkeil Arlene
Bushfield Walter
Bushfield Lucille
Bushfield Fred
Bushfield Allen
Bushfield A.J.

Bushfield Mary
Bushfield A.J. (Mrs.)
Bushfield Faye
Bussey Jessie
Bussey James
Caldwell Carrie
Cameron Grace
Campbell Gladys
Campbell Fred
Cardiff Betty
Carlson Bert
Carlson Margaret
Carpenter Merle
Carstens Doreen
Carstens Jeff
Carswell James
Cary Mary
Cary Paul
Chitwood Ken
Chitwood Doug
Chitwood Helen
Chitwood Ralph

Church Mary
Church Barbara
Church John
Church Charles
Church Peggy
Clapperton Hilda
Clapperton Dick
Clark Annie
Clark Peter
Clayholt Rheo
Clayton Dick
Clayton Margaret
Clayton Harvey
Clayton Cliff
Clayton Elinor
Clayton Alma
Clisdell Emily
Clisdell Bert
Collier Betty
Collier Bob
Colpitts Garth
Colpitts Janet
Cooper George
Cooper Eleanor
Cooper John
Copley Karen
Copley Don
Copley Robert
Copley Gwen
Cornwell Harry
Cowan John (Jock)
Cox Evelyn
Creaser Marilyn
Creaser Jim
Crighton Mabel
Davis W. (Mrs.)
Davis W.
Davy Donald
Davy C.R. (Robby)
Davy Lettie
Davy Margit
Duncan Jack
Duncan Emily
Dunn Annette
Dunn Harry
Echlin Irene
Edwards Lillian
Eitzen Agatha
Ekstrom Dorothy
Ekstrom Paul
Elliott Buster & Peggy

Epp Al
Epp Glenda
Evans Bobby
Evans Doug
Evans W.H.
Evans Jack
Evans Doris
Farish J. (Mrs.)
Farish J.
Farr Lambert
Farr Mary
Farr Myrtle
Farr Gordon
Farr Audrey
Fell F. Julien
Fenyvesis Margarite
Fletcher Gladys
Fletcher Norman
Forsythe Jim
Fowler John
Fowler Grace
Fowler Lorne
Fowler Chester
Fowler Rilla
Fraser Ken
Fraser Gail
Fraser Colin
Fraser May
Gadd David
Gault Betty
Gerlitz Dave
Goett Don
Griffith Arthur
Griffith Lois
Gross June
Hamilton Loreen
Hamilton Hugh
Hand Gerald
Hand Stella
Hanson Les
Hanson Marion
Hardy Fred
Harris Bruce
Harris Joyce
Harron Laurie
Hawkes Bill
Hawkey Margaret
Hawkey Marianne
Hawkey Frank
Hays Alice
Hays Jack

Hehr Dorothy
Heinzig Sarah
Henderson R. (Bob)
Hobbs Grace
Holden Helen
Holden Jim
Hollands Gary
Hollands Ann
Holmes Janet
Holmes Allan
Holmes Madelaine
Holmes Charlie
Holmes Bea
Holmes Dennis
Hupkes Mary
Hupkes Charlie
Jackson Lynn
Jackson Emory
James Earl
James Pearl
James Connie
James Cathie
James Ron
Jenkins May
Jensen Ellie
Jensen Lillian
Jensen Spens
Jobson Valerie
Jobson Herb
Jobson Hazel
Jones Ethel
Jones James
Jones Arnold
Jones Irene
Kerr Carrie
Kierman Irma
Kininmonth Leonard
Kininmonth June (Teddy)
Kinniburgh Edith
Kinniburgh Dave
Kinniburgh Margaret
Kirby Irene
Kirby John
Kirby Jean
Kirby Ellen
Kirby Harry
Kittle Bernice
Klitzke Louise
LaMarsh Wilbur
LaMarsh Trent
LaMarsh Marge

Larson Jim
Law Harvey
Law Joanne
Law Gerald
Lawson Bill
Lawson Erma
Leinweber Bud
Leinweber Jay
Leinweber Joyce
Longeway Fern
Loose Alma
Loose Henry
Lord Ted
Lovely Nellie
Lovely Ellen
Lubbers Warner
Lubbers Myrna
Makal M. Rae
Martin Ernie
Martinusen Milo
Martinusen Gladys
Maxfield Bernadette
May Irene
Mayhood D.
Mayhood E.S.
Mayhood R.B.
Mayhood W.
McCall Marilyn
McCall Ralph
McCreary Brian
McCreary Dorothy
McElroy Jean
McIntyre A.
McIntyre S.
Meyer Eleanor
Meyer Russell
Moen Walter
Morrison Glen
Morrison Margaret
Nesser Tiny
Nesser Fred
Nixdorff J.
Nixdorff Isabel
Nixon Nancy
Nixon Emily
Nixon Carroll
Northcott Ronnie

Northcott Stanley
Northcott Ruth
Northcott Ralph
Northcott Margaret
Northcott Veronica
Northcott Kathy
Northcott Earl
Northcott Charles
Northcott Chester
O'Neil Bernice
O'Neil Joe
Olson Arlene
Oosterhuis Hank
Osborne Merle
Osborne Helen
Osborne Jack
Osborne Bob
Osterman Connie
Perry Redvers
Perry Neil
Perry Dorothy
Perry Leighton
Perry Kingsley
Perry Mary
Pieschel R.J.
Pole R.J.
Pole Eunice
Pole Howard
Pole Marge
Pole John
Pole Harry
Pole R.J. (Mrs.)
Pole Gertie
Porter Agnes
Priest Dave
Priest Isabel
Raafloub Wynonna
Rankin Pat
Reid Jim
Reid Frank
Reid Margaret
Reynolds Floyd
Reynolds Nan
Riches Charlie
Roberts Dave
Roberts Jamie
Roberts Karen

Rogerson Elaine
Rosenberger Ed
Rosenberger Keith
Rosenberger Lois
Rush Margaret
Rush Clifton
Saville Arthur
Saville Nellie
Shuttleworth Grant (Jr.)
Shuttleworth Kathy
Shuttleworth Grant (Sr.)
Sterns Milo
Sterns Vera
Stevenson Anne
Stevenson Jim
Stewart Helen
Tilleman Dorothy
Tilleman Earl
Tocher Bob
Tocher Phyllis
Tubbs Tim (Mrs.)
Tubbs Tim
Turner Bobby
Turner Sunni
Vanderheide Evelyn
Veitch Joyce
Vroom Val
Waite George
Walker Florence
Walker Bill
Warhurst Roy
Warhurst Lynne
Watson Gertrude
Watters Harold
Watters Bernice
Webster Cena
Wilk Reta
Wilk Rev. Dr. Stephen
Williams Madge
Wolsky Tom
Woods Mary
Woods Bill
Woolliams Karen
Woolliams Harold
Woolliams Edith
Woolliams Cyril
Young Jack
Young George

The Making of this Anthology

(The Steps and Stages in the Production of this Anthology)

1. **The Idea** for the production of this book was proposed on November 8, 1994 by the editor on the occasion of receiving a Certificate of Appreciation for his many years of assisting the Nose Creek Historical Society in developing the history of the region.

2. **A Proposal** to have the book published was unanimously approved at the February Annual Meeting of the Society on February 1995. Encouragement was given at the same meeting to have the history book "One Day's Journey" re printed.

3. Several committee meetings developed policy and monitored the development of the book.

4. **A Mission Design** was developed by the editor to include the Goals and Objectives of the Society and the book project. The design included an estimated time-line and preliminary budget goal. These had to be revised as the project unfolded. Based on his professional fund raising experience he also developed a funding campaign with an appropriate brochure which gave interested corporate and individuals an opportunity to donate to the project.

5. **A Grant Application** with appropriate support documents was submitted to the Alberta Historic Resources Foundation and was accepted.

6. **Advertising Campaign** produced a wide interest of support and offers of manuscripts and photographs in telling the story of our heritage. There were two categories of materials for the project; (a) materials volunteered by interested persons and (b) topics assigned by the editor to a cross section of professional and non-professional historians as well as those who had primary historical information.

7. **The Research Phase** involved a study of a wide range of published and unpublished bibliographical information. This included the use of public and private historical collections such as, the University, Glenbow, Calgary Central and Museum Libraries together with private collections such as the Redvers Perry collection.

8. **Interviewing and Collecting** required many miles of travel and interview appointments together with revisits and follow up by telephone, fax and correspondence for verification and obtaining appropriate materials with legal permission in the use thereof.

9. **Photographs were collected** from a broad spectrum of sources such as the Redvers Perry, Ranchmen's Club, Glenbow, Pallesen, Tilleman and many others. A large number of photographs were taken by the editor.

10. **The Style of the Anthology** emerged from the vast collection of materials. It was decided that the materials for the anthology fell into specific themes and the 640 photographs permitted groupings into 200 pages of illustrations of the stories presented in the written text.

11. **Annual Historical Celebration** of twenty four themes provided ready written and illustrated brochures. These were edited and enriched with up-dated materials.

12. **Copyright Protocol** was carefully followed to conform to ownership and copyright laws. All written and quoted material was acknowledged and suitably footnoted. Photographs, maps and illustrations were used by written or verbal permission. Copyright was formally obtained for the publication together with the International Standard Book number (I.S.B.N.) with the publishers prefix. For ease of commercial handling a Bar Code was purchased and appears on the back cover.

13. **Book Sales Advertising** was started through local and provincial news vehicles. As a result over 500 copies of the 2000 first edition were pre-ordered or purchased prior to publication.

14. **As Publisher** the Nose Creek Historical Society engaged a smaller printing company which assisted in promoting small business. This provided a built-in advantage in that every stage of the creation and publishing was monitored by the editor on behalf of the project committee.

15. **Editorial Prerogative** was exercised in the standardizing grammatic and word usage throughout. Bibliographic material was acknowledged and Footnotes included along with an extensive index.

16. **Modern Printing Technology** required considerable updating of knowledge in the publishing and printing aspects of the book. As the printing industry was ushered into the latest high-tech computers for instance, the process language called for the following:

    (a) Camera ready script, maps, charts and illustrations were all done professionally by the use of computers, scanners and tapes.

    (b) Edited manuscripts were produced on compatible micro chip software with hard copies of the manuscripts.

    (c) Editor and publisher provided page making style, formatting, design and layouts with captions for the page maker.

    (d) Photographs were provided for modern scanning techniques. In some cases half-tones or original photographs and illustrations needed to be suitable for reproduction. Thus, assuring proper photo digital synchronization for maximum clarity and ultimate quality of production.

    (e) Proof reading and adjusting at various stages of the process was finalized by the editor and in some cases by other assistance.

    (f) Blue line checking was provided prior to final reproduction and printing process technology.

    (g) Prior to printing a prototype was supplied for approval and size of final product.

17. **Distribution and Sales** strategy had to be developed with proper business procedures of control, storage, audit, and distribution process. Book launching and signings are in process while this book is being printed.

Bibliography:

Unpublished Theses, Pamphlets, Private Papers, Videos
Airdrie Mutual Telephone Company minutes, in the possession of Margaret Carlson.
Balzac Mutual Telephone Company minutes, in the possession of Margaret Rush.
Balzac Rural Electrification Association minutes, in the possession of Margaret King.
Church Ranches. "Premium Water Supply". Pamphlet.
Goldeye Foundation Society. "The Barker Dinner." 1982. Program for a tribute dinner for Gordon Barker, Mary Dixon Barker, and Mabel Belyea Barker.
Head, Thomas. "Springtime at H.M.S. Balzac: Two Millennia of Bison Processing at a Stratified Campsite on the Alberta Plains." (M.A. thesis, University of Calgary, 1986)
Hill, David. Manuscript on the history of Crossfield
J.F. Macleod Family Papers, M776, Glenbow Archives.
Mayhood, Samuel E. "Recollections", in the possession of Cyril Woolliams.
Money's Mushrooms. "The Mushroom Growing Process". Pamphlet.
Nose Creek Valley Historical Society minutes, in possession of the Society.
Nose Creek Valley Museum Society minutes, in possession of the Society.
Perry, C. Redvers. Diaries.
_____. NCHS pamphlets. [Copies in the Local History Room, W.R. Castell Public Library.]
_____. Scrapbooks. [Copies in the Local History Room, W.R. Castell Public Library.]
Perry, C.W. Diaries, in the possession of C. Redvers Perry.
"The Ranchmen's Club" March 1993, Newsletter.
"The Ranchmen's Club: A Slight Historical Sketch" - booklet.
"Red Deer's First School 1887-1987". Red Deer?: sn, 1987. [In the Local History Room at the W.R. Castell Central Library in Calgary.
"A Short History of the Ranchmen's Club: A Light-Hearted Account" a Calgary Centennial Project, 1875-1975 - booklet, 1975
Shetson, I., "Sand and Gravel Resources of the Calgary Area", an open file report accompanied by a suite of maps, prepared for the Alberta Geological Survey, 1981.
Shortt, Mack W. "The Happy Valley Bison Kill." (M.A. thesis, University of Calgary, 1993)
Western Stock Growers Association. "The Great Centennial Cattle Drive 1896-1996." Video.
Wilk, Stephen. "A Critical Analysis of Metropolitan Mission Strategies for the Calgary Presbytery of the United Church of Canada." (Dissertation for Doctor of Ministry, San Francisco Theological Seminary, 1978.
_____. "The United Church of Canada in the Airdrie District." (Bachelor of Divinity thesis, Union College B.C., 1965)
Woods, Alan A., ed. "Petrogas Processing Ltd.: 25th Anniversary 1961-1986" compiled and edited by Alan A. Woods for the 25 Year Coordinating Committee, 1986

Newspapers and Periodicals
Airdrie Echo
Alberta History
Calgary Herald
Carstairs Courier
Community News [Airdrie and District People's Service Council.]
Crossfield Chronicle
Five Village Weekly [now *Irricana/Crossfield Rockyview Five Village Weekly*]
Fort Macleod Gazette
Morning Albertan [Calgary]
News Chronicle [Carstairs: serving Crossfield, Carstairs, Didsbury and districts.]
Prairie Forum
Rocky View Times
Saskatchewan Herald
Tri-Neighbour Press
Wheel and Deal

Reference Works
The Canadian Encyclopaedia, ed-in-chief, James H. Marsh, 4 vols. 2nd ed. Edmonton: Hurtig, 1988
The Canadian Encyclopaedia Plus CD-ROM. Toronto: McClelland and Stewart Inc., 1995.

The *Dictionary of Canadian Biography*, eds. George H. Brown, David M. Hayne, and Frances G. Halpenny, 12 vols. (continuing). Toronto: University of Toronto Press, 1966-.

The Gage Canadian Dictionary, eds. vols. : , 19.

World Book Encyclopaedia. Chicago: World Book, 1997. [Most recent edition.]

Government Publications

Calgary and District Telephone Directory 1903-1919. Microfilm #1 in the Local History Room, W.R. Castell Public Library.

Calgary Regional Planning Commission. *Airdrie: Census Results 1994*.

Canada. *Sessional Papers*. Annual Reports of the Department of the Interior. [includes Dominion Lands, Surveys, Geological Survey, and NWMP]

City of Airdrie. "A Special City Council Meeting". Brochure, 1987.

City of Airdrie. *Lifestyle: City of Airdrie Lifestyle Profile*. Economic Development Department, 1996.

City of Calgary. *1996 Municipal Handbook*.

_____. *Fort Calgary*. Text by Trudy Soby and D. Scollard. Calgary: The City of Calgary, 1978.

Dawson, G.M. "Report on the Region in the Vicinity of the Bow and Belly Rivers, North-west Territory." Montreal, Geological Survey, 1884.

Province of Alberta Historic Sites Service. "The Dickson-Stevenson Stopping House", and "MacPherson Coulee". Articles on wall panels at the Dickson-Stevenson Stopping House by Community Development Display Department, *circa* late 1980's.

Books and Articles

Alberta & Northwest Territories Conference Historical Society of the United Church of Canada. "Pioneer Missionaries Vie for the Loyalty of the West" in *Historic Sites & Archives Journal*, 7:1 (May 1994) pp.1-3, 21.

Anderson, N.R. *Oblate Fathers in Calgary: Roman Catholic Church, 1875-1889*. Calgary: Century Calgary Publications, 1975.

Artibise, Alan F.J. "Boosterism and the Development of Prairie Cities, 1871-1913," in *Town and City: Aspects of Western Canadian Urban Development*. ed. Alan F.J. Artibise. Regina: TheCanadian Plains Research Centre, University of Regina, 1981.

Baker, William M., ed. *Pioneer Policing in Southern Alberta: Deane of the Mounties*. Calgary: Historical Society of Alberta, 1993.

Barss, B.M. *Come 'n Get It: At the Ranch House*. Calgary: Rocky Mountain Books, 1996.

----------. *Come 'n Get It: Cowboys and Chuckwagons*. Calgary: Rocky Mountain Books, 1996.

Beattie, A.W. *Trails in the Sunset: A Tribute to People*. Alberta: Alberta Wheat Pool, 1983.

Beaty, Chester B. *The Landscapes of Southern Alberta*. Department of Geography, University of Lethbridge, 1975.

Bell, N. Fred. *My Fifteen Years with 4-H Clubs: 1944-1959*. Calgary: *circa* 1976.

Berry, Gerald L. *The Whoop-Up Trail: Early Days in Alberta...Montana*. [Applied Arts Products Ltd., 1953] Reprinted as Occasional Paper #29. Lethbridge: Lethbridge Historical Society, 1995.

Berton, Pierre. *The Last Spike: The Great Railway 1881-1885*. Toronto: McClelland and Stewart Limited, 1971.

Bott, Robert. *The University of Calgary: A Place of Vision*. Calgary: University of Calgary Press, 1990.

Breen, David H. *The Canadian Prairie West and the Ranching Frontier: 1874-1924*. Toronto: University of Toronto Press, 1983.

Brodrick, Richard N. "The Great Buffalo Migration" in *Canadian Cattlemen*. December 1939.

Buziak, Kelly. *Taking to the Road: Early Auto Touring and Camping in Alberta*. Wetaskiwin: Friends of Reynolds-Alberta Museum Society and Alberta Culture and Multiculturalism, Historic Sites and Archives Service, 1992

Byrne, T.C. *Alberta's Revolutionary Leaders*. Calgary: Detselig Enterprises, c.1991.

Canadian International Grains Institute. *Grains and Oilseeds: Handling, Marketing, Processing*. 3rd ed. (1st ed. 1973) Winnipeg: Canadian International Grains Institute, 1982.

Carter, Dean David J. "The Early Years of the Church of the Redeemer, Calgary" in *The Anglican Church in Calgary: Church Activities 1878-1974*. Calgary: Century Calgary Publications, 1975.

Cashman, Tony. *Singing Wires: The Telephone in Alberta*. Edmonton: Alberta Government Telephones Commission, 1972.

Chalmers, John W. *Schools of the Foothills Province*. Toronto: University of Toronto Press (for Alberta Teachers' Association), 1967.

Charyk, John C. *The Little White School House*. Saskatoon: Western Producer Prairie Books, 1968.

_____. *When the School Horse Was King*. Saskatoon: Western Producer Prairie Books, 1988

Cochrane & Area Historical Society. *Big Hill Country: Cochrane & Area*. Cochrane & Area Historical Society, 1977.

451

Cormack, Barbara Villy. *Perennials and Politics: The Life Story of Hon. Irene Parlby LLD*. Sherwood Park: Professional Printing Ltd, c.1960s?

Cote, B.D. "What Was Prairie Wool?" Strathmore, Alberta

Cunniffe, Richard. *Calgary in Sandstone*. Calgary: Historical Society of Alberta, Calgary Branch, 1969.

Dempsey, Hugh A. *A Blackfoot Winter Count*. Calgary: Glenbow Museum, 1965.

_____. *The Amazing Death of Calf Shirt, and Other Blackfoot Stories*. Saskatoon: Fifth House Limited, 1994.

_____. *Calgary: Spirit of the West*. Calgary: Glenbow and Fifth House Publishers, 1994.

_____. "The Calgary Edmonton Trail." *Alberta Historical Review*. Autumn edition, 1959.

_____. Ed. *The CPR West: The Iron Road and the Making of a Nation*. Vancouver: Douglas & McIntyre, 1984.

_____. *Crowfoot: Chief of the Blackfeet*. Norman: University of Oklahoma Press, 1972. Reprint. Edmonton: Hurtig, 1976.

_____. *Indian Tribes of Alberta*. 1979. Revised. Calgary: Glenbow Museum, 1986.

_____. "Launching Alberta History". *Alberta History*, 45:1 (Winter 1997).

_____. *Red Crow: Warrior Chief*. Saskatoon: Western Producer Prairie Books, 1980.

_____, ed. "Robertson-Ross' Diary: Fort Edmonton to Wildhorse, B.C., 1872." *Alberta Historical Review*. Summer edition, 1961.

_____, ed. *The Rundle Journals: 1840-1848*. Calgary: Historical Society of Alberta and Glenbow-Alberta Institute, 1977.

Denny, Cecil E. *The Law Marches West*. Ed. W.B. Cameron, 2nd edition. 1939; Toronto: J.M. Dent and Sons, 1972.

Dickason, Olive Patricia. *Canada's First Nations: A History of Founding Peoples from Earliest Times*. Toronto: McClelland & Stewart, Inc., 1992.

Eagle, John A. *The Canadian Pacific Railway and the Development of Western Canada 1896-1914*. Kingston: McGill-Queen's University Press, 1989.

Erasmus, Peter. *Buffalo Days and Nights*. As told to Henry Thompson; edited by Irene Spry. Calgary: Glenbow-Alberta Institute, 1976.

Ewers, John C. *The Blackfoot: Raiders on the Northwestern Plains*. Norman: University of Oklahoma Press, 1958

_____, ed. *The Horse in Blackfoot Indian Culture*. Bureau of American Ethnology Bulletin No.159. Washington, D.C.: Smithsonian Institute, 1955.

Foothills Historical Society. *Chaps and Chinooks: A History West of Calgary*. Vols 1 & 2. Calgary: Foothills Historical Society, 1976.

Foran, Max. *Calgary: An Illustrated History*. Toronto: James Lorimer & Company, Publishers and National Museum of Man, 1978.

_____. "The Making of a Booster: Wesley Fletcher Orr and Nineteenth Century Calgary," in *Town and City: Aspects of Western Canadian Urban Development*. ed. Alan F.J. Artibise. Regina: The Canadian Plains Research Centre, University of Regina, 1981.

Foran, Max, and Sheilagh Jameson, eds. *Citymakers: Calgarians After the Frontier*. Calgary: The Historical Society of Alberta, Chinook Country Chapter, 1987.

Foster, John, Dick Harrison and I.S. MacLaren, eds. *Buffalo*. Edmonton: The University of Alberta Press, 1992.

Fowke, V.C. *Canadian Agricultural Policy: The Historical Pattern*. 1946; Toronto: University of Toronto Press, 1950.

Francis, R. Douglas, Richard Jones, and Donald B. Smith. *Destinies: Canadian History Since Confederation*. Toronto: Holt, Rinehart and Winston of Canada, Limited, 1988. [Several revised editions since 1988]

Francis, R. Douglas, Richard Jones, and Donald B. Smith. *Origins: Canadian History To Confederation*. Toronto: Holt, Rinehart and Winston of Canada, Limited, 1988. [Several revised editions since 1988]

Friesen, Gerald. *The Canadian Prairies: A History*. 1984. Student edition. Toronto: University of Toronto Press, 1987.

Fryer, Harold. *Alberta: The Pioneer Years*. Langley, B.C.: Sunfire Publications Ltd., 1984.

Grant, John Webster. *Moon of Wintertime*. Toronto: University of Toronto Press, 1984.

Gray, James H. *A Brand of Its Own: The 100 Year History of the Calgary Exhibition and Stampede*. Saskatoon: Western Producer Prairie Books, 1985.

_____. *Men Against the Desert*. 1967. Reprint. Saskatoon: Western Producer Prairie Books, 1978.

_____. *The Winter Years*. Toronto: Macmillan , 1966.

Grinnell, George. *Blackfoot Lodge Tales*. 1892. Reprint. Lincoln: University of Nebraska Press, 1962.

Hallett, Mary, and Marily Davis. *Firing the Heather: The Life and Times of Nellie McClung*. Saskatoon: Fifth

House Ltd., 1993.
Hallworth, Beryl, ed. *Nose Hill: A Popular Guide*, Calgary, Calgary Field Naturalists' Society, 1988.
Head, Thomas. "Northern Plains Prehistory: The Late Prehistoric Period as viewed From the H.M.S. Balzac Site (EhPm-34)" in *Contributions to Plains Prehistory*, edited by David Burley. Occasional Paper No.26. Edmonton: Archaeological Survey of Alberta, Historical Resources Division, Alberta Culture, 1985.
Helgason, Gail. *The First Albertans: An Archaeological Search.* Edmonton: Lone Pine Publishing, 1987.
Hickey, Lynn, Richard L. Lightning, and Gordon Lee. "T.A.R.R. Interviews with Elders Program," in *The Spirit of the Alberta Indian Treaties.* ed. Richard Price, pp.103-112. 1979. Reprint. Edmonton: Pica Pica Press, 1987.
Holmgren, Eric, and Patricia M. *2000 Place Names of Alberta.* Saskatoon: Modern Press, 1972.
Holt, Faye. *Alberta: A History in Photographs.* Canmore: Altitude Publishing Canada, Ltd., 1996.
Huel, Raymond J.A. *Proclaiming the Gospel to the Indians and the Metis.* Edmonton: University of Alberta Press & Western Canadian Publishers, 1996.
Hungry Wolf, Beverly. *The Ways of My Grandmothers.* Reprint. 1980. New York: Quill, 1982.
Hurt, Leslie J. *The Victoria Settlement 1862-1922.* Occasional Paper #7. Edmonton: Historic Sites Service, Alberta Culture-Historical Resources, 1979.
Hutchinson, Gerald, and Stephen Wilk, eds. *McDougall Reflections.* Historical Booklet No.1. Calgary: McDougall Stoney Mission Society, 1996
Jackson, Lionel E. Jr., and Michael C. Wilson, eds. *Geology of the Calgary Area.* Canadian Society of Petroleum Geologists, 1981
Jackson, Lionel E. Jr., "The Quaternary History of the Calgary Area" in *Geology of the Calgary Area*, Lionel E. Jackson Jr. and Michael C. Wilson, eds. Canadian Society of Petroleum Geologists, 1981.
Jewish Historical Society of Southern Alberta. "Jewish Cattlemen Remembered" in *Discovery: The Journal of the Jewish Historical Society of Southern Alberta* 7:1 (Winter, 1997)
_____. *Land of Promise.* 1997.
Johnston, Alex, Howard MacDonald, J. Allen Campbell, and Wallace R. Hanson. "Range, Its Nature and Use." Publication #146, Alberta Lands & Forests and Alberta Agriculture. 2nd ed. Edmonton: L.S. Wall, Queen's Printer for Alberta, 1962. [A copy is in the Local History Room at the W.R. Castell Central Library in Calgary.]
Jones, David C., ed. *Empire of Dust.* Edmonton: University of Alberta Press, 1987.
_____, ed., with Nancy M. Sheehan and Robert M. Stamp. *Shaping the Schools of the Canadian West.* Calgary: Detselig Enterprises Limited, 1979.
_____. *We'll All Be Buried Down Here: The Prairie Dryland Disaster, 1917-1926.* Calgary: Alberta Records Publication Board, Historical Society of Alberta, 1980?
Karamitsanis, Aphrodite, ed. *Place Names of Alberta: Volume 2 Southern Alberta.* Edmonton: Alberta Culture and Multiculturalism, 1992.
Kelly, L.V. *The Range Men.* Toronto: Briggs, 1913.
Kirker, Jill and Diana Kary, *Exploring Nose Hill: A Hands-On Field Guide.* Calgary: Bare Bones Publishing, 1996.
Klassen, Henry. "Family Businesses in Calgary to 1939," in *Citymakers: Calgarians After the Frontier.* Max Foran and Sheilagh Jameson, eds. Calgary: The Historical Society of Alberta, Chinook Country Chapter, 1987.
Lamb, W. Kaye. *History of the Canadian Pacific Railway.* New York: Macmillan Publishing Co. Inc., 1977.
Larmour, Judy. *Making Hay While the Sun Shone: Haying in Alberta Before 1955.* Wetaskiwin: Friends of Reynolds-Alberta Museum Society and Alberta Culture and Multiculturalism, Historic Sites and Archives Service, 1992
Lavallee, Omer. "The Approach to the Mountains, 1883." Canadian Pacific Limited display, 1983.
_____. *Van Horne's Road.* Montreal: 1975.
Livingston, Donna. *Cowboy Spirit, Guy Weadick and the Calgary Stampede.* Douglas & McIntyre, 1996.
Long, H.G., ed. *Fort Macleod: The Story of the North West Mounted Police 1874-1904 Royal North West Mounted Police 1904-1920 Royal Canadian Mounted Police 1920 to present time.* Fort Macleod: Fort Macleod Historical Association, 1958.
Lysak-Martynkiw, Ruth. *Homegrown: Vignettes About Manufacturing Agricultural Implements in Alberta, 1890-1955.* Wetaskiwin: Friends of Reynolds-Alberta Museum Society and Alberta Culture and Multiculturalism, Historic Sites and Archives Service, 1992
McClintock, Walter. *The Old North Trail: Life, Legends, and Religion of the Blackfeet Indians.* 1910. Reprint. Lincoln: University of Nebraska Press, 1968.
McDougall, G.M. *Teachers of Medicine: The Development of Graduate and Clinical Education in Calgary.* Calgary: University of Calgary Printing Service, 1987.
McDougall, G.M. and S.C. Harris. *Medical Clinics and Physicians in Southern Alberta.* Calgary: University of Calgary Printing Service, 1991.

McDougall Stoney Mission Society. *McDougall Reflections: The Future of the Indians of Canada.* Prepared by Gerald Hutchinson and Stephen Wilk. Calgary: McDougall Stoney Mission Society, 1996. [John McDougall's speech was first published in 1905]

McDougall, John. *Opening the Great West.* Calgary: Glenbow-Alberta Institute Historical Paper No. 1, 1970.

_____. *Pathfinding on Plain and Prairie.* Toronto: William Briggs, 1898.

_____. *Saddle, Sled and Snowshoe.* Toronto: William Briggs, 1896.

MacEwan, Grant. *...And Mighty Women Too: Stories of Notable Western Canadian Women.* Saskatoon: Western Producer Prairie Books, 1975

_____. *Between the Red and the Rockies.* [First pub. University of Toronto Press, 1952] Saskatoon: Western Producer Prairie Books, 1979.

_____. *Blazing the Old Cattle Trail.* Saskatoon: Modern Press, 1962.

_____. *Fifty Mighty Men.* Saskatoon: Western Producer Prairie Books, 1958.

_____. *The Sodbusters.* Toronto: Thomas Nelson, 1948.

MacGregor, James G. *A History of Alberta.* Edmonton: Hurtig, 1972.

_____. *Blankets and Beads: A History of the Saskatchewan River.* Edmonton: Institute of Applied Art, c.1949.

_____. *Father Lacombe.* Edmonton: Hurtig Publishers, 1975.

_____. *Vision of an Ordered Land: the Story of the Dominion Land Survey.* Saskatoon: Western Producer Prairie Books, 1981.

Macleod, R.C. *The North West Mounted Police and Law Enforcement 1873-1905.* Toronto: University of Toronto Press, 1985.

MacPherson, Ian. *Each For All: A History of the Co-operative Movement in English Canada, 1900-1945.* Toronto, 1979.

Martin, Chester. *"Dominion Lands" Policy.* Canadian Frontiers of Settlement series. Toronto: Macmillan Co. of Canada Ltd., 1938.

Millar, Nancy. *Remember Me as You Pass By.* Calgary: Glenbow, 1994.

Millar, Rob and Nancy. *A History of the Calgary Co-op* or *Calgary Co-op: The First Twenty-Five Years.* Saskatoon: printed by Modern Press, 1981

Milton, Viscount, and W.B. Cheadle. *The North-West Passage by Land.* London: Cassell, Petter and Galpin, 1865.

Moir, Sean. *Perilous Journeys: Early Motoring in Alberta.* Wetaskiwin: Friends of Reynolds-Alberta Museum Society and Alberta Culture and Multiculturalism, Historic Sites and Archives Service, 1992.

Morris, Alexander. *The Treaties of Canada With the Indians.* Toronto: Belfords, Clarke & Co., 1877, reprint 1966.

Morton. A.S. *History of Prairie Settlement.* Toronto: Macmillan, 1938.

Morton, Desmond, and Glenn Wright. *Winning the Second Battle: Canadian Veterans and the Return to Civilian Life 1915-1930.* Toronto: University of Toronto Press, 1987.

Myers, Patricia. *When the Whistle Blows: Steam Threshing in Alberta.* Wetaskiwin: Friends of Reynolds-Alberta Museum Society and Alberta Culture and Multiculturalism, Historic Sites and Archives Service, 1992.

_____. *Facing the Land: Homesteading in Alberta.* Wetaskiwin: Friends of Reynolds-Alberta Museum Society and Alberta Culture and Multiculturalism, Historic Sites and Archives Service, 1992.

Nelson, Chris. "The Growth of a Legend" in *Calgary Stampede.* Calgary: Calgary Stampede, 1994.

Nesbitt, Leonard. *Tides in the West.* Saskatoon: Modern Press, c.1962.

Nix, James Ernest. *Mission Among the Buffalo.* Toronto: The Ryerson Press, 1960.

Nose Creek Book Committee. *The Nose Creek Story from 1792.* Calgary: Nose Creek Community, 1961.

Overholser, Joel. *Fort Benton: World's Innermost Port.* Helena: Falcon Press, 1987.

Owram, Douglas R. *The Formation of Alberta: A Documentary History.* Alberta Records Publication Board, Historical Society of Alberta, 1979.

Palmer, Howard and Tamara. *Alberta: A New History.* Edmonton, Hurtig Publishers, 1990.

_____, eds. *Peoples of Alberta: Portraits of Cultural Diversity.* Saskatoon: Western Producer Prairie Books, 1985

Peach, Jack. *Days Gone By: Jack Peach on Calgary's Past.* Saskatoon: Fifth House Ltd., 1993.

_____. *The First Hundred Years: The History of the Calgary Chamber of Commerce.* Calgary: Calgary Chamber of Commerce, 1990.

_____. *Thanks For the Memories.* Saskatoon: Fifth House Publishers, 1994.

Pearson, Bob. "March West...To Whoop-Up Country: Fort Whoop-Up, Fort Macleod and Fort Calgary" for Fort Regional Museums, Alberta.

Ray, Arthur J. *I Have Lived Here Since The World Began: An Illustrated History of Canada's Native People.*

Toronto: Lester Publishing and Key Porter Books, 1996.

_____. *Indians in the Fur Trade*. Toronto: University of Toronto Press, 1974.

_____. *The Canadian fur Trade in the Industrial Age*. Toronto: University of Toronto Press, 1990.

Read, Tracey. *Acres & Empires: A History of the Municipal District of Rocky View No. 44*. Printed Irricana: Tall-Taylor Publishing, *circa* 1983.

Red Deer District Local A.T.A. No. 24. *Schools of the Parkland*. Red Deer: circa 1966.

Reeves, Brian O.K. "Six Millenniums of Bison Kills." *Scientific American*. 249(4) (October 1983).

Roe, Frank Gilbert. *The North American Buffalo: A Critical Study of the Species in its Wild State*. (1951). 2nd ed. Toronto and Buffalo: University of Toronto Press, 1970.

Royal Tyrrell Museum of Palaeontology. *The Land Before Us: The Making of Ancient Alberta*. Red Deer: Red Deer College Press, 1994.

Sanders, Harry. "Calgary Timeline" in *Centennial City: Calgary 1894-1994*, Donald B. Smith, ed.

Schmidt, Joanne. "Chester Fowler" in *Sheep Canada*, Summer 1995.

Sharp, Paul. *Whoop-Up Country: The Canadian-American West 1865-1885*. 2nd ed. Helena, Montana: Historical Society of Montana, c.1960.

Sherrington, Peter, ed. *Calgary's Natural Areas: A Popular Guide*. Calgary: Calgary Field Naturalists' Society, 1975.

Silverman, Eliane Leslau. *The Last Best West: Women on the Alberta Frontier 1880-1930*. Montreal: Eden Press, 1984.

Smillie, Benjamin G. *Visions of The New Jerusalem: Religious Settlement on the Prairies*. Edmonton: NeWest Press, 1983.

Smith, Donald B., ed. *Centennial City: Calgary 1894-1994*. Calgary: University of Calgary, 1994.

Snow, John. *These Mountains Are Our Sacred Places: the Story of the Stoney People*. Toronto: Samuel Stevens, 1977.

Spry, Irene. "The Tragedy of the Loss of the Commons." In *As Long as the Sun Shines and Water Flows*, ed. Ian A.L. Getty and Antoine S. Lussier, pp. 203-228. Vancouver: University of British Columbia Press, 1983.

Thomas, L.G. *Rancher's Legacy: Alberta Essays by Lewis G. Thomas*. ed. Patrick A. Dunae. Edmonton: University of Alberta Press, 1986.

Thompson, Don W. *Men and Meridians: The History of Surveying and Mapping in Canada*. 3 vols. Ottawa: Information Canada, 1967, reprint 1972.

Thompson, John Herd. *The Harvests of War: The Prairie West, 1914-1918*. Toronto: McClelland & Stewart Ltd, 1978.

Tingley, Kenneth, ed. *For King and Country: Alberta in the Second World War*. Edmonton: Provincial Museum of Alberta, 1995.

_____. *Steel and Steam: Aspects of Breaking Land in Alberta*. Wetaskiwin: Friends of Reynolds-Alberta Museum Society and Alberta Culture and Multiculturalism, Historic Sites and Archives Service, 1992

Treaty 7 Elders and Tribal Council with Walter Hildebrandt, Dorothy First Rider and Sarah Carter. *The True Spirit and Original Intent of Treaty 7*. Montreal & Kingston: McGill-Queen's University Press, 1996.

Turner, John Peter. *The North-West Mounted Police 1873-1893*. 2 vols. Ottawa: King's Printer, 1950.

Van Kirk, Sylvia. *Many Tender Ties: Women in Fur-Trade Society in Western Canada*. Winnipeg: Watson & Dwyer, 1980.

Voisey, Paul. *Vulcan: The Making of a Prairie Community*. Toronto: University of Toronto Press, 1988.

_____. "Boosting the Small Prairie Town 1904-1931: An Example from Southern Alberta," in *Town and City: Aspects of Western Canadian Urban Development*. ed. Alan F.J. Artibise. Regina: The Canadian Plains Research Centre, University of Regina, 1981.

Warrack, Allan A. "The Development of Rural Gas Distribution Systems in Alberta". Bulletin 22, General Information. Edmonton: Dept of Rural Economy, Faculty of Agriculture and Forestry, University of Alberta: 1981.

Wilk, Rev. Dr. Stephen. *One Day's Journey*. Calgary: printed by Alcraft Printing Limited, 1963.

_____. *Pioneers of the Faith*. Calgary: The Albertan Job Press, 1962.

Wilson, Barry. *Beyond the Harvest: Canadian Grain at the Crossroads*. Saskatoon, 1981.

Wilson, C.F. *A Century of Canadian Grain: Government Policy to 1951*. Saskatoon, Western Producer Prairie Books, 1978.

Wilson, L.J. "Educational Role of the United Farm Women of Alberta" in *Shaping the Schools of the Canadian West*, edited by David C. Jones, Nancy M. Sheehan and Robert M. Stamp.

Woolliams, Edith. *My Neighbours and Yours*. Calgary: Printed by Friesen Printers, 1982.

_____. *Boots, Tents, and Miniskirts*.

Endnotes

One history book can never tell the whole story. Much more research can be done on topics mentioned in this book. The Glenbow Archives and other archives contain historical documents which tell fascinating stories. There is a growing collection of academic and popular publications about our history in Canada and Alberta. These endnotes provide a sampling of the sources available to anyone who wishes to do further research.

The endnotes name the sources of information used in writing each article, and give suggestions for further research, using the title and the author's name. The full reference is in the Bibliography, sorted into types of sources and then listed by the last name of the author or editor. The references follow the same order for each chapter: first, citations for quotations and specific information; then general references used in writing the article; then explanatory notes, if any: finally, suggestions for further research.

Some good general sources for Canadian history include *The Canadian Encyclopedia*, in the printed version or the CD; and the *Dictionary of Canadian Biography*. General histories of Canada include *Origins: Canadian History to Confederation* and *Destinies: Canadian History Since Confederation*, both by R.Douglas Francis, Richard Jones, and Donald B. Smith. General histories more specific to Alberta include *The Canadian Prairies: A History* by Gerald Friesen, *A History of Alberta* by James G. MacGregor, and *Alberta: A New History* by Howard and Tamara Palmer. The journal *Alberta History* contains articles on many aspects of Alberta's past, and *Prairie Forum* focuses on the prairie provinces.

Major sources for the history of the Nose Creek Valley include *One Day's Journey* by Stephen Wilk, *The Nose Creek Story* by the Nose Creek Book Committee, and *My Neighbours and Yours* by Edith Woolliams.

INTRODUCTION

p.xii about the naming of Deerfoot Trail: Hugh Dempsey, *The Amazing Death of Calf Shirt*, pp.168-

185; about the naming of Nose Hill and Spy Hill: Stephen Wilk, *One Day's Journey*, pp.116-119.

Further Reading: Wilk, *One Day's Journey*, Chapter 7, "What's in a Name?" pp.101-122, gives the origins of other local names. See also *2000 Place Names of Alberta* by Eric and Patricia M. Holmgren; *Place Names of Alberta: Volume 2 Southern Alberta*, edited by Aphrodite Karamitsanis.

PART I: CELEBRATING THE HISTORY OF NOSE CREEK VALLEY
CHAPTER 1: NOSE CREEK HISTORICAL SOCIETY

p.1 information about Alberta historians and Glenbow: Howard and Tamara Palmer, *Alberta: A New History* pp.339-40, 308.

p.1 books by Stephen Wilk: described in Chapter 50 of this book.

p.2 about *The Nose Creek Story*: see Chapter 47 of this book.

p.2 "...December 13th, 1960 - Fair..." from 1960 diary of C. Redvers Perry.

p.2 "...Saturday April 4th 1970 - Fair..." from 1970 diary of C. Redvers Perry.

p.3 it was Myrl Beaton's idea to start the Nose Creek Historical Society; from Edith Woolliams, *My Neighbours and Yours*, p.12.

General: sources include personal recollections of Nose Creek Historical Society members, minutes of Society meetings and pamphlets printed by the Society.

Further Reading: Hugh Dempsey, "Launching Alberta History" in *Alberta History*, 45:1 (Winter1997). Grant MacEwan published *Sodbusters* in 1948, and James MacGregor published *Blankets and Beads* in 1949.

CHAPTER 2: THE NOSE CREEK VALLEY MUSEUM

p.17 "...Sunny westerly winds, pleasant..." from 1988 diary of C. Redvers Perry.

p.17 "...To say the least..." from "Museum Officially Opened", Five Village Weekly, Vol.14, No.37 Tuesday, June 14, 1988

General: sources include personal recollection of members of the Nose Creek Valley Museum Society and minutes of Society meetings.

p.29 the list of capsule contents was published by *The Five Village Weekly* in June or July, 1988.

CHAPTER 3: HISTORIC RESOURCES PRESERVED

p.32 about Knud Jensen Park: see Chapter 32 of this book, p.209.

PART II: THE ORIGINS OF THE VALLEY

INTRODUCTION TO PART II

p.34 about winter counts: see Hugh Dempsey, *A Blackfoot Winter Count.*

CHAPTER 4: GEOLOGY OF NOSE CREEK AND ITS TRIBUTARIES

Further Reading: *Geology of the Calgary Area*, edited by Lionel E. Jackson Jr. and Michael C. Wilson; published by the Canadian Society of Petroleum Geologists in 1981; contains excellent coverage of the various glacial events and their effects on the landscape in an article entitled "The Quaternary History of the Calgary Area" by Lionel E. Jackson Jr. *The Landscapes of Southern Alberta*, by Chester B. Beaty of the Department of Geography, University of Lethbridge, 1975; contains delightful reading for the layman. Both of the above carry extensive references for more erudite follow-up. An open file report entitled "Sand and Gravel Resources of the Calgary Area", prepared by I. Shetson for the Alberta Geological Survey in 1981, is accompanied by a suite of maps which give details of surface deposits over the whole Nose Creek drainage area and beyond. (References provided by Desmond Allen.)

The Land Before Us: The Making of Ancient Alberta, by the Royal Tyrrell Museum of Palaeontology, is a brief, well-illustrated survey of Alberta's geological history over 4.6 billion years, with good maps.

Archaeology in the Nose Creek Area

p.37 "...the site is one of..." from the article "Northern Plains Prehistory" by Thomas Head, p.114.

General: Beryl Hallworth's "Archaeology and History of Nose Hill and Nose Creek" in *Nose Hill: A Popular Guide*, edited by Beryl Hallworth; Mack W. Shortt's M.A. thesis, "The Happy Valley Bison Kill", and Thomas Head's M.A. thesis, "Springtime at H.M.S. Balzac".

Further Reading: Gail Helgason's *The First Albertans: An Archaeological Search* is a good book for the general reader; the article "Six Millenniums of Buffalo Jumps" by Brian O.K. Reeves discusses several buffalo jumps in Alberta.

CHAPTER 5: THE INDIANS IN THE NOSE CREEK VALLEY

p.44 map of tribes and reserves is from Hugh A. Dempsey's *Indian Tribes of Alberta*, used bypermission

Further reading: Dempsey's *Indian Tribes of Alberta* has brief histories of each tribe, including the Tsuu T'ina (Sarcee) and Stoney tribes and the Blackfoot Nation. Other books about the Blackfoot, Blood, and Peigan tribes include *The Amazing Death of Calf Shirt, and Other Blackfoot Stories* by Hugh A. Dempsey; *The Blackfoot: Raiders on the Northwestern Plains*, by John C. Ewers; and *Blackfoot Lodge Tales* by George Bird Grinnell. (References provided by Hugh A. Dempsey.)

Canada's First Nations: A History of Founding Peoples from Earliest Times, by Olive Patricia Dickason is an excellent survey of the academic research on the history of our native peoples up to about 1990. *I Have Lived Here Since The World Began: An Illustrated History of Canada's Native People*, by Arthur J. Ray, is aimed more at the general reader, and stresses the different economic activities of the first nations in Canada's varied environments.

CONCLUSION TO PART II

p.47 for information on reasons for the settlement rate, see Gerald Friesen, *The Canadian Prairies*, pp.249-252; he also discusses the immigrant experiences of ethnic groups and the rural agricultural experience, pp.242-273, 301-338.

PART III: CELEBRATING 100 YEARS NORTH OF THE BOW

These chapters are based on the pamphlets produced by the Nose Creek Historical Society over twenty-five years. The information in the pamphlets was often based on recent history books and articles, which may have been superseded since then by new research. In some cases, the editors of this anthology did not know where specific information for a pamphlet came from, but have suggested possible sources for the topic.

Because the pamphlets were produced to celebrate aspects of the Nose Creek Valley's history, they naturally focus on events that were worth celebrating. A few of the darker parts of our history have been mentioned, such as the whiskey trade and natural disasters. Other issues have not been dealt with by this anthology, but a few references follow here: *Pioneer Policing in Southern Alberta*, edited by William M. Baker, contains reports of crimes by Mounted Policeman R.B. Deane; he mentions the red light district on Nose Creek near Calgary before World War I (pp.181-187). In *Patterns of Prejudice: A History of Nativism in Alberta*, Howard Palmer looks at Albertans' historical attitudes to immigration and behaviour towards ethnic, racial and religious minorities. W. Keith Regular discusses aspects of Indian reserve life in his MA thesis "'Red Backs and White Burdens'; a Study of White Attitudes Towards Indians in Southern Alberta, 1896-1911." *Alberta: A New History* by Howard and Tamara Palmer is a good general source of information on these issues, as well as major events such as the 1885 Rebellion, the World Wars, the Depression of the 1930's, and political development in Alberta. The journal *Alberta History* deals with all sorts of topics.

CHAPTER 6: THE JOURNEY OF COLONEL P. ROBERTSON-ROSS

p.49 "...Tuesday September 17th..." from "Robertson-Ross' Diary: Fort Edmonton to Wildhorse, B.C., 1872" edited by Hugh A. Dempsey, *Alberta History* 9:3 (Autumn 1961) pp.14-16.

p.50 The identification of "Writing Creek" as McPherson's Coulee was made by Dempsey in "Robertson-Ross' Diary", note 28, p.14.

pp.50-51 "McPherson Coulee as seen from Dickson Rest Stop" is from a panel at the rest stop made in the late 1980's by the Community Development Display Department, Historic Sites Service, Province of Alberta.

p.51 "...By the evening of the first day..." from *Opening the Great West* by John McDougall, edited by Hugh A. Dempsey, p.39. Note 23 on p.39 gives the additional information about McPherson.

p.51 statement by Mrs. Benars in *One Day's Journey* by Stephen Wilk, pp.241-242

p.51 "Not far from Fort McPherson..." from speech by Muriel Clayton; "The Story of an Alberta Town", *Calgary Herald*, January 28, 1939; also quoted in Wilk, *One Day's Journey*, p.241.

Further Reading: see Hugh A. Dempsey, *Calgary: Spirit of the West* pp.12-15, about the effects of the whiskey trade and traders turning respectable (more or less); and other references for Chapter 21; for the NWMP, see references for Chapter 8.

CHAPTER 7: THE ARRIVAL OF CATTLE IN THE CALGARY AREA

p.53 about McDougalls bringing cattle to Morley; *Blazing the Old Cattle Trail* by Grant MacEwan, p.70.

p.53 about first organized roundup; *Fort Macleod Gazette*, July 1, 1882.

p.53 about memorandum from the Brand Office; location is unknown. The Western Stock Growers Association Museum at Cochrane has brand books which can be researched; see also pp.404-405 of this anthology for some brands.

General: Stephen Wilk, *One Day's Journey*, p.53-71.

Further Reading: L.V. Kelly's *The Range Men* is an older classic; two of many academic works on ranching are *The Canadian Prairie West and the Ranching Frontier: 1874-1924* by David H. Breen, and *Rancher's Legacy* by L.G. Thomas, which includes essays about ranch life. B.M. Barss has written several cookbooks depicting pioneer life, including *Come 'n Get It: At the Ranch House*, and *Come 'n Get It: Cowboys and Chuckwagons*.

CHAPTER 8: THE HORSE IN ALBERTA

p.57 history of the horse; *World Book Encyclopedia*, year and edition unknown.

p.58 Robertson-Ross; see Chapter 6 reference.

pp.58-59 "...R.G. Robinson, who owned a lot..." from Samuel E. Mayhood Recollections, p.20-23.

p.59 "Tribute to the Horse and Horse Farmer"; from the Brisco Riding Club's scrapbook; author unknown

Further reading: in *The Horse in Blackfoot Indian Culture*, John C. Ewers describes the effect of the arrival of horses on Plains Indians. For the NWMP, see R.C. Macleod's *The North West Mounted Police and Law Enforcement 1873-1905*. Older histories are John Peter Turner's *The North-West Mounted Police* and *Fort Macleod: The Story of the North West Mounted Police 1874-1904 Royal North West Mounted Police 1904-1920 Royal Canadian Mounted Police 1920 to present time.* edited by H.G. Long; Cecil E. Denny's *The Law Marches West* is a personal memoir.

CHAPTER 9: THE JOHNSTON STEVENSEN STOPPING HOUSE

p.63 the NWMP history referred to may be John Peter Turner's *The North-West Mounted Police*, pp.238-243.

pp.64-65 "Johnston Stevenson Stopping House": see "The Dickson-Stevenson Stopping House" on p.66 for more recent information.

pp.65-66 "...as institutions offering welcome warmth..." from a column by Grant MacEwan in the *Calgary Herald*, January 2, 1988, "Whole community gathered in old livery stable".

p.66 "In the early years..." about the Dickson-Stevenson Stopping House is from a panel at the Dickson Rest Area, made in the late 1980's by the Community Development Display Department, Historic Sites Service, Province of Alberta.

Further reading: about the founding and naming of Fort Calgary and about Inspector Brisebois, see Hugh Dempsey's *Calgary: Spirit of the West*, pp.23-32; about Johnston Stevenson, see scattered references in Stephen Wilk's *One Day's Journey*, see index listings. Nancy Millar's *Remember Me As You Pass By* describes headstones from graves all over Alberta, with fascinating accounts of some of the history behind them.

CHAPTER 10: THE DEATH OF THE REVEREND GEORGE MCDOUGALL

p.69 John McDougall wrote several accounts of George McDougall's death, including in his last book, *Opening the Great West*, pp.30-36.

p.70 about early missionaries: "Pioneer Missionaries Vie for the Loyalty of the West" by the Alberta & Northwest Territories Conference Historical Society of the United Church of Canada; *Mission Among the Buffalo* by James Ernest Nix, pp.7-14; *The Victoria Settlement 1862-1922* by Leslie J. Hurt, p.13; *Moon of Wintertime* by John Webster Grant, pp.143-9, 151; *The Rundle Journals: 1840-1848*, edited by Hugh A. Dempsey, pp.116, 192-194, 260; and *Oblate Fathers in Calgary* by N.R. Anderson, pp.13, 35-41.

p.72 map and chronology about the McDougalls adapted from McDougall Stoney Mission Society, *McDougall Reflections*, pp.10-11.

Further reading: Grant's *Moon of Wintertime* is about missionaries and Indians in Canada; *Father Lacombe* by James G. MacGregor, a life of the famous Oblate priest. Raymond J.A. Huel's *Proclaiming the Gospel to the Indians and the Metis* is a recent book about the Oblates in Canada.

CHAPTER 11: TREATY NO.7 AT BLACKFOOT CROSSING

p.73 The title as quoted is a paraphrase, and it should say that the treaty is between the Queen and her Commissioners on the one part and the Blackfeet, Blood, Piegan, Sarcee, Stony, and other Indians on the other part. See Alexander Morris, *The Treaties of Canada with the Indians*, pp.368-375 for a version of the treaty, and pp.245-284 for reports on the treaty signing by Commissioner Laird and a newspaper reporter.

p.75 about the 1870 massacre in Montana; Hugh A. Dempsey, *Red Crow*, pp.64-65

pp.74-75 about Canada's preparations to settle the west; *Destinies: Canadian History From Confederation* by R.D. Francis, R. Jones and D.B. Smith, pp.24-32, 46-51. For differing interpretations of Treaty 7, see: *The Spirit of the Alberta Indian Treaties*, edited by Richard Price, which includes scholarly articles on Treaties 6, 7 and 8, and oral history accounts by Indian elders. A recent book, *The True Spirit and Original Intent of Treaty 7*, by Treaty 7 Elders and Tribal Council, with W. Hildebrandt, D. First Rider and S. Carter, uses a wide range of elders' accounts to explain how Indians understood the treaty. (The attitudes and actions of government officials and missionaries, however, need to be more thoroughly researched and explained). Other writers who have discussed Indians' views of the treaty include Chief John Snow, *These Mountains Are Our Sacred Places*, p.2; Irene Spry, "The Tragedy of the Loss of the Commons," p.204; Hugh A. Dempsey, *Crowfoot*, pp.93-107.

CHAPTER 12: 100 YEARS OF PRAIRIE FIRES

p.77 "...The state of affairs existing during the early part of the year..." is from "Appendix D North West Mounted Police" in the *Annual Report of the Department of the Interior*, 42 Victoria *Sessional Papers* (No. 52) A. 1879.

p.77 "...Then, during the winter of 1877-78 prairie fires raced across the Blackfoot hunting grounds..." in Hugh Dempsey, *Indian Tribes of Alberta*, p.16

p.78 about the Brushy Ridge Fire in Springbank on November 19, 1936: *Chaps and Chinooks* by the Foothills Historical Society, pp.25-28.

pp.78-79 article about dust devil by Paul Drohan, *Calgary Herald*, April 23, 1995. (See photo on pp.84 by Allen Browarny.)

pp.79-82 quoted from the "Recollections" of S.E. Mayhood, in the private possession of Cyril Woolliams, pp.1-6, 11-19, 31-36.

p.84 headlines from the *Calgary Herald* and other newspapers for various dates.

Further Reading: for a description of the 1930's drought and depression on the prairies see James Gray's *The Winter Years* and *Men Against the Desert*; for the drought in southern

Alberta in the 1920's, see *We'll All Be Buried Down Here* and *Empire of Dust*, both by David Jones.

CHAPTER 13: ANNIVERSARY OF MAIL SERVICE PASSING THROUGH THE AREA

p.85 "...Gus, the Bow River mail carrier, who left here with the mail...", *Saskatchewan Herald*, May 5, 1879.

p.85 information about Gus from Father E.O. Drovin, O.M.I. of Edmonton; there are records of the Oblate Fathers in the Provincial Archives of Alberta in Edmonton; see also Raymond J.A. Huel, *Proclaiming the Gospel to the Indians and the Metis.*

pp.87-88 an earlier version of the article on Balzac United Church, by Janie (Mrs.G.E.) Church, was published in *The Nose Creek Story*, pp.119-120.

pp.89-90 an earlier version of the article on the Anglicans was published in *The Nose Creek Story*, by the Nose Creek Book Committee pp.125-127.

CHAPTER 14: ALBERTA'S 75TH ANNIVERSARY

p.95 about the Sandstone Quarry Winch: reference to *Calgary in Sandstone* by Richard Cunniffe.

pp.95-96 about unmarked graves: see Nancy Millar's *Remember Me As You Pass By.*

p.96 about Alberta's 75th Anniversary: see *The Formation of Alberta: A Documentary History*, edited by Douglas R. Owram, which quotes significant documents about Alberta becoming a province in 1905.

pp.96-97 "Sandstone City", a pamphlet produced by the City of Calgary, is quoted and the photographs used courtesy of the Heritage Advisory Board, City of Calgary.

p.97 The Alberta Coat of Arms is reproduced from the First Edition of *The Canadian Encyclopedia*, courtesy of Mel Hurtig, and is used by permission of the Minister of Community Development.

CHAPTER 15: THE CALGARY-EDMONTON TRAIL

p.100 references to "The Calgary Edmonton Trail" by Hugh A. Dempsey, *Alberta Historical Review*, 7:4 (Autumn 1959), and "The Old Trail", Chapter 3 of *One Day's Journey* by Stephen Wilk.

p.104 map from *Pioneers of the Faith* by Stephen Wilk, p.110; based on maps at the Glenbow Library and Archives.

p.105 photo 6 is from *The North-West Passage by Land* by Viscount Milton and W.B. Cheadle; they were early tourists, who visited the North-West in 1862.

Further Reading: *The Old North Trail* by Walter McClintock; *The Whoop-Up Trail: Early Days in Alberta...Montana* by Gerald L. Berry; *Alberta: The Pioneer Years* by Harold Fryer; *Perilous Journeys: Early Motoring in Alberta* by Sean Moir.

CHAPTER 16: AGRICULTURE AND RANCHING IN THE NOSE CREEK AREA

p.106 about a century of agriculture in the Nose Creek country; *One Day's Journey*, by Stephen Wilk, p.59 re ranchers, p.77 re homestead rules.

pp.106-107 references to Peter Fidler and David Thompson in Stephen Wilk, *One Day's Journey*, pp.29, 33. See *The Nose Creek Story*, pp.84-86 about the Lewis family and pp.19-21 about the Nose Creek Literary Society.

p.111 map of sandstone quarries is from the pamphlet "Sandstone City" courtesy of the Heritage Advisory Board, City of Calgary.

p.113 map of ranch leases from Stephen Wilk, *One Day's Journey*, p.59.

Further Reading: about land policy and settlement, see Chester Martin, *Dominion Lands Policy*, and A.S. Morton, *History of Prairie Settlement*; about ranching, see Chapter 7 references; about agriculture, see Paul Voisey, *Vulcan: The Making of a Prairie Community*; James Gray, *Men Against the Desert*; V.C. Fowke, *Canadian Agricultural Policy: Th* *Historical Pattern*; and the Reynolds-Alberta Museum booklets on aspects of farming Kenneth Tingley, *Steel and Steam: Aspects of Breaking Land in Alberta*; Patricia Myers *Facing the Land: Homesteading in Alberta* and *When the Whistle Blows: Steam Threshin, in Alberta*; and Ruth Lysack-Martynkiw, *Homegrown: Vignettes About Manufacturin, Agricultural Implements in Alberta, 1890-1955.*

CHAPTER 17: ARRIVAL OF THE C.P.R. IN CALGARY

pp.114-115 "The Approach to the Mountains, 1883" by Omer Lavallee, Corporat Historian and Archivist, Canadian Pacific Limited was produced by the CPR in 1983 as pai of their 100th anniversary display; it was reprinted in the Nose Creek Historical Societ pamphlet by permission of Earl Olsen, Public Relations Canadian Pacific Railways; an printed in this anthology by the permission of Canadian Pacific Railways.

Further reading: about the CPR: W. Kaye Lamb's *History of the Canadian Pacifi Railway* is the best academic one; *The CPR West*, edited by Hugh A. Dempsey, has a interesting variety of articles; *Van Horne's Road* is an illustrated book by Omer Lavallee Pierre Berton's *The Last Spike: The Great Railway 1881-1885* tells some colourful stories *The Canadian Pacific Railway and the Development of Western Canada 1896-1914* b John A. Eagle is an academic study.

CHAPTER 18: THE 75th ANNIVERSARY OF AIRDRIE'S VILLAGE CHARTER

p.118 The population of Alberta increased from 73,000 in 1901 to 374,000 in 1911 Howard and Tamara Palmer, *Alberta: A New History*, p.78

p.119 "How Airdrie Got its Name" from Stephen Wilk, *One Day's Journey*, pp.102-10: see also Wilk, chapter 7, pp.101-121, for names of other local sites.

Further Reading: see Chapter 32 of this anthology for the more recent histor of Airdrie; for other place names see *2000 Place Names of Alberta* by Eric an Patricia M. Holmgren; *Place Names of Alberta: Volume 2 Southern Alberta*, edite by Aphrodite Karamitsanis.

CHAPTER 19: THE HAY TRAILS

p.122 general background information came from "What Was Prairie Wool?" by B.D. Cote Strathmore, Alberta.

Further Reading: the pamphlet "Range, Its Nature and Use" written by Alex Johnsto» Howard MacDonald, J. Allen Campbell, and Wallace R. Hanson for the provincial governmen and *Making Hay While the Sun Shone: Haying in Alberta Before 1955* by Judy Larmour.

CHAPTER 20: TRIBUTE TO THE SURVEYORS

pp.125-126 general background on surveyors, see James G. MacGregor, *Vision of a Ordered Land*; and Don W. Thompson, *Men and Meridians: The History of Surveying an Mapping in Canada*: Volume 2 covers 1867-1917.

pp.126-127 "Early Surveys of the Nose Creek Region" was a handout distributed b G.K. Allred, Alberta Land Surveyors' Association, at the Nose Creek Historical Societ interdenominational service held on November 16, 1986; published here by the permissio of the Alberta Land Surveyors' Association.

CHAPTER 21: THE FUR TRADERS' TRAIL

pp.131-132 excerpts from "The Great Buffalo Migration" by Richard N. Brodrick c Vulcan; it was published in *Canadian Cattlemen*, December 1939, pp.285, 308, 313.

pp.132-134 "Trails between the Forts" is adapted from "March West...To Whoop-U Country: Fort Whoop-Up, Fort Macleod and Fort Calgary", an article by Bob Pearso»

Coordinator, Fort Regional Museums, (Forts Whoop-Up, Macleod & Calgary), made available to us by the author. The added quotation, "...Most of the Indians would take it diluted, as long as it had some "kick"..." is from *The Whoop-Up Trail: Early Days in Alberta ... Montana* by Gerald L. Berry, pp.23-24.

Further Reading: about the fur trade, see Arthur J. Ray, *Indians in the Fur Trade*, and *The Canadian Fur Trade in the Industrial Age*; Sylvia Van Kirk, *Many Tender Ties: Women in Fur-Trade Society in Western Canada*; about the buffalo, see Frank Gilbert Roe's classic study *The North American Buffalo*, and the fascinating articles in *Buffalo*, edited by John Foster, Dick Harrison and I.S. MacLaren; about the whiskey trade, see Paul Sharp, *Whoop-Up Country*; Joel Overholser, *Fort Benton: World's Innermost Port*; and Hugh A. Dempsey *Calgary: Spirit of the West*, pp.11-15; about trails, see the references for Chapter 15.

CHAPTER 22: TRIBUTE TO LOCAL RURAL SCHOOLS

p.136 reference to records held at Red Deer, source unknown. There is a pamphlet called "Red Deer's First School 1887-1987" in the Local History Room at the W.R. Castell Central Library in Calgary; see also *Schools of the Parkland*, by Red Deer District Local A.T.A. No. 24.

p.136 about the first school in Nose Creek area opening in 1886; this is an error and should be 1896; Stephen Wilk, *One Day's Journey*, pp.117, 293-294.

p.136 letter from Lois (Church) Perry in possession of C. Redvers Perry.

p.139 reference is to *The Little White School House* by John C. Charyk.

p.147 bottom photo; the Rocky View Division School Board Office is in Calgary

p.148 map of Rocky View School Division from cover of *Acres and Empires* by Tracey Read; note that the district is wrapped around Calgary

Further reading: John W. Chalmers, *Schools of the Foothills Province*; John C. Charyk, *When theSchool Horse Was King*; and *Shaping the Schools of the Canadian West*, edited by David C. Jones, Nancy M. Sheehan and Robert M. Stamp.

CHAPTER 23: TRIBUTE TO LOCAL AND RURAL CHURCHES

p.151 "Church Beginnings in Eagle and Goldenrod": about student ministers, Stephen Wilk, *One Day's Journey*, p.201; about the community non-denominational church, Wilk, *Pioneers of the Faith*, p.65.

p.157 "The Bell Organ", quotation starting "The first service..." probably from Dean David J. Carter, "The Early Years of the Church of the Redeemer, Calgary" in *The Anglican Church in Calgary: Church Activities 1878-1974*.

Further reading: *Visions of The New Jerusalem: Religious Settlement on the Prairies*, edited by Benjamin G. Smillie.

CHAPTER 24: TRIBUTE TO BLACKSMITHING

p.159 reference to Stephen Wilk, *One Day's Journey*, pp.166-167.

p.163 from copy of blacksmith contract in the possession of Dorothy Tilleman. Dorothy Tilleman's great-grandfather was James Smith. His father had come from Scotland and received Empire Loyalist Grant land in Ontario in 1818; this land is still owned by the Smith family. The name "Smith" suggests that at least one of James' ancestors was also a blacksmith.

CHAPTER 25: TRIBUTE TO LAYING OF CALGARY-EDMONTON RAILROAD

Further Reading: about CPR, see Chapter 17 references.

CHAPTER 26: TRIBUTE TO LOCAL COMMUNITY HALLS

p.172 references to *The Nose Creek Story* and *My Neighbours and Yours*, see Chapters 48 and 52 of this book.

CHAPTER 27: TRIBUTE TO PIONEER WOMEN

p.175 "...Packing and unpacking dogs and horses..." from John McDougall, *Pathfinding on Plain and Prairie*, pp.12-13

p.176 "...Even the rough and ready teamsters..." from Grant MacEwan, *Between the Red and the Rockies*, pp.213-214.

Further Reading: for first-hand accounts of women's experiences see *The Last Best West: Women on the Alberta Frontier 1880-1930* by Eliane Leslau Silverman; about Plains Indian women, see *The Ways of My Grandmothers* by Beverly Hungry Wolf; about two of the Famous Five, see *Firing the Heather: The Life and Times of Nellie McClung* by Mary Hallett and Marilyn Davis, and *Perennials and Politics: The Life Story of Hon. Irene Parlby LLD.*, by Barbara Villy Cormack; for other biographies see *...And Mighty Women Too: Stories of Notable Western Canadian Women* by Grant MacEwan; for a study of U.F.W.A. activities see "Educational Role of the United Farm Women of Alberta" by L.J. Wilson.

CHAPTER 28: TRIBUTE TO THE TELEPHONE ERA

p.181 some historical information was provided in 1994 by A.G.T.'s Historical Records Department

p.181 "Telephone men here..." quotations from diary of C.W. Perry, in the possession of C. Redvers Perry

p.181 1913 *Calgary and District Telephone Directory* is on microfilm in the Local History Room at the W.R. Castell Central Library in Calgary.

pp.181-183 based on minutes of the Airdrie Mutual Telephone Company.

p.183 based on minutes of the Balzac Mutual Telephone Company.

Further reading: Tony Cashman, *Singing Wires: The Telephone in Alberta*.

CHAPTER 29: TRIBUTE TO PIONEER MEN

p.190 "The prehistoric hunter showed a lot more savvy..." from Gail Helgason, *The First Albertans*, pp.75-77, 94-96

p.191 story about James Macleod, Edgar Dewdney and mosquitoes, from a letter from James F. Macleod to Mary Macleod, August 15, 1879, in J.F. Macleod papers, M-766, file 14, Glenbow Archives.

p.193 "Men usually arrived in the west..." quotation from Hugh A. Dempsey, source unknown.

pp.193-194 about Bill Walker based on "Crossfield's Exemplary Citizen to Receive Canadian Citation in Ottawa", profile by Lorne Kosack, published in the *News Chronicle*, April 10, 1990, p.1.

Further reading: Grant MacEwan, *Fifty Mighty Men*; Peter Erasmus, *Buffalo Days and Nights*.

PART IV: URBAN CENTRES AND THE VALLEY
INTRODUCTION

Further reading: On boosterism, see the articles by Paul Voisey, "Boosting the Small Prairie Town 1904-1931: An Example from Southern Alberta," Alan F.J. Artibise, "Boosterism and the Development of Prairie Cities, 1871-1913," and Max Foran, "Boosting the Small Prairie Town 1904-1931: An Example from Southern Alberta," in *Town and City: Aspects of Western Canadian Urban Development*. ed. Alan F.J. Artibise. Most of the articles in the book deal with aspects of prairie urban growth.

CHAPTER 31: CROSSFIELD

p.202 some information came from an unpublished manuscript by David Hill

Further reading: *Prairie Sod and Goldenrod* by the Crossfield History Committee is local history of Crossfield; see Chapter 50 of this anthology.

CHAPTER 32: AIRDRIE

Further reading: earlier history of Airdrie and district is in *One Day's Journey* by Stephen Wilk; see Chapter 51 of this anthology.

CHAPTER 33: MILESTONES IN GROWTH OF CALGARY AND AIRDRIE

pp.248-250 information from "Calgary Timeline" by Harry Sanders, in *Centennial City: Calgary 1894-1994* edited by Donald B. Smith; and *One Day's Journey* by Stephen Wilk

p.250 population figures from the City of Calgary's *1996 Municipal Handbook*, and *Airdrie: Census Results 1994* by the Calgary Regional Planning Commission; weather facts from the City of Airdrie's pamphlet *Lifestyle: City of Airdrie Lifestyle Profile.*

Further Reading: there are many books about Calgary; see *Calgary: An Illustrated History*, by Max Foran; *Calgary: Spirit of the West* by Hugh A. Dempsey; *Days Gone By: Jack Peach on Calgary's Past* and *Thanks For the Memories* by Jack Peach; *Citymakers: Calgarians After the Frontier*, edited by Max Foran and Sheilagh Jameson; and *Centennial City: Calgary 1894-1994* edited by Donald B. Smith, which includes an extensive and useful bibliography on Calgary.

CHAPTER 35: MEDICAL CARE FOR CALGARY AND NOSE CREEK VALLEY

pp.252-253 information excerpted from *Teachers of Medicine: The Development of Graduate and Clinical Education in Calgary* by G.M. McDougall; and *Medical Clinics and Physicians in Southern Alberta* by G.M. McDougall and S.C. Harris.

p.253 information about Nose Creek Valley doctors from Stephen Wilk, *One Day's Journey*, pp.132-139

CHAPTER 36: HIGHER EDUCATION SERVES THE VALLEY

Further Reading: *The University of Calgary: A Place of Vision* by Robert Bott, is a brief illustrated history.

p.252 "the new hospital..." from *Macleod Gazette*, April 4, 1883.

p.263 map of Calgary 1883 adapted from Map #1 in Glenbow Library.

p.264 map of the growth of Calgary from Stephen Wilk, "A Critical Analysis of Metropolitan Mission Strategies for the Calgary Presbytery of the United Church of Canada."

pp.265-267 City of Calgary annexation map, crest, flag, floral emblem, list of mayors, and weather in Calgary, all from *1996 Municipal Handbook* published by the City of Calgary.

p.268 City of Airdrie crest is from the brochure "A Special City Council Meeting" about the twinning of Airdrie, Scotland and Airdrie, Alberta, which was proclaimed on July 22, 1987.

p.268 driving distances from *Lifestyle: City of Airdrie Lifestyle Profile*, published by the City of Airdrie.

PART V: BUSINESSES AND ORGANIZATIONS IN THE VALLEY

Many of the articles in Part V were written for this anthology, though in some cases we did quote from previously published works. The business histories were written by owners or employees, organization histories by members, and family histories by family members.

CHAPTER 37: WORKING AND SOCIALIZING IN THE VALLEY

p.277 "Premium Water Supply" from Church Ranches Information Booklet.

p.279 about farming in the area, Tracey Read, *Acres & Empires*, p.174.

p.279 "Don't talk about anyone..." quote from Edith Woolliams, *My Neighbours and Yours*, p.426.

pp.279-280 information about individuals from Edith Woolliams, *My Neighbours and Yours*, pp.209-215, and Nose Creek Book Committee, *The Nose Creek Story from 1792.*

p.282 Nose Creek Tree reproduced, with permission, from Edith Woolliams, *My*

465

Neighbours and Yours, p.425.

p.284 poster from M2382 BR/C212A, Glenbow Archives.

Further reading: about local histories, see Part VI of this book; about immigration and settlement by various ethnic groups, Howard and Tamara Palmer, *Peoples of Alberta: Portraits of Cultural Diversity*. There are many published histories about individual ethnic groups in Canada or parts of Canada; a new book about the local pioneer Jewish experience is *Land of Promise* by the Jewish Historical Society of Southern Alberta.

CHAPTER 38: GRAIN AND GRAIN MARKETING

p.293 reference to Beattie, A.W. *Trails in the Sunset: A Tribute to People*, pp.143-144.

Further Reading:about the Wheat Pool, Leonard Nesbitt, *Tides in the West*; about grain farming, V.C. Fowke, *The National Policy and the Wheat Economy* and Paul Voisey, *Vulcan: The Making of a Prairie Community*; about the effect of World War I on wheat farming, John Herd Thompson, *The Harvests of War: The Prairie West, 1914-1918*; about grain in general, *Grains and Oilseeds: Handling, Marketing and Processing* by the Canadian International Grains Institute; *A Century of Canadian Grain: Government Policy to 1951* by C.F. Wilson; *Beyond the Harvest: Canadian Grain at the Crossroads* by Barry Wilson.

p.302 photo is from "Jewish Cattlemen Remembered" in *Discovery*, published by the Jewish Historical Society of Southern Alberta 7:1 (Winter, 1997)

p.307 article was sent to C. Redvers Perry from Bill Lamport and Brad Lamport

p.307 photo is from "Jewish Cattlemen Remembered" in *Discovery*, published by the Jewish Historical Society of Southern Alberta 7:1 (Winter, 1997)

pp.309-310 article about Chester Fowler by Joanne Schmidt was published in *Sheep Canada*, Summer 1995; reprinted by permission.

p.315 "Calgary remained primarily a shipping point..." quotation about Pat Burns from Max Foran, *Calgary: An Illustrated History*.

CHAPTER 42: INDUSTRIES

p.341 "Our process begins..." quoted from pamphlet supplied by Money's Mushrooms

p.346 information about early history of ATCO from Stephen Wilk, *One Day's Journey*, pp.384-387.

pp.354 "They disembarked onto a platform..." from booklet "Petrogas Processing Ltd.: 25th Anniversary 1961-1986" compiled and edited by Alan A. Woods.

General information from Canadian Occidental Petroleum, including reply to Nose Creek Historical Society questionnaire, a brochure, and booklet by Woods.

p.357 about the number of furs shipped from Fort Benton, Joel Overholser, *Fort Benton: World's Innermost Port*.

Further reading: Henry Klassen "Family Businesses in Calgary to 1939," in *Citymakers: Calgarians After the Frontier*, edited by Max Foran and Sheilagh Jameson; *The First Hundred Years: The History of the Calgary Chamber of Commerce* by Jack Peach includes profiles of Amoco, ATCO, the General Hospital, the University of Calgary, and the Calgary Stampede.

CHAPTER 43: CO-OPERATIVES

p.362 about Buttes U.F.A., Nose Creek Book Committee, *The Nose Creek Story*, p.62; and Stephen Wilk, *One Day's Journey*, pp.334-336, about George Church and the U.F.A. Co-op.

p.364 information about Airdrie Rural Electrification Association was summarized from Stephen Wilk, *One Day's Journey*, pp.211-220.

pp.364-365 information from the Balzac Rural Electrification Association minutes.

pp. 367-368 extracts from "The Development of Rural Gas Distribution Systems in Alberta" by Allan A. Warrack.

pp.369-370 "...where modern co-ops got their start..." from Rob and Nancy Millar, *A History of the Calgary Co-op*, pp.6-7.

p.371 "Nellie Saville, now member #1..." from Rob and Nancy Millar, *A History of the Calgary Co-op*, p.40

pp. 371-372 "It is not exactly surprising...", about Keith Rosenberger by permission, Rob and Nancy Millar, *A History of the Calgary Co-op*, p.66.

Further Reading: Ian MacPherson, *Each For All: A History of the Co-operative Movement in English Canada, 1900-1945.*

CHAPTER 44: ORGANIZATIONS

p.382 references to *The Nose Creek Story* and *My Neighbours and Yours*, see Chapters 48 and 52 of this anthology.

pp.383-384 information about the Ranchmen's Club from pamphlets, "The Ranchmen's Club: A Slight Historical Sketch", and "A Short History of the Ranchmen's Club: A Light-Hearted Account" and a newsletter, "The Ranchmen's Club", March 1993.

p.386 "The Wolves' Den" from a wallhanging at the Ranchman's Club.

p.388 "Founders of the Ranchmen's Club" from a wallhanging at the Ranchman's Club.

Further Reading: about the World Wars and veterans, see *Winning the Second Battle: Canadian Veterans and the Return to Civilian Life 1915-1930* by Desmond Morton and Glenn Wright, and *For King and Country: Alberta in the Second World War* edited by Kenneth Tingley; about the Ranchmen's Club, see Hugh A. Dempsey, *Calgary: Spirit of the West*, pp 68-71.

CHAPTER 45: YOUTH ORGANIZATIONS

pp.390 "The Airdrie 4-H Beef Club was centred..." from N. Fred Bell, *My Fifteen Years with 4-H Clubs: 1944-1959*

p.391 "The Calf and Grain Clubs...", letter from Mrs. Bertram C. (Alexa) Church to Fred Bell, published in *My Fifteen Years with 4-H Clubs: 1944-1959.*

CHAPTER 46: THE CALGARY EXHIBITION AND STAMPEDE IN RETROSPECT

pp.397-400 "The Growth of a Legend" article by Chris Nelson in *Calgary Stampede*, pp.37-39, 43, printed here courtesy of the Calgary Stampede.

pp.403 reference to Donna Livingston, *Cowboy Spirit, Guy Weadick and the Calgary Stampede.*

pp.405-406 the brands were found in the brand books at the Western Stock Growers Association Museum in Cochrane; see also Chapter 7 of this anthology

Further Reading: *A Brand of Its Own: The 100 Year History of the Calgary Exhibition and Stampede* by James H. Gray.

CHAPTER 47: HISTORIC INTERPRETIVE CENTRES

p.407 see also photographs from the Grain Academy on p.296, and the list of museums near the end of this anthology.

p.412 about the caravan leaving Edmonton October 22, 1873, and quotation "It must have been an impressive..." from James Ernest Nix, *Mission Among the Buffalo*, pp.88-89.

p.412 "During the autumn and just prior..." from John McDougall, *Opening the Great West*, pp.26-27.

p.412 photos from Western Stock Growers Association video, "The Great Centennial Cattle Drive 1896-1996."

—by Valerie Jobson

468

Index of Names

Barker, George, 86, 285, 362
Barker, Ida, 85
Barker, John (Jack), 138, 173, 282
Barker, Lizzie, 88
Barker, Mary (née Dixon), 371, 373
Barker, Mrs., 150
Barker, W. Gordon, 291, 371, 373-4
Barkley family, 393
Barkley, Barbara, 393
Barkley, Donna, 392
Barkley, Ed, 216
Baron, Debbie, 377
Barrett family, 328
Bartnek, Andi, 228
Barvis, Jim, 132
Barwis, Colonel, 111, 263
Basso, Rino, v
Bateman, Don, 285
Baxter, Ina, 242
Baxter, Joanne, 425
Bayrack, Don, 329, 336
Bear Shield, 45
Bearspaw, Chief David, 319
Bearspaw, Johnnie, 319
Beaton family, 31, 33, 282
Beaton, Colin, 139
Beaton, Duke, 139
Beaton, Eileen, 2, 139
Beaton, Jerry, 139
Beaton, Mrs. N., 414
Beaton, Myrl, 3, 5
Beattie, A.W.
Beattie, Kathryn, 147
Beaudoin, Steve, 368
Beaupre, Joseph Antoine Aldous, 326
Beaupre, Victor Joseph, 326
Beck, Brenda, 228
Becker, George, 208, 320
Becker, Karen, 214
Beddoes, Leonard, 162, 285
Beddows, Don, 11
Bedford, Judy, 31
Bedingfeld, Mr., 132
Befus, Vern, 211, 243
Behrens, Mr., 220-1
Belcher, Colonel, 253
Belkin, Henry, 307
Bell, A., 285

Bell, Alexander Graham, 181
Bell, N. Fred, 285, 390-1, 395
Bell, Ray C., 291
Belshaw, Jim, 140
Belsheim, Thorstein T., 323
Benars, Mrs., 51
Benedix, Andrew, 18, 183
Benedix, H.F., 181
Benedix, Melva, 255
Benjamin, 49, 58
Bennett, Darrell, 12, 207, 221-2, 224, 226, 230, 237
Bennett, Everett, 270
Bennett, George, 293
Bennett, Hugh, 144, 185
Bennett, Mrs., 144
Bennett, Pat, 207, 222
Bennett, Robert, 144
Bennett, Wes, 385
Benzing, Karl, 357
Berry, Gerald L., 133
Berry, Harry, 358
Berthelot, Paul, 7
Bevan, Gordon, 212
Bevan, Vera, 212
Bews, Tommy, 403
Bezjack, Steve, 145
Bice, Bill, 213-4
Bice, Libby, 213-4
Big Snake, Chief, 45
Big Swan, 41
Bigstoney, Chief Jonas, 45
Bilben family, 282, 393
Bilben, Alfred, 355
Bilben, Bob, 174, 391
Bilben, Ken, 32, 223
Bilben, Liz, 174
Bilben, Norma, 391-2
Bilben, Rollie, 55
Biletski, Alex, 234
Bills family, 141
Bills, Evertt, 200
Birch, Cecil, 374
Bird, Lionel, 291
Bird, Dr. Charley, 432
Bischoff, Dr. George, 253
Bishop, Dr. George, 198, 253-4
Bishop, John, 142

Davis, Jim, 212
Davison, Andrew, 267
Davy family, 124, 282, 393
Davy, C.J. (Kelly), 2, 86, 91, 377-8
Davy, Danny, 271
Davy, Ellen, 90
Davy, Frank, 4, 89
Davy, H., 89
Davy, Joseph (Joe), 21, 184
Davy, Josie, 138
Davy, Margit (née Jensen), 271
Davy, Mark (Butch), 223, 225, 237, 271
Davy, Robbie, 271, 385
Davy, Soren, 271
Davy, Vi, 91
Davy, W.C., 89
Davy, W.J., 86, 89, 92, 171
Deane, Captain Richard Burton, 408
DeFehr, Dave, 218
DeFehr, Frank, 216
Delair, Gordon, 239, 297
Dempsey, Hugh A., 1-2, 41-46, 49, 51, 68, 77, 100, 190, 193, 417, 426
Denny, C.E., 263
Dewar, Garry, 292
Dewar, Peter, 326
Dewdney, J. Edgar, 191
DeWitt family, 143
DeWitt, George, 285
DeWitt, Richard, 232
Dewitt, Robert (Bob), 365
Dickinson, Al, 220
Dickson, John M. (or Dixon), 50, 64, 66, 118, 198
Diefenbaker, John, 259
Diertens, Steve, 216
Dillabaugh family, 282
Dillabaugh, Linda, 92
Dinning, R.J., 324
Disney, Walt, 399
Dmetrichuk, Metro, 211
Dobson, Mr., 138
Dodd, Edwin Jr., 149
Dodd, Edwin Sr., 149
Dodd, Estelle, 137, 211
Dodd, Mrs. Edwin, 149
Doherty, Margaret, 368
Doll, Guy, 210

Dollar family, 297
Dollar, Andrew, 396
Donald, Charles (Charlie), 161-1
Donoghue, Eric, 357-9
Dorval, Louise, 12
Doucet, Father Leon, 63, 70
Doucette, Andrew, 257
Dougan, G.A.C., 181
Dover, Mary, 432
Drebit, Don, 18
Drohan, Paul, 79
Drovin, Father E.O., 85
Drumheller, Mr., 132
Drummond, Mildred, 213
Dryden, Ki, 213
Dryden, Ward, 213
Duce, Gordon, 87
Duerr, Al, 267
Duggan, C.J., 122
Duhn, Robert, 291
Duncan, Eddie, 403-4
Duncan, Emily, 210
Duncan, Frances, 404
Dundas, Eastman, 381
Dunglison, Dawne, 211, 243
Dunglison, Ron, 211, 243
Dunn, Jim, 236, 396
Dunn, Lorne, 366, 372
Dunne, Dolly, 18
Dunne, Jim, 207, 220-2, 385
Dunne, Marilyn, 381
Durand, Michelle (later McKinnon), 274
Durnin, Patrick J., 291
Dyball, Alex, 227
Dyck, Herman, 231
Dyck, Jake, 222
Dye, Evelyn, 377
Dyrholm, David, 297
Eagleson family, 156
Eagleson, Angie, 377
Eaton, Lady Florence, 324
Eby family, 156
Echlin, Bob, 385
Echlin, Irene, 18
Echlin, Kelly, 84
Eckert, Eileen, 433
Edge family, 259

SUBJECT INDEX